Fourth Edition

EFFECTIVE BUSINESS COMMUNICATIONS

Herta A. Murphy
Professor Emeritus of Business Administration
and of Business Communication
University of Washington

Herbert W. Hildebrandt
Professor of Business Administration
and of Business Communication
University of Michigan

McGRAW-HILL BOOK COMPANY
New York St. Louis San Francisco Auckland Bogotá Hamburg
Johannesburg London Madrid Mexico Montreal New Delhi
Panama Paris São Paulo Singapore Sydney Tokyo Toronto

To my husband, Gene — H. M.
To my wife, Dee   — H. H.

EFFECTIVE BUSINESS COMMUNICATIONS

Copyright © 1984, 1980, 1976, 1972 by McGraw-Hill, Inc. All rights reserved. Printed in
the United States of America. Except as permitted under the United States Copyright
Act of 1976, no part of this publication may be reproduced or distributed in any form or
by any means, or stored in a data base or retrieval system, without the prior written
permission of the publisher.

3 4 5 6 7 8 9 0   DOCDOC   8 9 8 7 6 5 4

ISBN 0-07-044091-3

This book was set in Times Roman by Better Graphics.
The editors were Beth A. Lewis and Joseph F. Murphy;
the cover was designed by Rafael Hernandez;
the production supervisor was Diane Renda.
New drawings were done by Fine Line Illustrations, Inc.
R. R. Donnelley & Sons Company was printer and binder.

Library of Congress Cataloging in Publication Data

Murphy, Herta A.
    Effective business communications.

    Includes bibliographical references and index.
    1. Commercial correspondence.   2. Business report
writing.   3. Communication in management.
I. Hildebrandt, Herbert William, date
II. Title.
HF5721.M85   1984   651.7'4   83-11349
ISBN 0-07-044091-3

Preface

This fourth edition, like its popular, widely adopted predecessor, emphasizes that the purpose and the receiver of every message profoundly affect its content, organization, and style of presentation. In keeping with this theme, the book's broad subject matter is practical, ethical, and thorough. Condensed wherever possible, it is integrated with significant new materials, updates, and revisions. Its organization, visual aids, and clear conversational style make meaningful reading easy.

Purpose and Approach

Anyone preparing for or already in a business or management job that requires effective communication will find this book useful as both a text and a reference guide. Its goal is to help you communicate through sound, honest written and oral business messages that receivers can easily understand and to which they will react favorably. It is designed to develop a better understanding of human behavior and to improve abilities for analyzing, researching, organizing, writing, revising, dictating, speaking, and listening.

Abundant teaching and learning aids demonstrate key concepts for written and oral communications. In-depth explanations suggest *what* to do and *why*. Hundreds of examples—many with marginal notations—show *how*, and how not, to do. Chapter title pages list main topics, helpful for both preview and review. Footnoted bibliographies suggest sources for further readings. The unique, well-liked checklists provide concise summary guidelines for most types of messages. They are to be used only as *reminders*, *not* as *"recipe lists,"* because each message requires careful planning. End-of-chapter and appendix exercises range from simple to complex thought-stimulating activities for a wide variety of situations.

This book is suitable for students in universities and colleges, community colleges, business schools, continuing-education centers, and special training programs for executives, middle-management, or supervisory personnel. Whether you communicate as a business executive, professional person, government employee, administrative assistant, club officer, or an individual consumer, the text has useful material for you. It is ample for one- or two-semester courses, and adaptable for short courses that cover only selected chapters pertinent to particular student needs. The extensive learning aids—along with the thorough Instructor's Manual—are also timesavers for faculty.

Special Features

The fourth edition contains these features and changes:

1. A new section on nonverbal communication and a communication model in Chapter 2 help present a more detailed concept of the communication process. As in the previous edition, nonverbal impressions are mentioned also in several other chapters.
2. The business reports chapters have been strengthened by new or revised explanations of and examples on—among others—executive summary abstracts, short reports, title choices, an outline table, documentation, bibliographies, and editing procedure. Many other topics lauded by users of the previous edition are retained.
3. Oral communications—new and revised topics—occupies three chapters instead of two. One now includes various kinds of speeches plus specific suggestions on delivery, physical behavior, and vocal qualities; also listening—the common faults, desirable habits, and results. A new chapter on successful problem-solving meetings focuses on both leaders and participants. A third chapter features interviews—especially the employment interviewer's responsibilities; extended uses of modern electronic telephone equipment; and dictation methods. In addition, the book stresses that the 7-C principles, preparatory steps, and organizational plans apply also to oral messages.
4. A unique feature is the exceptionally thorough updated coverage on job application letters, résumés, interviews, follow-up messages, and legal aspects—in Chapters 12, 13, 21, and Appendix A. The wealth of options and specific aids are useful not only to graduates but also to experienced managers.
5. Three new chapters emphasize modern office technology, communication on social issues, and intercultural concerns—all matters increasingly important for the effective business communicator.
6. For increased emphasis on integrity and ethics, we have added new material, examples, and student exercises.
7. Recent cost figures on business letters, Mailgrams, telegrams, long-distance phone calls, E-COM mail, and losses on inadequately addressed mail help impress on students the importance of effective oral and written communications.
8. Discussion on "nonsexist expressions" has been broadened to "nondiscriminatory," including race, ethnic origin, and physical features—in keeping with laws.
9. To allow space for the new materials, several long chapters on letters have been condensed cautiously without sacrificing overall content.
10. Wherever desirable, all subject matter has been updated or revised. Though examples and exercises are based on actual business situations, most names, addresses, figures, and products mentioned in them have been changed—to protect anonymity.

Plan of Organization

This 24-chapter text begins with six background-for-communicating chapters, which constitute Part One. They introduce you to the importance, process, "C" principles, planning steps, deductive and inductive organization, costs, and media of written and oral business communications.

In Part Two each of the four chapters presents letters and memos organized by a basic pattern—direct request, good news, bad news, or persuasive request. Included are inquiries, claims, recommendations, adjustments, credits, orders, favors, announcements, and transmittals.

Part Three, five chapters, includes written and oral special messages—about sales, solicited and unsolicited; job applications, interviews, follow-ups by applicants and employers; collections; goodwill. You will see how the four plans for organizing are adaptable to these messages, depending upon their purpose and circumstances.

Part Four consists of three expanded chapters on various short and long reports and proposals. They cover planning steps, research, organization, visual aids, essential parts, documentation, format, and qualities.

In Part Five three chapters on oral communications present specific suggestions for conferences, oral reporting, platform speaking, listening, interviewing, telephoning, instructing, and dictating.

Part Six, three chapters, focuses on significant concerns—modern office technology, social issues, intercultural communication.

Appendixes include a brief discussion on legal aspects, writing mechanics, style, and symbols for marking letters, memos, and reports.

Acknowledgments

To the countless persons who have made suggestions and contributions we are heartily grateful. Our sincere thanks go to the executives and staff members who have provided hundreds of illustrative materials from business and industry; to students who have brought examples from their employment and organizational experiences; and to our American Business Communication Association colleagues, whose ideas, preferences, research, and writings along with those of other scholars through the years have influenced the scope of this book by enriching our knowledge during our combined more than 60 years' teaching and other responsibilities in communication.

Among those deserving special acknowledgment and thanks are the conscientious reviewers who offered constructive comments on the previous edition or the manuscript for this edition: Professors William J. Buchholz, Bentley College; Fay Beth Gray, Arkansas State University; Donna Kienzler, Iowa State University; Roberta Passenant, Berkshire Community College; Muriel Rada, Metropolitan Technical Community College (Omaha); Otto W. Taylor, New York State University; Dona Vasa, University of Nebraska; Judy West, University of Tennessee, Chattanooga.

Furthermore, we are thankful to the many instructors across the United States whose responses to our questionnaire gave helpful insights regarding their needs. Because courses necessarily vary in content and length, some topics that most instructors emphasize and value highly others must omit entirely. So we have tried to include in this comprehensive text as many useful materials as space allows for both basic and management-oriented courses.

To Professors Frank R. Jackle, American Graduate School of International Management, and Hilda Jones, Oregon State University, we express appreciation for their helpful, constructive opinions. Also we are grateful to four Cleveland State University professors—John E. Binnion, Bella G. Clinkscale, Kenneth R. Mayer, and Edward G. Thomas—who wrote challenging exercises for eight chapters. We thank as well three University of Washington colleagues: L. R. Goldberg for reviewing and improving the updated appendix on legal aspects; Virgil Harder for his suggestions; and Phyllis A. Needy, placement coordinator, for her views on current sensitive employment matters. We extend gratitude to Joanne Ripple, Shirley McCoy, and Robert Suh, University of Michigan, for their help in typing, editing, and research. Also, to the authors and companies that have given permission to quote from their publication and whose names are mentioned in footnotes, we express sincere thanks.

In appreciation of the thousands of students who have given reliable feedback about text content and assignments, we dedicate this revision to all its users who want to improve their oral and written communication ability.

Herta A. Murphy
Herbert W. Hildebrandt

Contents

PART FOUR   REPORTS

PART ONE
Background for Communicating

CHAPTER 1

Importance of Effective Communications in Business

If you can communicate effectively, orally and in writing, you have an important, highly valued skill. Executives of American business, industry, and government have repeatedly expressed their concern regarding the need for better communication. In numerous surveys business executives have ranked ability to communicate in first place among the personal factors necessary for promotion to and within management. And they have selected business communication as one of the most useful college studies in their work.

This chapter includes answers to the following questions regarding the importance of effective communication in business:

Why is effective communication the ''life blood'' of every organization?

How can it help you in your career and personal life?

What is the volume and cost of written business communication in the United States?

How can you meet the challenges of communicating for business?

''LIFE BLOOD'' OF EVERY ORGANIZATION

So important is communication that without it an organization cannot function. An organization is a group of people associated for business, political, professional, religious, athletic, social, or other purpose. Its activities require human beings to interact, react—communicate. They exchange information, ideas, plans; order needed supplies; make decisions, rules, proposals, contracts, agreements.

Because this book is concerned primarily with effective *business* communication, the discussions and illustrations you will read focus mainly on business messages. However, you can apply them also to other organizations, to the professions, and your personal communications.

Both within and outside the organization, effective business communication—oral and written—is its life blood.

Internal Communication

A vital means of attending successfully to matters of company concern is through effective *internal* communication—''downward,'' ''upward,'' and ''horizontal.'' It helps increase job satisfaction, safety, productivity, and profits as well as decrease absenteeism, grievances, and turnover.

Communicating Downward

When employees receive appropriate downward communication from management, they can be better motivated and more efficient. Furthermore, in some organizations—aviation, construction, medical, mining, oil drilling, others—inadequate instructions can result in loss of life and of millions of dollars.

Employees need and want not only clear job directions and safety rules, but also information about their companies. They desire facts about organizational goals, policies, and products and viewpoints on important controversial issues. They are concerned about relevant management and government regulations affecting employee benefits—health care, insurance, promotions, pensions, training, work environment, retirement. In all, the many pressures from employees force employers to be accountable for their decisions through effective downward communication.

Communicating Upward

Likewise, upward internal communication has become increasingly more significant. Many executives sincerely seek frank comments from employees—in addition to the usual periodic and progress reports. They listen more closely to opinions, complaints, problems, suggestions—especially when these are clearly and effectively stated. By recognizing employee needs and attitudes, a good company communication program can significantly help satisfy basic human wants and achieve favorable results.

Communicating with Peers

In organizations ranging from two to thousands of employees effective horizontal communication between peers is also essential. They must exchange ideas to help solve problems, perform job duties, prepare for meetings, and cooperate on important projects.

External Communication

Messages to persons outside the company can have a far-reaching effect on its reputation and ultimate success. The right letter, proposal, report, telephone call, or personal conversation can win back a disgruntled customer, create a desire for a firm's product or service, help negotiate a profitable sale, encourage collections, motivate performance, and in general create goodwill.

Furthermore, communications to the *public* regarding social accountability have become significantly more important during the past two decades.

Because of demands by many special interest groups (labor unions, environmentalists, government agencies, the press) reputable American organizations are seriously concerned about enhancing their public image. Important are well-planned public speeches by their executives, tactful replies to comments and criticisms from consumer groups, free informative pamphlets, annual reports, and interviews with news media. All these messages are transmitted with greater emphasis on honesty, openness, and concern for the public.[1]

In summary, effective communication within and outside the organization can contribute in various ways to its life blood. Successful messages help to enhance goodwill, safety, productivity, profits, and public credibility.

BENEFITS IN YOUR CAREER AND PERSONAL LIFE

Your jobs, promotions, and professional reputation often depend upon the success or failure of your written and oral communication. Also you will find that ability to communicate effectively is a valuable help during many activities in your personal life.

A Valuable Job Requirement

Especially if your career requires mainly mental rather than manual labor, your progress will be strongly influenced by how effectively you communicate your knowledge, proposals, and ideas to others who need or should receive them.

Preference for communication skills is found in the job descriptions listed by numerous companies wishing to employ college graduates. For example, Dr. Francis W. Weeks, executive director of the American Business Communication Association,[2] found in a six-year study of job listings at the University of Illinois Coordinating Placement Office that 340 jobs in 30 fields required communication ability. Among the specific descriptions were requirements like these:

Must be able to communicate effectively with all levels of management.

---

[1] Vernon M. Buehler and Y. K. Shetty, "Managerial Response to Social Responsibility Challenge," *Academy of Management Journal,* **19** (1): 66–78, March 1976; *Corporate Social Reporting in the United States and Western Europe:* U.S. Department of Commerce, Washington, D.C., 1979); Sandra L. Holmes, "Executives Should Be Seen and Heard," *Business Horizons,* April 1977, pp. 5–8; Rae Leaper, "CEO's of Nonprofit Organizations Agree: Communicate or Perish," *Journal of Organizational Communication,* **4**: 9, 1980; Gilda Parrella, "Are Newsletters Read? Are They Remembered? Are They Needed?," *Journal of Organizational Communication,* **9**: 26, 1980; John F. Steiner, "The Business Response to Public Distrust," *Business Horizons,* April 1977, pp. 74–81.

[2] The American Business Communication Association, organized in 1935, with its national office at the University of Illinois, Urbana, has members in major colleges and universities as well as in businesses across the United States and in 20 other countries.

Must have substantial experience and/or training in oral and written presentations and must demonstrate good writing skills.

Will prepare special analyses, research reports, and proposals.

Needs ability to compose effective correspondence.

Must have ability to communicate and "sell" ideas.

Must be able to cultivate and maintain good customer relationships.

Needs skills in gathering, analyzing, and interpreting data and in writing analytical reports.[3]

Job and career opportunities in which effective communication is the *main* responsibility are available in various areas, such as customer relations, labor relations, marketing, personnel, public relations, sales, teaching. Also, technical fields need editors, producers, researchers, and writers. Advancement can be made to management, research, training, and consulting positions. Furthermore, new job positions are being established in public offices. In demand are people who can work specifically on written communications and eliminate foggy "double-talk" from government reports.

Even if your work is mainly with figures, as in the accounting profession, the ability to communicate to those who read your financial reports is essential. The *Journal of Accountancy,* by an experiment cited in *Horizons for a Profession,* emphasized to the profession the importance of writing. A group of accountants who were considered "the most knowledgeable and forward looking segment of the accounting profession" ranked 53 subjects that a beginning CPA should be familiar with. First place went undisputedly to written and oral English—even over accounting theory and practice.[4]

An Essential for Promotion

The prime requisite of a promotable executive is "ability to communicate." Notice it is the top rung of the ladder in Figure 1-1.[5] Too often those who cannot communicate effectively remain "buried" in lower, dead-end jobs. Members of management spend about 90 percent of their working days communicating—receiving and sending messages.

[3] Francis W. Weeks, "Communication Competencies Listed in Job Descriptions," *The ABCA Bulletin,* September 1971, pp. 18–37, and December 1974, pp. 22–34.
[4] Betty Ann Stead, "Communication and the Accountant's Responsibility," *The Journal of Business Communication,* Spring 1977, p. 24; with citations from Editor's Notebook, "The CPA and the Second 'R,' " *The Journal of Accountancy,* November 1969, pp. 39–40, and Robert H. Roy and James H. MacNeill, *Horizons for a Profession,* American Institute of Certified Public Accountants, New York, 1967, pp. 14–15.
[5] John Fielden, "What Do You Mean I Can't Write?" *Harvard Business Review,* May–June 1964, pp. 144–145. Figure 1-1 adapted from original article.

Figure 1-1   Requisites for a promotable executive.

During the past 33 years, many surveys and articles have confirmed the statement that effective communication is essential for success and promotion in business. They have included, altogether, responses from thousands of executives and university business graduates across the United States. In answer to the question, ''What has been the most valuable subject you studied in college?'' such titles as Business Communications, Business Letter and Report Writing, and Written and Oral Expression were always listed among the top three. Respondents—including top, middle, and operations managers—have repeatedly asserted that business communication skills significantly influenced their advancement to executive positions.[6]

Do executives in the 1980s hold views similar to those expressed earlier? In a 1980–1982 survey of 2,819 persons newly promoted to vice president, president, or chairman of the board within the United States, respondents ranked Business Communication as their *first* choice among 13 curricular options preparing one for business leadership. These executives came from six major industry groups, including businesses under 10 million to over 10 billion gross operating revenue.[7]

As a trainee on a new job, you have opportunities to discuss problems with coworkers and to submit memos, reports, and letters that test your ability to communicate clearly and quickly. A frequent complaint of managers is the inability of college graduates to make themselves heard, read, or understood. Your messages can reveal how well you are doing a job. And they help management to evaluate your fitness for a substantial promotion. For example, imagine that you are one of several highly trained employees in an organization that requires everyone to submit frequent reports to clients or company personnel. If there is an opening for promotion and you each rate about the same except that you alone can write effective reports, then clearly you have the advantage over the others. One alumna who had five promotions in five years

[6] The following is a representative list of references: William Arthur Allee, "A Study of the Graduates of the College of Commerce. State University of Iowa, 1921–1951," Ph.D. dissertation, Iowa City, 1951; James C. Bennett, "The Communication Needs of Business Executives," *The ABCA Journal of Business Communication,* Spring 1971, pp. 5–11; Garda W. Bowman, "What Helps or Harms Promotability," *Harvard Business Review,* Jan.–Feb. 1964; William P. Carr, "An Evaluation of Accounting Curriculum Subjects" (Loyola University of the South, New Orleans), *Collegiate News and Views,* October 1952, pp. 5–10; Homer Cox, "The Voices of Experience: The Business Communication Alumnus Reports," *The Journal of Business Communication,* Summer 1976, pp. 35–46; Samuel D. Deep, *Human Relations in Management,* Glencoe Publishing Co., Encino, Calif., 1978, Chapter 1; H. C. Edgeworth, "Business Communication and Colleges of Business," *The ABCA Bulletin,* September 1978, pp. 34–36; William Grogg, "The Importance of Business Writing to the Student—A Businessman's Viewpoint," *The ABCA Bulletin,* June 1972, pp. 1–5; J. M. Hunter, Anthony Koo, and R. F. Voertman, "What Happens to Our Economics Majors" (Michigan State University, East Lansing), *Collegiate News and Views,* March 1954, pp. 11–13; R. R. Kay, "To Manage You Must Communicate," *Iron Age,* July 15, 1965, p. 55; Raymond V. Lesikar, *A Summary of Needs of Education for Small Business Based on a 1959 Survey of Louisiana Businessmen,* Louisiana State University Press, Baton Rouge, 1959; Charles E. Peck, "Survey of Curriculum Opinions of Business Administration," *University of Washington Business Review,* Seattle, 1958; Bill Rainey, "Professors and Executives Appraise Business Communication Education," *The ABCA Journal of Business Communication,* Summer 1972; C. Wilson Randle, "How to Identify Promotable Executives," *Harvard Business Review,* May–June 1956, pp. 122–124; Rollin H. Simonds, "Skills Businessmen Use the Most," *Nation's Business,* November 1960; J. B. Steinbruegee, T. J. Hailstones, and E. E. Roberts, "Personnel Managers Evaluate a College Business Program" (Xavier University, Cincinnati), *Collegiate News and Views,* May 1955, pp. 7–11; Stella Travaek, *An Opinion Report of the College of Business Administration, The University of Texas, 1917–1954,* Bureau of Business Research, University of Texas, Austin, 1954; Clarence E. Vincent, "Personnel Executives Examine the College Graduate," *Collegiate News and Views,* March 1966, pp. 12–16.

[7] H. W. Hildebrandt and others, "An Executive Appraisal of Courses Which Best Prepare One for General Management," *The ABCA Journal of Business Communication,* vol. 19, no. 1, Winter 1982, pp. 5–15.

emphasized that her success was based on her ability to prepare concise reports for senior management.

A Help for Meeting Personal Responsibilities

Effective communication—written and spoken—also helps you to better accomplish various aims in your personal activities. You will sometimes need to write letters, proposals, or reports or to present your views orally as committee chairperson, club officer, or private citizen. In these roles you might communicate with public officials; business, industrial, or professional people; or personal friends. Whatever your purposes, you will usually achieve them more effectively when you apply the same skills that help you communicate effectively in business.

Additional benefits that enthusiastic students of business communication have gained are better grades in some of their other college courses that require analytical problem solving and high-quality, well-organized reports.

VOLUME AND COST OF WRITTEN BUSINESS COMMUNICATION IN THE UNITED STATES

How many billions of dollars do United States businesses spend on communications? No one knows for sure, but the amount is enormous. Thousands of hours are devoted daily to interviews, conferences, memos, reports, employee manuals, letters, advertising, news articles, bulletins, and other messages.

The following discussion is intended to give you a general idea of factors affecting overall costs, estimates on one phase of communication—business letters, and possible savings by improvements.

Elements in Overall Costs

Time is the chief element in overall cost of written and oral communications. They require time of executives and assistants for researching, thinking, planning, dictating, typing, editing, revising, mailing (the written), presenting (the oral), and filing records. Among other costs are: materials (stationery, office supplies, postage) and fixed charges (heat, rent, light, depreciation, etc.). These elements likewise affect overall costs to the recipients who read or listen and respond to the messages they receive.

Still another significant fact to be considered is the wasteful cost of unclear, incomplete, inaccurate, inconsiderate, and unduly long or late communications. Poor messages are, indirectly, more expensive because they destroy goodwill, waste time, and alienate customers. Often they require several additional messages, though one message should have accomplished the desired result.

Furthermore, even one wrong important figure uncorrected in a proposal can cause the bidder to lose a contract or all profit on a project. In some industries incomplete instructions can cause loss of lives. Other communication inefficiencies may necessitate irritating, costly time lags, idleness of expensive equipment, or use of higher-paid employees than desirable for routine tasks.

Estimates on Business Letters in First-Class Mail

The Assistant Postmaster General's office, Washington, D.C., has reported:

> Americans sent 113 billion pieces of mail in 1982. Approximately 83% of the mail—93.8 billion pieces—originated in business offices and another 11% was mail individuals sent to businesses. Thus 94% of all mail was business-related. Of the total volume about 55% was first-class mail in 1982.[8]

Though totals may be different in the year when you are reading this book, these figures provide a basis for estimates. About 51.6 billion pieces of the first-class mail came from business offices in 1982. How much did these messages cost? The following figures are for letters only. (Some of those first-class envelopes may have contained other enclosures, but letters almost always accompany enclosures.) According to the Dartnell Institute of Business Research, the 1982 cost of a face-to-face dictated typewritten ''average'' business letter was $7.11. For an ''average'' letter transcribed from dictation equipment the cost was about $5.33. These costs are significantly higher than in previous years.[9]

Some cost consultants have asserted—after considering stopwatch timings, misuse of expensive machines, and the other elements mentioned above for overall costs—that too many business and government letters cost more than $20 each.

To get a conservative estimate on total annual cost of individually dictated business *letters* sent by *first-class* mail in the United States in 1982, we can multiply 51.6 billion by the Dartnell $7.11 average. The result is a staggering $366.8 billion total in one year.

Possible Savings by Improvements

If these $366.8 billion business letter costs were decreased even 10 percent because of improvements in message preparation and content, American busi-

---

[8] Figures courtesy of Barbara Moldauer, media relations officer, and Mary J. Layton, assistant postmaster general for public and employee communications, U.S. Postal Service, Washington, D.C. 20260-3100, January 1982.

[9] Costs of the average face-to-face dictated business letter climbed from 30 cents in 1930 to $3.31 in 1973, to $6.63 in 1981. (Of the secretaries surveyed in 1981, 77 percent reported taking face-to-face dictation at one time or another.) Costs of an average business letter using machine dictation rose ·from $4.47 in 1978 to $4.98 in 1981. Figures from *Dartnell Target Survey,* 1978, 1981, 1982, courtesy of The Dartnell Institute of Business Research, The Dartnell Corporation, Chicago.

ness could devote an estimated $36.68 billion annually to other productive services. The savings could benefit the companies, employees, customers, and ·general public.

We must realize too that the foregoing total estimates are for only business *letters* sent by *first*-class mail. Huge quantities of duplicated and printed messages are mailed by second-, third-, or fourth-class mail. Many documents are also sent by Express Mail and in ways other than by the U.S. Postal Service. In addition, memos and reports *within* companies and government offices are delivered by their own internal services.

Even greater savings could result from improvements in all these messages. Complex reports and proposals, which sometimes contain hundreds of pages, usually require more time for the elements listed under ". . . Overall Costs," pages 10 and 11. Here's one example of enormous volume: In 1982 when lawyers for one international United States company completed their paperwork complaining about certain price problems, they unloaded 400 cartons on the Federal Trade Commission dock in *one day!*

Many firms and government offices that have communication improvement programs report significant savings. For example, Mutual of New York reported saving an estimated $85,000 a year for 10 years by reducing both the number and length of letters written. (This report was made when average cost of a letter was only $2.32; savings could be proportionately greater in years when costs are higher.) A federal commission report to Congress regarding paperwork stated that for every $1,000 the federal government spent on correspondence management, it saved $32,000 in net operating expense. As discussed in Chapter 22, modern technology can also help considerably.

THE CHALLENGE OF COMMUNICATING FOR BUSINESS

Because communication plays such a major role in the operation of a firm and in possible promotion for the individual, communicating for business should be a challenge meriting your best efforts. Like any other worthwhile activity, the quality of communication is affected by the individual's attitude and preparation.

Developing the Right Attitude

The "personality" or image of your company is an extension of many individual personalities. You are one of these important personalities, whether you are an executive or a new clerk responsible for merely minor routine messages. With the right attitude, you—as well as other communicators—have opportunities to build goodwill and get favorable responses.

Help Your Company Image

Ask yourself if your company's image is a little better because of you. Some communications are so important to a firm that they can win thousands or even millions of dollars worth of business or goodwill. If you were working on such a message (for a letter, report, speech, or crucial interview), you would probably devote several hours—perhaps days or weeks—to your best thoughts, imagination, and planning. But what about the other messages—especially the minor, routine kind that you will handle daily? They may not be individually worth a million dollars, but each is part of the life blood of your organization. Each is an opportunity to build goodwill. Furthermore, such messages might lead to major business transactions. Collectively, the effect of thousands of routine messages is far-reaching.

"To the customer, you are the company," is good advice that public relations officials often give to their employees. AT&T's board chairman forcefully expressed this view when he urged all the firm's employees to be responsive to their customers' needs and concerns:

> If you were to sit at my desk and read and answer the mail I get about telephone service, you'd come to realize, if you don't already, how much "little things" mean; how sometimes lifelong impressions of the character of our business are formed on the basis of a single contact with just one employee. Rather significant, I'd say, when you consider that the Bell System employs more than a million men and women. . . .

> The key element in all the letters . . . I get is how the customer was treated by an employee of the company. . . . Intermixed with complaints are a goodly number of commendation letters . . . about how an employee treated the customer in a manner so unusually satisfying that the customer felt compelled to write to me about it.[10]

Be Enthusiastic and Capable

Doing an honest job enthusiastically and competently helps both the doer and the receiver. Answering even routine inquiries should and can be an interesting challenge. For example, an insurance company correspondent may often receive similar questions from policyholders who have lost their insurance policies. Instead of responding with an abrupt, impersonal, boring, routine-sounding message, the correspondent needs a different outlook. Though lost policy cases are familiar to him or her, they certainly are not routine to the reader. Thus the better approach is to send a personalized, helpful message considerate of the reader's viewpoint.

If you catch yourself sending stale, repetitive messages, try a new—and in

---

[10] John D. deButts, "When We Tell Customers, 'We Hear You,' We'd Better Be Listening," *Bell Telephone Magazine*, September–October 1973.

many cases a more personal—approach. Like any other job, written and oral communication can be more successful when the individual develops the right attitude.

Preparing Adequately

Most individuals can learn to communicate effectively for business if they desire to do so and are willing to devote whatever effort is necessary to prepare themselves adequately.

In addition to the right goodwill-building attitude, the following requisites are desirable:

Intelligent, sound judgment when choosing ideas and facts for each message.

Patience and understanding—even with unjustly insulting persons.

Integrity, backed up by a valid code of ethics.

Reasonable facility with the English language.

Applied knowledge of the communication process, principles, and successful methods for sending and receiving messages.

SUMMARY

Effective business communication is the life blood of every organization in its internal messages to and with employees as well as in its external contacts with customers, suppliers, and the public. It is also a key to success in your career and a help in your personal life. The volume and costs of business communications are great; so are challenges and opportunities for those with right attitudes and preparation. When you diligently apply the basics of effective business communications with common sense, you can continue to improve your communication ability.

In the following chapters and appendixes, you will study various principles, techniques, examples, cautions, and typical business communication situations. Your communications will involve thinking, analyzing, solving problems, gathering facts, planning, and organizing messages according to acceptable contemporary procedures for effective business communication. Through these experiences you should gain a better understanding of people, learn how to win favorable responses from them, and make friends for your company. The background provided should give you the confidence to tackle almost any task you might face when writing letters, memos, proposals, or reports and when communicating orally.

CHAPTER 2
The Process of Communication and Miscommunication

Communication is a process of transmitting a message so that the recipient understands it. The communication is considered effective when it achieves the desired reaction or response from the recipient. Simply stated, communication is a two-way process of exchanging ideas or information between human beings.

In actual practice, however, the communication process is not simple. It involves more than sender——message——receiver. Sometimes quite complex and imperfect, it malfunctions easily and may result in miscommunication. This chapter includes a brief overview of communication elements, concepts, and problems regarding verbal and nonverbal communication. The information presented is adapted from various studies in such fields as psychology, sociology, semantics, communications, and human relations.

ELEMENTS OF COMMUNICATION

The process of communication involves five elements or factors:

- Sender/encoder
- Message
- Channel/medium
- Receiver(s)/decoder(s)
- Feedback

The model in Figure 2-1 illustrates partly how these factors interact in the communication process, affected by various conditions and decisions.

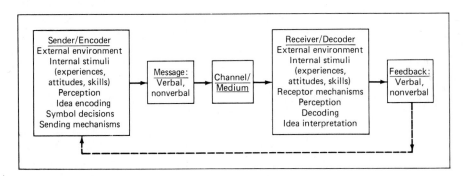

Figure 2-1   A communication model.

Role of Sender/Encoder

When you send a message, you are the writer or speaker, depending upon whether your communication is written or oral. You are likewise the "encoder." You try to choose symbols—usually words—that will correctly, tactfully express your message so the receiver(s) will understand it and react with the response you desire. Both external and internal stimuli affect message encoding and sending.

First, an external stimulus prompts you to send a message. Perhaps the stimulus is a business transaction, a written question, a meeting, a past-due bill, or an unexpected favor. As you think of ideas for the message, you react also to various conditions in the external environment—physical surroundings, weather, noise, discomforts, cultural customs, and others.

Next, internal stimuli have a complex influence on how you translate ideas into a message. When you encode, your choice of symbols is affected by your own world of experience—mental, physical, psychological, semantic. Attitudes, opinions, biases, emotions, past experiences, and communication skills influence the way you communicate your ideas. Also especially important are your perception of and consideration for the receiver's viewpoint. In all, you decide which symbols best convey your message and which sending mechanism to choose among the available written and oral media.

Message

The message consists of both *verbal* (written or spoken) *symbols* and *nonverbal symbols* to convey ideas from the sender to the receiver(s). Examples are discussed later in this chapter and others.

Whenever you compose a message, you need to consider what content to include, how the receiver(s) will interpret it, and how it may affect your relationships. A simple "thank you" message will be relatively easy. In contrast, to inform 200 employees of bad news about salaries or to bid on a $30 million industrial building will require much more complicated, carefully planned messages.

Channel and Medium

How will you send your message? Should it be communicated through a written channel—by word or graphic symbols on paper, or through an oral channel—by oral words through the medium of sound?

Like message content, the choice of channel and medium is influenced by interrelationship of sender and receiver. If your message requires an immediate answer or if it contains bad news for the receiver, an oral channel may be the better choice. But if the message contains complicated details and figures or if its subject requires filing for future reference, a written communication is necessary. Furthermore, whether your message receiver is inside or outside your organization affects your choice not only of channel but also of medium.

Inside Your Organization

For internal communication, written media may be memos, reports, bulletins, job descriptions, posters, notes in pay envelopes, or employee manuals. Oral communication may be by staff meeting reports, face-to-face discussions, speeches, audio tapes, telephone chats, or teleconferences. Another oral channel, though unplanned by the sender, is the "grapevine," through which news and rumors often travel quickly—sometimes accurately, sometimes inaccurately.

Outside Your Organization

External written communication media may be letters, reports, proposals, telegrams, cablegrams, Mailgrams, postcards, contracts, ads, brochures, catalogs, news releases. You may also communicate orally—face-to-face, by telephone, or by speeches in solo or panel situations—personally before groups or via teleconferences, video conferences, or TV.

Receiver(s)/Decoder(s)

The message receiver is your reader or listener—also the decoder. Some messages, of course, may be directed to many readers or listeners.

As Figure 2-1 indicates, the receiver(s) as well as the sender are influenced by external environment and internal stimuli. They receive messages through eyes and ears (sometimes through touch) and decode according to their experiences. A problem is that all of us do not have identical experiences with the subject or the symbols a sender uses. Attitudes, abilities, opinions, communication skills, and cultural customs vary. Hence, misinterpretations occur; personal biases intervene, as each receiver through his or her recepter mechanisms perceives the intended meaning of the sender's idea.

Ultimately the receiver reacts, either with a response based on clear interpretation of the symbols or an incorrect response because of miscommunication.

Feedback

Most often we expect responses—oral or written feedback—to our sent messages. What we receive may be a "yes" or "no," a request for further clarification, an undesirable decision, or a detailed, helpful report. If the receiver incorrectly perceived (decoded) our message, we have miscommunicated. The success or failure of the communication is indicated by the feedback we get.

SOME GENERAL COMMUNICATION CONCEPTS AND PROBLEMS

No two people in the world are alike mentally, physically, or emotionally. Thus the innumerable human differences plus cultural, social, and environmental differences may cause problems in conveying the intended messages.

Each person's mind is a unique filter. What is already in this mental filter affects the meanings a person places on messages and, to some extent, determines the new ideas the person chooses to accept or reject. Communication difficulties are more likely to occur when the communicators' filters are sharply different. The message sender's meanings and the receiver's response are affected in numerous ways. Among them are their:

Interpretations of words

Perceptions of reality

Attitudes, opinions, and emotions

The consequences of miscommunication may range from mild or humorous to extremely serious and costly, as revealed in the following examples and suggestions for improvement.

Interpretations of Words

A fundamental general communication principle is that the symbols the sender uses to communicate messages must have essentially the same meaning in both the sender's and the receiver's minds. If the symbols are misunderstood or misinterpreted, miscommunication results.

Another basic truth is that meanings are in people. The knowledge a person already has in mind regarding any given subject affects the meaning placed on words. Different word interpretations are often especially noticeable in *"bypassed" instructions* and in reactions to *denotations, connotations, and euphemisms.*

"Bypassed" Instructions

When the message sender and receiver attribute different meanings to the same words or use different words though intending the same meanings, bypassing often occurs. Many words have several dictionary definitions; a few have over 100. For example, in one abridged dictionary the little word *run* has 71 meanings as a verb, another 35 as a noun, and 4 more as an adjective. Moreover, for some words people have their own unique meanings which are not in a dictionary. Thus, confusion sometimes arises easily, as these incidents illustrate:

1. An office manager handed to a new assistant one letter with the instruction, "Take it to our stockroom and burn it." In the office manager's mind (and in the firm's jargon) the word "burn" meant to make a copy on a company machine which operated by a heat process. As the letter was extremely important, she wanted an extra copy. However, the puzzled new employee, afraid to ask questions, burned the letter with a lighted match and thus destroyed the only existing copy!

2. An equipment supervisor told a new night-duty employee, "You'll have to crack all the valves before you clean the settling tank." The next morning the supervisor found a floor full of smashed castings. "Crack" to the supervisor meant opening each valve just enough to allow minimum flow. You may be surprised that the supervisor was discharged because of the inadequate instructions that resulted in costly miscommunication.

3. A superintendent (John) said to Tim, a maintenance worker, "Plant 2 is having trouble with its automatic control. Whatever the trouble is, go out there and get rid of it." The next day, after receiving angry complaints from Plant 2, John berated Tim for yanking out completely and discarding the entire control unit and installing a new one, even though Plant 2 had purchased the original unit only five months before. The company had a new, rigid cost-cutting program with rules to repair, rather than replace, all salvageable equipment whenever possible. But John had failed to inform Tim of that rule. Thus Tim thought that because the control unit was causing the trouble, that's what he should "get rid of." John had wrongly assumed that his instructions were clear, but Tim's meaning was entirely different from John's.

Bypassing occurs not only in business and industrial offices but also among government officials, professionals, and all of us in our everyday contacts. To avoid communication errors of bypassing when you give instructions or discuss issues, be sure to ask yourself whether the words and sentence structure you are using will convey the intended meaning to the recipient. What that person thinks the message means is of crucial importance, regardless of what you think it should mean. Also, when you are the recipient of unclear instructions, before acting on them, ask questions to determine the sender's intended meaning.

Reactions to Denotations, Connotations, and Euphemisms

Almost everyone has at some time been surprised that a remark intended as a compliment, matter-of-fact statement, or joke was interpreted by the receiver as an insult. A statement intended as a good deed can be distorted into something evil or self-serving. Some of these communication problems may occur because words have both denotative and connotative meanings, and the sender has not been thoughtful of the receiver's probable interpretations and reactions.

Denotations. The denotative meaning is the literal word meaning on which most individuals will probably agree. It informs the receiver, and it names objects, people, or events without indicating positive or negative qualities. Such words as *car, desk, book, house, water* convey denotative meanings (provided, of course, the communicators understand the English language).

Connotations. In addition to the literal denotative meanings, connotations arouse qualitative judgments and personal reactions. The term *meeting room* is denotative. *Director's lounge, executive suite, rickety firetrap, rat-filled joint*— though they each denote a meeting place—also have connotative meanings. The word *student* is denotative; *book worm, scholar, dropout, school dummy* are connotative. They tell how the sender evaluates the subject. Some words— such as *efficient, gentle, prompt*—usually have only favorable connotations. Others—such as *lazy, cowardly, rotten, delinquent*—usually have only unfavorable connotations. Some words have favorable connotations in some contexts, but unfavorable meanings in other instances. Compare, for example, *fat check* and *fat girl; free enterprise* and *free* (rude, bold) *manners; sucker* (customer) and *sucker* (candy); *cheap product* and *cheap price.* In common usage, words which usually have opposite meanings can sometimes have the same meaning, as in the two expressions *slim chance* and *fat chance.*

The connotative meanings for words and labels are also affected by the communicators' different backgrounds and interests. Words such as *amnesty, unions, generation gap, speed, grass, hippies, gay, fair wages, women's liberation* may arouse mixed feelings and arguments, depending on people's associations with them.[1]

Euphemisms. Tactful writers and speakers use euphemisms whenever possible to replace words that might have blunt, painful, lowly, or distasteful connotations. Euphemisms are mild, innovative expressions with which most people do not have negative associations.

Expressions like the following have obvious connotative advantages: *maintenance worker* or *staff member* instead of *janitor; slender* instead of *skinny; Salisbury steak* or *hamburger* instead of *choice ground dead steer.* Instead of saying an employee was *fired* a communicator may use such euphemisms as *laid off, terminated,* or *victim of reorganization* or *staff cutbacks.*

Euphemisms and any expressions that have pleasant associations for the recipients are especially helpful in advertising and selling. Usually, mass-produced consumer items—like soap, lotions, toothpaste, soft drinks—have similar functions and ingredients though made by different manufacturers. Advertisers then market their products by associating them with pleasant experiences the users will gain—popularity at social functions, physical at-

---

[1] For additional examples of connotations, see also the discussion on "slanting" in this chapter and "nondiscriminatory expressions" in Chap. 4.

tractiveness, enjoyment at sports events, etc. Advertising slogans or labels can help make or break a product's effectiveness. For example:

> One basically sound product—a vibrating mattress, which could have been a great help to sufferers of insomnia and industrial fatigue—failed mainly because the advertisements stressed, "Shake yourself to sleep." The connotation of the word *shake* was the deathblow to the marketing effort.

To communicate effectively you need to be aware of the usual connotative meanings of various terms and also to realize that some people may have their own unique meanings because of their experiences and background. Thus, choose your words carefully, considering both their connotations and their denotations to convey the idea you want and to achieve the desired results. Whenever possible, choose words with positive (favorable) rather than negative connotations.

Perceptions of Reality

The world of reality is complex, infinite, and continually changing. Also, human beings' sensory perceptions—touch, sight, hearing, smell, taste—are limited and each person's mental filter is unique. Therefore, people perceive reality in many different ways. Our statements about an object, event, or person are necessarily incomplete—and sometimes also inaccurate. We make various kinds of *abstractions, inferences,* and *evaluations*.

Abstracting

The process of focusing on some details and omitting others is *abstracting*. In countless instances, abstracting is necessary and desirable—for both written and oral communication. However, the alert, honest communicator should also be cautious about at least two semantic traps of abstracting—the "allness" fallacy and "slanted" statements.

Justifiable Abstracts. Whether you write a memo, letter, or report, or converse by telephone, you will be limited somewhat by time, expense, space, and/or purpose. You will need to select—honestly—facts that are pertinent to accomplish your purpose and to omit the rest (as you do, for example, in a one-page job application letter about yourself). Also, when preparing a business report you may—after gathering perhaps a "mountain" of data—have to abstract and condense it into a "molehill."

The chapter you are now reading is also necessarily an abstract; it condenses into these few pages some highlights of numerous studies relating to communication and miscommunication.[2]

You, as the communicator, must also anticipate the likelihood that others may not be abstracting as you are. Their points may be as important as yours though they select differently from the infinite details in reality. For example:

> When reporting on an event—a firm's new-store dedication ceremony, a factory explosion and fire, a football game, a traffic accident—no two witnesses give *exactly* the same descriptions. Their knowledge and backgrounds affect what they perceive. The participants will have a different view than the observers, and all those within each group will perceive different details or parts, though some parts of the whole may be mentioned by all or several observers.

Differences in abstracting occur not only when persons describe events but also when they describe objects, animals, projects, people. No two people perceive reality exactly the same way or choose exactly the same points when they abstract.

"Allness" Fallacy. We should not yield to the *allness fallacy*—the attitude that what we know or say about something or someone is all there is to know or say. The more we delve into some subjects, the more we realize there is so much more to learn and to consider. Semanticists suggest that we at least mentally add "etc." to remind us that statements are incomplete and to keep from making incorrect, unfounded judgments.

Even authorities on certain subjects humbly admit they don't know all the answers. Though they sometimes disagree among themselves on various topics, they continue to study all available facts. So do conscientious, open-

---

[2] If you wish to read more details about communication and human relations, semantics, processes of speaking, listening, writing, reading, or group dynamics, you might begin with the following books plus any bibliographies they contain: Kurt Baldinger, *Semantic Theory,* St. Martin's, New York, 1980; Ernest Bormann, *Communication Theory,* Holt, Rinehart & Winston, New York, 1980; David K. Berlo, *The Process of Communication: An Introduction,* Holt, Rinehart and Winston, New York, 1960; Richard W. Budd and Brent D. Ruben, *Approaches to Human Communication,* Hayden, Rochelle Park, N.J., 1972; James H. Campbell and Hal W. Hepler, *Dimensions in Communication: Readings,* Wadsworth, Belmont, Calif., 1970; Stuart Chase, *Power of Words,* Harcourt, Brace, New York, 1954; William V. Haney, *Communication and Organizational Behavior,* Irwin, Homewood, Ill., 1973 (comprehensive bibliography pp. 529–570); Thomas A. Harris, *I'm OK–You're OK,* Avon, New York, 1973; S. I. Hayakawa, *Through the Communication Barrier:* Harper & Row, New York, 1979; Richard C. Huseman, Cal M. Logue, and Dwight L. Freshley, *Readings in Interpersonal and Organizational Communication,* Holbrook, Boston, 1977; Wally D. Jacobson, *Power and Interpersonal Relations,* Wadsworth, Belmont, Calif., 1972; Alfred Korzybski, *Science and Sanity,* Institute of General Semantics, Lakeville, Conn., 1948; Irving J. Lee, *Handling Barriers in Communication,* Harper & Brothers, New York, 1957; Gail E. Myers and Michele T. Myers, *The Dynamics of Human Communication,* McGraw-Hill, New York, 1973; T. C. Pollock and J. G. Spaulding, *General Semantics: A Theory of Meaning Analyzed,* Institute of General Semantics, Lakeville, Conn., 1981.

minded business executives, government leaders, educators, scientists, and students.

Unfortunately, it is true of some people that "the less they know, the more sure they are that they know it all." Perhaps you have worked with such persons.

> A conspicuous example is that of the high school sophomore chatting casually with a man who (unknown to the student) was a distinguished scientist devoting his lifetime to studying botany. The smug sophomore commented, "Oh botany? I finished studying all about that stuff last semester." As Bertrand Russell stated, "One's certainty varies inversely with one's knowledge."

Thus, it is best for us to avoid assuming we know all about any subject or circumstances simply because we have a few facts. Otherwise we will have an inadequate, erroneous impression of the whole, as did the six blind men who each felt only one part of an elephant. The one who felt only the swinging tail thought an elephant was like a rope. The others' ideas of an elephant—based on the part they felt (shown here in parentheses)—were: a spear (its tusk), a wall (its broad side), a snake (its trunk), a tree (its knee), a fan (its ear).

"Slanted" Statements. Conscientious communicators—as both senders and receivers of messages—should try to determine whether the facts they are acquainted with are truly representative of the whole. Are they slanted with intentional bias and opinion? Slanting is unfair in factual reporting. The reporter should be careful to include quoted statements in context and exclude connotative expressions of personal approval or disapproval of the persons, objects, or occurrences being described. For example:

> The reporter is not permitted to write: "A small crowd of suckers came to hear Superintendent Jones yesterday noon in that rundown hotel that disfigures the central area." Instead, the write-up may state: "Between 100 and 150 people heard an address yesterday noon by Superintendent Jones in the auditorium at the Edgemont Hotel on Center Street."

Likewise, the voting secretary who writes minutes of meetings must be careful to avoid slanted reporting. To omit some items merely because they may seem less important or are contrary to the secretary's personal biases is both unfair and inaccurate. He or she must not allow personal preferences to influence perception and reporting.

Inferring

Every day most of us find it necessary to act on some inferences. We make assumptions and draw conclusions even though we ourselves do not (or cannot) directly see, hear, feel, taste, smell, or otherwise immediately verify the evidence. Statements that go beyond the facts our senses report and conclusions made by reasoning from evidence or premises are called *inferences.* Some inferences are both necessary and desirable; others are risky, even dangerous.

Necessary, Desirable Inferences. For business and professional persons inferences are essential and desirable in analyzing materials, solving problems, and planning procedures. Systems analysts, marketing specialists, advertisers, architects, engineers, designers, and numerous others all must work on various premises and make inferences after they have gathered as much factual data as possible. Even our legal procedures allow inferences from experts as acceptable evidence. However, when nonexperts attempt to argue on professional matters about which they have no facts, they—deservedly—get into communication troubles. Also, as consumers in our daily activities, we may make inferences that are necessary and usually fairly reliable.

> When we drop an airmail envelope into a mailbox, we infer it will be picked up, flown by plane(s), and ultimately delivered to our intended reader(s). We assume that the gas station attendant pumps gasoline (not water) into our car's tank, that the restaurant's kitchen is sufficiently sanitary (and free from poisons!), that the elevator in our building is capable of taking us to the desired floor, and so on.

When we base our inferences on direct observation or on reasonable evidence, they are likely to be quite dependable; but even so, there are disappointing exceptions. Conclusions we make about things we have not observed directly may be true or untrue.

Risks of Inferences. As intelligent communicators we must avoid faulty inferences. We must realize that inferences may be incorrect, unreliable, and the causes of miscommunication. We need to anticipate risks before acting on the bases of inferences.

> Suppose that a personnel manager notices that Sue Jones, a new management trainee, has been staying at least an hour after closing time every evening for the past two weeks. He might infer that Ms. Jones is exceptionally conscientious, that she is incapable of doing the required work within the regular time, that she has been given more responsibility than should be expected of a new trainee, or even that she is snooping around for confidential materials after others have left the office. Before acting on any of these inferences, the manager should get more facts!

In some industries executives may make a disastrous decision that ultimately causes loss of lives as well as money if they assume wrongly that an inference in a report is a verifiable fact.

On any job you do—for an employer or others—be sure to consider the bases of inferences. Inform those who may be acting on your inference what portions of your statements are mere assumptions. If you are presenting or receiving a report on which an important executive decision may rest, be especially careful to distinguish clearly among verifiable facts, inferences based on facts, and mere "guesstimates."

Making Frozen Evaluations

Another drawback to effective perception is the *frozen evaluation*—the stereotyped, static impression that ignores significant differences or changes. Stereotyping is often based on faulty generalization. To help assure that your comprehension of reality will be correct, you need to recognize that any person, product, or event

May be quite different from others in the general group

May have significant differences today when compared with characteristics yesterday or some time ago

May deserve more than a two-valued description

Individual Differences within Groups. In reality no two elements of a general group or classification are exactly alike. When people ignore significant individual differences and consider all parts of a group to be the same, they have formed a frozen—stereotyped and unfair—evaluation. Even manufactured assembly-line products differ under a microscope. Flashlight $\#F320_1$ is not exactly the same as $\#F320_2$ or $\#F320_{1020}$. Though you may have trouble with one F-brand flashlight, that does not necessarily mean all flashlights of that brand are also defective.

The same caution applies emphatically also to human beings. Some people adhere to their faulty stereotypes about all members of a group merely because of an experience with one member's promptness, honesty, or appearance. Such stereotyped generalizations—based merely on assumptions that all parts of a whole are alike—unjustly disregard important differences in individual characteristics.

Differences within Time Periods. Frozen evaluations are also made when people disregard the possible changes that may have occurred over a period of time. Everything and every person in the world changes. No one, no thing remains static; neither should our evaluations remain static.

Perhaps you've known a customer who asserts, "I'll never again buy any coat with the Realex label! The one I bought last year came apart at the seams." He or she should realize that (1) probably not all Realex coats last year ripped at the seams; Realex coat$_1$ is not exactly the same as Realex coat$_{10,500}$; also (2) Realex coats last year may not be the same as Realex coats this year or next year.

A customer's payment record this year is not necessarily exactly the same as last year. Nor can you be sure that a successful sales campaign this month will again be successful next month. Furthermore, though a certain area may have been ideal (or disappointing) for skiing the past several weeks, its weather may be quite different next week.

In all, we should remember to avoid frozen evaluations made on the basis of what was true at one time. Changes occur in products, people, laws, business conditions, organizations, environment, and so on.

Differences in Degree. The communication practice of making only a strict, two-valued, "either-or" evaluation may be a source of miscommunication. If communicators designate people, products, or statements as either good or bad, strong or weak, honest or dishonest, hard or soft, large or small, fast or slow, black or white, true or false, they may be *polarizing*. They are overlooking important areas in between the extremes. To be fair and accurate, communicators should be specific in each case, using details and figures whenever possible.

In short, to be discerning communicators, we must consider significant differences for a unit of any group—and also changes in any one unit during a period of time. We must ask *which* person, *which* product, *which* event, exactly *when* and *to what extent* any particular statement is true. This caution is useful for all communicators. It is also especially applicable for report writers, who must be able to identify their sources, dates, and specific details of important facts.

Influence of Attitudes and Opinions

Communication effectiveness is influenced also by the attitudes and opinions the communicators have in their mental filters. People tend to react favorably when the message they receive agrees with their views toward the information, the set of facts, and the sender. In addition, sometimes unrelated circumstances affect their attitudes, emotions, and responses.

Favorable or Unfavorable Information

The effective communicator should be considerate of the receivers and whenever possible emphasize—honestly—points they will regard as favorable or beneficial. Rejecting, distorting, and avoiding are three common undesirable, negative ways receivers react to information they consider unfavorable. For example:

> Suppose some employees perceive that a recently announced change in company policy is contrary to their beliefs or benefit. In reacting, they may reject or resent the company and/or their boss, perhaps falsely accusing them of being unfair. Or they may, instead, distort the meaning and misinterpret the true purpose of the policy change. Or they may avoid the message, situation, or people by putting off acceptance, hoping that the delay will somehow prevent the change and protect them.

Inadequate Information

Some individuals have a closed mind toward receiving new information, or their attitudes are based on an incorrect set of facts.

Closed Mind. The *closed-minded* person is one of the most difficult to communicate with. Typically, this person has only inadequate and mainly incorrect knowledge of the subject. Yet he or she refuses to consider any new facts, even from an expert who has made a long, careful study of the problem and the proposed change. The closed-minded person says in essence, "My mind is made up. Don't bother me with facts. I want what I want." Sometimes this type of individual goes a step further and before reading or hearing the documented facts—unjustly labels them or the sender's views as distorted, or calls the sender a liar. In all, closed-minded individuals stubbornly reject, distort, and/or avoid a viewpoint before they know the facts.

Sometimes there is hope for better communication if these adamant persons can be encouraged to state their reasons for rejecting a concept. They may reveal deep-rooted prejudices, opinions, and/or emotions. However, if they react only with anger and refuse both to give reasons as well as to consider the other person's facts, effective communication will be impossible. To settle such a dispute, the intervention of a mediator or even a court of law may be necessary.

A Set of Facts. Occasionally individuals react according to their attitude toward a set of facts, rather than to the facts themselves. For instance, a customer may be happy over an adjustment or a loan which a company extends, but angry when learning that a neighbor received a better deal for what the customer assumes (perhaps wrongly) to be the same circumstances. This person may have inadequate information.

Sender's Credibility

Often, people react more according to their attitude toward the *source* of facts than to the facts themselves. A staunch Democrat will be more likely to accept an idea from a fellow Democrat than the same idea from a Republican. A conservative executive may be less likely to accept statements from the "office grapevine" than from the department manager.

Stated positively, employees, customers, and people in general will react more favorably when a communicator has credibility—when they respect, trust, and believe in the communicator. Also, when an adult must present a disagreeable message to another adult, the recipient will usually be more open to suggestions and less defensive if the sender communicates on an adult-adult basis instead of like a critical parent to a child, for such communications often arouse negative responses.

Other Circumstances Affecting Attitudes, Emotions, Responses

When personal or business or environmental upsets occur, emotions and attitudes toward various messages may be adversely affected. Worry, anger, fear, despondency, hatred—even when due to circumstances entirely unrelated to the particular message, can adversely affect it. On a day when everything at home is wrong and disturbing, a person's written and oral communications at the office might sound unusually gruff, gloomy, or uncooperative. On the contrary, when everything is rosy in an individual's personal life, that person's business communications may also reflect this better emotional condition. In an emotionally charged situation, words must be chosen extremely carefully, for even one slip may trigger an emotional reaction and ruin the success of a message.

To be good communicators we must realize that people may react inconsistently when they are influenced by their emotions. We will have better communication when we catch people in the right frame of mind. Admittedly, it is often difficult or impossible to know just when is the best time. We need also to try not to allow our own personal emotions and sore spots to affect our attitudes and messages.

If you can predict the probable attitude, opinion, or prejudice the receiver already has about a certain matter or person, you can better focus your communication in ways to reduce tension and resistance. Also, if you are the receiver, try not to let your personal, biased viewpoints affect your perception of a message. Observe, read, and listen to various sources, because useful information may come from almost anyone.

When both sender and recipient are open-minded, each may find areas in which the other person is right, so that a compromise can be reached. In the words of an old Indian prayer, "Let me not criticize my neighbor until I have walked a mile in his moccasins."

NONVERBAL COMMUNICATION

The preceding sections about the communication process and problems focused mainly on *verbal* communication—by written or spoken symbols, usually *words*. As Figure 2-1 indicates, we also communicate *nonverbally*—*without words*. Sometimes nonverbal messages contradict the verbal; often they express true feelings more accurately than the spoken or written language.

During the past two decades numerous articles and books have been written on the importance of nonverbal messages. Some studies have found that from 60 to 93 percent of a message's overall effect comes from nonverbal cues. This section presents a brief general overview, in these broad categories:[3]

Appearance

Body language

Silence, time, and sounds

How Appearance Communicates

Appearance conveys nonverbal impressions that affect recipients' attitudes toward the verbal messages even before they read or hear them.

Effect on Written Messages

The envelope's overall appearance—size, color, weight, postage—may impress the receiver as important, routine, or "junk" mail. Telegrams, Mailgrams, and Express Mail also have distinctive envelopes that signal urgency and importance. Next, the letter communicates nonverbally even before its words are read. Important is appearance of its stationery and of its length, format, and typing. The enclosures—quantity and attractiveness (with or without charts, graphs, pictures)—also give significant nonverbal impressions.

Effect on Spoken Messages

Whether you are speaking to one person face to face or to a group in a meeting, personal appearance and appearance of the surroundings convey nonverbal stimuli that affect attitudes—even emotions—toward the spoken words. Communication success can be profoundly influenced.

---

[3] For further reading on nonverbal communication you might begin with these articles and books: D. Archer and M. Akert, "Words and Everything Else: Verbal and Nonverbal Cues in Social Interpretation," *Journal of Personality and Social Psychology*, **35:** 443-449, 1977; M. Argyle and J. Dean, "Eye Contact, Distance and Affiliation," *Sociometry*, **28:** 289-304, 1965; J. E. Baird, "Nonverbal Communication Can Be a Motivational Tool," *Personnel Journal*, September 1979, pp. 607-610; Ray L. Birdwhistell, *Kinesics and Context:* University of Pennsylvania Press, Philadelphia, 1970; Albert Mehrabian, *Nonverbal Communication:* Aldine-Atherton, Chicago, 1971; M. Bond and D. Sheraishi, "The Effect of Body Lean and Status of an Interviewer on Nonverbal Behavior," *International Journal of Psychology*, **9** (2): 117-128, 1974; Julius Fast, *Body Language:* M. Evans, New York, 1970; Edward T. Hall, *The Silent Language:* Doubleday, Garden City, N.Y., 1973; Mark L. Knapp, *Essentials of Nonverbal Communication:* Holt, Rinehart & Winston, New York, 1980; Michael Korda, *Power! How to Get It: How to Use It:* Random House, New York, 1975; Dale G. Leathers, *Nonverbal Communication Systems:* Allyn and Bacon, Boston, 1976; Pavel Machotka and John P. Spiegel, *Articulate Body:* Irvington, New York, 1980; Robert W. Rasberry, "A Collection of Nonverbal Communication Research: An Annotated Bibliography," *ABCA Journal of Business Communication*, **16** (4): pp. 21-29, Summer 1979.

Personal Appearance. Clothing, jewelry, hair styles, cosmetics, finger nails, neatness, stature are parts of personal appearance. They convey impressions regarding occupation, age, sex, nationality, social and economic level, job status, and good or poor judgment, depending upon the circumstances.

Appearance of Surroundings. These include room size, location, furnishings, machines, architecture, wall decorations, floor (carpeted or bare?), lighting, windows, view, and other related aspects wherever people communicate orally. How does appearance of surroundings affect attitudes toward and interpretation of spoken words?

Here is one example, among hundreds. Why will an executive or professional whose office is a luxurious top-floor suite with a panoramic view convey a different nonverbal message (about status, success, advice, size of bill) than if that same person's office were in a dingy, poorly lighted basement room?

In some factories and business firms, lower-status employees may work in small, crowded, unattractive areas. Without expressing their feelings in *words,* they may communicate nonverbally by their actions. Thoughtful managers can help improve morale and efficiency when they perceive employee attitudes toward appearance of surroundings and follow suggestions for improving appearance.

How Body Language Communicates

Included under this heading are: facial expressions, gestures and posture; smell; touch; voice. All are noticeable nonverbal communication symbols. Sometimes they are more meaningful than words, but always we must be careful when interpreting them.

Facial Expressions

The eyes and face are especially helpful means of communicating nonverbally. They can divulge hidden emotions—anger, annoyance, confusion, enthusiasm, fear, hatred, joy, love, interest, sorrow, surprise, uncertainty, and others. They can also contradict the verbal statements.

For instance, a new employee may answer "yes" hesitatingly, ashamed or embarrassed to tell the truth when asked if she or he understands the supervisor's oral instructions. Yet that employee's frown or red face and bewildered expression in the eyes should prompt the observant supervisor to consider restating the instructions more clearly.

Direct eye contact (but not icy staring) is usually desirable when two honest people converse face to face. The person whose eyes droop or shift away from the listener is thought to be shy or perhaps dishonest and untrust-worthy. But we must be careful not to overgeneralize! Because people differ, there are exceptions on individual nonverbal cues, as shown in the following example:

> Some folks assume, wrongly, that they can tell what individuals have been doing just by looking into their eyes. However, a person's eyes may be misty and red because he or she has been ill, or crying, laughing, lying, drinking heavily, smoking, sleeping, suffering from infection, walking in the wind, swimming, or working near harmful vapors.

Moral? Get more facts before judging anyone's facial expressions conclusively.

Gestures and Posture

Do actions speak louder than words? They do in some occupations, as well as in many interpersonal situations. Employees who direct traffic on crowded streets or in noisy stadiums, or guide huge trucks when backing up in narrow places, can effectively communicate by pointing arms or fingers in the desired directions—without uttering any words. And, of course, deaf people communicate silently by hand and finger movements.

Clenched fists pounding on a table or podium may indicate anger or emphasis. Continual gestures with arms while speaking may signal nervous-ness; they may also distract listeners' attention from the spoken words. Hand-shakes reveal attitudes (and sometimes handicaps) by their firmness or limpness, promptness, and movements.

Legs, too, communicate nonverbal messages. For instance, consider the possible attitudes of these people: a sitting man whose legs are stretched on top of his office desk during an interview; a quiet person with head bowed and knees on the floor; a standing person who shifts weight from one leg to another in a rhythmic motion while humming—or who paces back and forth while speaking.

Posture nonverbally conveys impressions of self-confidence, status, and interest. Confident executives may have a relaxed posture and yet stand more erect than a timid subordinate. Interested persons occasionally lean forward toward the speaker, while those who are bored or annoyed may slump—as well as yawn and repeatedly glance at their watches.

Smell and Touch

Various odors and artificial fragrances on human beings can sometimes convey emotions and feelings better than spoken words. (Some odors on equipment can indicate smoke, fire, decay, or dangerous leaks in containers or pipes, thus helping to save lives if detected early.)

Touching people in different ways (and places) can silently communicate friendship, love, approval, hatred, anger, or other motives and feelings. A kiss on the cheek, pat on the shoulder, or slap on the back are prompted by various attitudes and emotions. Also, ''touching'' in a crowded bus in which passengers are squeezed closely is offensive to many North Americans.

Voice

Perhaps you have heard people speak words that were pleasant but in a tone of voice that betrayed their true feelings? *Paralanguage* is a term denoting the subtle variations in meaning between *what* is said and *how* it is said.

> The words ''Wow! How prompt you are today!'' could be a compliment. But if the tone of voice is sarcastic and said to someone who arrived an hour late, the true meaning is criticism, perhaps anger.

You can also convey different meanings by the rate, pitch, and volume of your voice. Speaking fast may indicate nervousness or haste. A soft voice soothes and calms; a loud, shouting voice may foretell danger, urgency, a serious problem, joy, or anger. A sobbing or crying voice conveys sorrow or fear. Furthermore, by emphasizing different key words in a sentence you can purposely indicate your feelings about what is important, as in the following example:

> Consider the sentence ''Tom completed two reports.'' If you accent *''Tom,''* you are stressing who deserves credit for the reports. If, instead, you emphasize the word *''completed,''* or *''two''* or *''reports,''* you can change the meaning of your message with each different voice emphasis.

How Silence, Time, and Sounds Communicate

Silence

Though at first thought silence may seem unimportant, it can actually cause serious hard feelings, loss of business, and profits.

> Suppose you wrote an urgent letter to the customer relations manager of a large company, stating why you need a reply by March 5. If you receive no answer by that date and none for a month after that, what is your reaction to the silence? Do you worry whether your letter was lost? Do you angrily assume the manager is rude and just considers your request unworthy of his or her time? Do you wonder if the manager is annoyed by something in your letter, or if your envelope is perhaps at the bottom of a stack under other priority mail?

Time

Waiting when an important appointment or request is ignored causes problems and attitude changes. In the preceding example, after the long silence should you write again, telephone, wire, or just drop the matter and buy from a competitor? You should also consider whether in your request for "a reply by March 5" you gave the manager enough time to reply. Time is important also when sending announcements of policy changes or events. Be sure to allow ample time before the effective date.

Sounds

In addition to a speaking person's voice, other human sounds—clearing the throat, sighing, laughing, sneering—communicate nonverbally. Also nonhuman sounds—of bells, whistles, steamshovels, cars, trains, airplanes—all can be significant nonverbal communicators. Many people set their watches by certain whistles, rush off to work or to catch their transportation when they hear certain signals. Sounds can also indicate leaky pipes or defective machines that need immediate attention. And they can sometimes serve as convincing evidence—contrary to the written or spoken words of a mechanic—that the repair work just completed is unsatisfactory!

SUMMARY

Effective communication depends to a large extent on insights into human nature and on the ability to get desirable responses. It is a complex art which involves sender/encoder, message, channel/medium, receiver/decoder, and feedback. This chapter has included merely an introduction to the complex process of communication. Its aim has been to give you helpful ideas of why communication problems can occur and how, in general, they may be decreased or avoided.

To be an effective communicator, realize that human beings' mental filters differ. Their experiences, attitudes, abilities, skills, and cultural customs vary.[4] What is already in their mental filters affects the meanings individuals place on messages and, to some extent, the new ideas they choose to accept or reject.

Try always to consider differences in word (and sentence) interpretations, keep an open mind for getting as many accurate facts as possible about reality, admit there is always more that can be said, and allow for the influences of attitudes, opinions, and emotions. Remember also the importance of nonverbal communication—by appearance, body language, silence, time, sounds. Above all, try to better understand the people with whom you communicate. This ability will be useful and developed further as you apply the principles in the remainder of this book.

---

[4] To help you understand cultural variables when you communicate with people in other nations, see Chap. 24.

EXERCISES

1. Divide your paper into five columns with the following headings: Sender/Encoder, Message, Channel/Medium, Receiver(s)/Decoder(s), and Feedback. Under each column list possible causes of miscommunication, problems that contribute to the breakdown of communication. Also include examples from your own experiences, if possible.

2. Consider three of the following names: John, Eleanor, Barbara, Ronald, Jackie, Liz, Virginia, Mary, Jimmy, Walter. Prepare to share with the class your thoughts, opinions, experiences (and emotions, if any) about each. Using communication terms in this chapter, explain how and why details of your reactions are different from those of classmates.

3. The comment "Harold Joiner is a member of five business clubs and two athletic clubs" may be intended as a compliment. Why might some listeners interpret it as derogatory?

4. Give two examples of how the opinions and prejudices in your mind affect your communication.

5. Choose a national government officer whom you consider to be a good or poor communicator, and state specific reasons for your opinion.

6. Discuss whether each of the following statements is an inference or a verifiable fact based on observation:
   a. The boss is a "swinger."
   b. Employees under 20 and over 65 are inefficient.
   c. The union requested double pay for each hour of overtime.
   d. The union requested too much money.
   e. XYZ skis are no good.

7. What general communication principles do the following statements and incidents illustrate? Discuss each briefly.
   a. A friend of yours states: "I'll never buy our groceries from Tiptop Market. Haven't been there since the first week after they opened four years ago. Their produce department is a mess and prices are too high."
   b. In a public utility, an order went out setting up a new procedure; on the basis of that order, five different powerhouses set up five different procedures.
   c. An article in tonight's newspaper states that a nationwide strike appears all but certain after union negotiators walked out of contract talks and accused management of forcing a strike. But the chief negotiator said he couldn't "conceive how anyone could say what we gave them was a provocation for a strike."

8. Suppose you see Helen (the tenant who lives alone in an apartment directly above you) leaving at 8 p.m. from the front of the building. You have observed that she leaves at the same time each weekday evening. Yesterday she told you she is a doctor in a downtown hospital and her shift starts at 8:30 p.m. Tonight at 8:55 you hear footsteps in the apartment above you.
   a. Name three spontaneous inferences you could make.
   b. Discuss possible reasons why those inferences may be right or wrong. What action, if any, should you take?

9. Discuss two examples of how your nonverbal communications contradicted your spoken words.

10. List six nonverbal messages you have noticed business people convey by body language or appearance. Do you consider them favorable or unfavorable? Why?

11. Bring to class an example of a written message that conveys an unfavorable nonverbal message. State specific reasons for your evaluation.

12. A popular humorist and actor has stated that sometimes the same jokes which cause one audience to laugh spontaneously don't even get a chuckle another night in a different town. Discuss this comment in terms of a communication principle.

13. Can you share with the class an example of (a) bypassed instructions, (b) a closed-minded person, or (c) judging the whole by a part? Discuss the causes and consequences.

CHAPTER 3
Business Communication Principles I

To help you compose effective messages you need to apply certain specific communication principles. They tie in closely with the basic concepts of the communication process and are important for *both written and oral communications*. They provide guidelines for choice of *content and style of presentation—adapted to the purpose and receiver of your message*. Called "the seven C's," they are: completeness, conciseness, consideration, concreteness, clarity, courtesy, correctness. This chapter discusses the first four C's and Chapter 4, the remaining C's. (You will find the C's in other chapters too.)

COMPLETENESS

Your business message is "complete" when it contains all facts the reader or listener needs for the reaction you desire. To achieve both the specific purpose of your message *and* the long-term purpose—maintaining goodwill—you need to consider carefully just how much information is enough for each person. Remember that communicators differ in their mental filters; they are influenced by their backgrounds, viewpoints, needs, attitudes, and emotions.

Completeness is necessary for several reasons: First, complete messages are more likely to bring the desired results without the expense of additional messages. Second, they can do a better job of building goodwill. Third, they can help avert costly lawsuits which may result if important information is missing. Last, papers that seem inconsequential can be surprisingly important if the information they contain is complete and effective. In high-level conferences, in courtrooms, and in governmental hearings, the battle often centers around an ordinary-looking message that becomes important because of the complete information it contains.

As you strive for completeness, keep the following guidelines in mind:

- Answer all questions asked.
- Give something extra, when desirable.
- Check for the five W's and any other essentials.

Answer All Questions Asked

Whenever you reply to an inquiry containing one or more questions, answer all questions—stated and implied. A prospective customer's reaction to an incomplete reply is likely to be unfavorable. The customer may think the respondent is careless or is purposely trying to conceal a weak spot. In general, "omissions cast suspicions," whether you are answering an inquiry about your product or recommending a former employee for a new job. If you have no information on a particular question, you must say so clearly, instead of omitting an answer. If you have unfavorable information in answer to one or more questions, handle your reply with both tact and honesty.

The replies in situation 1 and 2 were incomplete because the respondents omitted the answers to one or more questions or omitted important information in an explanation that answered a question.

Situation 1

A distributor of model trains, when replying to an inquirer's letter, answered only three out of seven questions. Because they were unnumbered and somewhat buried in five long paragraphs, the respondent apparently overlooked or disregarded four questions. The reply, which was both incomplete and unfriendly, caused the distributor to lose the business and goodwill of a potential customer.

Sometimes before you can answer an inquiry, you need certain specific information from the inquirer. Then it is a good idea to list the needed details on a reply form which the inquirer can fill out and return to you. In this way both your answer and that of your respondent will be complete. In situation 2 the eight messages about one transaction resulted in delay and annoyed, disappointed customers. Had the bank supplied a reply form, the desired sale could have been completed promptly with four messages: the first inquiry; the bank's reply with an enclosed form to be filled out; the owner's authorization (on the form); and the bank's final liquidation notice and check.

Situation 2

On August 8 the owner of mutual fund stock wrote to a New York bank's investment department that he wanted to sell his shares. He asked "Just how does your bank want me to authorize this sale?" and he received the following reply:

```
If you wish to terminate Account #99998 and liquidate the shares
held by this bank, we need a letter of instructions signed by both
you and your wife just as the account is registered. Please be sure
to give us the name of your fund, your account number, and to whom
proceeds are to be mailed.
```

The customer's reply, signed by both himself and his wife, included the fund name, account number, and this statement:

```
Please sell our 37 shares effective this date (August 23, 19__) and
send proceeds to us.
```

On August 28 they received the following telegram:

```
RE MLF FUND A/C 99998 UNABLE ACCEPT INSTRUCTIONS TO LIQUIDATE ON A
SPECIFIC DATE FORWARD NEW SIGNED INSTRUCTIONS.
```

In their reply the customers wrote essentially the same letter as their second but they omitted the words "effective this date. . . ." A week later they received from the bank another request—this time to include in their reply both the name and address to which the proceeds were to be mailed! (The bank had not asked *specifically for the address, and the customers assumed the proceeds would be mailed to their home address.) The next day they wrote their fourth letter. Finally—on October 8, two months after the original question—they received a formal notice of liquidation with an attached check for the proceeds. However, during the delay, the price of the stock had fallen considerably, and they lost money on their sale.*

Give Something Extra, When Desirable

The words "when desirable" are essential here. Sometimes you must do more than answer the customers' specific questions. They may not know what they need, or their questions may be inadequate. For example, suppose you are president of the regional business executive's league for your industry and receive the following inquiry from an out-of-town member:

```
I think I'd like to attend my first meeting of the League, even
though I'm not acquainted in your city. Will you please tell me
where the next meeting will be held?
```

If you answered only this one question, your letter would be incomplete. Realizing that your reader is a newcomer to your city and to your league's meetings, you should include in your reply a welcome plus such needed details as directions for reaching the building; parking facilities; day, date, and time of meeting; and perhaps also the program for the next meeting. Your message will then have the "something extra" that a reader really needs and appreciates.

Sometimes the "something extra" is a detailed explanation instead of a mere brief statement. The last paragraph of letter 1, below, contains an invitation that is meaningless for any new depositor who does not know what "facilities" are at his or her disposal. Letter 2, on the contrary, clearly explains the services offered and thereby makes the invitation meaningful. (If a writer can enclose a descriptive brochure, the letter can be shorter and still complete if it merely mentions the services and refers to the enclosure for details.) The following examples show only the message of each letter (without address and salutation).

Letter 1

Incomplete letter to a new savings depositor.

```
Thank you for the confidence you have shown us by the account you
recently opened.
```

All our facilities are at your disposal, and any time we can be of service please feel free to call upon us. Our appreciation is best expressed by our being of service to you.

Letter 2

Revised, complete letter to the new savings depositor.

Thank you for the confidence you have shown in First Federal by the savings account you recently opened. Our goal is to make all our services to you both pleasant and helpful.

Among the conveniences and services available to you at First Federal, you may be especially interested in these:

YOUR PASSBOOK DEPOSITS earn 5½% interest compounded daily.

BETTER-THAN-CHECKING service helps you pay bills by phone, earn interest on your spending money, and use our 24-hour Cash Machines.

MORTGAGE LOANS help you to buy, build, or refinance a home or to borrow for property repairs and improvements.

With our MONEY MARKET CERTIFICATES you can earn interest at various current high rates, depending upon time and amount of your investment. The enclosed leaflet gives you more details about these and other services available to you at First Federal.

FREE CUSTOMER PARKING is provided in the lot north of our office. The teller stamps your parking check, entitling you to free parking while doing business here. Office hours are 9:30 a.m. to 4:00 p.m. weekdays except for Friday, when the doors remain open until 6:00 p.m.

You are most welcome to come in whenever we can assist you. Please consider this association your financial headquarters for your savings and borrowing needs.

Check for the Five W's and Any Other Essentials

Another way to help make your message complete is to answer, whenever desirable, the "five W" questions—*who, what, where, when, why*—and any other essentials, such as *how*. The five-question method is especially useful when you write requests, announcements, or other informative messages. For instance, to order (request) merchandise, make clear *what* you want, *when* you need it, to *whom* and *where* it is to be sent, and *how* payment will be made. To reserve a hotel banquet room, specify type of accommodations needed *(what),* location *(where),* sponsoring organization *(who),* date and time *(when),* function or event *(why),* and other necessary details *(how).*

For some letters—especially those that bring bad news, make an unusual request, or announce a special meeting—answering the question *why* may be important. Remember this general communication principle:

> A message that tactfully answers the question *why* is more likely to motivate the receiver to take the desired action than one that does not explain why. But not everyone is motivated for the same reasons.

When you must refuse customers' requests for a refund or ask them to pay a higher bill than they expected, they will probably be less angry if you explain *why*, from *their* viewpoint.

To sell a product by mail, you need also to answer these five W's and the H *(how)*. The example below shows one way a costly sales campaign can fail because of incompleteness.

The sales department of a retail company decided to sponsor a direct-mail campaign to 100,000 prospects. Each sales letter was to be personalized with a typed inside address and personal salutation. A special-price offer was to be good for a limited time only. The letter ended with this request:

So that you can enjoy the advantages of (product) at this special price, send your order—but no money—today. Just take these two easy steps—

> Write your initials in the upper right-hand corner of this letter.
> Then mail it back to us in the addressed, stamped envelope that is enclosed.

However, to save the expense of inserting the 100,000 inside addresses and personal salutations, a budget-minded official requested that the entire message be printed and that all inside addresses be omitted. And the salutation was changed to the general, printed, "Dear Customer." The result was that the company received over 11,000 of the letters back, but no one had the slightest idea to whom the 11,000 initials in the upper right-hand corners belonged! Because all inside addresses had been omitted, the letters were incomplete for the action requested; they failed to answer the questions who *and* how.

An attempt to find out from whom the orders had come would have necessitated the expense of a second letter to the same 100,000 people and the embarrassment of admitting the serious slipup. Instead, the decision was made to abandon the entire campaign. No one knows the resulting disappointment and perhaps ill will caused among the 11,000 prospects who received neither a reply nor the product they had ordered. In addition, the company wasted the cost of the first 100,000 letters and lost the profits from 11,000 orders.

In summary, make your messages complete by answering all questions asked, giving something extra when desirable, and checking for the five W's and H (who, what, when, where, why, how) as well as any other essentials.[1]

CONCISENESS

A concise message saves time and expense for both sender and receiver. Conciseness is saying what you have to say in the fewest possible words without sacrificing the other C qualities. Conciseness contributes to emphasis. By eliminating unnecessary words, you help make important ideas stand out.

To achieve conciseness—the opposite of wordiness—try to observe the following suggestions.

- Shorten or omit wordy expressions.
- Include only relevant statements.
- Avoid unnecessary repetition.

Shorten or Omit Wordy Expressions

By observing these suggestions you can help decrease wordiness in your messages:

1. Use single-word substitutes instead of phrases whenever possible without changing meanings.

Wordy	*Concise*
along the line of (salary)	about (salary)
at this time	now
consensus of opinion	consensus
date of the policy	policy date
due to the fact that	because
during the time that	while
during the year of	during
few and far between	seldom, scarce
for a price of	for
for the purpose of	for; to
for the reason that	since; because
from the point of view of	as
have need for	need
in accordance with your request	as you requested
in due course	soon
in many cases	often; frequently

---

[1] To make your *action request* complete in various types of letters, follow suggestions concerning the five W's and the H discussed under Closing Paragraphs, Chap. 5.

in most cases	usually
in order to	to
in some cases	sometimes
in spite of the fact that	although
in (for) the amount of	for
in the city of	in
in the event that	if
in the neighborhood of $60	about $60
in view of the fact that	because
please don't hesitate to write	please write
under date of	dated
under the circumstances	because

2. Eliminate "which" and "that" clauses whenever possible.

Wordy: She ordered desks which are of the executive type.
Concise: She ordered executive-type desks.
Wordy: Tom said that he heard the news.
Concise: Tom said he heard the news.

3. Avoid overusing "it is," "there is," and "there are" at sentence beginnings.

Wordy: There are four rules which should be observed.
Concise: Four rules should be observed.
Wordy: It is known that we must reduce the . . . .
Concise: We must reduce the . . . .

In the following examples each concise sentence eliminates from half to two-thirds of the words in the wordy sentence, yet the meaning is clear and courteous.

Wordy: At this time I am writing you to enclose the postpaid appointment card for the purpose of arranging a convenient time when we might get together for a personal interview. (30 words)

Concise: Will you please return the enclosed card and name a convenient time for an interview? (15 words)

Wordy: We hereby wish to let you know that we fully appreciate the confidence you have reposed in us. (18 words)

Concise: We appreciate your confidence in us. (6 words)

Include Only Relevant Statements

The effective concise message should omit not only unnecessarily wordy expressions but also irrelevant material. To be sure you include only relevant facts:

1. Stick to the purpose of the message.
2. Prune irrelevant words and rambling sentences.
3. Omit information obvious to the receiver; don't repeat at length what that person already told you.
4. Avoid long introductions, unnecessary background material or explanations, excessive adjectives, pompous words, gushy politeness.
5. Get to the important point tactfully and concisely.

The next example shows how writers can prune so much that they remove relevant facts and overlook the purpose of the message.

Once upon a time, a fish dealer was planning a new sign for his store. It was to read: Fresh Fish for Sale Here Today. *A critical friend, however, had some suggestions:*

"You don't need the word 'here,' " she said. "People can see where the store is. And you don't need 'for sale' either. They know you're not giving things away."

The friend continued: "And how about 'fresh fish' and 'today'? Do you want customers to think this is the only day you have fresh fish? That you sell old fish on other days? Take out 'fresh.' And while you're at it, take out 'today.' People know you wouldn't be open if you weren't selling something today.

"You might as well drop 'fish' too. Anyone within half a mile can smell what you're selling."[2]

The moral of this fish story? Write concisely, but don't destroy your message.

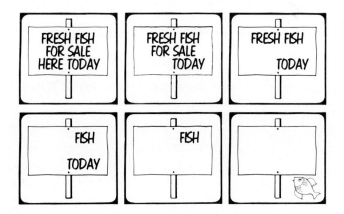

The following overly wordy letter is the opposite extreme of the preceding example. This is to the Business Administration Placement Office from a person who graduated from a university the previous year and had difficulty

[2] From *Effective Letters Bulletin,* New York Life Insurance Company, Spring 1967, p. 1.

finding a satisfactory job. Notice his pompous words and irrelevant material. If he talked and wrote this way to employers or customers, would they probably react negatively toward him? Compare his letter with the revised example below it.

```
The university Placement Office has sent me at periodic intervals a
form inquiring as to my current employment status.  As you may recall
from our discussion last spring I was most desirous of making a fa-
vorable change in vocational locale.  After following up several
recommendations made by your office (Goodwin, etc.) I was unable to
negotiate an immediate change, and upon receiving suave assurances
of rapid promotion from my superiors promptly regressed into the
torpid complacency which characterized my thinking upon graduation.
However my present intention to move is more than a harbinger of
that most fragrant of seasons but rather stems from a feeling of
disillusionment and inadequacy with my vocational environment.

May I once again prevail upon you to assist me in this undertaking
by informing me at your convenience of any job opportunity for which
you think I would be well suited.  As indicated in my last reply to
your office, I no longer look to accounting as my forte but instead
am seeking a selling situation which is both challenging and re-
munerative.

Thank you for your patience and understanding in this matter.  You
may reach me at 555-1234 during the day or at 564-4321 in the eve-
ning.
```

Concise Revision with Only Relevant Statements

```
Will you please tell me about any sales opening which is both chal-
lenging and remunerative?  I am no longer interested in an accounting
job.

You can reach me at 555-1234 during the day or at 564-4321 in the
evening.  I will appreciate your suggestions.
```

Avoid Unnecessary Repetition

Sometimes repetition is necessary for emphasis. But when the same thing is said two or three times without reason, the message becomes wordy and boring. Here are three ways to eliminate unnecessary repetition:

1. Use a shorter name after you have mentioned the long one once: Instead of the "Thomson Product Manufacturing Company," use "Thomson Company."
2. Use pronouns or initials rather than repeating long names: Instead of "North Central Auto Insurance Company, Inc." again and again, use "it" or "they" or "NCAI."

3. Cut out all needless repetition of phrases and sentences. For example, the following letter from a business executive to a firm the company had dealt with for five years shows unnecessary repetition at its worst:

```
Will you ship us sometime, any time during the month of October, or
even November if you are rushed, for November would suit us just as
well, in fact a little bit better, 300 of the regular 3" by 15" blue
felt armbands with white sewn letters in the center.

Thanking you to send these along to us by parcel post, and not ex-
press, as express is too stiff in price, when parcel post will be
much cheaper, we are . . .
```

The writer took 81 words to say what is said in 25 below:

```
Please ship parcel post, before the end of November, 300 regular 3"
by 15" blue felt armbands with white sewn letters in the center.
```

In summary, a concise message includes all necessary ideas and facts in the fewest possible words without sacrificing the other C qualities. You can shorten or omit wordy expressions by using single words instead of certain phrases, eliminating "which" and "that" clauses whenever possible, and avoiding overuse of "It is," and "There is (or are)" for sentence beginnings.

The message should include only facts relevant to its purpose. Sentences should omit pompous words, irrelevant details, excessive adjectives, and statements the receiver already knows. You can avoid unnecessary repetition of long names by using pronouns, initials, or shorter names. The concise message helps emphasize important points and save costly time for both sender and receiver.

CONSIDERATION

As discussed in Chapter 2, the interrelationship of the message sender and receiver profoundly affects communication effectiveness. Consideration means that you prepare every message with the recipient in mind and try to put yourself in his or her place. Try to visualize your readers (or listeners)—with their desires, problems, circumstances, emotions, and probable reactions to your request. Then handle the matter from *their* point of view. This thoughtful consideration is also called "you-attitude," empathy, the human touch, and understanding of human nature. (It does *not* mean, however, that you should overlook the needs of your organization.)

In a broad but true sense, consideration underlies the other six C's of good business communication. You adapt your language and message content to your receiver's needs when you make your message complete, concise, concrete, clear, courteous, and correct. However, in four specific ways you can indicate you are considerate:

- Focus on "you" instead of "I" and "we."
- Show reader benefit or interest in reader.
- Emphasize positive, pleasant facts.
- Apply integrity to your messages.

Focus on "You" instead of "I" and "We"

Your receivers are usually more concerned about themselves than about you or the company you represent. They are more likely to read your message when they see *their name* and the pronoun *"you"* rather than "I, we, us."

Usually it is desirable to get your reader into the first paragraph. (Exceptions are presented later in this section.) If psychologically desirable, begin with "you" or "your," and keep your reader in the message (tactfully) until you finish. The opposite of the you-attitude is the we-attitude, in which the writer views every matter from his or her own (or the organization's) standpoint rather than from the reader's:

We-attitude	*You-attitude*
I want to send my congratulations . . .	Congratulations to you on your . . .
We will ship your May 4 order today.	You should receive the Apex screen you ordered May 4 on or before May 9.
We have enclosed a reply envelope.	Just mail your check in the enclosed envelope.

The we-attitude department store letter, below (letter 1), contains 20 "we-our-us-I-my" pronouns (underlined) and only three "you's" (in italics).

Letter 1: We-attitude

May I take this opportunity to express my thanks for the account *you* recently opened with our store. We are pleased to furnish a wide variety of products for the home or individual customer.

We want *you* to take full advantage of our store services, for we have the largest stock in the city. Also we make deliveries of our customers' purchases free of charge within 30 miles of our store.

(The next two paragraphs—omitted here to save space and reading—have four "we's," three "our customers," and no "you." The last paragraph is:

We welcome *you* to Bekinson's. If we can be of additional service in any manner, please call on us.

In contrast, letter 2—rewritten for more you-attitude—contains 18 "you's" and "your's" (in italics) and only two "we-our-us" pronouns (underlined):

Letter 2: You-attitude

Thank *you* for the account *you* recently opened at Bekinson's. Serving *you* with *your* needs for clothing and home furnishings is a pleasure.

You will find 32 departments at Bekinson's stocked with a variety of quality items. And courteous sales clerks are here to assist *you* in selecting the merchandise that best meets *your* requirements.

If *you* prefer to shop within the comfort of *your* home, instead of coming to the store, *you* need only to telephone 882–5555 and ask for "Personal Shopping Service." A Personal Shopper will gladly take *your* order for any number of items, answer *your* questions about brands and sizes available, and see that the goods *you* order reach *you* by store delivery within a few days.

When *you* shop at our store downtown, *you* are invited to use the free customer parking privilege provided just across the street.

You are always welcome at Bekinson's. Please call on us whenever *you* need additional services.

As the foregoing examples illustrate, a letter is likely to have better you-attitude when it contains more "you's" than "I's." But there are notable exceptions! An extreme example is the collection letter with "you" or "your" in almost every sentence; yet if those sentences are insulting, sarcastic, tactless, or untrue accusations and threats against the debtor, the letter surely lacks you-attitude.

In two kinds of situations it is advisable *not* to use "you."

1. When the reader has made a mistake:

Poor:	You failed to enclose your check in the envelope.
Better:	The envelope we received did not have a check in it.

Poor:	Your contract tells you plainly that . . .
Better:	I am glad to explain more fully the contract terms.

2. When the reader has expressed an opinion different from your own:

Poor:	You are entirely wrong in your attitude.
Better:	The proposed plan has three aspects which are extremely important and which we need to explain now.

Show Reader Benefit or Interest in Reader

Whenever possible and true, show how your readers will benefit from whatever the message asks or announces. They will be more likely to react favorably and do what you suggest if you show that benefits are worth the effort and cost. In situations where actual direct reader benefit is impossible or irrelevant to the subject matter, the message should at least show interest in and concern for the reader's needs or viewpoint.

Even a simple request gets better response when a reader-benefit plug accompanies it. For example, an insurance company that wanted to update its address files sent to one-half of its policyholders a double postcard with this message:

> Since we haven't written you in some time, please help us bring our records up to date by filling in and returning the other half of this card.

Only 3 percent of these cards came back. To the remaining half of its policyholders the firm sent the same request—reworded to show reader benefit:

> So that dividend checks, premium notices, and other messages of importance may reach you promptly, please fill out and return the other half of this card.

This request brought 90 percent of the cards back in a few days!

Merely inserting the word *you* does not ensure you-attitude, as shown in this sentence:

> You will be glad to know that we now have a Walk-Up Window open 7-9 a.m. and 3-8 p.m. every weekday.

The reader may wonder, "So what?" The revised sentence includes reader benefit:

> You can now take care of your banking needs also at our new Walk-Up Window, open to serve you 7-9 a.m. and 3-8 p.m. Monday through Friday.

Reader-benefit appeals help collect payments on bills, soften the blow in a turndown, and sell products. Though your company is in business to make a profit, you omit that selfish-sounding idea; the reader assumes it anyway and is motivated only by what benefits he or she receives. Reader-benefit appeals are desirable also in job applications, favor requests, and announcements to your customers, prospective buyers, stockholders, and employees. Whether you are writing to one person or to large numbers, try to personalize the reader benefits (as in Letter 2, page 49) instead of stating them in a general way ("our customers," as in Letter 1, page 48).

If your organization provides employee benefits—such as health insurance and various retirement plans—management should make every effort to assure that all employees understand and appreciate those benefits. Many may be unaware that their employer spends more than one-third of the total payroll on employee benefits. To inform employees effectively, management can use such media as memos, employee manuals, bulletins, policy statements, company magazines, news sheets, reports, posters, films, and notes in pay envelopes.

Emphasize the Positive, Pleasant Facts

A third way to show consideration for your reader (or listener) is to accent the positive. This means (1) stressing what *can* be done instead of what cannot be done and (2) focusing on ideas your *recipient can view favorably*.

Statement of What Can Be Done

The reader (or listener) wants to know what you *can* do for him or her. For most people negative words like *no, won't, cannot, never, impossible* trigger unpleasant emotional reactions. By making clear what you *can* or *will do*, you (by implication) often make clear what you *cannot do*, without using a single negative word. Furthermore, whenever possible and helpful, tell the recipient why or how.

Negative–Unpleasant	*Positive–Pleasant*
It is impossible to open an account for you today.	As soon as your signature card reaches us, we will gladly open an . . .
We don't refund if the returned item is soiled and unsalable.	We refund when the returned item is clean and resalable.
When you travel on company expense, you will not receive approval for first-class fare.	When you travel on company expense, your approved fare is for tourist class.
To avoid further delay and inconvenience, we are sending this report by special delivery.	So that you will get this report as soon as possible, we are sending it special delivery.

Ideas Your Recipient Can View Favorably

Among the *positive* words to which people react *favorably* are: benefit, cordial, happy, help, generous, loyal, pleasure, thanks, thoughtful. Words with *negative* connotations that often arouse *unfavorable* reactions include: blame, complaint, failed, fault, negligence, regret, reject, trouble, unfair, and many others. For example, in the following opening of a letter the negative words (underlined) focus on ideas you'd rather not have the reader think about.

```
We regret that, since you closed your account, your name will be
missing from our long list of satisfied customers.  We sincerely hope
that, despite the best efforts of our fine staff, there were no oc-
casions on which you felt we failed to serve you properly.
```

A better opening expresses appreciation for the customer's patronage in the first paragraph, as shown below. Then the second paragraph welcomes him or her to other services.

```
It was a pleasure to have had you as a member of Federal Savings.
Thank you for giving us the opportunity to serve you.

We noticed recently that you closed your account with us.  Perhaps
you reached that particular goal for which you were saving, or it
may be that an emergency arose which called for a large outlay of
cash.  Whatever the reason, we are happy to have played some small
part in your financial program.  You are cordially invited to use our
other profitable, timesaving services as occasion may require.
```

Apply Integrity and Ethics

To be truly considerate, you need also to apply integrity—high moral standards, personal honor, truthfulness, sincerity—to your written and oral messages. Integrity is indispensable in our jobs, in business transactions, in social and political activities, in everything we do. Without it, business communications would prove worthless and our confidence in people would be shattered.

Ethics is concerned with what is right human conduct. Codes of ethics provide standards enabling us to determine the fundamental distinction between right or wrong human behavior. Often "gray" areas involve fine decisions between complete truth and a partial falsehood. An honest business person needs a strong conscience as well as knowledge of communication principles and company policies.

The following statements, adapted from "Honest Communication," an essay by the Royal Bank of Canada, express well several important basic concepts:

> Honesty is not a simple subject, because it goes to the very heart of human nature. Honesty is born when one perceives what is right and wrong and chooses to do what is right. . . . Confidence in one's honesty cannot be established simply by avoiding only what is illegal. . . . The rules of ethics are far wider than mere legality. . . .
>
> Promises made in speeches, letters, and advertising should be fulfilled scrupulously. . . . Honesty in business communication reaches its most visible public testing point in advertising, labeling, and selling. . . . Half-truths, exaggerations, and misleading descriptions of products or services are not honest communications.[3]

Because you are an agent of your company, you help build your company's image. To make this image one of integrity and ethical conduct requires consistently fair standards and honesty in communications with persons outside and inside your organization.

Integrity with Persons outside the Organization

When you show consideration for your customers, you try to let them know you are aware of and are doing something about their interests and needs. This does *not* mean, however, that you yield to the temptation of showing favoritism, allowing deviations for one customer that you would not allow for all other customers in similar circumstances, or arranging money kickbacks and bribes to obtain government or commercial business. If customers insist that "everyone else does it," the temptation to comply with their wishes may be difficult. Nevertheless, widespread existence of evil does not make evil right. High ethical standards may require *"doing the harder right instead of the easier wrong."*

Studies have shown that the behavior of superiors and pressures from top management to meet competition and increase profits was the number one factor influencing executives to make unethical decisions. Typical examples include: misrepresenting contents of products, substituting materials without customer knowledge after the job contract has been awarded, scheduling inaccurate delivery dates to get a contract, and so on. Therefore, an ethical boss can be an important influence for ethical employee communications.[4]

Among ten examples of behavior that advertising and/or marketing executives considered most unethical (in a 1981 study by Lewis and Reinsch) were these dishonest communications to persons outside the firm:

> Making false product or service claims to a potential customer in order to obtain $1,000,000 (or $500,000 or $1,000).

---

[3] Royal Bank of Canada, "Honest Communication," *The Journal of Business Communication,* vol. 10, no. 2, Winter 1973, pp. 19–27.

[4] Steven N. Brenner and Earl A. Molander, "Is the Ethics of Business Changing?" *Harvard Business Review,* vol. 55, no. 1, January–February, 1977, pp. 59–64.

Shading the truth in published financial statements.

Divulging confidential data to persons outside the company.[5]

Needed Ethical Communication within the Organization

Employees must also be fair to their employer and to each other. Weak ethical standards, economic pressures, and competition for promotions or increased income have tempted many to unethical behavior.

Dishonesty toward Employers. Employee internal thefts and dishonest messages like the following are estimated to cost businesses billions of dollars yearly:

Wasting time on the job—by taking excessive lunch and coffee breaks, "snoozing" in the stockroom, claiming sick leave when not ill, and so on. One survey of 325 employers revealed (according to a report in the *Star,* December 21, 1982) that a worker steals an average of more than four hours a week from the boss.

Failing to report an employee error that will cost the company losses ranging from $10 to $100,000.[6]

Unfairly padding expense accounts with dinner dates and travel items far above the actual costs to the reporting persons.

Purposely ordering larger quantities of supplies or equipment than needed so that employees who order can take valuables home for their own use.

Unfair Communications with or about Coworkers. Examples of dishonest behavior by employees toward each other include these—and many others:

Issuing false instructions to a coworker in order to make that person look bad or perform poorly.

Giving false information to a superior in order to improve the giver's position in the department.

Falsely reporting high work evaluations for personal favorites so they will get unjustified promotions.

Spreading false rumors against a competitor for a promotion in the department or company.[7]

---

[5] Phillip V. Lewis and N. L. Reinsch, Jr., "The Ethics of Business Communication," *ABCA National Convention Proceedings 1981,* p. 9.
[6] Lewis and Reinsch, "The Ethics of Business Communication," pp. 16–17.
[7] Lewis and Reinsch, "The Ethics of Business Communication," pp. 16–17.

How do unethical practices affect you and all other business communicators? Pertinent suggestions are in the following excerpts from "Corporate Morality and the Crisis of Confidence in American Business" by Phillip I. Blumberg:

> Corrupt practices corrupt personnel, impair the integrity of the corporation, challenge the corporate chain of command, and threaten the free-market system itself. . . . Corporations should establish internal codes of honest conduct for the guidance of company personnel and internal procedures for their effective enforcement. It should be made plain by the board and by management that economic results will not excuse violations of the code. . . .

> In the end, the problem comes down to individuals and their personal sense of morality. . . . All acts are those of individuals, although they may be acting in the name of, and on behalf of, corporations. As individuals, they are subject to the inescapable imperative of morality. . . . There is no obligation to shareholders that requires management to steal or bribe for them. . . .

> Further, we must recognize that unless this moral imperative is generally accepted by business leaders, business will inevitably suffer further decline in the confidence of the public. . . . Honesty is not merely the best policy. It is the *only* policy.[8]

In summary, consideration means you are genuinely thoughtful of your message recipients and consider their probable reactions to your messages. You can indicate you-attitude by focusing on "you," the reader or listener; by showing benefit to or interest in the receiver; by emphasizing positive, pleasant facts; and by applying integrity and ethics—consistently fair treatment, honesty, and sincerity. Consideration involves the golden rule—showing to others the same fairness and honesty we expect for ourselves. Remember, both your own integrity and that of your company are revealed in your business messages.

CONCRETENESS

Communicating concretely means being specific, definite, and vivid rather than vague and general. The following guidelines should help you compose concrete, convincing messages:

• Use specific facts and figures.
• Put action in your verbs.
• Choose vivid, image-building words.

---

[8] Phillip I. Blumberg, dean of the School of Law and professor of law and business at the University of Connecticut, from his *Invited Essay to Beta Gamma Sigma,* "Corporate Morality and the Crisis of Confidence in American Business," January 1977. Beta Gamma Sigma, national scholastic honorary for students pursuing degrees in business and management, has endeavored to foster integrity in business practice since its founding in 1913.

Use Specific Facts and Figures

Whenever you can substitute an exact fact or a figure for a general word to make your message more concrete and convincing, do so.

Vague, general, indefinite	*Concrete and convincing*
These brakes stop a car within a short distance.	These Goodson power brakes stop a 2-ton car traveling 60 miles an hour, within 240 feet.
Our product has won several prizes.	(Name) product has won first prize in four national contests within the past three years.
This computer reproduces campaign letters fast.	This computer types 1,000 personalized 150-word campaign letters in one hour.

Often vague, general words are *opinion words;* they may have different meanings to the sender and the receiver. For instance, how fast is *fast?* A bicycle rider and a racing-car driver will have different meanings for this word. How large is *large?* A person reared in a village of 150 people may consider a population of 15,000 large; yet to a native of a city with 10 million inhabitants, 15,000 is very *small.* The list that follows gives additional words which can lead to uncertainty, misunderstanding, or confusion.

a few	high	low	more	quick	soon
early	long	many	most	slow	tall

Using plenty of examples, prefixed by phrases like "for instance," "for example," "such as," also helps make your writing concrete as well as clear. (You will notice that this book uses this technique often.)

In certain cases it is, of course, permissible—and even desirable—to use general expressions. *Exceptions* to the "facts and figures" rule occur:

1. When it is not possible to be specific, for you may not have nor be able to get definite facts or figures.
2. When you want to be diplomatic. Thus, instead of saying, "We have sent you four notices of your overdue payment," you may be more tactful (to a usually prompt paying customer) by saying, "We have sent you *several* reminders of this. . . ."
3. When you want to allow the person to form his or her own opinion, or when exact figures are unimportant, as in: "A *few* (or *many*) of our employees attended the parade."

Put Action in Your Verbs

Strong verbs can activate other words and help make your sentences definite. To compose strong sentences, you should (1) use active rather than passive verbs and (2) put action in your verbs instead of in nouns or infinitives.

Active versus Passive Voice

When the subject *performs* the action which the verb expresses, the verb is said to be in the *active* voice. In "Mr. Jones *repaired* the computer," the subject (Mr. Jones) did the repairing; the verb *repaired* is active.

When the subject benefits from or otherwise *receives* the action the verb expresses, the verb is said to be in the *passive* voice. In "The computer *was repaired* by Mr. Jones," the verb *was repaired* is passive.

A passive verb has three characteristics: (1) The subject doesn't do the acting; (2) the verb consists of *two or more* words, one of which is some form of "to be" (is, is being, am, are, was, were, will be, has or have been, had been, or will have been); and (3) the word *by* is expressed or implied ("by whom" or "by what"). The examples below show the difference between passive and active voice.

Passive (Subject receives the action)	*Active (Subject performs the action)*
Tests were made by us.	We made tests; or Tests showed that . . . .
A full report will be sent to you by the supervisor.	You will receive a full report from the supervisor; or The supervisor will send . . . .
These figures are checked by the research department.	The research department checks these figures.

Generally you should use *active* rather than passive verbs because active verbs help make your sentences more:

1. *Specific.* "The board of directors decided" is more explicit than "A decision has been made."
2. *Personal.* "You will note" is both personal and specific; "It will be noted" is impersonal.
3. *Concise.* The passive requires more words and thus slows both the writing and reading. Compare "Figures show" with "It is shown by figures."
4. *Emphatic.* Passive verbs dull action. Compare "The child ran a mile" with "A mile was run by the child."

Sometimes, however, you may prefer the *passive* voice instead of the active, as in the following situations:

1. When you want to avoid personal, blunt accusations or commands. "The July check was not included" is more tactful than "You failed to include. . . ." "Attendance at the meeting is required" is less harsh than "You must attend. . . ."
2. When you want to stress the object of the action. In "Your savings account is insured up to $40,000," you have intentionally stressed "your account"—not the firm that does the insuring. Also, "You are invited" is better than "We invite you."
3. When the doer isn't important in the sentence. In "Three announcements were made before the meeting started," the emphasis is on the announcements, not on who gave them.

Action in Verbs, Not in Nouns

Seven verbs—*be, give, have, hold, make, put,* and *take* (in any tense) might be designated as "deadly" because the action they introduce is hidden in a "quiet noun." The examples below show how these "deadly" verbs can be changed to action verbs which shorten the sentences.

Action hiding in a "quiet noun"	*Action in the verb*
The function of this office <u>is</u> <u>the collection</u> of payments and the <u>compilation</u> of statements.	This office <u>collects</u> payments and <u>compiles</u> statements.
Mr. Jones will <u>give consideration</u> to the report.	Mr. Jones will <u>consider</u> the report.
The contract <u>has a requirement</u> that	The contract <u>requires</u> that . . . .
They <u>held</u> the <u>meeting</u> in the office.	They <u>met</u> in the office.
He <u>made</u> his first installment <u>payment</u>.	He <u>paid</u> his first installment.
The chairperson <u>puts</u> her <u>trust</u> in each committee member.	The chairperson <u>trusts</u> each committee member.
We will <u>take a look</u> at your record.	We will <u>look</u> at your record.

Action in Verbs, Not in Infinitives

Action can also be concealed by infinitives. Notice, in the following example, that both main verbs in the left-hand sentence follow "is" (or some form of "to be") plus the preposition "to," and they don't convey much action.

<table>
<tr><td align="center">Action hiding in infinitive</td><td align="center">Action in the verb</td></tr>
<tr><td>

```
The duty of a stenographer is to
check all incoming mail and to
record it.  In addition, it is
his or her responsibility to keep
the assignment book up to date.
```

</td><td>

```
A stenographer checks and records
all incoming mail and keeps the
assignment book up to date.
```

</td></tr>
</table>

Choose Vivid, Image-Building Words

Among the devices you can use to make your messages forceful, vivid, and specific are comparisons, figurative language, concrete instead of abstract nouns, and well-chosen adjectives and adverbs.

Comparisons

Sometimes adding a comparison helps your recipient to build a meaningful picture. Consider the vague "sense" images you get from the sentences in the left-hand column below as contrasted with the vivid impressions gained from those at the right.

<table>
<tr><td align="center">Vague</td><td align="center">Vivid</td></tr>
<tr><td>

```
There are a great many solder
joints in the spacecraft,
and each must have just the
right amount of solder.
```

</td><td>

```
The spacecraft has 2½ million
solder joints.  If an extra drop
of solder had been left on these
joints, the excess weight would
have been equivalent to the
payload of the vehicle.
```

</td></tr>
<tr><td>

```
This is pure clover honey, made
by honeybees.
```

</td><td>

```
Honeybees have gathered nectar
from approximately 4½ million
clusters of clover and traveled
about 150,000 miles—or equal to
six times around the world—to
deliver this package of Bradshaw
honey to you.
```

</td></tr>
</table>

Figurative Language

Figures of speech often express an idea more vividly than literal language.

Literal (and dull)	*Figurative*
She is usually the one who gets things started in the organization.	Jean Jones is the spark plug of the organization.
X product helps you lose your double chin in four weeks, if you use X as directed.	If two chins quarrel constantly for a place on your collar, X product helps settle the argument. Only one chin remains after you use X just four weeks as directed.

Concrete Instead of Abstract Nouns

Still another way to enliven your message is to use concrete nouns instead of abstract nouns, especially as subjects of your sentences. Concrete nouns represent subjects your recipient can touch, see, smell, feel, hear, or taste. Abstract nouns as subjects bring only vague, if any, "pictures" to a person's mind.

Abstract	*Concrete*
Consideration was given to the fact that. . . .	The committee considered. . . .
Termination of the insurance contract will be in June.	The insurance contract ends in June.
Analysis of the situation suggests that Mr. Smith is right.	I think Mr. Smith is right.

   Be exact in your titles, subjects, and references. Don't force your receiver to guess. One more caution: If you are referring to an *inanimate object,* avoid using the neutral word *thing* whenever possible. Use a *more specific word* that is related to the "thing"—such as *event, element, fact, idea, condition, method, plan, purpose, principle.*

Adjectives and Adverbs

You can often build a more realistic and interesting word picture by adding well-chosen adjectives and adverbs. In the following list, adjectives are underlined; adverbs, in capitals.

Colorless	*Realistic, vivid, interesting*
The camera has a system that gives you <u>good</u> pictures.	The <u>Poney</u> camera has an UNCANNILY <u>precise metering</u> system that assures you PROPERLY <u>exposed</u>, <u>true-color</u> pictures.
This cookware is guaranteed to withstand changes in temperature.	Creston cookware withstands <u>extreme</u> changes in heat and <u>cold</u>—from <u>zero</u> to <u>450</u> degrees Fahrenheit. The guarantee assures you that you can SAFELY move any piece from your freezer to your <u>microwave</u> oven.

In your search for vivid, picture-building words, be careful not to go to extremes with adjectives or with superlatives such as ''the most,'' ''the largest,'' ''the greatest,'' and ''the best.''

In summary, good concrete writing and speaking include specific facts and figures, with examples. Generally you should use active rather than passive verbs and place action in verbs, not in nouns or infinitives. To help make messages vivid and specific you can use comparisons, figurative language, and concrete instead of abstract nouns, plus well-chosen adjectives and adverbs.

EXERCISES

1. Discuss orally how to make each of the following requests complete, concise, and concrete:

   a. Please send me c.o.d. five more shirts exactly like those I bought from you three months ago. (*From a cash customer.*)

   b. The coat you had in your window last Thursday is exactly the style I would like to have. Please send it to me on my charge account.

   c. I am interested in the portable TV you advertised in yesterday's newspaper. Will you please tell me more about it? (*The firm advertised one television set in the city's morning paper and a different set in the evening paper.*)

   d. Please reserve three seats for the opera <u>Turandot</u> on Saturday evening.

   e. My daughter and I wish to repaint two bedrooms, each of which is 10' × 12'. Please send us the right amount of paint—in pink—to do this job, and charge my account.

2. Choose an active verb to replace each ''deadly'' verb hiding in some of the following nouns.

   a. Be of assistance.

    b. Make substitution.
    c. Have intention.
    d. Held a meeting and had a discussion.
    e. Improvement in quality has been made.
    f. Evaporation of the liquid takes place.
    g. Make a decision.
    h. Take action; take a look.
    i. We will give thought to your proposal.
    j. Put on a demonstration.
    k. It is my intention to.

3. Which of the following verbs are passive and which are active voice? Revise the sentences that have passive verbs so they will have active verbs.

    a. Each member was given a copy of the annual report.
    b. The printer is planning to expand operations on Monday.
    c. Each courteous clerk wins goodwill for Mace Department Store.
    d. Final preparation will be made by the planning committee.
    e. The finance committee has been making a careful study.
    f. By January, the committee will have interviewed all applicants.
    g. Mr. Thom's secretary has completed the assignment.
    h. The contract will be signed next week.
    i. A farewell banquet has been planned in honor of Miss Bray.
    j. Many customers are reached by television advertisements.
    k. An account was opened by Mrs. Simms.
    l. It is suggested that you come early.

4. Revise the following sentences to eliminate the negative aspects.

    a. To avoid the loss of your good credit rating, please send your $130 check this week.
    b. This information is being sent to you now so that we will avoid later misunderstandings about our credit terms.
    c. We know you will agree that our prices are not any higher than those of competitors.
    d. On c.o.d. orders we require a 20 percent deposit to safeguard ourselves against loss in case of refusal of merchandise.
    e. We will hold shipment of this hardware until we receive your confirmation.
    f. Unfortunately, I will not be able to give you any definite price until you let me know the size and quantity of cartons you need.
    g. We are sorry that we cannot add a car to the policy without a specific description of the vehicle.
    h. There will be a delay of four days in filling your order because the material for your coat has to be ordered from Chicago. We are sorry about this delay, but there is nothing we can do about it.
    i. Because of shortages of material, we will not be able to ship before June 10.
    j. I am sorry I cannot send you the booklet you requested, as we have not received it from the publishers.

k. Your bicycle has been repaired and we hope you will have no further trouble with it.

l. We regret that we cannot extend your payment date for more than two months.

m. You won't be sorry you made this decision.

5. Change the following sentences so that they emphasize "you-attitude" instead of "we-attitude."

a. We allow 2 percent discount for cash payments.

b. This is just the kind of job I am looking for, since it offers me a chance to get practical experience in personnel work.

c. We value your patronage, for satisfied customers are the foundation of our success.

d. Since we have our own obligations to meet, we must ask your immediate attention to your past-due account.

e. We do not send receipts because of the extra work involved for us; of course, you have your canceled checks anyway.

f. Our pamphlet is designed to help its readers get the most out of raising beautiful roses.

g. We hope to have the pleasure of showing you what we think is the finest assortment of Italian boots in the city.

h. To help us improve our production schedule, we would appreciate your ordering two weeks in advance.

i. I wish to tell you that we are sending your new coat tomorrow.

6. Revise the following sentences to eliminate wordiness and other errors.

a. The picture which is enclosed will give you an idea of the appearance of this home. (*Whenever possible, talk in the present tense.*)

b. In the event you would wish to schedule playings of there anniversary records to certain or all of you're employees, arrangements for these programs may be made by getting in touch with Lon Jones. As you probably know, his phone extension is 562. (*Can you cut these 43 words to 22?*)

c. Their would still be continuation of the controversy, I must say, after the new plan is instituted.

d. You will note when you study the cost of stationery that the expenditure of stationery gradually and steadily increased for 1976, 1977, 1978, and 1979.

e. I have your letter of October 14 and wish to say that we'll be glad to give you a refund for the blouse you bought here last week.

f. Permit me to take this opportunity to call your attention to the fact that we have brought your account up to date.

g. For your information we are attaching hereto a carbon copy of the letter sent to Mr. Ava Knocash under date of April 25.

i. Please find enclosed herewith a copy of the report which is 15 pages in length.

j. I wish to take this opportunity to sincerely acknowledge receipt of your order for one bushel of Washington Red Delicious apples and thank you for placing it with our company.

    k. Please be assured that we are now rechecking and reviewing all of our specifications as it is our earnest and most sincere desire to be certain and for sure that this machine gives you satisfaction and good service in every possible way in the future.

    l. In addition, will you please permit me to state in this letter that we will welcome any suggestions or comments that you may have any time if you think of any methods for the improvement of our service to our customers.

7. Regarding ethics and integrity choose one or more of the following:

    a. Bring to your class for discussion a specific example of ethical conduct in a difficult predicament, and an example of behavior you consider shady or downright unethical. Your examples may be from business, industry, government, or other situations and may include ethical dilemmas on which your classmates can express conflicting opinions.

    b. Discuss an action or statement that is not illegal but is unethical.

    c. How can corporations help encourage honest conduct?

    d. Evaluate the following actions that have occurred in business:

        (1) A manager wrote to a customer:

        "Your request will be given our careful attention, and we assure you our objective is to be fair." (*This writer merely threw the case into a file folder, and told his secretary he had no intention of working on it or assigning anyone else to do so. He hoped that after a long wait the customer would forget.*)

        (2) An advertisement stated:

        "Nationwide, three out of four people prefer this amazing new product." (*Actually, the product was not nationally known, and only three persons in each of four states were surveyed.*)

CHAPTER 4
Business Communication Principles II

The preceding chapter discussed four of the seven business writing principles: completeness, conciseness, consideration, concreteness. To make your writing easily understood, friendly, and accurate, you should also apply the remaining C principles: clarity, courtesy, and correctness.

CLARITY

Clarity means getting your message across so the receiver will understand what you are trying to convey. You want that person to interpret your words with the same meaning you have in mind. Accomplishing that goal is difficult because, as you know, individual experiences are never identical; and words have different meanings to different persons, as discussed in Chapter 2.

Here are some specific ways to help make your messages clear.

1. Choose short, familiar, conversational words.
2. Construct effective sentences and paragraphs.
3. Achieve appropriate readability.
4. Include examples, illustrations, and other visual aids, when desirable.

Choose Short, Familiar, Conversational Words

When you have a choice between a long word and a short one, use the *short, familiar* word, since you can usually be more sure your reader or listener will understand it.

Say:	*Not:*	*Say:*	*Not:*
after	subsequent	home, house	domicile
big, large	substantial	pay	remuneration
error	inadvertency	show, uncover	disclose
issue	promulgate	use	utilize

Instead of Latin terms unfamiliar to your message receivers, *use synonyms.*

Say:	*Not:*	*Say:*	*Not:*
about	circa	that is	i.e.
following	sequent	for example	e.g.

Avoid technical jargon whenever possible when you talk or write to a person who is not acquainted with such words. If you must use technical words, define them briefly and clearly. If you don't, you'll confuse, embarrass, or irritate the reader, and perhaps be forced to explain later, as in the following story:

A plumber wrote the National Bureau of Standards to tell them hydrochloric acid is good for cleaning out clogged drains. (Before you go any further into the story, visualize the plumber. Assume you don't know him or have never exchanged correspondence. It is a pretty good guess he isn't a college graduate—maybe he didn't finish high school. But he probably is a good plumber—at least conscientious—because he's writing to the bureau to tell them something he thinks will help other people.)

In reply to the plumber's message, a technical specialist of the bureau wrote:

```
The efficacy of hydrochloric acid is indisputable, but the corrosive
residue is incompatible with metallic permanence.
```

The plumber then wrote to thank the bureau for agreeing with him—when, of course, the bureau was actually disagreeing with him. Sensing the plumber didn't understand, another member tried to set the man straight by writing:

```
We cannot assume responsibility for the production of toxic and nox-
ious residue with hydrochloric acid and suggest you use an alterna-
tive procedure.
```

Again the plumber thanked the bureau. Then, in desperation, the head of the department wrote:

```
Don't use hydrochloric acid. It eats hell out of the pipes.
```

The moral of this story is to write or speak on the *receiver's level of understanding*. Here are a few technical words used by mortgage loan firms—and the synonyms a layperson is more likely to understand:

Technical jargon	*Expressions familiar to the layperson*
abstract	history of the property
annual premium	annual payment
assessed valuation	value of property for tax purposes
charge to your principal	increase the balance of your loan
easement for ingress and egress	agreement allowing passage in and out
escrow account	reserve account for taxes and insurance
maturity date	final payment date
per diem	daily

Construct Effective Sentences and Paragraphs

Arranging your words in well-constructed sentences and paragraphs is also an important task that requires adaptation to your reader. Generally, the *average* length for sentences should be about 17 to 20 words; for paragraphs, about four to five lines in letters (eight to ten maximum). Even more important than length is quality. *Aim for unity, coherence, and emphasis.*

Unity

In a sentence—whether simple, compound, or complex—unity means that you have one main idea, and any other ideas in the sentence must be closely related to it. "I like Jim, and the Eiffel Tower is in Paris" obviously should not be in the same sentence.[1]

In a paragraph, unity likewise means you have one main idea or topic. A *topic sentence* expresses the main idea, usually at either the beginning or the end of the paragraph. The preferred position for the topic sentence in most business writing is at the beginning, where it receives the best emphasis. The sentences that follow it contain details to help develop the main idea. However, if you think that your main topic will be considered unfavorable or unclear by your reader, you may be wise to place the supporting details first and then lead up to the topic sentence at the end.

The following 69-word sentence to an insurance agent is confusing because it is too long and the main point is not emphasized clearly. Isn't the revised paragraph clearer—with topic sentence at the beginning—and with shorter sentences?

```
We have been advised that the allotment for the above-numbered pol-
icy was filed effective April 1984, but inasmuch as the premium due
March 1, 1984, of $90.91 has not been remitted and inasmuch as al-
lotment payments are not applicable to premiums due and payable in
advance of the effective date of allotment, we hereby request that
you contact the insured directly and request payment of this premium
due.
```

Revision:

```
Allotment payments can be applied only to premiums falling due after
the effective date of allotment. Since the allotment did not become
effective on this policy until April 1984, it cannot pay the March
1984 premium of $90.91. May we ask you to collect it?
```

---

[1] If you'd like a review on sentence structure or other essentials of correct English, see footnote 8, p. 81.

Coherence

In both sentences and paragraphs, coherence is the quality of hanging together in such a way that the intended meaning is clear. It involves showing the reader the relationships within a sentence, as well as pointing the way from one sentence to another. Place every modifier as close as possible to the word it is supposed to modify; otherwise, the meaning may be unclear. (See also Dangling Participles, Appendix B.)

Unclear:	Walking into your office, a bus hit the east wall.
Clear:	Walking into your office, I saw a bus hit the . . . .

Unclear:	Being a top lawyer, I am sure you can help us.
	Being a top lawyer, you can surely help us.
	or
Clear:	As you are a top lawyer, I am sure you . . . .

Emphasis

The quality that gives force to important parts of your sentence is *emphasis*. You can emphasize by position, space, and repetition. For instance, important ideas deserve the most important position in the sentence—at the beginning or at the end; they should not be buried in the middle. You can also emphasize important ideas by: giving them extra space, underlining them, stating them in short sentences and paragraphs (some as short as one line), or repeating significant words or phrases. Too much repetition, however, can result in a wordy sentence; too little repetition or the use of indefinite words such as *it* and *there is* can result in an unclear sentence.

Unclear:	Our association recommends Mr. Johnson's article on credit, but it says that in it he makes it seem easier than it is.
Clear:	Our association recommends Mr. Johnson's article on credit, but says that in the article he makes credit seem easier than it is.
	(*In a letter promoting a laundry's special dry cleaning process that practically eliminated ironing by the customer.*)
Unclear:	When your clothing is returned, there is very little left to iron. . . . We don't mangle your clothes by machinery; we do it carefully by hand.
Unclear:	It is necessary, for technical reasons, that these warheads should be stored upside down. That is, with the top at the bottom, and the bottom at the top. In order that there may be no doubt as to which is the bottom, and which is the top, for storage purposes it will be seen that the bottom of each warhead has been labeled with the word "TOP."

Achieve Appropriate Readability—and "Listenability"

Besides aiming for qualities of unity, coherence, and emphasis, you should adapt your business messages so that their word-and-sentence level will be appropriate for your recipient's general education level.

Among the guides that measure readability is Robert Gunning's well-known Fog Index.[2] It is based on two factors: length of sentence and percentage of hard words. By using the Fog Index, you can determine the educational level of your writing (and speaking—if you write your speech before presenting it).

1. *Find average sentence length.* Use a sample at least 100 words long (beginning preferably with the first word of a paragraph).[3] Divide the total number of words in this passage by the number or complete thoughts. (A simple or complex sentence has one complete thought; a compound sentence contains two complete thoughts.) Your quotient gives the average sentence length.
2. *Figure the percentage of "hard" words.* Count the number of words of three syllables or more. Include any unexplained abbreviations (CMO, BSD), but don't count words:
   a. That are (correctly) capitalized
   b. That are combinations of short, easy words (like *bookkeeper*).
   c. That are verb forms made into three syllables by adding *ed* or *es* (like *created* or *trespasses*)
   Divide the number of hard words by the total number of words. Your quotient is the percentage of hard words.
3. *Add the average sentence length and the percentage of hard words and multiply by 0.4.* The product, called the Fog Index, is the reading level required for the same number of years of education.

This readability formula can indicate whether your messages are on a level your receivers can easily understand. Everyone appreciates easy reading and listening with a Fog Index of between 8 and 12 (eighth- to twelfth-grade level). (*Reader's Digest* and *Time* have indexes between 9 and 10; *Scientific American* averages 11 or 12.) If your writing level to the average person is on the thirteenth level or higher, your message runs the risk of being ignored or misunderstood.

[2] Robert Gunning, *The Technique of Clear Writing,* rev. ed., McGraw-Hill, New York, 1968, p. 38. Used with permission of author, copyright owner.

[3] These additional guides from Robert Gunning may help you: (1) Count anything as a word that has space around it. Thus *March 1, 1986,* is 3 words; *one thousand dollars* is 3 words; *5 1/4* is 2 words; *five and one quarter* is 4 words; but *5¼* is 1 word; *twelve-month* is 1 word; *$5,000* and *$9,752,461* are each 1 word; if spelled out, the latter figure is 10 words. Exception: Do not count the numbers (I, II, 1, 2, 3) or alphabetic letters (A, B, a, b, c) that precede items or paragraphs. (2) Count hyphenated words as polysyllables only if one part is a word of 3 syllables or more. For example, *seventy-two* is 4 syllables. (3) Do not regard numerals as polysyllables regardless of pronunciation. Example: $987,652,431.50 is 1 syllable.

Among the writings and documents that especially need simplifying to be understood by the average reader are those from legal, insurance, medical, and government offices. Their messages sometimes have a Fog Index of 26 or more—at least 14 school years beyond a high school graduate. Also, in many other large companies the employee grapevine has indicated that management's messages are too often misinterpreted.

As you read the following portion of a letter, try to guess its readability level. (The underlined words have three or more syllables.)

Thank you for your nice letter of March 1, 198_____. Since you will be moving back to Pomona in the future, we look forward to meeting you then. To answer your questions regarding a savings plan, we have two types for your consideration.

1. Regular passbook savings yield 5 1/2 percent dividends compounded quarterly. You can make deposits and withdrawals by mail, with postage paid by us both ways.
2. Our Savings Certificates yield 12 percent dividends. Minimum amount for opening this type of account is $5,000 and then upward in amounts of $1,000. They can be six-month or twelve-month Certificates and are automatically renewable unless you advise us to the contrary. (110 words)

This example has 110 words in the first 8 sentences, or an average sentence length of 13.8 words. The 13 hard words (underlined) are 11.8 percent of the 110 words. From these figures, you can compute the Gunning Fog Index—10, the educational level of a high school sophomore.

Words in example	110
Sentences	8
Average sentence length (110÷8)	13.8
Percentage of hard words (13÷110)	11.8
Total	25.6
Multiplier	0.4
Grade level (Fog Index)	10.24

Though average sentence length should be about 17 to 20 words, a pleasing variety of length is desirable. You can use a range of, say, from 3 to 40 words; but when a sentence exceeds 40 or 45 words, ask yourself how you can rewrite it into more than one sentence. Also, if *all* sentences are short (for instance, under 10 words) the result is monotonous, primerlike language—choppy and undesirable.

Mr. Gunning considers his Fog Index a "simple warning system"—not a cure-all for any writing problem. He wants you to use this formula "to check to see if your writing is in step with that which has proved easy to read and understand."[4]

[4] Robert Gunning, "The Fog Index after Twenty Years," *Journal of Business Communication,* vol. 6, no. 2, Winter 1968, p. 3.

Readability formulas[5] are popular and helpful in improving clarity, but there are limitations and cautions. First, a person must be careful not to use too many simple words and short sentences, for the message would be monotonous, elementary, choppy. Second, some ''long'' words really aren't as difficult as some two-syllable words (for example, *employee* versus *avid*). Also, you must count the same word as many times as it appears in the passage. Finally, a message with crude, harsh, unethical, insulting words may still get a desirable Fog Index. Used with discretion, however, the formula will serve the purpose of a *guide* to the readability of letters, reports, books, magazine articles, or any other business writing—and speaking.

Include Examples, Illustrations, and Other Visual Aids, When Desirable

When you have a complicated and/or lengthy explanation in a letter, speech, or report, you'll often find you can improve the clarity by giving your recipient an example, an analogy, or an illustration. Furthermore, visual aids—such as headings, tabulations, itemizations, pictures, charts—are definite aids to clarity and easy understanding. Throughout this text—especially the section on reports—are examples of messages that use illustrations and visual aids to help clarify the material for the reader.

In summary, make your message clear by using words that are familiar to your receiver. Aim for unity, coherence, and emphasis in your sentences and paragraphs. Have *average* sentence length around 17–20 words; average paragraphs 4 to 5 lines in letters, 7 to 8 lines in reports. Itemize and tabulate figures to make them stand out clearly. And give your reader helpful examples with appropriate, easy-to-read headings whenever you need to explain complicated material.

COURTESY

Courteous messages help to strengthen present business friendships, as well as make new friends. Courtesy stems from sincere you-attitude. It is not merely politeness with mechanical insertions of ''please's'' and ''thank-you's.'' To be courteous the considerate communicator should follow—in addition to the four guidelines discussed under Consideration (Chapter 3)—these suggestions regarding *tone* and *promptness* of messages:

- Be sincerely tactful, thoughtful, and appreciative.
- Omit expressions that irritate, hurt, or belittle.

[5] See George Klare, *The Measurement of Readability,* Iowa State University Press, Ames, 1963, for a discussion of 31 different kinds of readability formulas.

- Grant and apologize good-naturedly.
- Answer your mail promptly.

Be Sincerely Tactful, Thoughtful, and Appreciative

Tact instead of Bluntness

Though few people intentionally want to be abrupt or blunt, these traits are a common cause of discourtesy. Sometimes they stem from negative personal attitudes; sometimes from a mistaken idea of conciseness. A time to be especially wary of bluntness is on those days when everything seems to go wrong. At such times, you are in danger of allowing your pent-up feelings to come through in your messages. Avoid expressions like those in the left-hand column below; rephrase as shown in the right-hand column.

Tactless; blunt	*Tactful*
Your letter is not clear at all; I can't understand it.	If I understand your letter correctly, ...
Obviously, if you'd read your policy carefully, you'd be able to answer these questions yourself.	Sometimes policy wording is a little hard to understand. I'm glad to clear up these questions for you.
Apparently you have already forgotten what I wrote you two weeks ago.	As mentioned in my May 15 letter (or memo) to you, (continue with the facts) . . . .

Writing a letter to a customer generally requires more conscious "niceties" than writing a memo to someone within your organization. A one-sentence memo like the following is all right to an employee or colleague if it adequately covers your particular message:

Tom,
Please call me (Ext. 312) to tell me the casting number on the side of the trunk safety lock you need for that '83 Ford.

But in letters to customers, you usually avoid a one-sentence body because it sounds blunt. Instead, you need to add a few tactful words, as in this example:

We will gladly replace the safety lock on the trunk of your 1983 Ford.

So that we can know the right lock to fit your trunk, please send the casting number. You'll find it imprinted on the side of the lock.

Thoughtfulness and Appreciation

Writers who send cordial, courteous messages of deserved congratulations and appreciation (to persons both inside and outside the firm) help build goodwill.[6] The value of goodwill or public esteem, can be recorded on the balance sheet in thousands (or even millions) of dollars. Much money is spent on advertising to attract new customers and to keep desirable old customers. While advertising may bring buyers into the front door of your firm, discourteous letters can drive customers out the back door! Even for routine payments "Thank you" or "We appreciate your prompt payment" can be added to your bill marked "paid" before you return it to the customer.

Omit Expressions That Irritate, Hurt, or Belittle

The thoughtful business communicator should avoid expressions that might offend the reader. Such expressions are discussed here in three groups: irritating, questionably humorous, and belittling statements.

Irritating Expressions

The following list contains irksome expressions to be avoided, particularly when used with "you" and "your."

contrary to your inference	you are delinquent
delinquency (delinquent)	you are probably ignorant of the
due to your questionable credit	fact that
we are unable to	you claim that
I do not agree with you	you did not tell us
if you care	you failed to
I'm sure you must realize	you forgot to
inexcusable	you have to
irresponsible	you leave us no choice
obnoxious	you neglected to; (overlooked)
obviously you overlooked	you say
simply nonsense	you should know
surely you don't expect	you surely don't expect
we are confused	your apparent disregard of our
we don't believe	previous request leaves us no
we expect you to	alternative
we find it difficult to	your complaint
believe that	your failure to
we must insist	your insinuation
we take issue	your neglect
why have you ignored	your stubborn silence

---

[6] For examples of goodwill messages see Chap. 15.

Questionable Humor

Humor is often quite effective in business writing. However, before you try to be funny, be sure your humor is good-natured and appropriate for the situation. A flippant attitude can be in poor taste, as letter 1 indicates. Letter 2 conveys the same message informally but courteously.[7]

Letter 1: Offensive rather than humorous

```
Dear Mr. and Mrs. Smith:

    We were mighty happy to learn about the package the stork brought
you.  And what a distinguished tag you put on him. . .Joshua Gerald
Smith II.  You tell Josh:  that as soon as he's ready, his Prudential
agent will be around to help him set up his insurance program.

    In the meantime, I guess it's up to us to take care of the little
fellow's insurance needs for a while--you know, educational funds
and a little nest egg to help him start his journey through life.

    I'll phone you in a couple of days to find out when it will be
convenient for you to talk about insurance for your new bundle of
joy.  Till then, keep his powder dry!
```

Letter 2: Courteous

```
Dear Mr. and Mrs. Smith:

    Congratulations on the birth of your son, Joshua.

    Like other thoughtful parents, you no doubt want him to have a
happy, well-protected future.  It may seem early to be concerned
about financing his college education.  But we at Prudential have
seen too many youngsters miss out on college because their parents
put off the problem too long.

    If it is convenient, I would like to call at seven o'clock Friday
evening to show you how Prudential can help you solve this problem.
I'll phone Thursday to confirm the appointment or to arrange a dif-
ferent time that you prefer.
```

Belittling Statements

Talking down to or belittling a person is another form of discourtesy that can have a profoundly unfavorable effect, as in the following case:

---

[7] From *Dear Sir*, vol. 3, no. 1, Correspondence Improvement Section, Public Relations Department, Prudential Insurance Company of America, Newark, N.J., 1961-1962.

To substantiate a railroad claim, the accountant of the AMC company needed the exact charges on certain returnable drums in which the XYZ Chemical Company annually shipped thousands of dollars worth of chemicals to AMC. AMC's accountant checked with the local representative of XYZ Company for this information, but was asked by him to contact Mrs. Lancaster in Diamond, California. After writing to her, the accountant received the following reply, which he said caused "a much greater explosion within our department than could have all XYZ chemicals combined."

> In reply to your letter of October 10th addressed to Diamond, California, attention Mrs. Lancaster, you made two mistakes. In the first place we have no Mrs. Lancaster, and in the second place Diamond is not a place to send mail.
>
> We make a charge of $8.50 on the Carbon Bisulphide—Carbon Tetrachloride Mixture drum to AMC Company, in your city. That is for the drum only. We trust this is what is meant.

Grant and Apologize Good-Naturedly

Whenever you grant a customer's request, begin your letter with the best news first and inject a courteous, ungrudging tone. Notice the difference in tone of the following two paragraphs:

Grudging:

> You request causes a great deal of extra paper work to change monthly payments. However, in compliance with your request we hereby reduce your monthly interest and principal payments called for in our note to $_____, plus $_____ for taxes and insurance; effective (month–day–year) your total monthly payment will be $_____.

Good-natured:

> As you requested, we will reduce the monthly interest and principal payments called for in your note to $_____, plus $_____ for taxes and insurance. Thus, starting (month–day–year) your total monthly payment will be $_____.

If a request has caused you extra work, you may tactfully tell the customer somewhere in the letter—but not the first paragraph—to notify you by a certain time if he or she again wishes to change something.

Occasionally you may get a "nasty" letter from a customer who is wrong in his or her accusations. A courteous reply can lead not only to an apology from the customer but also future staunch loyalty as a booster for your organization.

When someone in your organization makes a mistake, you can apologize and correct the error perhaps even before the customer discovers it. Sometimes a small, courteous printed form is useful to admit an error promptly and to explain how (and when) you are correcting it. Of course, if the matter is serious or complicated, a special letter will be more appropriate, as you will see in later chapters.

Answer Your Mail Promptly

For courtesy as well as better results one should answer a business inquiry promptly—in a few days if possible. Even a reply on the bottom of the inquiry or a handwritten note on a postcard is usually better than a late (or no!) reply. If you need time to gather information, or have a stack of other urgent work, before you can answer a request, send a short note to acknowledge the reader's letter and state about when the requested material will be mailed.

In summary, the courteous communicator is sincerely tactful, thoughtful, and appreciative. In both written and oral messages courtesy requires omitting expressions that irritate, belittle, or have questionable humor. The courteous person also grants and apologizes good-naturedly and answers mail promptly. Tone and promptness are special qualities of courtesy.

CORRECTNESS

The correctness principle comprises more than proper grammar, punctuation, and spelling. A message may be perfect grammatically and mechanically but still insult or lose a customer and fail to achieve its purpose. The term *correctness,* as applied to a business message, means the writer should:

- Use the right level of language
- Include only accurate facts, words, and figures
- Maintain acceptable writing mechanics
- Choose nondiscriminatory expressions
- Apply all other pertinent C qualities

Use the Right Level of Language

The three levels of language—formal, informal, and substandard—overlap because of our ever-changing language. English, with almost a million words, has the richest, largest vocabulary on earth. Some words once considered substandard have moved into the informal level, and some once informal words are now acceptable on a formal level. The first two—formal and informal language—are both correct; but they are quite different from one another, have different uses, and should not be interchanged.

The *formal level* of language is used for writing scholarly dissertations—master and doctoral dissertations, legal documents, top-level government agreements, and other materials in which formality is expected. The expressions used are often long, unconversational, and impersonal—just what the term *formal* implies.

In contrast, the *informal level* refers to the language of business—for letters, reports, newspapers, and other business communications. Instead of formal words, you will use short, well-known, and conversational words, as the following list illustrates:

Formal	Informal	Formal	Informal
anticipate	expect	endeavor	try
ascertain	find out	interrogate	ask
conflagration	fire	procure	get
deem	think (believe)	terminate	end
edifice	building	utilize	use

The following poem by Enid C. Stickel provides a humorous example of how people try to formalize their language.

Readability Gap
Colleges aren't schools,
They are learning institutions;
Problems don't have answers,
They have viable solutions.
People don't spend money,
They re-allocate resources.
Newsmen don't use tipsters,
They rely on informed sources.

Speakers don't make speeches,
They give oral presentations.
Bosses don't set quotas,
They just indicate objectives.
Workers don't take orders,
Though they implement directives.

Machinery can't break down,
But components can malfunction.
A court does not command
It just issues an injunction.
Programs don't have failures,
They have qualified successes.
And jargon doesn't hurt you—
It just constantly distresses!

The third level of language—*substandard*—is the one you want to avoid, because people generally don't accept it. If you use words on this level in writing (or in speaking), your reader(s) will begin to question your ability to use good English. Here are a few examples:

Substandard	Acceptable	Substandard	Acceptable
ain't	isn't, aren't	haven't got	don't have
between you and I	between you and me	in regards to	regarding
		irregardless	regardless
can't hardly	can hardly	nohow	anyway
hadn't ought	shouldn't	should of	should have

The following sentences illustrate the three levels of language discussed above:

Formal:
```
Although item 21 is enumerated in this report, the
writer has ascertained that it is currently not in the
organization's inventory or in the writer's posses-
sion.
```

Informal:
```
Although item 21 is listed in the report, it's not in
our stock now and I don't have it either.
```

Substandard:
```
Irregardless of the report that item ain't on our
shelves now, and I haven't got it either.
```

Include Only Accurate Facts, Words, and Figures

Absolute accuracy is essential for effective written messages. One erroneous digit (for example, $25,000 instead of $75,000) can make a difference of thousands of dollars. Even small errors of a few cents can be annoying to customers and undermine goodwill, as various examples in this text will show. And a wrong figure in an account number muddles up records and leads to untold problems.

To be sure of the accuracy of your facts, you should verify all statements before writing and again before you sign or approve the message. Of course, you also need to be up-to-date on laws that affect your organization. Guessing or assuming that you are right can be costly. Just because a certain fact was true about a customer last year—or even last month—does not assure it is true now, as the following case illustrates:

Mr. Henry Simson sent in a claim for medical benefits to his insurance company. In turn, the correspondent handling the case wrote back to Mr. Simson, saying, "We are pleased to enclose a check for $277.54 for benefits due you because of your confinement at the Mountain View Hospital." Unfortunately this correspondent shouldn't have sent the check because that hospital was not certified as a full "general" hospital, a requirement under the terms of Mr. Simson's policy. Innocently, Mr. Simson cashed the check.

A month later the mistake was discovered and a notation made on Simson's file to the effect that no future payments were to be made because of confinement to the Mountain View Hospital.

Two months afterward Mr. Simson again sent a claim for medical benefits because he once again had been a patient in that same hospital. The person who handled the claim this time consulted Simson's file, found the notation, and wrote a letter refusing the claim.

However, this refusal was wrong because between Simson's two admissions the Mountain View Hospital had been certified as a full "general" hospital. Had the correspondents at the insurance company checked all the facts, such a mix-up would not have happened.

The good business writer must be continually alert to accuracy because of changing rates, regulations, laws, and conditions locally, nationally, and within his or her organization.

Also, like most things in life, English is ever-changing. Even the dictionaries can't keep up with its fast pace, but they can usually help you choose correct words to convey your intended meaning. Below are a few of the many words that are often confused in usage.

a, an	Use *a* before a word that begins with the consonant sound or long ''u'' sound. Use *an* before a word that begins with a silent ''h'' or a vowel sound.
amount, number, quantity	Whenever you count the units, use *number*. *Amount* and *quantity* refer to bulk, weight, or sums.
anxious, eager	*Anxious* implies worry, whereas *eager* conveys keen desire.
between, among	*Between* involves two people or two groups; *among,* three or more.
biannually, biennially	*Biannually* means two times a year; *biennially,* every two years.
continual, continuous	*Continual* means to recur regularly (like lapping ocean waves). *Continuous* means without stopping.
counsel, council	*counsel* (verb) means to advise, and (noun) means lawyer, advice. *Council* (noun) is an advisory or governing group.
data	*Data,* plural of *datum,* is now used informally with a singular verb (This data *is*) when all the facts are considered as a unit; but the plural (These data *are*) is the more appropriate in formal usage.
effect, affect	In business usage only *effect* is a noun; it means result, condition, or influence. Both words are verbs—to *effect* is to bring about, to *affect* is to influence.
imply, infer	*Imply* means to insinuate, or suggest; *infer* means to conclude. A writer *implies;* the reader *infers.*

lay, laid, laid lie, lay, lain	A person or a rug *lies* on the floor, but a person *lays* the book on the table or *lays* oneself on the floor. If you can substitute *place(s)* and answer *what?*, use the proper tense of *lay*.
principal, principle	*Principal* means "chief," "main," or (noun) sum of money, head of a school; *principle*, rule or basic truth.
which, that, who	*That* refers to persons or things; *who* to people; *which* only to things.

Maintain Acceptable Writing Mechanics

Acceptable writing mechanics includes correct punctuation, capitalization, syllabication, and spelling—plus correct sentence and paragraph structure already mentioned under Clarity. This area also includes using correct format for letters, memos, reports, and envelopes—as discussed in other chapters of this book.

If you need review on the dangling participle, numbers as words or figures, abbreviations, punctuation, and other details that seem to plague writers, you'll find helpful suggestions in Appendix B. And if you need help on the parts of speech and sentence structure, be sure to consult an excellent, up-to-date grammar book.[8]

Two common weaknesses in writing mechanics deserve special, though brief, mention here: the inability to spell correctly and careless omissions.

Spelling Errors

Business executives and customers expect you to spell correctly and may begin to question your overall ability if you misspell—especially the customer's name and everyday words like *convenience, questionnaire, stationery, personnel,* and *accommodation.* Errors of transposition (*nad* instead of *and* or *recieve* instead of *receive*) are also spelling errors that show carelessness.

If you are one of the many educated men and women who are better able to solve complicated business problems than spell correctly, you can take two precautions: refer to a dictionary often, and hire a top-notch assistant who's a whiz at spelling! English spelling does have many inconsistencies. Among them

---

[8] Any of the following contain helpful material on grammar and English for business communication: Greta Henderson and Price R. Voiles, *Business English Essentials,* 6th ed., McGraw-Hill, New York, 1980; Celia Millward, *Handbook for Writers: Grammar, Punctuation, Diction, Rhetoric, Research,* Holt, Rinehart & Winston, New York, 1980; Norman B. Sigband, Theodore W. Hipple, Lois J. Bachman, *Successful Business English,* Scott, Foresman, Glenview, Ill., 1983; and William Strunk and E. B. White, *Elements of Style,* 3d ed., Macmillan, New York, 1978.

are also short words like these—pronounced the same yet spelled differently: made, paid; rule, school; say, weigh; dough, blow; sign, line; trend, friend. Inconsistencies in plurals are highlighted in this anonymous poem:

Pluralistics
We'll begin with a box and the plural is boxes,
But the plural of ox should be oxen not oxes.
Then one fowl is a goose but two are called geese,
Yet the plural of mouse should never be meese.
You may find a lone mouse or a whole set of mice,
But the plural of house is houses not hice.
If the plural of man is always called men,
Shouldn't the plural of pan be called pen?
If I speak of a foot and you show me your feet,
And I give you a boot would a pair be called beet?

If one is a tooth and whole set are teeth,
Why should not the plural of booth be called beeth?
Then one may be that and three would be those,
Yet hat in that plural wouldn't be hose.
And the plural of cat is cats and not cose.
We speak of a brother and also of brethren,
But though we say Mother we never say Methren,
Then the masculine pronouns are he, his, and him,
But imagine the feminine, she, shis, and shim.
So English I fancy, you all will agree.
Is the funniest language you ever did see.

Careless Omissions

Another way to maintain correct writing mechanics is to double-check for any careless omissions of punctuation marks or words needed for grammatical accuracy. Sometimes even small omissions can lead to costly miscommunication, as this example illustrates:

A traveling client had instructed his stock broker to buy for him as many shares of a certain company's stock as was possible and desirable. One day the broker found an opportunity to purchase 3,000 shares. Because the price had risen considerably, he asked the client to wire his decision—whether or not to buy. The client considered the price exorbitant. He wired:

NO. PRICE TOO HIGH.

Unfortunately, the period was omitted after the first word; and the broker bought the unwanted shares.

Choose Nondiscriminatory Expressions

Another important requirement for correctness is "equal treatment of the sexes" and nonbias toward people of different races, ethnic origins, or physical features. Conscientious business communicators (as well as authors) should be continually alert to use nondiscriminatory expressions whenever possible. The suggestions selected here are guidelines that can be particularly useful for your written and oral business communication. Try to choose nondiscriminatory language when you refer to occupational roles and achievements, personal characteristics, physical and mental attributes, humanity at large, names, and various title designations.[9]

Occupational Roles and Achievements

People should not be stereotyped or arbitrarily assigned to a leading or secondary role because of their gender, race, ethnic group, or some physical "handicap." Individuals can be in a variety of professional work at all levels— doctors and nurses; principals, professors, and teachers; lawyers, judges, and social workers; bank presidents and tellers; accountants, pilots, plumbers, computer operators, and many others.

Personal Characteristics

Women and girls of any race or ethnic origin should be shown as having the same ambitions, abilities, mental strengths and weaknesses as men and boys. Both sexes include some people who are industrious, active, strong, independent, courageous, competent, decisive, assertive, persistent, serious-minded, successful. Both include logical thinkers, problem solvers, and decision makers pursuing career goals.

Stereotypes of the logical, objective male and the emotional, subjective female are to be avoided. Among them are: scatterbrained female, henpecking shrew, apron-wearing mother, frustrated spinster, and nagging mother-in-law clichés. Also taboo are biased words when used against all or most members of any race, age, disability, or ethnic background. Examples include such words as: aloof, pagan, untrustworthy, lazy, useless, stingy, hot-tempered, insane, dull.

In descriptions, the smarter, braver, or more successful person should be a woman or girl as often as a man or boy. Characteristics that have been traditionally praised in women—such as gentleness, compassion, sensitivity— should also be praised in men. Characteristics that have been praised in men— such as boldness, initiative, assertiveness—should also be praised in women.

---

[9] The discussion in this section is adapted mainly from "Guidelines for Equal Treatment of the Sexes in McGraw-Hill Book Company Publications." For a bibliography of 16 publications about sexist and nondiscriminatory communication, see "Some Guidelines for Nondiscriminatory Communication," *The Journal of Business Communication,* vol. 16, no. 2, Winter 1979, pp. 75–76. See also International Association of Business Communicators, *Without Bias: A Guidebook for Nondiscriminatory Communication,* ed. by Judy E. Pickens, Wiley, New York, 1982.

Physical and Mental Attributes

Men and women should be treated with the same respect, dignity, and serious-ness. Neither should be trivialized or stereotyped. Women should not be described by physical attributes when men are described by mental attributes or professional position.

Not this:	Henry Harris is a shrewd lawyer and his wife Ann is a striking brunette.
But this:	The Harrises are an attractive couple. Henry is a handsome blond and Ann is a striking brunette.
OR:	The Harrises are highly respected in their fields. Ann is an accomplished musician and Henry is a shrewd lawyer.
OR:	The Harrises are an interesting couple. Henry is a shrewd lawyer and Ann is very active in community (church; civic) affairs.

Here are suggestions for changing some other undesirable expressions into acceptable ones:

No	*Yes*
girl, as in: I'll have my *girl* check that.	I'll have my *secretary* (my *assistant*) check that. (Or use the person's name.)
female-gender word forms, such as *authoress, poetess, Jewess*	*author, poet, Jew*
the better half; ball and chain	*wife*
career girl or *career woman*	name the woman's profession: *Attorney Ellen Smith; Marie Sanchez, a journalist (editor; business executive; doctor; lawyer; or agent)*
Housewives are feeling the pinch of higher prices.	*Consumers (customers* or *shoppers)* are feeling the pinch of higher prices.

In descriptions of men, especially men in the home, references to general ineptness should be avoided. Men should not be characterized as dependent on women for meals, or clumsy in household maintenance or self-care.

Humanity at Large

In references to humanity at large, language should include women and girls. Common problems encountered when trying to meet this goal stem from "*man*-words" and singular pronouns.

Man-Words. The word *man* has long been used to denote not only a male person, but also, generically, humanity at large. However, to many people today the word *man* has become so closely associated with "a male human being" that they consider it no longer broad enough to be applied to any person or to human beings as a whole. In deference to this position, alternative expressions should be used whenever such substitutions do not produce an awkward or artificial construction. The following are some possible substitutions for man-words:

No	*Yes*
mankind	humanity; human beings; human race; people
If a man drove 50 miles . . .	If a person (or driver) drove 50 miles . . .
the best man for the job	the best person (or candidate) for the job
man-made	synthetic; manufactured; artificial; constructed; of human origin
manpower	human power; human energy; workers; workforce
grow to manhood	grow to adulthood; grow to manhood or womanhood

In cases where man-words must be used, special efforts should be made to ensure that pictures and other devices or a footnote makes explicit that such references are meant in their generic sense—to include all human beings and both sexes.

Singular Pronouns. Because the English language lacks a generic singular pronoun signifying "he or she," it has been customary and grammatically sanctioned to use masculine pronouns in expressions such as "anyone . . . *he*," and "each customer . . . *his* bill." Nevertheless, we should avoid whenever possible the pronouns *he, him,* and *his* when referring to the hypothetical person or humanity in general. Here are possible alternatives to consider:

	Alternative	*No*	*Yes*
1.	Reword to eliminate unnecessary gender pronouns.	The average American drinks *his* coffee black.	The average American drinks black coffee.
2.	Recast into the plural.	The average *American* drinks *his*. . . . The shopper . . . *she*	Average *Americans* drink *their* coffee . . . Shoppers . . . *they*
3.	Alternate male and female expressions and examples.	Supervisors often say, ''*He's* not the right man for the job,'' or ''*He* lacks the qualifications for success.''	Supervisors often say, ''*She's* not the right person for the job,'' or ''*He* lacks the qualifications for success.''
4.	Replace the masculine pronoun with *one, you, he or she, her or his*. (Use *he or she* and its variations sparingly to avoid clumsy prose.)	This sale benefits every charge customer. He may purchase up to. . . .	This sale benefits every charge customer. *One* (or *he or she*) may purchase up to. . . .
5.	Repeat the noun (or a similar noun) if at least a few words intervene.	The executive benefits from this policy every month. *He* may choose from. . . .	The executive benefits from this policy every month. Each *executive* (or *manager*) may. . . .
6.	Sometimes change to passive voice instead of active voice.	Every employee has an assigned parking place. *He should park* his car in. . . .	Every employee has an assigned parking place. Each car *should be parked* in. . . .

7. In long reports, to avoid severe problems of repetition or inept wording, it may sometimes be best to use the generic *he* freely. But you should add, in the preface and as often as necessary in the text, emphatic statements that the masculine pronouns are being used for succinctness and are intended to refer to both men and women. Each communicator must use good judgment regarding which alternatives to choose.

Names, Titles, and Parallel Language

Expressions used to designate men and women should, whenever possible, treat the sexes equally—by using their own names, nonsexist titles, and parallel language.

Own Names. Women should be referred to by their own names in the same ways that men are. Both should be called by their full names, by first or last name only, or by title. Unnecessary reference to a woman's marital status should be avoided. Whether married or not, a woman may be referred to by the name by which she chooses to be known, whether her name is her original or her married name, or a combination (Smith-Jones).

No	*Yes*
Ron Smith and Helen	Ron Smith and Helen Brown
Helen and Smith	Helen and Ron
Mrs. Brown and Smith	Ms. Brown (because she prefers Ms.) and Mr. Smith
Miss Kohn and David Green	Hilda Kohn and David Green or Miss Kohn and Dr. Green

Occupational Titles Ending in "Man." Whenever desirable, occupational titles should be nonsexist. Terms ending in "man" may be replaced by terms that can include members of either sex unless they refer to a particular person.

Yes, for men	*Yes, for men and/or women*
businessman	business executives; business person; manager
cameraman	camera operator, photographer, technician
chairman	chairperson, chairman and chairwoman, head, leader, coordinator, moderator, person presiding at (or chairing) a meeting, presiding officer, or the chair[10]
congressman	member of Congress; representative (but Congress*man* Koch and Congress*woman* Swanson)
mailman; postman	mail carrier; letter carrier
salesman	sales representative; salesperson; sales clerk; sales agent

Parallel Language. Words like the following should be expressed in parallel terms:

---

[10] For decades the accepted procedure at meetings when addressing a woman presiding officer has been "Madam Chairman." Ardent nonsexist communicators have asked, humorously, how a man presiding officer would feel if he were addressed as "Sir Chairwoman."

No	*Yes*

men and ladies   men and women
gentlemen and ladies, girls and boys

man and wife   husband and wife

The foregoing discussion and examples have introduced you to ways you can reconstruct, substitute, or omit expressions in order to correct discriminatory communication. However, always remember that good judgment is necessary. Before you change any words, check their meanings and roots to be sure they need to be changed. For some expressions changes could be unnecessary and ridiculously incorrect.

In summary, for overall correctness in business communications you should always watch for the little things as well as for the big things. And never leave checking for correctness solely to your secretary. Once you sign your name or initials to the message, you assume responsibility for everything on the page—correct language level, facts, figures, words, mechanics, nondiscrimination, and also all the other pertinent C qualities discussed in this book.

SUMMARY CHECKLIST OF BUSINESS
COMMUNICATION PRINCIPLES

Completeness: Answer all questions asked
Give something extra, when desirable
Check for the five W's and any other essentials

Conciseness: Shorten or omit wordy expressions
Include only relevant statements
Avoid unnecessary repetition

Consideration: Focus on "you" instead of "I" and "we"
Show reader benefit or interest in reader
Emphasize the positive, pleasant facts
Apply integrity and ethics

Concreteness: Use specific facts and figures
Put action in your verbs
Choose vivid, image-building words

Clarity: Choose short, familiar, conversational words
Construct effective sentences and paragraphs
Achieve appropriate readability—and "listenability"
Include examples, illustrations, and other visual
aids, when desirable

Courtesy:	Be sincerely tactful, thoughtful, and appreciative
	Omit expressions that irritate, hurt, or belittle
	Grant and apologize good-naturedly
	Answer your mail promptly
Correctness:	Use the right level of language
	Include only accurate facts, words, and figures
	Maintain acceptable writing mechanics
	Choose nondiscriminatory expressions
	Apply all other pertinent C qualities

EXERCISES

1. Correct the following sentences so that meanings are clear. If necessary, use more than one concise sentence.

   a. From an employee news bulletin:
      Remember next Friday's paper drive! Bring your papers (and your neighbors). Put them in paper bags and tie them, if possible.
   b. During a job interview the executive wants to hear what you can do in a few seconds.
   c. Enclosed are your contracts on Gary Green in triplicate.
   d. Mr. Jones visited the factory yesterday and lectured on "Destructive Pests." A large number were present.
   e. Your Memorial Day speech will be followed by the firing squad.
   f. From the mayor of a city to the county engineer:
      I have reviewed the plans of Metro, their ability to finance, and in some areas, realizing a great number of years may elapse, because of financial conditions and the build-up of areas, before construction is warranted of sanitary trunk lines for sewers, I think it is very appropriate at this time that the county enter into a study and possibly use their ability given to them under the County Services Act of operating lagoons and serving areas that can develop only if sanitary sewers are constructed.
   g. From one insurance company to another insurance company:
      Frankly, the information we have while it may disclose some contributory negligence on our assured's part which, of course, is questionable, we still feel that your assured had he not been driving at the high rate of speed that he was could have swerved to his right and avoided our assured's vehicle but due to the fact he was coming down a hill at such a tremendous rate of speed with no control over his car and struck our assured, there was enough room to the right of your assured to have turned slightly and, therefore, avoided the accident.
   h. Working in a grocery, several professors chat with him daily.
   i. She wanted a policy for her house that cost $100 a year.
   j. Although working full time on an outside job, Tom's grades remained good.

```
    k. Thank you for your letter concerning the 10 pianos we received by
       airmail this morning.
    l. When only four years old, this customer's mother died.
    m. As an experienced certified public accountant, I would like to
       ask your help with a problem my high school bookkeeping instruc-
       tor assigned to us today.
```

2. Check the Fog Index of two pieces of business writing—one that you consider easy to read and one that is difficult. Then tell the class how the Fog Index of each agrees with your readability level. Use examples from this list:

   a. Letter from a company to a customer
   b. Annual report
   c. Magazine read by the masses or members of a certain profession
   d. *The Wall Street Journal*
   e. Article on front page of your daily newspaper
   f. Report or textbook. One sample selection for a 500-word report, article, or booklet is sufficient. In long reports (or books) five or six separated samples may be desirable.

3. Assume you are writing to the average citizen. What synonyms for the following words would be better understood?

accelerate	contingent	rescind
aggregating	default	validity
allegation	discrepancy	terminate

4. Using your dictionary, find the meaning of the following words that are similar in sound but have different meanings:

extinction, distinction	eminent, imminent
ingenious, ingenuous	receipt, recede
historical, hysterical	moral, morale

5. Correct the errors in the following message from a savings association to a real estate corporation:

```
In rgard to your letter of the fifteenth, let me explain our policy
on our Certificates of deposit.  Your certificate comes due on
November 9, 198___.  At this time the interest check will be dis-
persed as you indicated at the time of your initial deposit and the
certificate will be automaticly renewed unless you give us instruc-
tions to the contrary.

In your letter you asked that the certificate be "rolled over for
another 30 days."  As I have explained our certificates have a life
of 6 months, if you want the certificate renewed it will automat-
```

```
icaly be done. If you wish the certificate to be dispersed please
contackt us prior to the experation date.
```

6. *Exercises on choice of words:* Choose the word or words that should be used in each sentence listed below. (For choice of words in some sentences you might need to consult a dictionary or grammar book in addition to the rules for word usage in this chapter.)

```
  a. This act will not (effect, affect) my confidence in you.
  b. I am (anxious, eager) to (tell, advise) you that you are cor-
     rect.
  c. (Continuous, continual) rains are drenching the fields.
  d. We assure you (its, it's) a pleasure to do as you suggest.
  e. Enclosed (please find, is) my check for ($100.00, $100).
  f. We have a large (quantity, amount, number) of suits on hand.
  g. The dissension (between, among) the five departments has been
     settled by a (well known, well-known) authority.
  h. The man (who, which, that) was crossing the street was struck by
     a car (who, which, that) Mr. Smith was driving.
  i. (A, An) university regent held (a, an) one-hour meeting with (a,
     an) honor society (council, counsel).
  j. We sold (fewer, less) fans last month.
  k. We had (already, all ready) received the suit when your letter
     arrived.  I am (already, all ready) to write this customer.
  l. Your rug should (lie, lay) (smooth, smoothly) on the floor.
  m. Please (lay, lie) the files on my desk.
  n. The (principal, principle) officer of this company is Ms. Jones.
  o. The (principal, principle) of honesty should be evident in our
     letters.  Now that you've been paying on your house for three
     years, how much (principle, principal) have you accumulated?
  p. The (principle, principal) of the school criticized the boy be-
     cause he didn't know the (principal, principle) river in the
     United States is the Mississippi.
  q. Of the two plans, the second is (least, less) expensive.
  r. Do you know (who, whom) the manager promoted yesterday?
  s. I never knew anyone could be so slow in answering when a person
     wrote to (them, her or him).
  t. Just between you and (I, me), that package is for Helen and (I,
     me, myself).
  u. Be courteous to (whomever, whoever) comes to your desk.
  v. A large number of bills (is, are) outstanding.
  w. The large number of employees (prevent, prevents) us from adher-
     ing to this suggestion.
```

7. Assume the following words appear in the letters and reports your secretary has typed for your signature. Without the help of any source, determine which words are misspelled and correct the errors. Then check all words (in a dictionary or in class) to see how many you had right.[11]

---

[11] If you need a handy pocket-size dictionary to help you spell correctly, try *20,000 Words*, compiled by Louis A. Leslie, McGraw-Hill, New York, 1978.

1. accommodation
2. aquainted
3. attatched
4. attendence
5. attornies
6. batchelor's degree
7. benefited
8. brosure
9. compliment
   (meaning supplement)
10. catalog
11. childrens'
12. colledge
13. consede
14. concensus
15. congradulate
16. convience
17. correspondant

18. defendent
19. descendant
20. develop
21. dissadvantage
22. disatisfaction
23. envelop
24. excellant
25. existance
26. Febuary
27. heighth
28. incessent
29. insistance
30. interupt
31. it's (possessive)
32. knowlege
33. labled
34. manageing
35. mispelled

36. occured
37. oppurtunity
38. paralel
39. preceed
40. prefered
41. proceedure
42. proceed
43. questionaire
44. recieve
45. referance
46. referred
47. recind
48. reccomodation
49. resistence
50. sargeant
51. seperate
52. servicable
53. stationary (paper)

8. Assume that you received from a leading corporation a complicated, unclear letter to stockholders. You wrote the chairperson suggesting the need for simplifying communications to the average stockholder, and for stating clearly the purpose of the meeting. The following is the chairperson's reply. Is it courteous and clear? Why or why not?

```
Yours is the first criticism we have had from the many thousands of
stockholders who have already sent in the proxies saying that the
purpose of the meeting was not understandable to them. I do not
see how I can state the facts any more clearly and simply than was
done in my letter of January 18.
```

9. Suggest acceptable nonsexist alternatives, if desirable, for the following words:

bellboy
checkroom girl
committeeman
craftsman
deliveryboy

foreman
furnaceman
layman
lumberman
maiden name

manhole
man-hours
repairman
showmanship
workman

10. For the following interdepartmental memo (a) list all sexist statements and (b) opposite each statement write a nonsexist version. Number the paragraphs and your corrections in each.

```
To:      Mrs. Erica Cosmos              DATE: May 10, 198___
FROM:    Tom Grant
SUBJECT: CPC Staffing Requirements
```

I would like your support along with that of Charles to serve as co-chairmen of our Staffing Requirements Committee for the Communications Planning Centers. As you know, the CPC's are a most important sales tool and we need highly qualified manpower with top salesmen.

The other committeemen I have appointed to work with you are: Scott Durke, Fred Picker, Miss Helen Jaynes, and Mrs. Thoms.

One of the important jobs at the centers is that of a professional sales demonstrator, which requires many man-hours of work. This man will be an entry-level group manager, responsible for all equipment sales demonstrations. He must of course be extremely knowledgeable about all our products and services. Currently this assignment is being handled by Miss Carolyn Mayer at our XY Center and by Kermit Smith at ABC Center. Both are doing a superior job.

We would like this task to be a one-year rotational assignment and be filled with the best available candidate--man or lady. This job experience can greatly benefit the assigned individual and make him more valuable to our company on future reassignments. Please get your committee together this week to begin an extensive search for good people that are available for these assignments. If you need help typing announcements or other materials, I've asked the gals in the typing pool to be available for you.

11. Encircle the correct choice of "a" or "an" before each entry in the following list.

a	an	hotel	a	an	heroic effort
a	an	honorary degree	a	an	hour
a	an	unit	a	an	heir
a	an	historical event	a	an	union
a	an	honest opinion	a	an	unanimous decision
a	an	unique method	a	an	humble opinion

CHAPTER 5

Planning, Organizing, Editing before Communicating

Whether you are preparing a written or an oral business communication, you need to plan, organize, edit—and revise when desirable—before transmitting that message. These steps are essential for successful communication. Remember, your goal is to gain the desired reaction or action from the recipient.

Your letter on company stationery or your telephone call as a company representative to a customer can create in the receiver's mind a favorable or unfavorable attitude toward your entire organization. Even after you have communicated orally on an important matter, you are often asked to "put it in writing." Your message then becomes a permanent record which the recipient can reread anytime. Also, if geographical distance separates you and the person with whom you are communicating, or if the material is complex, technical, or lengthy, writing is often the only effective means of communication. A well-organized letter is like a bridge that spans the gap between you and the receiver of your message.

This chapter discusses the planning steps; basic organizational patterns; openings and closings; and preparing, editing, and revising steps. Though the suggestions presented here can be useful for both written and oral communications, the discussion and examples focus on written messages—especially letters and memos.

FIVE PLANNING STEPS

To communicate effectively, you should go through the following steps before you write your message:

- Know the purpose of the message.
- Visualize your reader (or listener).
- Choose the ideas to include.
- Get all the facts to back up these ideas.
- Outline—organize—your message.

Know the Purpose

Your first step when planning your communication is to determine your main purpose. For instance, is it to get an immediate replacement for defective articles? Or is your main purpose to announce your firm's new location? Or to apologize for a serious error? Or to persuade prospects to buy your product? Or to explain why you are not granting a customer's requested refund?

In addition to the specific purpose of each message, all communications have, of course, an underlying general purpose—to build goodwill. For example, in a refusal or a collection letter, the purpose should be twofold—not only to refuse a request or ask for money, but also to maintain the customer's goodwill.

Visualize Your Reader

After reading about the communication process and principles (Chapters 2–4), you realize how important it is to adapt your messages as much as possible to the recipients' views and mental filters. If you are well acquainted with your readers—or even if you have met them at least once—you can actually visualize each individual. Most of your writing, however, will probably be directed to people you have never met.

If you are sending a message to one person, you should try to picture that person the best ways you can—business or professional person or laborer; superior (boss), colleague, or subordinate; man or woman; young, middle-aged, or elderly; new or longtime customer; and so on. If you are addressing a form message to many people, remember the caution that every person within any group has a unique filter and special interests! You should try to discover characteristics common to all of them and then imagine you're talking to one individual within that group. In all communications consider the areas on which your readers are likely to be well informed or uninformed, pleased or sensitive, positive or negative.

Choose the Ideas

With your purpose and recipient(s) in mind, your next step is to choose the ideas for your message. If you are answering a letter, you can underline the main points to discuss and jot your ideas briefly in the margin or on a memo pad. If you are writing an unsolicited or a complex message, you can begin by listing ideas as they come to you.

The ideas you will include depend upon the type of message you're considering. For example, in a welcome letter from a savings and loan association to new customers, is your purpose only to welcome them? If so, then one or two sentences should suffice. They might merely thank new customers for selecting your association and welcome them. But should the purpose of this message be *only* to welcome? Shouldn't you also help them know your policy concerning savings accounts, the overall services available to them, and your association's eagerness to be their financial headquarters? Thus, the five ideas listed below should be included in the welcome letter. (After you have gathered all the facts and outlined your message, you might write a letter like letter 2, page 41.)

- Welcome the customers and thank them for opening an account.
- State some of your services—free parking, save-by-mail, mortgage loans, special accounts.
- Tell them the hours you're open to serve them.
- Mention percentage of interest they earn.
- Assure them you're ready to help with their problems or wishes.

Get All the Facts

Having determined what ideas to include, ask yourself if you need any specific figures, facts, or quotations. Be sure you know your company policy, procedures, and product details if this message requires them. Perhaps you should check with your boss, colleague, subordinates, or the files for an exact percentage, name of an individual, date, address, figure, or statement. Sometimes you need also to enclose a useful brochure, table, picture, or product sample.

Outline—Organize—Your Message

Before you write the message, outline it (in your mind or on paper). The order in which you present your ideas is often as important as the ideas themselves. Disorganized writing reflects a disorganized, illogical mind.

Choose the organizational plan after you have determined your purpose, collected all needed facts, and asked yourself "How will the reader react to these ideas?" The basic plans are discussed briefly in the next section, and more specifically in other chapters.

BASIC ORGANIZATIONAL PLANS

Your choice of organizational plan depends upon how you expect your reader (or listener) to react to your message. And that reaction, of course, depends to some extent upon what is already in that person's mental filter, as well as on the content of your message.

For letters and memos you can choose one of four basic organizational plans: the *direct-request, good-news, bad-news,* or *persuasive-request.* The first two of these use the direct (deductive) approach, which begins with the main idea; the last two, the indirect (inductive) approach, which states the main idea later.

Direct (Deductive) Approach
for
Direct-Request
and Good-News Plans

Indirect (Inductive) Approach
for
Bad-News and Persuasive-
Request Plans

All these plans are to be considered as flexible guides only, not as rigid patterns. Your own judgment must help you decide the best organization and content of each message. (Other chapters discuss various ways you can use these plans.)

Direct (Deductive) Approach

When you think your reader (or listener) will consider your message favorable or neutral and the information understandable (without any obstacle), you can use the direct approach. You *begin with the main idea or best news. After* the opening, you include all necessary explanatory details—in one or several paragraphs—and end with an appropriate, friendly paragraph.

The direct-request and good-news plans both have three basic parts. Notice their similarities as you compare the brief outlines shown side by side in the frame below.

Use the direct-request plan when the main purpose of your message is to make a request that requires no persuasion, because the reader will say "yes" readily.

Use the good-news plan for messages that grant requests, announce favorable or neutral information, and exchange routine information within or between companies.

ORGANIZATIONAL PLANS USING THE DIRECT (DEDUCTIVE) APPROACH

Direct-Request Plan	*Good-News Plan*

1. Main idea
  a. Request, main statement, or question
  b. Reason(s) if desirable
	1. Best news or main idea

2. Explanation
  a. All necessary and desirable details
  b. Numbered questions, if helpful
  c. Easy-reading devices
	2. Explanation
	  a. All necessary and desirable details
	  b. Resale material*
	  c. Educational material
	  d. Sales promotion material*

3. Courteous close, with motivation to action	**3.** Positive, friendly close, including, if appropriate:

a. Clear statement of action
   desired
b. Easy action
c. Dated action, when desirable
d. Appreciation and goodwill

a. Appreciation
b. Clear statement of action
   desired, if any
c. Easy action
d. Dated action, when desirable
e. Willingness to help further
f. Reader benefit

Resale material is usually favorable information about a product or service the reader has already
bought or is planning to buy. *Sales promotion material* usually includes suggestions for additional
products or services the customer may find useful.

Indirect (Inductive) Approach

When you think your reader (or listener) will probably react unfavorably
(negatively) to your request or information, you should usually *not* spring the
main idea in the first paragraph. Instead you will need to begin, preferably, with
some relevant pleasant, neutral, or receiver-benefit statements; then give adequate explanation *before* you introduce the unpleasant idea(s).

Thus the bad-news and persuasive-request plans both use the indirect
approach. Notice—in the side-by-side framed outlines below—that each has
four instead of three parts. You need to take a little longer to present bad news
and to persuade.

ORGANIZATIONAL PLANS USING THE INDIRECT (INDUCTIVE) APPROACH

Bad-News Plan

1. Buffer (pleasant or neutral
   statements to "get in step"
   with reader)

2. Explanation
   a. Necessary details, tactfully
      stated
   b. Pertinent favorable, then
      unfavorable, facts
   c. Reader-benefit reasons

Persuasive-Request Plan

1. Attention
   a. Reader benefit
   b. Reader-interest theme

2. Interest
   a. Descriptive details
   b. Psychological appeals
   c. Reader benefits

3. Decision (implied or expressed), along with offer of additional help or suggestions

3. Desire
   a. Statement of request
   b. Conviction material to help create reader's desire to grant request

4. Positive, friendly close
   a. Appreciation
   b. Invitation to future action
   c. Clear statement of action desired
   d. Easy action
   e. Dated action, when desirable
   f. Willingness to help further
   g. Reader benefit and goodwill

4. Action
   a. Clear statement of action desired
   b. Easy action
   c. Dated action, when desirable
   d. Special inducement
   e. Reader-benefit plug

The bad-news message is one of the most difficult to prepare because your receiver will consider it unfavorable. Likewise, in the persuasive request you expect resistance from your receivers. They will probably find obstacles and react negatively unless they are persuaded. So you try to show them how they or someone in whom they are interested will benefit from granting your request.

BEGINNINGS AND ENDINGS

Two of the most important positions in any business message are the opening and closing paragraphs. You have probably heard the old sayings: "First impressions are lasting" and "We remember best what we read last." Whenever possible, place the main favorable ideas at the beginning and ending of a message. (This advice applies also to business sentences and paragraphs.)

Because openings and closings are so significant, this section gives you an overview so you can concentrate on common essentials before studying various message types in later chapters.

Opening Paragraphs

Often the opening of a written message determines whether the reader continues reading, puts the message aside for later study, or discards it. The following checklist includes suggestions for good openings that help make favorable impressions. Sections 1a–c, 3a, and 4b in this checklist apply especially to openings. The other sections include qualities that are important for openings and also for all other paragraphs, as discussed in Chapters 3 and 4.

CHECKLIST FOR OPENING PARAGRAPHS

1. Choose an opening appropriate for the message and reader. You can begin with:
   a. Main idea or good-news subject—for direct-request, neutral, and good-news messages.
   b. A buffer—for bad-news messages.
   c. Attention getting statements relevant to letter's purpose—for persuasive requests.
2. Be considerate and courteous.
   a. Get reader into opening.
   b. Focus on the positive.
   c. Use courteous, never irritating, expressions.
3. Make the opening concise and interesting.
   a. Keep first paragraph relatively short.
   b. Use conversational words.
   c. Avoid unnecessary repetition.
4. Check for completeness
   a. In sentence structure.
   b. Regarding date of letter you're answering.

Choose Openings Appropriate for Message and Reader

Main Idea or Good-News Subject First. Begin directly with the main idea or subject when (1) doing so does not unfavorably affect the relationship between reader and writer, and (2) you are sure the information is considered favorable or neutral by the reader. It is, of course, also important that the reader will understand the main idea if it is in the first paragraph.

Request:
So that the account of Mr. A. B. Smith, deceased, can be transferred to your name as Executor, will you please return to us the following:

Good news:
Three copies of *Brown's Garden Book* were sent to you today by parcel post as you requested.

Announcement (five W's):
You and your family (*who*) who are invited to a machinery demonstration (*what*) next Saturday from 10 a.m. until noon (*when*) in the ballroom of the Statler Hotel (*where*). The purpose of this demonstration is to show and explain to management the operation of the latest data processing equipment (*why*).

Buffer First. When you have bad news for the reader, begin with a buffer—some statement on which you can agree. Don't spread gloom with your first words; try to get in step first.

Poor: We regret your loan application did not meet our regulations and board policies for approving a loan.

Good: Your application for a loan has received our careful
attention. It is evident you are doing your best to
provide a comfortable home for your family.

Attention-Getting Statements First. When you have a persuasive request (sales letter), begin with relevant statements that will induce the recipient to read further, as in this opening to a licensed dog owner:

Like most conscientious dog owners, you know that proper food is
just as important to a pet as it is to a human being. And you know,
too, that if you are trying to make up a scientifically balanced
diet for your dog, it involves more time and effort than you can
spare. And that's where Muskies can help!

Make the Opening Considerate, Courteous, Concise, Interesting

Get your reader into the opening whether your message is good or bad news, a direct or persuasive request. Don't emphasize the writer. Focus on the positive, what *can* be done. Use courteous expressions, avoiding anything that might anger the reader.

Keep the first paragraph relatively short—five typewritten lines or less—to entice the reader to start reading. The sentences should average about 17 words. As in all paragraphs, use conversational words—in clear, concise sentences. Avoid unnecessary repetition of what the reader told you.

Check for Completeness

Avoid opening with an incomplete sentence like:

Reference your letter (*or* Received your letter) of March 26, 198___,
concerning Ms. Helen M. Smith's application.

Usually, subordinate the date of the letter you are answering, but include it if doing so is beneficial to either the reader or you—generally, for record keeping.

Poor: As per your letter of October 10, we have shipped your
order today by Railway Express.

Good: The five dozen Conform hats you ordered October 10
were shipped to you today by Railway Express.

Closing Paragraphs

The closing is more likely to motivate the reader to act as requested if it is appropriately impressive. Here you have the opportunity to bring final focus on the desired action and leave a sense of your courtesy with the reader. What you say in the closing depends upon the purpose of the letter and the ideas in previous paragraphs.

The checklist and examples below again focus on ways to apply the C qualities in closings for various letter and memo situations.

CHECKLIST FOR CLOSING PARAGRAPHS

1. Make your action request clear and complete with the five W's and the H if you want your reader (or someone else) to do something.
   a. (*What* and *who*) Clearly state what action you desire and who should do it.
   b. (*Where* and *how*) Make action easy.
   c. (*When*) Date the action, if desirable.
   d. (*Why*) Show reader benefit, if possible.
2. End on a positive, courteous thought.
   a. Include any apologies and negatives before last paragraph.
   b. Be friendly.
   c. Show appreciation.
   d. Occasionally add a personal note.
3. Keep last paragraph concise and correct.
   a. Avoid trite expressions.
   b. Omit discussion and worthless details.
   c. Use relatively short and complete sentences.

Make Action Request Clear and Complete with Five W's and H

Whenever you are requesting action by your reader or someone else, your closing paragraph will usually be more effective if you make clear *what, who, how, where, when,* and (if appropriate) *why.*

1. ***What and Who?:*** *Clear statement of the action you desire your reader (or someone else) to take.*

   Should the reader: Phone your office for an appointment? Sign a card or a document? Return it? To whom? Come to your office in person? Send you certain details, merchandise, forms, payments, or opinions? Ask another person to do something?

2. *How and Where?: Easy action.*

Include your phone number (with area code) and extension if you want the reader to phone you.

Enclose a form (card, order blank, questionnaire, document) and an addressed reply envelope (perhaps with postage paid) if you want the reader to furnish information or sign and mail something.

Give complete instructions regarding *where* and *how* if you don't include a form and/or an envelope.

State your office hours and location if you want the reader to come to you in person. When, if at all, is your office open evenings? Do you have a free parking lot? Where?

3. *When and Why?: Dated action; special inducement to act by a specified time.*

Name the date (and the time, if pertinent) whenever you need the reply by a certain time. Tactfully state the reason you need it then—perhaps to meet a report or printer's deadline or for a speech you are giving at a certain meeting.

When appropriate, mention some benefit(s) the reader will gain by prompt action. A reader-benefit plug in the ending paragraph(s) is a stimulus to action.

In the following example, notice how the vague action request is improved by inserting some or all the W's and the H:

Vague:	Please take care of this matter at your earliest convenience.
Better:	So that we can discuss suitable arrangements for your meeting, please call me at 323-9900, Ext. 25, before Thursday, June 2.

End on a Positive, Courteous Thought

Include Any Apologies and Negatives before Last Paragraph. Finish with positive statements.

Negative:	I regret we cannot be more helpful in the study you are making.
Positive:	The best of success with your term paper. You have an interesting topic to research.

Be Friendly. Offer to help the reader further or again if that is appropriate. Words like *please* or *will you* help soften commands.

Good:	If you have further questions about this method, please write or call me. My number is 555-4422.
Poor:	Send us your check today.
Good:	To keep your credit in good standing, please send us your check for $123.94 today.

Show Appreciation. Everyone likes sincere praise when earned. But don't thank people in advance for doing something before they have agreed to do so.

Avoid:	I thank you in advance for your cooperation in informing your employees of these tours.
Say:	I will appreciate your cooperation in informing your employees of these tours.

Occasionally Add a Personal Note. When unrelated to the subject discussed in the message, a personal note is appropriate sometimes as a last paragraph or preferably as a postscript.

You're fortunate to be at Estes Park this month.
The thermometer registered 103° at 3 p.m. here yesterday.

Keep Last Paragraph Concise and Correct

Trim your last paragraph to five or fewer lines of complete sentences. Avoid trite expressions and worthless repetition.

Poor:	Again, we thank you for your inquiry. Enclosed you will find a self-addressed stamped envelope. Hoping to hear from you soon about your preference, I remain (*or I am*) . . .
Good:	Please fill out this form and return it in the enclosed envelope by (*date*). Then you can soon begin to enjoy the comfort of . . . .

PREPARATION OF THE MESSAGE

Composing First Draft

When you have completed the five planning steps and considered your openings and closings, you are ready for the first draft of your message.

For the routine, short communications, you will usually be able to dictate or write quite easily with little or no revising. Try to compose from your outline and choose words to express your ideas. Temporarily forget about mechanics of spelling, punctuation, sentence structure; you can check on them after the first draft is finished.

For other writing—especially complex, longer messages and reports, new form letters, and any communication that is to be published—you should expect to edit and revise, sometimes substantially.

Editing and Revising

After you have finished the first draft of a complex message, you will need to evaluate its content, organization, and style.

To edit effectively, you must read your draft objectively, from the viewpoint of your recipient. Make sure the message meets all principles of good business communication. Is it *complete, concise, considerate, concrete, clear, courteous, correct*—in content and all mechanics? Read paragraph by paragraph for the continuity of ideas. Then check sentence by sentence and every word, figure, and punctuation mark for the C qualities. Check your message for organization. Does it logically, clearly, concretely present the facts with consideration for your reader? Are opening and closing paragraphs appropriate?

On complicated, long reports and proposals (also important letters or memos addressed to many readers) you may need to talk over some aspects with colleagues. Whenever desirable, consider suggestions from knowledgeable associates. Be willing to revise drafts several times.[1] Occasionally you may feel like the doubtful report writer who remarked to his supervising editor: "You mean you want the revised revision of the fifth revised revision revised?"

Top correspondents and authors have confirmed again and again that the best writers rewrite and rewrite and rewrite. Tolstoy revised *War and Peace* 5 times; James Thurber rewrote his stories as many as 15 times; Franklin D. Roosevelt's speeches often went to 18 drafts.

Proofreading

Careful proofreading is also essential after your best revised business message is typewritten. Before it is mailed you or other dependable persons should read it. Any error should be corrected so that your paper will reflect favorably on you and your company. Remember, some uncorrected errors in mailed messages can be not only embarrassing but also extremely costly—in loss of goodwill, sales, income, and sometimes even lives.

---

[1] Time-wasting retypings can be eliminated by using a machine such as the word processor on which you can make changes or additions easily without having an entire report draft retyped. Text as originally draft-typed is "played out" automatically to each point of revision. Changes or additions are typed manually, and then automatic playout of the corrected copy resumes.

SUMMARY

Before composing any message, consider carefully the five planning steps; they furnish the basis for an effective message. Choose a direct or indirect organizational plan, *depending upon your reader's (or listener's) probable reaction to the message*. And when expressing your ideas, pay particular attention to the opening and closing paragraphs because of their strategic importance. After preparing your message, edit it for *content, organization, and style*—according to the 7 C's and various pertinent checklists (which are for suggestions but not rigid patterns).[2] Wherever desirable, revise your draft(s). Then see that the finished typewritten message is proofread and any errors are corrected before you transmit your message.

EXERCISES

1. What is your reaction to each of the openings below: Is it good, fair, or poor? Why? If two openings are given (indicated by *versus*), which do you prefer? Why?

   a. You made several errors on the reply form you submitted, and you neglected to answer three questions.

   b. Jean Doe, about whom you inquired in your July 6 letter has kept an account with us since August 18, 1975.

   c. We regret to learn from your letter of September 10 that you found a foreign object upon opening a can of Seacrest oysters.

   versus

   Thank you for taking the time to tell us about your experience when opening a can of Seacrest oysters.

   d. You have failed to correct the existing delinquency on the above-captioned loan, and furthermore, you have made no arrangements for repayment.

   e. We are in receipt of your note regarding the two toaster ovens which you say are defective.

   f. Good news! After reviewing the facts again, we are issuing the desired policy.

   versus

   This is in reply to your letter of March 19, requesting us to review the application which was previously declined.

   g. We will be pleased to consider issuing the desired policy provided you submit a new application by November 15.

   versus

   A new application must be submitted by November 15; otherwise we cannot consider issuing the desired policy.

[2] For a quick overview of the C qualities, see checklist on pp. 88–89 (and pp. 485–490 for reports).

h. Congratulations on making the final payment on your home improvement loan #4-5555. We are sure that you had a real happy feeling
of satisfaction when you could finally say to yourself, "Well,
that debt is paid in full."

versus

Our records show that the balance on the loan account above has
been paid off.

2. What is your reaction to each of the closings below? Is it good, average,
or poor? Why?

   a. We hope our error has not inconvenienced you too much.
   b. When it is convenient, please let me know your decision.

   versus

   I trust you will avail yourself of the opportunity of making either of these changes and when your decision is reached, notify
   me at your earliest convenience. I await the pleasure of your
   reply.
   c. Please let us know when we can help you again.
   d. We appreciate your interest and will keep you informed of all developments.
   e. Hoping to hear from you, I remain . . .
   f. Fill out this form and return to me.
   g. As soon as you return the four completed forms, I'll airmail one
   to Chicago for prompt rating. In this way you will receive the
   renewal as quickly as possible.
   h. Again, let me repeat how sorry I am to have not answered sooner.

3. The following two letters consist of an inquiry from a church to a bank and a
reply to the inquiry.
   a. Which organizational plan does the inquiry follow?
   b. Evaluate the opening and closing paragraphs of the inquiry.
   c. What is the purpose of the reply? What organizational plan should be
   used?
   d. Evaluate the opening and closing paragraphs of the reply.
   e. Does the reply include the ideas necessary to fulfill the purpose? Are the
   ideas organized effectively? What improvements can you suggest?

Inquiry

Gentlemen

We would like to request your permission to post a church directional sign (First Christian Church) with directional arrow at the
edge of your property parking lot on First Avenue, near Central.

This is an attractive, small sign on a neatly painted post. This is very important to our church because of the fact that Central Street is probably the shortest street in (*city*). The size of the sign is about 15″ × 15″.

The exact location of the sign will be specified to us as soon as we bring written permission from you from our office to Mr. Smith at City Hall. He will then advise us as to how and where to place the sign so that it will give a good appearance and not interfere with either traffic or your business operations.

Please indicate your permission hereon and return your reply to this office as soon as possible.

We appreciate your cooperation.

Reply

My dear Reverend Glouster

Thank you for your recent letter requesting permission to post a church directional sign in the corner of our parking lot on First Avenue near Central.

Unauthorized parking in the lot during our business hours has been a continuous problem for our bank. The parking lot already has several signs posted for different purposes. An additional sign in this corner of the parking lot could cause the public confusion regarding the use of the parking area. We, therefore, find it necessary to decline your request.

Your parishioners are welcome to continue to use this parking lot on Sundays and at other times that you have church services which do not conflict with the business hours of the bank. We appreciate and wish to continue the cordial relationship with you and members of your church.

4. The following reply is from the Blank Oyster Company, Anytown, to an out-of-state customer who complained that she found two "ugly specimens" in her favorite brand of canned oysters.
   a. What is (should be) the purpose of this message?
   b. What organizational plan should be used?
   c. Evaluate the opening and closing paragraphs and the explanation.
   d. Point out the portions that are "resale" material and "apology." Are they well placed? Discuss.
   e. Do you think the letter helps restore the customer's confidence? Why?

Thank you for giving us the opportunity to reply to your experience with Blank Brand oysters. We appreciate your thoughtfulness in writing.

Your enclosure turned out to be small pieces of the root section of a common seaweed which grows on the oysterbeds in great abundance. We are stumped how this substance could stick to an oyster through three successive washings and inspections in the canning process and still escape detection by our packers. But it did, and we are sorry that it happened.

It is of little help to explain that this harmless vegetable substance became totally sterile when the oysters were cooked in the can. You did exactly the right thing when you wrote about the incident.

Today we are sending you by parcel post two cans of Blank Brand oysters with our compliments. You are the discriminating consumer we want to please.

5. Assume that the following wordy memo from an auditor of disbursements in your city was sent to the auditor of disbursements in another branch. Both work for the same organization. Your job is to revise this monstrosity. Can you make the revision no longer than four or five sentences? (A *rear support* is a metal holder for a large ledger or dictionary you usually find only in libraries.)

We previously sent you copies of our correspondence with the Albert M. Hunter, Inc., relative to the Hunter Wage Charts. Particular attention is directed to our comments relative to the rear supports $4\frac{1}{2}$ inches in length, which in our opinion were too long, in our letter dated April 8. As a result of our comments, Albert M. Hunter, Inc., developed rear supports $2\frac{1}{2}$ inches in length which they furnished us to replace supports $4\frac{1}{2}$ inches in length.

On July 19 we sent you by express 26 sets of the rear supports $2\frac{1}{2}$ inches in length. We are of the opinion that the rear supports $2\frac{1}{2}$ inches in length are a considerable improvement over the rear supports $4\frac{1}{2}$ inches in length and have accordingly replaced the rear supports $4\frac{1}{2}$ inches in length on the Hunter Wage Charts in use by us with rear supports $2\frac{1}{2}$ inches in length.

We assume that you will also wish to replace the rear supports $4\frac{1}{2}$ inches in length on the Hunter Wage Charts in use by you with the rear supports $2\frac{1}{2}$ inches in length. If you make the replacement, please return the rear supports $4\frac{1}{2}$ inches in length to us in order that we can return them to Albert M. Hunter, Inc., in accordance with their request.

For your information, the rear supports $2\frac{1}{2}$ inches in length to replace the rear supports $4\frac{1}{2}$ inches in length were furnished by Albert M. Hunter, Inc., free of charge with the understanding that the rear supports $4\frac{1}{2}$ inches in length would be returned to them.

If you prefer to continue using the rear supports $4\frac{1}{2}$ inches in length, please return the rear supports $2\frac{1}{2}$ inches in length to us in order that we can return them to Albert M. Hunter, Inc.

6. Revise the following letter—from a college bookstore to a small manufacturer. Though the purpose is stated at the beginning, the letter rambles and seems artificially friendly. Improve it wherever desirable.

> Once again with your kind permission, will you please make for us four armbands, blue felt, white sewn letters, and white chain stitching as per the attached layout, and if you please Mr. Cowell, we have marked on the layout for the operator to kindly make these up just as we show them, and not change them. What we mean by that, in a most friendly way, this is a little order which you made up for us a few days ago, and the operator, thinking it would be perfectly all right, transposed the position of some of the lettering, so that they were not uniform all the way, and too, inadvertently on one or two of them left one or two of the letters out, and we are not complaining about that at all, all we want to say sincerely is that we are grateful for your taking care of these little things for us, and we are not registering any complaint at all, for we are using them for samples and do not expect you for one moment to do this again without your regular charge, for you make nothing on it, and you are just like us, we know, doing this to satisfy a customer, we being a customer, for other things, and if we weren't we would not have the nerve to ask you to make these, so therefore, if you please, this is for a bunch of women and they are a little bit more particular than men, and if the operator will just follow what we have laid out everything will be fine.
>
> Thanking you so much, and with best wishes and kindest regards, we are . . .

7. Discuss the purpose and weaknesses in each of the following letters. Then revise one to improve it in every way you can.

Letter A

Reply from a motel manager to a husband and wife who requested accommodations for two weeks starting one month from today.

> Dear Sir and Madam
>
> Your letter of the 23d. inst was received on the 25th, and in reply will say, I can give you two rooms for time you desire them, and can make you very comfortable with the exception of hot water.
>
> My wife is away on a vacation and shut off the gas water heater, but the few guests here at present find the water warm enough for a shower bath. Sea bathing is close by, and we are in a very desirable location and very central. You could come and stop with me for a day or so and if it meets with your approval stay for the two weeks.
>
> The price would be $25.00 per person per day or $149.00 per week each. Please let me know if you decide to be my guest and the time you expect to arrive. Thank you kindly.

Letter B

Reply from a sardine cannery in Canada to a college student who wrote that he especially liked the sardines but to please improve the can.

We thank you for your letter of April 28th and might say that we have a letter before us from our broker in (*city*) wishing to purchase a carload of our sardines. After we received your letter we were a little uneasy about shipping him another car; however, on thinking the matter over if you had not liked our sardines we presume you would not have taken the trouble to write us.

We know the cans do not open right; it seems they will go alright for awhile and then we get a run of cans that everything seems to be wrong; the last thing we found out was that the grain in the tin-plate had been changed without our knowledge. We have a special dye maker chasing this trouble all the time but let me tell you it is a headache. Don't think for a minute that you are the only one that writes in; we have good customers all over the country and when we get a run of cans that don't open right you can bet your life we get a lot of letters but we are going to keep trying and we hope in the meantime our customers will not be too hard on us.

We are going to send you a few tins from the new pack and will just pray that the dye maker has got the cans opening alright. With kindest regards.

8. The sales manager of Right Fite Hanger, Inc., recently wrote to three television stations asking if they would like to handle her product on a commission basis. She had heard that some stations occasionally used their open time in this manner. Which of the three replies below do you think adheres best to the writing principles for business? Why? Compare your choice with the other two replies.

Reply A

I don't know where you got your information as stated in the opening sentence of your letter, "I have been informed that your station promotes items on a commission basis," and we don't appreciate it. If you want to do business with us, buy; if you don't, don't write us.

Reply B

This will acknowledge your recent letter of offering your all plastic clothes hanger on a commission basis.

I am quite sure that you did not run your advertisement in the Sunday newspaper supplement on a commission basis. By the same token, we will not accept business on a percentage or per inquiry basis.

For your information, I am attaching our rate card.

Reply C

Your information must have been somewhat misleading inasmuch as NUTZ has never promoted items on a commission basis.

We would be delighted to handle the Right Fite hanger, and I personally think it is an item of great demand.

Enclosed is our rate card so that you can choose the time, frequency, and length of message which will promote your product as you wish it. As soon as your reply to these points reaches us, we will be glad to put all our resources at your disposal.

9. Revise the following memo announcement so it has better you-attitude and more active than passive verbs. Correct any other errors. This company employs both men and women to sell its products.

TO: Customer Service Personnel   DATE: March 1, 198____
FROM: Tom S. Powers
SUBJECT: Deposit and Cash Receipt Books

Effective March 1, 198____, the following changes will be made in the use and care of deposit and cash receipt books by our salesmen:

1. The deposit and/or cash receipt book(s) issued to a salesman will be used only by the client to whom the book is issued.

2. Whenever a deposit or other monies are collected, the salesman will remove from the receipt book(s) the customer's copy(s) and give this to the customer as is now done. In addition, at the end of his shift, each salesman will no longer turn in the receipt book(s) with the money and tickets for those transactions.

3. Deposit and reciept books are not to be left laying around in a vehicle or other places. They are to be under the strict control of the individual the book(s) is issued to.

Normally a salesman will have one deposit book and one cash receipt book. Additional books may be issued by a service supervisor. All used up books are to be returned to the supervisor for forwarding to the accounting department.

CHAPTER 6

Appearance and Uses
of Business Message Media

Among the various media you can choose for your written messages are letters and memorandums—plus such special timesaving media as memo-letters, postcards, Mailgrams, telegrams, radiograms, and cablegrams. This chapter focuses on the appearance and uses of these media and on form messages—discussed from the writer's viewpoint.

BUSINESS LETTERS

The medium used most often for written messages to persons outside the firm is the business letter. It is judged on content, presentation, and physical appearance. Planning the content and presentation is your responsibility; typing the message so that it is neat, accurate, and attractive is usually your secretary's job. But when you sign your name at the bottom of the letter, you assume responsibility for everything—mechanics, proper layout, content. If the message contains misspellings or grammatical errors, or if its appearance is poor, the reader judges you unfavorably. Therefore, you and your secretary must work as a team to produce effective and attractive messages.

Elements of appearance that help produce favorable reactions are appropriate stationery, correct letter parts and layout, and properly addressed envelopes. In addition to these elements, neat typing also helps make favorable impressions. Strikeovers, dirty keys, light ribbon, smears, or poor erasing and overall appearance convey significant nonverbal impressions even before recipients read the message.

Stationery

If you have an opportunity to choose or suggest a change in your organization's stationery, keep the following guidelines in mind.

Quality, Size, Color

To help build an image of quality and stability, the paper you use for general correspondence should have at least 25 percent rag content and usually 16- to 20-pound weight (based on actual weight of four reams of standard-sized paper). The standard-sized sheet is 8½ by 11 inches, but other sizes are also appropriate for various uses. White is most popular, though many firms achieve a distinctive warm touch with pastel stationery.

Letterhead

Every business, even if it is a one-person operation, should use letterhead stationery for the letter's first page. Only when writing a business letter for yourself (not as an agent or representative for any organization) will you use paper without a letterhead.

The modern letterhead (see Figure 6-1) usually occupies no more than two inches at the top of the page. Printed, embossed, or engraved are the firm's name and address, ZIP code, and sometimes telephone number, cable address, nature of business, and name of department or branch office sending the correspondence. Optional details are names of officers and directors, trademark or symbol, slogan, starting date of the firm, and an appropriate picture—perhaps of the building, product(s), or a familiar landmark.[1]

[1] The expanded ZIP code—ZIP + 4 figures—began officially in October 1983. Its use is optional. According to the U.S. Postal Service, ZIP + 4 has various advantages.

Figure 6-1   Illustrations of letterheads. (All these are printed in black, except TWA initials, circles, and horizontal lines, in red; Weyerhaeuser outer triangle, in dark green; Allenite, all in medium green.)

Standard Parts of the Letter

Most business letters have seven standard parts: (1) heading, (2) inside address, (3) salutation, (4) body, (5) complimentary close, (6) signature area, (7) reference section, as shown in Figure 6-2.

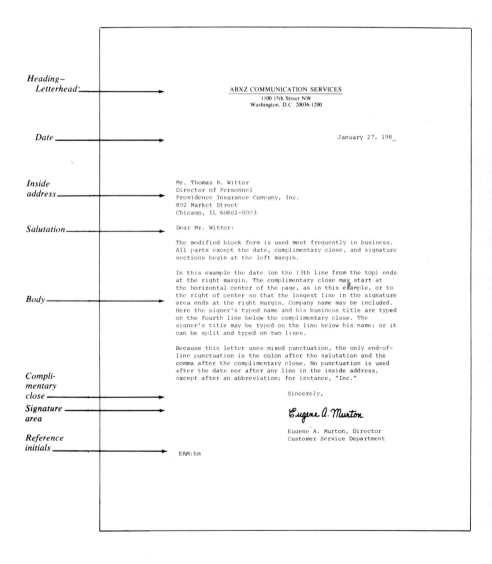

Heading–
Letterhead:

ABXZ COMMUNICATION SERVICES
1100 15th Street NW
Washington, D.C. 20036-1200

Date

January 27, 198_

Inside
address

Mr. Thomas R. Wittor
Director of Personnel
Providence Insurance Company, Inc.
892 Market Street
Chicago, IL 60601-0003

Salutation

Dear Mr. Wittor:

The modified block form is used most frequently in business. All parts except the date, complimentary close, and signature sections begin at the left margin.

Body

In this example the date (on the 13th line from the top) ends at the right margin. The complimentary close may start at the horizontal center of the page, as in this example, or to the right of center so that the longest line in the signature area ends at the right margin. Company name may be included. Here the signer's typed name and his business title are typed on the fourth line below the complimentary close. The signer's title may be typed on the line below his name; or it can be split and typed on two lines.

Because this letter uses mixed punctuation, the only end-of-line punctuation is the colon after the salutation and the comma after the complimentary close. No punctuation is used after the date nor after any line in the inside address, except after an abbreviation; for instance, "Inc."

Compli-
mentary
close

Sincerely,

Signature
area

Eugene A. Murton

Eugene A. Murton, Director
Customer Service Department

Reference
initials

EAM:hm

Figure 6-2 Modified block; mixed punctuation. Length, medium; side margins, 1½"; line length, 5½".

Heading—Letterhead and Date

The heading shows where the letter comes from and when it was written (or dictated). Usually the date is typewritten two to six lines below the last line of the letterhead—at left margin, or centered, or begun at center, or placed so it ends with the right margin. The preferred date sequence in American business is: month day, year—March 5, 1984, with the month spelled out. In memos figures may be used: 3/5/84. However, these figures would be interpreted 3 May, 1984, in the U.S. military, Europe, and Latin America because their sequence is: day, month, year. Thus, spell out for clarity!

When you type a business letter on blank paper (for yourself, not an organization), your return address, but *not* your name, is typed directly above the date about two inches from the top, as in Figure 6-3 on page 124.

Inside Address

Always blocked at the left-hand margin, the inside address includes name and address of the individual, group, or organization to whom you are writing. The person's name is preceded by a courtesy title and followed by a business or executive title, if any.

Courtesy Title and Name. If the addressee has no professional title—such as "Doctor," "Reverend," or "Professor"—the traditional courtesy titles are "Mr.," "Mrs.," "Miss," or "Ms.," which stands for either "Miss" or "Mrs." When you write to a married woman who prefers "Mrs." and her husband's name ("Mrs. John Jones"), address her that way. When in doubt about a woman's preference, use "Ms." plus her own first name and surname. The trend is to use "Ms." as the courtesy title for all business and professional women, regardless of their marital status, unless of course they have a professional title that takes precedence.

After the courtesy title include your addressee's full first name or two initials plus surname—for the first line of your inside address. When you do not know whether the initials are for a man or woman, you can use "Mr. or Ms." for the courtesy title—or omit it. Avoid duplication of titles.

Wrong: Dr. Herbert Moore, M.D. (*or Ph.D.*)
Right: Dr. Herbert Moore or Herbert Moore, M.D. (*or Ph.D.*)

Business or Executive Title. Depending upon relative length of lines, the business or executive title may be typed (1) on the same line as the addressee's name, (2) on the second line preceding the company's name, or (3) on a line or two by itself. These are illustrated in the next section, below.

Order of Arrangement. The various elements of the inside address are arranged like a pyramid. On the top line you place the smallest unit (an individual's name). The remaining items progress downward to the largest unit, as the pyramid below illustrates. The number of lines usually ranges from three to six.

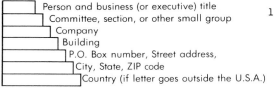

```
                                                          1. Mr. John Stassen, President
                                                             Central Construction Company
                                                             Harton Building
                                                             1399 Adams Street
                                                             Chicago, IL 60622-1111
```

```
2. Ms. Marietta R. Worthington          3. Mr. Harry M. Fitzsimmons
   Treasurer, Ace Credit Company           Vice President and Manager
   P.O. Box 91467                          Building Services, Inc.
   Augusta, GA 30915                       1120 Royal Trust Tower
                                           Edmonton, Alberta T5J 2Z2
                                           Canada
```

Salutation

The salutation is the friendly greeting that precedes the body of the letter. It is typed on the second line below the inside address, two lines above the body and even with the left margin.

Acceptable Salutations. The following list includes both traditional and comparatively recent salutations, all of which must be *appropriate for the first line of the inside address.* You have these choices:

1. Dear Mr. (or Ms., Mrs., Miss) Doe: when the first line of an inside address is the name of an individual.
2. Dear John (or Mary or nickname): when you'd address the individual this way in person and when it is appropriate for you to do so in your letter on this occasion. (See, for example, the salutation in Figure 6-3.)
3. Dear Manager (or Executive or Director) or Dear Mr. or Ms. Doe or Dear Sir or Madam or an appropriate variation: when the first line is a position within an organization and you have no person's name, or the name includes only initials.

```
Manager, Service Department          R. L. Macon
. . . . . . . . .                    . . . . . . . .
. . . . . . . .                      . . . . . . .
. . . . . . . .                      . . . . . . . .

Dear Manager:                        Dear Ms. or Mr. Macon:
(or Dear Mr. or Ms. Manager)
(or Dear Madam or Sir)
```

4. Ladies and Gentlemen (or reverse, or Gentlemen and Gentlewomen, or Dear Members of . . . , or Dear People, or Gentlewo/men, or Gentlepersons, or Gentlepeople, or other innovations): when the first line is a committee, company, or group of men and women; "Gentlemen" if all are men, and "Ladies" if all are women.

ABC Toy Company   Public Relations Committee
. . . .
. . . .
                                        . . . .
Ladies and Gentlemen:
(*or others, as above*)   Dear Committee members:
                                        (*or others, as above*)

Professional Women's Club
. . . . . .   XYZ Fraternity
. . . .
                                        . . . . . .
Ladies: (or
Dear Professional Women:)   Gentlemen:
                                        (or Dear Members of XYZ)

Most of the suggestions under item 4 are innovations since the women's rights movement has advocated eliminating the all-male plural salutations when females may be within the group. Some of these new salutations are not yet widely used. If you don't like them, or you feel your recipients may dislike any of your choices, *omit* the salutation and get right on with the message. In general it is courteous to address people the way they feel comfortable. Some are less likely to miss an omitted salutation than they are to be annoyed by one to which they object.

5. Dear Customer, Dear Homeowner, Dear Executive, or Dear Student (or Occupant or Member of name group), or similar expressions: for messages that omit the inside address—as in sales letters, announcements, or other identical letters to more than one person.

Salutopenings. Some business executives prefer "salutopenings" when they feel a salutation such as "Dear Mr. Brown" is not appropriate because he is a stranger, or "Dear" just seems unnatural, or they merely want a change. When you use a salutopening, type it on the salutation line, but omit "Dear" and begin with the first few words of your opening paragraph plus reader's name. After the name, the sentence continues a double space down to the first line of the letter body, as below:

Salutation line   What do you think, Mr. Brown,

Body   of the enclosed suggested arrangement for. . . ?

If you use the Administrative Management Society (AMS) "simplified letter" (see Figure 6-6), you *omit the salutation line* and place the reader's name near the beginning of the first sentence (as in a salutopening).

Body

This book discusses in detail the content and presentation of the message body; thus only general guidelines are summarized here. In the body you try to:

1. Organize according to an appropriate plan.
2. Keep your first and last paragraphs short—preferably less than 5 lines.
3. Vary the intervening paragraph lengths; maximum 8 to 10 lines.
4. Make the average length of your sentences about 17 to 20 words.
5. Achieve the C qualities.
6. Set long quotations, numbered items, tables, and special ideas in attractive ways for emphasis—by indenting, underlining, using dots or dashes or designs, and leaving extra space around them.

Generally all letters should be typed single space, with double spacing between paragraphs, before and after the salutation, and before the complimentary close.

When the body of a letter is two or more pages, each page beyond the first is headed by a combination of addressee's name, page number, and date. This information is typed 1 to 2 inches from the top of the sheet in any of these ways:

```
Mr. John Jones              2              May 3, 198_
         or

Mr. John Jones-2-May 3, 198_

      or

General Supply Corporation
Attention Mr. John Jones
Page 2
May 3, 198_
```

Complimentary Close

Most business letters use one of three key words in the complimentary close—*sincerely, cordially, or truly*. Only the first letter in the first word is capitalized, as shown in the following complimentary closes:

```
Sincerely, (most popular)
Sincerely yours, Yours sincerely,
Very truly yours, Yours very truly,
Cordially,
```

When an informal salutation like "Dear Tom" (Mary or nickname) is used, the preferred complimentary closes are:

```
Sincerely, Cordially, Warm regards, Best regards
```

Signature Area

You can include in the signature area three or four identifications—name of your company, your signature, your typewritten name, and your business title.

Company Name. If printed on the letterhead, your company name need not be typed after the complimentary close. The company is considered responsible for the content of the message written by one of its agents (only when it concerns business the agent is *authorized* to handle). However, if you wish to include the company name (some firms require it), type it in capital letters a double space under the complimentary close, as in the BRONSON COMPANY example below.

Signature, Typewritten Name, and Business Title. Your signature is penwritten above your typed name, which appears three to five lines under either the company name (if included) or the complimentary close. The typed business title usually follows the typed name.

Very truly yours,   Sincerely,   Cordially yours,

Thomas L. Sutton   *Roy*

                        BRONSON COMPANY

Thomas L. Sutton   *Mary P. Tracy*   Roy Layton, President
Manager, Plant 2

                        Mary P. Tracy
                        Personnel Manager

Usually the signature is the same as the typed name. An exception is that if you have used your reader's first name for the salutation, you will usually sign only your first name above your typed name, as Roy Layton did in the example above.

If you prefer, instead of having your name typed under the complimentary close, it may be typed flush with the left margin, usually on the same line with your title, as in Figure 6-5.

For business and professional women unnecessary reference to their marital status is avoided. In the signature area a married woman always signs *her* first name and not her husband's. Thus for Mary P. Tracy, Personnel Manager (example 2 above), though she is the wife of William R. Tracy, her professional messages are never signed (nor addressed to her as) "Mrs. William R. Tracy." If her name before marriage was Mary Pullman, she may sign either "Mary P. Tracy" or "Mary Pullman Tracy." (Of course, when she writes about a personal charge account, for instance, that is listed as "Mr. and Mrs. William R. Tracy," she should include the latter name in parentheses so as to correctly identify herself.)

It is also noteworthy that many married women, especially professionals, do not use their husbands' surname. Their signatures continue as before marriage, and they prefer the title "Ms."

Usually both men and women omit the courtesy title from their typewritten names and their signatures. However, if a man or a woman uses only initials before his or her surname, or the first name is not clearly male or female (for example, Chris, Robin), then it can be helpful to the recipient for the man to include ''(Mr.)'' and the woman to include ''(Ms.)'' in front of their typewritten names.

Reference Section

Your initials as dictator of the message, and those of your typist, usually appear at the left margin on the same line with the last line of the signature area (your name or title) or one or two lines below that. If your name is typed at the left margin instead of in the signature area, the typist's initials follow it. Among the common forms used are:

```
KLM:tr            KLM:TR           klm/tr                     tr
K.L.Morning:TR    KLMorning-tr     K. L. Morning:tr
```

If someone other than the signer of the letter composes it, practice varies regarding reference initials. Many firms show at least on the file copy the initials of signer, writer, and typist (KLM:JC:tr). The original, to the addressee, may omit all or the writer's initials, to avoid showing that the signer did not dictate the letter.

Optional Parts of the Letter

When appropriate, any of these optional parts can be included: (1) attention line, (2) subject line, (3) enclosure(s), (4) copy notation, (5) file or account number, (6) mailing notation, and (7) postscript.

Attention Line

Considered part of the inside address, the attention line directs a letter to a particular person or title or department when the letter is addressed to a company. It is useful when the writer (a) doesn't know an individual's name but wants the message to go to a particular title (sales or adjustment director) or department (personnel), (b) knows only the individual's surname and thus cannot use that name on the first line of the inside address, or (c) expects that the addressee travels often, and the writer wants the letter to be attended to promptly by whoever takes care of the addressee's business.

Because the first line of the inside address is to a company (or group), the salutation should be plural. The intervening attention line does not change the salutation.

The usual placement of the attention line is between the inside address and salutation (a blank line before and after it), flush with the left margin as in Figure 6-5, or indented with the paragraphs, or centered.

Subject Line

Considered part of the body of the letter, the subject line helps to tell your reader at a glance what your letter is about. It also helps in filing. The subject line may include or omit the word *subject*. It can be placed either on the same line with the salutation or double-spaced below the salutation and centered (Figure 6-3), or flush with left margin (Figure 6-6) or indented.

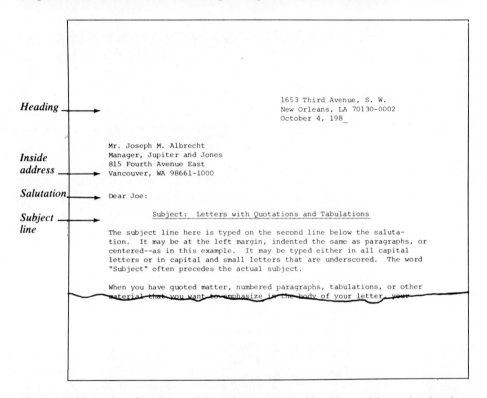

Heading

Inside address

Salutation

Subject line

```
                                              1653 Third Avenue, S. W.
                                              New Orleans, LA 70130-0002
                                              October 4, 198_

            Mr. Joseph M. Albrecht
            Manager, Jupiter and Jones
            815 Fourth Avenue East
            Vancouver, WA 98661-1000

            Dear Joe:

                     Subject:  Letters with Quotations and Tabulations

            The subject line here is typed on the second line below the saluta-
            tion.  It may be at the left margin, indented the same as paragraphs, or
            centered--as in this example.  It may be typed either in all capital
            letters or in capital and small letters that are underscored.  The word
            "Subject" often precedes the actual subject.

            When you have quoted matter, numbered paragraphs, tabulations, or other
            material that you want to emphasize in the body of your letter, your
```

Figure 6-3   Illustration of heading on plain stationery; also, inside address, nickname in salutation, and centered subject line. (This example is the beginning of a 2-page letter; side margins are 1″; line length, 6½″.)

Enclosure Notation

To remind whoever prepares your envelope for mailing that something is to be enclosed, the enclosure notation is usually typed a single or double space under the reference initials. This notation also alerts the addressee's incoming mail department to check for enclosures. An enclosure is anything in the envelope other than the message itself. One enclosure is a unit that can consist of one or more pages (for example, a two-page résumé with an application letter is only one enclosure). When more than one item is enclosed, your secretary should indicate the number: ''Enclosures 3'' (see Figure 6-5) or ''Enc. 3'' (Figure 6-6).

When the enclosures are especially important (checks, legal documents, or blueprints), it is desirable to list in the enclosure notation exactly what the enclosures are:

```
Enclosures 2-Policy #95999 and #23805.
```

Copy Notation

When you want other persons to receive a copy of the letter you have written to the addressee, the names of these persons—arranged in order of importance or alphabetically—should be typed after ''cc'' (carbon copy, as in Figure 6-5), ''xc'' (Xerox copy), or a ''copy'' notation just below the reference initials or the enclosure notation, if any. If you do not want the addressee to know that other recipients are getting a copy of the letter, your secretary can type ''bc'' (blind copy) and the recipients' names *on the carbon copies only.*

File or Account Number, and Mailing Notation

To aid in filing and quick recognition for both the sender's and the reader's company, some firms require that file, loan, or account numbers be typed above the body of the letter in a conspicuous place.

Mailing notation words such as *Special Delivery, Registered,* or *Certified Mail,* when applicable, may be typed either below the copy notation or whatever is the last notation (as in Figure 6-4), or on the second line below the date.

Postscript

To emphasize a point already in your letter or to include a personal brief message unrelated to the letter, a postscript (typed or handwritten) may be added—below everything else typed on the page. However, if you forgot to include an important idea in the letter body, it is usually better to retype the letter than to add the information in a postscript. (See Figure 6-4.)

If you have occasion to use several notations after the signature area, the initials RECMP may help you remember the proper order for arranging them vertically at the left margin: reference initials, enclosures, copy notation, mailing notation, postscript.

Letter Layout

Although layout of the letter is primarily the typist's responsibility, it is covered briefly here to give you a basis of choosing the style(s) you prefer. Many companies have adopted a format so that all their letters contribute to an attractive, uniform image—regardless of dictator, department, or secretary.

Punctuation Styles

The two forms of punctuation most used in business letters are "open" and "mixed." In open punctuation, no line of any letter part (except the body) has any punctuation at the end unless an abbreviation requires a period. Mixed punctuation—the most popular style today—is like open except that a colon follows the salutation and a comma follows the complimentary close.

Letter Styles

Business letters are usually arranged in one of the letter styles described briefly below. You will find additional details discussed in the letters illustrated in Figures 6-2 to 6-6.

1. *Full block* begins every line at the left margin. This is the fastest style to type. To offset a lopsided appearance at the left, some firms use a letterhead with most of its printing at the right side, as in Figure 6-4.
2. *Modified block* form is currently the most popular style. The date, complimentary close, and signature sections may begin near the center of the page; attention and subject lines may be indented; the other parts begin at left margin. (See Figures 6-2 and 6-3.)
3. *Modified block with paragraphs indented* is also popular. (See Figure 6-5.)
4. *AMS simplified style,* adopted by the Administrative Management Society, uses full block and open punctuation; omits the salutation and complimentary close; and includes a subject line without the word *subject,* typed in all capital letters a triple space after the inside address. The first paragraph contains the reader's name. (See Figure 6-6.)

Tips for Letter Placement

In general, an attractive letter is placed like a picture in a frame. The easiest way to achieve a pleasing appearance for all your letters is to have a competent secretary. However, most students—and even many young businesspersons— find it necessary to type some letters themselves. To save time and money, some firms use the same line lengths—usually 5 inches—for all messages, regardless of length. (In short messages they double-space the message and triple-space between paragraphs.)

Nevertheless, for the most attractive-looking letters, it is advisable to use line lengths adapted to letter length and paper size. When using 8½- by 11-inch stationery you may find these suggestions helpful for short, medium, long, and 2-page letters:

Letter length	Words in body	Side Margins —Width in in inches	Line Length in inches	Number of lines between date and inside address	Examples
Short	Under 100	2	4½	4–10	Figure 6-4
Medium	100–200	1½	5½	3–8	Figures 6-2 and 6-6
Long	200–300	1	6½	2–6	Figure 6-5
2-page	Over 300	1	6½	2–6	Figure 6-3

Regency Office Equipment Company
312 Zero Street
Somecity, NY 10002-0000

June 22, 198_

Ms. Jeanette Darlene, Consultant
Intermountain and Coast
  Telephone Company
456 Exchange Building
Sometown, Anystate 98888-4000

Dear Ms. Darlene

In this full-block letter, every line begins at the
left margin. The letter is preferably typed single
space, with a blank line between paragraphs.

Many firms prefer open punctuation with this form,
but mixed can also be used. The writer's company
name may be typed under the complimentary close,
as here, or omitted.

Other accepted forms or reference initials could,
of course, be used with this letter style. Also
the "Registered Mail" or other special service
(such as "Special Delivery") notation could be
typed in full capitals two lines below the date
instead of under the reference initials.

Sincerely yours

WESTERN OFFICE EQUIPMENT COMPANY

James Briggs

James Briggs, Manager
Adjustment Department

JB/jd

REGISTERED MAIL

P.S. *Best of success on your speech!*

Figure 6-4 Full block; open punctuation. Length, short; side margins, 2″; line length, 4½″.

LETTERHEAD

- -

                                                    December 1, 198_

        Accounting Department
        Eastern Register Company
        1969 Fourth Avenue NE
        Sometown, Anystate 99999-2000

        Attention Mr. Johnson

        Ladies and Gentlemen:

            This modified block form is like that in Figure 6-2 except that its
        paragraphs are indented five or more spaces. The date may be centered or
        placed so it does not extend into the right margin. In this example the date
        begins at the horizontal center of the page.

            The attention line here is at the left margin, two lines below the inside
        address, and underlined. It could also have been centered and typed in all
        capital letters without underscoring. If you wanted Mr. Johnson's name in the
        salutation, you would type his first name (or two initials) and his surname
        above Accounting Department. Then you would omit the attention line and use
        "Dear Mr. Johnson" (or "Dear Bill") in the salutation.

            In this example the complimentary close, like the date, begins at the
        center of the page. The company name is omitted, but it could have been
        included. Also the signer's name--instead of being at the left--could have
        been typed above the "General Manager" and reference initials (like "MM:hw")
        could then have been used at the left margin.

            The term "Enclosures 3" in the reference section shows that three
        additional items are being enclosed in the envelope. Each different item is
        counted as one, regardless of the number of pages it may have.

            The notation "cc" indicates that a carbon copy is being sent to Mr. Jami
        and Miss Krown. Names are in alphabetical order or by rank. The address of
        each may be included if doing so will help the typist in sending the carbon
        copy or if it is needed for filing information.

                                                    Very truly yours,

                                                    Millard M. Morrison

                                                    General Manager
        Millard M. Morrison/hw

        Enclosures 3
        cc: Mr. Thomas Jami
             Ms. Helen Krown

Figure 6-5 Modified block with paragraph indentions; mixed punctuation. Length, long; side margins, 1″; line length, 6½″.

```
                              LETTERHEAD


- - - - - - - - - - - - - - - - - - - - - - - - - - - - - - - - - - - - - - - -

      July 26, 198_


      Mrs. Lary Burl
      P. O. Box 9152
      Sometown, Anystate 66666-1234

      FORMAT FOR SIMPLIFIED LETTER

      This letter form, Mrs. Burl, has been recommended by the
      Administrative Management Society as an important timesaving step
      when typing business letters.  This letter setup saves about 19
      key strokes. Here are its features:

      1.  It uses full block form and open punctuation.

      2.  It omits the salutation and the complimentary close, but--to
          personalize--uses the reader's name at least in the first
          sentence.

      3.  The subject line is in all capitals, omits "subject," and has
          at least one blank line both before and after it.

      4.  The signer's name and business title are typed in all capi-
          tals, starting at the left margin at least four blank lines
          below the last line of the letter body.

      5.  Only the typist's initials are typed at the left margin two
          lines below the signer's name. Enclosures are indicated below
          the initials. Names of persons receiving carbon copies are
          typed below the initials and enclosures.

      Mrs. Burl, the Simplified Letter not only saves time but also
      avoids the need for a correct salutation.  Furthermore, the sub-
      ject line tells the reader immediately what the letter is about.

      Paul A. Mullins

      PAUL A. MULLINS - RESEARCH DIRECTOR

      hm
      Enc 4
      Messrs. Ronald Scharf, Mike Luberts, Erich Wittor
```

Figure 6-6 AMS simplified style; full block; open punctuation. Length, medium; side margins, 1½″, line length, 5½″.

Envelopes

The quality of the envelope paper, and pictures and slogans, if any, all contribute to your organization's image. Each envelope should—in the upper left corner—show the sender's return address, usually printed like the letterhead, or, if necessary, typewritten. The addressee's address (which is the inside address of the letter) should be placed on the envelope according to U.S. Postal Service published guidelines for location, legibility, and format of information.

Address Location and Legibility for Optical Character Recognition

To quicken the processing of mail at the post office, the addressee's name and address on the envelope must be completely in the *"OCR read area"* because the electronic mail sorters—Optical Character Readers (OCR)—are programmed to scan this area automatically. (See Figure 6-7.) The address should be clearly imprinted with dark print or typewriter type on a light background, parallel (within five degrees) to the envelope's bottom edge; slanted or crooked lines can confuse OCR recognition.

Address Format for OCR

1. Addressee's address on the envelope must be blocked (not indented). Upper case (CAPITAL) characters are preferred but *not* required. Italic, artistic,

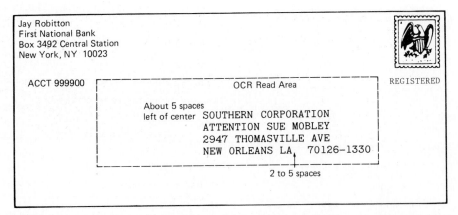

Figure 6-7 Large business envelope (9½ by 4⅛ inches) properly addressed for Optical Character Recognition.

and scriptlike fonts cannot be read by the OCR. Punctuation is not required. (See Figure 6-7 and examples under 2.d. below.)

2. Line sequence should be:
   a. *Top line*—NAME OF RECIPIENT.
   b. *Next 1 or 2 lines*—INFORMATION/ATTENTION; includes name of company, agency, department, or other identifying information and attention line, if needed (Figure 6-7).
   c. *Line above last*—DELIVERY ADDRESS; includes street number and name or route number and box number. Unit, apartment, office, room, or suite numbers are placed *after* the street address on same line or, if necessary, on the line above (never below or in front of) the street address.
   d. *Last line*—POST OFFICE/STATE/ZIP CODE. The standard 2-letter state abbreviation should be used, followed by 2 to 5 character spaces before the ZIP code. Mail to a foreign country must have full name of post office in that country; postal delivery zone number, if any; and country name as last item in the address.

```
MR H M JONES
ACCOUNTING DEPT
ABC CORPORATION          MS KATHY STEVENS        MR EARL BROWN
3645 E INDUSTRIAL PKWY   CLIFTON TOWERS APT 952  342 HIGH DRIVE
CLEVELAND OH 44106-1537  3900 53D AVENUE WEST    LONDON W1P 6 HO
                         SACRAMENTO CA 95816-1437 ENGLAND
```

3. Mail notations such as *Special Delivery* or *Registered* should be typed in all capitals below the stamp position.

4. On-Arrival Instructions such as *Confidential, Hold for Arrival, Please Forward,* and *Account Numbers* should be typed in all capitals a triple space below the return address near the left edge of the envelope.

Some firms use the "all-capitals no punctuation" layouts only for monthly billings and large quantity mailings. When appearance is more important than speed, you may prefer to have envelopes addressed in the usual format—consistent with each letter's inside address—with upper- and lower-case typewritten characters (NOT all capitals), with punctuation, and few if any abbreviations except states. Such envelopes can also be sorted accurately and efficiently.

To give you an idea of the wastes that occur from inadequately addressed mail, here are some figures from Mary J. Layton, Assistant Postmaster General, Public and Employee Communications, U.S. Postal Service, Washington, D.C.: Approximately 44.5 million pieces of mail went to the dead-letter office and its branches in 1982. The Postal Service found—in 1982—$1.2 million in cash enclosed in 159,000 letters sent to the dead-letter office. Approximately $579,000 of the $1.2 million cited above could not be restored to rightful owners because of lack of information on or within envelopes. The Postal Service spent approximately $4.3 million in 1982 trying to find correct addresses for inadequately addressed mail.

MEMORANDUMS

In contrast to the letter, which is directed outside your organization, the memorandum (memo) goes within your organization. It is an informal, written communication from one person or department to another person, persons, or department. The stationery, parts, layout, and envelopes of the memo are somewhat different from those of the letters described in the preceding section.

Stationery

Memo stationery often differs from letter stationery in quality, color, size, and printing. Usually it is of a much less expensive quality paper than that for regular letters; also, instead of white, memo paper is often in pastel colors—yellow, cream, pink, blue—for easy identification. Sizes of sheets range from the standard 8½ by 11 inches to small slips 4 by 5 inches. Printing usually includes OFFICE MEMORANDUM and the company's name (but not address); also words naming various memo parts.

The combination *message-and-reply memorandum* form is an especially good time- (and expense) saver for both sender and recipient. A packet of three or more perforated sheets (white and colored), plus carbons (unless special "carbonless" paper is used), makes up a message-reply packet. Printed instructions at the top or bottom tell the sender and the reader how to use the sheets. Printed lines may aid those who communicate in handwriting. Each sheet is divided into two sections—MESSAGE and REPLY. These two sections may be side by side or one above the other. (See Figure 6-8.)

Parts of the Memorandum

The standard memo parts are: to, from, subject, date, and body. Optional are such items as reference initials, enclosure(s), file number, routing information, and the department and telephone number of the sender. Most of these parts are printed on the memo stationery. Unlike the letter, the memo requires no inside address, salutation, complimentary close, or full signature. The combination message-reply forms do, however, provide lines for both the writer's and the reader's signatures. (See Figure 6-8.)

What you write after the TO, FROM, and DATE will vary with the situation and your organization's practices. A courtesy title—Mr., Mrs., Miss,

ABC Company	INTEROFFICE COMMUNICATION	
TO		PLANT/DEPARTMENT
FROM		PLANT/DEPARTMENT
SUBJECT		DATE

M E S S A G E

SIGNED

R E P L Y

DATE	SIGNED

PERSON RECEIVING COMMUNICATION · RETAIN THIS COPY FOR YOUR RECORD (1st page: white)

ORIGINATOR:
DETACH THIS COPY. SEND REMAINING SET, CARBON INTACT, FOR USE OF REPLIER. (2d page: yellow)

REPLIER: RETURN THIS COPY TO SENDER (3d page: pink)

Figure 6-8 Interoffice memorandum packet containing carbons under sheets of paper (white, yellow, pink) with sections for both the message and the reply.

Ms.—before your reader's name (after TO) may be used or omitted, depending upon your relationship with the reader (superior or subordinate) and the degree of informality within your organization. You omit the title before your name. Also, if the memo is a temporary message, not to be filed, and if you and the writer work together regularly, you may merely use initials, first name, or nickname after TO and FROM, and all figures or abbreviations for the date. Place your handwritten initials above or to the right of your name.

TO:	J.E.H.		**TO:**	Jack
FROM:	T.R.M.	*or*	**FROM:**	Ted *Ted*
DATE:	2/10/8_		**DATE:**	Feb. 10, 198_

However, if the memo will be filed, these parts should be spelled out:

TO: Mr. (optional) James E. Hill, Personnel Manager
FROM: Theodore R. Murdock, Accounting Department *TRM*
DATE: February 10, 198_

If you are sending the same message to several persons, their names and/or titles should be typed after TO. If you write to the same persons often, you might have a form prepared with their names printed (or dittoed, Xeroxed, or mimeographed) after the TO. When you have only one copy of a document, book, or other important papers that you want everyone in a certain group to read and comment on, circulate a covering memo—the single original, with no copies for readers to keep—among those on your list. Brief instructions (printed or typed) tell the readers what to do. Their names are listed alphabetically or in order of importance.

DATE: May 2, 198_
TO: Tom Brehm_____   Please initial and pass on; last
            James Brown_____   reader please return memo and attach-
            Anita Jones_____   ment to sender.
            Searl Lichen_____
            Harry Green_____
FROM: Kermit Hobson, Personnel *K.H.*
SUBJECT: Your suggestions on attached Procedures Manual

Layout of the Memorandum Body

The body of the memo, as for the letter, is its most important part because it contains your message. *In general, you can use the same guidelines, principles, and organizational plans for the memo as for the letter;* the few differences are pointed out in succeeding chapters.

The memo body, unlike that of a letter, is not centered on the page. The first line usually begins a triple space under the subject line regardless of message length. Left margins are usually lined up evenly below the TO. The body is typed single space, with double spacing between paragraphs. For memo pages beyond the first, headings are the same as those for the business letter: reader's name, page number, and date. Reference initials are typed a few spaces below the body, at the left margin. Copy notations (cc or "copy") may be placed after the reference initials (as in letters) or near the top of the memo between the TO and the FROM. If only your business title appears in the FROM line, or if the FROM line is omitted, you should sign your name a few spaces below the memo body.

Envelopes

How your memo is routed to the addressee depends partly upon where you and the reader are located. If you are in the same building, the memo might be inserted into the reader's mailbox, put on her or his desk by a messenger, or routed through compressed-air tubes. If you are in different buildings, your memo may be mailed in a manila or regular company envelope. The envelope address contains your name and department in the upper left corner and the reader's name, department, and address according to your organization's procedures.

SPECIAL TIMESAVING MESSAGE MEDIA

Included in this section are various message media that save time for both the sender and recipient. They can be useful in certain situations when speed is essential *and* the messages are relatively short (though, of course, there are exceptions). The media that merit at least a brief discussion here are memo-letters, postcards, Mailgrams, telegrams, cablegrams, radiograms, and form messages.

Memo-Letters

In the interest of speed and lower costs, many firms (especially wholesalers, publishers, and manufacturers) use a combination message-reply or memo-letter form for routine short messages directed *outside* their organization. Compare the memo-letter packet in Figure 6-9 with the interoffice memorandum shown in Figure 6-8. The main differences are that in the memo-letter: (1) after the FROM, the full name and address (perhaps also phone number) of the sender's company are printed (sometimes in the same format as the firm's regular letterhead); and (2) after the TO, a larger space is provided so that the typist can insert the full name and address of the recipient, because he or she is outside the sender's firm.

A further timesaver is the printed request-for-information form, as illustrated in Figure 6-10. Notice that besides the printed 28 requests this firm commonly uses, the form leaves spaces for 6 others to be inserted if desired. The bottom of this memo-letter form allows space for comments by both the sender and the receiver. This form also is a packet of three sheets with carbons preinserted.

The memo-letter is mailed in the same kind of envelope as a regular business letter or in a window envelope (in which the address after the TO serves also as the envelope address).

Postcards

For short messages that are not confidential, you can often save time and expense by using postcards. These media do not require folding, sealing, or inserting in envelopes.

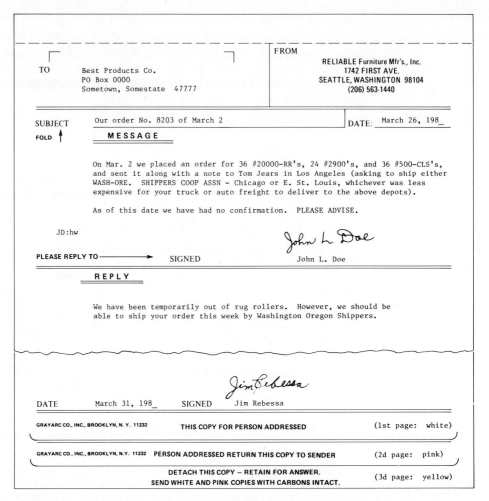

Figure 6-9 Memo-letter stationery for routine short messages—usually going outside your company. (Jagged lines indicate a portion of actual sheet removed here only to save space.)

On the stamped side of the card, usually only the reader's name and address are typed. The message side includes the name and address of the sender, the date, salutation, message, complimentary close, and signature. (To save both space and time, some business firms have their names and address *printed* in one line, usually across the top of the postcard's message side.)

As a customer you can use a postcard, for example, to inquire, to request a free advertised booklet, or to order a product that is to be charged to your account. As a representative of a business firm you can send postcards and reply cards for a wide variety of uses, two of which are illustrated in Figures 6-11 and 6-12.

J. W. MICROELECTRONICS CORPORATION
REGIONAL TECHNOLOGY PARK - BLDG. C
4901 STENTON AVENUE • PHILADELPHIA, PENNSYLVANIA 19144 • PHONE 215-329-8681

REQUEST FOR INFORMATION

TO: _____   DATE _____   REQUEST NO. _____
_____   P.O. NO. _____   INV. NO. _____
_____   INV. DATE _____   INV. AMOUNT _____

PLEASE REPLY TODAY VIA   ☐ THIS FORM   ☐ WIRE   ☐ TELEPHONE   ☐ RETURN ENVELOPE ENCLOSED

☐ 1. PLEASE ACKNOWLEDGE OUR ORDER AND GIVE SHIPPING DATE
☐ 2. PLEASE CHANGE ORDER AS NOTED BELOW AND ACKNOWLEDGE
☐ 3. PLEASE ADVISE WHEN ORDER WILL BE SHIPPED
☐ 4. MUST HAVE MORE SPECIFIC SHIPPING DATE
☐ 5. CAN YOU MEET OUR SHIPPING DATE?
☐ 6. GOODS NOT RECEIVED, PLEASE TRACE SHIPMENT
☐ 7. IF SHIPMENT HAS BEEN MADE, PLEASE MAIL INVOICE TODAY
☐ 8. WHEN WILL BALANCE OF OUR ORDER BE SHIPPED?
☐ 9. PLEASE RUSH PRICES REQUESTED
☐ 10. PLEASE SEND A SHIPPING NOTICE
☐ 11. PLEASE SEND A RECEIPTED FREIGHT BILL
☐ 12. PLEASE SEND A CERTIFIED WEIGHT SLIP
☐ 13. PLEASE SEND ACCEPTANCE COPY OF OUR P.O.
☐ 14. RELEASE SHIPMENTS AS SHOWN UNDER "REMARKS" BELOW
☐ 15. PUT OUR P.O. NUMBER ON ALL SHIPMENTS
☐ 16. SHIP THIS ORDER TO ADDRESS BELOW
☐ 17. WE HAVE NO RECORD OF TRANSACTION COVERED BY YOUR INVOICE. PLEASE GIVE US ORDER DATE, DATE SHIPPED, P. O. NUMBER, NAME OF PERSON PLACING THE ORDER AND/OR SIGNED DELIVERY RECEIPT.

☐ 18. YOUR INVOICE IS RETURNED FOR REASON CHECKED:
☐ 19. WE REQUIRE_____COPIES OF EACH INVOICE
☐ 20. PRICES DO NOT MATCH YOUR QUOTATION
☐ 21. TERMS DO NOT MATCH OUR P.O.
☐ 22. QUANTITY DIFFERS FROM OUR P.O.
☐ 23. UNIT PRICE IS INCORRECT
☐ 24. EXTENSION PRICE IS INCORRECT
☐ 25. OUR P.O. NUMBER IS LACKING OR INCORRECT
☐ 26. SALES TAX DOES/DOES NOT APPLY
☐ 27. ORDER SHOULD BE BILLED F.O.B. DESTINATION
☐ 28. ORDER MUST BE SHIPPED VIA _____
☐ 29. _____
☐ 30. _____
☐ 31. _____
☐ 32. _____
☐ 33. _____
☐ 34. _____

OUR REMARKS   **YOUR REPLY**

Form R-R113 The Drawing Board, Inc., Box 505, Dallas, Texas

Figure 6-10 Printed request-for-information packet (three sheets) with numbered requests for easy check-off; also spaces for remarks and for recipient's reply.

ORDER CARD

Please send me

_____copies of *Two Studies in Automobile Franchising*   @ $9.50 = $ _____

_____copies of *Institutional Holdings of Common Stock*   @ $9.00 = $ _____

_____copies of *Antitrust Policy and Economic Welfare*   @ $8.00 = $ _____

and charge my account for........................total $ _____

Name_____

Address_____

City_____State_____Zip_____

Figure 6-11 Business reply order postcard. The reverse side is addressed to the seller; the firm's name, address, and postage permit number are printed in appropriate places for address and stamp.

Figure 6-12 Seller's "miss-you" postcard, asking to serve customer soon.

Mailgrams

When you need to reach any number of people predictably, simultaneously, in writing, with impact, the *next business day*—you can use Mailgrams. These media have urgency and prestige value similar to telegrams, but at much lower cost.

Uses and Appearance

You can use Mailgrams in many ways—to announce important news to sales representatives, distributors, stockholders, employees—speedily, simultaneously; quote special prices; acknowledge orders; congratulate; collect delinquent payments. Figure 6-13 illustrates Mailgram format and tells some advantages.

Methods of Sending

Mailgrams may be sent by various means, including phoning a Western Union toll-free number. Direct input into the Western Union Mailgram system may be done by customers who have Telex I, Telex II, INFO-COM services, or word processing terminals with capability of transmitting information telegraphically. Also, some direct computer transmission or magnetic and paper tape reels may be accepted at certain Western Union locations.

Each message is routed electronically by the Western Union network to a post office near your addressee and printed out individually. It is delivered in a Western Union blue and white Mailgram envelope the next regular mail, usually the day after it's sent, sometimes the same day. The price structure and manner of counting words or characters differs for each type of Mailgram filing. Costs are also lower for quantity mailings ranging from 100 to over 25,000 messages.[2]

Telegrams, Cablegrams, Radiograms

You can send a message by telegram within the continental United States and by cablegram or radiogram for overseas communication. The format of telegrams and cablegrams is similar to that of the Mailgram. Most telegrams today

[2] Information in this section is from Western Union brochures and courtesy of Marlene Parry, administration manager, Western Union, Seattle, Washington. Cost of a Mailgram originating by phone or over-the-counter and destined to points within the United States including Alaska, was (in 1982) $3.90 for 50 words or less and $1.25 for each additional group of 50 words or less. Rates for identical messages with multiple addresses are less. Mailgrams sent from a Telex I, Telex II or INFO-COM subscriber are charged a rate for usage and service. Mailgrams filed by direct computer transmission, magnetic and/or paper tape reel, are charged by number of words and quantity of messages.

```
WESTERN UNION TELEGRAPH CO
ONE LAKE STREET
SADDLE RIVER, NEW JERSEY 07458
```

western union **Mailgram**

```
0-001012U056003 4/5/8_  ICS NY 14233          MLTN

                                       ***BUSINESS REPLY***

L. B. JONES
32 SOUTH MAIN STREET
MAPLEWOOD     PA 15219


HERE'S THE RESPONSE GETTER
YOU'VE BEEN WAITING FOR......

IT'S BUSINESS REPLY MAILGRAM...DELIVERING YOUR MESSAGE WITH THE IMPACT
OF A TELEGRAM (AT A FRACTION OF THE COST)...ALL WITH A BUILT-IN REPLY
SLIP...A BUSINESS REPLY ENVELOPE FOR IMMEDIATE TURNAROUND.

IT LETS YOU REACH HUNDREDS OR THOUSANDS OF PEOPLE IN THE NEXT BUSINESS
DAY'S MAIL...TO:

        ...GENERATE SALES LEADS
        ...COLLECT ON DELINQUENT ACCOUNTS
        ...OFFER SALES PROMOTION MATERIAL
        ...SOLICIT CONTRIBUTIONS OR PROXIES
        ...TAKE READER/CONSUMER AUDITS/SURVEYS
        ...RELEASE PRICE CHANGE INFORMATION

OR TO SEND ANY OTHER ANNOUNCEMENTS AND REQUESTS.  YOU'LL GET GREATER
RESPONSE FASTER.

YOUR PROSPECTS AND CUSTOMERS NEED MERELY FILL OUT THE REPLY FORM AT THE
BOTTOM OF YOUR MAILGRAM, AND REFOLD IT SO THAT YOUR RETURN ADDRESS AND
PERMIT NUMBER SHOW THROUGH THE WINDOW OF THE BUSINESS REPLY ENVELOPE.
NO POSTAGE NEEDED.

WESTERN UNION WILL GLADLY ASSIST YOU IN PREPARING YOUR MESSAGE AND LIST
FOR TRANSMISSION IN VOLUME ORDERS SO THAT YOU MAY OBTAIN THE LOWEST COST
POSSIBLE.  FOR FURTHER INFORMATION CALL WESTERN UNION TOLL FREE.

MAILGRAM IS THE FASTEST WAY TO GET THE WORD AROUND...AND BACK.


WESTERN UNION TELEGRAPH CO
ONE LAKE STREET
UPPER SADDLE RIVER, NEW JERSEY  07458

06:14 EST

MGMCOMP MGM
```

Figure 6-13   Mailgram.

are delivered by telephone; cablegrams are transmitted by transoceanic cable; radiograms are wireless messages (usually delivered to ships).

Telegrams

For domestic telegraphic service, you can choose full-rate telegrams or overnight telegrams. The fastest domestic service, for transmission within two hours, is the full-rate telegram. The minimum charge is for 15 words. The more economical overnight telegrams are messages accepted up to midnight for delivery not earlier than the following morning.[3] If your firm sends numerous telegrams, you should be sure to get a copy of Domestic Telegraph Service Rules. These sheets contain highly useful, money-saving, specific details on how to count words, figures, forms of money, symbols, and punctuation.[4]

Cablegrams and Radiograms

Because transmission of messages outside the continental United States is necessarily costly, it is extremely advisable to be well informed on rules for international word count. If you communicate frequently with representatives overseas, you might develop mutually understood code symbols to save costs. For example, notice how the following cable text from an insurance agent in Greece to her home office in the United States can be cut from a word count of 25 to only 10 words. (Words in the address count extra.)

(25 words)   CUSTOMER HAS TODAY ACCEPTED A NEW INSURANCE POLICY IN-
              CLUDING FIRE EXTENDED COVERAGE AND VANDALISM ALSO PUBLIC
              LIABILITY AND PROPERTY DAMAGE AS WELL AS WORKMEN'S COM-
              PENSATION

(10 words)   CUSTOMER TODAY ACCEPTED NEW POLICY INCLUDING FECVM PLPD
              AND WC

Form Messages

Whenever you want to send an identical message to at least two persons, you can write what is called a ''form letter'' or a ''form memo,'' based on a master draft. These messages can help save time and money because they can be duplicated by various automatic processes, be used again and again, speed up correspondence, and make possible wider mass mailings.

Four kinds of form messages are: complete form, fill-in form, guide form, and paragraph form.

---

[3] Cost of an interstate 15-word telegram (in 1982): $7.45, if delivered by telephone; $13.20 by messenger; 23 cents for each additional word over 15. Cost of an interstate overnight telegram: $6.05 for 15 words or less, if delivered by telephone; $11.85, by messenger; 18 cents for each additional word over 15. Only words in the message (not the address or signature) are counted. Intrastate nightletter: $5.50 for first 50 words; over 50, 12 cents per word.

[4] Chargeable words in a domestic telegram are a total of (a) dictionary words, (b) full words in proper names, and (c) matter subject to the five-character word count. Under the five-character rule, combined figures, signs, or alphabetic letters count one word for each five characters or fewer. For example: these are one word: urlet (your letter), 9-16-84, 415(A). Punctuation marks—including, . ; : - ( )—though transmitted, are neither counted nor charged for. Spaces automatically separate matter into word groups: AT&SF is one word; A. T. & S. F. is five words. These are counted as one word each: # $ % & / " indicating inches or seconds; thus these are each two words: 112-3/4 and 15".

Complete Form

Messages identical in every word are *complete forms,* especially useful for announcements, some collection reminders, and large-scale campaigns when being *impersonal* is desirable. They may be reproduced on a printing press, computer, multigraph, mimeograph, ditto, Xerox, or other types of duplicating machines.

In a complete form *memo* the word TO is followed by such terms as ''All Employees'' or ''Management Personnel.'' In *letters* a general salutation (Dear Customer, Homeowner, Sports Buff, Student) is chosen to fit the type of individuals getting the letter. Sometimes the first few words of the opening sentence are placed where the inside address and salutation usually are:

''Faked'' *inside* *address*	`The last time you had` `a chance like this` `to get World and Home News`
''Faked'' *salutation*	`at a big savings . . .`
Body	`. . . business was coasting along without any serious` `worries, the war in _____ seemed to be cooling off,` `the President had . . . .`

Fill-in Form

A message prepared in advance to meet a specific kind of situation may have spaces left for filling in variable information. The date, customer's name and address, account number, payment due date, and so forth are inserted in the right spaces on each individual letter. The fill-ins should be made on a machine with matching type and ribbon.

Some fill-in forms—for example, Figure 6-10—are obviously forms. They are useful in routine situations when both the writer and the reader consider forms acceptable.

However, when it is desirable to personalize each letter, fill-in forms can be reproduced by computer, automatic typewriter, or other high-speed automatic machines with magnetic tape capacity for inserting variable information at the time each form is reproduced. Thus, each person on your mailing list will receive a letter containing his or her name in one or more places and all the specific variables that apply to his or her case. The ''fill-ins'' are almost unnoticeable. If your firm uses a word-processing system, form letters can be run automatically at 1,000 wpm.

Guide Form

Sample letters prepared in advance for various situations can be kept on hand (usually in an office correspondence manual) and referred to whenever a communicator writes similar messages. The communicator uses any sample as a guide only, inserting personal phrasing wherever desirable.

Paragraph Form

An office booklet or a magnetic disc for storing paragraphs to meet various situations is often an efficient way to save the letter writer's time. The writer does, however, need to use good judgment in selecting appropriate paragraphs.

The booklet or disc usually contains various sections covering the frequently written messages. An airline, for example, may group its paragraphs under Passenger Fares, Flight Schedule Inquiries, Air Cargo, Adjustments, Charter Flights, and Goodwill. Each section contains numbered pages with various opening, closing, and intervening paragraphs that answer often-asked questions. Each paragraph may be marked by a number and a letter of the alphabet.

Thus, after choosing the appropriate paragraphs for your message, you need merely dictate the paragraph numbers; for instance, "2C, 5A, 9C, 15E." If you need a special paragraph that is not in the booklet (or on the disc), you dictate it. Your transcriber arranges the designated paragraphs and adds your specially dictated paragraph in the right order. (If a word processor or automatic typewriter with magnetic tape or card is used, a letter can be completed in a few seconds.) Each customer gets an attractive, personalized letter composed of form paragraphs that exactly answer his or her questions and needs.

SUMMARY

Letters and memos are the most used written business message media. In addition, for special situations, memo-letters, postcards, Mailgrams, plus other telegraphic and wireless media and forms are also effective.

Attractive appearance of a business letter is an important aid to the reader's favorable first impression. Stationery, parts and layout (format), and envelope addressing should follow certain guidelines. For memorandums (sent within the organization) the stationery, parts, layout, and envelopes are different from those of letters. Memo-letters have a format more similar to a memo than to a letter. Postcards have certain timesaving features. Though the formats of Mailgrams, telegrams, and cablegrams are similar, these messages differ in methods of transmittal, word count, and costs. All convey the impression that your message is important and urgent. To get the most economical rates, study the telegraph company's rules governing these services.

The four kinds of form messages offer advantages in time, cost, quality, and quantity mailings; but they must be used with good judgment to avoid possible disadvantages.

This chapter is your guide for *formats* of business letters, memos, postcards, telegraphic media, and form letters and memos. In Chapters 7 to 14, which focus on *content,* most illustrations include only the message *body*—to save space. Therefore, when typing your complete messages, you may want to refer regularly to this chapter for correct layouts.

EXERCISES

1. What are the standard and optional parts of a business letter?

2. **a.** What is the most popular layout style for business letters?
   b. Describe it and compare it with other popular styles.
   c. Which do you prefer and why?

3. How do the standard parts of the memo differ from those of the letter?

4. What are the advantages of using postcards, when desirable, for business messages? What disadvantages can you name?

5. Describe briefly five features of the AMS Simplified letter.

6. Name three differences between a modified-block form and a full-block form of letter. Consider all standard and optional parts of these letters.

7. What are the advantages—and possible disadvantages—of (a) form messages? (b) Mailgrams? (c) telegrams? (d) cablegrams?

8. Each of the following parts of a letter has one or more faults. Treat each part as an independent unit. Correct errors and change all obsolete forms.

   In the heading (stationery that doesn't have a letterhead):

   a. 3 April 198_
   15,447 E. 5th St.,
   Seattle, Wn. 98155

   b. Mr. Ray F. Byfield
   15 Mt. Vernon Ave.
   New Orleans, La. 70145
   Jan. 5th, 198_

   In the inside address:

   c. Mrs. John E. Henning,
   4317-18 Avenue N.E.
   Chicago,
   Illinois

d. Professor Lee Stephenson, Ph.D.
School of Business Administration
University of California
BERKELEY 94700

e. Campbell and Morris Furniture Co.,
1,496 Westlake Ave.
City (*Sender is in same city as addressee.*)

In the signature and reference section

f. (open punctuation)   Very Truly Yours,
                                             State Federal Savings Assn.,
D.E.S./A.R.F.   Mr. Donald E. Smith
INCLOSURE   President

g. (mixed punctuation)   Sincerely Yours,
Richard E. Scroggs:ab   Credit Manager

h. (mixed punctuation)   Cordially yours
                                             MEURER & HOHANNES, INC.
RAJ:AF   Raymond Jensen
cc: Thomas Brown   Prod. Mgr.

In the inside address, salutation, and complimentary close (assume mixed punctuation for parts i through n):

i. Gladyne Lucchesini
Des Moines, Ia. 50320

Dear Miss Gladyne Luchesini

                     Yours truly

j. Dr. William Knapp, M.D.
618 Wrigley Bldg.
Chicago 14, Ill. 60667

Dear Carl,

                     Sincerely yours

k. B.K. Renshaw
17,672 3rd St., N.E.,
New York City 10011

Dear Sir:-

                     Yours

l. Veterans Adm.
644a Liberty Bldg.
Detroit, Mich. 48256

Attention: Dr. Chester Allen Powers

Dear Dr. Chester Powers

                     Respectively yours,

 m. Northwest Company, Inc.
   Accounting Department
   Phila, Penna. 19133

   Dear Ms. Swanson

          Your faithful friend

          Pasco & Co.

   Incl.   Clifford D. Bergerson
   al; cdb:TR   Personnell Mgr.

 n. HAVDAHL MANUFACTURING COMPANY
   Attention: Miss Helen Burgess
   Eleven South Fifteenth St.
   Kansas C'y, Mo. 64143

   Dear Sirs: RE: February Sale

9. Which of the following three memorandums is best? Why? How does even this memo need improvement? In your evaluation, be sure to consider the probable purpose of the message and whether the memo is likely to be filed.

 a.

```
Jack to Bob, 4-23-8_

B O O K L E T   S C H E D U L E
Johnson now says Saturday sure.
```

 b.

```
TO:      RJL
FROM:    JS
April 23, 198_
HEALTH BOOKLET SCHEDULE

I checked with Johnson and now have a definite promise that
the 6,000 Standard "Your Health" booklets will be delivered
Saturday, April 26.

This rescheduling will not affect our other production sched-
ules.
```

 c.

```
TO:        Dr. Robert Lawson, Vice President
FROM:      John Spam, Managing Editor
April 23, 198_
RESCHEDULING OF STANDARD "YOUR HEALTH" BOOKLETS

I talked with Thomas Johnson this morning in an effort to re-
schedule production of 6,000 Standard "Your Health" booklets
to permit delivery Saturday, April 26.
```

```
He indicated at first that such a rescheduling would delay
either the "Travel Plans" or the "Vacation Hints" booklets,
but after talking with his production manager he agreed to
make the schedule change without delaying our other produc-
tion.

Thus we can definitely count on delivery of "Your Health"
Saturday.
```

10. If you have an employer or know an organization that is willing to furnish the following specified materials, ask for them and then answer the questions:

   a. Bring to class a sample of a firm's letterhead stationery and envelopes and be prepared to evaluate them orally. If the firm has several sizes, qualities, and colors of stationery, evaluate them all and discuss briefly the uses of each.

   b. Bring to class a sample of memorandum stationery and any intra-company envelopes used for memos. Be prepared to evaluate them orally. Can you suggest improvements—perhaps timesaving additions or changes?

   c. Which of the standard styles of letter layout does the firm use? If the firm has not adopted a uniform style for all letters, try to collect—from various secretaries—as many different styles and layouts as you can. Be prepared to:

   (1) Illustrate those you like best and tell why.

   (2) Discuss those you like least and tell why.

   (3) Find out, if possible, why the secretaries and/or their bosses prefer the style they use.

   d. Be prepared to discuss the following aspects of memos in the firm you visited:

   (1) How frequently are memos used rather than telephone conversations?

   (2) Who writes memos? Only department heads? Nontitled employees? Others?

   (3) To whom do employees write memos?

   (4) Are memos usually routed through a superior? If so, through whom?

   (5) What is the average length of memos?

   (6) What standard and optional parts do the firm's memos contain?

PART TWO
Major Plans for Letters and Memos

CHAPTER 7
Direct Requests

When the main purpose of your message is to ask the reader to do something, you are writing a *request* letter or memo. Whether you organize your message according to the *direct-* or the *persuasive*-request pattern depends upon the nature of the request and, most of all, upon how you think the reader will react to that request. Generally when you make a simple inquiry or a routine request, you will *not* have to persuade your reader to do what you ask. You can usually handle the following types of messages with the direct-request plan:

Inquiries

Claims (complaints) and requests for adjustments

Requests, regarding routine business or public causes

Invitations, orders, reservations

Early-stage collection messages

This chapter presents the direct-request organizational plan, discusses the first four types of requests, then compares them briefly in capsule checklists. Chapter 14 discusses early-stage collection messages.

ORGANIZATIONAL PLAN

For a routine inquiry or request you assume that the reader will do as you request, once he or she understands what you want and why you want it. Thus you use the direct approach—introduce your main idea in the first paragraph. The direct-request plan has three basic parts:

1. Main idea
   a. Introduce your request, major statement, or question.
   b. State reason(s), if desirable, justifying the request.
2. Explanation
   a. Include details necessary to help the reader respond to your request correctly.
   b. Consider numbering your questions (if more than one) for easy reading and answering.
3. Courteous close with motivation to action
   a. State clearly what action you want the reader to take—and when.
   b. Make action easy, if appropriate, by including a postpaid reply envelope, your telephone number, office hours, or any other appropriate, helpful information.
   c. Express appreciation and, if appropriate, include a statement of goodwill or reader benefit.

INQUIRIES

To get facts that you need and cannot conveniently or economically obtain yourself, you write inquiries requesting information. The questions asked are important in all inquiries, whether they are in a letter or a long survey questionnaire. Thus, this section begins with suggestions about phrasing and arranging questions. Then follows a discussion of direct-request messages that seek information about persons and messages inquiring about products, services, and other matters requiring no persuasion.

Wording and Arrangement of Questions

So that you can get exactly the information wanted, you must be especially careful when planning the questions to be included in your inquiries.[1] The following suggestions apply to all kinds of direct-request inquiries:

1. Make your questions specific. If the product about which you inquire is technical, include specific physical dimensions, technical specifications, exact intended use of the item, architectural drawings, or whatever else will help the respondent. A single general question such as "Will you give us any information you can on this applicant (or product)?" will probably bring a reply so general that it will be almost useless.
2. Use a separate paragraph for each main question if the questions require explanation.
3. If you have more than one question, consider numbering them. If you have only two or three questions, you may place them in the body of your letter, but it is generally better to list your questions on the same sheet below the body or on a separate sheet or sheets; and be sure to allow enough space for adequate answers.
4. Word your questions to get more than "yes" or "no" answers if you need a detailed opinion or description. For example a yes or no answer to: "Did the applicant have duties that required responsibility?" would probably be inadequate. To obtain a more helpful answer, you might ask: "What kinds of duties requiring responsibility did the applicant perform especially well?" In contrast, a yes or no answer would be adequate for such a question as: "Does the applicant have an account with you?"
5. Word some questions for simple checking of "Yes," "No," or "Don't know" if you plan to tabulate numerous answers (say, 50 or more).
6. Cover only one topic in each question. "How long is your product guaranteed, and do you accept C.O.D. orders?" should be in two separate questions.

[1] See also Stanley L. Payne, *The Art of Asking Questions* (especially Chap. 14, which lists 100 considerations), Princeton University Press, Princeton, N.J., 1980; and Lyndon O. Brown, *Market Research and Analysis,* Ronald, New York, 1969.

7. If you wish the respondent to "rate" a person, product, or service, it may be better to define each category on your rating scale. For instance, the following example shows one of eight questions on an employer's questionnaire about an applicant for employment. Notice how both the squares and the definitions make responses easy. The best choices may be at the right (as in the example) or at the left, but consistent placement of best choices is more convenient for both the reference and you—especially if you must compare many replies.

```
ABILITY TO GET ALONG WITH OTHERS:
    Is the applicant a likable, friendly, and tactful individual, or
    an egotistical, unpleasant, or thoughtless individual? Will this
    person attract the people with whom he or she deals or keep them
    at a distance? Is he or she poised in normal social situations?
    (Check one.)
```

☐	☐	☐	☐	☐
Egotistical, unfriendly or tactless	Somewhat neutral, does not easily attract friends	Approach-able	Likable, friendly, and tactful	Exceptionally pleasant and agreeable; will attract others

8. Carefully arrange your questions—generally with the easiest to answer first.
9. Word your questions in a neutral way so you will not influence the answers.

Inquiries about Persons

When you need information about a person, you usually direct your request to a reference—a responsible source of information. You ask the reference to give information about an applicant for a job, a loan, credit, membership in an organization, an award, or some kind of special training or insurance protection.

Inquiries to a reference may be written by the applicant or, more frequently, by the person who seeks information about the applicant.

Applicant's Request to a Reference

Sometimes an applicant asks references if they will send a recommendation direct to someone who needs confidential information about that applicant. For instance, suppose you are seeking admission into a graduate school that requires at least four confidential recommendations. Perhaps you can approach some of your selected references in person or by telephone. To others, however (if they are out of town or if you have a questionnaire they need to fill out), you will have to write a letter.

In the first paragraph it is courteous to state why you are writing to this person and what the recommendation is for. If you haven't been in touch with the references for some time, you may need to refresh their memory about who you are.

The explanation should include a brief summary of pertinent facts about yourself. If, for example, the reference is a former professor, you might include:

1. The course you studied under the reference—when, where, and your grade.
2. Your major, and your grade point average (GPA) in the major.
3. Your overall GPA in college.
4. Positions you held, and dates employed.
5. Honors, honor societies (Phi Beta Kappa, Beta Gamma Sigma, etc.), studies in any special honors programs, scholarships awarded.
6. Leadership qualities; for example, offices held in living group, on campus, in political groups.
7. Activities—tutoring, United Nations Model Congress, etc.
8. Guidelines, if possible, for the recommendation. Enclose, if you can, a form or letter from the graduate school, stating what information it seeks from the reference about you—distinguishing intellectual traits or abilities, leadership capacity, quality of work done, character, integrity, or other personal traits.
9. Statement of your goals; objectives.

Your closing paragraph should state to whom the letter or form is to be sent. Be sure to state the full name and address, unless this information is printed on the form. And, of course, include a statement of appreciation. (Many colleges now supply preprinted forms for the applicant and the recommender to complete. The recommender's statement is sent to the college placement office, then duplicated for prospective employers or graduate schools.)

If it is necessary for you to obtain recommendations about your work in specific courses or jobs in which your work was just mediocre, be sure to provide an explanation regarding the quality of your work, if possible. In inquiry 1 the applicant shows consideration for the reader by courteous tone, by the facts included about courses she studied, by mention of factors that influenced the quality of her chemistry studies, and by the reasonable time allowed for response.

Inquiry 1

An applicant's well-written request to a former professor.

Dear Professor Brown:

Introduction of request and reason
This letter is to reintroduce myself to you and to ask a favor of you. The University of (*name*) Dental School has asked for a recommendation from my Organic Chemistry professor.

*Explanation:
details about
past relationship*

Almost four years ago—in winter and spring quarters of (*year*)—you were my chemistry professor here at the University of (*name*). The courses I took from you were Chemistry 241 and Chemistry 242, both of which met at 3 p.m. daily. The grades I received were C's, but I believe I could have done better if circumstances had been a little different that year.
 Besides the lapse of two years between my inorganic and organic studies, there was my part-time job in the Applied Physics Laboratory until 3 p.m. four days a week. Because this work caused me to come to your class about 15 minutes late, I sometimes missed important laboratory work, a fact which necessarily affected my grade. In our several conferences, however, you often commented very favorably on my work.

*More details,
leading to reason
for this request*

Currently I am a senior, graduating this quarter with a grade point average of 3.02 (out of 4.0) in Business Administration. I am applying for admission to the Dental School at the University of (*name*). To this date I have completed successfully all the predental requirements, and would like to begin dental studies next fall.

*Easy and
dated action*

The enclosed form is one the Dental School requires regarding my studies in organic chemistry. Professor Brown, will you please fill out and return this form in the enclosed envelope to the admissions officer? I will appreciate very much your mailing this information within the next two weeks—before the admissions deadline, March 1.

Inquirer's Request to a Reference

The most frequent requests to references are those written by persons who need confidential information about the applicant. Suppose, for example, that you are the employer, lender, creditor, insurance underwriter, or officer of any organization that is considering an applicant for a special reason. The letter of inquiry you write to each reference the applicant has listed can be organized according to the direct-request pattern.

Your opening paragraph usually includes the applicant's full name, and why you are writing to the reader.

The explanatory section should include:

1. Sufficient details about the requirements of the job, loan, credit, scholarship, or membership for which the applicant is being considered.
2. If appropriate, a few pertinent facts the applicant has already told you—such as length of time worked for the reference, job title, achievements. This way you can check on the applicant's accuracy and honesty.

3. Clearly stated questions (preferably numbered) asking exactly what you want to know about the applicant—including relevant information about unique capabilities, character, special qualities. Be sure preemployment questions meet legal requirements. (Appendix A has suggestions.)

The ending paragraph usually includes appreciation, promise of confidential treatment of the reply, and (if appropriate) provisions for easy action,[2] and an offer to reciprocate.

The letter below (inquiry 2) from a hardware store manager to a department store manager is an example of such an inquiry.

Inquiry 2

Personalized request listing numbered questions in letter.[3]

Name; why being considered; a few facts he has told	Mr. Victor L. Dryer, one of your former employees, has applied here as assistant manager of our electrical supplies department. He states that he was in charge of your electrical appliances section for about a year, and he has given your name as a reference.
Request	We need a qualified person who can, in about two years, become department manager. I will appreciate your frank answers to the following questions and any other pertinent facts you can include:
Questions:	1. When was he in your employ and why did he leave? 2. How satisfactory were his services as a section head in your store? 3. Do you know of any personal habits or characteristics that might hinder or help his success in a position of responsibility?
A promise	Your statements will, of course, be kept confidential.

Inquiry 3 below is an exceptionally thorough, individually typed inquiry which interweaves explanation and unnumbered questions for each qualification. It is reproduced here as an example of the care that a reputable firm takes in placing an outstanding candidate. (Also, some questions might occur over the telephone.)

---

[2] When you write to a business executive at a business address, you can usually omit the enclosed reply envelope because many business executives prefer to use their own firm's stationery. However, when you write to a reference at home (for instance, to a personal reference whose business address is unknown to you) or to someone who may be in a one-person office or in a nonprofit organization, it is appropriate to enclose a stamped reply envelope.

[3] To save space, most examples in this and succeeding chapters include only the body of each message, without the letterhead and other parts. You can assume the salutation is the usual "Dear Mr. (Mrs., Miss, Ms.) plus the reader's surname; and the complimentary close is one of those illustrated in Chap. 6, unless otherwise indicated.

Inquiry 3

Personalized request interweaving explanations with questions in the letter.

Full name;
reason for request

We are seriously considering Ms. Barbara Rankin for a position in our research department here. She has given your name as a reference.

Details—
applicant's work

As you may know, Ms. Rankin has been working in a clerical position for us part-time for about a year in our branch office in your city. Now she has expressed interest in getting into more professional work and pursuing her career in writing for our head office.

Details; specific
request and
explanation

Because of Ms. Rankin's outstanding record in college, to say nothing of the fine work she has done for us, we are making every effort to find, or create, a position for her here. And for that reason I am asking for help in finding out as much as possible about her relative strengths and weaknesses. In this way we can do a better job of fitting her talents to our needs and in assigning her work which is neither beyond her present capacity nor out of line with her interests and skills.

Two implied
questions

I understand that Ms. Rankin worked about two years part-time in your advertising office, and I will welcome information about how effectively and concisely she writes, particularly how readily she can compose business letters to advertisers.

More questions
with details

In addition, we would like to have your impressions of the attitudes and skills that Ms. Rankin can carry over from school to the business world—her ability to organize her work, her originality, initiative, reliability, and ability to work smoothly with others while under pressure. Under what degree of supervision and guidance is she likely to do her best work?

A promise

Any and all comments you may care to make will be a great help and, of course, confidential.

Easy action
(phone)

Your schedule is probably particularly heavy at this time of year—and I hesitate to call you when you may be busy. Perhaps it would be simplest for you to telephone me collect *(area code and phone number)* when convenient for you. I am usually at my desk between 9:00 and 11:30 Monday through Friday.

For a personnel department that needs references on hundreds of new applicants, sheer volume will require a duplicated form that can be used again and again. Some paragraphs may then have spaces for typewritten fill-ins:

M _____*(name)*_____ of _____*(city)*_____ states that he or she was
employed by you as _*(type of work)*_ from _*(date)*_ to _*(date)*_ . Your
name is listed as a reference.

After the explanation of what is needed and the courteous request, the questions are stated. These may be open-ended with space for detailed comments, and/or similar to the illustration in suggestion 7, page 154, or to the example below:

	Superior	Good	Average	Below Average	Unsatis-factory	Comments
Potential ability to sell a quality product (your estimate) _____						
Personality _____						

At the end of the questionnaire form, lines are provided for the reference's signature, title, and date of reply.

Inquiries about Products or Services

Both as a consumer and as a business or professional person, you will have many occasions to seek information from the seller of products and services or from customers, employees, and others.

Direct Request to the Seller

When your inquiry goes to a seller—whether a manufacturer, retailer, investment broker, or hotel clerk—the addressee's self-interest should make him or her glad to comply with your wishes. Perhaps you want a free catalog, price list, or booklet about products, deliveries, or payment plans. At such times your complete direct request need be only one sentence, such as:

> Please send me your latest sporting equipment catalog and the descriptive folder you advertised in the April issue of Sportsman Illustrated.

If, however, you have a unique individual problem, you may need to ask questions for which the recipient does not have prepared answers. Following the direct-request plan, present your main idea (request and/or reason) in the first paragraph. For most inquiries to a seller concerning a product or service, it is entirely optional whether to present request or reason first. But if you think your request is somewhat unusual or will be time-consuming for the reader to answer, state the reason first. After the opening paragraph, include all needed explanations and/or questions. The final paragraph contains the action request.

Inquiry 4 is written by a purchasing manager requesting information from a manufacturer about a product he is considering buying. Notice that the letter begins with the major request; but if you prefer to begin with the reason, you might interchange paragraphs 1 (request) and 3 (reason).

Inquiry 4

Inquiry about an advertised product; numbered questions within the letter.

Major request	Your ads in <u>Good Business</u> magazine have attracted our attention, and we will appreciate your answers to the following questions:
Specific numbered questions	1. What is the price of each Quiktyper? 2. How long does it take an average typist to learn to operate this machine? 3. To what extent can your experts estimate how much money a company can save in a year with Quiktyper, if it uses—for instance—25 different one-page form letters and mails a total of 270,000 letters a year? 4. What guarantee do you offer?
Reason for request	Before deciding whether our firm should invest in one or more automatic typewriters, we should like as much information as possible about leading brands.
Suggested action	If you have a factory agent in this area, we welcome a demonstration any time within the next two weeks, preferably after receipt of your written reply to these four questions.

Direct Requests to Customers, Employees, and Others

As the seller of products or services, you can often use direct-request inquiries to win back "missed" customers who have not bought from your firm for some time or to obtain information about your firm's products or services.

"Miss-You" Messages. Many firms have revived hundreds of unused accounts by mailing a series of direct requests—ranging from colorful postcards to form letters on specially designed stationery. Such messages concentrate on telling readers that they are missed, appreciated, and important, and asking them to come back. Some may go a step further and ask what is wrong, as in inquiry 5. Then if the former customers have a complaint, they feel they can express it; if they have none, they will probably say so and perhaps place another order. Either way the silence has been broken, and a dead account may be revived. Also, your firm may have gained useful information about its products or services.

Inquiry 5

A miss-you inquiry aiming mainly to get a reply that answers: "What is wrong?"

Main idea	Perhaps you have the answer to a question that has worried us. For a long time we have received no order or mail from you; and as we do not know why, we are concerned.
Explanation	We have missed the privilege of serving you—a good business friend. Often we have asked ourselves: "What did we do or say to offend this good customer"? What causes this absence? We've checked all the orders and correspondence from you plus our shipment schedules and prices to you—and everything looks OK. But something must be wrong, to keep you from us so long.
Request and easy action	Please tell us about it frankly. Let us help if possible. Just write your note on the margin or back of this letter and mail it in the postpaid envelope addressed to me. I'll very much appreciate your reply.

Other Inquiries about Your Firm's Products or Services. Often you will need information from employees, colleagues, or other persons. Whenever questions are easy to answer and no persuasion is necessary, messages like inquiry 6, a *memo* launching an employee survey, can be adapted to other readers—inside or outside your organization.

Inquiry 6—Memo

A memo seeking employee needs and preferences about parking on company premises; questionnaire attached.

	TO: All employees DATE: May 1, 198___. FROM: Parking Division, Personnel Department SUBJECT: <u>Your preferences about parking permits</u>
Reader-benefit reason	In an effort to improve the parking situation for all employees, your parking division is conducting a survey of your needs and preferences.
Request and dated action	Will you please fill out the questionnaire below and return it, unsigned, to your supervisor by Friday, May 1, at 5 p.m.? Then you will be sure that your feelings are included in the survey. The results of employee opinions and suggestions will be tabulated and announced at the next employee meeting, May 15.

CLAIMS (COMPLAINTS) AND REQUESTS FOR ADJUSTMENTS

Whenever you are dissatisfied with a product, service, or policy, it is to your advantage—and the company's—to communicate with the right person promptly about the desired correction. Oral complaints to sales representatives or clerks often do not bring results; a much better procedure is to write an effective letter to the proper company official who does care when a problem exists and who can and will do something to correct it.

When you state your complaint, you usually make a claim or request for some kind of adjustment. All such requests are grouped together in this section and labeled *claim letters*. Claim letters should be organized by the direct-request pattern whenever they involve a routine matter that is covered by a guarantee or by established procedures for customer relations.

Typical situations for direct-request claims about merchandise involve defective materials or workmanship, malfunctioning parts, soiled or shopworn items, or products not as represented. Claims about services include delivery mix-ups, broken promises, discourtesy, carelessness, clerical or bookkeeping errors, and minor inconveniences relating to violation of published company policies. (For those claims that involve controversial issues, substantially large sums of money, repeated errors, and other serious matters, you will need to write a persuasive request, as discussed in Chapter 10.)

Characteristics of Well-Written Claims

To be fair to the seller, product or service, and yourself—write promptly. Also, be sure your letter has all the C qualities. Show by your attitude and wording that *you have confidence in the readers' fairness*—confidence that they will make the adjustment after they get the facts. Omit any statements that sound like appeals or threats.

When you complain about the poor condition of a product, for instance, state all the pertinent facts logically, courteously, and impersonally, without exaggeration or irrelevant material. Guesses and opinions about who may be to blame are unwise and unhelpful. Let the reader determine causes; you present facts as you see them. And when your purpose is to call attention to employees' poor service, make clear you are doing so because you think the behavior is not representative of the firm's usually good customer relations policies. Cite phone-call records of dates and times each call was made as well as the name of the person spoken to.

Anger and name-calling are, of course, taboo. Antagonizing the recipient merely lowers the chances of satisfactory adjustment—or at least of being considered a reasonable person. One extra caution: When you write as an agent for your employer or business, you must be even more careful to avoid tactless, intemperate accusations. Such outbursts not only reflect unfavorably upon you *and* your company, but they also may place you in danger of a libel suit.[4]

---

[4] See Appendix A, about legal aspects of letters.

It is often a good idea to state both sides of the case—for example, you might comment on something you *like* about the firm's products or service. Such a statement can be in the opening paragraph or in the explanation. Even humor (not sarcasm) is appropriate when the matter is relatively small.

Organization and Content of the Simple Direct Claim

 Begin your direct claim with the main idea—namely, the need for an adjustment or correction of an error.

In the explanatory paragraph(s) include all facts the reader will need to understand your claim clearly. For instance, if you wish free repairs on an item that is malfunctioning within the guarantee period, present evidence of the date of your purchase, make clear that you followed carefully the operating instructions (if you did), and state clearly what is wrong.

In your action paragraph, ask for what you want or leave the decision to your reader. Depending on circumstances, you will usually request one or more of the following. (The numbers in parentheses after each request refer to the claim-letter examples illustrated in this section.)

1. Refund—for all or part of purchase price (1).
2. A new shipment with the correct item(s) ordered (1).
3. Free replacement of defective part(s), the whole item, whole shipment, or service (2). Often it is better not to return goods until you have the seller's instructions.
4. Free repairs (3).
5. Reduction in the price (because of a product or service defect) (3).
6. Free inspection, leading to redecorating, complete overhaul, etc.
7. Explanation and/or change in policy or procedure (3).
8. Credit to your account (or a credit slip).
9. Cancellation of an order or part of an order.
10. Correction (and perhaps explanation) of a billing error.

Claim 1

A courteous claim (dated June 9) to a sportswear-department manager from an out-of-town cash customer who needs an exchange or a refund.

Main idea; request

```
Enclosed is the sweater which Nelson's delivery truck
left yesterday and which I wish to exchange for the
correct size or a refund.
```

Explanatory details

```
When I selected and purchased this Hudson sweater in
your department last week (for $30.50 cash), I asked
that a size "L" be sent to my home. The size I re-
ceived is only an "S", and of course I can't wear it.
My sales check is #7902, dated June 4, written by
salesclerk #801.
```

Specific request   Will you please send me the correct size "L" in ex-
                          actly this same style and color or, if this is not
Dated action   available now, a cash refund of $30.50? As I am leav-
                          ing on a one-month trip June 17, it is necessary that
                          I receive the sweater or the check before that date.

The next two examples are written by business executives for claims concerning their companies. Claim 2 concerns faulty products; claim 3, faulty service. Notice that in both letters the writers present all needed facts without anger and with a good you-attitude.

Claim 2

A considerate complaint from a gift store owner to a wholesaler, about faulty merchandise.

Main idea; request   Our shipment of Swedish tumblers was checked in yes-
                         terday and put on sale, then hurriedly withdrawn when
                         the stock room reported it to be a completely defec-
                         tive shipment. We are asking you for an adjustment on
                         these tumblers.

Details   The news about this shipment was especially disap-
                         pointing to me because we had already advertised that
                         the sale was to begin today. I personally washed and
                         examined a dozen glasses of each size, four each (and
                         not necessarily the worst) of which we are sending you
                         by express for your examination and comment.

                         There is no regularity in the mars, scratches, and
                         abrasions, or whatever the defects should be termed,
                         to indicate faulty moulds. In fact, I've never seen
                         anything in domestic or imported glass to equal the
                         variety of imperfections apparently present to some
                         degree in every glass of this shipment.

You-attitude   I realize fully that you had no opportunity to check
                         this merchandise and that it is only through your cus-
                         tomers that you learn of its condition and can in turn
                         seek an adjustment from the factory.

Action   We are withholding sale of the glasses and payment of
                         the bill until we hear from you.

Claim 3

A considerate complaint (May 18) from a restaurant manager to a laundry, about faulty service.

Main idea:
something is wrong;
compliment too

What has happened to Spic's starching and mending service? You may recall my April 19 letter complimenting
you on the neat appearance of the uniforms Spic sent
then. But the last three shipments have contained
both torn and incorrectly starched garments.

Details

On May 10, nine of our twenty waitresses' uniforms
came back as limp as though they had not been starched
at all. On May 14, all twenty uniforms came back
again limp——in collars and cuffs. Also, four had un-
mended rips. That morning, on our outgoing laundry
bag I pinned a note for the driver, asking if the
laundry would please again observe the following request, which had been overlooked the previous week:
EXTRA HEAVY STARCH ON ALL COLLARS AND CUFFS.

More details

Good-natured
attitude

Today——same thing happened. All collars and cuffs
were limp. But this time five of the cotton slacks of
our men waiters were so stiff they stood up alone! It
took a bit of persuading to get the men to wear them;
we had a good laugh each time.

More you-attitude

Yet all this mix—up hurts the image of our restaurant.
We like our employees to look neat. As you know, I'd
much rather compliment than complain. But the change
has been so abrupt that I'm sure you want to know.
Will you please:

Specific request

Reduce your charges for the 49 unstarched uniforms and
the overstarched five pairs of slacks,
Make free repairs on the four torn uniforms, which we
will return to your driver on his next call, and
Let me know whether we can count on the usual good
mending as well as starching service in the future.

REQUESTS REGARDING ROUTINE BUSINESS OR PUBLIC CAUSES

The messages in this section include business or professional people's requests
that are directly related to routine business or to public issues that affect their
firm or industry. The discussions and examples are grouped in two categories—
according to whether the requests go to persons outside or within the organization.

Requests to Persons outside Your Organization

As a business or professional person you may need to ask your customer,
supplier, transportation company, or others to sign an enclosed signature card
or document. Or you may need missing answers on a customer's credit application, or a correction of an irregularity in a check sent to your firm. Also, you
may have requests for public officials about concerns that are in the best

interests of your community, business, or industry. These and numerous other matters may be handled by the direct-request plan.

You can use form letters, but it is often a good idea to personalize the letter by individual typing, as in request 1 below. However, even processed form messages—for example, request 2—are satisfactory when the messages are clearly the same for all recipients in a group.

Notice that the following letters are concise, clear, courteous. And they begin with the reason or the request (or a major statement that leads to the request) either in the first paragraph or at the beginning of the second.

Request 1

A bank's trust department asks the executor of an estate to return an affidavit, signature card, and passbook; individually typed message.

Reason; request	So, that we can transfer the account of Mr. R. S. Roe, deceased, to your name as Executor, will you please do the following:
Numbered specific requests	1. Sign the enclosed affidavit. 2. Fill out the enclosed card and sign it. 3. Return to us the signed affidavit, card, and your passbook #222-222.
Reader benefit; easy action	The same day these important materials reach us, we will transfer the funds to a new account, with no loss of earnings. Please use the enclosed airmail envelope to speed your reply.

Request 2

Request from a mortgage loan company to a borrower regarding insurance premium payments; personalized form letter signed by the company's president.

Main idea	The valuable benefits your Homeowner's Mortgage Protector Plan provides become effective on the date the certificate indicates—if you have paid the insurance premium for the plan.
Request, with specific payment amounts	In case you have already mailed your mortgage installment for the month in which your protection is to become effective, please send the premium—$ —to us now so that you will be fully protected for the month.
Request, with specific payment amounts	Next month and for all future payments please be sure to combine your mortgage and insurance payments into one check for $

Reader benefit
We are pleased you have secured this protection for yourself and family. Many of our customers have found this is a very valuable and worthwhile program. After you have read the certificate carefully, please file it with your other valuable papers.

Whenever certain requests occur frequently among your customers or suppliers, sometimes a well-worded form like Figure 6-10 (not a letter) is a time saver.

In letters to public officials the opening should preferably begin with a sentence expressing the main idea, as in the following examples, then continue with adequate explanation, and end with your frank request.

1. *From a business executive to a Senator in Washington, D.C.:*

The proposal to increase the truck weight and sizes on the interstate highway system deserves your serious consideration. I believe such an increase would be extremely unwise and wish to join the many others who ask that you oppose such a measure.

2. *From a store owner to the City's District Engineer:*

This letter protests the proposed underpass at 60th Street and Highway 409. This change would cause an undue hardship on small-business owners who have invested their savings to build businesses convenient to the community in this area.

Requests to Persons within Your Organization

The memos included here are straightforward requests exchanged between employees, colleagues, supervisors and subordinates, and others, such as stockholders, who are part of an organization. (Most memos of authorization for special studies and reports also fall in this direct-request group.)

The next example illustrates a well-written request to persons within the writer's organization. As you read request 3, notice its good features—the six numbered details for easy reading and the definite, courteous instructions about the desired action.

Request 3 (Memo)

A division manager's memo asking field representatives to send monthly reports.

```
TO:  Jim Inkley      Emma Koontz
     Ruth Lindquist  Dick Dubuque
     Tom Sedlock
```

```
                          CC:  Ralph Smith
                               B. J. Loners

                        FROM:  James Pearson

                     SUBJECT:  Monthly Reports DATE:  September 10, 198___
```

Request

```
Starting October 1, will each of you please submit to
this office on the 21st of the month a monthly report
including:
```

Numbered details

```
1.  Major orders received during the month
2.  Anticipated major orders for the following month
3.  New business activity
4.  Lost orders
5.  Industrial trends
6.  General comments
```

Helpful sample

```
A copy of the form I would like you to use is at-
tached.
```

Clear statement of where and when report should be sent

```
By no later than the 21st of every month, please mail
your monthly report to me, with copies to:

1.  Each of the other sales representatives
2.  Gail Rankin, Sales Manager

I will appreciate your cooperation.
```

INVITATIONS, ORDERS, RESERVATIONS

Though quite different from each other, invitations, orders, and reservations are similar in that the reader is asked for participation, merchandise, or facilities.

Invitations

Invitations that require no persuasion can be classified as both good-news announcements (Chapter 8) and simple requests. Regardless of how you classify them, they are organized according to the same three-part plan: main idea, explanation, action.

The main idea in the first paragraph is the invitation request, and you should try to include in it as many of the five W's as you can. The following sample openings are representative of two kinds of invitations you may need to send in business.

Memo

To all employees (from the company's house-organ editor).

> Do you have an item of news or a suggestion you would like to share with other employees in our company? If so, you are invited to submit it for inclusion in our Semiannual Company House Organ before March 1.

Letter

To all customers (from an administrative officer).

> You are cordially invited to attend the open house of our Topname Airplane Company . . .
>
> > Sunday, June 10, from 2 to 5 p.m.
> > in Plants 2 and 3.

In the explanation paragraph of your direct-request invitation, include all details that your reader(s) will appreciate and need. The ending paragraph clearly states the desired reader action and makes the action easy. If you need a reply by a certain date, be sure to say so, as in the following letter to business executives.

Dear ALTRUA member:

Request
The next meeting of Altrua is one you are especially invited to attend. As your yearbook shows, this is

What
Who
> The FORUM LUNCHEON, sponsored jointly by
> the Chamber of Commerce and our club
>
> > to be held

Where
> at Lake City Community Hall, (*address*)

When
> on Thursday, April 21, 198_, 12:15 p.m.

A detail about the program
A highlight of the program is the panel discussion on the topic, "Problems of the Small Business Executive in King County." You will find the discussion timely, challenging, and thought provoking.

Easy action
To make your reservation, please call either Trish Norden (823-7777) or Mike Browne (349-9999) before Tuesday, April 19, 5 p.m. How about phoning right now while you think of it?

Reader benefit   For your convenience, free parking is available on the north side of the Hall. We look forward to seeing you April 21 at the luncheon.

Orders and Reservations

When you are ordering supplies or equipment and do not have an order blank or purchase form of the company with which you are placing the order, you can accomplish your purpose by writing a letter according to the direct-request plan. The same is true when you wish to reserve hotel accommodations, a meeting room, parking facilities for a conference, or any other premises.

Order letters include three kinds of facts: details about *what you are ordering or reserving, directions for shipment,* and *manner of payment.* In both order and reservation messages, the main idea in the first paragraph is that you are ordering or reserving something. Your explanatory paragraphs give whatever details the order or reservation requires—about quantity, color, style, size, price, payment, location, shipment date, place—plus any special instructions your reader might need. The last paragraph invites prompt shipment and dated action, if desired.

The following letter illustrates the organization and content of an order letter with items tabulated for easy reading. You can use a similar organization for reservations.

Request   Please ship the following supplies to reach our main office at 9251 Grand Avenue (*City, State, Zip*) by Wednesday, June 3:

	Description (and or	Unit	
Details	Quantity	catalog number)	Price	Total
		Total	$ _____

Payment   These items are to be charged to our account on the usual 2/10, net 30 terms.

Shipment; courtesy   As we plan to distribute the ball-point pens for customer gifts on the opening day of our new branch, June 5, it is imperative that this shipment arrive on time. We count on your company's usual promptness in filling orders.

SUMMARY

The Capsule Checklists on pages 187 and 188 provide a quick summary of each type of direct request discussed in this chapter—inquiries; complaints; requests about routine business or public concerns;[5] and invitations, orders, reservations that require no persuasion. As you study these direct-request plan lists, notice that you introduce your main idea at or near the beginning, include whatever details your reader needs, and end courteously with easy and dated action, if appropriate.

Caution: Remember that these Capsule Checklists—and all others in this text—are to be used *only as guidelines and reminders, NOT as "recipe lists."* In every message, use your best judgment for planning and content after you have considered purpose, reader, and pertinent circumstances.

EXERCISES

Inquiries about Persons, Products, Services

1. Comment orally on the good and poor qualities of the following inquiries about persons (sent to references). Which ones do you think will best accomplish their purpose? Why?

   a. From a national oil company:

   > We are considering Mr. Larry R. Terrill, for a position with this company, and he has given your name as a personal reference.
   >
   > May we have your frank comment both as to his ability and personal qualities? Do you know of any reason for our not giving him full confidence? We shall appreciate any additional comments which will help us in reaching a correct decision, and also in adapting him to our organization if we employ him.
   >
   > Since this matter is very active at present, we shall appreciate a prompt reply and are enclosing a stamped and self-addressed envelope for this purpose.

   b. From the Big Brother volunteer service organization of a city:

   > Dear Mr. Willman:
   >
   > About: <u>Robert Zurbach</u>
   >
   > The above-named gentleman has applied to us to serve as a Big Brother. He has given your name as a reference.
   >
   > We feel you, in your contacts with him, would be able to advise us as to his stability and moral character. As a Big Brother, he

---

[5] For every direct request pertaining to a civic cause or public officials, follow the checklists on whatever type of situation best applies. If you prefer, merely follow the *Direct-Request General Plan* in the first column and use your good judgment about what details to include.

will be working with a young, fatherless boy, establishing a friendship and offering moral and character guidance to the boy.

We would like your frank appraisal, which will be held in strict confidence. Since your evaluation is necessary to complete the application, we will appreciate hearing from you soon.

c. Night letter telegram from a regional utility company:

ROBERTA R ADSEN BEING CONSIDERED FOR POSITION AS MANAGEMENT TRAINEE, ULTIMATE ASSIGNMENT TO KEY STAFF IN PUBLIC RELATIONS. HAS GIVEN YOUR NAME AS REFERENCE. WE WOULD APPRECIATE IMMEDIATE NIGHT LETTER COLLECT STATING TO WHICH DEGREES (A. OUTSTANDING, B. VERY GOOD, C. ADEQUATE, D. UNSATISFACTORY) APPLICANT POSSESSES THE FOLLOWING QUALITIES: (1) MENTAL ABILITY--ALERTNESS, OPEN-MINDEDNESS, FLEXIBILITY. (2) SOCIAL ADJUSTMENT--COURTESY, TACT, COOPERATIVENESS. (4) SELF EXPRESSION--CLARITY, COHERENCE, SENTENCE CONSTRUCTION, SPEECH DIRECTNESS. (5) APPEARANCE, BEARING, MANNER. PLEASE ADD ANY OTHER PERTINENT INFORMATION INCLUDING MATURE JUDGMENT, STRENGTHS, OR WEAKNESSES BASED ON HER ACADEMIC STANDING OR YOUR PERSONAL KNOWLEDGE.

2. Messages a and b are forms used by two law schools to get information about the many applicants who seek admission. Compare them for completeness, clarity, information sought, and ease of action. Which will probably be more effective?

   a. The above named person has applied for admission into (school name) Law School. Because your name was listed as a reference, we will appreciate a letter of recommendation from you.

   No special form is required. Letters should be detailed, with frank appraisals of the applicant as to (1) qualities of intellect, (2) communication skills, (3) character, (4) maturity, (5) personality. Comparisons of the applicant with other students known by you to have been admitted to law school are helpful.

   b. Mr.
   Ms.
   Mrs. _____
   Miss (LAST NAME)   (FIRST NAME)   MIDDLE NAME)
   is an applicant for admission to the (school name) Law School. Each year the number of applicants to the school far exceeds the number that can be accepted. You will greatly assist this applicant and the school by providing specific and candid answers to this inquiry. The information you provide will be treated as confidential. Prompt completion of this form will be appreciated by both the applicant and the school, for the application cannot be acted on until this form is received from you. Thank you for your cooperation.

1. How well do you know the applicant? _____

2. Has the applicant performed in an honorable and trustworthy manner in academic work and social relationships? _____

3. Has the applicant been the subject of disciplinary action or proceedings (for misconduct) or of academic censure (for deficient scholarship)? _____
   If so, please explain. (Please use the reverse side if this space is insufficient.)

   _____

   _____

4. Has the applicant any physical handicap or any illness, physical or mental, that in your opinion bears on his or her ability to do law school work? _____
   If so, please explain. _____

   _____

5. In classes with you, how have you graded the applicant's academic performance (percentile, if possible)? _____

6. What is the applicant's approximate rank for all work taken in your college?

   _____

7. To what degree did the applicant's scholastic achievement measure up to capacity? _____
   ☐ Fully realized capacity.   ☐ Had capacity to do considerably
   ☐ Performed reasonably in   better.
      view of capacity.   ☐ No basis for judgment.
   Remarks: _____

   _____

8. Please furnish any other information that will be of assistance to a consideration of the applicant's transcript and college record as a whole. Helpful remarks can relate to, but need not be limited to, unusual time-consuming extracurricular activities, leadership performance, motivation, capacity for interpersonal relations, and significant participation in outside employment. We will also appreciate your estimate of the applicant's grades, courses taken, and major field as a reliable measure of academic capacity. (Please use the reverse side if this space is insufficient.) _____

   _____

9. Do you recommend the applicant for admission to the (name) Law School?
   ☐ I recommend with   ☐ I recommend with reser-
      enthusiasm.   vation.
   ☐ I recommend.   ☐ I do not recommend.

Signature _____

Name (Please type or print) _____

Title _____

Date_____ Address _____

3. Prepare to discuss orally the strengths and weaknesses of the following
letters designed to get information. Comment particularly on organization,
clarity, completeness of explanations, and motivation for action.

   a. To subscribers of a magazine (salutation is "Dear *Journal* Reader"):

   > You're right. Another questionnaire.
   >
   > But we feel it's an important one, and the short time required
   > to complete it should be well spent, for it will help shape the
   > course YOUR magazine, the <u>Journal,</u> will take in the important
   > years ahead.
   >
   > We say YOUR magazine because it's written and edited with
   > readers like you in mind. That's why the editors would like to
   > take stock of what you like and dislike about the <u>Journal.</u> What
   > parts are good? What needs improvement? What might be cut down
   > or eliminated? What might be added?
   >
   > Your answers will help the <u>Journal</u> keep in step with the
   > rapidly changing field of (*name of field*).
   >
   > You will note that we have not provided a space for your sig-
   > nature. This is by design. We believe that anonymity will produce
   > more straight-from-the-shoulder opinion and constructive criti-
   > cism. Thank you for your help.

   b. From a firm of research counselors in New York to an addressee in a
   state 2,500 miles away. Addressee is an employee of a city light company
   (letter is an obvious form with a "Dear Sir" salutation):

   > May we ask a favor that takes only a minute of your time?
   >
   > We are conducting a special study to help determine how familiar
   > people in industry are with one of our clients.
   >
   > We would appreciate it very much if you would answer the ques-
   > tions on the attached sheet and return the questionnaire to us in
   > the enclosed stamped envelope. Your reply will be confidential,
   > of course, and the results of the study will be shown in statis-
   > tical form only.

4. Assume the role of purchasing manager for an industrial firm with over 2,000
employees. You have a desire to install a word processing center in your
company to cut down on the cost of processing your daily paper load. You

will need equipment to take care of (1) *original input* (longhand, shorthand, machine, handwritten, or central dictation); (2) *reproduction* [spirit, fluid (ink); offset; carbon copy; composer systems such as magnetic tape typewriters, magnetic card typewriters, paper tape typewriters; or copying machines]; (3) *delivery system* (personal, messenger, PBX, dial system, private wire, telephone, or machine dictation options); (4) *storage file* [magnetic tape, magnetic cards, paper tapes, computer storage (punched cards, discs), microfiche, microfilm, or office storage file cabinet (alpha numeric, geographic, library indexing system or mechanized system)].

Select several equipment suppliers that handle word processing equipment. Request the following information, to be presented to your board of directors one month from the date of your letter: different models available; special features of each model; estimated price of equipment; service policy cost; in-service training availability; portability; facility needed to house equipment; and noise level when in operation.

You are to prepare the information you have requested from the various suppliers, make a decision in two months on what equipment you will purchase for your firm, and present this to your board of directors. Write a letter that can be sent to several companies, requesting the information you will need.

5. As executive administrator of staff personnel at City Hospital, you are currently searching for the right person to be chief pharmacist. One of the applicants you interviewed yesterday is Helen Bensor (age 35), who worked at the Excello Pharmacy in Omaha from January 1979 until July 1983. She has given the name of Jason Morgan, chief pharmacist at Excello, as a reference.

Your hospital, one of the leaders in the country, established a new 300-bed teaching and research wing two months ago and now plans to open a new pharmacy five months from today. Both personal qualifications and technical skill are important for the responsible job of chief pharmacist. You need to know whether Ms. Bensor has the ability or potential to organize from scratch a pharmacy in your modern, well-equipped hospital. You need a frank evaluation of her as a worker, because this job will demand a tremendous amount of initiative, drive, and sustained working capacity. Also, because she will have people working under her direction, she must be able to organize them into a tightly knit and happy working group. You'd like to know if she is liked and respected by subordinates, associates, and supervisors. Also, it would be helpful to know what duties she performed at Excello Pharmacy. Write a tactful, well-organized inquiry to Mr. Morgan for the information you need. Keep your questions within the laws regarding fair preemployment inquiries.

6. You are an assistant marketing manager for a manufacturer of pharmaceuticals. Your sales staff markets prescription drugs to drug stores, hospitals,

and physicians and dentists in private practice. Every year from five to seven new sales representatives must be trained in your two-month sales instructional program. Experienced sales representatives are brought back to the main office for periodic one- or two-day professional development workshops.

One training procedure which has been effective is the videotaping and playback of sales role-playing situations and sales presentation simulations. Training lectures are other items which are taped for viewing by sales trainees. Your organization has one videotape recorder, a tripod-mounted black-and-white camera, and a 19-inch monitor—all of which are scheduled for replacement. The marketing manager has authorized you to investigate new videotape equipment and recommend replacements.

In the latest issue of *Pharmaceutical World* you noticed an advertisement for equipment manufactured by Video-Eye Corporation, 1980 South Michigan Avenue, Chicago, IL 60616. Write them requesting product, service, and price information. You are considering switching to color equipment for more realism but are wary of cost and dependability. You are interested in converting from reel-to-reel to cassette equipment; however, you are concerned about higher cost, capability of tape cassettes, and reliability of the mechanically more complex cassette equipment. Finally, service is extremely important because you have no backup equipment and require minimum downtime.

Indicate to the Video-Eye Corporation that you will be trading in your present equipment. An equipment choice decision must be made within three weeks, so you must request specific follow-up to this request. Create other relevant supporting details, if necessary.

Claims (Complaints) and Requests for Adjustment

1. Evaluate the following opening paragraphs of claim letters, and tell how to improve the poor ones. Which one(s) do you consider effective? Why?

   a. In line with your policy on consumer satisfaction published in your recent catalog, I am requesting a cash refund of $45.38 for a toaster I purchased two weeks ago for cash. The reason I have directed this request to your office is that your department manager said such a refund would not be possible. (*Written to the adjustment department manager.*)

   b. In the past year I have ordered nearly $200 in goods from your store, by mail. Two weeks ago I came there in person and bought a gray overcoat. As I was heavily loaded with packages, I asked the clerk to send the garment to me by store delivery. When the overcoat arrived, I was busy and so I didn't open the package until two days ago.

   c. Never in my life have I been treated so rudely as I was the other day in your store, by two jerks you call employees. I tell you,

the way I was insulted gave me a good indication of what kind of
people you're hiring these days. I'm so mad I will never go back
to your store again.

2. Comment on the following claim letters. Consider tone, organization, clarity, accuracy, and probable effectiveness in getting the desired result. What changes, if any, do you recommend? Please be specific. Try to determine first what each writer really wants.

   a. From a business firm in Detroit to an air freight corporation in Pittsburgh:

   Re your Airbill #54663, we originally shipped this same amount of
   mdse. to Cincinnati UPS (United Parcel Service), got overnight
   delivery, and it cost only $15. Now your shipment from Cincinnati
   to us took over 15 days to get to us and you want $48.36. Now if
   you want to rebill and charge ICC surface rates, we will pay you,
   but if you think 15-day delivery is Air Express. . .better check
   the rubber bands on your airplanes or start feeding those pigeons
   better.

   b. From a charge customer to a department store with five branches: [This handwritten letter had merely the date at the top and the writer's signature ("Mrs. Joan M. Smith") at the end. Her envelope had no return address. (The store has 250 Smiths and no Joan M. Smith.)]

   I cannot understand your statement each month showing that our
   account has a past due payment. This is very irritating since our
   payments have been:

   ```
   1/10/8_ - $25.00
   2/3/8_  - $30.00
   3/4/8_  - $25.00
   4/3, 5/6/8_ - each $50.00
   ```

   It is my understanding that our payments each month are to be
   only $20.00 per month. As you can see ours have been much more
   than that--so where do you get this "overdue" bit?

   I am at this time sending another $50.00 check, which I'm sure
   you will agree does not make my account past due. Please get my
   records straight as I don't believe this makes my credit rating
   look too good.

   c. From a landlord to apartment tenants:

   It seems some of your typing late at night disturbs some tenants.
   Perhaps when all is quiet it is easier to hear.

   I was wondering if you type on the nook table--as that is bad because the table is fastened to the building. A felt pad will help

```
if you do not already have one. The university bookstore has them
just for that purpose.

I know your typing is important to your schoolwork, however I
would like to keep everyone happy.
```

3. Your local chapter of Zeta Theta Omega national sorority has planned to do a dramatic skit presentation at their regional conference in order to invite the convention to their city next year. This requires that all members wear the uniform dress. Therefore, as chairperson of the sorority social committee, you were given the assignment of ordering twenty-five floral pink dresses from the Arts Company in California. You placed your order for these dresses and requested the following sizes: five dresses in size 9; two in size 10; four, size 12; four, size 14; five, size 16. This is a total of twenty dresses.

   The other five dresses you ordered were in special sizes, as follows: two in size 18½; one, size 7; and two, size 9 for tall girls.

   When you received the shipment, you discovered that the order had been partially filled.Twenty of the twenty-five dresses ordered were shipped to you, and the other five dresses were promised within one week. Today, one month after arrival of the first shipment, you received the other five dresses; but they are all damaged so much that the girls cannot wear them. An explanation for the delay was enclosed with the order, stating that because of the irregular sizes, the dresses had to be specially made. There are now only two days left before your convention, and you do not have time to return the dresses to the company for replacements.

   The members, disappointed, have voted to return all twenty-five dresses. You have packed and shipped them back to the Arts Company today. Now it is your responsibility to write the claim letter requesting refund for the complete order—the twenty dresses in excellent condition and the five that are damaged. After discussing the circumstances and reasons in class, decide whether you should also ask for reimbursement on the shipping charges.

4. Last Saturday you took a 7:40 a.m. Transcontinental bus to Mount Vernon, a city 200 miles from where you live. The bus was scheduled to make five stops along the way and to arrive in Mount Vernon at 11:40 a.m. This would be just in time for you to attend an important regional luncheon at the Marlborough Hotel, starting at 12 noon. (You were to be a panel speaker at this function and had accepted the appointment two months ago. You planned to return the same afternoon on the 5 p.m. bus.)

   At about 10 a.m. the driver of your 7:40 a.m. bus, after making four scheduled stops to pick up passengers, turned off the freeway for an *unscheduled* stop at a roadside snack bar—a 6-foot open-air counter with no chairs and no roof. He told passengers they would be there "a few minutes to stretch and have a snack if they wished." As your hands were sticky after eating a candy bar, you stopped in the rest room to wash them. About two minutes later when you came outside, the bus was gone! The driver had apparently left without a warning toot or a count of noses! Thus you were stranded off the freeway, 15 miles from any scheduled bus stop; and no other bus was to pass on the freeway ½ mile from the snack bar for three hours. You would surely miss the entire function. What could you do?! (You're not a hitchhiker.) The snack bar operators stated this was the second time in a week that the same bus driver had left a passenger stranded at the same place. Rather than have you miss your luncheon, one of the two operators generously offered to drive you in her car until she caught up with the bus. You both hoped it would be just a few miles, because she had to get back to her job. However, after 25 miles you reached the next town—at the fifth scheduled stop—just as the bus driver was starting the motor, ready to leave for the last lap of his trip. You hurriedly pressed $12 cash into the hand of your Good Samaritan and hopped on the bus. Not one word of apology came from the bus driver! At the luncheon all your friends agreed with you that the driver should be reported.

Write an effective letter to the customer service manager at Mount Vernon requesting whatever adjustment (and explanation) you think is fair. Send a copy to the bus company's head office in Chicago. Make your message as concise as possible; assume whatever is necessary for completeness.

5. Last Tuesday you took an interesting tour with a group of 15 other business-people through the Ray Lumber Mills. All of you had attended a conference and the tour was scheduled as part of the conference. After walking from one building to another, you happened to be the target for a glob of tar that dripped from a roof of one of the mills as you entered. It fell on your left shoulder, on your new suit. One of the employees suggested that after the suit was cleaned you should send the bill to that lumber mill. Now you have had the suit cleaned and you want reimbursement. Write a courteous letter to get the desired refund ($9.75).

6. As the chairperson of your company's social committee, you called several committee meetings to decide on the entertainment for your company's annual Valentine Day dance. After considering several suggestions, the committee voted to contract with a new local company for the evening's music. The company, called Dance Shows, Inc., specializes in providing recorded music and a special light show for parties and dances.

Specifically, the company brings in a sound system with records and tapes for any type of music desired. Two disc jockeys are provided so that you may have continuous music with commentary; the D.J.'s also provide some special events, such as dance contests. In addition, the company also has a computerized light show which is synchronized to the music for added effect.

You asked Dance Shows for the names of two clients who have used them for parties. When you checked with the references, the reports were good. Apparently, the company had delivered everything as promised and the clients were completely satisfied. You signed a contract with Dance Shows for their standard service (recorded music, professional quality sound system, two disc jockeys, and the light show). You stated your preferences as to the music to be provided and agreed to make the meeting room (the ballroom of a large local hotel) available five hours prior to the scheduled starting time for the dance. Your contract with the hotel guaranteed that your event would be concluded by a specific time and, because of union agreements, hotel cleanup personnel would be entitled to overtime pay if you exceeded your time limit. The company, in turn, agreed to have the equipment set up and checked out at least one hour prior to the starting time.

On the day of the dance the company's technicians arrived only two hours before the scheduled starting time for the dance. Consequently, the equipment was still being set up when the first party-goers arrived. Also, while checking the sound levels, the technicians generated high-pitched squeals (feedback) through the speakers, causing considerable irritation to the guests. A tall technician named Mike seemed to be in charge. When you asked him how long it would require to complete the preparations, he gave you a menacing look and growled "Leave us alone, Mac. We'll be done when I'm satisfied with the sound." The disc jockeys arrived on time, but the dance got started 35 minutes late.

Among the party-goers who arrived on time was the president of your company. He remarked that he hoped things would soon begin to run more smoothly. He also commented that because the dance was delayed, he thought you should get some adjustment in the fee charged by Dance Shows. After the equipment problem was solved, the dance started and the evening was enjoyed by everyone. The disc jockeys were professionals who were able to generate excitement and make the attendees forget the earlier problems.

Because of the delay, the dance was not over by the deadline, and you were subsequently billed by the hotel for $65 in overtime charges for the cleanup personnel. You believe that the overtime charges were the direct result of Dance Shows' failure to have the equipment set up and operating properly by the agreed-upon time and that you are justified in asking Dance Shows' manager for an adjustment in the fee to compensate for the overtime charges. Also, because you had to listen to several complaints about the late start and the irritating noises made by the technicians, and because the sharp comments made by the head technician were overheard by several of your company colleagues, you feel some apology from Dance Shows is in order. After all, you kept your part of the bargain and booked the hotel ballroom early enough to provide sufficient time for Dance Shows' technicians to do their work.

Make sure the tone of your letter is correct. Remember that the company's reputation indicates that this is not their usual mode of operation. Also, you should remember to praise the disc jockeys for their professionalism and their ability to salvage what could easily have become a disaster. Address your claim to Mr. Edwin C. Lyons, Manager, Dance Shows, Inc., 1722 E. 20th St., Toledo, OH 43615.

7. You are accounting department manager of Flowers by Hardley, a reputable florist. Today (April 5) you received a $106.50 bill from Airway Freight Corporation, 947 Columbus Building, Indianapolis. The bill shows two deliveries—Airbill #18694 and #25479—unpaid since January 20 and February 9, respectively. You have canceled checks and invoices showing that both these shipments were paid when delivery was made. In fact, your firm always pays freight when it arrives. You resent the computerized statement across the bottom of today's bill: "THIS IS OUR FINAL REQUEST BEFORE REFERRING THIS TO A COLLECTION AGENCY. REMIT NOW." This is the first billing you have received. Your firm's general manager has decided that as of today he is switching to another airfreight company that takes better care in bookkeeping. He says that any company this careless in keeping records probably is no less careless in handling freight. Write to the general manager of Airway Freight Corporation after you have determined your purpose and what evidence you need to enclose with your message. Use good judgment in the tone and content of your letter.

Miscellaneous Requests, Orders, Invitations

1. The following messages deal with routine business situations. Analyze each situation and then decide whether the message is adequate. Suggest improvements.
   a. A printed form letter from the manager of a savings association to customers; it has no salutation, but customers' names and addresses are inserted at the top:

   _____ Please sign the enclosed withdrawal slip and return to us.

   _____ Would you please send us your signature card. _____

   _____ Would you please send us your social security (reporting) number.

   _____ We need your *original* hazard (fire) insurance policy (with extended coverage) in at least the amount of $_____.

   _____ An error was made on your last transaction, which has already been corrected on our records (we'll correct your passbook the next time we have it).

   _____ We are returning your check because _____.

   _____ Your construction interest payment starts _____
   19_____, in the amount of $ _____; thereafter, interest payments will be $ _____until regular payments

($ _____) start _____ , 19 . YOU
MAY MAKE FULL PAYMENTS AT ANY TIME AND RE-
CEIVE CREDITS TOWARD FUTURE PAYMENTS.
Thank you.

b. *Memo* from the company's social director to all supervisors.

SUBJECT: Christmas gifts for our departmental secretaries

With Christmas just around the corner, it's time for me to raise
my ugly head above ground once again to remind you it's time to
consider our departmental secretaries.

If you wish to contribute toward a gift for each gal, please
leave your donation in my box by December 10. A buck from each
of you will be adequate.

2. *(Memo)* Your employer encourages young executives to enroll for additional university training whenever possible, and the firm pays tuition for
desirable programs. You (assistant personnel manager) would like to attend the Graduate School of Business Administration Management Program at the *(name)* University (in your city). Because most classes meet
Monday evenings and a few on Saturdays, they will not interfere with your
job. You believe the course will definitely make a graduate more knowledgeable in the management field, thereby increasing his or her worth to
the company. Some of the topics you foresee as particularly valuable to
your present job are: Management Communication, Performance Appraisals, and Basic Human Motivation. The course, over one academic
year, costs $1,500; $300 required to be submitted with your application and
the remaining $1,200 by October 8. Today is August 15. Enclose your
application with your memo to Mr. D. J. Helwick, Executive Vice President, for his approval.

3. *(Memo)* You are area coordinator for your company's blood bank. Last
year, through the cooperation of various departments, your blood bank had
ample credits to provide the 289 withdrawal units requested by employees.
Now the annual drive is approaching again. On March 5 and 6 your
company's employees are to participate in this worthwhile cause, from 10
a.m. to 5 p.m. (You decide on the place and on other necessary details.)
You want donors to sign up for the time most convenient for them. Provide
sign-up sheets in convenient places, and write a memo to all 200 employees, attaching a folder about the blood bank and on donor qualifications.

4. *(Memo)* To conserve fuel, because of the current fuel shortage, you—as
operations manager of a large company—want to request all employees to

observe certain simple fuel-saving steps. Without fuel your plant cannot operate; so it is to everyone's interest that as much gas and diesel fuel be saved as possible.

You ask that all vehicles must be shut off when idle. Examples include: during lunch periods and break times; when chip trucks are under bunker for any time (diesel manufacturers recommend engines should not idle for more than five-minute periods); when trucks are being loaded with lumber, logs, or other materials; when trucks are standing idle at any other times not in use. Also, you want all employees having company cars to obtain fuel at outside sources. And you request that operators run machines in such a manner as to conserve fuel without loss of efficiency. Excessive speed where not necessary consumes more fuel. You believe that cooperation of all employees could result in a 5 to 10 percent savings. Ask the superintendent and shop stewards to make sure proper steps are being carried out. Mention in your memo that you will make personal inspections periodically. Plan an attractive, easy-to-read format for your requests.

5. *(Invitation)* You are the local sales manager for an office equipment company which has a new line of word processing machines. Since this is your company's first entry into the word processing field, you have decided to display your new equipment at a business show sponsored in your city by the Administrative Management Society. An admissions fee is charged to defray the expense of the show, but you have purchased a block of tickets to distribute to your regular customers and to other good prospects for your products. The three-day event starts one month from today. At the show, you will display your company's new Wordpro I electronic disc typewriter; the Wordpro II Computerized CRT machine; and your new line of dictating equipment, the Wordbank machines.

Write a letter, which will be personalized and typed on your new Wordpro I machine, to invite your customers to see your machines at the business show in your city's convention center. The letter will go to purchasing agents, office managers, administrative managers, and word processing supervisors. Enclose a ticket to the show and give them the exact dates and exhibit times. You will be happy to furnish more tickets if there are others from a company who wish to attend. All they need to do is call your office (give your number). You will send the extra tickets immediately.

6. The following is the first draft of a form letter request from a mortgage loan company to borrowers. The revision which was mailed is illustrated in request 2, page 166. Which do you think should be more effective and why? Compare the two letters' organization, openings and closings, paragraphs, action requests, clarity, completeness, and consideration. Be specific.

```
Dear Homeowner:

We wish to inform you that the Homeowner's Mortgage Protector Plan
Certificate which you recently received is to be read carefully and
then filed with your other valuable papers. The benefits provided
by the plan are very valuable.

The protection will become effective on the date indicated on the
certificate after the premium has been paid. The premium which is
shown on the enclosed certificate should be added to your future
monthly payments.

If your mortgage payment has already been made for the month the
protection is to become effective, the premium should be sent now
so that you will be fully protected for the month. Next month,
combine the payments.

We are pleased you have secured this protection for yourself and
family. The acceptance of this plan by so many of our customers
indicates to me that it is certainly a valuable and worthwhile
project.
```

7. *(Memo)* You are the owner of a small retail business which specializes in household appliances and the repair of those appliances (mixers, vacuum cleaners, waffle irons, toasters, and similar items). When you started your business about five years ago, you operated the store yourself and received help from your wife in keeping records and waiting on customers during busy times.

Business has been good, and you have expanded your stock of sales items. You now have one full-time salesclerk and one part-time repairperson to help. Even the bookkeeping and accounting records are now done by an outside firm on a part-time basis. (The firm that does your accounting comes in once a month for routine affairs, does your year-end closing, prepares tax returns, and is responsible for the annual inventory.)

In recent months you have been wondering about the advertisements you have read in the newspaper and heard on radio and television about "small computers" and their value to a small business. All that you have heard sounds good, but you really know little about computers and will need some advice on how you could use them.

Write a memorandum to your accountants (the Apex Accounting and Management Service) and ask them to investigate this matter for you. You will want to know the cost of such a small computer, what specific bookkeeping and accounting functions it can perform for you, what special training your employees will need in order to be able to use it, how it can help Apex, and other business matters. You will also want to be certain that the accountants understand that you are not trying to replace them—that you only want to know if the small computer will provide you with more information than is currently possible and, if so, whether the additional information is worth the cost of the equipment, maintenance, and training. Be specific in your request for information.

8. As administrative assistant to the president of Renton Savings Association, write a letter inviting customers and their families to be your special guests at a grand opening of your new quarters on Thursday, Friday, and Saturday, the last three days of this month. There will be handsome gifts for both ladies and gentlemen, special door prizes with drawings every two hours, and refreshments. Children will receive balloons. Also, each current passbook holder will receive a special present. Your new building is graciously furnished, with a number of authentic period antiques. A SPECIAL GUEST name tag which you will enclose with your invitation letter entitles customers to their gifts.

9. *(Memo)* You are assistant director of your company's regional office. You need to write a memo to all 15 plant managers asking them for a report by June 30 of this year. In this report—for the past fiscal year, June 1 through May 31—you want them to be sure to cover the following points: the major accomplishments of their plant during the past year, major problems facing them for next year, objectives for their plant for next year, plans for accomplishing them, and anticipated difficulties. Also, you want a brief summary—one paragraph on each subject—covering their plant's operations last year in the areas of: organization planning, quality performance, production and scheduling performance, community relations, personnel management, costs of operation, health and safety, product development, and any other matters they think significant. If they will please organize their report in this manner, they will be especially useful to you in preparing your Annual Division Report and in making plans for next year. You feel the company has had a good year and you look forward to an even better one next year.

   Arrange your request in an easy-to-read format (perhaps consider some tabulating?) and achieve a pleasant tone.

10. One of your duties as circulation manager for *Hike and Bike,* a special interest monthly magazine aimed at hiking and biking enthusiasts, is to control the spiraling costs of delivering this magazine to your 50,000 subscribers all over the country. Some magazine publishers have been experimenting with alternative home-delivery methods which are less costly and faster than the third-class mail service that *Hike and Bike* has always used.

   Compose a memo of authorization to your administrative assistant requesting an informational report. Ask your assistant to gather and organize data on the following: types of alternative delivery modes, such as private mail carriers; publishing companies which have experimented with or adopted alternative delivery methods; and an analysis of their experience, examining such factors as reliability and promptness of delivery; coverage of urban, suburban, and rural subscribers; cost, etc.

At a staff meeting in 30 days you will need to make conclusions and recommendations based on the report's contents. Suggest that the report be based on information gathered from recent articles in trade and business publications (provide several leads) and from telephone and in-person conversations with circulation staff members of similar periodicals (suggest the names of a few of your professional contacts).

11. Assume you are the new assistant manager of the Tower Life Insurance Company's office in your city. Your company will be holding interviews on a nearby college campus January 30 for winter and spring quarter graduates. You want to send a concise, personalized form letter to graduating seniors inviting them to sign up for an interview (whenever you specify) or to call you for further information. You will also grant off-campus interviews. You believe your company has jobs that graduates might be interested in. They can be in the fields of accounting, marketing, computer programming, personnel, and administration. Graduates can build a business career with no capital investment, they can get comprehensive training to develop their talents, and a monthly life income after 20 years of qualified service. Is there anything else you should include?

12. As customer relations director of Executive Services, Inc., you now have the pleasure of announcing your firm's three-day management seminar. Your letter is to be a form, individually addressed to local and regional directors of large firms that have supervisors and assistant managers in various departments. Make clear that from each firm one or more of these managers may attend. Enclose with your announcement a formal seminar folder, giving cost and detailed program. Make clear in your letter the place, dates, and highlights of the training sessions, and create a pleasant, goodwill-building tone.

CAPSULE CHECKLISTS FOR DIRECT REQUESTS*

I Direct-Request General Plan	II Inquiries about Persons		III Inquiries about Products or Services
	To Reference by Applicant	To Reference by Person Interested in Applicant	

1. MAIN IDEA
  a. Request, main statement, or question
  b. Reason(s), if desirable
	1. Main idea
	  a. Reason for writing to this person
	  b. Introduction of request
	  c. Memory refresher
		1. Main idea
		  a. Applicant's full name
		  b. Why you are considering this applicant
		  c. Why you are writing to this reader
			1. Main idea
			  a. Major request and/or
			  b. Reason(s) for interest in product or service

2. EXPLANATION
  a. All necessary and desirable details
  b. Numbered questions, if helpful
  c. Easy-reading devices
	2. Explanation
	  a. Summary of pertinent facts about yourself: courses, major, GPA, outside work, tests, scores, honors, scholarships, leadership
	  b. Guidelines for the recommendation: kinds of information the inquirer needs
	  c. Enclosure of form(s) and résumé, if helpful
		2. Explanation
		  a. Requirements for job, loan, credit, scholarship, membership (legal?)
		  b. A few pertinent facts applicant told you about him- or herself
		  c. Specific questions for:
		    (1) More than "yes, no" answers
		    (2) Explanations if necessary
		    (3) Itemization—in body, underneath, or on separate questionnaire
			2. Explanation
			  a. Specific questions
			    (1) More than "yes, no" answers
			    (2) Explanation, whenever necessary
			    (3) Itemization if more than one and desirable for clarity and/or ease of response
			  b. Promise of anonymity, if desirable

3. COURTEOUS, CLOSE, WITH MOTIVATION TO ACTION
  a. CSAD[1]
  b. EA[2]
  c. DA[3]
  d. Appreciation and goodwill
	3. Courteous close
	  a. CSAD,[1] to whom recommendation should be sent
	  b. EA[2]
	  c. DA[3]
	  d. Appreciation
		3. Courteous close
		  a. Appreciation
		  b. Promise of confidential treatment
		  c. EA[2]
		  d. DA[3]
		  e. Offer to reciprocate, if appropriate
			3. Courteous close
			  a. Suggested or specific action desired
			  b. DA[3]
			  c. EA, when appropriate[2]
			  d. Appreciation and courtesy

* All lists include possible content. For any one message, choose only the pertinent, appropriate items.
[1] CSAD = clear statement of action desired.
[2] EA = easy action.
[3] DA = dated action, if desirable.

CAPSULE CHECKLISTS FOR DIRECT REQUESTS*
(Continued)

IV Complaints, Claims, Requests for Adjustment	V Requests regarding Routine Business or Public Causes	VI Invitations	VII Orders and Reservations

1. Main idea
  a. Purpose(s)
    (need for adjust-
    ment or correction
    of error or pro-
    cedure)
	1. Main idea
	  a. Reason and
	  b. Request (inter-
	    changeable)
		1. Main idea
		  a. Invitation request
		    with all pertinent 5
		    W's: who, what,
		    when (day, date),
		    where, why
			1. Main idea
			  a. Statement of order
			    or reservation

2. Explanation
  a. Something good
    about reader, prod-
    uct, or service, if
    true
  b. All facts pertinent
    to claim
  c. Omission of anger,
    threats, sarcasm,
    exaggeration, per-
    suasion
  d. Desirable qualities:
    promptness; faith
    in reader's fairness;
    good humor, when
    appropriate
	2. Explanation
	  a. Desired details
	    and, if helpful,
	    instructions
	  b. Itemization, prefer-
	    ably when more
	    than two items are
	    requested
	  c. Reader benefit,
	    if any
		2. Explanation
		  a. All necessary de-
		    tails—if to a
		    function: program,
		    time, apparel,
		    costs, refresh-
		    ments, location,
		    directions, parking;
		    if to submit mate-
		    rial: length, meth-
		    od, format, etc.
		  b. Setup and en-
		    closures as needed
		    for easy reading
			2. Explanation
			  a. Details about:
			    (1) Needed items
			      or facilities—
			      quantity, size,
			      color, style,
			      catalog num-
			      ber, price (or
			      rate)*
			    (2) Payment—
			      method, time,
			      deposit (if any)
			    (3) Shipment—
			      date and place
			    (4) Special instruc-
			      tions, if any
			    *If reservation:
			    function, number
			    in expected attend-
			    ance, requirements

3. Courteous close
  a. CSAD:[1]
    Free replacement,
    free repairs, re-
    fund, credit, price
    reduction, inspec-
    tion, explanation,
    apology or change,
    new shipment, or
    adjustment left up
    to reader
  b. EA[2]
  c. DA[3]
  d. Appreciation and
    courtesy
	3. Courteous close
	  a. CSAD[1]
	  b. EA[2]
	  c. DA[3]
	  d. Courtesy
		3. Courteous close
		  a. CSAD[1]
		  b. EA[2]
		  c. DA[3]
		  d. Courtesy
			3. Courteous close
			  a. CSAD[1]
			  b. EA[2]
			  c. DA[3]
			  d. Courtesy

* All lists include possible content. For any one message, choose only the pertinent, appropriate items.
[1] CSAD = clear statement of action desired.
[2] EA = easy action.
[3] DA = dated action, if desirable.

CHAPTER **8**

Good-News and Neutral Messages

A message that conveys good news is usually easy to write, because you are giving or telling your reader something that is pleasant. A neutral-reaction message is also relatively easy to write, because it is about something the reader considers neither good nor bad news—just information that may be useful. This chapter discusses the good-news organizational plan, and the following kinds of letters and memoranda you can organize with this plan:

Favorable replies

Answering inquiries about individuals

Granting adjustments on claims and complaints

Approving credit

Acknowledging orders

Granting favors and other requests—pertaining to business, government, and organizational procedures or individual needs

Favorable unsolicited messages

Announcements about:
    Sales and events
    Procedures, policies, and responsibilities
    Honors and activities of people

Transmittals

Additional illustrations of other messages adaptable to the good-news plan are included in later chapters.

ORGANIZATIONAL PLAN

You can use this direct-approach good-news plan whenever you answer a request or initiate an unsolicited message yourself, if the news will be *favorable or neutral–at least not unfavorable–to your reader*. As with direct requests, the plan has three parts:

1. Best news or the main idea
2. Explanation, which includes one or more of the following, when desirable:
    a. All necessary details
    b. Educational information

  c. Resale material
  d. Sales promotion
  3. Positive, friendly ending
   a. Appreciation
   b. Clear statement of action desired and motivation to action
   c. Willingness to help further

Because the items in the explanation section form the basic core of your message, you must use good judgment in deciding which items to include. The following discussion highlights the content and uses of four items:

1. *All necessary details:* Include whatever facts, terms, reasons, and other explanations pertain directly to the best news or the main idea. Consider, for instance, whether the reader needs specific details on the why, what, when, who, where, and how of the news or main idea.
2. *Educational information:* Include instructions for use and other educational facts about a product or service the customer has bought if such information is necessary to help the customer get the utmost benefit from the purchase or from the relationship with your firm. If you enclose an instruction book- let, a short paragraph within the letter may call special attention to certain pages in that booklet.
3. *Resale material:* Include appropriate favorable information about a product or service the reader has already bought or is planning to buy, or about your organization. Such material usually answers the question, "What will this do for me?" and strengthens the reader's confidence.
4. *Sales promotion:* Include suggestions about other products or services related to those the customer has bought or is considering buying. When- ever you do so, you indicate your desire to be of further service to the customer. This material should be presented without sales pressure; the emphasis should be on what the customer may need or appreciate and not on a desire to get more business.

FAVORABLE REPLIES

To help build goodwill, any progressive organization replies to all reasonable requests courteously, helpfully, promptly (within four days, if possible). If you know there will be a delay, a brief acknowledgment should state why and then tell the inquirer approximately when to expect a complete answer. In such a message you can still begin with the best news first—information that is useful to the reader or shows you are doing something. Don't start with such negative statements as: "We are sorry we cannot answer your request here. . . ." Emphasize the positive, for example:

> Your request for information about solenoids has been forwarded to our Chief Systems Analyst, Mr. Richard Hacket, in our Chicago offices.
>
> You can expect to receive his helpful comments regarding your special needs soon after he returns from Alaska next week.

In every good-news reply your compliance with the reader's request is more important than any expression of gratitude or pleasure. Depending upon circumstances, you can begin by saying that you have done it (the preferred beginning), that you are doing it, or that you will do it. Thereafter the material you select for the explanation and ending varies significantly with the circumstances.

The discussion in this section includes guidelines and examples of favorable replies to requests for information about individuals, requests for adjustment, credit, orders, and favors, and provides a basis for deciding how to answer other types of good-news replies.

Answering Inquiries about Individuals

Among the most frequent nonsales-related inquiries you might need to answer are requests for information about personnel and credit applicants. The following section focuses on recommendation letters about personnel for jobs, but also briefly discusses replies to inquiries about applicants who are considered for reasons other than jobs.

When you furnish pertinent information about an applicant's qualifications, character, and/or general conduct, you are writing a recommendation. It should preferably be addressed to the specific person interested, instead of "To whom it may concern."[1]

You have a fourfold responsibility when you write recommendations. You must be fair (1) to the applicants, so they can get what they are best qualified for, (2) to the inquirers (prospective employer, creditor, landlord, or whoever), for they are depending on your frank comments, and (3) to your own conscience and reputation for integrity. Also, (4) you must abide by civil rights laws and be aware of possible legal problems. Discussed below are the expanded good-news outline, recommendation letters on outstanding candidates, and recommendations on candidates with shortcomings.

Expanded Good-News Outline for Recommendations

The following suggestions serve as a basis for confidential recommendation letters when facts are mainly favorable or neutral.

---

[1] A to-whom-it-may-concern letter is sometimes given to a satisfactory employee before she or he leaves the company; but because it must necessarily be general and not confidential, it carries much less weight than the confidential, specific recommendation.

1. Main idea
    a. State the applicant's full name and what his or her relationship was to you—employee, customer, friend, tenant, club member. Mention dates, length of time, and type of job, credit, tenancy, or whatever is pertinent that he or she held under you. Use facts; don't guess.
    b. Include an expression of pleasure, if sincere, in your statement of purpose for the letter: *replying confidentially to a request*. A subject line can cover part of item b with such words as "Confidential report by request, on Thomas W. Jones as a prospective field representative."
2. Explanation
    a. Answer all questions—direct or implied—unless doing so would be legally risky.
    b. Arrange answers in the best psychological order, depending upon facts.
    c. Back up your statements of evaluation (excellent, outstanding, and so on) with specific facts about performance record. For a job applicant:
        (1) Tell specific job duties that applicant performed.
        (2) If the inquiry states requirements of the job for which the applicant is being considered, talk about those duties that will be significant.
        (3) When desirable, mention work habits that show personality characteristics.
    d. Be honest and fair with negative material.
        (1) Include it *only* if pertinent to the inquiry and likely to affect the applicant's fitness to perform the particular job.
        (2) Embed and subordinate it through amount of space and word choice.
        (3) Know the legal aspects of recommendations (see Appendix A).
        (4) If you prefer to omit pertinent negatives, invite the reader to phone you; then present the facts orally and discreetly.
3. Ending
    Include if possible a candid statement of your personal opinion about the applicant's probable fitness for the position (or whatever the applicant is being considered for— a lease, credit, membership) and your recommendation, qualified or unqualified.

Recommendation Letters for Outstanding Candidates

When everything you want to say is favorable, the recommendation is easy to write, as in letter 1 below.[2]

Letter 1

A Marine Corps commanding officer writes a good solicited recommendation to the regional manager of a nationally known business firm about a corporal seeking a management trainee position.

---

[2] Regarding salutations and complimentary closes used for examples in this and following chapters, please see footnote 3, p. 157.

Pleasure; purpose; name; job; length of time

I am glad to answer your inquiry about Wayne S. Prochas. Because Wayne has worked with me nearly two
years as a correspondence clerk, I know him well.

Answers to questions

Duties performed

During this time he has demonstrated outstanding abilities in both general office and management work. In
twenty years of military service I have only once before made such a high recommendation, and presently I
have over 800 officers and men in my command. With
speed and efficiency Wayne has attended to the administrative correspondence of more than 800 men attached
to this command, and he has never once complained of
the work load or poor conditions under which he has
had to work.

Personality

and

I recognize in this man a great potential because he
is intelligent, industrious, and so well liked by all
who come in contact with him. Corporal Prochas does
his work with no supervision and can be relied upon to
deliver a finished product at all times. Also I get
the very definite impression that he could, if placed
in a position to do so, generate ideas as well as
process those of others.

character

As to conduct, personal habits, and ability to handle
himself properly this man has no faults, to my knowledge. He doesn't appear to have to work at being a
gentleman. It seems to come natural to him. His loyalty is unquestionable and by his practices he has
influenced others to a great extent.

Unqualified recommendation

I have two regrets: first, I can not take this man to
my next command and, secondly, I do not possess the
word power necessary to describe this man. But I do
say this; my information is accurate and I am sincere.
He will make a real contribution to any organization
which he may choose to join. I recommend him very
highly without any reservation.

Though the statement following "secondly" in the last paragraph above
seems overdone (and could be revised), this commanding officer is to be
commended for his sincerity and for including more than mere glowing adjectives to describe a man he considers outstanding.

Recommendations for Candidates with Shortcomings

You must decide whether to include or omit negative material. If the candidate
has the needed good qualities, you may be able to give a qualified or even an
unqualified recommendation without stating the shortcoming. In any case, you
should mention a weakness only if it meets these conditions:

1. It is pertinent to the job (or credit, etc.) for which the candidate has applied.
2. *It is sufficiently serious* to affect the applicant's probable fitness for that responsibility.
3. It is true (not hearsay or stated because of your personal prejudice, jealousy, malice, or discrimination).
4. It occurred often enough (and recently enough) to be worth mentioning.
5. It answers a specific question asked or implied, and/or you mention it in a spirit of goodwill based on items 1 to 4.

Recommendations are misleading and useless as personnel reports if they omit truthful, pertinent, helpful information. Nevertheless, many employers have been reluctant to make any negative—though truthful—statement (in writing or orally) for fear of a costly lawsuit or unfavorable publicity if the applicant should sue. Others, however, feel they have a moral duty, when responding to a legitimate inquiry, to state what they honestly and in good faith believe to be true and pertinent to the questions asked about a former employee. Basically, one should have no fear of stating the *truth prudently.*

For instance, an applicant who was discharged, after warnings, because he was caught three times stealing from the cash drawer should probably not be employed in a job handling company funds. But he may be a fine employee in other work. Likewise, such serious shortcomings as the following, unless corrected, will probably affect an employee on the next job, too: excessive drinking or drug use, poor health causing frequent absences, unwillingness to cooperate or to obey laws, dishonesty, extreme emotional instability. If you prefer not to present them in writing, you can write a short letter acknowledging the request and inviting the reader to call you. To protect yourself whenever you must make negative statements, you should know the legal aspects of recommendations.

If you are writing a recommendation letter about a candidate who, apart from one serious shortcoming, is satisfactory (or excellent), organize your letter so that you establish the applicant's more favorable characteristics before you mention the defect. In letter 2, for example, the negative facts answering two questions are embedded; the message ends with a candid, qualified recommendation. (Three lawyers and an assistant attorney general have declared this letter "absolutely legal.")

Letter 2

A department manager comments on a former employee who had a serious shortcoming. (This letter, dated July 28, answers inquiry 2, page 157.)

Confidential Appraisal by Request on Victor L. Dryer

Full name and brief summary

Mr. Dryer worked hard for us as a salesperson in the electrical appliances section for about a year. He was such a dependable salesperson that when the sec—

Answer to part of question 1

tion manager resigned to go to the East, we placed Vic in charge and found him well qualified for the job. He was with us 22 months--until June 30 this year.

Answer to question 2

As section manager, Vic had much responsibility. Besides ordering all merchandise for the section, he was also in charge of the five salespeople working under him. He was well liked by subordinates and customers. He had a knack of being tactful and thoughtful with every customer. Because of his personality and his knowledge of the stock, he pleased a good many steady patrons and helped increase total sales within his section.

Favorable comment before and after the negative answer to part of questions 3 and 1

Vic's work at the store was entirely commendable for about 16 months. Then he developed a personal problem, which noticeably affected his disposition and his attendance. When I talked with him about the change, he mentioned serious worries. He tried to lick the problem and did so for three weeks. But after he had missed at least a day's work every week for six months, I regretfully had to let him go.

More about question 3

Vic's other personal habits are good. His personality, honesty, and physical appearance are an asset to any company. He takes an active part in outdoor sports and, except for the problem I mentioned, is in fine health. It is quite probable that his move to your town will be a definite advantage to his family and himself.

Qualified recommendation

Vic is intelligent and well educated (a marketing graduate of Broadway College). Because he knows the electrical appliance business well and has so many other fine qualities, he can be a top-notch department or section manager especially in the electrical field.

Besides recommendations of job applicants, you may sometimes be asked to recommend people for other reasons. Whether the inquirer is considering a person as a tenant on leased property, or for membership in a distinguished organization, or for credit, or an honorary award, you can adapt the Expanded Good-news Outline for Recommendations to help you write honest favorable recommendations.

Granting Requests for Adjustment

An *adjustment letter* is the reply to a complaint (called a claim letter). In general, the best attitude is to give the customer the benefit of any doubt. Most persons are honest in their claims, and it is usually better to make the desired adjustment than to risk losing a customer.

Even though your firm's adjustment policy may be generous, the ultimate success of your good-news adjustment letter depends upon not only *what* you say but also *how* you say it. The discussion in this section concerns (1) the tone of adjustment-granting messages, (2) organization and content when the seller is at fault, (3) variations when the buyer or a third party is at fault, and (4) organization when the fault is not yet determined and will be investigated.

Tone of Adjustment-Granting Messages

Consideration and courtesy are exceptionally important when you grant an adjustment. Because your reader has been inconvenienced, irritated, and perhaps angered, he or she is especially sensitive to the tone of your message. Even when the letter grants a request, it can lose a friend and destroy goodwill if its tone is poor. Compare, for example, the following ''poor'' sentence (in which the antagonizing expressions are underscored) with the suggested ''better'' version:

Poor: Nevertheless, so that we can keep you as a satisfied customer, we are willing to allow you to exchange these toys. (*The motive sounds selfish; "willing to" and "allow you" sound condescending and grudging; the sentence lacks you-attitude.*)

Better: Because we want you to be completely pleased, we will gladly exchange the toys for you.

When you (or anyone else in your firm) are definitely at fault, saying ''I'm sorry,'' ''We apologize,'' or even ''Please forgive us'' is quite disarming. You are more likely to lose face by *not* apologizing than by doing so. One apology (preferably in the *explanation* section) is enough, for most situations.

Organization and Content When Seller Is at Fault

You should, of course, always grant the adjustment when your company is at fault. In general, the best organization is:

Begin with the best news—what is being done about the claim.

Include whatever explanation and details are desirable concerning the cause of the mistake; resale on the product, service, or your firm; sales promotion and/or educational material.

End courteously, showing a desire to cooperate, please, and assist.

The following discussion aims to help you plan carefully. After reading about various parts and paragraphs of adjustment grants, you will see examples of complete letters.

Opening Paragraph. Try to begin with whatever you think the reader will consider the best news. If the customer asked for something specific—like a refund, exchange, credit memo, or speedier service—you should grant or promise immediately. However, if the nature of the request or attitude makes a "granting" opening inadvisable, you will try to get in step with the customer in some other appropriate way. For example, if a customer has found a bug in a jar of oysters and vows never to buy your products again, you can't very well *begin* by saying you're sending another jar of oysters to replace the faulty one! Instead, you might express appreciation for the thoughtfulness in writing and/ or agree with a comment made in the complaint. In the following examples, the first two grant immediately and the last three open with various statements to get in step with the reader.

Customer's request or complaint	*Suggested opening*
1. That you "eliminate the delays" in your merchandise shipments or risk losing business.	You will be glad to hear that we have found a new way to speed deliveries of fresh vegetables to you. From now on your produce can reach you within two hours after we receive your order.
2. That you replace immediately five defective copies of a book needed by May 15.	Today five copies of (*book title*) were sent to you by air express, shipping charges prepaid. You should receive them three days before May 15.
3. That you refund to a friend the $40.50 purchase price because of your firm's error. (Your customer bought a wedding gift for a friend. Instead of charging it to your customer's account, your store incorrectly sent the "gift" to the friend c.o.d. That was two months ago; the friend does not yet know about the mix-up.)	(*To the customer's friend*). You have had the unusual experience of paying for your own wedding gift— much to the embarrassment of our mutual friend, James L. Lamson. The mix-up is due entirely to our error, for which we extend to you our sincere apologies. (*Note: In this case the refund check is mentioned only after the explanation.*)
4. That two special toys ordered four weeks ago did not arrive in time for Christmas.	We have disappointed you and your children at what is usually the happiest time of year, and we are truly sorry! Now I want to do the best we can to make amends.
5. That the service of a certain waiter in your restaurant was disappointing, and the customer's guests were embarrassed.	You are perfectly right to feel that you should receive prompt and courteous service from our waiters. That is exactly our goal for every guest, and we thank you for taking time to write us.

Explaining What Caused the Mistake. When your firm is at fault, admit it frankly. How much explanation to include depends upon the kind of mistake and the customer's probable interest. Don't say, "mistakes are bound to happen" or that because of the size of your firm there will naturally be frequent errors. Don't promise the error will *never* happen again. If it *does*, the situation will be doubly embarrassing. Generally it is desirable to include at least *some* explanation. Paragraphs like the following—from two adjustment grants—help the reader understand how the error occurred:

1. You guessed correctly. Apparently all the shipping papers, including the original ones that should have been kept for our use,
   were sent to you. As a result, we have no record of the ordered
   paint. We are certainly sorry that you were inconvenienced by our
   slipup. We always try to be careful in processing every customer
   request accurately and promptly.
2. Sometimes we find that a package miscarries in the mails. This
   occasionally happens because of an error in addressing the label,
   or damage to the label in the mail, obliterating the address. Apparently that's what happened with your parcel.

Resale. If the person complaining seems to be losing faith in your firm, resale is desirable. If possible, include concrete evidence of your efficient service, safe and correct shipments, and/or your care in producing or selecting high-quality products. If certain steps have been or will be taken to prevent recurrence of whatever the customer is complaining about, mention them. Sometimes you can honestly state that a new procedure is developed "on the basis of helpful comments like yours."

Sometimes it is desirable to resell the customer on keeping both the replacement you are sending *and* the original slightly defective shipment. (You save return-shipping charges and the bother of processing the damaged merchandise.) A consumer may be glad to keep slightly damaged articles if you substantially reduce their price. Likewise, a dealer customer may be willing to accept a below average shipment which can be used for a special sale and quick profits if you give sufficient inducement—price reduction, consignment terms, or perhaps longer payment time.

Sales Promotion Material. If a retailer sells only one type of costly product (like furnaces, home insulation, or roofing), which the average consumer buys only once in a great while, sales promotion material would be out of place. On the other hand, if the seller carries a variety of often-replaced items, sales promotion may be desirable. Without sounding greedy, you want to encourage the customer to continue to buy other goods from you. Also, if the customer returned the original shipment and is receiving credit or a refund, she or he really needs a different replacement. Sales promotion material is then appropriate.

Ending Paragraph. For a pleasant close you may (1) tie suggested action in with sales promotional material; (2) comment on the pleasure the reader will gain from the high-quality new article you have sent; (3) express appreciation that the reader took time to write; and/or (4) issue a cordial invitation that the customer continue to come to your firm for top service. Omit negative thoughts, such as an apology or a reminder of the inconvenience the mistake caused. Don't suggest future trouble or imply that the customer may stop buying from your firm.

Now that you have read about the parts of adjustment grants when the seller is at fault, you are ready to analyze and compare complete messages.

Letter 3 concerns a situation in which the seller is at fault. The disappointed customer stated the intention of never buying this canned food product again. Notice that the writer does not begin by "granting" or even giving the free assortment; the main idea is appreciation and resale. The assumption is that only after reading the explanation—and more resale—will the customer be in a mood to accept the replacement. The last paragraph effectively ties in a gift with a hint of sales promotion.

Letter 3

A good adjustment-granting letter from the assistant manager of the quality control department of a national packing corporation to an out-of-state customer who found a fly in the can.

Main idea:
thanks; resale

Thank you for writing us of your experience upon opening a can of DeMona spinach. We are very concerned about this because of the particular care taken in the preparation of all DeMona products to assure you of receiving a wholesome and high-quality food item.

Explanation,
with resale

Upon arrival at the packing plant, the spinach is run through a large perforated cylinder where it is tumbled and shaken apart to eliminate particles of soil, etc. From there, it is transferred to wide traveling belts where inspectors remove all imperfect leaves and any other defects present. The spinach then goes into the washers in which a series of paddle wheels keeps it in a state of constant agitation while high-pressure jets of water wash, rewash, and rewash. After that, it is subjected to a further careful inspection as it is placed in the cans; therefore, you can see we do everything possible to produce a clean, wholesome product.

Easy action;
apology

To further investigate this incident, we will appreciate your sending us the code mark which was embossed on the lid of the can in question. This will enable us to refer the matter directly to the plant where the spinach was packed. If you made a note of it, please send it to us on the enclosed reply card. We appreciate your bringing this situation to our attention and offer you our sincere apology.

Gift to regain goodwill and promote sales

Within a few days you will receive an assortment of DeMona fruits and vegetables. We want you to enjoy them so thoroughly that you will continue to be a regular DeMona satisfied customer.

Variations When the Buyer or a Third Party Is at Fault

When someone other than the seller is at fault, you may be justified in refusing—instead of granting—the request. Nevertheless, firms will occasionally grant a buyer's claim even though the buyer or a third party is at fault.

Buyer at Fault. If you decide to grant the adjustment claim though the buyer is at fault, you have two choices for letter organization. You can begin with the best news (granting the claim) and continue with the usual pattern. Or you can begin with a statement that gets in step with the reader (perhaps something on which you both agree, or your appreciation of the customer's promptness or whatever is appropriate). Then explain the mistake, and after that grant the claim. The reason for the latter alternative is that sometimes the psychological effect on the reader is better if you allow the claim *after* you have shown tactfully that the buyer, not your firm, is at fault.

The writer of letter 4 chose the first alternative.

Letter 4

A sales manager grants a refund on a blouse that faded because someone washed it incorrectly; best news first.

Best news; refund

Because we want you to be completely pleased with your purchases at Bon's, you are receiving the enclosed refund. It covers the original price of your Barlow blouse, plus sales tax, totaling $41.50.

Resale, with tactful (impersonal) explanation of necessary washing care

The Barlow is one of the finest lines of blouses made. The synthetic fibers and the special dyes which make possible the beautiful colors in these blouses do, however, require special care. Whenever these blouses are laundered, washing by hand in a solution of very mild detergent and lukewarm water gives the best results. As the instruction tag on every blouse states, these garments are very sensitive to heat and should therefore always be dried at room temperature, never in an automatic dryer. Furthermore, any staining substance which comes in contact with the material must be loosened in cold water, because hot water often causes a chemical change that loosens the dye and results in fading.

Resale; additional emphasis on care; educational enclosure

Although the Barlow line does require special care, I'm sure you will agree that its beauty and elegant fashion lines outweigh the special care required by the fine fabric. Because of the many new materials on the market, I think you will find the enclosed booklet on the laundering of all types of synthetics both interesting and educational.

Sales promotion, with implied action and courtesy

As you are one of our regular customers, we invite you to our upcoming June sale. A complete line of summer fashions, including new pastel and print blouses, will be waiting for your inspection. The sale begins June 12, but the general public will receive an announcement on June 14.

It's been a pleasure to help you.

Third Party at Fault. Sometimes merchandise is damaged or lost while it is in the warehouse or truck of a third party—distributor, broker, shipper, or someone else. Then the third party has the legal responsibility to adjust the claim, and many sellers prefer not to get involved.

However, some wholesalers that sell to small retailers assist them in the claim-filing procedures, or they even file the claim directly on behalf of the dealer. Letter 5, from a retailer to an individual customer, is unusually generous and considerate.

Letter 5

A gift shop owner replaces a lamp damaged in shipment.

Best news: replacement

A new Brighton lamp should reach you in a few days to replace the one you received in damaged condition. We sent it today by prepaid express.

Explanation showing seller not at fault

As the Ace Truckline gave us a receipt acknowledging that they received the original lamp in perfect condition, the porcelain base must have been cracked in transit. We are sorry this happened, for we know how much you want this beautiful gift for your cousin's wedding anniversary. Although our responsibility ended when the truckline accepted the package, we are glad to make this replacement for you.

Suggested action to help claim with carrier

Will you please give the original lamp to the express driver when the second lamp is delivered? We will then enter a claim with the truckline.

Courtesy; resale

Thank you for writing promptly. Our concern now is that you receive the lamp in time for the anniversary, and in perfect condition.

Organization When the Fault Is Not Yet Determined

Sometimes the final adjustment decision cannot be made until the seller determines who is responsible for the mistake. In such cases, let the buyer know promptly that you want to investigate the claim. Your letter should have a neutral effect on the reader, for you are neither granting nor refusing the request. The best organization is: express interest in the problem, assure the customer you are looking into the matter, include brief resale if desirable, and courteously state that you will give the facts as soon as they are available.

Letter 6

A hatchery manager promises to investigate.

Interest in problem

Thanks very much for your report on the N&H "Nick Chick" Leghorn pullets delivered to you on March 29. I sympathize with you, for pullets you buy from Nerving's should meet the high standards of previous lots. We want to do everything possible to cooperate with you.

Possible causes of problem; promise of investigation

Tints, egg size, broodiness are characteristics both genetic and environmental. That fancy phrase simply means pullets can be influenced by both breeding and rearing, management, etc. Because there are so many factors involved in the conditions you describe, we are asking our Oregon field representative, Mr. Vern Jackson, to call on you within the next few days. You will find him cooperative and helpful.

Resale

Most hatcheries would be satisfied if 90% of their stock were good 90% of the time. Not Nerving's. We are aiming for 100% on both counts and won't rest until we reach that goal. Of course, when you are dealing with "life", there are numerous variables making this difficult. But, we keep trying. That's why letters such as yours help in pointing out where improvements can be made.

Courtesy

We want you to be a satisfied customer, Mrs. King. If we are at fault in any way, you are assured we'll do our level best to make amends. Thanks again for writing; you help us take steps to make things right.

Approving Credit

The message telling the customer of your granting credit[3] often includes all parts of the basic good-news plan—best news first, then terms, resale, sales promotion, and appreciation. Most firms have preset letters acknowledging credit approval and containing all needed information.

Decision or Shipment in First Paragraph

If the customer has not yet ordered any merchandise on credit, begin with the credit-granting decision and a cordial welcome. If an order was sent with the request for credit, begin with the date and method by which the goods are being shipped (thereby implying the credit grant). Make clear the purchase details (name and quantity of goods sent, item prices, freight, and total charge); for more than two or three items, attach an invoice copy. Mention cordially that the shipment has been added to the customer's new account.

Explanation of Credit Terms

In your explanation section, mention briefly the basis on which credit was earned, and clarify the terms.[4] If, for instance, an applicant's references all speak highly of prompt-pay habits, it is psychologically a good idea to mention them. The applicant is then encouraged to continue this good reputation in dealing with you.

Clear explanation of the credit terms helps reduce collection problems later. Suppose, for example, your wholesale firm's terms are 2/10, net 30. You must be sure that every new credit customer (dealer) knows whether your terms are based on invoice date, shipping date, delivery date, or from the end of the month (e.o.m.). Misunderstanding on this important detail can cause a customer's payments to be as much as a month off. Compare these vague and clear statements regarding credit terms.

Vague:	Our credit terms are the usual 2/10, net 30.
Vague:	Under our credit terms of 2/10, net 30, you earn a 2 percent discount if your payment is made in 10 days. (*10 days after what?*)
Clear:	Our credit terms are the usual 2/10 net 30, based on invoice date.

---

[3] Every city has a credit bureau—an association of credit grantors (stores, banks, car dealers, credit unions, and so forth). The function of the credit bureau is to collect the credit records of their customers and consolidate the information of each individual. Then, when a credit grantor receives a request for credit, it asks the credit bureau for the applicant's record and forms its own conclusions. The larger credit grantors are linked to the bureau by teletype, which enables them to get a printed record in seconds.

[4] You can place the terms either before or after the resale and sales promotion. If before, you're more certain the reader will notice them because you're emphasizing the terms; if after, you seem to be stressing the other person and not ''what's in it for me.''

In a retail firm you will make clear what kind of account you are opening for the consumer—monthly, flexible, major-purchase (furniture, appliances, etc.) with fixed payments, or other. Explain the billing procedures,[5] the consumer's payment obligations, and the finance charges.

Be tactful in telling the customer when payments are due. Compare, for example, the poor tone in, "We expect you to pay" or, "You are expected to pay" with the improved tone in, "Payments are due within 10 days after the billing date" or, "Please send your payment within 10 days after. . . ."

Resale and Sales Promotion

The credit-granting message should include customer-benefit resale information on the firm's services. Also, it is sometimes desirable to include sales promotion material (in the next-to-last or last paragraph) about such news as a forthcoming sale, new seasonal merchandise, or products allied to those ordered (if any). Such news encourages the customer to use credit. To keep your letter short, you can enclose a leaflet describing *departments and services* such as the following:

For the consumer
Free parking, mail and telephone shopping, personalized services for men, home-planning bureau, bridal consultants, tearoom, other restaurants, child-care, gift wrapping, free and frequent deliveries, special discount or purchase privileges.

For the intermediary (retailer or wholesaler)
Nearby warehouses, factory representatives, quantity discounts, free window or counter displays, national advertising, cuts and mats for newspaper and other advertising, repair services, manuals, factory guarantees, prompt and speedy deliveries, research department.

Future-Service Ending

Close your credit grant with statements which indicate your desire to serve the customer well in the future, or which specify particular services. Inviting readers to a special sale, for example, helps to get them to use their accounts. The tone must in no way sound greedy for orders, and you must observe the usual suggestions for easy action and courtesy.

---

[5] Some retailers mail all statements the same day each month. Others use *cycle billing* according to account numbers or names. This method helps to level out the billing department's load over a 30-day period. For example, customers whose names begin with A–C may be billed for 30-day purchases through the 5th of a month and statements may be mailed on the 10th; those whose names begin with D–F may be billed through the 8th and statements mailed on the 14th; etc.

Letter 7

A retailer uses a processed form letter to grant credit to a consumer; the applicant's name and address are typed in the inside address and salutation.

Best news: welcome; new account

We welcome you as a Nelson credit account customer. Your new charge plate is enclosed and we invite you to use it often. This plate will identify you at all Nelson stores; so please sign it in ink before putting it into your wallet or purse.

Credit terms

You will receive your statement soon after the first of each month, showing purchases up to the 23d of the preceding month. Bills on this monthly account are payable by the 10th of each month. (Unpaid bills are subject to a 1½ percent finance charge.)

Resale on store services

As one of our regular charge customers, you will receive announcements of all our sales before they are advertised for the public. If you should wish sometimes to shop in the comfort of your own home without a trip to town, you can do so conveniently by phone. Just ask for "personal shopping services," tell your needs to the shopping assistant, and then just say, "Charge it to my account."

Invitation to future use of account

The enclosed leaflet explains the numerous Nelson services available for your convenience. Do use them often to save yourself both time and money. We look forward to giving you friendly, courteous service in any of our colorful stores . . . for many years to come.

Acknowledging Orders

An order acknowledgment performs several important functions. It lets the buyer know that his or her order has been received, is appreciated, and is given attention. It helps to build goodwill. Furthermore—and very important—by identifying and accepting the order, the acknowledgment completes a valid contract between buyer and seller. For these reasons the acknowledgment must be definite and complete, in keeping with the situation.

Orders that your firm can fill immediately fall into two types—first orders and repeat orders. Although the acknowledgment for both types should identify the shipment and show appreciation, the message contents will be quite different.

Acknowledgment of First Order

The new customer needs to know that his or her order is being filled promptly and correctly, that it is appreciated, and that—because of your products and services—dealings with your firm will be pleasant and profitable.

Sending the Ordered Items. Usually the best beginning for your first-order acknowledgment is to state what, when, and how you shipped. If possible, state approximately when the shipment should reach its destination. Express appreciation for both the order and remittance (if you received the latter).

Then take care of any needed details about shipping charges and payments. If you opened a new credit account for this customer, you will of course explain the credit terms.

Here are a few overworked expressions to avoid in first-order acknowledgments; they are followed by comments and/or suggested revisions:

Vague, trite, and a little inaccurate: "We have shipped your order. . . ."
Comment: The order is really a piece of paper on which the customer authorizes you to send requested items; your firm fills the order and ships merchandise, groceries, livestock, or whatever was ordered.

Better: "The bedspread (#204) and the electric blanket (#B43) you ordered September 4 were sent to you today by parcel post. You can expect them in a few days. Thank you for your order and your enclosed $65.20 check in full payment.

Trite: "Welcome to our long list (or family) of satisfied customers."
Comment: Omit such statements and show elsewhere in your letter by actions—prompt service, reader-centered resale, sincere thoughtfulness— instead of by empty words that you appreciate the order and want to please the customer.

Specific Resale Material. For the first-order acknowledgment, resale on company *services* is appropriate for both the consumer and the retailer. Resale on *products* ordered is usually more desirable for the consumer than for the retailer. Before ordering, the business manager who will resell your products has usually studied their merits carefully—through sales literature, catalogs, and perhaps information from your sales representative—and you generally need not repeat what has already been read. However, the manager may appreciate a few additional facts and any special product features he or she can emphasize to customers.

To a consumer, resale material from the "home office" is sometimes extremely helpful. After placing a large first order with a firm (either by mail or through a house-to-house sales representative), the consumer may regret having signed the contract—especially when the item purchased is a luxury. But the order acknowledgment from headquarters with detailed reader benefits about the product and warranty helps reinforce the buyer's confidence in the purchase.

Looking Forward to Future Orders and Reader Satisfaction. To end the first-order acknowledgment, you can tie your suggested action in with resale or sales promotion. Be sure your reader has order blanks or whatever else is needed for easy action. If you wish, you may invite the cash customer to fill out and return a credit application form; but avoid suggesting that credit will be automatic.

Letter 8

A wholesaler's personalized acknowledgment of a first cash order from a dealer.

Best news: shipment	You can expect to receive the two dozen Topskill lawn edgers, #L592, and the five manual mowers, M 687, in time for your garden sale Monday, May 15. They were shipped by prepaid express this afternoon.
Appreciation; check acknowledgment	Thank you for your order and for your $425.50 check, which exactly covered the items as priced in your new dealer catalog. As you know, the suggested markup on these items is 30 percent.
Resale on services for dealer; customer benefit	Your customers will be pleased with these highly popular Topskill tools. Currently they are advertised in special 1/2–page, two–color ads in House and Home and Western Garden magazines, April through July. You can assure your customers that every Topskill is factory guaranteed according to the contract that accompanies each tool. A special feature of the Topskill edger is its ability to trim neatly within one inch of flower beds and rockeries. On the mower, a simple twist of the dial knob adjusts both wheels and roller for precise cutting height and ease of operation.
Services to dealer	Illustrations of counter and window displays and other free sales helps are sent with this letter. Just let us know your needs on the enclosed checklist.
Suggestion for credit	You may be interested in our regular credit terms of 2/10, net 30 on future orders. If so, just fill in and return the enclosed form; we will gladly consider your credit application. Also, if you have any ques-
Courtesy	tions with which we might be able to help, just write us. We'll do our best to serve you promptly.

Acknowledgment of Repeat Orders

Most orders come from repeat customers who know and like a firm's products and services, and who don't expect a typewritten letter acknowledgment. Usually the goods can be sent as quickly as an acknowledgment can be mailed. In some cases standard purchase order forms give complete instructions about terms and delivery date, and they stipulate that the buyer will be notified only if the order cannot be filled as requested. In others, an adequate good-news order acknowledgment is an inexpensive (perhaps printed) form, a carbon copy of the shipping invoice, or a postcard.

Though most repeat orders are filled without letter acknowledgments, an unusually large order may occasionally warrant a personalized letter. This may include appreciation, a statement of how the order is being handled, and perhaps a few cordial comments about your past relationship and future plans to supply the customer's needs.

Granting Favors and Other Requests

Whenever you decide to grant a favor, you have a comparatively easy letter to write. Whether the favor is serving on a committee, speaking without pay at a convention, donating money, or lending your firm's equipment without charge, the good-news plan is the best to use. Usually all you need is the acceptance first, pertinent comments or explanation, and a cordial ending.

By following the good-news plan plus the suggestions and cautions discussed in this section, you can also write effectively favorable replies to other kinds of requests—from customers, employers, employees, friends, government officials, or anyone else. Good judgment is necessary, of course, to adapt your messages to the circumstances and your readers.

UNSOLICITED FAVORABLE MESSAGES

The previous section considered messages that are written because someone inquired. This section discusses *unsolicited* favorable and neutral-reaction messages—specifically, announcements and transmittals.

Announcements

Favorable and neutral-reaction announcements should follow the good-news plan—best news or main idea first; then adequate explanation, resale, or educational material; and, finally, the appropriate ending. Some messages combine an announcement with an invitation. How should you classify them? Either way. Whether you call them announcements (discussed in this section) or invitations (Chapter 7), you use the same three-part organizational structure.

Included in this section are group and personal announcements about sales and events; procedures, policies, and responsibilities; and honors and activities of people.

Announcing Sales and Events

Whenever you wish to announce a sale or an event (luncheon, conference, celebration, meeting, or other function) about which you need merely to inform your readers, you can use the good-news plan. The opening paragraph usually includes as many of the five W's as possible.

An excellent way to build and strengthen goodwill with regular customers is to let them know you appreciate them. For example, message 1 announces a sale before newspaper publication.

Message 1–Letter

A store's preannouncement to charge customers about a forthcoming sale; a processed form without an inside address or salutation, but with a "Cordially" complimentary close and the signature of the district manager.

Reason:
best news;
five W's

Because you are a regular (*store name*) customer, we are glad to announce to you a special sale of an unusual collection of spring coat values . . . in one of the Designer Room's greatest coat events. This announcement comes to you now so that you can make your selection during a three-day period before newspaper ads appear.

Displayed items
for emphasis

PREANNOUNCEMENT SELLING
Wednesday, Thursday, and Friday
February 6, 7, and 8
NEW SPRING COATS BY OUR FOREMOST MAKERS
all priced far below regular
$75 $115 $160

Details

FINE COATS FROM OUR BEST MAKERS . . . IN MISSES AND PETITE SIZES. Coats such as you'll see at much higher prices after this great selling. Every one a new, just-arrived 198_ fashion!

EXCITING FASHIONS AND COLORS including whites, neutrals, bright colors, town tweeds, dressy and casual styles, various shapes, coats that wrap or button.

Easy action

TAKE ADVANTAGE OF THIS OPPORTUNITY FOR FIRST CHOICE AND SUPER SAVINGS! Come in early . . . February 6, 7, 8 . . . to choose your coat. Prices will return to regular immediately after this outstanding coat event.

Announcing Procedures, Policies, and Responsibilities

Some business firms commonly use "directives" to announce to employees official statements of company policy, procedures, and employee responsibilities. They provide loose-leaf policy manuals for all employees to file every current directive (usually typed in memo form) and to remove those that are outdated. The manual may cover a wide variety of topics ranging from assigned parking facilities and office hours for employees to policies about salary increases, retirement benefits, overtime, handling inflammable goods, and treatment of customers.

Two cautions to remember when you write directives are: (1) be sure your statements are absolutely clear to all levels of your employees, from the top executive to the part-time janitor, and (2) avoid a bossy or threatening tone. Show confidence that all will cooperate if they understand what they are supposed to do.

Of course, many messages about procedures, policies, and responsibilities are not directives. They can be processed announcement letters to customers (and others) or memos like message 2, to employees.

Message 2—Memo

Announcement to all employees about enrollment for company insurance plans.

TO: All Kenmore employees DATE: Feb. 22, 198_
FROM: John K. Wood, Retirement and $\mathcal{J}\,\mathcal{K}\omega$
          Insurance Officer[6]
SUBJECT: Open Enrollment Period for Company Insurance
          <u>Plans</u>

The annual open enrollment period for employee insurance plans will be between March 4 and 27 at the
retirement and insurance office. During that time,
Why; when; you may
for whom;
where; what
(itemized) 1. Enroll in medical, life, salary continuation, or
                 accident insurance plans for the first time,
              2. Transfer from one basic medical plan to another, or
              3. Add previously uninsured dependents to medical in-
                 surance plans.

Effective date Changes and additions made during the open enrollment
                  period will take effect April 1, 198_.

                  Please refer to the attached individual Insurance Pro-
                  gram Summary, which shows the premiums, company
                  contributions, and payroll deductions for the plans in
Enclosure;   which you are presently enrolled. Then refer to the
instructions   rest of the attached material, which explains just
                  what to do if you wish to make changes in your
                  coverage.

                  Brochures describing the plans and individual counsel-
Offer of more help ing services are available at the retirement and
                  insurance office, 4th floor; or phone extension 987 if
                  you wish one mailed to you.

Announcing Honors and Activities of People

To inform employees and customers about promotions, awards, honors, new appointments, retirements, and other recognition-deserving activities of various persons, it is thoughtful to send announcements.

The first paragraph—which states the good news—often begins with words like "We are pleased to announce that . . . ." or "It is with great

---

[6] Some officers omit the FROM line and sign above their typed signature and title at the bottom.

pleasure that we inform you . . . ." The second paragraph gives details about the new officer, award, or whatever pertains to the announced honor or activity. Suggested action may be that all join in congratulating and/or wishing the person success and happiness.

Transmittals

As the name implies, the main purpose of transmittals is to transmit something, which is usually mentioned in the first paragraph. Transmittals, also called "covering letters," have many uses. They range from short (5- to 10-line) notes to official letters that accompany, explain, or justify documents. In general, they follow the good-news plan.

For routine business to a consumer, employee, or other persons a cordial short note is sufficient to transmit one or more items—such as a check, policy, passbook, warranty deed, or map. Often processed fill-in forms are used, with various listed items and spaces for checking those that are enclosed.

Transmittals that accompany official documents, bids, applications, proposals, or formal reports should be carefully worded letters. (Three are illustrated in Chapter 18.)

SUMMARY

Whenever you answer favorably a request or announce news that will be favorable or neutral to your reader, keep in mind the three-part organizational good-news plan. The Capsule Checklists on pages 221 to 223 give you a review of both the basic plan and various adaptations when you answer requests for information, adjustment, credit, order filling, favors, and when you announce or transmit something.

EXERCISES

Favorable Replies to Inquiries about Individuals

1. *(Memo)* As staff supervisor in the test support division of MAX factory, you have been asked by the personnel department to write your recommendation on James P. Rockman, Clock #4-509. Today is August 31. Your statement about Jim's summer employment will become part of the permanent personnel records. A carbon copy of your memo is to be sent to Jane Taber and Mark Saylor, both department heads in your firm. Jim arrived in your department on June 10 this year and was assigned to your most tedious job—#8477 (you can decide what this job is)—which lasted two months. Jim is returning to college next month, as agreed when he was hired in June. Jim reasons well and has the ability to organize his work load. Should he apply for reemployment next summer, you would gladly welcome him into

your group. Tom learns quickly and has adapted himself to your methods with minimum difficulty. His attitude, attendance, and cooperation are excellent. He is highly thought of by his lead personnel and supervisors. Write a recommendation, using correct *memo* format.

2. *(Telegram)* You—personnel manager for Trustline Insurance Company—have just received the night letter telegram in Exercise 1c, page 172, about Roberta R. Adsen. She worked in your claims department 20 hours a week for two years while attending the university, in the school of business administration. She was meticulously accurate with figures, conscientious, courteous, friendly. Although only a part-time employee, she earned two promotions during the two years. She thrives on responsibility. She was intelligent, thorough, honest, resourceful, receptive to suggestions, always eager to correct any shortcoming. Her letters and oral explanations to customers were clear, tactful, effective. You recall she took two university courses in Business Communication and she happily showed you her grades—A and B. She was poised, self-confident, neat in her work. You know of almost no adverse information except that while working in the claims department filing section she usually dressed quite shabbily. Also her spelling was sometimes inaccurate. Write your night letter telegram, choosing only pertinent facts. (See footnotes 3 and 4, page 141.)

3. You are assistant manager of the loan department of the Central National Bank, your city, and you have received a letter of inquiry from Ms. Janet Tonn, Public Relations Director of the National Environmental Council. She is considering Emmet Gart for a field representative job and asks your recommendation of Gart, who worked for your bank as a field collector of unpaid loan installments. Gart's job was to call at debtors' homes and collect their payments which were past due. In the new job he would work with business executives to upgrade environmental conditions.

   Emmet worked for your bank from April 5 to November 16 last year and quit on impulse with one week's notice after a disagreement with an immediate supervisor. This supervisor happens to be the strictest of all your supervisors in his collection policies. He insists that every item of property should be promptly repossessed when a debtor is delinquent in his payments. Emmet Gart, on the contrary, believed in the gentle "soft sell" method. He was pleasant, honest, and extremely patient with customers, often much more so than the supervisor wanted. With one customer in particular, Emmet and the supervisor clashed; it was finally the cause of Emmet's leaving. The customer had borrowed $7,000 to lease a fleet of trucks for an out-of-state construction job. Although he was financially able to pay the monthly installments, he was habitually late; furthermore, he threatened to transfer all his business—including his checking and savings accounts—to a competing bank unless the collection department stopped harping about his late payments. Gart sided with the customer, arguing that as long as the customer cheerfully paid extra interest on all his late payments and because he always did pay (though late), the bank should "go easy" in its dealings with him, to save his goodwill. One day the supervisor angrily told Gart to repossess his customer's trucks or quit; Gart chose the latter, for he refused to compromise what he thought was the right course of action.

When you heard about the incident, you called Emmet back to your office and tactfully told him that his record had been very satisfactory with the bank and you hoped he would reconsider and stay. Emmet's collection record for the six months he was with your bank was second to the top of your 10 collectors in the field. He was exceptionally well liked by customers and fellow employees. Gart thanked you for your invitation to return and said he would like to; but, because he would have to remain under the same stern supervisor, he thought it best to return full-time to his university studies and give up the job until another opening might occur the following summer.

Emmet is a sociology and English major at the university, and an ardent supporter of social justice. He spoke occasionally about his desire to do something worthwhile in the community to help improve environment and help the underprivileged. You honestly believe he will be happier in the type of work for which Ms. Tonn is considering him. Write a tactful, frank recommendation, after you have sorted out the important and the irrelevant facts.

Granting Adjustments

1. Evaluate the following adjustment letters. What do you like and dislike about each? Suggest specific improvements where needed—in the tone, organization, accuracy, and adequacy of explanation and resale.
   a. From the Chicago (head office) Service Department of a national electrical appliances firm to a customer in a city 1,000 miles away. The letter is mimeographed; the customer's name and "Coffeemaster" (at the bottom) are obvious typewritten fill-ins.

   We are concerned with your report about your appliance.* Our service work is guaranteed and if our service person failed to repair the appliance correctly, we want to see that the proper repairs are made without further expense.

   We would suggest that you return the appliance* to us and use the enclosed shipping label on the package so that it will be connected with this correspondence when it arrives here. If we failed to make the correct repairs, we will not only take care of that for you without charge, but we will also pay the postage both ways.

   * Coffeemaster

b. From a manufacturer to a retailer.

Thank you for telling us of the problem you have had with the coats you purchased.

Some time ago, a batch of material having bad formulation escaped detection by our quality control people. The line inspectors caught most of the finished coats before they were invoiced. However, some were shipped. Apparently your order was among them.

The situation has since been corrected and we don't believe you will have this problem with a replacement. Accordingly, a special shipping label is enclosed for returning your defective merchandise to us. It will be promptly exchanged upon receipt. Please let us know if we may be of further service.

2. You are the sales manager of a local hotel which is a member of a large, national chain of hotels and motels—the Hudson Inns. The Langdon chapter of the Administrative Management Society (AMS) was host to the annual spring district meeting; approximately 90 officers and spouses were present. The meeting started on Thursday night for the early arrivals, but the main meetings began on Friday and lasted until Saturday noon.

   In making preliminary arrangements the Hudson Inn agreed to provide two suites for the meeting (one for the international president and his wife and one for the district president and her husband) at a special price of $240. As these were connecting suites, with a large meeting room between, complete with meeting tables, a beautiful view, and a wet bar, the price was most attractive.

   The meeting was a success and everything was fine until the final accounting from the Hudson Inn was presented to the Langdon chapter. The charge on the suites was $290 and there was also one long distance telephone charge of $2.75 billed to AMS which was made in the afternoon after a member checked out in the morning. The treasurer of the Langdon chapter, of course, appealed the two charges.

   As sales manager of the local Hudson Inn, write a letter to Mr. Waldo Samuel, treasurer of the Langdon chapter of AMS, admitting to the error and telling him to disregard the two charges ($50 for the suite and $2.75 for the phone call). Remind him of the excellent facilities, good meals, extra service, and other good reasons for the Langdon chapter to use Hudson Inn for another AMS meeting sometime in the future.

3. Assume that two months ago Mrs. Joseph Key, one of your long-time good customers, bought a dual-control, four-slice, chrome-plated electric toaster from your store and asked that it be sent as a wedding anniversary gift to her out-of-state friends, Mr. and Mrs. Herbert Norton. Since then she has found no charge for the $49.50 on her monthly statements from your store; neither has she received a thank you from the Nortons. Last weekend, as a guest at

the Norton home, she noticed they were using the exact toaster she had sent them. To her chagrin they called it their "mystery toaster" because it had reached them c.o.d., although neither of them had ordered it. Because they needed one, they kept it. Mrs. Key then told them of her gift. She is furious with your store and wants you to make a proper adjustment immediately. This situation requires two letters—one to the Nortons and one to Mrs. Key. Will you send her a copy of your message to the Nortons? Also, should your letter to the Nortons mention the refund in the opening paragraph? Why or why not? The salesclerk forgetfully omitted Mrs. Key's name on the sales slip. Finding only the name and address of the Nortons (who have no account at your store), the shipping department sent the toaster to the Nortons c.o.d.

4. As assistant manager in the customer service department of Finecraft Company, "jewelry's finest craftsmen," in Hartford, Connecticut, you need to answer today (January 5) a special delivery complaint from Ben Greene, vice president of Beta Gamma Sigma, business honorary, at the University of Missouri chapter. He asks what happened to the order he mailed to you almost three months ago (October 6). The chapter needs 38 crested pins for an initiation to be held three weeks from today. Your records show you received his official order and that the pins were shipped to him November 10 by first-class mail. Since the package has not been returned to you unclaimed, you can only assume it was lost in the mail. Company procedure requires that the customer complete the enclosed insurance affidavit so that you can file a claim and tracer with your insurance company. Upon receipt of the affidavit properly executed, you will immediately enter a no-charge replacement order. Write a goodwill-building adjustment. (This chapter has bought jewelry from you for many years.) You'll rush the pins to reach him before initiation.

5. From Ms. Katy Orth you (customer service manager) received today a complaint letter that the boots your store sent by mail last week are too small. These boots were on special sale for $38.50. The usual store policy is to accept no returns on special sale merchandise. (This rule is one reason that you can offer goods at such low prices.) However, in this case you will make an exception to the rule because she did not know (and your store did not inform customers) that this style of boot must be larger than for dress shoes. You'll be glad to take the boots back and you will credit her account for $38.50. Ask her to pack them in the same box in which they came and to mail them with your name on the address label. If she wants a larger size, you will send it to her for the sale price. Make action easy for Ms. Orth so the package will come to your attention with all the information you need to benefit both Ms. Orth and your store.

6. You are correspondent for National Commemorative Stamp Society, Philadelphia, PA 19122, an organization which sells first-day covers and albums.

A *first-day cover* is an envelope bearing a commemorative stamp and related illustration postmarked on the first day of issue at a designated post office. Prepare a response to this letter from a novice stamp collector:

> I am returning this album because it is not suitable for my first-day covers. Please credit my account for the $24.40 which I was charged. A copy of the invoice is enclosed.
>
> The album holds my U.S. covers but not my British covers. I looked through the album catalog again, but I am still not sure which album would best accommodate all my first-day covers—the U.S. and British covers I now own and additional future covers I may purchase which may be of assorted sizes.
>
> What National album would best store my growing collection of covers of different sizes? Do you have a suggestion?

Indicate that you will credit the customer's account immediately. Even though the customer received exactly what he ordered, it is National's policy to accept returns and refund the purchase price if the item is undamaged and does not suit the collector's needs.

You can give the customer a choice of two suitable albums. One is the Lafayette, which holds 98 first-day covers in crystal-clear vinyl pockets arranged in two tiers of 49 covers each. It is bound in tough, simulated Morocco leather, comes with a matching dustcase, and is available in either blue or chestnut brown. The other is the Jackson, a convenient loose-leaf binder with fingertip controls for ease of opening and 25 clear vinyl pages which will hold 50 covers. It, too, is bound in simulated Morocco leather in either black or emerald green. Both are described in the album catalog you are enclosing. The Lafayette is $22.50; the Jackson, $15.75. Make ordering easy. Because this is a relatively new customer, include appropriate resale material about National first-day covers, display albums, and customer service. Assume any other pertinent details consistent with the facts of the case.

Other Favorable Replies about Credit, First Orders, Favors

1. You are a correspondent in the credit department of the leading department store in a city of 150,000 population. Several weeks ago Mrs. Vera Rick wrote you, saying she just moved to town from a distant city and wants a credit account with your store. In turn, you sent her an application form to fill out because the local credit bureau had no information available on Mrs. Rick. She filled out the form and returned it to you promptly. You checked her facts—including the references—and find she has an excellent credit reputation. The references complimented her for prompt payment throughout the years she traded with them. Your assignment is to notify her that you have granted her credit with your store. Assume your department store has the services you'd expect in a city of 150,000. In preparation for this assignment, you (or a representative from your class) might want to find out

what services are available at a comparable department store and also the type of message the store sends to an individual like Mrs. Rick.

2. You are credit manager of the Recreational Supply, Inc., a wholesale firm in Rochester, New York. Today (January 20) you approved a credit request from Mr. Raymond Bryce, owner-manager of Ray's Sporting Goods in Toledo, Ohio. He has ordered:

20 Little League baseball bats, Catalog #BB897	$2.60	$ 52.00
30 baseballs with cork centers, BC2125	2.10	63.00
10 Deluxe table tennis sets, #TT8126	9.00	90.00
Total		$205.00
Shipping charges		10.50
		$215.50

This is his first order to your firm. It came to you through your field representative, Betty Giori, who reports an exceptionally favorable location of Ray's Sporting Goods—within two blocks of both junior and senior high schools and in the heart of a residential shopping area catering to young families with children. Mr. Bryce (a college graduate seven years ago, majoring in recreation) bought the store three years ago with savings and a small inheritance. Although his capital investment is limited, he is a well-liked manager with progressive ideas. As a former captain of his college football team and as a Little League coach for four years, he is widely known and respected in the community. His character and ethical standards are above reproach. His references report that he has always paid his bills, although often payments have run past the 30-day periods. You decide to grant him credit on your usual 2/10, net 30 terms based on invoice date, and to give him a little "education" (tactfully) on what he gains from paying within the discount period. You are setting a credit limit of $250 until you see how well he keeps his account up to date. The items he ordered were sent by Railway Express today; delivery will be within two days. The Little League bats (of white ash) are approved by the American Baseball Association; the Deluxe table tennis sets (with five-ply basswood paddles and sure-grip vinyl handle bindings), as well as the bats, are nationally advertised in *Sports Parade* and *Parents* magazines. You're enclosing with the shipment some counter and window displays, plus the needed order lists and blanks and your new spring catalog.

3. Assume that in the five years since you graduated from college you have become active in the local chapter of a national business organization relating to your major work. (Assume a pertinent name.) Last month you were presented with the "Executive of the Month" award, and a short article appeared about you in this organization's national magazine. Today you receive a complimentary letter and invitation from the president of the organization's chapter in another city (100 miles away) to be dinner guest (6 p.m.) and banquet speaker (20 minutes) on Thursday evening, one month

from today. Your spouse or a friend will also be a welcome guest, and the organization will provide for your car expenses and hotel overnight costs. There is no fee for speaking. After thinking the matter over, you decide to accept, even though you must be back at your office at 8 a.m. the next (Friday) morning. The topic suggested for your talk is one that's dear to your heart. Write your pleasant acceptance and make clear any details the president will need to know. Assume any additional necessary facts. The chapter's publicity will go to press 10 days from today, so of course you need to respond fairly soon. The earliest you can get to the banquet is 6:30 p.m.

4. You are the newly elected vice president and membership chairperson for your college alumni association. Your first form letter is to the alumni who have paid their membership dues for the current year. Welcome them and express your personal appreciation for their interest and support. Encourage each member to participate fully in the various alumni programs available (name them). Solicit suggestions at any time concerning your association. Address your sample form letter to Ronald Irby, 890 Miller Avenue, your town (city). All future letters you mail to members for this same purpose will have a body identical to the one you write today, but each will be typed on an automatic typewriter and will have a personalized inside address and salutation.

Good-News and Neutral Announcements

1. *(Memo)* You have recently been appointed chairperson of your company's employee finance committee. One of your long-time employees—Ken Maxwell—will retire June 30 this year after serving the company in various capacities for one-third of a century. For the past two years he has been editor of the employee newsletter, which goes to 100 employees. Known for his witty columns and good-natured humor, Ken is generally well liked. Last month when he returned from a trip to France he wrote (and told) ribald mouse stories to the delight of the office grapevine. His enthusiasm for improving the employee newsletter caused him to spend the whole biennial operations budget in the first year, but by special "know-how" he has done well this second year.

   To honor his years of dedicated service there will be a reception from 3 to 4:30 p.m. in a company meeting room you select. Your committee plans goodies, punch, and a minimum of maudlin speeches. To help "punch up" the punch, pay the caterer, and if possible, present a little token to Ken, you must now write a memo to all "friends of Ken Maxwell." Let them decide how much to give, but tactfully set a suggested minimum. Some past and present department chairpersons will perhaps recall how Ken extricated them from problems from time to time. Spouses are welcome, too, at the reception. If you can, add a little light humor to your memo.

2. You are accountant for D&M Distributors. Today (January 13) you have discovered an error you made regarding freight bill #720015, dated October 3 last year, from Mason Carloading Company, 708 Central Avenue, Oakland, CA. Through your oversight you have not yet paid this bill, though payment was due last October 13! Your firm tries always to pay its bills on time. It was an honest mistake and you want to apologize for it. You received freight bills 720015 and 71129 from Mason on the same day. Since these two freight bills were identical except for the bill number, you had put them together assuming that one was a copy of the other. You hope this incident will not hinder any future good relations your firm may have with Mason Carloading. Write an appropriate letter with which you transmit your check for the $90.98 that was due 3 months ago.

3. You are chairperson of the chamber of commerce second annual spring luncheon, and you've been working hard on plans for the past two months. A senator of your state, the Honorable Nancy T. Roe, has accepted your invitation to be principal speaker. Because you anticipate that recent events in the state capitol will generate a high level of interest, you have moved the luncheon to a larger room at the local athletic club. You have decided to permit each member to bring one nonmember guest. The purpose of these luncheons is to provide an opportunity to get reacquainted with other business executives in your community and to hear a challenging and provocative message from a prominent public figure. The program this year should provide both. The date is Thursday, April 10, 198_. The total number you can accommodate is 180. Your cutoff date for reservations is April 6. Luncheon will begin at 12 noon. Write the letter announcing this event and make action easy for reservations. Be specific.

4. You are employed as assistant director in the school of drama on your campus. At the end of the present academic year (June 8) two popular professors, Mary Larson and Jean Scher, have elected to retire after a combined total of 57 years' dedicated service to your university. They have both directed numerous productions in the community and been active in the field of children's drama. The director has asked you to write a letter to their friends (both on and off campus) telling them about a bound volume of letters your school would like to present to each of them. Ask your recipients to send you any letter of appreciation they would like to write to either or both of them—only if they feel moved to do so. They could mention the influence the work of these people had in their own life. Give specifications of the paper size and due date for these messages. Today is May 12; so time is short.

CAPSULE CHECKLISTS FOR GOOD-NEWS MESSAGES*

I Good-News (and Neutral): General Plan	II Answering Inquiries for Information about Individuals —Letters of Recommendation

1. BEST NEWS or MAIN IDEA	1. Best news or main idea
	  a. Applicant's full name and relationship to you, or how you know applicant—job(s) held, tenant, customer, club member . . . ?
	  b. Reason for writing (by request)

2. EXPLANATION
  a. All necessary details
  b. Resale material
  c. Educational material
  d. Sales promotion
	2. Explanation
	  a. Answers to all questions—direct or implied
	  b. Best psychological order for fourfold responsibility to:
	    (1) Applicant
	    (2) Person considering applicant
	    (3) Your conscience
	    (4) Civil rights laws
	  c. Specific facts about
	    (1) Applicant's job, duties, conduct
	    (2) Applicant's work or other habits
	    (3) Personality, etc.
	  d. Honesty and judgment about negatives
	  e. Caution on legal aspects
	  f. Confidentiality
	  g. Offer, phone call

3. POSITIVE, FRIENDLY ENDING
  a. Appreciation
  b. CSAD[1]
  c. EA[2] and motivation
  d. Willingness to help further
  e. DA[3]
  f. RB[4]
	3. Courteous close
	  a. Candid statement of your personal opinion about applicant's probable fitness for whatever he or she is being considered for
	  b. Positive (not negative) attributes at end

* All lists include possible content. For any one message, choose only the pertinent and appropriate items.
[1] CSAD = clear statement of action desired
[2] EA = easy action
[3] DA = dated action, if desirable
[4] RB = reader benefit

III Granting Requests for Adjustment		IV Approving Credit
Seller at Fault (A)	**Buyer or Another at Fault (B)**	

1. Best news
  a. Whatever will please buyer most
  b. Courtesy
	1. Best news or buffer
	  a. Same as IIIA, 1 a
	     or
	  b. Get-in-step-with-reader, courteous comment and concern
		1. Best news
		  a. Credit grant (if no purchase)
		  b. Shipment (if goods ordered)
		    (1) Description
		    (2) Quantity
		    (3) Prices, costs
		    (4) Method, charges
		  c. Courtesy

2. Explanation
  a. Brief resale with tactful explanation of error (if desirable)
  b. Instructions for buyer action, if needed
  c. Concrete resale on firm, services, or goods, if desirable
  d. Cautions
  e. Sales promotion on replacement of returned item(s) or on allied goods
	2. Explanation
	  a. Brief resale with tactful explanation of error, showing seller not at fault
	  b. (If use of 1 b above, best news after explanation)
	  c. Concrete resale on firm, services, or goods, if desirable
	  d. Cautions
	  e. Sales promotion on replacement of returned item(s) or on allied goods
		2. Explanation
		  a. Basis for credit; compliment
		  b. Credit terms; payments, discounts, limits
		  c. Resale on services:
		    (1) *Consumer:* parking, shopping services, departments, conveniences, deliveries, price benefits
		    (2) *Middleman:* (Intermediary): warehouses, discounts, selling aids, advertising, guarantees, repairs, deliveries
		  d. Resale on product choices
		  e. Sales promotion?

3. Courteous close
  a. Suggested action and forward look to future pleasant use of goods and services
  b. EA[2]
  c. Positive, idea; help
  d. RB[4]
	3. Courteous close
	  a. Suggested action and forward look to future pleasant use of goods and services
	  b. EA[2]
	  c. Positive idea; help
	  d. RB[4]
		3. Courteous close
		  a. Forward look to pleasant service and orders (not greedy)
		  b. Suggested action
		  c. EA[2]
		  d. RB[4]
		  e. Courtesy; suggestion of further help, if pertinent

[1] CSAD = clear statement of action desired
[2] EA = easy action
[3] DA = dated action, if desirable
[4] RB = reader benefit

CAPSULE CHECKLISTS FOR GOOD-NEWS MESSAGES (Continued)

V Acknowledging First Orders	VI Granting Favors	VII Announcements	VIII Transmittals

1. Best news
  a. Shipment details
    (1) Description
    (2) Quantity
    (3) Prices, costs
    (4) Method, charges
  b. Thanks for remittance and/or order
	1. Best news
	  a. Acceptance of favor, request
	  b. Courtesy
		1. Best news; main idea
		When appropriate:
		  a. Five W's (all or most); reader in first and all other paragraphs
		  b. Statement of pleasure, compliment, congratulations
		  c. Admission of error, with good news
			1. Best news; main idea
			  a. Transmittal of specific item(s)
			  b. A concise reason
			  c. Courtesy

2. Explanation
  a. *For credit customer,*
    (1) Basis for credit; compliment
    (2) Credit terms; payments, discounts, limits
  b. *For cash or credit:* Resale on services same as IV, 2c(1) and (2)
  Resale on products ordered; highlights on special features—adapted to buyer
  c. *For cash customer:* Perhaps credit application form enclosed, with invitation to return it for consideration.
	2. Explanation
	  a. Pertinent comments, and details regarding favor— what is being or will be done, etc.
	  b. Questions, if necessary, pertaining to favor
		2. Explanation
		  a. Details to emphasize, reader benefits, if possible
		In admission of error:
		  b. Explanation apology; emphasis on sincere desire to serve well
		  c. Resale on firm, products, or services, as appropriate
			2. Explanation, if needed:
			  a. Comments
			  b. Instructions

3. Courteous close
  a. Forward look to pleasant service and orders (not greedy)
  b. Suggested action
  c. EA[2]
  d. RB[4]
  e. Courtesy, suggestion of further help, if pertinent
	3. Courteous close
	  a. Cordial, pertinent comment; perhaps a forward look, good wish, compliment, or request
		3. Courteous close
		  a. CSAD[1]
		  b. EA[2]
		  c. DA[3]
		  d. RB[4] and/or offer of further help
		  e. Courtesy
			3. Courteous close
			  a. CSAD[1]
			  b. EA[2]
			  c. DA[3]
			  d. Offer of further help or other items or RB[4] about items transmitted

[1] CSAD = clear statement of action desired
[2] EA = easy action
[3] DA = dated action, if desirable
[4] RB = reader benefit

CHAPTER 9
Bad-News Messages

Whenever you must send a message that your reader will consider disappointing or unfavorable in some way, the situation requires special planning and careful choice of words. A competent communicator can actually win or keep a friend for his or her company even when refusing an inquirer's request or transmitting other unfavorable facts.

Many of the bad-news letters and memorandums you may have to write can be grouped under the following unfavorable replies and unfavorable unsolicited messages:

Unfavorable replies

Answering non-sales-related inquiries when the information is undesirable

Refusing adjustments on claims and complaints

Refusing credit

Acknowledging orders you can't fill now or at all

Declining requests for favors

Unfavorable unsolicited messages

Announcing bad news about prices and/or services

Penalizing for nonconformity with rules and procedures

Conveying other bad news

This chapter discusses the right attitude for transmitting bad news, suggests plans for bad-news messages, presents various examples of unfavorable replies and unsolicited messages, and provides capsule checklists.

THE RIGHT ATTITUDE

Everything you learned in preceding chapters about the communication process, consideration, and courtesy toward your reader applies to bad-news messages. In such messages it is especially important that the *tone* of your letter be appropriate. Because the right attitude toward your recipient will improve the tone and thus the effectiveness of your letters, keep the following additional suggestions in mind when you write bad-news letters:

1. *Remember that every letter you write can be considered a sales letter.* You are trying to sell your reader on the idea that your decision, though contrary to his or her request or action, is fair, necessary, and reasonable—and possibly even to his or her advantage in the long run.

2. *Try honestly to see things from the other person's point of view.* A statement such as, "It will be advantageous to you if you work it out this way. . . ." is much more effective than the selfish, "It would be inconvenient for us (or against our policy) to do as you ask."

3. *Avoid leaning on company rules or policy;* it seldom soothes your reader. Include, if possible, the *customer-benefit reasons* that are behind your rules and procedures.

4. *Look for the best in the other person.* Although a customer may be mistaken, try to have confidence that she or he honestly wants to do the right thing. The following expressions show faith in the reader:

```
We are confident that you . . .
You are probably wondering how you can . . .
You will agree, I believe, that . . .
```

5. *When praising a person, single him or her out; when criticizing, put the person in a group; and mention mistakes impersonally.*

Single out:	You certainly made the right decision, Mr. Brown.
As a group:	Sometimes people, unknowingly, make the wrong decision.
Impersonal:	Some figures in this list need to be rechecked for errors.

6. *Shield the reader's pride.*

Tactless:	If you had read the instructions I gave you, you would have noticed that they specifically state you had to sign the acceptance form within 30 days.
Tactful:	Our commitment was good for 30 days. In the instructions that you received with the . . . you will find. . . .

7. *Talk with the reader; do not talk down to him or her.*

Condescending:	We are willing to look into this matter for you.
Agreeable:	Thank you for taking the time to tell us about . . . . We always appreciate . . . .

PLANS FOR BAD-NEWS MESSAGES

The underlying purpose of every bad-news message is to present the unpleasant facts with you-attitude—in such a way that the reader will consider you fair and reasonable and, preferably, remain a friend of the organization you represent. Your choice of message plan is influenced by the circumstances—your purpose, your relationship to the reader, and the particular facts in each case. You have two choices of plans: the indirect or the direct.

Indirect Plan

Before you read the suggested indirect pattern for stating bad news, try an experiment on yourself. Suppose you, as a customer, have been waiting for a reply to your request for something you want very much from a business firm— a refund or perhaps a loan important to you. How would you react if the reply began with a negative statement similar to these:

```
We regret (are sorry, wish to state) that we are unable to refund
the $300 down payment you made on the car.
```

or

```
Your application for a loan (refund) has been denied (refused, re-
jected).
```

Wouldn't you feel more receptive toward the firm and its bad news if the reply had opened with at least a brief agreeable statement—like the following—and then presented an explanation *before* the bad news?

```
We appreciate your letter telling us how you feel about the 198___
hard-top Mercury you purchased from us three months ago.
```

or

```
Thank you for giving us the opportunity to consider your loan ap-
plication for financing your proposed home purchase.
```

Most people appreciate hearing at least some explanation before the bad-news decision, especially if it seriously affects them. Usually a good rule to consider is: "Be quick to give good news, but take longer to tell the bad news." Thus, whereas the good-news message uses a direct approach, the bad-news message usually follows the indirect approach. Using this approach, the bad-news plan has the following four-part suggested organizational structure:

1. Buffer
2. Explanation and analysis of circumstances
3. Decision—implied or expressed—with resale and/or constructive suggestions
4. Friendly, positive close

1. Buffer.
If possible, fill your first paragraph with mainly reader-interest information—to get in step with your reader. However, your buffer must begin close to the general subject of your letter; avoid irrelevant material. Also, avoid statements that might mislead the reader into thinking you are grant-

ing the request; such statements merely build the reader up for a sad letdown! Apologies are unwarranted if your firm is not at fault. One or more of the following buffers can help put your reader in a more receptive attitude:

   a. *Agreement.* Agree with your reader on something, if possible (perhaps a matter-of-fact comment on which there is general agreement—business conditions, costs, or any other pertinent item).

   b. *Appreciation.* Thank the reader (for a check, information, application, request, inquiry, cooperation, or whatever applies).

   c. *Assurance.* Assure the reader of careful consideration and explanation of all available facts about the problem.

   d. *Compliment.* Try to compliment the reader on something good about his or her past record or request (sincerity, careful listing of all pertinent facts, etc.).

   e. *Cooperation.* Show a sincere desire to be as helpful as possible.

   f. *Good news.* If you can grant any part of a request and you think your reader will be pleased, begin with that good news.

   g. *Neutral courtesy.* Keep your opening paragraph noncommittal. For instance, if you must announce an unfavorable price increase or service decrease, use neutral words such as "needed change."

   h. *Understanding.* Show you understand or sympathize with the reader's problem (desire to have a dependable product, to pay at least a partial amount due, etc.).

2. Explanation and Analysis.

Include honest, convincing reasons why under the circumstances the matter must be handled differently from the way the reader wants it. In two types of situations, however, stating a reason is unnecessary: (1) when the matter is routine and obvious (clerical error) and (2) when you'd get mired in negative or confidential material if you tried to explain. When you decide to include an explanation, place it *before* the decision and remember these suggestions:

   a. Try to convince the reader you are acting in his or her best interests in the long run, or at least according to a law that is enforced equally for all. Avoid the insincere: "Much as I would like to . . . however . . ." Also avoid reasons that suggest benefit only to your firm.

   b. Explain courteously all pertinent facts behind your decision. Mention first the favorable factors, then the less favorable ones.

   c. If the reason is confidential or too complicated to explain, then show—as a substitute—that the request has been carefully and sincerely considered (for the reader's benefit as well as your company's).

3. Decision—Implied or Expressed—with Resale and/or Constructive Suggestions.

Make the decision clear, positive, concise; embed it in favorable material, if possible. You have these alternatives:

   a. If the reasons are so sound that your reader will conclude you *must* refuse the request, payment, or such, you can omit the negative entirely and make the bad-news decision clear by implication. For example, if you are already scheduled as luncheon speaker in Chicago on May 6, omit saying, "Therefore, I cannot attend your luncheon in St. Louis that same day."

b. If an implied decision might be misunderstood, express your decision briefly and clearly, near the end of the explanation. Be careful never to mislead or cause your reader to be uncertain about your decision. The best place for a negative decision is in the middle—not the beginning—of a paragraph, and never in a paragraph by itself. Avoid "must refuse," "cannot grant," and similar negatives.

c. If you can, offer a constructive suggestion, counterproposal, compromise, alternative course of action, or a ray of hope for the future. By emphasizing what *can* be done, you may clearly imply what can*not* be done, without actually using the negatives. For instance, if you must refuse requested credit, you can offer a lay-away plan; instead of a requested personal interview, you can enclose a helpful booklet to answer questions.

d. If desirable, resell the reader on your company's services and/or practices and policies.

4. **Friendly, Positive Close.**
   End on a positive note, with one or more of these ideas:
   a. Assure the reader he or she is appreciated as a customer (or as an interested inquirer and possible future customer).
   b. Invite future patronage, cooperation, suggestions, and/or compliance with the decision. Include mild, no-pressure sales promotional material if you think your reader is in the right mood for it.
   c. If you are awaiting his or her approval or if he or she should take some action, make clear what the customer is to do, when to do it, and how to do it easily.
   d. Express continued interest, service, and reader benefit.

Direct Plan

Though you can use the indirect bad-news plan for most unfavorable messages, there are situations that may warrant the direct approach. Again, the choice depends upon the particular circumstances. You may decide to begin directly with the bad news if you have:

A routine or small matter on which the reader is likely not to be seriously disappointed or personally emotionally involved—especially a message between employees of two business firms or within the same firm (and perhaps also to a person who is known to prefer reading the bad news in the first paragraph!).

or

An urgent message that should be called to the reader's attention forcefully—as in the late stages of a collection procedure.

If you use the direct approach, the pattern is essentially the same as the direct good-news plan, except that the opening contains bad instead of good news.

---

1. Bad-news decision (with or without a brief buffer)
2. Explanation
3. Appropriate courteous ending

Most examples of bad-news replies and unsolicited messages in this chapter are organized by the *indirect* approach (hereafter referred to as the bad-news plan). For examples of messages organized according to the direct approach, you will find the words *direct plan* in the title.

UNFAVORABLE REPLIES TO REQUESTS

This section focuses on unfavorable replies to requests for information about non-sales-related subjects, adjustment, credit, orders, and favors.

Answering Non-Sales-Related Inquiries When the Information Is Undesirable

Occasionally you may have to write bad-news answers to non-sales-related inquiries. Whenever you send bad news to anyone outside your firm, it is usually better to follow the bad-news plan.

When you receive a request for a recommendation on a person about whom you have only unfavorable information, and whom you honestly cannot recommend, you have four alternatives:

1. Call the inquirer on the telephone and discuss the matter (with prudence).
2. Write a brief refusal similar to the following:

   On the basis of my experience with Tom Dawson, I am sorry to inform you that I do not have sufficient favorable information to recommend him for the position (credit) for which you are considering him.

3. Omit the applicant's name throughout the reply (use: "the person about whom you inquire in your letter of April 10")[1] and include whatever facts are pertinent regarding employment, credit, or personal record.

---

[1] Omitting the applicant's name is acceptable if you are sure your reader knows whom you are writing about. However, such a practice could be extremely confusing and lead to mix-ups if the same two firms happen to correspond about two or more persons on the same day! Employers who exchange information frequently might set up a file number for each person on whom they seek information. Replies would then be about a file number (known to the employer and respondent as a specific person).

4. Include both the applicant's name and an honest, frank report, as in message 1. Because of libel laws it is imperative to be cautious and scrupulously accurate. (See also the five conditions on page 195 and Appendix A.) The following letter to a counselor uses the bad-news plan. Notice the first paragraph is basically a buffer of neutral courtesy; it does not reveal the bad news. Only after stating facts does the writer state a decision. This person may become a truly desirable employee with benefit of a counseling service.

Message 1–Letter

A frank confidential nonrecommendation of an unsatisfactory former employee.

Full name; work

Tom Zoe, about whom you inquire, was on our payroll five months—from April 198_ until two months ago. He was hired as a messenger and a sign painter's helper.

Facts

Because his job with our firm was his first since he quit high school, we tried to be more understanding about his personal problems that affected his work. I must tell you confidentially that Tom had been victimized by unfortunate home experiences which caused him to drift into careless habits from the standpoint of responsibility and reliability.

Unfavorable work

Decision

His attendance record with us shows an average of one absence every six days. As both a messenger and helper he abused rules and privileges. Because each time he promised to do better, we gave him several extra opportunities to straighten himself out. Unfortunately the pattern became worse instead of better and we finally had to replace him. Thus, on the basis of our experience with him, I am sorry I cannot recommend him for responsible work. I am glad to see that he is now getting the help of your counseling service and sincerely hope he will develop right attitudes.

Hope for the future

Perhaps in time he will be able to establish himself with really worthwhile activities. You have my sincere good wishes.

The best overall policy is: be honest, tactful, and aware of your fourfold responsibility—to the applicant, to the addressee, to yourself, and to civil rights laws.

When you're writing to someone in your own organization about a relatively small matter with which the reader is not emotionally involved, you probably should use the *direct* refusal plan, as in the following memo.

Message 2–Memo

A bad-news direct-plan memo about company equipment.

TO: Ann Brown, Purchasing
FROM: Harry Mills, Plant 2
SUBJECT: New ventilating fans needed

Bad news

Today Fred Jones, representative of Ace Electric, told me that the noisy fans you asked about can't be repaired or adjusted again. He says they're a total loss. The only thing possible for ventilation is to buy new fans.

Details

Three fans, model XA22, should do the job well. They'll cost us $80 apiece installed. Jake says he can install these fans this coming Saturday.

Action request

If you approve, I'll go ahead and make arrangements. Fred needs two days' notice, because he'll order what we need from the factory. Will you give me a jingle by Wednesday afternoon?

If your firm is a nonprofit organization that gets large numbers of requests for free information—and if you often need to send bad-news replies—you may, to cut correspondence costs, even devise a form letter listing the most recurring negative facts.

Message 3–Letter

Printed form letter to handle a nonprofit organization's multiple inquiries for which many answers may have to be bad news.

Buffer: thanks

Thank you for your recent inquiry. In the interest of economy your request is being answered by this form letter. Check marks and the comments below indicate the action taken.

Facts; implied decisions

1. The item or information you requested is
   (a) enclosed _____,
   (b) out of print. Copies are in many libraries _____.
   (c) not yet available _____; will be sent later _____; related material is enclosed _____.
   (d) not a publication of this organization _____.
2. Your request will be filled as soon as our supply is replenished _____.
3. The free supply of this report is exhausted _____. Copies may be purchased from (name and address) for _____ cents a copy.

4. Your request has been referred to _____
_____ .

Suggestions for future action

If you write us again in regard to this request,
please return the enclosed correspondence, since we
have retained no record of it.

(Printed name and title of writer)

Comments:

Refusing Adjustments on Claims and Complaints

When you refuse a request for adjustment, realize that the customer is probably
disgruntled and even irritated, and be particularly tactful when "selling" on the
fairness of your refusal. Especially important material to include—besides
your buffer and explanation—is resale material, constructive suggestions, and
even sales promotion when appropriate.

This section discusses two kinds of unwarranted customer claims on which
you may have to write a refusal: (1) when the customer is at fault regarding a
product, (2) when the customer is mistaken in a complaint about an account or
a service.

When the Customer Is at Fault regarding a Product

Often, customers who claim free replacement or repair of a "malfunctioning"
product are at fault because they violated instructions for using it. Or a
customer might return as "new" an article which cannot be resold because of
something the customer did wrong. Also, many customers seek a refund or
credit on items simply because they have changed their mind. The next three
examples illustrate satisfactory adjustment refusals in such cases.

Misuse of a Product. Notice that in message 4 the writer calls attention to
the user's mistake indirectly and that she shields the reader's pride. She
doesn't say, "You violated the instructions" or, "You obviously failed to read
the directions." Instead, the message includes a tactful, logical explanation and
an implied but clear refusal, followed by a constructive suggestion and easy-
action, reader-benefit ending.

Message 4–Letter

A mail-order house refuses to replace free a broken, misused garden hose.

Buffer: agreement, appreciation

When you buy a Widgeon product, you are right to expect high quality. We appreciate your returning the
hose for our inspection so that we can meet our
goal—satisfying your needs.

Resale; assurance about honoring guarantee

To provide each of our thousands of Widgeon customers with the specific hose he or she needs, we carry a wide selection. Each type of garden hose described in the Widgeon catalog is guaranteed to give you the service it was designed for. We are always glad to replace a hose provided its defect lies with assembly or materials.

Reason for hose breakdown

Implied refusal

As stated in the catalog, the Opaque Plastic Hose you bought is recommended only for use in mild climates and also it is not to be shut off at the nozzle. Since Mount Vernon's weather ranges in temperature annually from −15 to +105°F, you can see how these extremes may have affected the splitting of the hose. Laboratory analysis indicates that the damage was caused by excessive water pressure resulting from either shutting the hose off at the nozzle or from water pressure greater than that normally found in most cities. Because Mt. Vernon has the normal water pressure of 60 pounds per square inch, the split occurred because someone shut the hose off at the nozzle.

Constructive suggestion

Two Widgeon hoses——the Gold-Line Plastic and the Neoprene Rubber——are especially recommended for shutting off at the nozzle. In addition, you can use the Neoprene Rubber Hose even in harsh weather. Both are described on the enclosed copy of catalog page 977.

Easy action; reader benefit

After you have decided which hose best meets your needs, fill out the enclosed order form and mail it in the envelope with your check or money order for $9.97 or $11.98, which includes shipping costs; or indicate that you wish c.o.d. shipment. Either way you can be watering your garden again just three days after we receive your order. And you can be sure of many years' dependable service.

Unsalability of Returned Product. Some products (for instance, prescription drugs and undergarments) cannot—because of state or national statutes—be accepted for return after they have left the store. In such cases the explanation is easy. However, sometimes a customer may try to return a product he or she has damaged or owned for so long that the store can no longer resell it. Then a tactful detailed letter like message 5 may be necessary.

Message 5–Letter

A retail-clothing-store adjustment manager refuses to accept a returned evening gown.

Buffer: assurance; thanks

To please our customers is the foremost aim of Bon-James. Thank you for writing us explaining your wishes about the evening gown you purchased here last month.

Reader benefit facts about exchange policy in general

We want you and all our other customers to enjoy the confidence of knowing that any purchase from us is for merchandise of outstanding quality and style and that it is absolutely clean, fresh, and new. Wearing apparel may be returned for full credit anytime within 30 days provided the garment is in clean, resalable condition.

Findings in this case

Implied decision

To maintain the high standard on the goods we sell, we carefully check returned merchandise before it is again placed for sale. This examination of the gown you mailed to us disclosed facial makeup at the neckline and several brown spots near the hemline. Because cleaning would render the garment "used" to anyone wishing to repurchase it, the gown is unacceptable for resale.

Helpful suggestions

You can be sure that the skillful touch of our fitter will make the sleeves of your Dior evening gown just the length you like best. For this reason, we suggest that you stop in to see Mr. Davis, who served you when you purchased the gown. He will hold it for you until you can come in for a fitting; or, if you want us to send it to you without any changes, he will arrange its prompt return.

Easy action

Resale

Please check and mail your preference on the enclosed card. You can depend upon us to do everything possible to help you feel pleased with the gown. You can wear it for several years with confidence that it is a highly fashionable evening garment. As you may recall, it was an outstanding success in the designer show held in New York on June 2.

When the Customer Is Mistaken in a Complaint about an Account or a Service

In addition to refusing adjustments on returned merchandise, you may also have bad-news for customers who make erroneous claims resulting from a variety of intangible grievances. Among them are unwarranted claims about their account balances and unjustified gripes about various aspects of your firm's service. Many firms now handle most of these complaints by telephone whenever possible.

Unwarranted Claims about Account Balances. When customers think you have made an error and you find your records are correct, you must give the customers the bad news that they owe more than they claim. You need to assure them that you have carefully rechecked their records and want to cooperate fully. Be sure to explain each additional charge clearly, for your readers may have forgotten that a purchase or late charges were added or that some past checks were returned by the bank for various reasons. If the matter is too complicated for a phone explanation, a letter will be more helpful—with a tabulation of figures or a photostatic copy of the record.

Unjustified Gripes about Company Services. Careful and tactful explanation is desirable to establish your company's accuracy and resell the reader on its usual high-quality service. For instance, the printer who is wrongly accused of misspelling a name on the customer's stationery may have to send a copy of the customer's original handwritten order showing the identical spelling. Professional cleaners may reduce customer gripes by sending a printed note like the following, with a cleaned garment or rug that has unremovable stains:

> We've tried and tried, but find that the stains on this (*item name*) cannot be removed without possible injury to the color or fabric. This has been called to your attention so that you will know it has not been overlooked.

If a customer does complain, a detailed oral or written explanation may have to include specific facts about the extra care and time devoted by the experienced workers skilled in modern spot-removing processes. Likewise, similar procedures are desirable in all other types of business regarding their services. The message should tactfully convince the customer that the firm has well earned the fee and in fairness must charge for an honest job.

Refusing Credit

Even when you are refusing a credit application, you want to try to keep the reader's goodwill. A person's credit reputation is quite important. Thus, a credit manager has responsibilities to make sound, informed decisions. In fact, there are federal laws concerning credit. If someone makes a wrong decision, his or her company could be involved in a lawsuit and unfavorable publicity. A credit manager must be careful about what he or she writes and how reasons are expressed.[2] Refusals of both retail and mercantile credit are organized by the bad-news plan, though their contents differ.

Retail Credit Refusals

For various reasons, approving credit purchases of some customers may be undesirable or impossible. Also, sometimes a customer who has credit established must be told that further credit purchases will be stopped until a current balance is reduced or even paid in full. Other decisions may involve those people who move into the city and want credit immediately; unsettled divorce actions which bring different problems; young people who are just getting started in married life and who may be good risks, but yet have no established credit record; and others.

Opening Paragraph. The refusal usually begins with a buffer that refers to the firm's appreciation or careful consideration of the reader's request for credit and/or to his or her interest in the store.

---

[2] Some credit departments use the telephone for all their refusals. Even if you work in such a department, you will find that you can apply many of the writing principles in this chapter to your oral refusals.

Explanation. These parts of retail credit refusals vary considerably, but four ways of handling the *reasons for refusal* are in common use:

1. Reason is omitted entirely (see letter 1).
2. "Insufficient information" is the only reason given (see letter 2).
3. Factors generally considered in evaluating credit applications are stated without indicating specifically which apply to the reader (see letter 3).
4. Specific reasons are stated (see letter 4).

The first three of these methods can be easily adapted by credit departments that find it necessary to use form letters because of a large number of applications (often over a wide geographic area). Because of similar names among the thousands of individual requests, mix-ups and errors do occur. Thus credit managers for firms which handle numerous requests find it safer to omit specific reasons, especially those that pertain to undesirable character and poor pay habits. From the customer's standpoint the refusal which omits the reason entirely is the least helpful (although it may save some embarrassment). The "insufficient information" reason is considered by some customers to be artificial and insincere; nevertheless both methods 2 and 3 are popular and usually acceptable under certain circumstances, provided the constructive suggestion is tactful and helpful.

Letter 1

No stated reason. An unhelpful retail credit refusal.

Buffer: appreciation	Thank you for your confidence in us as expressed by your recent credit application.
Decision	After careful consideration, we find that at this time it would be better for you to continue your purchases from us on a cash basis.
Forward look (weak)	We hope you will give us frequent opportunities to serve you from our wide selection in each of our stores.

Letter 2

Insufficient-information reason. A popular retail credit refusal inviting a conference as well as cash purchases.[3]

Buffer: thanks	We sincerely appreciate the preference you have shown Mack's by your application for a charge account.

---

[3] The last paragraph of letter 2 refers to buying on a cash basis. Because some customers consider this suggestion obvious—maybe even offensive—you can avoid reference to cash by wording the last paragraph in a way similar to that in letter 3.

Explanation: insufficient information

Decision

Suggestions: conference

As you know, the usual custom before opening a new account is to get information which will serve as a
basis for credit. Such information as we have thus
far obtained is insufficient for us to pass favorably
upon your request at this time. If you feel there are
other details which would favorably affect your
credit, you are welcome to call on us so that we can
consider all the facts.

Cash buying. Resale

In the meantime, please let us supply your needs on a
cash basis. We will make every effort to serve you
well with high quality merchandise and friendly service.

Letter 3

List of factors (general reasons) usually considered. A popular retail credit refusal inviting reapplication and layaway (with no reference to cash buying).

Thank you . . .

Buffer: thanks

for your recent inquiry regarding the status of your
credit application.

Explanation: list of factors considered

A number of factors are taken into consideration when
reviewing an application. Length of time at one residence and employment are of vital importance—as well
as income, assets, and the paying record of current
and past obligations.

Implied decision; assurance; invitation

You are assured that all the above available information has been carefully analyzed in your case.
Circumstances may improve in the future, at which time
we would be pleased to reconsider your new request for
credit.

Reader benefit invitation to purchase; no mention of cash

In the meantime, we invite you to save on your household and clothing purchases at Ranney's regular
everyday low prices and frequent sales. Also, of
course, you're welcome to use our easy layaway plan
for bigger purchases.

The fourth method of refusing credit—stating specific reasons—is desirable when the following conditions exist:

The situation requires an individually typed reply (as in an application for a
large loan).

The reason does not involve poor (dishonest, unreliable) personal character.

The desired relationship between the credit department and the applicant
is somewhat personal.

The applicant cannot come for a personal interview and is likely to be offended with anything but an individual helpful letter.

Such letters are usually longer—and harder to write—than the first three types, but when tactful and accurate they are highly appreciated by the recipient because they indicate what must be done to earn (or restore) a good credit standing.

Some large firms use printed forms with courteous opening paragraphs and then a list of perhaps 20 possible reasons for credit refusals. In front of each is a small square. The sender checks only the reason(s) applicable to the reader. These forms may also state (at the bottom or reverse side) the applicant's rights according to law.

Decision, Resale, Suggestions. In stating your decision, avoid such negatives as "did not approve," "unfavorable," "does not meet," "must decline." Instead of stressing what is wrong, suggest (whenever possible) how the situation can be improved. Often you can combine resale and constructive alternatives with either the decision or the ending paragraph. In line with circumstances, the applicant may be invited to take one or more of these steps:

1. Come to an office to discuss the case if he or she has questions or thinks an error has been made.
2. Apply again later when conditions have improved
3. Contact another lender or credit agency that you name
4. Examine his or her record at the credit bureau and write any needed corrections[4]
5. Use the layaway plan or another suitable credit plan
6. Continue buying from the company on a cash or c.o.d. basis

Ending Paragraph. The suggested action ties in with one of these suggestions and, if possible, includes a reader benefit. Compare letters 2, 3, and 4.

Letter 4

Specific reasons: inadequate income. An individually typed loan refusal.

Buffer: compliment; favorable aspects

You are to be complimented on your desire to provide the best possible housing for your family. Also, both your loan application and credit report indicate that you have maintained a steady employment record. This too is commendable.

---

[4] See footnote 3, p. 204, about functions of city credit bureaus. The Fair Credit Reporting Act gives rejected applicants certain rights to request from consumer reporting agencies disclosure of adverse information and correction of errors. Also, for a small fee, they may see their credit bureau report if they merely want to check its accuracy. If you are moving from one city to another, it is an excellent idea to check your current report, then request that it be sent to the bureau nearest your new home.

Explanation: reasoning from general to specific

Reader-benefit decision

In mortgage lending, however, extensive studies have revealed that a certain relationship between a person's income, fixed monthly expense, and loan amount should exist to make a loan advisable. Our maximum loan is 2½ times the annual income, or payments may not exceed 20 percent of the monthly income. Since your income at present meets neither of these requirements, you can understand why we feel that an additional financial burden will not serve your best interests.

Suggestion

If you would like to stop in my office, I will be glad to go over with you the minimum requirements for a smaller loan. This discussion might help you in setting and planning your desired goal for home ownership. As time goes on and your income increases, you will be able to improve your financial position to the point where we can help you buy a newer and larger home.

Future help

Feel welcome to come in any day between 9 and 5. We sincerely want to help you reach your desired goal.

Mercantile Credit Refusals

Wholesale or mercantile credit is that which is extended by one business firm to another. The preferred organizational pattern for these credit refusals is the bad-news plan.

For the buffer you have choices similar to those used in retail refusals—appreciation and assurance of careful consideration.

The most noticeable difference between retail and mercantile credit refusals is that the latter are generally more forthright in the reasons for refusal and are individually typewritten. The decision is based on the firm's financial statement plus other credit ratings (by Dun and Bradstreet, special rating agencies, creditors, and sales agencies of the wholesaler or manufacturer considering the applicant). As with retail credit, the emphasis should be on the positive—the desirable goal—rather than on what is wrong now.

A mercantile credit refusal can include one or more reader-benefit suggestions:

1. Reduction of apparently excessively high inventory by special means
2. Ways to build up customer's volume of sales (and working capital, if pertinent); perhaps offering assistance of your firm's sales representative
3. Advantages of modest buying, local financing, and cash discounts
4. Cash purchases—smaller, more frequent orders
5. Cash on delivery or cash with orders earning discount privilege
6. Review of the applicant's credit situation at a future time

One good test for any letter is what your reaction to it would have been if you had received it. Would you feel offended if you were the retailer? Would you buy from the wholesaler? True, you're not getting credit, but does the writer seem sincere and interested in helping you?

Acknowledging Orders You Can't Fill Now or At All

Whenever you get an order which you cannot fill immediately, your acknowledgment will be at least temporarily bad news to your customer. The customer is expecting the goods ordered, and any intervening message from you may delay delivery and cause some inconvenience. This section discusses bad-news acknowledgments regarding incomplete or vague orders, back orders, and substitution orders.

Many firms handle routine and repeat orders by preprocessed forms. These are acceptable when the firm sells cataloged, small, or low-profit items and when the situation does not require much detailed explanation. One common timesaving way to indicate portions of routine orders that cannot be filled as requested is to use rubber-stamped (or typewritten) comments inserted on printed acknowledgments (like the stamped S7 comment regarding a substitution in "letter" 1 that follows).

"Letter" 1

A printed order acknowledgment with stamped comment (S7), used by a national retail mail-order firm.

COMPANY NAME OF SELLER		INVOICE NO. ____	
Thank you for your order. It received our careful attention. Any changes necessary in filling your order are explained by stamp impressions or by letters.	Catalog Number L5021 Current Price $3.85	VALUE OF GOODS	
PLEASE DO NOT DESTROY THESE PAPERS until you are satisfied that your order is all right in every respect.		TAX	
	Catalog Number L5053 Current Price $4.95	SHIPPING CHARGES	
	(S7) OUR SELECTION IS THE NEAREST TO YOUR CHOICE THAT WE CAN FURNISH. IT IS BETTER MERCHANDISE AT NO INCREASE IN PRICE.	TOTAL AMOUNT	
IF YOU WRITE US about this order, please be sure to return ALL these papers with your letter. It will help us give you prompt service.			
IF YOU RETURN ANY PART of this order, please glue the envelope containing these papers and your letter to the outside of the package and apply additional mailing postage for the envelope.	This is the amount charged by the post office for c.o.d. service. The delivering postmaster also collects a fee to pay for the money order sent to us. You can save the c.o.d. fee expense by including total remittance with future orders.	←U.S. MAIL C.O.D.–FEE	
		TOTAL AMOUNT OF C.O.D.	

Though processed form letters are time-savers, they are impersonal and cold. Many times the customer expects or deserves a more detailed explanation. Situations that require phone calls or personal letters are discussed below.

Incomplete or Vague Orders

If an order that omits necessary information comes from a customer who has never before ordered the items in question, you probably cannot guess what is wanted. It is always better to telephone the customer than to risk errors and annoyance. Your main goal is to keep the customer sold on your goods and to get whatever information is missing so you can fill the order soon.

If the order lists some items that you are sending now, mention them first, of course. If not, begin with a buffer—usually short resale on the product about which the order is incomplete, appreciation for the order, and, if a first order from a customer, welcome. Then, before you request the missing information or payment, state a reader-benefit reason—that you want to be sure to send exactly what will be liked best. Shield the reader's pride by omitting such words as "you forgot" or "you failed to." Be sure to include explanatory facts the customer needs to complete the order, such as sizes or color choice available. If a letter (instead of a phone call) is necessary, include pictures, catalog numbers, sketches, swatches, and other helpful items when appropriate. Make customer action easy, and assure prompt shipment, if true.

Orders for Out-of-Stock Items to Be Back-Ordered

If your stock of an ordered item is temporarily depleted and you expect a new shipment within a reasonable time (one or two weeks), you can usually back-order and assume the customer would rather wait than cancel the order.

As with the incomplete-order acknowledgment, your main goal in the back-order letter is to keep the customer sold on your goods and to serve him or her well. Because of the necessary delay in waiting for the return of the out-of-stock item, your message should again be organized by the bad-news plan.

Your buffer can be resale on the ordered item (to reinforce the customer's confidence in her or his choice), appreciation, and (if appropriate) a welcome.

Your explanation should focus on the positive aspects—the date the goods will or can reach the customer. Be sure to omit such negatives as "cannot send," "out of stock," "exhausted," "Won't have any . . . until." Instead, say something like this:

```
We will be able to ship these radios to you by May 15, when our re-
ordered new shipment from the factory is expected here.
```

Your explanation should preferably include a reason for your being out of the item, so the customer won't think your firm is inefficient. If such reason(s) pertain to high popularity or exceptional demand, this even strengthens your resale and the customer's desire for the item. In your action-getting close, positive suggestion is again useful. The easiest way for the customer to "show" approval of the back order is to take no action. Thus back-order acknowledgments often include the positive:

Shipment will be made as soon as we receive the new supplies, unless you instruct us to the contrary.

If the wait might be unreasonably long, you should ask the customer to let you know (perhaps by an easy-action reply card) whether he or she approves of your shipping on the later date. Your emphasis whenever possible should be on acceptance, not cancellation. Sometimes a bit of sales promotion material on seasonal or related goods is appropriate, if it is included clearly for the customer's benefit—as a service to the customer rather than just another sale for your firm.

A short message like letter 2 is sufficient for one temporarily out-of-stock item.

Letter 2

Acknowledging an order from a long-time charge customer on an item to be back-ordered.

Buffer: thanks; acknowledgment	Thank you for your order for one dozen Perkup 26—inch Window Fans, at $42 each.
Resale; explanation	The demand for this newest three—speed reversible fan has far exceeded our most optimistic expectations at this time of year, with the result that we have twice reordered from the factory. The manufacturer has assured us that our new supply will be delivered within 10 days.
Decision: expected delivery date; reader benefit	You may plan on receiving a rush shipment of your fans before March 20. Your customers will like the way these automatic thermostatically controlled Perkups enable them to enjoy cool breezes indoors regardless of the heat outdoors.

Orders for Out-of-Stock Items on Which You Suggest a Substitute

When you get an order for a certain model or brand that you cannot supply soon enough by back-order or that has been discontinued, you can often suggest a substitute by telephone—provided you honestly think it will meet the customer's needs.

Usually it is safer to ask permission to substitute before you ship, as in letter 3, especially if the customer must pay a higher price for the newer line and if the items are breakable or otherwise costly to ship. (Unfortunate ship-

pers who have sent large substitute shipments without permission have sometimes had to pay many dollars in express charges both ways for rejected
merchandise returned by a displeased customer.)

Letter 3

Suggesting a substitute in place of an ordered discontinued item.

Buffer: brand resale, thanks	You can be sure that your decision to buy a Semco was a decision to buy the finest. Many thanks for your order on June 27 for a Semco office storage cabinet.
Explanation for new model (substitute) *Where ordered item might be obtained*	Early this year, in line with business executives' increasing need for better internal security, the Semco factory came out with a new model storage cabinet, the C-402. Because it has all the features our customers have been asking for, we now stock this model exclusively. Though it's possible that George's Supply in North Center may still have the model C-302 you ordered, we are sure you will want our newest after you check these improved features of the C-402:

√ . . . HEAVIER GAUGE STEEL than any other cabinet on
the market assures extra heavy duty for extra
safety.
√ . . . REINFORCED DOORS and BASE provide added
sturdiness.
√ . . . DEPENDABLE YALE LOCK makes cabinet tam-
per-proof for stored articles.

Reader-benefit features of substitute

√ . . . ADJUSTABLE SHELVES--six of them--allow easy
storage for almost any size supplies.
√ . . . NEW COLORS blend with your office decor:
mint green, fog grey, or walnut brown.

Easy action	For all these advantages the C-402 is inexpensively priced at only $94.95 delivered to your office. To give me your "OK" for shipment, just call me at (555)873-9999 any weekday between 8 and 5. I'll have your new Semco cabinet on its way to you the same day.
Reader-benefit resale	We'll be happy to deliver it on open account, giving you a full 30 days for payment. You'll be glad you bought the newest Semco: C-402.

Notice that the buffer begins with appreciation and general resale—emphasizing the strongest point of reader appeal that the two articles have in common—
the Semco brand. It omits any point of difference (model number, in this case)
between ordered and substitute items.

The explanation and bad-news decision stress what the firm *does* have
instead of what it does not carry. The new substitute—model C-402—is introduced with one of its merits *before* the bad news that the ordered item—model

C-302—is unavailable. One good way to do this is to state that you now stock the substitute *exclusively* (if true), but don't use the word *substitute* because of its negative connotation. If the substitute is a different brand instead of merely another model of the same brand, do not mention the ordered item by brand name more than once (or at all), because you want the reader to focus attention on your product. However, don't knock your competitor's product; sell your product on its own merits. If you can mention where the ordered product may be obtained, subordinate your statement in a dependent clause, as in letter 3. If the price of the substitute is higher, be sure to state adequate selling points to justify the difference.[5] If your substitute is lower in quality but an excellent value because of price or other reasons, stress these benefits.

Your ending asks for authorization to send the substitute—or tells why you have already sent it. Then make clear that the item comes to the customer on trial or subject to approval. Although you are safer to get approval before sending a substitute, many sellers (such as mail-order firms) substitute quite regularly in orders from repeat customers whose preferences they know. Sometimes substitution is also made in rush orders for very similar same-price inexpensive items or when the company absorbs the price difference.

Declining Invitations and Requests for Favors

Customers, noncustomers, and employees may extend invitations or request various privileges or favors, other than information, which you have to refuse. The bad-news plan is usually the safest to use in most of these refusals. However, in some instances you may use the direct plan, placing the refusal in the first paragraph. This section illustrates a variety of favor refusals, both business-related and personal.

Declining Business-Related Favors

Among the numerous favors that customers ask and that you may have to refuse are: changing requirements or payment due dates, borrowing your company's equipment or premises, seeing your firm's confidential material, getting special reduced rates, or skipping several payments on a contract (as handled by the message below).

Message 1–Letter

A loan officer refuses a customer's request to skip several loan payments.

Buffer: *cooperation;* *thanks*	Accommodating customers is one of our main objectives. Thank you for telling us your viewpoint regarding your loan payments during the summer.

[5] Instead of "is inexpensively priced at," you might write, "is well worth the small additional $5," or "is an excellent value even at $5 more than the older model," if you think your reader would appreciate knowing the price difference.

Explanation; appeal to fair play

Our services involve fair treatment to every borrower with accepted business practice that also protects the investments of our depositors. Exceptions granted to one customer could rightfully be expected of others too, and thus eventually disrupt the entire credit structure. Therefore, the long-established rule is that all payments not made within 10 days of the due date are subject to an added "late payment" charge. When a loan becomes 90 days past due, the law requires that foreclosure action be started.

Implied refusal

Mr. Howe, when you obtained the loan last December, you agreed to repay it in regular monthly payments. Though you were a schoolteacher then (as now), there is no indication in our file that you requested any deviation from the usual 12-month payment schedule. Because most of the high school teachers in this area get their salary each of 12 months, we assumed the same was true for you. However, even on a 9-month basis a teacher does know in advance that he will receive no paychecks during the summer. Many other people have little or no advance indication when their source of income will cease.

Reader-benefit suggestion

The enclosed leaflet was prepared for persons who need to allocate earnings over a 12-month period. You will find it useful, I believe. For the present, you will save the late-payment surcharge if your check reaches us by June 10.

Action request

If you feel that mailing your June check before that due date would impose an extreme hardship on you, please call me at 772-7222. At that time we can make an appointment so that we can work out your problem with you.

On somewhat routine matters between departments of the same firm it is quite permissible to begin directly with the bad-news decision, as in this memo:

Message 2—Memo—Direct Plan

An acceptable direct-plan refusal of a specification change in an airplane factory.

```
TO:         J. R. Lander
FROM:       T. M. Jepson
SUBJECT:    Food and Beverage Elevator
REFERENCE:  RPD-5244-12 dated 6-15-8_
```

Refusal

As shown on page 5 of the specifications, paneling for elevator walls remains a valid requirement. Thus the referenced request to use paint instead of vinyl paneling is unacceptable.

Explanation	Because of the particular uses for this elevator and the expected altitudes for flights, it is necessary that all walls have the extra protection of the exact vinyl as in the specifications instead of mere coats of paint.
Request	Will you please, therefore, see that the paneling requirement is met, according to specifications?

Declining Nonbusiness and Personal Favors

Requests concerning nonbusiness activities may involve donations of your time, money, property, or other assistance. In refusing a nonbusiness favor, include an appropriate buffer, reason(s) before your decision, and (if possible) a helpful suggestion.

Message 3—Letter

A refusal to accept the office of regional director.

Buffer: agreement; compliment; appreciation	XYZ Club has a great deal to offer businesspeople. I've always found it worthwhile. And so I appreciate even more the compliment you expressed in nominating me for the office of regional director.
Reasons	To perform this job adequately, I realize I should travel to the three State Days this coming year and correspond regularly each month with the 22 chapters in this region, before sending monthly reports to our national office. I've given your invitation a good deal of thought, in the light of my present responsibilities as executive trainee at the ABC Company here. My job requires that I devote long hours to the program daily. Often I work Saturdays, too. In addi-
Implied refusal; emphasis on positive	tion, Sally and I must spend a great deal of time with our 3-month-old son. Considering everything, I'm convinced the job would be better filled by someone else for the coming year.
Suggestion	If you'd like a suggestion, you might find Albert J. Smith would be interested in this type of chapter office. He's been active in XYZ for 10 years, two of them as our excellent president. He's an established accountant at the National Gadget Company and is unmarried. AJ enjoys being involved and in my opinion would be a perfect regional director. I'm enclosing a card with AJ's address in case you would like to contact him.
Cordial wishes	You have my best wishes, Jim, for getting the right person. You're doing a terrific job for the organization.

At times you may honestly feel that a request is extremely unreasonable and you're tempted to tell the reader so. If you must get some negative thoughts off your chest, go ahead and write the grumpy letter. But don't mail it immediately. Chances are that the next day you'll decide to soften the tone and improve the message.

UNFAVORABLE UNSOLICITED MESSAGES

You may sometimes have to send unpleasant messages which are not in response to an inquiry. This section illustrates unfavorable announcements about prices and services, rules and procedures, plus miscellaneous bad news. You are generally wise to use the bad-news plan whenever you think your readers will be seriously disappointed or even angered by your bad news. However, when you write to employees or other business associates on routine matters, you may use the direct plan.

Announcing Bad News about Prices and/or Services

When your firm finds it necessary to increase prices and/or curtail services to customers, a buffer opening followed by reasons before the unhappy decision will help break the news gently, as in message 1.

Message 1–Letter

A clear, acceptable announcement by a wholesaler, regarding limitations in services.

Buffer:
neutral courtesy

In reviewing 198_ business and trying to plan for a future in which we can continue to give you good service, it has become evident that some modifications must be made.

Reasons

Decision

Our problems are not unlike yours or anyone else's in business today. All items of expense in business have been constantly increasing without a corresponding increase in profit margin on goods and services. Rather than increase prices in general, the following changes as an alternate plan will become effective July 1 this year:

(1) Free local delivery will be continued only on orders of at least $15. Orders for a lesser amount, if received by 1 p.m. can be delivered the next business day by United Parcel Service or can be sent by our regular delivery service if the customer wishes; but the actual cost of this service will be added to the invoice.

Details on
the decision

(2) Out-of-town shipments will continue to be shipped as instructed by the customer, or instead of instructions, will be routed by the least expensive of Parcel Post, United Parcel Service, or Auto Freight. Actual shipping costs will be added to the invoice.

(3) Collect telephone calls will be accepted only in cases where we have been in error.

Fairness to
customers;
courteous invitation

A decision on these three changes was made after a very careful analysis of our costs in relation to service. We are sure you will agree that these changes are minimal and fair to our customers. If you have any suggestions on how we may improve our service to you, we will greatly appreciate your writing or calling us right now.

In contrast to the *buffer opening* of message 1, to customers, you can use *bad-news direct-approach openings* similar to the following when you announce the same decisions in *memos* to your employees. The first is an opening for a memo about a laundry's increased prices:

Because of increased costs of all materials and operations, TRIM now finds it necessary to increase prices of laundry services. The following new prices will go into effect for all customers May 1, 198_.

And an opening for a memo about the wholesaler's limited services might be:

So that Gray's can continue to give good service without a general increase in prices to our customers, the following restrictions in delivery and telephone services will become effective July 1 this year.

Even for employees, however, you should follow the bad-news plan and begin with a buffer when they are likely to be personally affected or seriously disappointed by your bad-news decision. Suppose, for instance, that your company management has decided to close the employee cafeteria food service mornings and evenings and to keep it open only during noon hours. To partially offset this decrease and to provide for changing employee food preferences, the snack bar service will be increased. Message 2 illustrates a poor way to announce these changes to employees; message 3, a good way. Notice the difference even in subject lines.

Message 2—Memo—Direct Plan

A poor negative, incomplete bad-news announcement to employees about decreased cafeteria service.

```
TO:       All employees of ABC      January 25, 198_
FROM:     Karen Whitson, Food Services Director
SUBJECT:  Closing of Cafeteria for Breakfasts and Suppers
```

Starting next Monday, February 1, there will be no more breakfasts or suppers served in the cafeteria.

This facility will hereafter be closed every morning and afternoon. Lunches will be served in the cafeteria only between 11 a.m. and 2 p.m.

However, to provide continuing service to our employees, the snack bar will be open from 8 a.m. to 5:45 p.m. and offer a wider selection of food.

Message 3–Memo–Indirect Plan

An improved version of the preceding bad-news announcement to employees.

```
TO:       All employees of ABC      January 25, 198_
FROM:     Karen Whitson, Food Services Director
SUBJECT:  Changes in Company Snack Bar and Cafeteria
          Service
```

Buffer: reader-benefit; noncommittal statement

To keep food prices at their present level, in spite of rising costs, and to meet your changing needs——the snack bar and cafeteria services will be modified starting Monday, February 1.

Reasons

Employee benefits

Changes are necessary because during the past three years fewer employees have been eating breakfasts and suppers in the cafeteria and costs of operating it have steadily increased. So that you can continue to benefit from both low prices and good-quality food, we are altering the services and we believe you will like them.

Decision: favorable changes first

Snack Bar Services——The snack bar will be expanded to offer a wider selection of food than ever before. From the semi-self-service counter and the vending machines you can choose:

Packaged Cereals	Fruits and Juices	Sandwiches
Doughnuts	Soft Drinks	Hamburgers
Rolls	Ice Cream	Salads
Coffee, Tea, Milk	Pies and Cakes	Potato Chips
Hot Chocolate	Candy Bars	Soup

Decision: emphasis on the positive

Cafeteria Service——Each day a lunch special consisting of a hot main course, salad, dessert, and drink will be served, as before, for less than $2. The cafeteria will serve only lunches.

New Hours--The new hours effective February 1 are:
Snack Bar --   8 a.m.—5:45 p.m.
Cafeteria -- 11 a.m.—2:00 p.m.

Employee benefits

In addition, the cafeteria doors will remain open be-tween 8 a.m. and 6 p.m. for those of you wishing a meeting place during work breaks or to enjoy food brought from home or the snack bar.

*Forward look:
employee benefits;
invited action*

You are invited to use these facilities whenever you can. They are available to you at no extra price on snacks or lunches. If you have any suggestions on the new cafeteria or snack bar services, please jot them on a slip of paper and drop them into the suggestion box, at the cafeteria door.

Penalizing for Nonconformity with Rules or Procedures

Announcements about penalties for deviating from required procedures or disregarding previous notices quite often begin with the bad news. The direct plan should be used especially when the situation is urgent or when the writer wants the reader to be sure to read the main idea, as in this letter signed by a bank's branch manager:

Message 4–Letter–Direct Plan

Processed announcement about dormant savings accounts; typewritten inside address and salutation.

Main idea

A new (*name*) state law will definitely affect the status of your inactive account #111-2222.

Explanation

Effective March 1, 198_, accounts will be considered dormant after two years of inactivity. The dormant fee will be $10 a year, and dormant accounts earn no interest unless they are activated. Our records indi-cate that there has been no activity on your account for several years.

*Suggestion;
easy action*

Having your passbook updated to reflect the 5½% inter-est earned from past quarters will prevent your account from becoming dormant. At your earliest con-venience before March 1 please complete and return this form in the enclosed postage-paid envelope.

Pleasant close

If you have any question concerning your account, please come in or call me at 222-2222. We are here to serve you.

The form below this letter asks the saver to check an answer to one of two questions: (1) whether he or she is enclosing the passbook for updating, or (2) whether it is lost and thus a Lost Passbook Affidavit should be sent by the bank. Lines are provided for the saver's signature and address change, if any.

Conveying Other Bad News

You may have to write other bad-news unsolicited (and solicited) messages. As a rule, you can handle most of them well by the bad-news plan.

However, one exception to the usual rule for customer bad-news letters is when you must announce that you made a mistake which is not in the customer's favor. In such cases it is often better to admit your error in the opening, as in the next example.

Message 5—Letter—Direct Plan

Announcement of an error that unfavorably affects the reader.

Tactful lead to bad news	We always appreciate the opportunity to be of service to our customers, but I'm sorry to tell you that last month we did you—and ourselves—a disservice.
Details	The correct amount of your February, 198_ premium was $125.61, and we billed you for only $120.55, a difference of $5.06. We overlooked the difference in insurance premium between your former policy and the new policy, which has given you additional coverage since January 1.
Request; easy action	May we ask you to sign the attached form and send it to us with your check for $5.06? Just slip it into the enclosed envelope and mail it.
Goodwill	You can be sure we'll do our best to see that you get accurate service in the future.

The letter of resignation is another bad-news announcement you may have to write. It should include your reason for resigning (ill health, better position, or whatever), appreciation and pleasant comments about the people you are leaving, perhaps a statement of regret, a definite effective date for the resignation, and a sincere, cordial ending. Whether you resign from a job for which you have been paid or from an elective office, you consider your reader(s) and your relationship to them before you decide to organize by the indirect or direct plan.

Message 6—Letter

An indirect-plan letter of resignation (to a board of directors).

Buffer: agreeable statements

During the past four years I've greatly enjoyed working with the many fine people of our state organization. Civil defense is an important and challenging cause.

Reason

Recently I received unexpected news that will seriously affect my activities. Because I have developed a heart condition, my doctors have instructed me to move on a slow bell and particularly emphasized my giving up civil defense. While the condition is not dangerous at present, it is of the "warning" type.

Decision and date of resignation

As you may guess, this is pretty much of a blow to me, but it isn't smart to ignore the advice of our doctors. Thus with much reluctance and regret I must ask to be released from my position as state director of civil defense. It is difficult for me to request that you accept my resignation to become effective immediately after your next month's board meeting.

Good wishes

I assure you that my good wishes will continue to be with you and the great work you are doing.

If this writer had felt that the busy board of directors would prefer reading the main idea in the first paragraph (though it is bad news), he could have chosen the direct plan. The letter might then begin with a sentence like the following and continue with reason, pleasant comments, resignation date, good wishes.

With reluctance and regret I must ask to be released from my position as state director of civil defense.

SUMMARY

Whenever you must write unfavorable news—whether you are replying to a request or initiating an unsolicited message—you are usually safe to follow the indirect, four-part bad-news plan. If you use the direct plan, be sure that the type of message, the situation, and the relationship between yourself and your reader warrant that approach. The Capsule Checklists on pages 266–269 review both plans (column 1) and adapt the indirect plan to nine kinds of bad-news messages.

EXERCISES

Answering Non-Sales-Related Inquiries When the Information Is Undesirable

1. Your new assistant has just laid on your desk the following letter he wrote (to a long-time customer) for your signature as customer service manager of

your firm, Research Consultants. He admits he hasn't had much training in letter writing and says he'd appreciate your comments on his attempt. You decide to rewrite this one for him and let him compare the two versions of this bad-news message. Improve the letter in every way you can—especially the organization and you-attitude. Emphasize positive instead of negative aspects, and maintain goodwill toward your firm. Because you aim to assist this good customer as much as possible, you have asked your staff to contact other sources in addition to your own company files. Those sources may have some materials on plans that do fall into the group the customer discussed. As soon as they have something definite, you will write the customer again.

```
I am sorry to say that, unfortunately, our editors did not find any-
thing in our plan files that would apply to your problem regarding
pension plan summaries for trade association staff employees.
```

```
We have also not yet found any plan elsewhere that would fall into
the class you discussed.
```

```
I wonder if, when you looked through the reports, you did not notice
that there is a pension plan for the Employee Association League of
New York State? I found this plan on pages 106-112. I am not cer-
tain whether this is the type of plan you are interested in.
```

Refusing Adjustments on Claims and Complaints

1. You are the manager of the adjustment and claims department in a small department store with a relatively low volume of business. Therefore, it is the store's unwritten policy to grant few refunds and replacements on items returned 30 days after purchase.

   A customer, Mr. Larry Rimer, recently returned a cardigan sweater with which he was dissatisfied. The sweater was blue knit, size 44, and contained a label which indicated that the sweater was wash and wear but must be washed by hand using a mild detergent. Mr. Rimer decided to return the sweater because after he had washed it in his washing machine, using the wash and wear cycle, the sweater would no longer fit. He had no record of when it was purchased because he had misplaced his sales slip. However, when he came to the store, he stated that he bought the sweater over two months ago. He also indicated that he had washed it on several occasions, using the wash and wear cycle on his washing machine. The sweater, as returned, now appeared to be a size 42 instead of a size 44.

   The customer argued that the label on the sweater said wash and wear and that the store should be accountable. The settlement was not made when the customer came into the store, but you promised to respond to him in writing in a few days.

   Write a letter to Mr. Rimer refusing the request for a refund or a free replacement on the knit sweater, because the instructions said specifically to wash the sweater by hand and with a mild detergent. You believe the garment was not properly laundered. However, provide some other alternatives in your reply so that Mr. Rimer will be inclined to forget about the requested adjustment. You might offer an inducement such as an invitation to a special customer sale or a discount on another purchase.

2. As consumer service assistant manager of the Bleachex Company, in St. Louis, you have today received a complaint from Mrs. R. A. Jeffry, of Portland, Oregon. She writes that after using your Bleachex liquid to remove a stain from her new white nylon car seat belt, she found the belt turned "an ugly yellow." She wants you to pay the $15 for a new belt. However, from her description of the yellow discoloration, it appears that the nylon had been treated with a resin (for soil resistance and "body") that is not compatible with any dry or liquid chlorine bleach. Your label states that Bleachex removes fruit, vegetable, etc., stains from washable cotton, linen, nylon, and other synthetic materials. But you do not advocate Bleachex for stain removal unless the entire item can be immersed in the properly mixed solution and then rinsed well, which is important to stop the bleach action. Thus, Bleachex should not be used on a car seat belt because of the inconvenience of removing the belt and all metal trimmings before immersing the material in the right solution. Though you can't guarantee 100 percent results, she may wish to immerse the belt for a few minutes in a solution of 1 gallon water, 2 tablespoonfuls of sodium sulfite (from a drugstore or photo supply shop), and ½ cup of white vinegar, and then rinse thoroughly. Although you must refuse her claim, make your reply tactful, helpful, and positive.

3. You are customer service director for the telephone company in your region. One of the letters you must write today is a refusal to Lars Clint, a student at Central Community College (about 50 miles from your office). Here is his letter:

The enclosed bill from you for $79.80 contains long-distance calls that I won't pay for. Apparently someone in your office got numbers screwed up and charged my account instead of someone else's. I know I made eight of the calls on this bill, but the other two I didn't make. I don't know anyone in those towns and therefore I refuse to pay the $18.75 charges on them.

Your bill says I supposedly made those calls on March 18. Well, that day I'm sure I didn't make any long-distance calls, because I was busy planning for the little celebration party I had that same night. It was a special event. I didn't see anyone using my phone that night, either. Anyway, whoever made the calls should have to pay for them, not me.

Enclosed is my check for $61.05, which I think is in full payment of what I owe you.

Your operations staff members have thoroughly investigated this claim. Your highly accurate equipment registers every call—whether it is directly dialed, or placed through an operator as a collect call. If it is the latter, the operator makes a definite, written report on each call. The two calls Mr. Clint questions were placed at 9:35 p.m. and 10:03 p.m. March 18; each was directly dialed; one was 15 minutes long, $7.60, and the other, 25 minutes, $11.15. The number from which these calls originated is definitely that of Lars Clint. As every phone book states near the front under "long-distance information and rates," any calls dialed must be billed to the number from which the call is made. Thus Lars must pay for the entire bill, including the $18.75 unpaid balance. Can you include one or two helpful suggestions for him? (Perhaps, now that he knows the date, time, town, length of each call, and the cost of each, he should check among his March 18 guests to see who placed the calls.) Your staff even checked all equipment and operations records, and found no equipment problems recorded for March 18.

Write Lars Clint a tactful refusal that will keep his goodwill and, you hope, get his full payment before your company has to disconnect his telephone! Remember to emphasize positive aspects.

4. Your firm repairs cameras and electronic equipment. One of your out-of-town customers sent you for repair a GRAPHLIX camera, Model 612, bearing the serial number 69865. She claims the camera is defective and asks for free repairs, because she has had it only six months on a one-year guarantee. Examination shows that the camera is not defective, but it has been dropped and badly misused. These repairs are needed: replace broken lens, $45; repair range finder, $8.50; repair and readjust electronic eye, $9. These repairs will put the camera in first-class shape; it cost originally $285. Write to the customer, Ms. Joan A. Horley, letting her know why and what she will have to pay for these repairs. You are customer service manager. Your guarantee accompanying all cameras states they are guaranteed for workmanship and materials under normal operating (use) conditions, but *not* when immersed in water, dropped, or given other unusual "shock" treatment. Make action easy for Ms. Horley.

5. An out-of-town customer returned his Superfonic automatic record changer, Model 990, for service to Stereo Precision, in your city. He wants the phono needle replaced and the turntable mechanism checked for speed fluctuations. The changer, which was purchased 18 months ago, is covered by a 24-month limited warranty, which states in part: "This warranty does not cover the cabinet, plastic parts, or phono stylus furnished with the set." (These parts deteriorate through normal wear and must be replaced periodically by the owner, for correct maintenance.)

Your service technicians have examined the changer and determined that only one of the required repairs is within the scope of the warranty. As service manager, write the customer, notifying him that the deteriorating sound quality was caused by normal wear of the phono stylus. A new needle (stylus) can be installed for $29.50, including labor. The replacement stylus (Model No. 519X) also incorporates technical improvements which result is a noticeable improvement in sound quality over the original-equipment stylus. It is designed to serve well during 750 hours of playing time. It provides truer fidelity than the original stylus on this customer's Superfonic changer. After your technicians inspect and adjust the entire turntable, repair the drive mechanism and replace the needle, the customer can have the best possible audio reproduction available in modern technology.

Tell the customer that the speed fluctuations were caused by a defective drive mechanism which can be repaired under warranty terms. Interweave resale, on turntable quality, throughout the letter. Convince the customer that $29.50 is a small investment to return his record changer to like-new condition. Make it easy and convenient for the customer to indicate his instructions.

Refusing Credit

1. Mr. and Mrs. Glen R. Feld, 2190 Olivett Lane, Tulsa, OK 74192, have been your credit customers for the five years they have lived in your city. Their account shows that average monthly purchases are about $50 and until two years ago their account was almost always paid on time. During the past two years, however, the payments have not been made when due. The account balance is now more than $600 and no payments have been received for four months.

In your today's mail was a letter from Mrs. Feld which said that she had tried to purchase some furniture last week and the salesclerk told her that the items could not be charged. She left the store in an angry mood, and this letter from her is the result. Among all the things mentioned in the letter are two which are of importance: (1) she threatened to take the matter up with the local better business bureau and the local credit bureau; and (2) she said that she would never again purchase anything at your store.

Write to Mrs. Feld and explain, in a tactful manner, why her recent credit purchase was turned down. Remind her, for example, of the current balance in the account; of the credit terms that she agreed to when the account was first opened; that neither the better business bureau nor the credit bureau will take any action, because your store has broken no laws; and anything else that will support your position. You will not, of course, resort to threats but will encourage immediate payment of the account so it can be reopened for her future convenience.

You will also want to include, as best you can, some statement of goodwill or concerning her future as a customer of your store. This is not, of course, the time to try to sell her anything; but you can remind her of the quality products you sell, the several convenient locations in the area shopping centers, the customer announcements which go out several days before sales are announced to the general public, and similar points. Tact and firmness are both important, but so is your effort to regain the Feld family's goodwill. Can you show your concern by willingness to help her work out an agreeable, beneficial solution?

2. You are the assistant credit manager of Commercial Plumbing Supply Company, wholesalers of bathroom fixtures and plumbing hardware. Compose a credit refusal to Mr. Rick Keller, owner of Midway Plumbing and Heating, 3950 Empire Boulevard, Columbus, OH 43265.

   After examining the business's financial statements, credit ratings from Dun and Bradstreet and the credit bureau of Columbus, and reports from two of Midway's creditors, you must tactfully deny the credit application because of a slow open account payment record and the firm's low working capital ratio. Midway has been making an average of $260 cash purchases monthly, and you want to keep them as a cash customer. You also feel that in a year or two the company may have improved its credit worthiness to meet your credit standards. The company has grown steadily since it was organized four years ago.

   Carefully consider these factors and use the most appropriate organizational pattern—direct or indirect. Provide several reader-benefit suggestions for strengthening Midway's credit eligibility. Assume, as needed, other pertinent and realistic facts regarding Midway's financial position.

3. You are the manager of a wholesale fabric business. You distribute fabrics to many stores in your state. You allow them 30 to 90 days to pay for goods and sometimes longer if necessary. Just recently you have run into a very difficult situation. You extended credit to one small fabric shop that was run by a very personable fellow, Mr. Mesher. He has come in several times to your warehouse and ordered and picked up fabric. He seems quite at home with all the personnel in your company and everybody likes him. For these reasons, when he was unable to pay his bill in 90 days, you gave him an indefinite extension. He continued to place orders and his bill has become larger and larger. It has now been a year since he has paid for anything. Of course part of the blame is yours for letting it go on as it did, but you have decided that you can no longer extend credit to this man until he starts paying his past bill. You had explained that you had to stop credit and he said he understood, but when he called up on what he termed ''emergency'' situations, you always said, ''Well, only this time.'' The situation is now out of hand, and you want your money. Decide on a course of action and write an effective letter.

4. As credit manager of the Fair Department Store, you have received a credit application from Mrs. Ross Webb, who seems to be doing a noble job of making the family ends meet on her $750 monthly wages. She and her husband and four children rent a $130-a-month cottage. Her husband has been unable to work for three months because of illness, but he hopes to get a job within two or three more months. You honestly feel that a charge

account is not what this family should have now. Unexpected emergencies in their financial position could cause them serious problems. Cash purchasing from your complete catalog, where they pay as they go, lets them know where they stand at any time. Also you have end-of-month sales regularly, with savings up to 50 percent. Send Mrs. Webb a catalog supplement with all the news about your sales. Perhaps when Mr. Webb is working you will reconsider her application for your monthly payment plan. Make your letter specific and genuinely helpful.

Acknowledging Orders You Can't Fill Now or At All

Incomplete Orders

1. As customer service representative for Evans Department Store, Glendale, CA 91220, you have today (Tuesday, June 6) received an order from Ms. Lora Fretwell, 835 Fifth Avenue, Burbank, CA 91547. She writes that last Saturday evening on her way to a theater in Los Angeles, she happened to pass your store windows on the west side. In the center window she saw a suit that she would like you to send her in size 12: in "white and blue. I think the price was $72.50; just charge it to my account. It's just the thing I'd like to take with me on a trip; we'll be leaving Tuesday, June 13. Will you please send it to reach me no later than Monday?" In checking with your window decorator, you learn that six suits were displayed in the center-west window last Saturday. Worse yet, three of them were in blue and white: (1) horizontal stripes in the jacket top, with navy blue skirt, (2) vertical stripes for both the jacket and slacks, and (3) light blue jacket with navy trim on the collar, and white skirt. Which does she want? Your secretary tried today to reach her by phone, but discovered that Ms. Fretwell has either an unlisted number or no phone. You must now write her a letter which goes in the 5 p.m. mail pickup and should reach her tomorrow or Thursday morning. If she will get her answer to you by no later than Friday noon, you can be sure to send the right suit to her on the store delivery truck Monday morning. Devise easy action for Ms. Fretwell, and also make sure you will get all the information you need to fill her order immediately.

2. From Mr. Jonathan Lamb, assistant manager, Silver Marine and Pool Supply, 825 Arnold Avenue, Detroit, MI 48294, you receive an order for:

```
10 Boarding ladders, 3 steps                  @ $10.50 each
50 ft. #6424 Marine Mat and Dock Runner, red  @  4.20 per ft.
3 doz. deluxe #98145 Chaise pads, floral       @  4.00 each
```

These items are to be shipped freight charges collect and billed on the firm's usual credit terms of 2/10, net 30. You can't ship two of these items, however, until you get more information. The boarding ladders come with 7- and 11-inch hooks—so they can clamp securely to boats, rafts, pools, or docks. Which size does he want? It is even possible that he might want five of each, but you think it is risky to guess. The ladder prices are the same for both sizes of hooks. These white vinyl-covered hooks turn a full 360 degrees for fast and easy fitting, and they fold so that the ladder is flat for convenient storage. The steps are varnished oak hardwood, 16 inches wide.

The Mat and Dock Runner #6424 is in aqua color, not red. The red is listed in your catalog (which Silver Marine has) as #6425. Though he probably wants the red and just wrote the wrong catalog number, you want to be sure before you ship this heavy roll. (Shipping weight is 3 pounds per foot!) This is an excellent runner for deck or dock. It is made of all-weather, nonslip, brush-action polyester pile with heavy rubber backing and is 36 inches wide.

You do have the chair pads and can ship them today. They are a durable, waterproof vinyl floral pattern, ideal for outdoor patio use. Today is May 12. Decide whether you should ship the pads today or wait until you can send the other items too. Write for the needed information, make action easy, and cover all pertinent details. You are assistant sales manager for Pool and Patio Wholesale Company, Oakland, CA 94621.

Back Orders

3. Mr. Thurston Roldo, a charge customer at 945 Sound Drive, Portland, OR 97216, orders five more rolls of the #WP4662 gold color, flocked, raised damask wallpaper ($17.95 a roll). He writes that he just finished papering the dining room with this pattern and his family likes it so much that they now want the hall to match. Your store (Milli's Interior Design Shop, Tacoma, WA 98422) is completely out of this pattern; you sold your last roll three days ago. You are the exclusive dealer for these distinctive wallpapers in the Northwest and get them direct from the Dayberry Mills in Massachusetts. A wire from the mills yesterday promised that your special order of #WP4662 would reach your shop in 10 days. Write Mr. Roldo the appropriate letter to keep him convinced that this choice wallpaper is well worth waiting for. It is one of the most elegant you carry. Its beautiful flocked damask pattern has the lovely look and feel of velvet. Textured to simulate fine silk, all on tough vinyl, it is strong and won't tear even when wet. Also, it's prepasted and pretrimmed, and can be cleaned with soap and water. Shipping time between Portland and Tacoma is one day.

4. In your Wholesale Camera Supply Company (Charleston, WV 25369) you have just received an order from Cline's Photo Shop, 831 Stevens Avenue, Huntington, WV 25701, for parts to repair a Model #36 box camera. Mr. Cline stated that his customer cherishes this old camera as an heirloom and wants to get it into good working order. Facts: This model of American camera is obsolete and new parts are no longer available. If Mr. Cline's customer desires, you will try to obtain these parts on special order; however, there will be a delay from four to six weeks and the parts may be used.

The price also may be considerably higher than current material prices on similar parts for newer models. At this moment you have no way of knowing just what the prices may be. Write to Mr. Cline to get his approval of the back order and an understanding about what his customer considers the maximum she would be willing to pay. You will, of course, try to get them for the lowest price possible and assure Mr. Cline that such an old-model camera in top working order will be a possession to be proud of. Make action easy.

Substitution Orders

5. You are the hotel reservation clerk for an ultramodern, very popular hotel in New York City. Every Thanksgiving holiday various tourist groups of holiday shoppers make plans to come into the city and want to stay specifically at your hotel. Your facility offers the finest restaurants, great entertainment, attractive meeting rooms, indoor shopping facilities including the leading department store outlets, health spa, swimming pool, ice skating rink, etc. This is a facility for any season in the year. Therefore, the name is the Four Seasons Hotel.

    A request has been received from a group of "Golden Agers" who would like to stay at your hotel. They have done so in the past, but are late in sending their reservations for this year. Although your records show that this particular group has been your guest for the past five years, you must write them that your hotel cannot provide them with all the reservations they have requested. Offer them 35 of the 60 rooms requested, and confirmation on the other 25 rooms in another hotel close by. Give a deadline date for their response.

6. You are sales manager of National Confectionery Supplies. Your assistant has just composed the following draft of a bad-news message, which needs your signature before it is sent to Ms. Susana White, White Candy Company, Muncie, Indiana:

```
Thank you for your special delivery letter of January 11 ordering a
rush shipment of another supply of our Exel Cherry Syrup.

May we suggest item 10-B on page 12 of our catalog? This is in stock
now and ready to be shipped to you immediately. Item 10, "Jumbo
Ann," which you inquired about has been completely sold out; we will
be unable to fill any more orders for this particular item until
early February, about the 9th. The two syrups, 10-B and 10, are sim-
ilar except that the former has a heavier syrup. We have found that
many of our customers prefer the heavier syrup since, by dilution,
they have been able to supplement their other syrups without appre-
ciably altering the original. As you will note in the catalog, the
price of item 10-B is 11 cents a case higher than the cherry syrup
which was the subject of your inquiry.

We believe you would be completely satisfied with the substitution
and shall await further instructions from you.
```

Today is already January 13. This letter overlooks the fact that Ms. White stated in her "rush order" letter that she needs the syrup by January 17 at the latest, because the factory has exhausted its supply and must fill large candy orders from stores before the Valentine Day rush. Shipment time between your warehouse and Muncie is two days minimum. Thus there is insufficient time for an exchange of information by even special delivery. You need to get your message to her faster. If you can get White's reply of approval by January 14 (tomorrow), you will ship 10-B in time to reach her by the 17th. Now try your skill in expressing the above letter in these timesaving ways:

a. A 15-word telegram. (See footnote 4, page 141, for word-cutting suggestions.

b. A 100-word Mailgram. (See pages 139–140.)

Declining Favors, Invitations, and Miscellaneous Requests

1. Assume you receive the following letter from Mrs. Eugene Hewsen, chairperson of the local United Way campaign for this year:

   Dear Mr. (or Ms.) (your name)

   As you know, our city conducts a United Way fund drive annually. Many people volunteer their help to coordinate the campaign. Will you be willing to serve as a captain this year?

   Captains are responsible for a particular geographic area. Yours would be a 10-block area bounded by _____ Street on the west, _____ Street on the east, _____ Street on the north, and _____ Street on the south. You would be responsible for selecting workers in each block, who in turn will canvass each house in their particular block.

   Needless to say, your effort will be for a most worthy cause. Will you drop me a line . . . soon, saying you'll accept?

   Unfortunately you must decline the request. Since the campaign is kicked off in September and you will be out of the state on vacation (or company business) that month, you won't be around to do your duty. Write a considerate reply.

2. As the sports editor of the daily morning newspaper of a large city, you are the recipient of a large quantity of mail. Some of the letters are important; others could just as easily be answered by the writer, if that person would devote just a little time to the question. So it is with the current letter in your hands.

   Specifically, the writer wants to know how many times the Boston Red Sox have played in the World Series, how many times they have won, and in which year was their last win. There is obviously much information you could provide, but the writer (a boy of 12) should know where such information can be found so that he could look it up himself.

Answer the young person in a polite manner, and tell him where he can easily find those answers and additional information about baseball: World Series games and scores, Cy Young Award winners, home run leaders, members of the Baseball Hall of Fame, and much more. One of the more common almanacs would be a place to start, but his librarian could also provide additional information, plus some interesting books about baseball.

Be polite and wish him well. If you wish, you might answer one of his questions. But remember that you are doing him a favor by giving him information about source material that he will be able to use for years to come. You might even want to give him the names of several references. Above all, you want to retain him as a reader of your column and your newspaper.

3. As chief clerk of the traffic department of the Washington State Ferries, you have to answer a request you received two days ago from Miss Amy Jones, Star Route 2, Box 956, Spokane, WA 99230. She asks if you would please make a special search for a small camera (Ektol 5) she lost on the ferry from Winslow to Seattle July 10. It was a special gift from her fiance, who had her initials (ARJ) engraved on it, and she will be heartsick until it is found. She was sitting by a window seat in about the middle of the ferry on the right-hand side and she thinks the camera dropped out of her bag that was on the floor under her seat. As she doesn't mention the name of the ferry nor the exact time of her trip, and as you have four ferries on this route, you had to search on all four ferries. So far no camera has been found. But you'll keep this a matter of permanent record and if the item is found or turned in, you will notify her immediately. Write the bad news to Miss Jones; send copies of your letter to: Information Booth, Colman Ferry Terminal; Dock Superintendent, Colman Ferry Terminal; and Agent, Winslow—and indicate these copies on your letter to Miss Jones.

Bad-News Announcements

1. *(Memo)* Your company cafeteria, built 16 years ago to serve about 1,000 employees, is definitely too small for your 1,800 employees. As a remedial step you (vice president for food services and finance), together with the board of directors, have decided upon a temporary solution. You will close the directors' lounge as a lounge facility, starting November 1, 198_, and will no longer serve just officers and guests there. The plan is to convert the directors' lounge—which is a table service dining room of very limited capacity and use—to an employee vending-machine food service room, supplemented by short-order counter service during peak demand hours. Present patrons of the directors' lounge are mainly a few officers and a few guests; the average patronage daily has been less than 30 during the three

hours a day the present table service is open. Economically this is a marginal operation that cannot be justified. This lounge is conveniently located so that it can easily be used by your swing shift during evening hours without keeping the rest of the building open.

This planned change will of course greatly alleviate the pressing demands for additional food service facilities for employees. But the table service will be missed by the few who enjoyed it before. To them this announcement will be bad news. Word your announcement so that every loyal officer will accept your decision with understanding, and even approval. The new plan should help decrease employee lunch-hour tardiness and improve morale. The officers still have the officers' dining room on the twelfth floor. To partially offset the loss of table service from the directors' room, this officers' dining room now has additional private seating space. The recent enclosure of the south porch has been equipped with comfortable lounge facilities in the latest decor, and a modern sliding partition is usable for those officers who want a separate space for private conferences. Write your memo to all management members.

2. For many years your company has been sending free copies of a glossy magazine, *Improving Your Correspondence,* to anyone who requested to be on your mailing list. Seldom do you hear from your readers. The cost of this little publication is about $2.90 each. In an effort to try to pare unnecessary expenses, your firm's directors have suggested that the mailing list be revised to include only those persons and firms that still read and appreciate the publication. They realize that after a passage of years those who originally requested to be on the mailing list may no longer be reading the magazine. Write a pleasant, positive-sounding, processed message that will offend no one, even though it is basically bad news. Your goal is to find out which readers wish to keep the magazine coming. They'll help you keep your mailing list up to date by taking a certain action that you request. Can you word your announcement in such a way that the readers will be dropped from your mailing list if you don't hear from them?

3. You are president of the Central Building Garage, Inc. Your company manages a 400-car garage used by business executives who occupy the Central Building. Because of steadily increasing operating costs (mainly wages) you have found it necessary to increase the monthly parking rates to $105 a month (instead of the former $95), plus the state sales tax. This increase will become effective February 1, 198_.

For the past two years you have been absorbing the increased operating expenses, but cannot continue to do so any longer. After several conversations with Mr. P. L. Brown, vice president of Commercial Properties, Inc., and with the Central Building's owners, who lease to the business firms in the building and from whom you lease your garage facilities, you received permission for the rate increase. Now that you have decided on the rate and date, you will write two messages:

a. A letter to Mr. Brown, telling him your final decision regarding the monthly rate and the effective date. Inform him that you will notify all your parking customers before a certain date. You might restate to him briefly the reason for this increase, refer to your previous conversations, and show appreciation for his understanding. Will you organize this message by the direct or indirect plan? Why?

b. A letter to all customers who have been renting monthly parking space from your garage. This increase comes to them as a bad-news surprise. Give them whatever details you think they will appreciate having. Will you organize the same way as for message a? Why or why not?

CAPSULE CHECKLISTS FOR BAD/NEWS MESSAGES*

I Bad News		II Answering Non-Sales-Related Inquiries When the Information Is Unfavorable
General plan (A) (indirect)	Exception (B) (direct)	

1. BUFFER
  a. Agreement
  b. Appreciation
  c. Assurance
  d. Compliment
  e. Cooperation
  f. Good news
  g. Neutral courtesy
  h. Understanding
	1. Main idea
	  a. Bad-news decision, some-
	    times with a brief buffer
	    and/or reason
		1. Buffer
		*For unfavorable recommenda-
		tions:*
		  a. Applicant's name; relation-
		    ship
		  b. Reason for writing; reply by
		    request
		For other inquiries:
		  a. Appreciation
		  b. Assurance
		  c. Understanding

2. EXPLANATION
  a. Necessary details—general
    to specific
  b. Favorable, then unfavorable
    facts
  c. RB[4] reasons
  d. Emphasis on desired goal
	2. Explanation
	  a. Necessary details—general
	    to specific
	  b. Emphasis on desired goal
		2. Explanation
		  a. Answers to all questions
		  b. Pertinent facts (favorable
		    and unfavorable)
		  c. Caution on legalities
		  d. Confidentiality
		  e. Offer, phone call

3. DECISION—implied or ex-
  pressed—WITH RESALE
  AND/OR CONSTRUCTIVE
  SUGGESTIONS
  a. Embedded statement of bad
    news—with suggestion of
    what CAN be done
  b. Helpful counter-proposal,
    plans, alternatives
  c. Resale
  d. Sales promotion
	3. Decision omitted (already in I
	  B, 1). Resale and suggestions
	  often unnecessary and omitted;
	  sometimes:
	  a. Helpful counter-proposal,
	    plans, alternatives
		3. Decision—with constructive
		  suggestions
		About applicant:
		  a. Honest nonendorsement
		  b. Possibility of changes since
		    you last saw applicant
		*About other non-sales-related
		inquiries:*
		  a. Same as I A, 3a and b

4. POSITIVE, FRIENDLY,
  APPROPRIATE CLOSE
  a. Appreciation
  b. Invitation to future action
  c. CSAD[1]
  d. EA and motivation[2]
  e. DA[3]
  f. Willingness to help further
  g. RB[4]
  h. Good wishes
  i. Courtesy
	4. Positive, friendly, appropriate
	  close. Sometimes:
	  a. Appreciation
	  b. Invitation to future action
	  c. CSAD[1]
	  d. EA and motivation[2]
	  e. DA[3]
	  f. Willingness to help further
	  g. RB[4]
	  h. Good wishes
	  i. Courtesy
		4. Positive, friendly, appropriate
		  close
		  a. Ray of hope for improve-
		    ment
		  b. Willingness to help further
		  c. Good wishes

* All lists include possible content. For any one message, choose only the pertinent appropriate items.
[1] CSAD = clear statement of action desired
[2] EA = easy action
[3] DA = dated action, if desirable
[4] RB = reader benefit

CAPSULE CHECKLISTS FOR BAD/NEWS MESSAGES (Continued)

III	IV Refusing Credit	
Refusing Adjustments on Claims and Complaints	Retail Credit (C)	Mercantile Credit (D)

1. Buffer
  a. Agreement
  b. Appreciation
  c. Assurance
  d. Cooperation
  e. Neutral courtesy
  f. Understanding
  g. If granting a part is good news, opening is on that part
	1. Buffer
	  a. Agreeable comment
	  b. Appreciation
	  c. Assurance
	  d. Brief resale on product and/or firm
	  e. Incidental reference to the order, if any
		1. Buffer
		  a. Agreeable comment
		  b. Appreciation
		  c. Assurance
		  d. Brief resale on product and/or firm
		  e. Incidental reference to the order, if any

2. Explanation
  a. Logical statements of reasons
  b. General RB[4] procedure, policy, instructions, guarantee
  c. Resale interwoven
  d. Education on use
  e. Impersonal facts on buyer's mistake
	2. Explanation
	Choice of:
	  a. No reason
	  b. "Insufficient-information" reason
	  c. List of all usual reasons
	  d. Specific reason(s): with RB[4] and emphasis on desired goal
		2. Explanation
		  a. Specific reasons
		  b. Favorable, then unfavorable facts
		  c. Emphasis on desired goal

3. Decision—with resale and/or suggestions
  a. Impersonal, expressed or implied, but clear refusal; positive language, perhaps RB[4]
  b. Clear indication if you are returning product
  c. RB[4] suggestion(s) for using rejected product and/or another
  d. Resale on product, service, and/or firm
	3. Decision—with RB[4] counterproposal and suggestion(s)
	  a. Embedded statement of bad news—with suggestion of what CAN be done
	  b. Suggestions:
	    Conference
	    Other lenders
	    Future review
	    Other credit plans available
	    Layaway
	    Cash or c.o.d. buying
		3. Decision—with RB[4] counterproposal and suggestion(s)
		  a. Embedded statement of bad news—with suggestion of what CAN be done
		  b. Suggestions:
		    Inventory reduction
		    Sales or capital increase
		    Local financing
		    Cash or c.o.d. buying: smaller, frequent orders
		    Help of sales representative
		    Future review

4. Positive, friendly, appropriate close
  a. CSAD (tactful suggestion without urging)[1]
  b. EA[2]
  c. Positive forward look
  d. RB and satisfaction[4]
  e. Courtesy
	4. Positive, friendly, appropriate close
	  a. Invitation regarding a suggestion; CSAD[1]
	  b. Forward look
	  c. Resale
	  d. RB[4] and EA[2]
	  e. Courtesy
		4. Positive, friendly, appropriate close
		  a. Invitation regarding a suggestion; CSAD[1]
		  b. Forward look
		  c. Resale
		  d. RB[4] and EA[2]
		  e. Courtesy

[1] CSAD = clear statement of action desired
[2] EA = easy action
[4] RB = reader benefit

CAPSULE CHECKLISTS FOR BAD-NEWS MESSAGES (Continued)

V Acknowledging Orders You Can't Fill Now or at All			VI Declining Invitations and Requests for Favors
Incomplete or Vague (E)	Back Orders (F)	Substitutions (G)	

1. Good news, if any, and buffer
  a. Shipment details, if sending anything
  b. Buffer: short resale on vaguely described item(s)
  c. Brief order acknowledgment (date, item)
  d. Appreciation
  e. Welcome, if new customer
	1. Good news, if any, and buffer
	  a. Same as V E, 1a
	  b. Buffer: specific resale on ordered depleted item; no mention of depletion
	  c. Brief order acknowledgment (date, item)
	  d. Appreciation
	  e. Welcome, if new customer
		1. Good news, if any, and buffer
		  a. Same as V E, 1a
		  b. Buffer: broad resale embodies both substitute and ordered item; omits differences
		  c. Brief order acknowledgment (date, item)
		  d. Appreciation
		  e. Welcome, if new customer
			1. Buffer
			  a. Appreciation
			  b. Compliment (to reader)
			  c. Assurance
			  d. Agreeable comment

2. Explanation
  a. RB[4] reason for requesting missing information
  b. Facts about choices available (sizes, colors, models)
  c. Descriptive enclosures
	2. Explanation
	  a. Approximate date goods expected to reach buyer
	  b. Reason unavailable now (RB?)[4]
	  c. Resale
		2. Explanation
		  a. One or two merits of substitute (S)[5] before revealing unavailability of ordered item (O)[5]
		  b. Sales point on why we carry S exclusively
			2. Explanation
			  a. Facts and (sometimes personal) reasons leading to refusal

3. Decision—with resale and/or suggestions
  a. See E2a, above—implied decision
  b. Perhaps brief resale on the item(s) in general
	3. Decision—with resale and/or constructive suggestions
	  a. See F 2a above—implied decision
	  b. Possibly mild sales promotion on allied item(s) to be shipped with back-ordered item
	  c. Perhaps brief resale on back-ordered item
		3. Decision—with resale and suggestions
		  a. Unavailability of O[5]—in positive terms (exclusively stock S[5]—if true)
		  b. Passive statement on where O may be bought
		  c. Price and quality justification of substitute; RB[4]
		  d. Sales promotion
			3. Decision—with resale and/or suggestions
			  a. Clear, tactful decision, implied or stated; emphasis on the positive aspects (desire to help, etc.)
			  b. RB,[4] suggestions—when, how you *can* help
			  c. Alternate sources of help to reader

4. Positive, friendly, appropriate close
  a. CSAD[1]
  b. EA[2]
  c. DA[3]
  d. RB (prompt delivery?)[4]
  e. Courtesy
	4. Positive, friendly, appropriate close
	  a. If shipment in reasonable time: no action; assumption that back-order is OK
	  b. If longer: CSAD[1]; EA[2]; DA[3]
	  c. RB[4]
		4. Positive, friendly, appropriate close
		  a. If S[5] is already shipped: assurance of money-back "shipment on approval"; RB[4]
		  b. If S is not yet shipped: CSAD[1]; EA[2]; DA[3]; RB[4]
			4. Positive, friendly, appropriate close
			  a. CSAD[1]
			  b. EA[2]
			  c. DA[3]
			  d. Good wishes
			  e. RB[4]
			  f. Courtesy

[1] CSAD = clear statement of action desired   [3] DA = dated action   [5] S = substitute; O = ordered item
[2] EA = easy action   [4] RB = reader benefit

CAPSULE CHECKLISTS FOR BAD-NEWS MESSAGES (Continued)

VII **Announcing Bad News about Prices and/or Services**	VIII **Penalizing for Nonconformity with Rules or Procedures**	IX **Conveying Other Bad News**

1. Main idea or buffer
  a. If routine (or reader not emotionally involved), 1 B, 1— (Direct plan)
  b. Otherwise, I A, 1 buffer:
    (1) Agreeable comment
    (2) Neutral courtesy
    (3) Brief resale
	1. Main idea or buffer
	  a. If routine, urgent, or reader not emotionally involved): Bad-news decision, sometimes with reason (Direct plan, I B, 1)
	  b. Otherwise, I A, 1 buffer:
	    (1) Agreeable comment
	    (2) Neutral courtesy
	    (3) Compliment on past
	    (4) Hint of urgency or need for change
		1. Main idea or buffer
		  a. Same as VIII 1a
		  b. Same as VIII 1b

2. Explanation
  a. RB[4] reasons and analysis of increasing costs, etc.
	2. Explanation
	  a. Details about the requirements
	  b. Reasons leading to the penalty
		2. Explanation
		  a. Details on what is wrong

3. Decision—with resale and suggestions
  a. Effective date of new plan
  b. Clear statement and itemizing if needed
  c. Enclosures or examples if helpful
  d. Resale on your firm's products, services, prices
	3. Decision—with resale and suggestions
	  a. Clear, tactful statement of what will happen unless reader meets requirements
	  b. Suggestions for eliminating penalty in future
	  c. Forms and deadlines
		3. Decision—with suggestions
		  a. What needs to be done
		  b. How to do it

4. Positive, friendly, appropriate close
  a. Forward look
  b. Resale
  c. Invitation to action
  d. CSAD[1]
  e. EA[2]
  f. RB[4]
  g. Courtesy
	4. Positive, friendly, appropriate close
	  a. CSAD[1]
	  b. EA[2]
	  c. DA[3]
	  d. RB[4]
	  e. Assurance
	  f. Good wishes
	  g. Courtesy
		4. Positive, friendly, appropriate close
		  a. CSAD[1]
		  b. EA[2]
		  c. Goodwill
		  d. Courtesy

[1] CSAD = clear statement of action desired
[2] EA = easy action
[3] DA = dated action, if desirable
[4] RB = reader benefit

CHAPTER 10

Persuasive Requests

Besides situations in which mere *asking* is sufficient (routine direct requests), you will face situations in which you need to *persuade*. The favor or action you ask—the reader's time, money, support, or agreement—is such that you anticipate some objection. To persuade your reader to take the requested action, you develop rational and/or emotional appeals. Analysis of and consideration[1] for your reader's circumstances, needs, and emotions are especially important for effective persuasion.

This chapter discusses the persuasive-request plan and how you can adapt it for the following kinds of messages:

Requests for favors that:
        Require time, knowledge, and/or effort
        Ask donations of money or other valuables
        Urge cooperation on goals and projects

Other nonroutine requests:
        Adjustment
        Credit
        Changes in policy or performance

The persuasive-request plan is also used for job application, unsolicited sales, and some collection letters, as discussed in Chapters 11 to 14.

ORGANIZATIONAL PLAN

The persuasive request, like the bad-news letter, uses the indirect approach. You assume that if your request were stated directly at the beginning, it would be bad news to your reader, who would then react unfavorably. Thus, before you mention the specific request, you will have to prepare the reader for it, and, when possible, present facts to indicate that your proposal is beneficial or useful. Remember, your reader is not expecting your message, and you should attract his or her attention and arouse interest *before* revealing what you'd like done.

The basic structure for persuasive letters usually has four parts, commonly known as the AIDA formula for sales presentation:

A—Attract the reader's favorable *attention*.
 I—Arouse the reader's *interest*.
D—Create *desire* and convince the reader.
A—Make clear the *action* the reader needs to take.

[1] For a review of general ways to show consideration, see pp. 47–55.

Although attention, interest, and desire are listed here as distinct steps, they are usually combined or blended so smoothly in the well-written persuasive message that it is difficult—and unnecessary!—to separate them. Also, the parts do not always occur in the sequence given here; for example, it is possible to omit or deemphasize those points that have been covered in earlier letters, advertising, or personal contacts with the prospect. *You-attitude content and reader benefits are most important.* What you call the parts and whether you have three or four is unimportant. In fact, the persuasive-request plan is sometimes called the four P's—promise, picture, prove, and push—or discussed under *three* parts—star, chain, and hook. In the AIDA persuasive-request expanded outline below, other names for the parts are indicated in parentheses.

1. **Attention** *(promise; star)*

   Attract favorable attention with a reader-interest or a reader-benefit theme. Begin with a relevant statement or a challenging question that entices the recipients to read on because they want to know: "What's in this letter for me?" Highlight a point that is close to the reader's interests or needs, instead of talking about yourself or your organization.

   Because many people throw away envelopes that look like part of bulk mailings, even the envelope plays an important part in getting favorable attention. Among the devices used with varying degrees of success on envelopes are color, handwritten addresses, contest announcements, questions, and a few enticing words from the message printed on the envelope.

   The letterhead can also be an effective, important attention getter. For favor and sales letters that are sent to numerous readers, letterheads can and do deviate from the usual simplicity suggested for other business letterheads. Some contain different pictures and colors to tie in with each favor or sales message. (Advertising agencies and stationery design specialists can help you with these needs.) The discussion in this text concentrates on the written message itself.

2. **Interest** *(picture; chain)*

   Build upon the theme started in the attention-getting opening. Begin to tell what your project, product, or service is and what it will do for the reader. Describe it clearly and specifically in two ways (not necessarily in this order):

   a. Its physical description—important features, construction, appearance, performance, beauty, functions (any or all of which may be omitted for a long-established subject well known to the reader).

   b. Its value or benefits to the reader or others in whom the reader is interested. Of the various features and uses that the project, product, or service has, emphasize the central selling point—that point you think is most likely to make the strongest appeal to the prospect. For instance, will your proposal bring comfort? entertainment? health? recognition?

security? Show the reader how your proposal gives one or more benefits like the following:

Appreciation (by others)	Pleasure
Approval (by others)	Popularity
Beauty or attractiveness	Position of authority
Cleanliness	Prestige
Comfort	Pride
Convenience	Profits
Cooperation	Protection for family,
Customer satisfaction	business, self, or others
Distinctiveness	Provision for the future
Efficiency	Recognition
Enjoyment	Reduced work
Entertainment	Respect
Extra earnings	Safety and security
Fair treatment	Satisfaction of helping others
Friendships	(altruism)
Good reputation	Savings
Health	Self-preservation
Improvement	Solution to a problem
Love of home, family, others	Success
Money and other valuables	Thrift habit
Peace of mind	Usefulness

3. **Desire and Conviction** *(prove; chain)*

   So that your readers will desire to do as you request and be convinced they (or others in whom they are interested) will benefit from your proposal, you usually present proof. Give evidence that your statements are true. Include needed facts, pictures, figures, testimonials, tests, samples, guarantees, or any other proof your proposal may call for. Be aware of your legal responsibilities for truth.

   A descriptive folder permits you to avoid cluttering your letter with many details. However, if you have an enclosure, mention it only after stating most of your selling points and then motivate your reader to read further details in the folder. Link your reference to the enclosure with a sales point. Don't depend on the enclosure to do your selling.

4. **Action** *(push; hook)*

   Clearly state what the reader should do to comply with your request and thus to gain the benefits. Make action easy—by including a reply form, envelope, phone number, office hours, location, and so forth. Induce the reader to act now or within a certain time, and end on a reader-benefit plug, which may tie in with your opening statement.

PERSUASIVE REQUESTS FOR FAVORS

As a conscientious business or professional person you probably participate actively in various committees and organizations. And you have numerous opportunities to write (as well as to answer) favor requests that seek the recipient's donation of something—time, knowledge, effort, money, or cooperation. The AIDA plan helps you to ask a favor effectively, as described below.

Getting Attention for Favor Requests

To begin your favor request with something close to your reader's interest or benefit, consider what appeals are likely to be most meaningful to her or him. Try to introduce a direct or indirect benefit that you can develop as a central selling point more fully later in the letter. You want to get the reader's attention *before* stating your request, but you need to use good judgment in introducing benefits. Be careful that your statements don't sound like high-pressure appeals or bribes, as in this poor opening for a letter inviting a political candidate to speak: "How much would it be worth to you to influence the views of 2,000 voters?"

Effective openings you can use—with discretion—for various favor requests are:

1. Comments or assertions with which the reader will agree
2. Compliments—if sincere
3. Frank admission that your message is a request for a favor
4. Problem(s) that are the basis of your favor request
5. Question(s)—one or two rhetorical questions
6. Statement(s) of what is being done or has been done to solve or lessen a problem

Agreeable-Comment or Assertion Openings

To speak to students majoring in advertising:

Advertising is the spark plug of any business and a challenge to the creative thinker. Yet what advice can you give to the many students who cannot decide what area of advertising to enter?

To help in getting community support:

One topic in which you and I share a special interest is the education of our children. The success of our school levy will determine the quality of education received by Bellevue students.

Sincere-Compliment Openings

Request to speak, without fee, to a local chapter:

Ever since your stimulating speech last year to delegates at KSA national convention in Atlanta, our TriCity chapter members here have
wanted to meet you personally. We believe you could be a profound
influence on our future program and growth.

Request to accept an important chairperson position:

Your exceptionally fine work in People-to-People projects, as well
as your present council position, emphasizes that you deserve a
place on this year's East Coast conference program of the National
Personnel Association.

"Frank Admission of Favor" Opening

To be moderator at a national convention:

To get and keep our 198_ NRMA convention program on the beam, we
shall need three top-grade people to serve as moderators. You can no
doubt guess why I am making this appeal to you.

To fill out and return a questionnaire:

WILL YOU HELP DMAA?
--AND HELP YOURSELF, TOO?

   I'd like to ask a favor of you. It concerns the gathering of
important facts and information regarding postal rates. Here, in a
nutshell, is the story:

Basic-Problem Openings

To contribute to a lab fund:

DIAGNOSTIC LABORATORY IN DANGER!
INDUSTRY STANDS TO LOSE $60,000!
Contributions for the new diagnostic lab in (*town name*) **have stopped
coming in. Unless we can immediately raise $11,000, we will lose the
$60,000 appropriated by the last legislature, on the condition we in**
the industry match it with $35,000. Only $24,000 of the necessary
$35,000 has, so far, been pledged.

Question Openings

Request to participate in a six-month research project:

```
Have you ever had the fun of participating in a market research
study? As you know, market research is the study of consumer reac-
tions and attitudes to products. This research is extremely useful
to manufacturers in helping them to give you and your family prod-
ucts to better suit your needs.
```

Request to become a member of a university YWCA:

```
WHAT'S THE USE?
"What's the use of getting an education?"
    "What's the use of planning ahead?"
        "What's the use of living thoughtfully?"
            "WHAT'S THE USE OF ANYTHING?"
```

"What Has Been Done about a Problem" Openings

To send a gift to the Fund for the Blind:

```
Thousands of blind Americans wait eagerly each month for their cop-
ies of the Braille or Talking Book edition of The Reader's Digest.
It is the only magazine of its kind available in Braille or Talking
Book form (long-playing records) which is exactly like the ink-print
edition read by their sighted friends. This means something very
special to them.
    With the help of friends like yourself, we can supply these. . . .
```

Arousing Interest and Creating Desire to Do the Favor

When you have decided on an opening that sets the theme and encourages the recipient to read on, you can continue to build on your idea. To get both the reader's interest and desire, you need to (1) include all necessary description—physical characteristics and value of the project, (2) present facts and figures through which the reader can determine direct or indirect benefits he or she may derive, and (3) handle negatives positively. This material comprises the greater portion of your persuasive request.

Physical Characteristics and Value of Project

If your reader is not a member of your organization or familiar with it, you need to give brief, but adequate information about its purpose, scope, and members. But be sure not to *begin* your letter by talking about your organization, especially if the reader is an outsider! Place this material after a you-attitude opening.

In addition, you need to describe to all readers the problem or project to which the favor relates and to establish its values. For instance, if you are asking for funds to send underprivileged children to summer camp, you might describe (perhaps with the use of a folder) the physical camp facilities, size and number of buildings, surroundings, recreation areas, and number of children and counselors. Then you show the value of these facilities to the children—character-building, friendships, appreciation of nature, fun, and so forth. Sometimes you can effectively get readers to visualize themselves in the shoes of those their funds can help and in this way arouse their interest in your project.

Direct and Indirect Reader Benefits

Usually near the middle of your letter you explain how the reader is to take part in the project. So that readers will desire to do as you ask, be sure to include all necessary facts and figures to convince them that their contribution will be enjoyable, easy, important, and of benefit to them (as much as is true and possible). Try to show direct and/or indirect benefits.

Direct Benefits. To a person who does a favor, vary direct benefits with the type of favor. For example, if a person is to speak (without a fee and perhaps even without a traveling expense allowance) at a widely publicized convention, he or she may gain direct benefit from the favorable publicity as well as from personal contacts with the audience. If other prominent speakers are on the same program, say so; for this fact is an additional compliment to your reader. Be sure to tell the reader when he or she is to speak, where (date, day, hour), on what topic (or if the speaker is to choose it), for how long, to whom, and to how many people.

Direct benefit may also come to the company that donates merchandise to, for instance, a charity or well-attended event. The people who see the company's name on the donated product will feel goodwill toward the donor and tend to buy its products when they need them. It is better, however, not to state such benefits specifically, but to let your readers determine them themselves.

In some favor requests the direct benefit offered may be a premium or gift or other small reward or token of appreciation. Those who participate in a questionnaire survey may gain, because the results will ultimately lead to improvements that make their work easier or help them to save money.

Indirect Benefits. The participant who helps the members of a group he or she is interested in or a member of may receive indirect benefits. For instance, you can use indirect-benefit appeals to get a sales manager to speak (without a fee) to your school's marketing club or an auditor to talk to an accounting club. In each case, your reader's contribution may benefit him or her or the profession at least indirectly, because the reader helps a group of listeners whose interests are in a field of work he or she is interested in. Similarly, when you want to urge a busy person to accept a time-consuming office without pay, you can appeal to a sense of loyalty to the organization and the benefit his or her leadership can provide. Such indirect reader benefits are often persuaders.

In still other cases you can get a reader's cooperation by appealing on the basis of *altruism*—selfless devotion to the welfare of other human beings (or even animals). When persons contribute to a charity drive, for instance, they benefit by knowing they have helped bring happiness and hope to less fortunate people.

Positive Handling of Negatives

With the persuasive-request plan you must not only use appeals and stress reader benefits, but you need to ask yourself, "To what will my reader probably object?" Then stress the positive aspects—what *can* be done—to minimize the negatives, as in the following examples:

Probable objection	*Possible points to stress*
1. Allowance for traveling expenses and/or speaker's fee is inadequate	a. Will you gladly meet her at the airport or any other location? b. Will she be guest of honor at a banquet? Maybe her spouse too? c. Will a car and/or parking be available for her use in your city? d. Is her part on the program so important that her employer will want to take care of her expenses? e. Can you arrange overnight accommodation?
2. Expected pledge or contribution is too large	a. Will you accept contributions in small installments? b. May he pledge now and pay after a future date? Can you show the great relief his gift will bring to those who need it?
3. Requested questionnaire looks long	a. Are the questions easy to answer? Why? b. Is taking part in the survey fun and important because . . . ? c. Can the entire questionnaire be finished in *x* minutes? d. Will the ultimate gain or reward be an incentive?

Asking for Action

Having included necessary facts, benefits, and positive aspects, you can confidently ask for the reader's acceptance. Make action clear, easy, and dated if necessary. If you need the reply by a certain date, tie this request in with reader benefit whenever possible—prominent billing on the program, adequate time for publicity, and so forth. Omit such negative statements as, "*If you can donate anything*, please. . . ." Better say, "To make your contribution, just return. . . ." Your last sentence often can tie in with a statement featured in the opening paragraph, as a last reader-benefit plug.

Asking Favors That Require Time, Knowledge, and/or Effort

By using the persuasive-request AIDA plan, you can urge a busy person to be speaker at an important banquet or conference for little or no pay—and even partly or entirely at his or her own (or employer's) expense. You can encourage people to accept time-consuming chairmanships or to serve without pay on long-term committees and boards. You can obtain answers to research questionnaires which require more than routine effort by the recipient. You can give employees or club members a pep talk about attending certain functions; and you can increase membership in a business, professional, social, or religious organization. All these favors require time, knowledge, and/or effort, as the next two examples illustrate.

Request for a Speaker

In message 1, the president of an aircraft owners and pilots association invites an author (who is a member of the same nonprofit association in another city 500 miles away) to be principal speaker. The letter includes all needed details about date, time, place, audience, length and topic of talk. The underlying appeal or central selling point is the reader's ability to help in a serious crisis those of similar interests.

Message 1—Letter

Inviting a speaker to address a banquet, without an honorarium.

*Attention;
reader-centered;
compliment*

The article you wrote in the March issue of <u>Flying</u> has been of great interest to us in the Viewmont chapter of AOPA. We are currently involved in a battle to ac-quire a surplus Naval air station for general aviation use and find your ideas on airport facilities just the approach we need to convince those not familiar with general aviation problems.

*Interest;
the problem*

Three months ago we learned that the Highpoint Naval Air Station would be surplus in August of this year. It seemed at first that general aviation would easily acquire this badly needed airport. But recently much opposition has developed. The area residents simply do not understand why another airport for "small planes" is needed. We have planned a banquet for the leaders of the community to convince them of the genu-ine need for this facility and would very much like you as our dinner guest and speaker. Your views on

And the request   the general crisis of airport congestion would be extremely helpful in presenting our case. Will you tell
us how you put the new program into effect last year
in your city?

Reader benefit   You will enjoy, I'm sure, the dinner and entertainment
we have planned. The banquet will be held at the new
Century Hotel, Monday, June 20, at 7 p.m.; but the
time can be changed if another hour is more convenient
for you. You will, of course, be reimbursed for your
traveling and overnight hotel expenses; and I personally will see that you are picked up and returned to
Desire;   the airport at your convenience. We expect about 100
conviction details   persons to attend. After two local speakers present
their views, we would like you to speak for twenty to
thirty minutes to conclude the arguments with an expert's opinion which will add much strength to our
cause.

Dated action   A brief letter from you indicating acceptance will assure the success of this function. Also, please
include your preference as to dinner hour. Because
the program goes to press in three weeks, will you
send your decision by May 20? The members in this
Value of   area will sincerely appreciate the contribution you
reader's talk   can make to our obtaining another urgently needed general aviation airport in this area.

Request for Help in a Survey

Whether you are a student gathering firsthand information for a report, a
business executive surveying your employees, or a research consultant working for numerous clients, you will get better cooperation from your readers
when you write persuasively.

Message 2, for example, stresses reader benefit throughout. This letter
also illustrates one way you can save money if you have a slim budget and a
long mailing list: in place of the personalized inside addresses and salutation,
you can use a reader-centered attention-getting statement or question. A letter
similar to the one below gained a 79 percent response.

Message 2—Letter

*A persuasive, effective request for return of a questionnaire by college teach-
ers.*

Attention;   Would knowing what other college teachers are doing in
reader benefit   their business communication courses help you?

Perhaps you, like many others, have wondered how the
content, emphasis, and assignments of your basic

Reader benefit or interest

course compare with those in other colleges that offer courses similar to yours in credit hours, size of sections, and prerequisites. Or you may have considered changing your courses and you could use tips on what others are including.

Interest; description of project

To gather this information about this rapidly expanding field of study, we are making a nationwide survey of business communication courses taught in schools holding membership in the American Association of Collegiate Schools of Business (AACSB). This study is planned to get specific details on the subject matter and written assignments in 19XX-19XX courses.

Desire; facts; reader benefit

You are the only teacher in your institution receiving this letter and the enclosed form. All names of participants will remain confidential in the report of this study. By completing the questionnaire and returning it, you will be helping expand knowledge about the teaching of this vital subject matter. Also, you'll know how your courses compare with others. You will find the questions easy to answer, we believe, because most of them require only your check mark.

Dated, easy action; reader benefit

To make sure that your college is included in this study, please mail the form by May 1, in the stamped envelope provided. In appreciation of your cooperation in this study, you will receive a summary of the findings, if you wish,[2] before the information appears in print.

The benefits offered to the college teachers for mailing the questionnaire enclosed with message 2 are mainly intangible, yet they are adequate because the readers are expected to have a keen interest in helping to improve their profession. On the other hand, when you ask information from persons who have no built-in interest in your questionnaire, you may—if your budget allows—also have to offer a tangible inducement. For instance, the director of consumer panels for a national market research firm, in a request to "Dear Homemaker," included a tangible gift (tableware), as well as intangible benefits (enjoyment, usefulness, safety, and anonymity).

Asking Donations of Money or Other Tangible Valuables

Many people are even more reluctant to part with material goods than they are to donate their time. Thus all you have learned about persuasiveness, appeals, factual presentation, and reader benefits is even more important for requests to donate valuables.

---

[2] The respondent could indicate his or her wish—and also protect anonymity—by returning his or her name and address on an enclosed separate slip.

If you want your reader to donate money, describe the problem and tell what is being or has been done, what needs to be done, and what your organization is doing about the problem. After stating meaningful facts, tell what it will cost to do what your organization wants to do—and how the reader can help.

If the donation is for a cause from which the reader benefits directly—as in improved recreation facilities for a club of which he or she is a member—you can choose from appeals such as comfort, enjoyment, friendships, health, love of family. However, if the donation goes to charity, your main appeal is usually altruism—helping others. Action paragraphs like the following help the conscientious reader who wonders how much he or she should give:

1. A gift of $10 will buy vitamins for 25 children . . . $25 will provide a cup of milk to 400 children . . . $45 may keep a father and mother alive to care for their own children . . . $250 sends 800 pounds of medicines to our hospitals.
2. "What is a thoughtful contribution?" You can best answer this question, BUT we suggest that an amount approximating two hours' pay would be justified in light of . . . .

Message 3—Memo

An executive's persuasive request to employees to contribute generously to an annual fund drive.

TO: All Members of the Wigget Staff
FROM: Alberta Jones, President
SUBJECT: An appeal for the UGN Fund
         DATE: Oct. 15, 19___

Attention: problem

All of you are aware that this year our community has a larger number of needy, desperate, afflicted people of all ages, creeds, and races.

What is being done

You know also of the fine work that the United Good Neighbors Fund does to provide community services through 82 Good Neighbor agencies. Hundreds of persons volunteer freely of their time and money to make this drive successful each year, with no thought of tangible rewards.

Reader benefit

Request

Your one contribution helps in many ways, and you are spared from being dunned by separate agencies. I would like to make a personal appeal this year that all of us reassess our values of this program and make an honest effort to give just a little bit more. Each of us sets the figure our conscience dictates, but I sincerely hope you can find it in your hearts to join

me in increasing our donation this year. Our company's goal is $52,900.

Appeal to
altruism
We are all most fortunate in not being on the receiving end of this program, and one way to count our
blessings is by helping those less fortunate, as described in the enclosed leaflet.

Easy
action
Remember, UGN pledge cards make it possible to contribute in small monthly or quarterly installments, or
if you choose, you may pay by payroll deductions.

Appeal
to pride,
altruism
Let's give serious consideration to the amount we contribute this year and try to make it one of which to
be proud. Your support will be received with appreciation by the many agencies within UGN.

Urging Cooperation on Goals and Projects

As a committee chairperson or officer you may sometimes need your readers'
support for various goals and projects your organization considers important.
Messages 4 and 5, sent to members and voters respectively, illustrate how
persuasive requests can help move readers to action toward which they would
otherwise be indifferent.

Message 4–Letter

A membership chairman appeals for help in boosting membership

Attention:
agreeable
comment
and question
NPRA MEMBERSHIP
JUMPS 100%

Wouldn't you be delighted to see that headline in the
NPRA Journal? And you can . . . for it can be done
easily . . . without gimmicks or strings or expense to
you.

Reader-benefit
goal
Increased membership will strengthen our effectiveness
and benefit each of us as well as the entire field of
public relations. If you—each member—will find us
one new NPRA member, our size can double.

Easy-action
request
The method is simple and effective. Go over your
firm's executive roster, your list of business associates. Think of everyone you know who might be
interested in public and customer relations. Write
the names and addresses on the enclosed card and drop
it into the mail. That's all you need to do! Our
secretary, Mr. Jim Ark, will take it from there.

Tie-in with
opening

Isn't that easy? Find one new member for NPRA . . . and
look for that headline soon . . . NPRA MEMBERSHIP
JUMPS 100%.

Message 5—Letter

Four citizens (one expert each in engineering, medicine, business leadership,
and law) persuade citizens to vote for a bond issue.

Dear Southside resident:

Attention:
reader-benefit
comment

Each of us has the opportunity on May 19 to leave a
legacy for the future when we vote on the Forward Move
bond issue--rapid transit. This program will substantially improve the quality of your environment for
many years to come.

Interest:
reader benefits

Rapid transit will reduce traffic congestion and air
pollution, both of which are becoming increasingly
difficult problems in the Southside area. In addition, it will be of enormous benefit to you as a
resident of Southside. To you and the employees in
this area rapid transit brings easy access to plants
and businesses plus increased mobility from the south
side to all parts of the greater *(city name)* community.

Two paragraphs for "interest and desire" include reader-benefit facts
about two new underground bus transfer stations and low taxpayer costs (less
than 6 cents a day).

Reader-benefit
request

On the basis of the compelling need and an opportunity
to preserve and strengthen your area, we ask you to
vote "yes" with us on May 19.

OTHER PERSUASIVE NONROUTINE REQUESTS

Adapting the AIDA Plan

You can also use the AIDA plan effectively when you must persuade your
reader to grant your request for adjustment, credit, or a change in a policy or
performance. For your attention-getting opening you can use any of the suggested six kinds discussed for favor requests (pages 274 to 276). However, to
present a concise, logical argument, it is usually best to begin with an assertion.
This statement often is a principle—a major premise on which both you and the
reader agree or about which you wish to persuade the reader; for example,
these two (which can also be considered agreeable-comment openings):

No doubt you expect your authorized dealers to uphold the good name
of your products.

I am sure you want your company to have a reputation for fairness
and honesty.

You will get the reader's interest and desire when you state all necessary
facts and details—interwoven with reader benefits. Include whatever description the reader needs to see that his or her firm is responsible (if this applies)
and that your request is factual, logical, and reasonable. Your action request
should be a logical conclusion based on the major premise and the clearly
stated facts.

Persuasively Requesting an Adjustment

When a product or service from a reputable firm is unsatisfactory but you know
that your claim for an adjustment is outside the warranty or otherwise unusual,
your message should follow the persuasive-request instead of the direct-request plan. You also need to be persuasive when your request is *not* unusual
but the seller disregarded your first direct request.

In letter 1, because of unusual circumstances, the customer persuasively
asks for a new camera and certain other expenses—even though the printed
guarantee includes a statement that the firm will service the camera but "cannot assume responsibility for loss of film, for other expenses or inconveniences, or for consequential damages occasioned by the equipment." This is an
unusually long letter, but the details included are necessary to achieve the goal.
The writer did get essentially what she wanted, though in slightly different
form—six free rolls of film with processing mailers and an exchange of her
camera with one owned by the manager of the local Picturetronics, Inc.

Letter 1

*A consumer writes persuasively to a manufacturer's adjustment manager,
requesting an unusual adjustment.*

*Attention:
assertion of
major premise*

"Let your Wessman camera preserve those precious moments for you." This appealing advertising slogan,
plus your company's good reputation, helped me to
choose a Wessman camera for my once-in-a-lifetime trip
to South America. Because of unusual circumstances I
now find it necessary to appeal to you.

*Interest; facts
about purchase*

Six months ago I purchased my Wessman Instanshot camera from a reputable store here. That was two months
before my trip, so that I would have time to become
thoroughly familiar with the camera before traveling
in a foreign country. (I was a member of a group representing the Foundation for International

Understanding, and our long-planned trip was a good-will tour which I wanted to preserve in good pictures.)

For Conviction, a paragraph states facts on malfunctioning and repairs of the electronic eye, bar indicator, and flash attachment by an authorized dealer twice before the trip.

Conviction: more on the problem

Two days before my departure they called to report my camera was "now in excellent working order." Little did any of us guess the picture problems ahead. Nevertheless, the camera was again a disappointment only two days later—on my first attempt to take a picture before leaving the airport. Twice the flash did not go off. Because it was Sunday morning and only a few minutes before plane departure, there was of course no way to have further repairs then. Perhaps you can imagine how you would feel at this moment. I had depended upon your authorized dealer's word that my camera was in excellent condition! (Incidentally, I always handle a camera with care according to instructions, for I know it is a delicate precision instrument.)

Reader in writer's shoes; writer's care and trust

Tie-in with major premise

Throughout my trip there were numerous "precious moments" I wanted to preserve with my new Wessman camera. Most of these were on indoor occasions—receptions, dinners, and other functions with people. I can buy postcards of buildings and nature. But no one sells pictures of the precious moments with other human beings who assembled just for our group! Yet these moments are lost forever because the flash attachment failed numerous times. These failures also resulted in my ample supply of Wessman film being exhausted much too soon. I thus had to purchase additional film plus flashbulbs in foreign stores, at much higher prices.

Writer's losses

When my developed film was returned I found that 72 negatives were total blanks. I other words, 72 times that flash attachment failed; 72 precious moments are lost instead of preserved, as your slogan advertises.

Appeal to fairness and pride

Picturetronics, Inc. have said they can't understand what is the matter with this camera and they've done all they can. Even they suggest that my camera must be one of the very rare defective products from your usually dependable high-quality stock. Thus I am returning this camera to you for your inspection. But after all the heartaches it has given me—in losing instead of preserving precious moments—I ask that you please keep this camera and send me instead a new de-

Request

```
pendable Instanshot camera.  Also, will you please
reimburse me for the $49.20 I paid for wasted film,
processing, and flashbulbs.  Copies of sales slips are
enclosed.
```

Tie-in with
major premise

```
By making these fair replacements you will help to re-
store my faith in Wessman.  Also, not only I, myself,
but friends who share my disappointments, will again
believe that Wessman does "preserve those precious
moments."
```

Retailers also sometimes encounter serious situations that require persuasive requests to their wholesalers or manufacturers after previous direct requests have failed. In such cases the attention-getting assertion in the first paragraph may even be a negative appeal: loss of reader benefits. For example, a retailer who sold a certain manufacturer's tools exclusively threatened he would go to competitors' products if the manufacturer would not immediately improve both the quantity of tools and the promptness of deliveries sent to this distributor. The opening of his letter introduces the fear appeal:

```
Repetition is an accepted mechanism for achieving emphasis. Al-
though we have stated to you before our situation with respect to
Crown tools, we are writing again now to emphasize to you the prob-
able sad consequences of your current performance and allocations.
```

In seven additional paragraphs the letter reviews specific facts regarding order backlogs, manufacturer's broken promises, disappointed construction contractors, cancellations by 69 customers lost to competitors, and further risks of lost reader benefits. After appeals to fairness, the letter closes with this reader-benefit request:

```
Therefore, please do everything you can this month to step up your
shipments to fill the backlog of orders while you can still save
this excellent market!
```

Persuasively Requesting Credit

Most credit applications are direct requests, made in the routine course of business. However, sometimes you may seek a special credit privilege which on the surface you appear to be unqualified for. In such cases a persuasive request is more effective. For instance, if you are just starting your own first store and your capital, inventory, and current income are barely adequate, you will need to convince prospective creditors that they can depend upon you to pay regularly. Or you may wish to ask for 120-day credit terms instead of the usual 30-day period. Whatever your unusual request may be, be sure to include sufficient facts and figures to show how you have planned carefully and perhaps how the reader will benefit—for example, from your expected expanding market.

Sometimes credit applicants' first direct request is turned down and they cannot understand why. If they still want credit with that firm, a persuasive request such as letter 2 may help accomplish that purpose. This letter brought a prompt, pleasant phone call, an apology, and the granting of a revolving credit account "gladly."

Letter 2

A persuasive request for credit after a turndown.

Attention: assertion	Your form letter of January 31 refusing my request for the Blank's Revolving Credit (BRC) account and suggesting I consider an Easy Payment Account came as a mild shock.
Interest; applicant's work and knowledge	Blanks, without a doubt, maintains certain policies regarding credit applications from individuals. In my occupation as a bookkeeper and assistant manager of City Paint and Hardware Company, I process many applications for credit. Therefore, I feel that when you considered my application, either sufficient information was not given or the fact that I am renting a house, rather than buying, was regarded as grounds for listing me as a person of "questionable" credit standing. In either assumption, I believe the following information will give you a clear picture of my "present circumstances."
Conviction facts	Employment and Income (*7 lines*) Assets and Liabilities (*8 lines*) References (*11 lines*)
Reader-benefit request	The Easy Payment Plan you suggest is an expensive way to buy merchandise. To buy on this plan partially defeats the purpose of "SHOP AT BLANKS AND SAVE!" Small easy payments <u>do</u> <u>not</u> appeal to me. Nor does dragging out payments over a long period of time. Your BRC account would be one I would use frequently. And you can be sure that you will receive prompt payments. BRC fits my present needs and my ability to pay. Your extending this privilege to me will be greatly appreciated.

Persuasively Requesting Changes in Policy or Performance

Besides requesting nonroutine adjustment or credit, you may at times need to persuade a company to make other exceptions from its usual policy. Or you may wish to persuade individuals to change their actions; or to give employees a written pep talk, hoping to improve their future performance. The basic persuasive-request pattern is again applicable here.

Changes in Policy

In letter 3, an advertising consultant tries to persuade the public relations officer of ABC Company to divert from its usual policy of not giving away or lending products. An outstanding magazine feature writer (renamed "Jake Edlis" in this example) had written for permission to borrow, free, ABC Company's new XX boating equipment—to use, photograph, and mention in his new series of feature stories on outdoor life.

Letter 3

An advertising consultant's persuasive request to change from the usual no-loan policy regarding company equipment.

Attention: assertion	Though I know it is ABC's policy not to loan or give away its products, I think sticking to it in the case of Jake Edlis would be a mistake.
Interest; conviction	There are very few writers in the recreation field for whom I'd take a stand on this issue. Among them are _____, _____, _____, and Jake Edlis.
Company benefit	First, lending your boating equipment is a relatively small expense for the publicity ABC is bound to receive in return. The space value could, conceivably, amount to tens of thousands of dollars. As you know, his write-ups reach about 16 million readers each month.
More company benefit	Second, ABC is a big league now. Big leaguers play the game by getting respected writers like Edlis to use their products (many of them carrying big price tags) and write about them.
More company benefit	Third, as a member of the Outdoor Writers Association of America and a well-known feature writer, Edlis is bound to talk to a lot of other "influentials" in the field. He could, intentionally or not, start word that ABC is willing to take lots of free space, but unwilling to extend the accepted courtesy of letting legitimate feature writers try its products without charge. Ultimately, this could lead to poor press relations and a resulting drop in our publicity lineage.
Risk of harmful results if change is not made	
Company-benefit request	In the interest of maintaining exceptionally good press relations, please reconsider your company's "no giveaway" policy when someone with the stature of a Jake Edlis offers his services. I'm sure you'll be glad you did.

Changes in Performance

Persuasion is necessary whenever you need to convince individuals to change their performance (which may include personal appearance and habits as well as business practices) and if direct requests have been or would be unheeded.

The next two examples[3] illustrate how important the right tone and use of appeals are for getting reader cooperation. As you read letter 4, note these faults:

1. Overemphasis on negatives—"disturbed," "horrified," "will have to be removed," "senseless," "punishing," "destroying"
2. Overuse of "we"—meaning "Landlord, Inc.," rather than "all people (us) in the neighborhood"
3. Manager's domineering, threatening, discourteous attitude, which places all parents on the defensive and seems to blame their children, although the vandals may have been outsiders
4. Total lack of reader appeals

Letter 4

A poor, negative, unpersuasive request from a building manager to tenants.

```
TO ALL PARENTS LIVING IN 100 OAK AVENUE AND 50 ELM AVENUE

    We have become seriously disturbed because of the recent vandal-
ism in your neighborhood. Every day now, storage room doors are
being broken, tires removed from bicycles, parts of baby carriages
are taken off, etc. etc.; but today we were horrified to see a beau-
tiful living tree (in front of 50 Elm Avenue) completely cut in
half. Now the tree will have to be removed.

    We would like all the parents to have a good talk with their
children in order to stop this senseless destruction.

    We will start patrolling this section very closely from now on,
and if necessary, we will call in the municipal and school au-
thorities of Metropolis, in order to start punishing children who
are found destroying property.
```

In contrast, letter 5 eliminates the main faults of letter 4. Its tone is friendly, courteous, and positive. Equally important, this letter emphasizes community spirit, mutual concern, and cooperation. Letter 5 appeals to the parents' pride, love of family, health, and desire for security; and it includes the young people as citizens instead of accusing them indirectly of being vandals.

Letter 5

An appealing, improved version of letter 4.

[3] Courtesy of New York Life Insurance Company, *Effective Letters Bulletin*, Summer 1965.

TO ALL FAMILIES IN THE ELM AVENUE SCHOOL DISTRICT:

Attention:
a mutual problem

I know you will be as sorry as I was to learn that the lovely old elm tree which gave our school its name was destroyed today. Its beauty and grace are now lost to us forever, and all of us regret this tragedy.

Interest; need for
mutual effort

The destruction of our landmark appears to be another in a recent series of acts of vandalism in our neighborhood--a problem which can affect all of us unless we make a mutual effort to rid ourselves of it.

Conviction; appeals
to safety, health,
security, and civic
pride

A number of residents of our community have volunteered to do patrol duty in their off-hours, protecting the safety of our families and our property. Though we appreciate their desire to help, we need to ask ourselves if a patrol is what we really want. Do we want our neighborhood to be a prison for our children or a place of freedom and healthful growth?

Shall we instead face this problem frankly and constructively? Let us consider a few facts. Does our community have adequate provisions for recreational activities, or should we be contributing more to the creativity, growth, and culture of Metropolis? Have we done everything possible to make this the city in which our young people will be proud to grow up?

Request

It has been suggested that we discuss these things both in our own homes and then together as a community. Will you meet with us next Monday evening, January 18, at 7:30 in the auditorium of Elm Avenue School so that we may plan a constructive program of progress? Perhaps we can form a Civic Pride Committee comprised of both young people and adults--a committee

Appeals to pride
and cooperation

which can investigate our needs and help us plan a calendar of events to appeal to everyone. Our mayor and council members share our enthusiasm and have agreed to be present.

Reader benefits

Let's make Monday evening "Family Night." Fill the auditorium with families, ideas, and appetites for cake, coffee, and sodas. See you at 7:30!

SUMMARY

The Persuasive Request Plan has a four-part ''AIDA'' structure—consisting of attention, interest, desire-conviction, and action paragraphs. You can adapt this plan whenever you need to request favors that require the readers to donate time, knowledge, effort, cooperation, money, or other intangibles. You can also adapt this plan when you need to persuasively request an adjustment, credit, or changes in policy or performance.

The Capsule Checklists on page 299 give a summary of the general plan and two main kinds of persuasive requests. (Following chapters discuss other messages using this plan.)

EXERCISES

Requests for Favors

1. Assume that you are the state president of a group of professional people who will attend a meeting in Washington, D.C., May 21, and would like to go through the White House together. There will be about 45 in your group, and you expect to have all the names and an exact number of attendees by May 1.

    You are aware that any member of the United States Congress— senator or representative—can assist you in visiting the White House when in Washington. This assistance is commonly referred to as a Congressional White House Tour because you are given a special pass and a specific time to be at the entrance gate. Others who are not aware of this often stand in line for hours to make the visit, whereas those with the Congressional Tour tickets can walk in at the proper time.

    Write to a member of Congress (preferably the one who represents you) and ask if an afternoon tour at about 3:30 can be arranged. Explain the name and purpose of the association, at what hotel the group will be meeting, and any other pertinent information. Assume a reason why this request for May 21 requires persuasion, and include appropriate appeals. Ask for specific instructions about picking up the tour tickets prior to the date you will be using them.

2. Assume that you are program chairperson for your college chapter of a national organization composed of students whose major is the same as yours. For the past two years the members have repeatedly mentioned their desire to hear this organization's national vice president, Ms. L. F. Conison. She is known to be an outstanding, dynamic speaker. Two of your members who heard her at the organization's national convention last June also have been enthusiastic about her. Because she lives 2,000 miles from your school and your chapter's treasury is small, everyone has just assumed that getting Ms. Conison would be almost impossible. Fortunately, in yesterday's newspaper you happened to read that Ms. Conison will be attending a one-day business conference in Somecity (you insert a city name), which is only 210 miles from you—just the day before your chapter's annual Founders' Day Banquet.

    Now you want to persuade Ms. Conison to accept your invitation to be principal banquet speaker. You cannot pay her any speaker's fee, but your budget enables you to pay traveling expenses equal to round-trip plane fare from (Somecity) to yours. Six planes daily fly between these cities; if she prefers a bus, buses run on an hourly schedule. A scenic ride by freeway takes about four hours, in case she prefers to drive a private car. Ms. Conison will, of course, be your chapter's dinner guest. Maybe you can think of an inexpensive, courteous way to take care of her if she wishes to stay overnight after her talk? Assume any other necessary details that will make your letter complete—with you-attitude. Consider carefully the best appeal(s) to use.

3. *(Memo)* Assume International Valve Corporation is the largest industrial employer in your city. Over the last five years, IVC has been the object of much unfavorable publicity, stemming from violation of water and air pollution regulations and controversy over discriminatory hiring practices. Its corporate image has suffered.

   To increase its contributions as a responsible corporate citizen in the city's economic and social life, IVC has launched a drive to increase the participation of its employees in social service, civic, and cultural organizations. As a participant in one phrase of this new direction, you have been delegated the responsibility of writing a form memo to all IVC executives. You are to secure volunteers to serve as business advisers for Tomorrow's Managers. This is an organization which sends businesspeople into area high schools to assist students in forming and managing business enterprises to manufacture and market goods or services. The students thus obtain firsthand experience in how the free enterprise system functions.

   IVC is sponsoring three advisors for Tomorrow's Managers. Each will devote two evenings a month to working with one of these groups at a city high school during the school year. There is no pay; the only benefits each volunteer receives come from working with young people, helping to develop their business skills and understanding of business enterprises. And, of course, International Valve will benefit from improved visibility in the community as an involved, public-spirited business organization.

   Write a memo which will get at least four volunteers for this project. Select and develop appeals focusing on benefits to IVC, the executives, and the high school students they will be advising. Anticipate and overcome objections which your readers might have. Date the memo August 8—schools open in one month.

4. Point out the weaknesses, errors, and good points in the following letter. Then—as program chairperson—rewrite it, applying the principles you have learned, to make your request so appealing that the reader will want to accept. Address it to Mr. Loren Greene, Director of Public Relations, KNRO Television, in a city about 80 miles from you. If your instructor approves, you may choose another topic instead of air pollution.

   What are you plans for Saturday evening, March 8? The members of our (*city name*) Business Leaders' Club feel it would be a pleasure to us to have you as the principal speaker for our annual banquet that night.

Ways to fight air pollution is a topic that our members are concerned and realize the need of practical advice from experienced
executives. Your many editorial comments on Channel 15 KNRO have
shown us your sincere interest and extensive study on this subject.
Our members and their spouses want to hear you in person. This banquet is our biggest function of the year, and we would be honored to
have you and your spouse as our guests.

The banquet will be held in the Marlbron Room of the Plaza Hotel at
7 and will be informal. A varied entertainment program and an excellant dinner at $12.50 per person have been arranged.

Your traveling expenses would be provided, and I hope that you can
take advantage of a visit to our city to settle any personal affairs
you may have here. The Plaza Hotel is equipped with excellant facilities in the event you decide to extend your visit.

I shall appreciate your assent to this request so that I can welcome
you on your arrival if feasible.

5. Assume you graduated from the university five years ago and you have
become an active member of a certain professional (or business, social, or
religious) group that owns the building in which meetings and activities take
place.

You have just been elected treasurer of your organization for a two-
year term. For about 15 years this organization has been saving money to
build a much needed extension to its building. (Assume specific reasons why
the addition is necessary and beneficial to members.) It has been planned
that construction will begin next July 1—three months from today—and be
completed by October 1. (Assume today is April 1.) The addition, as
sketched by architects and approved by your executive board, will cost
about $105,000. Your books show $49,000 cash in the building fund; your
organization can get a $50,000 mortgage. You need to raise $6,000 cash
between now and about May 5 or construction cannot begin. Your task is to
try to raise this money. After several meetings with the executive board, it is
decided that, rather than asking your members to put on several fund-raising
events (which are time-consuming), or assessing them a definite amount,
you will urge them to make a donation. The board members want you to
head this fund-raising campaign.

Write a letter, remembering that it is a form letter, to be sent to all
members. Assume a mailing list of 650. Try to keep your letter to one
typewritten page. Select the appeals (loyalty, pride, self-interest, and so
forth) that you think will be most effective in moving your readers to take
the requested action. Set May 1 as the deadline for donations, because
adequate time must be allowed for making financial arrangements before
construction begins. Make action easy and include any reasonable inducements for your readers to act now. Naturally, you'd rather have checks
returned with each reply; however, for those members who would rather

sign a pledge now and pay later—before completion of construction—plan an easy-action reply form you can depend on in your financial calculations.

6. *(Memo)* As the new systems manager for the National Insurance Co., you have considered numerous ways to increase company efficiency and decrease costs. Your firm sends 1,850,000 letters and notices each year. Recently, after checking correspondence procedures, you were surprised to find several wasteful, unnecessarily time-consuming methods that you'd like to change. However, before authorizing any changes, you have decided to survey the preferences of the management staff in your home office and 60 branch offices. You have prepared an easy-to-answer two-page questionnaire asking for their reactions to eight money- and timesaving suggestions. Now write a persuasive, courteous memorandum urging these executives to fill out your enclosed form and return it to you by a certain date, so that you can complete a needed report on their replies. Promise anonymity to all respondents. Include appropriate appeals to urge their cooperation. Three of your money-saving suggestions may require a little explanation and "selling" before your readers approach the questionnaire.

   a. You advocate using window envelopes instead of individually addressed envelopes for the approximately 160,000 monthly messages your company sends to policyholders, prospective customers, suppliers, and stockholders. You think window envelopes could save thousands of hours of typing time annually, because the inside addresses on the letters or forms within the envelopes could serve for the envelopes too.

   b. You are considering adopting a standardized companywide letter format—blocked, open punctuation, with or without salutation and complimentary close. Such standardization, you feel, would give the company an image of uniformity and at the same time save stenographic time. (For examples, see Figures 6–4 and 6–6.)

   c. With each company letter that asks the recipient for a brief answer, you would like to enclose a courtesy carbon for reply. The recipient would then merely type the reply at the bottom of your letter, return to you the carbon copy (showing both your letter and the reply), and keep the original for his or her files. Such an enclosure would bring speedier answers to company requests and would cut down the need for second or third requests to get replies, thus saving postage and labor costs.

   As you write your memo, remember that your readers are in management, just as you are, even if you do probably outrank many of them. Watch your tone and try to build pleasant relations and high morale.

7. *(Memo)* As building manager of your company's three-story structure, you have just received an unusual report from your sanitation engineer. He has found that at least two rats have been attracted to the building recently. The employee practice of leaving food on bookshelves, desks, and other open locations will have to be discontinued or watched very carefully. Each office occupant must be made aware of the problem and the possibility that he or

she is part of the cause. As rats will not bother to infest an area unless there is good reason to do so (food), the best way to maintain rat-free premises consists of denying them food, water, and safety. It would be economically unfeasible to make the needed structural changes for rat-proofing the entire building. (The cafeteria is, however, rat-proofed.) About four months ago you wrote a simple announcement (without appeals—merely a "direct request") to all employees. But apparently some (or most?) have forgotten about it. Now again two rats were seen, but many more, still unseen, could come into the building. Thus you must write a persuasive request in a memorandum to all employees, urging them to cooperate on preventive action. Instruct them to exercise utmost care with lunches or other food brought into the building. Instruct them not to leave any food in their offices overnight. Also request them to be alert for signs indicating rodent or insect activity: droppings; gnawed food, odor; dark rub marks along wall, ceiling, under door, ventilator, which indicate a runway. Request that employees inform a certain office as soon as such evidence appears. Watch the tone of your memo, and be sure to consider the attitudes of your readers.

8. Assume you graduated from college two years ago and became an active member of a business, professional, social, or religious organization. You have just been elected vice president and have been asked by the executive board to see if you can increase attendance at meetings for next year. Assume that the organization has a potential membership of 200, but that during the past three or four years only 20 to 30 have been attending monthly meetings regularly. You would like to have at least 55 or 60.

   Plan a letter to send to the 200 potential members, aiming to find out in a friendly, tactful way why so many have not been attending meetings and what types of programs, arrangements, or methods would get them to the meetings. Be careful to keep the tone positive and cheerful, filled with you-attitude. Suggestions: Perhaps more would come if they had transportation; if the meetings were held at a more central location, on different days, or during different hours; if the business portion were shorter and the programs more entertaining; or if someone would phone them shortly before meetings. In the past, written announcements have been sent to all members a week before a meeting. Devise some method which will make it easy for each member to answer your letter, giving you specific information about what is preferred in topics, speakers, activities, dates, times. Assume that your letter will be reproduced by Xerox or offset printing.

Nonroutine Requests for Adjustments, Credit, or Changes

1. You are manager of Larry's Men's Wear in Sometown, Nebraska. You have two stores—one situated in the downtown area and one two blocks from a college campus. For years you have carried exclusively Van Doner shirts, which you buy direct from the manufacturer. On June 2, only four days after

this firm's fall catalog came out, you again ordered a complete Van Doner line for your two stores. You asked for delivery by September 2. But today (September 9) you have noted with alarm the many changes the manufacturer made in your fall order. Back-to-school goods scheduled by your sales staff for early delivery have been pushed to October and November. You haven't a plaid in stock and college opens next week. You've had to switch to other brands because you can't get all the Van Doner merchandise you'd like. You have faith in Van Doner merchandise; it's your preference of all brand shirts on the market. But this is the third time in four years that they have changed delivery time on your orders.

While you were in Springfield, Missouri, just a few days ago, you noted that the Lester Men's Store (a retail store for this shirt manufacturer) was stocked with everything in the Van Doner book, and Lester could not have ordered any sooner than you did. Just how does this manufacturer expect to keep good customers like you with that kind of treatment? Unless they can find some way to supply your stores adequately and promptly—by no later than September 21—you may have to find a replacement for Van Doner shirts. You feel you have helped considerably to build this manufacturer's business the past five years. (Your store's total Van Doner purchases were $220,000.) Right now you feel like giving your business to a competitor. Address your message to Mr. Harry Nomad, sales manager of Van Doner Manufacturing Company, Chicago. Be tactful, firm, appropriately persuasive, and clear in your request.

2. Assume you have just received a credit turndown for a charge account with a local store. The reason stated for the refusal is correct. (Assume a legitimate reason such as under age 18, presently unemployed, or a similar one.) However, for various other reasons—perhaps a steady trust fund income you receive from a regular source, a verifiable record of integrity, or any other good reason(s) that might outweigh the shortcoming—you know that you will be a prompt-paying customer. You always take care of all obligations you have. Write to the store's credit manager an honest, persuasive request for credit. Make your reasoning logical and appealing, so that your reader will be convinced that she or he should make an exception for you and grant you a charge account.

3. About three months ago you received a letter from a magazine publisher offering a special subscription rate to members of the National Business Association. (You are a member.) Because you think the magazine is an excellent source of current information in your major field, you decided to take advantage of the special offer—$8.50 for a one-year subscription, $16 for two years (24 monthly issues). Using the convenient order form provided, you indicated that you wanted the two-year subscription and that you enclosed your payment. You attached your personal check #552 to the order form and mailed it in the envelope provided.

The order was mailed exactly three months ago today and your check cleared the bank the following month. You received your first issue of the magazine four weeks ago, along with an invoice for $16 for the subscription. The notice indicated that no further issues would be sent until payment was received. As you have your canceled check clearly showing that it was deposited by the National Publishing Company (the magazine's publisher), you realize that the company was in error. The same day you wrote a letter to Ms. Anne Plumb (Circulation Manager, National Publishing Company, 902 Broad Street, Philadelphia, PA 19108), explaining the facts and asking her to see that your account (#0147392) was credited for the $16 and that the remaining 23 issues of the magazine were sent promptly.

Today you received a second invoice, stating that you still owe $16. The computer-printed bill had the following message: "We have not heard from you." Obviously, they should have heard from you: not once, but twice. Because your letter to Ms. Plumb seems not to have led to any action, you have decided to write a persuasive request for an adjustment directly to the party in power—the computer. Explain the situation again and ask for the appropriate action. A little humor may be acceptable, but remember the main purpose of your letter.

CAPSULE CHECKLISTS FOR PERSUASIVE REQUESTS*

I Persuasive Requests—General Plan	II Persuasive Requests for Favors	III Other Persuasive Nonroutine Request

1. ATTENTION (promise; star)
  a. Introduction of relevant reader-benefit or reader-interest theme—centered on reader, not on writer's organization
  b. Envelopes and letterheads sometimes specially designed for the message
	1. Attention
	  a. Sincere compliment
	  b. Questions
	  c. Agreeable comment or assertion
	  d. Basic problem
	  e. What has been done about a problem
	  f. Frank admission of a favor
		1. Attention
		  a. Preferably an agreeable assertion or a principle used as major premise
		  b. Sincere compliment
		  c. Question
		  d. Basic problem
		  e. Frank admission of a favor

2. INTEREST (picture; chain)
  a. Introduction of project, product, service, or problem: description, central selling point
  b. Appeals—direct or indirect reader benefits: appreciation, approval, beauty, cleanliness, comfort, convenience, cooperation, customer satisfaction, distinctiveness, efficiency, enjoyment, entertainment, extra earnings, fair treatment, friendships, good reputation, health, improvement, love of home and others, money and other valuables, peace of mind, pleasure, popularity, position, profits, recognition, safety, satisfaction of helping others, savings, self-preservation, and others
 	
3. DESIRE (prove; chain)
  a. Development of description, benefits, central selling point, request, appeals; perhaps with an enclosure
  b. Appropriate handling of possible objections
  c. Conviction:
    (1) "Outside" proof; perhaps with enclosures
    (2) Price and terms when needed and appropriate; perhaps in enclosure
	2. Interest and
	3. Desire
	  a. Necessary physical description of project
	  b. Facts, figures, and reader benefits to convince reader that his or her contribution will be enjoyable, easy, important, beneficial—directly or indirectly
	    (1) In request for speaker: date, day, hour; place; function; topic; talk length; audience size, interests; honorarium; expenses; special attractions; appeals.
	    (2) In request for donation: problem; needs; past, present methods of meeting needs; costs; reader contribution: benefits; appeals.
	    (3) In request for cooperation: problem; facts, suggestions, committee, etc. to help meet goal; reader's part; benefits; appeals.
	  c. Positive handling of negatives and probable objections for favors that:
	    (1) Require time, knowledge, or effort
	    (2) Ask donations of money or other valuables
	    (3) Urge cooperation on goals and projects
	  d. Enclosures (brochures)
		2. Interest and
		3. Desire
		  a. All necessary facts and details pertaining to request for adjustment, credit, or changes in policy or performance—interwoven with reader benefits and appeals
		  b. Description as needed by the reader to see that his or her firm is responsible (if applicable) and that the request is factual, logical, and reasonable

4. ACTION (push; hook)
  a. CSAD[1]
  b. EA[2]
  c. DA when desirable[3]
  d. Special inducement when desirable
  e. RB[4] (often tied in with opening statement)
	4. Action
	  a. CSAD[1]
	  b. EA[2]
	  c. DA when desirable[3]
	  d. Special inducement when desirable
	  e. RB[4] (often tied in with opening statement)
		4. Action
		  a. Logical conclusion based on the major premise and the clearly stated facts; then same as II. 4

* Lists include possible content. For any one message, choose only pertinent and appropriate items.

[1] CSAD = clear statement of action desired.   [3] DA = dated action, if desirable.

[2] EA = easy action.   [4] RB = reader benefit.

299

PART THREE
Special Messages

CHAPTER 11
Sales Letters

Every year millions of dollars' worth of goods and services are sold to consumers, businesses, and industries—by means of sales letters, both solicited and unsolicited. These kinds of messages are grouped in this chapter according to the organizational plans used.

Solicited sales letters

Good-news replies to sales-related inquiries
Bad-news replies to sales-related inquiries

Unsolicited, persuasive sales letters

Making direct sales
Serving as stimuli to future sales
Bringing back lost customers

SOLICITED SALES LETTERS

Requests for information about services or products you sell are inquiries related to sales. Included are questions about catalogs, prices, terms, discounts, deliveries, products, manufacturing methods, types of accounts available, sources of supply, and similar information.

Replies to many of these inquiries are actually sales letters and are called *solicited,* or *invited,* sales messages. The inquirer is often already your customer, or a potential buyer, who may become a steady, satisfied customer *if* you send a reply that impresses favorably.

Good-News Replies to Sales-Related Inquiries

When the information you can send in answer to an inquiry brings favorable or neutral information, you will use the Good-News Plan. This section discusses content of the three parts and suggestions for handling inquiries prompted by advertising.

Positive Opening Paragraphs

The best way to begin these letters is by courteously doing one of the following:

1. *Sending the requested material*

```
Enclosed are three samples of the nylon materials you asked about.
We are glad to send these to you with our compliments.
```

2. *Answering favorably one of the inquirer's questions*

    a. Yes, Ms. Jones,
You can use Latex Enamel paint in your bathroom with complete assurance that it is washable.

    b. You're right! Model XL2, about which you inquired, can easily become an exceptionally good profit maker for you. Our dealers have reported it to be their most popular do-it-yourself maintenance kit.

3. *Introducing the main idea(s) that your letter will cover*

    a. Thank you for giving us the opportunity to tell you about the two insured savings plans available to you at First Federal.

    b. I am glad to explain to you the differences in the three Portable Vibration Monitors you asked about in your May 5 letter.

Helpful Explanation Answering All Questions

In your explanation section, you should answer all questions—direct or implied. In many cases, you will also provide educational, resale, or sales promotion information. Arrange your answers so that the favorable responses are at the beginning and end of your explanation section, to accent the positive and "embed" the negative aspects. Maintain a you-attitude; keep the reader in every paragraph if possible.

    Embedding the negative does not mean that you should omit or twist the truth. It means that you can emphasize what something *is* rather than what it is *not*. Like a good salesperson, you try to determine what the customer really needs. Contrast, for instance, the negative and the positive answers to the following questions:

1. *Question:* Is the raincoat sprayed with ABC liquid so it is waterproof?

Negative reply:

No, I'm sorry to say the raincoat is not sprayed with ABC liquid. However, the material itself is made of durable vinyl which is completely waterproof.

Positive reply:

The material in this raincoat is made of a durable vinyl which is permanently and completely waterproof. Thus you need never bother with any spray even after the garment has been cleaned many times.

2. *Question:* Do you carry Bronson tape recorders? If so, how long would it take for you to send one to my office if I should decide to order it? (*The inquirer lives 500 miles from the seller, and only 100 miles from the factory. The seller is out of the item today, but notice that the inquirer has not yet ordered it.*)

Negative reply:

```
We are temporarily out of stock of the Bronson, and so we couldn't
send you one right away. If we reorder especially for you, it will
take 10 days after we receive your request.
```

Positive reply:

```
Yes, we do carry the Bronson tape recorder, and we can usually send
it to you within one day after we receive your order. As it is an
extremely popular model, we sometimes run out of it temporarily. In
such a case, we will gladly reorder immediately so you can expect
delivery within 10 days. Occasionally, for a rush order, we could
have the item sent to you direct from the factory within two days
after your request reaches us.
```

When quoting prices, be sure to use the same positive psychology by considering your reader's needs and circumstances. Unless the price of a particular product is a bargain, mention it only *after* you have stated most selling points and reader benefits. (Additional suggestions for quoting prices honestly and effectively are on pages 321 and 322.)

Effective Action-Getting Paragraphs Leading to Sales

To get the desired action from your invited-sales reply, remember to make action clear, easy, dated if necessary, and beneficial to the reader when possible. Sometimes, numbering the steps the reader should take is effective.

Letter 1 below is a helpful reply to an inquiry related to sales. It can be sent to any consumer who writes to this manufacturer for information and prices on the firm's interior home furnishings products—floor coverings, ceiling materials, furniture, and wall coverings. Notice that the consumer services manager includes specific suggestions for finding helpful retail merchants who can give the consumer needed information. The letter focuses on positive aspects instead of on negative regrets that the manufacturer can't quote retail prices.

Letter 1

A well-written reply that answers questions tactfully, encloses a booklet containing decorating ideas, and suggests where to go for additional help.[1]

---

[1] Courtesy of Armstrong Cork Company, Lancaster, Pa.

*Best news first;
reader benefit*

Thank you for your recent request for information about Armstrong products. We appreciate your interest and are enclosing for you various pamphlets showing how these products can help make a home easier to care for as well as more attractive.

*Further help
available*

For retail information and addresses of nearby Armstrong merchants, we suggest that you refer to the Yellow Pages of your telephone directory. You will find Armstrong products listed under "Floor Materials," "Carpet," and "Ceilings." For additional information on our Thomasville and Founders furniture, please write to Thomasville Furniture Industries, Inc., P.O. Box 339, Thomasville, NC 27360. Retail sources for Armstrong Cork Wallcovering can be obtained by writing to Katzenback and Warren, 950 Third Avenue, New York, NY 10022.

*Educational
information*

Your local retail firms selling our products will gladly supply retail cost information. We do not establish retail prices. Because of shipping and other considerations, prices necessarily vary in different zones of the country. In addition, when floors, carpet, or ceilings are professionally installed, your real cost is the "installed" cost, which, again, we cannot anticipate. We suggest that you obtain such information from local retail firms selling our products. Most of them will gladly give you estimates without obligation to you.

Suggested action

So that you can see the newest in products, designs, and colors, visit Armstrong retail merchants near you. From them you can get complete and up-to-date information on current offerings. We wish you every success with your selections.

Suggestions for Handling Inquiries Prompted by Advertising

Whenever a firm advertises, it should be prepared in advance for various kinds of inquiries. To save time and expense, you (or the marketing department) can compose pertinent form paragraphs, and entire messages, to answer the most asked questions. Some messages should look personalized and individually typewritten, even though the body may be essentially the same for other inquirers who asked the same questions. Costs of personalized messages can be decreased considerably by using word processing equipment.

On the other hand, many favorable replies do not need to be personalized—especially in routine situations when you are sure your reader will not object to a processed form. Most readers would rather receive promptly a high-quality, courteous, complete form than a poor, personalized letter that is late, incomplete, or perhaps even inaccurately—and hurriedly—typewritten. Letter 2 is typical of the well-written processed sales-oriented replies that accompany booklets, samples, or other free information sent in response to a coupon or inquiry.

Letter 2

Processed sales promotion reply (without inside address) with easy action order form.

Good news with courtesy; no salutation	Here is your . . . Foremost Radio catalog to aid you in your selections. Thank you for requesting information on Foremost communication receivers.
Resale	You will find much useful data in the section on "precision construction and advanced design." Other sections show you why Foremost sets are the world's finest receivers. They are the choice of radio amateurs, shortwave listeners, industrial and scientific
Reader benefit	users. A Foremost set places the whole world at your fingertips.
Reader benefits	All communication receivers listed in your catalog are in stock now for prompt shipment at the prices shown. You can get liberal trade-in allowances on standard communications receivers (Hallicrafters, National, Apex, and Howell). If you prefer a time-payment plan, the attached sheet gives you details.
Easy action	To assure delivery within 10 days, just enter your order on the enclosed order form and mail it now in the postage-free envelope. Your order may be accompanied by a deposit as low as 10%, with shipment to be made c.o.d. for the balance due, or you may include full remittance if you prefer.
Reader benefit	You can begin to enjoy the unusual reception of a famous Foremost set by placing your order now.

Bad-News Replies to Sales-Related Inquiries

If you have no honest favorable answer to your reader's direct question(s) regarding catalogs, prices, terms, products, and similar sales-related information, your reply should be organized by the bad-news plan. In some situations all four parts of such a message may be expressed adequately in four or five sentences.

When the inquiry is about a complex or more serious matter, however, much more detail may be necessary—especially in the explanation and resale portions. Letter 3—from the president of a wholesale cement firm to a contractor who had asked why the firm's prices were so high—illustrates how tact and specific details can help to retain a reader's goodwill despite bad news. Notice how it adapts to the *four parts of the bad-news plan: buffer; explanation; decision, with reader benefit and resale; positive friendly close, with offer of further service.*

Letter 3

A goodwill-retaining bad-news reply to an inquiry about high prices.

Buffer: thanks for inquiry and business

Thank you for your inquiry regarding the amount we charged you for your concrete. Because your business is very much appreciated and we understand your concern, it is important to me as well as to you that you understand why we billed you $528.08 instead of $465.13.

Explanation

Decision

Fairness to all; reader benefit

Due to the $1.44 hourly employee wage increase, the increase in the price of cement, and overall increases in direct and indirect operating expenses, it was necessary to increase the price of our concrete. For the past 11 months our prices for 5 sacks of our concrete have been $21.90 to individuals and $21.40 to all contractors. If we lower the price to one contractor, all others would rightly expect equal treatment. By maintaining our price, we treat everyone equally and can assure you that you are getting the quality of material you order and expect.

Resale

I realize you were able to buy concrete at a lower price in the past, but the company you bought the concrete from is no longer in business just because their price was not sufficient to cover their direct costs and expenses. Neither you nor we would want this condition to happen to us. We are proud of our reputation for quality products and service and want to continue to serve you in the future.

Pleasant close: thanks; further service

Your letters are always welcome. Also, if you have questions or need supplies, please call me between 7:30 a.m. and 5:30 p.m. at 999–3333, or call evenings at 666–6666.

UNSOLICITED SALES LETTERS

Also known as ''prospecting'' and ''cold turkey'' letters, unsolicited sales letters are initiated by the seller for various reasons and are not direct answers to inquiries. Direct mail[2] successfully urges people to buy products ranging from mail-order cataloged items to real estate. Not only large retail chains such as Montgomery Ward and Sears, but also thousands of lesser-known big-city and small-town merchants, wholesalers, and manufacturers sell effectively by mail. Many firms sell exclusively by mail. Even managers of shops selling services (for home and auto repair, health, beauty, protection, and others) stimulate their businesses by sales messages.

Although enormous potential income is possible using well-written sales letters, you need to be aware of the strong resistance many people have toward such messages. Common criticisms from readers who look unfavorably on sales letters are these: insincerity, appeals to the wrong group, hidden gimmicks, lack of personalization, excessive length, exaggeration.

In general, your success in sales letters will depend upon three factors: the mailing list, the right appeals, and the presentation. The first two of these factors are *pre-writing* steps. The remainder of this chapter discusses the steps to take before writing unsolicited sales letters, gives suggestions for writing them, and offers examples of various kinds of unsolicited sales letters. Appendix A includes various cautions regarding the seller's legal responsibilities in written and oral statements about the product or service. They can strongly affect the success of your sales messages.

Steps before Writing the Unsolicited Sales Letter

Because your sales letter may go to hundreds—even thousands—of people, you need to do exceptionally careful planning before starting to write it. The five planning steps—about purpose, reader, ideas to include, fact gathering, and organization—are especially important. Usually you first gather facts on your product, the competition, and your prospective buyer. Then give extra thought to the purpose, appeals, and presentation of your entire sales message.

Gathering Facts about Your Product

Before you write a sales letter, you first analyze thoroughly the product you want to sell. (The word *product* as used here includes both tangible products and intangible services.) You gather information through reading, observing, testing, using, comparing, questioning, researching.

If yours is a tangible product, what are its physical characteristics—size, color, shape, content, composition? How is it made and where did raw materials come from? How does it operate? What is its performance record? How does it compare with and differ from competitors' products in durability, efficiency, appearance, price, terms? What are its weaknesses? Strengths?

---

[2] In general, the term *direct mail* refers to any printed matter, other than periodicals, that attempts to sell or promote sales by mail. It includes—in addition to letters—postcards, manuals, brochures, order blanks, pamphlets, leaflets, gadgets, and reply forms. These items usually supplement the letter and help create a favorable seller-buyer relationship.

For your future buyers, benefits (psychological description) are usually much more significant than physical description. What will the product do for each user? What human needs or desires does it fulfill? For instance, a magazine may be a certain size, with *x* number of pages, on glossy paper, with hundreds of half-page pictures. But what information and enjoyment—even profits—does it bring to the user? What good does it do the buyer in business, home, family, and community contacts?

Whatever your product, you must know all its physical features and its reader benefits before you can confidently and effectively sell it.

Considering Your Reader and Mailing Lists

To sell your product effectively by letter requires also some knowledge of your readers and a selective, up-to-date, accurate mailing list. You'll use the mailing list both for a test mailing and for the entire mailing of one or several sales letters. *Testing* means mailing the letter to a small percentage (perhaps 5 to 10 percent) of the names on your list to see whether the letter brings the percentage of response necessary for you to make a profit.

When your product has almost universal use, you may have several different, reasonably homogeneous groups of prospects. Thus if you want to sell lighting fixtures by mail, you need to know the tastes, problems, preferences, and conditions of your various prospective users—homeowners, architects, store or office managers, plant or hospital or school superintendents, and so forth—and you'll write a different letter to each group.

Selectivity. Even an excellent sales letter about the best product in the world will not sell if the message goes to the wrong readers. You would not sell office filing cabinets to outdoor laborers, fishing boats to low-income people in a desert area, or Cadillacs to pensioners.

You can buy, rent, or make up a mailing list that includes the best potential buyers for your product. The more similar their characteristics and circumstances, the better. You can buy names and addresses of almost any kind of specialized group of people—classified by income level, age, marital status, sex, number of children, occupation, geographic location, color of eyes, height, education.

If you wish to make your own list, you will find one or more of these sources useful: telephone books, directories, membership lists, vital statistics, newspaper articles, and replies to your advertising. Furthermore, many firms have found that sometimes best of all are the prospect names from their own company records (on customers, stockholders, suppliers).

Up-to-Dateness and Accuracy. Postal authorities tell us that over one-fourth of all addresses change within one year. Names and titles may change too. The mailing list must be correct in addresses, spelling of names, use of prefixes (such as Mr., Miss, Mrs., Ms., Dr.), and titles (such as vice president or executive vice president). No matter how selective the list may be, it is good only when it is updated and correct.

Deciding on Purpose

The purpose of an unsolicited sales letter may be to make a direct sale, to serve as stimulus for future sales, or to win back lost customers.

To Make a Direct Sale. For relatively inexpensive convenience items or services the purpose of the sales letter is usually to make a direct sale. Sometimes even for more expensive or complex items your purpose may be to sell with only one letter, as you will see later in this chapter. More often, however, for such products the direct-sale letter follows previous groundwork laid by former letters (in a campaign series), by demonstrations, by advertising, or by sales representatives.

To Serve as Stimulus for a Future Sale. The long-range purpose of sales promotion messages may be to help build goodwill, supplement advertising, or give pep talks to distributors. Or they may serve as part of a campaign series involving complicated costly products (like factory machinery) or services (like mortgage lending) that require planning and/or individual consultation with a company representative before purchase. In these letters the purpose may be to introduce the product and then follow up with a salesperson. The requested action may be that the customer should: ask for a booklet, catalog, or other information; invite a representative to call; or come to the salesroom.

To Win Back Lost Customers. In other sales letters the purpose is: to let customers who haven't bought anything for some time know you miss them, to find out why they haven't been buying from you, and to sell them on coming back. The requested action is usually that the customer return a questionnaire; often an enclosed order blank brings a direct sale. And good follow-up can help bring in future purchases by presently dissatisfied customers.

Choosing Ideas and the Central Selling Point

After you have collected facts on your product, obtained a mailing list of likely prospects, and determined your purpose, you are ready to decide on ideas to include in your sales letter. Instead of cluttering your letter with a long list of facts about your product, you should select for emphasis a *central selling point* and translate it into user benefits. You stress *whatever appeal is most likely to convince the prospect that he or she should buy your product*. Often this is the feature or benefit that differentiates your product from competitors'. After you have stressed the central selling point, you can introduce other appeals about your product. *(For a list of reader-benefit appeals, see pages 272–273.)*

Your central selling point is always based on what you estimate are the prospect's needs. Will the product cut his or her costs? protect him or her? make him or her more attractive? If your product will appeal to different groups of prospects for different reasons, you will write a different sales letter to each group. In each letter you will feature the central selling point and appeals that you estimate are most pleasing to the readers for whom you write it. For example, to dealers who expect to resell your product, you will emphasize quick turnover and profits. To consumers you may feature comfort, pride in personal appearance, safety, or any other appropriate appeals. Remember also that individuals within any group have different mental filters and situations, and may thus be motivated for different reasons (perhaps another central selling point which you stress in a later letter).

Suppose, for instance, you want to sell by mail vinyl jackets that are water-repellant, fully lined—with removable warm inner lining, fashionable, and easily cleaned with a damp cloth. To readers living in rainy areas you might feature year-round comfort (dry in any downpour). To readers in arid regions your major appeal may be convenience (easily cleaned and wearable the year around). For students you might focus on both attractiveness (in style) and saving money (infrequent replacements, factory prices, no dry-cleaning bills).

Organizing and Planning the Sales Presentation

The fifth planning step—outlining and organizing—involves much more than deciding upon the organizational plan and letter content. Your letter is part of an entire sales presentation, whether it is to be a single sales effort or part of a campaign series. Thus you will consider—perhaps with other executives and a consultant—its length, appearance, timing, and enclosures along with your budget and expected returns.

Your presentation must move readers to take the desired action—and yield a satisfactory profit. The percentage of response needed for profitable returns may range from less than one percent to a much higher figure, depending upon various factors. For instance, the Mercedes-Benz letter mentioned in footnote 4 successfully achieved its goal, though only three-tenths of 1 percent of the readers purchased a car. The returns the mailing brings must be sufficiently greater than its total cost—for the list, plus planning, consulting (with direct-mail specialists),[3] writing, revising, reproducing, testing, and mailing the letter with all its enclosures.

Number and Kinds of Enclosures. Before writing your sales letter, plan the enclosures. Will the envelope contain any descriptive pamphlet, separate testimonials, pictures, samples, gimmicks, gadgets, order blank, and/or reply enve-

---

[3] Many firms (except those with specially trained direct mail staffs) ask outside specialists to write their sales letters and plan the enclosure.

lope? Gadgets and gimmicks should be used only if they help to dramatize a point, not if they merely attract attention. (Some readers dislike them; others become absorbed in them and fail to read the letter.) The usual enclosures are leaflet, order blank, and reply envelope.

Length of Sales Letter. If the enclosures adequately take care of all needed details, the letter should preferably be only one page. This is especially true if its purpose is to get action other than a direct purchase. If a catalog or booklet is to be sent later upon request, or if a demonstration or sales representative is to follow, these methods will help make the sale. But if you do not have an enclosure—and especially if you want to make a direct sale—your letter may have to be longer than one page. Just be sure it is as concise as possible!

Many conflicting ideas exist about the desirable length of sales letters. However, direct-mail experts have proved again and again that long copy works—if it catches and holds the reader's interest and is sufficiently convincing.[4]

Appearance of Sales Letter. To a prospect a company is what it appears to be in its printed mailing. You need to decide (usually with the help of experts in direct mail, advertising, and/or processing) on the quality and color of paper to be used and also whether the printing will be in one or more colors. Among other factors to be considered in your planning are these:

Should special pictures, designs, handwritten "teaser" statements, or other attention-getting devices or gimmicks be used on the outside envelope and the letterhead?

What about the sizes of the letterhead, envelopes, and other enclosures? Should any be oversize? Transparent? With what size and kind of type?

Should the letter be personalized with the reader's name and address?

Should the letter have occasional underscoring, capitalizing, "inked" lines, arrows, or other marks to emphasize important ideas?

Timing of Sales Message. Consider what is likely to be the best time of the week, month, season, and year to launch a certain sales campaign. The time of your mailing will naturally affect the wording of your sales letter and sometimes your choice of appeals (as for certain seasons, holidays).

Figures released by the National Association of Manufacturers show that 80 percent of orders are placed after the sales representative's fifth call.

---

[4] One of the more startling success stories is the case of the Mercedes-Benz company that sold 1,500 Model 190D Sedans for $4,068 each, one summer before Labor Day (1965)—entirely through a five-page letter which their advertising agency designed and mailed to 500,000 people. This letter's success was remarkable for another reason: these cars used diesel fuel, a hurdle because diesel fuel stations were scarce at the time. (Courtesy of Mercedes-Benz of North America, Inc., Fort Lee, N.J.)

Remember that a sales letter is a "sales representative" too. Some firms have effectively sent the same letter (perhaps on paper of a different color) to the same prospects two or three times and received orders only after the last mailing.

Suggestions for Writing the Unsolicited Sales Letter

After you have completed the prewriting steps about your product, mailing list of prospects, choice of ideas and main appeals, and the planned presentation—you are ready to develop the sales letter itself. This writing and revising will probably take hours, even days. If time and budget permit, you may decide—with the help of a consultant—to prepare several versions of your letter to test their pulling power before mailing one to the entire mailing list.

Your basic guide is the AIDA organizational plan—attention, interest, desire, action. Although the discussion below focuses separately on each part of the AIDA plan, the parts need not always be in this sequence, nor need all parts be in every letter. Some sales letters begin with desire-creating material such as testimonials or guarantees. Some start with action-inducing statements such as special offers or free trials. Some may skip product description and uses (the interest section) and devote most of the letter to proof—if, for example, the reader already knows the description and uses but needs conviction material to reinforce interest and create desire to buy the product. Circumstances vary—and so do sales letter content and organization.

Attracting Your Prospect's Attention

The best way to catch the attention of a busy reader is by promising—or implying a forthcoming promise—*to benefit him or her by satisfying a need. Mention what the reader gains from the product before* you name it. Even before the opening paragraph you can attract the reader's attention by inserting a benefit in place of the inside address.

Though the letter may go to thousands of people, each copy must "talk" in a natural, sincere, friendly way to an individual human being. The opening should be appropriate, fresh, honest, interesting, specific, and relevant to the central selling point. Avoid tricky, exaggerated openings, which have been so overused that the American public is unmoved or annoyed by them. Of course, if you can think of a novel, catchy opening that honestly relates closely to your central theme, go ahead and use it.

Also be careful to avoid openings that may outdate your letter soon. For instance, one letter addressed to "Dear Graduate" began "Now that you are out of school for three months . . ." Readers who had been out of school longer than that were of course annoyed by the inaccuracy.

Keep the first paragraph short, preferably two to five lines, sometimes only one. Short paragraphs look easy to read and thus are more likely to get the reader started. If unusual circumstances require you to have a long opening paragraph, it should be set up in an easy-to-read way—sometimes with double spaces between sentences or with some lines indented from both margins.

For your opening, you can choose reader-benefit attention getters like these:

1. A Comparison or a (Short!) Story

Selling a secretary's handbook along with a free *kit:*
(Pictures of a cluttered and a tidy desk at top of letter)

```
It's really amazing!  Betty and Sue work side by side in the same
office.  They have the same secretarial training and skills . . . both
have identical workloads--yet Betty is usually putting away her
typewriter by 4:45 everyday, while Sue usually can't even find her
newspaper under the clutter of unfinished work still on her desk.
   And not only the janitor notices!  Their boss has noticed the dif-
ference too.  So besides the sheer delight of an easier day with
much less pressure, let's face it, Betty will be in line for promo-
tions, pay raises, and all the "fringe benefits" that go with them!
```

2. An Event or Fact in the Reader's Life

Selling car insurance:

```
The fact that you are a college senior specializing in medicine and
attending a well-respected university like (name) tells people about
your character.
   For instance, it may qualify you for a special low-cost auto in-
surance program that might not otherwise be available to you.
```

3. A Problem the Reader May Face

Urging use of a catalog to shop by mail:

```
During the next few weeks you and people all over the country will
be doing Christmas shopping.  Some will be early birds.  Others will
wait until the last minute; and if they are shopping in the stores,
they will be pushed around and have to take what is left instead of
being able to purchase the items they had in mind.
```

4. A Significant Fact about the Product

Selling TV cable service:

```
More than 4,000,000 viewers in the UNITED STATES . . .

                        . . . and . . .
```

over 10,000 people in the (*city*) area alone enjoy sharp, clear, multi-
channel television reception by means of C.A.T.V. (Community
Antenna Television).

5. A Solution to a Problem

Selling hospital insurance:

You can receive a check like this, or even up to $5,000, when you or
a member of your family goes to the hospital . . . IF you are protected by ABC Hospital Plan.

6. A Surprising Question or Challenging Statement

*Offering a special paint sprayer on 15-day free trial for homeowners, do-it-
yourselfers, and professional painters:*

How would you like to beautifully paint a 9 x 12 room—walls and
ceiling—in less than one hour including clean-up time? To paint
400% faster than with a 4" brush and 222% faster than a 9" roller?

For some sales letters the attention-getting opening might be a testimonial,
guarantee, special offer, or free trial—parts that are usually in later sections.

Arousing the Reader's Interest

Having attracted the reader's attention, you now arouse interest by beginning
to "picture" your product and telling what it will do for the reader. You begin
to develop the central selling point.

You can picture your product in two ways—physical description and
reader benefits. You can place the benefits first—as in example 1 below—or
later, but usually they are interwoven with physical description, as in example 2.

Example 1

Stating benefits before physical description.

When you use Family Investments you find hundreds of ways to make
your money earn more and go further—for your home, clothing, food,
travel, taxes, and pleasure. You get a rich source of advice from
accountants, automotive specialists, real estate agents, tax consultants, life insurance experts, bankers, stockbrokers, lawyers.

This leatherbound book contains 467 pages, divided by subject into
15 chapters, 165,000 words. Sturdily built for continual use, the
book has 310 drawings, graphs, and tables to illustrate points and

clarify meanings. In essence, using the book will be like taking a fascinating course in managing your family's money——from highly paid professionals.

Example 2

Interweaving benefits and physical description.

The "heart" of your outfit is Bell & Howell's great Zoom-Lens Electric-Drive Super 8 Camera. You just pop in the Kodak cartridge of Super 8 color film (it's fast and simple) . . . <u>aim</u> . . . and <u>shoot</u>. That's all there is to it. And this camera is <u>electrically</u> powered—— no winding whatsoever. Pop the cartridge in and you are ready to shoot a full 50-foot movie without interruption.

Just consider how every step virtually takes care of itself: the camera sets itself automatically for different types of film——it even adjusts automatically for indoor or outdoor filming——and the Optronic Electric Eye sets the lens (also automatically), measuring only that light reaching the film.

Creating Desire and Convincing the Reader

After getting your readers interested in one or several of your product's benefits, you need to create in them a desire to own it. Furthermore, if your purpose is to make a direct sale, you need to convince them that they should buy your product. Like the personal sales representative, your letter leads the prospective buyers through a ''mental demonstration'' so they imagine themselves already the owner—and it offers proof whenever necessary.

The reader's progression from interest to desire to conviction is usually gradual. It is not necessary to worry about exactly where one step begins or ends; these steps are parts of an integrated whole. Together they develop your central selling point and help urge the reader to take the requested action.

Desire for Your Product. Desire-creating material within the letter ranges from one paragraph—in a one-page letter with descriptive brochure—to several paragraphs if the letter itself it two or more pages long, with or without an enclosed brochure.

The following example illustrates desire-creating paragraphs that develop the central selling point and benefits. Example 3 here follows example 2. Notice how it continues to stress the central theme—convenience—in order to increase the reader's desire. These paragraphs are part of a three-page letter.

Example 3

Developing the central selling point and benefit–convenience.

Breathtaking ZOOM Shots from Wide-Angle to Close-Up[5]

And with this camera, the special fingertip-control ZOOM lens makes it possible for you to get the same kind of breathtaking zoom shots TV and movie directors use. You can actually shift from wide-angle shots to dramatic close-ups (and back again) while you're shooting. And there is still another tremendous design advance: you actually view through the lens while you're filming—you get exactly what you see. And for extra fun, you can get in the act yourself: you just set the camera's special "Automatic Run Control."

Bell & Howell Super-Bright Super 8 Projector Threads Itself

With this Bell & Howell Super 8 Projector, threading is, at last, outmoded—this projector does it all for you—easily, in just five seconds! Just press a button, insert the film, and the film automatically winds itself through—and you sit back, relax and enjoy your movies—up to 400 feet of film without interruption of any kind.

And this projector has other top-quality abilities: Imagine being able to run your movies backward. You can! Simply flip a lever and divers bounce backward onto the board or the family goes backward into the car after just getting out.

Just flip a lever again and this projector practically turns into a slide machine! Now you can view the hundreds of motion picture frames you have taken one at a time—and look at them individually.

You get a complete HOME MOVIE "ENTERTAINMENT CENTER"—all these extras are included: (*The letter continues to list nine extras.*)

Evidence to Convince. The main proof about your product's features and benefits comes preferably from evidence that persons outside your company determine. These outside sources include *satisfied users; recognized testing laboratories, agencies, and disinterested persons;* and *the prospect himself or herself.* Seven popular kinds of proof are illustrated below.

From Satisfied Users:

1. Facts about Users' Experience with the Product
These include verifiable reports and statistics from users.

The green page in the enclosed brochure itemizes the savings which 203 contractors have realized from EASI-POUR concrete mix. Notice that their actual savings range from 45% to 85%. As you study the table, note its specific facts about the size of each job. Then compare the figures with your own average costs for similar projects.

---

[5] The headings in this letter were green, in contrast to the blue print used for the rest of the letter; in a subsequent mailing of the same letter, headings were orange and the rest of the letter, brown.

2. Names of Other Buyers and Users

State how many persons or firms already are using the product. Better yet, when appropriate, give the names of satisfied well-known users, or offer to send names and addresses upon request.

```
Among the hundreds of business firms that are pleased with their use
of ABC equipment are: Marshall Field and Company, Alcoa Aluminum,
Ford Motor Company, United Airlines, and Chase Manhattan Bank.
```

3. Testimonials

Because testimonials have been abused (with phony quotations by nonusers who are paid to make them), many people distrust them. To establish credibility of the testimonials you use, select persons or firms that are bona fide users of your product and whose judgment the reader respects. Be specific. Get their permission. Avoid exaggerations.

```
"Since we've been using EASI-POUR concrete mix, six of our workers
can place and finish a section of concrete street with curb—12 feet
wide and a football field long—in only one hour. Its paving abil-
ity and its quality surpass any concrete mix we've used during our
twenty years of operation." Gene Aimes, Project Superintendent,
East Contractors, Inc.
```

From Recognized Testing Laboratories, Agencies, Disinterested Persons:

4. Performance Tests

Whenever recognized experts, testing laboratories, or authoritative agencies in a field relative to your product have made satisfactory performance tests on it, their evidence offers convincing proof. Also effective are statements, reports, and statistics compiled by impartial, reliable witnesses.

```
a. Learnfun electric toys have earned the endorsement and Seals of
   Approval from Underwriters Laboratories, Good Housekeeping In-
   stitute, American Medical Association, and National Safety
   Council.
b. In every performance test by the United Automotive Association,
   ALERT batteries ranked at the top of the list. Read in the en-
   closed brochure the details of qualities tested, and decide for
   yourself why ALERT is the battery for you.
```

From the Prospect:

5. Free Trial

If you have so much confidence in your product that you're willing to let the prospect try it on a free trial basis, your offer provides a very effective form of proof. The mail-order customer thus has the same opportunity to examine the product carefully as he or she would have before buying in a store. In fact, the customer gets the added privilege of using it before buying or paying for it.

a. For your use alone, we have enclosed a Reservation Certificate giving you the privilege of using the <u>Bell & Howell</u> <u>Super 8 Complete Home Movie Outfit</u> <u>for 30 full days</u>—<u>free</u> and <u>without obligation</u>. We supply the color film—a 50-foot Kodak Cartridge—and the movies you make are yours <u>free</u>—to show and to keep.

b. You'll have a full 10 days to use your new coats . . . to wear them walking, driving, working—without actually spending a single cent. . . . If for some reason, any reason at all, you don't like them, just send them back to me within 10 days, and we'll forget the whole thing. What could be fairer?

6. Guarantee

With the guarantee, the customer pays for the product before using it, but gets a written promise that if not satisfied he or she will get a refund (or credit), free repairs, or free replacement of the entire article.

With every ARTEX product you buy you get this firm, money-back guarantee: "ALL ARTEX products are Unconditionally Guaranteed to please. If you are not completely satisfied with any ARTEX, return it for full refund within 30 days."

7. Samples

Let the prospect examine, try, and/or use the samples that you send (for instance, swatches of clothing or drapery materials; pieces of wire, rubber, or fireproof insulation) or that he or she calls for personally (such as gasoline for the car, or a food and beverage made fresh daily). The prospect is asked to perform some suggested action to convince him- or herself that the product meets the writer's claims.

Just pick up the enclosed STICK-UP page, pull back the hardy Celanar protective sheet. Then place an assortment of odd-sized clippings, ads, photos on the STICK-UP sheet in any arrangement you choose. Finally, return the protective covering and press down gently.

Note how <u>sharply</u> and <u>clearly</u> you see every word through the transparent sheet, every shading of the material you've mounted on the STICK-UP page.

<u>But note this, too</u>: If the arrangement you've set up doesn't please you, all you have to do is pull back the Celanar cover, pick up the clippings or photos, and rearrange them any way you desire . . . as often as you wish and there's no mess, no fuss, no sloppy paste pot! You save time and. . . .

Price of Your Product. Your presentation on the selling features, benefits, and proof may have convinced the prospect that your product meets the need and he or she should buy it. But is the product worth the price and can he or she pay for it?

If your price is a bargain, you might feature it as an attention-getting opening. If the price doesn't justify this emphasis, state it only *after* you have presented most of the selling features, benefits, and proof. Of course, if your letter is part of a campaign series to sell a costly item, the price might not be mentioned until near the end of the series. Sometimes price is not mentioned in the letter at all. If the product or service varies with the customer's needs (as for insurance or a complex heating installation in an industrial plant), the exact price quotation is given only after consultations with sales representatives.

If your prospect is likely to consider your price a drawback, try to bring the price within reach. For example, in addition to stating the full price, you can use the following methods to help convince the prospect that he or she can pay it:

1. Break it down into "easy" weekly or monthly payments.
2. State it in terms of unit prices ($9 each book) instead of case lots, dozens, or sets ($210 for the encyclopedia set).
3. Interpret it on the basis of the benefits to be gained.
4. Emphasize its cost on a daily, monthly, or yearly basis—depending upon the product's estimated life and service (only 3 cents a day).
5. Compare it with the amount the average reader spends daily (monthly) for nonessentials or luxuries.

The discussion of price is usually presented just before the action paragraph(s)—if price and action are clear-cut and distinct. Sometimes, however, they blend, as do interest and desire. In some letters you will include price inducements with conviction details; in others, with action. Because offers of easy payment (as well as "no money down now" and credit card use) more often serve as special inducements to action, they are discussed in the next section.

Getting Action

Having convinced your reader that your product is valuable, needed, and worthy of purchase, you now must encourage the most important step—performing the action you request.

All previous discussions in this book about handling negatives, overcoming price resistance, and inducing action are applicable to sales letters and are not repeated here. You also already know that a complete action section should:

State clearly the action you desire.

Make action easy.

Date the action (when desirable).

Offer special inducement to act by a specified time (when desirable).

End with a last reader-benefit plug (when appropriate).

To induce the reader to act within a certain time instead of procrastinating, you can use one or more of the following methods (arranged here alphabetically):

1. Credit Cards

The convenience of merely charging a purchase to a nationally accepted credit card–bank, national oil company, travel agency, diners' club, or other cards–is an effective inducement to action. The holder of such credit card(s) need not write a check or send a money order now, but merely return an order blank listing a credit card number.

```
Send no money now. To order, just check on the enclosed form that
you wish this purchase charged to your account with one of the ac-
ceptable national credit firms listed. Then be sure to fill in your
account number as shown on your credit card.
```

2. Easy Payments and/or "No Money Now"

A budget plan or a future-payment plan by which the prospect pays nothing down now may serve two purposes–to convince the reader that he or she can afford to buy your product and to induce him or her to take the requested action. Thus, though the prospect may not have the entire price of the product, he or she will be able to order right away if the entire amount (or anything) is not required at once.

```
For as little as $10 down you can begin to reap the benefits of this
useful encyclopedia before school starts. Easy monthly payments as
low as $8 a month can be arranged at your convenience.
```

3. Free Gift[6]

If the prospect buys one item, two may be received for the price of one; or he or she may receive a free gift that is different from the item you are selling.

```
Agree to try them for 10 days on our No-Money-Down offer, and I'll
send you a matching leather-look vinyl Tote Bag FREE. This gift is
yours to keep, even if you later return the jackets.
```

---

[6] Sweepstakes and other games of chance have been powerful action inducements. The prospect may be "eligible for winning any one of 5,000 prizes" if an enclosed card is mailed before midnight of a certain date. However, some states prohibit such methods. Furthermore, studies have shown gross inconsistencies between the prizes some companies advertise and the number they actually award. See "Games People Shouldn't Play," *Sales Management,* December 1969, pp. 17-18.

4. Free Trial

The free trial serves two purposes—to convince the reader of your sincerity about the product's merits, and to induce action now. The reader has nothing to lose; no money is spent now and he or she need pay later only if the article is found satisfactory.

5. No Obligation to Buy

When the purpose of your letter is to get the prospect to ask for more information, to come for a demonstration, or perhaps to ask a sales representative to call, he or she is more likely to act if you promise there is no obligation to buy.

```
Mailing the enclosed card does not in any way obligate you to buy
insurance, and no salesperson will call on you unless you invite him
or her. To receive full details about this plan, with specific fig-
ures at your present age--and your free portfolio--just return the
postpaid card above.
```

6. Premium

A promise of higher earnings if the reader acts before a certain date is also a good incentive.

```
By sending your deposits in the enclosed envelope, so they reach us
by the 10th of May, you earn 6% dividends from the 1st of the month.
```

7. Special Price for a Limited Time

Setting a time limit for bargain prices (perhaps on out-of-season items or limited supply), or for introductory prices on new items or to new buyers, effectively induces action. Offer a discount on the purchase price if the reader buys before a certain date or if cash in full is sent with the order.

```
This special introductory rate (for new subscribers only) brings you
40 big news-packed issues of World Reports for only $9.97. That is
down to half-price for 40 issues if you bought them a copy at a
time. You get this special rate if your order is postmarked before
May 1.
```

Writing an effective sales letter is a lot of work, but it can be greatly rewarding. Many a sales letter mailed to thousands of prospects has brought thousands—even millions—of dollars in returns. Even the expert writers "agonize" over their copy. Good selling presents the benefits and the proposition in such a way that the readers become convinced and "sell themselves." On the other hand, if the letter sounds like a high-pressure sales pitch, the readers may become defensive. To achieve your goal may require meticulous editing and rewriting, but the results will be worth the effort.

Examples of Unsolicited Sales Letters

This section illustrates letters that aim to: (1) make a direct sale, (2) serve as stimulus to future sales, and (3) bring back lost customers. As you read them, notice how description is mixed with and reinforces reader benefits, how the central selling point (labeled CSP) is developed, and how reader-benefit appeals are emphasized.

Making a Direct Sale

The letter below, sent to business owners, illustrates one way to sell relatively high-priced items successfully by one letter and detailed enclosures. The two items sold were priced at $170 and $295 (prices, though omitted in the letter, were in the enclosures). On a mailing of 4,500 this one-page letter brought in $45 in direct sales for every single dollar of costs.[7]

Letter 1

Selling radiator cleaning tanks to service-shop owners.
CSP: Less time to clean tanks.
Appeals: Reduced work; higher profits.

Attention	IF THREE RADIATOR REPAIR EXPERTS WALKED INTO YOUR SHOP THIS AFTERNOON . . .
	And the first one, the owner of Midtown Auto Radiator Service of New York City, said: "We are cleaning 10 to 12 radiators in our tank and find that it requires only 20 minutes to get them thoroughly clean."
Interest	And the second person, proprietor of the Bronx Radiator Service, said: "We clean nine radiators in one tank in half the time it used to take to clean two."
	And the third person, owner of Goldberg's Auto Service of St. Johnsbury, Vt., said: "We have found this the most satisfactory way to clean radiators that we have ever used."
Desire	. . . you'd certainly feel that you owed it to yourself to find out just what they used to bring those people such new speeds and profits, wouldn't you?

[7] Courtesy of Aeroil Products Company, West New York, N.J., and The Dartnell Corporation, *The Dartnell File of Tested Sales Letters.*

Conviction

```
Well, here is how they——and YOU——are in a position to
make such claims!

You will find their explanations of exactly how they
do it (along with reports of other leading radiator
specialists from coast to coast) in the enclosed Bul-
letin #308. In addition, you will find complete
specifications on two sizes of radiator cleaning tanks
that will enable you to clean up from 4 to 12 radia-
tors at a time——probably in LESS time than it now
takes you to clean ONE!
```

Conviction; action

```
Don't just take our word for it———read the genuine
letters and see the actual, unretouched photographs in
the enclosed bulletin. Then prove these new speeds
and savings in your own shop by mailing the Guarantee
Order Form TODAY!
```

Serving as Stimulus to Future Sales

Many sales letters urge action other than an immediate order for a direct purchase. Some of these sell products or services which are complicated or expensive, or which must be specially tailored to fit the buyer's particular needs. Others sell continual use of the customer's credit card which enables her or him to buy not only the firm's products but also other conveniences.

To Sell Complicated, Expensive, or Specially Designed Items. For some products the buyer will need more time, information, and personal observation. In this category are real estate, industrial equipment, insurance, costly installations, pleasure boats, cars, and products or services the reader may have considered unnecessary.

A campaign series of letters is a popular means of stimulating ultimate sales of such products and services. You decide in advance how many letters you should send, the time intervals, and the content of each. Some might ask the customer merely to request further information. In other letters you might request that the reader call your office or store for a demonstration, or ask for a sales representative to visit, as in letter 2.

Depending upon the kinds of products you sell, you can sometimes get a highly satisfactory return by mailing only a relatively few letters. For instance, a manufacturer of bulldozing equipment mailed one sales letter to only 58 business executives. To the requested action "Write, wire, or phone for further details" 30 readers replied; they bought $250,000 worth of equipment. Letter 2 was also an effective single letter. Though mailed to only 100 sales managers, the letter sold one million caps! Each letter was individually typewritten on one page.

Letter 2

Urging sales managers to request a sales representative to give more information about an advertising gadget.[8]
CSP: Adjustable, lightweight, low-cost Paperlynen service caps for distinctive advertising.
Appeals: Appearance, savings, comfort, distinctiveness.

Dear Mr. Gates:

Attention

Literally and figuratively you can hit the top with your advertising.

How? With Paperlynen Adjustable Service Caps.

Interest

Paperlynen Caps offer the ideal medium for placing your name constantly before the public eye. Worn by storekeepers and your own employees, these caps will not only help sell your products but are a constant goodwill reminder. And, as a means of cooperative advertising, they're excellent. In addition, Paperlynen Adjustable Service Caps are preferred because of their:

Appearance
Adjustable to any and every head size; always fit; look like linen; sanitary-clean

Low Cost
Cost less than expense of having ill-fitting cloth caps laundered; this saving in addition to saving of initial cost of cloth caps

Desire

Comfort
Light in weight; porous nature of crown permits free, filtered ventilation

Distinction
Offer the opportunity of distinction through imprinting your firm's name or trademark in a manner not possible on ordinary caps. With cooperative advertising or as a dealer help, the storekeeper's name may also be added.

Conviction

Several samples of Paperlynen caps are enclosed. Look at 'em, try 'em, test 'em. We're sure you'll like 'em.

[8] Courtesy of S. Posner Sons, Brooklyn, N.Y., and The Dartnell Corporation, *The Dartnell File of Tested Sales Letters.*

Action   When you are ready for more information, call
              XX3-628-1030 and one of our salespeople will be up to
              see you promptly.

To Sell Continual Use of the Customer's Credit Card. From time to time you may need to show the benefits that can be gained from the credit card. By encouraging regular use of the card, you also help increase your future sales. Besides the convenience of buying on a pay-later basis, your credit customers receive additional benefits. Among them may be: coupon discounts, special sales not announced to the general public, low-cost insurance policies, free gifts on various occasions, and others.

Benefits differ, of course, depending on the nature and scope of a business. For example, a national company's travel club included these extra credit card benefits in a sales letter:

    You can charge a stay at any one of some 2,000 really good hotels
      all over America.
    If you ever run into trouble on the road, you can use your card to
      charge car repairs up to $100 . . . and
    You can reduce the amount of money you must carry, reducing the risk
      of loss or theft.

Bringing Back Lost Customers

Many businesses spend thousands of dollars on advertising to attract new customers and yet neglect regular customers. Studies have indicated that *indifference* on the part of the seller is the main reason customers leave one company for another. At least two-thirds of such customers drift away because they feel their business isn't appreciated, because they are treated discourteously, or because some grievances were unadjusted.

The best way to find out why customers haven't bought from you for, say, six months or more, is to ask them—either in person or by mail. Warm, sincere, friendly letters can help you to learn why you lost customers and can also help you win them back. (Of course, it is important that after you know customers' reasons, you take steps to correct any weaknesses!)

The secret for winning back lost customers is to tell them that you miss them—and to keep telling them. Patience and persistence do pay off. For instance, one department store in Chicago reopened 2,724 accounts with sales totaling $73,001.34; a retail store in Long Beach, California, brought in $30,000 from lost customers; and a Buffalo merchant regained 47 percent of his lost accounts with 30 mailings over a period of five years.[9] Numerous other firms have also had rewarding results (sometimes even with one letter!).

[9] *The Reporter of Direct Mail Advertising,* September 1965, pp. 49-50. Though business conditions are different in the 1980s, persuasive sales letters can still bring back lost customers.

Your first miss-you letters may be simple (direct-request) **inquiries** without appeals. However, when direct inquiries bring no response, **you need** to mail persuasive requests that say, in essence:

We miss you.

Here are the benefits you get by coming back to us.

Please come back.

Sincerity, imagination, appropriate appeals, and sometimes good-natured humor characterize these messages, as illustrated below in letter 3.

Letter 3

A unique letter to win back "lost" hotel guests.[10]
CSP: High standard of personal service to "special guests."
Appeals: Enjoyment, comfort, convenience, prestige.

	Dear Mr. Morgan:
Attention	Today we registered an ex-president; two senators; a congressman; several assorted corporation presidents; a foreign personage with party; generals by the one, two, and three star; plus a group of tourists. But not you.
Interest	I suppose you thought we'd be too busy to notice that you were among the missing. But that's not true. We haven't made The Mayflower the standard of personal service by forgetting our special guests the moment they leave the checkout desk.
	What happened?
Desire	Have you sworn off roast beef when it's as succulent as our Rib Room specialty? Are you punishing yourself by giving up really comfortable, handsome, airconditioned guest rooms for lesser accommodations?
	Do you feel guilty about staying at a hotel so perfectly located and so completely dedicated to your convenience? Or have you just not been in Washington lately?
	We hope it's the latter.

---

[10] An award-winning letter created by Spiro & Associates, Inc., Philadelphia, for the Mayflower Hotel in Washington, D.C.

Action
```
Please write and end our suspense as soon as possi-
ble. Or, better yet, come back for a visit. Old
friends are best friends. And busy as we are, we miss
one of our very best friends: you!
```

With good judgment, sincerity, and imagination, you can develop a variety of appealing miss-you letters. If you prefer, you can buy special-theme messages from advertising specialists, with or without gadgets symbolic of various holidays, seasons, products, and services. Be sure, however, that they relate closely to your company's business.

SUMMARY

Sales letters may be either solicited (invited) or unsolicited. When you answer inquiries that are related in some way to your sales—regarding prices, terms, discounts, deliveries, products, manufacturing, types of accounts available, and so on—you have opportunities to write solicited sales letters. Follow the good-news plan if your information is favorable for the inquirer, the bad-news plan if it is unfavorable.

Use the persuasive-request plan for unsolicited sales letters—those you initiate yourself to make direct sales, encourage future sales, or win back lost customers. Begin with an attention-getting appropriate opening; arouse interest through physical description and/or reader benefits; create desire and conviction by developing your central selling point and benefits, by offering proof, and by handling price in a positive way; then ask for action. If appropriate, offer special inducements so that the reader will act within a certain time.

The Capsule Checklists on page 339 give a summary of how to adapt the good-news and the bad-news plans for replies to sales-related inquiries, and how to use the persuasive-request plan for solicited sales letters.

EXERCISES

Good-News Replies to Sales-Related Inquiries

1. Letters **a** and **b** below are replies to routine, direct requests. Suggest improvements where needed in opening and closing paragraphs, you-attitude, and adequacy of resale material. Which of the two do you like better? Why?
   a. Individually typed reply from a steam specialty company:

   ```
   Gentlemen:

       Replying to your letter of 30 Sept. 198_, please be advised
   that we are mailing to your attention, under separate cover, four
   ```

copies of our current #57 General Catalog describing products of our manufacture, at no charge to your company.

Appreciating your inquiry and hoping to be favored with your orders, we remain. . .

b. Processed form reply from a clock manufacturer;[11] personalized address and salutation:

Here is the Seth Thomas booklet which you recently requested.

As you look over the wide variety of styles offered for your choice, we are sure you will find the Seth Thomas clock you have always desired—either for your own home or for that certain someone who appreciates an outstanding gift. There are distinguised period designs, charming colonial reproductions, and smart moderns for those who appreciate this mode of furnishing.

All clocks illustrated represent the finest in designing achievement and are truly the creations of experts in the craft of fine clockmaking. Their friendly presence in your home is a tribute to your appreciation of fine living.

May we suggest that you visit your local Seth Thomas dealer. Many appliance stores handle Seth Thomas self-starting electrics— while keywound and electrics are offered by better jewelry and department stores.

For gifts that will surely become treasured possessions, select Seth Thomas clocks—they are always appropriate. And, for finer, friendlier living in your own home, be sure to choose an authentic Seth Thomas—"The Finest Name in Clocks."

2. A motel manager in a resort town sent the following reply to a young man who inquired about rates and accommodations. He wrote that he and his wife were planning a three-week automobile trip and they expected to stay four nights in the town (Lagina) "sometime in July."

Comment orally on the good and poor qualities of this reply. How many errors can you find? (The crossed-out words appeared that way on the mailed letter.) Rewrite it so that it is accurate and contains appropriate you-attitude and resale material. Make any necessary assumptions.

Thank you for your postal card regarding rates for Summer.
Our rates for two are $185.00 per week & ~~xxxxxxxx~~ ~~xxxxxxxx~~ Ocean-view are $195.00 per week.
These Apartments consist of Bed Sittling room, fully equipped kitchen, bathroom and Shower and Garage.

---

[11] Courtesy of Seth Thomas Clock Company, Thomaston, Conn.

```
      We are located in the North section of Lagina about a mile from
the main business District.  The market is a block away and we are
about two hundred yards from Crescent Bathing Beach.
      We do not allow Pets.
      On receipt of $15.00 deposit we will be pleased to reserve the
accomodation you require.
      Thanking you for your courtesy, I am,
```

3. As customer service manager of Topco Business Forms, Inc., you just received an inquiry from Amy C. Ball, Purchasing Agent, Tomson Machinery Company, 2110 Lakeshore Blvd., Erie, PA 16593. Ms. Ball wants to know if your company prints custom stationery (letterhead and envelopes). If so, she would like to know how a customer submits the design, what types of paper are available, what your prices are, and how long it will take for delivery.

   Topco Business Forms does sell custom stationery so the customer may be its own "image maker." The customer may choose a logo from your stock selection or Tomson Machinery may submit its own design. (You will accept a sketch or a printed sample.) The customer has a wide range of choices in paper and ink color.

   The best idea is for the customer to send a sketch or sample of the exact letterhead and/or envelope format desired and let you do the rest. Your answer to Ms. Ball will include a catalog which shows all the choices and the exact prices. You should direct the customer to page 23 for information on custom stationery. Remind the customer that you have a minimum order quantity of 1,000, but prices for larger quantities are discounted.

   Make sure that Ms. Ball knows about the order form and postpaid envelope in the catalog. Also, let her know that orders may be called in on your toll-free number (1-800-572-2978). Finally, your company has a 30-day free trial policy. If, for any reason, a customer is not completely satisfied, she or he need only return the merchandise within 30 days and the payment will be refunded or the invoices canceled.

4. As correspondent for the Safety Electric Products Company, manufacturers of electric mixers, toasters, and other kitchen appliances, you need to answer an inquiry from Barto Electric Company, one of your new distributors in Tucson, Arizona. They carry your complete line of eight products in their two stores, and they need the free newspaper mats to use in their local advertising campaign and also window display materials. Also, they would like to see a sample of the envelope stuffers (illustrative sales leaflets) that they might enclose with their customers' monthly statements. These leaflets are not free, although of course the one sample you're sending today is free. These colorful leaflets, which are revised periodically, cost $9.90 per thousand, but customers get good ideas from them. This is the first inquiry you have had from this new distributor since the welcome letter you sent 10 days

ago. Your company advertises on TV in four states and in two national magazines.

5. Assume you work in the passenger department of Central Airlines, whose planes fly in and out of your city, Dallas, Texas. Answer the following letter from Mrs. Teresa Oldtime who lives in a rural area about 50 miles east of Dallas.

> For several years now I've been wanting to get up courage to take an airplane trip from Dallas to San Diego. I have saved up the money and the bus to downtown Dallas goes right by our house. Now I'm 81, but I'm still in pretty good shape. My family has been urging me to come. My favorite grandson is getting married in S.D. and I want to attend his wedding, and I want to go the safest and fastest way. How long does the plane take?
>
> There are a few things I want to know first. I imagine that lots of people get sick on airplanes. I also hear that you serve alcohol and I can't drink anything but milk or tea. I suppose, too, that nothing but cold food is served, and I have to have hot meals. Oh, and one more thing, would we be too high up to see objects on the ground?
>
> If you can clear up these points, I think I'd like to take the trip.

Here are the facts: Fewer people get airsick than get sick in trains or autos. You don't serve cold meals. Hot meals are prepared and served individually by the attendants—not just lunches but full dinners (depending on flight times). Also, there is no extra charge for the meals or for soft drinks, tea, milk. You don't serve alcohol free in economy and tourist classes. Champagne cocktails are served free in first-class travel, but for those who don't want champagne, there's tomato or fruit juice. Jet planes between Dallas and San Diego fly at between 30,000 and 39,000 feet altitude, from which passengers can see the ground when the weather is clear. One stop is made in Los Angeles, California—the plane swoops down smoothly before it lands. Scenery is gorgeous along the way. Flying time is about three hours. Airport bus picks up passengers at Sleepeze Hotel in downtown Dallas and takes them to the Dallas Airport in 35 minutes; the charge one way to the airport is $3.50. Give all the information Mrs. Oldtime needs to make a reservation. Your goal is to try to encourage her to travel by air *on your line*. Skillfully combine reader-benefit sales talk with your answers to all her questions, implied and stated. Assume any other needed pertinent details.

Bad-News Replies to Sales-Related Inquiries

1. The following letter from a national manufacturer of party favors has several weaknesses. Rewrite it (to Jim Shyre, chairperson of a college football

banquet) to improve it in every way you can. Assume additional pertinent facts, if necessary, and try to be more helpful to this banquet chairperson. He wants individual souvenirs (''about 3 or 4 inches wide'') to use as favors or place cards for the 250 persons expected to attend the banquet, five weeks from today. Although your factory does not have any such souvenirs in stock, you do manufacture special items to order. All you need is a design and three to four weeks' time; your skilled workers turn out really attractive novelties. Assume that your reader (the chairperson) lives 2,000 miles from your factory. Time is short. It is possible that the L. G. Paltwin Company (a retail supplier about 1,000 miles from Jim Shyre's city) may have football souvenirs in stock. What can you say to be helpful?

```
Dear Sir:

We have pleasure in acknowledging your letter of 20 September con-
cerning your inquiry about small individual football souvenirs for
your banquet.  Though we note that you had been advised by Marcus
Company to approach us in this connection, we are sorry to inform
you that we do not have football novelties and thus cannot supply
the material which you need.

We regret we cannot be of service to you for this occasion.
```

2. Your new assistant has just laid on your desk the following letter he wrote (to a long-time customer) for your signature as customer service manager of your firm, Research Consultants. He admits he hasn't had much training in letter writing and says he'd appreciate your comments on his attempt. You decide to rewrite this one for him and let him compare the two versions of this bad-news message. Improve the letter in every way you can—especially the organization and you-attitude. Emphasize positive instead of negative aspects, and maintain goodwill toward your firm. Because you aim to assist this good customer as much as possible, you have asked your staff to contact other sources in addition to your own company files. Those sources may have some materials on plans that do fall into the group the customer discussed. As soon as they have something definite, you will write the customer again.

```
I am sorry to say that, unfortunately, our editors did not find any-
thing in our plan files that would apply to your problem regarding
pension plan summaries for trade association staff employees.

We have also not yet found any plan elsewhere that would fall into
the class you discussed.

I wonder if, when you looked through the reports, you did not notice
that there is a pension plan for the Employee Association League of
New York State?  I found this plan on pages 106-112.  I am not cer-
tain whether this is the type of plan you are interested in.
```

Unsolicited Sales Letters

1. Your company publishes sports books and how-to manuals for sales directly to consumers. Just off the presses is your newest book, *Everything You Always Wanted to Know about Running, but Couldn't Slow Down to Ask*. Because of the popularity of jogging and marathon running you feel that this book will be highly successful.

   The book was coauthored by Mr. Jeff Long (an Olympic gold medal winner in the 10,000 meter run) and Dr. Gary C. Lane (an expert in the physiology of running and a consultant to the United States Olympic Team). Contained in the book are chapters on "The Beginning Runner," "The Physiology of Running," "Developing the Running Attitude," "Dietary Rules for Runners," and "Selecting Jogging and Running Shoes and Accessories." Other chapters cover the history of marathons, and Olympic track events, plans for developing speed and stamina, and information on avoiding injuries while running.

   Because you think this book will be widely accepted you have, for the first time, arranged for its sale through selected book stores in several large cities. And, to promote the book, the authors will travel to each city to conduct running seminars and autograph copies of the book. You, as regional sales manager, have been asked to write a letter to a prospect list which your company has purchased for this purpose. Describe the book in detail and invite the prospects to attend the free seminars. Mention the time and location of the seminar and the name of the local stores where the books will be sold. If they take a copy of the book to the seminar, the authors will autograph it. The book will also be sold at the seminar. A runner's refreshment buffet (Perrier water, granola snacks) will be served.

2. As sales manager of the AABBB Insurance Company of Illinois, which is licensed to do business in your state and in 44 of 50 states, you have a special offer which you believe is attractive. No salesperson will call on prospective customers; no one who applies will be turned down if the application form is completely, accurately, and honestly filled out; the policy cannot be canceled for any reason if the premiums are paid on time; and the applicant can examine the policy in the home for a full 30 days and then cancel it if not satisfied. There are other features, too, which will be included in a brochure from AABBB if the prospective customer will just fill out the initial application-for-information blank.

   Best of all, the policy will pay, IN CASH TO THE FAMILY, $42 per day for the period of hospitalization plus certain other fees which are listed in the policy. No matter what other coverage one might have, the $42 per day will still be paid for as long as one full year.

   Cost of hospital room occupancy and care is extremely high and many families do not have adequate insurance coverage. If illness should strike such a family, the results could be disastrous—debt, loss of savings, emergency bank loans, mortgages, possible bankruptcy, and similar financial problems would have to be faced.

Write a letter which will be sent to the employees of the Acme Iron and Steel Company, in your city. You know that these employees have some health and hospitalization coverage, but the amount is insufficient for most serious illnesses. Although you will not mention this, you will also send a second letter four weeks later if the first one is not answered. After that—no more letters.

3. As sales manager for EXELL Manufacturing Company, Columbus, Ohio, you want to send—to retail store managers who have been your regular customers—a letter that ties in with your national advertising campaign. During November and December your company's all-purpose folding card tables with four matching folding chairs will be featured in two consumer magazines in full-page three-color ads. These ads will be read by 24 million people. You consider this the most powerful selling story you have ever put across. Now (October 1) you want to be sure that the 510 retail store managers that carry your products are sufficiently stocked with a variety of these table-chair sets to meet the expected consumer demand. Wholesale price of each five-piece set is $69.50. Retail price is $95; separate folding tables are $30 each and each chair is $19.50. Thus, by buying the combination set, consumers save $13. Each table is 36 inches square, with vinyl covered top and bronze-tone finish steel frame 28 inches high; shipping weight, 21 pounds. The matching folding chairs have 1-inch thick padded vinyl seats, steel legs, and steel backs; shipping weight 12 pounds each. Colors for both tables and chairs, green or mushroom beige in plain or floral patterns. These beautiful, practical, and low-priced items are just what consumers will need for Christmas, and will find useful throughout the year for many years. In your sales letter, provide easy-action order blanks and promise prompt shipment; be as specific as possible. Orders you receive by October 18 can be filled and the sets shipped in time to be in stock by November 1.

4. You are a part-time employee for Mod Man, Inc., a men's clothing shop "For men who think young." Your employer, knowing you are a college senior and that you're studying business communications, has just offered you a challenging opportunity to try your skill on a sales letter. After you write it, she will pay all expenses for reproducing and mailing it—plus a 10 percent commission to you on the direct sales your letter brings in.

Here is her proposition: The store's men's formal wear rental department is sponsoring a special Senior Ball promotion. Your letter is to be mailed to all men in your college class. (If your college does not have a Senior Ball, assume you are writing to any other group of young people that do have an annual ball.) Assume at least 1,000 on your mailing list. Your employer has made arrangements with a local automobile dealer to have a brand new 198_ convertible on display right in the store starting this week-end until two days before the ball. Someone who registers will win the free use of this car for the night of the ball, courtesy of Ron Kane Auto Sales, Inc. In addition, there will be four other big winners, each of whom will get: Senior Ball tickets for two; a corsage of their choice; a $25 gift certificate for dinner for two at (name) restaurant (the best in your city); and their formal wear rental at no charge. All the readers have to do to get a chance to win is to register and choose their formal wear from your store. You have the largest and most fashionable collection in the city: everything from white dinner jackets to full-dress tails, with 22 styles in between including double-breasted coats, turtlenecks, and ruffled shirts, and all at Mod Man's low rental rates.

Your one-page letter will be processed in any way you choose—mimeographed, by computer, or printed—and will be on the store's letterhead. There is to be no enclosure. You may send the letter over your own signature, if you prefer. Design its layout in any way you choose. If you wish, you can give this promotion a special name (such as, "Your Prom Night on Us").

5. As manager of a large company that deals exclusively in mail-order clothes for executives, you have come up with a new idea to promote your product. You plan to let your customers sample your product before they decide to buy.

Sample clothes that you will offer include business suits for men and women, shirts, shoes, ties, belts, dresses, pantsuits, and top coats for men and women.

Since the high prices of clothes continue to rise rapidly, you have developed a plan to offer a variety of coordinated executive outfits to men and women at reduced prices. You can make this offer at such a low price because you deal in volume, and with low overhead.

For your plan, you have obtained several prepared lists of executives and have in your possession more than 1,500 names. Write a letter to the people on the lists. They should know that the plan is exclusively for executives; that the clothes can be worn for two weeks on a trial basis; that any outfit can be returned if the customer is not satisfied. With your letter include brochures about your clothes and samples of material used to make the clothes. Enclose also a postage-paid envelope and a card on which the executive checks brief information you need so you can send the right outfit.

6. You are relocation director for a real estate firm in a large city (use your city or select a large city with which you are familiar). One of your primary activities is working with the management of companies, helping employees being transferred to your area find appropriate housing. Companies and other contacts provide you with the names of people who will be moving to your city within the next one to three months.

Write a personalized form letter in which you welcome the recipients as prospective residents of your city. Acquaint them with the many attractive qualities it boasts (comfortable climate, modern transportation facilities, renovated downtown area, quality schools, museums and orchestras, diversified recreational facilities, pleasant residential areas within easy commuting distance, etc.). Mention the special real estate services your company offers to individuals who are house-hunting in an unfamiliar city. One of your agents can pick up the prospect (and members of his or her family) at the airport, take them to their hotel or motel, escort them on a tour of the city, and show them homes in city and suburban residential areas which will satisfy their housing requirements.

Remember that other firms in your city will be offering similar services to relocating executives. Therefore, choose your appeals carefully and develop them imaginatively and concretely so as to set your relocation service apart from those of your competitors. Perhaps you can send prospective clients descriptive materials about the city and your real estate services. Indicate that you will call to discuss relocation plans within 10 days. Because your firm is a member of a multiple listing network, it also helps find buyers for the transferred persons' former homes.

CAPSULE CHECKLISTS FOR SALES LETTERS*

I Solicited Sales Letters		II Unsolicited Sales Letters
Good-News Replies to Sales-Related Inquiries	**Bad-News Replies to Sales-Related Inquiries**	**Persuasive Requests**

<table>
<tr>
<td>

1. Best news or main idea
   a. Positive opening with
      one of these:
      (1) Requested material
      (2) Favorable answer to
          a question
      (3) Introduction of main
          idea(s)
   b. Courtesy; appreciation

2. Explanation
   a. Answers to all ques-
      tions—direct or implied
      (1) Positive, helpful tone
      (2) Embedded negatives
      (3) Emphasis on what
          something *is*, what
          you can do or have
      (4) Reader benefits
      (5) Prices after most sell-
          ing points (unless
          price is a bargain)
   b. Resale (with reader bene-
      fits), when appropriate
   c. Educational material on
      product use, if pertinent

3. Courteous close
   a. CSAD[1] (sometimes);
      itemized steps, if desir-
      able
   b. EA[2]
   c. DA[3]
   d. RB[4] and courtesy; offer
      of further help, if appro-
      priate

</td>
<td>

1. Buffer
   a. Appreciation
   b. Assurance
   c. Resale
   d. Understanding

2. Explanation
   a. Answers to all questions
   b. Pertinent facts and de-
      tails
   c. RB[4] reasons for com-
      pany policy

3. Decision—with resale
   and/or suggestions
   a. Embedded statement of
      bad news with suggestion
      of what CAN be done
   b. Ideas for help
   c. Possible future changes
   d. Resale on firm, products,
      services, if appropriate

4. Positive, friendly, appropri-
   ate close
   a. Good wishes
   b. Appreciation
   c. CSAD[1]
   d. Willingness to help
      further

</td>
<td>

1. Attention (promise; star)
   a. Introduction of relevant reader-benefit
      theme by:
      Comparison or short story
      Event or fact in reader's life
      Problem reader may face
      Significant fact about product
      Solution to a problem
      Special offer or gift
      Surprising question or challenging state-
      ment
      Testimonials
   b. Envelopes, letterhead, maybe special
      designs

2. Interest (picture; chain)
   a. Beginning development of physical de-
      scription, benefits, CSP
   b. Appeals: approval, beauty, cleanliness,
      comfort, convenience, customer satis-
      faction, distinctiveness, efficiency,
      enjoyment, entertainment, friendships,
      health, improvement, love of home and
      people, money and other valuables,
      peace of mind, pleasure, popularity,
      profits, safety, savings, self-preserva-
      tion, and others

3. Desire-Conviction (prove; chain)
   a. Full development of needed description,
      reader benefits, central selling point
   b. Proof by users, laboratories and agen-
      cies, prospect:
      (1) Users' experiences with product
      (2) Names of users
      (3) Testimonials
      (4) Performance tests
      (5-7) Free trial, Guarantee, Samples
   c. Price presented psychologically
   d. Enclosures to strengthen desire-convic-
      tion

</td>
</tr>
</table>

* Lists include possible content. For any one message, choose only
pertinent items.
[1] CSAD = clear statement of action desired.
[2] EA = easy action.
[3] DA = dated action.
[4] RB = reader benefit

4. Action (push; hook)
   a-d. CSAD[1] b. EA[2] DA[3] RB[4]
   e. Inducements
      (1) Credit cards
      (2) Easy payments or no money now.
      (3) Free gift   (4) Free trial
      (5) No obligation to buy
      (6) Premium
      (7) Special price for limited time

The Written Job Presentation

Sometime in your life—perhaps several times—you will probably seek a job through a written presentation. If you answer advertisements or choose companies that do not send recruiters to your campus, you will usually need to write and mail your application. Also, even if you interview a firm's representative on your campus, you may still be asked for additional, written information. Furthermore, several years after you graduate from college—if you desire to change jobs—the ability to write a good presentation of yourself will help you get a better, more satisfying job. Thousands of applicants have found that the best way to get interviews and desired jobs is through the direct-mail approach.

Actually, when you apply for a job you are selling a "product"—yourself. The research before you write, as well as the planning and writing of your "sales promotion" job presentation, should be as thorough as for selling any other product by direct mail. This chapter discusses the "product" analysis, market research, résumé, and application letter.

"PRODUCT" ANALYSIS: EVALUATING YOURSELF

Whenever you are selling something, you want to be sure you are representing the product fairly. You need to analyze it to know *what* you are selling before you can start investigating *where* and *how* to sell it. The same is true when you are selling your services. For an adequate *self-appraisal*, take an *inventory* of your employment qualifications. Begin by listing—on several sheets of paper—your specific achievements, capabilities, interests, and characteristics. You might write them under various general headings and subheadings like the following:

1. *Work experience, skills, aptitudes*

   Your part-time and full-time jobs (paid and volunteer) since high school—dates, employer and supervisor names and addresses; your title(s), duties, responsibilities, successes, promotions.

   Your specific skills and aptitudes—speaking ability, report-writing ability, shorthand, etc.; also machines (office, industrial, craft) you can operate well.

   Military service—dates, responsibilities, achievements.

2. *Education—evidence of intelligence and knowledge*

   Schools (colleges, technical, military, high, other) you attended—dates, names, locations; your degrees, major(s), scholastic standing in each.

   Courses—in major, core, and useful electives; grades; significant reports written.

3. *Activities, achievements, social development*

Extracurricular and professional organizations—memberships, offices held, and noteworthy accomplishments in clubs related to your major, or in sports, church, social, community projects; coaching, student teaching, tutoring.

Achievements, honors, awards—scholarships, honor rolls, and other recognitions.

Travel, foreign language facilities, hobbies, personal business ventures, publications, attendance and responsibilities at conventions, and so forth.

4. *Interests, preferences, and attitudes*

Which courses in my schooling did I enjoy most? In which did I earn high grades?

Do I prefer to work with people, figures, machines, or ideas?

Would I rather sell, create, or design? Lead or follow?

In which locality do I prefer to live? Have I strong preferences?

How well do I work under pressure?

Am I a good listener? planner? leader? follower? (List evidence.)

What are my strongest skills?

Which hobbies do I enjoy most? Do they relate to the job I'd like?

What have I done to correct my shortcomings?

What are my goals and priorities?

5. *Personal characteristics–self-appraisal checklist*

Rate yourself on the following characteristics considered important by employers who seek college graduates. Notice that "integrity" heads the list.

	Excellent	Good	Fair	Poor
• Integrity, sincerity				
• Ability to think logically				
• Enthusiasm, initiative, drive				
• Dependabilty				
• Ability to communicate: orally				
in writing				
• Intelligence				

	Excellent	Good	Fair	Poor
• Maturity				
• Analytical ability				
• Ability to get along and cooperate with others				
• Emotional stability				
• Evidence of good judgment				
• Ability to make decisions				
• Health and energy				
• Physical appearance				
• Capacity for leadership				
• Self-confidence				
• Courtesy, tact, diplomacy				
• Adaptability				
• Sense of humor				
• Neatness of work				
• Determination				

An objective self-analysis like the foregoing inventory is strictly for your own use. It will not be mailed to anyone, but it helps you see patterns emerge regarding your capabilities, desires, interests, and achievements that are unique to you.

MARKET RESEARCH: FINDING WHO CAN USE YOU AND WHAT THEY PREFER

The next phase of your job-getting campaign is to determine which jobs and employers require what you have to offer. This section includes suggestions to help you in these phases of your job-market research, whether you are a recent or upcoming graduate or a person who has worked a number of years and now wants to change jobs or career.

Information Sources for Careers and Jobs

Various information sources can be helpful. Bear in mind, of course, that because supply and demand in the employment market change from year to year, it is best to get the most current information on both careers and job opportunities.

Publications regarding Careers

To get ideas about various occupations and careers you will find useful printed materials such as the following in libraries and perhaps your campus career placement office:

Books. Among many books available, these six give a broad overview:

Career Planning Handbook; A Guide to Career Fields and Opportunities, U.S. Civil Service Commission, U.S. Government Printing Office, Washington, D.C.

Dictionary of Occupational Titles, U.S. Department of Labor, U.S. Government Printing Office, Washington, D.C. Summarizes characteristics, abilities, and skills contributing to success in various occupations and careers. Includes 23,000 occupations.

Occupational Outlook Handbook, U.S. Bureau of Labor Statistics, U.S. Government Printing Office, Washington, D.C. Highlights employment opportunities in various fields.

Guide to Career Education, by Muriel Lederer, Quadrangle/The New York Times Book Company, New York, 1976.

What Color Is Your Parachute? A practical manual for job hunters and career changers, by Richard Bolles; Ten-Speed Press, Berkeley, Calif., 1982.

SRA Occupational Briefs, Science Research Associates, 259 East Erie Street, Chicago. Consists of 210 four-page briefs (of which 70 are revised each year) about major job areas.

Magazines and Newspapers. For lists of recent articles on careers you are considering, consult one or more of these periodical indexes: *Applied Science and Technology, Business Periodicals, Public Affairs Information Service, Readers' Guide, Standard and Poor's Industrial Index, Standard Register of Advertisers.* Among the magazines that occasionally devote a part or an entire issue to occupations are: *American Journal of Sociology, Fortune* magazine, *M.B.A. Magazine, Wall Street Journal,* and *Time.*

Publications and People regarding Employers and Jobs

After deciding on the kind of career you want, you will need information about employers and various types of jobs available in your chosen field. Published materials and various people can inform you about openings, products, services, geographical locations, sizes, problems, and/or facts about the employers. Among them are the following:

College Placement Annual, College Placement Council, 35 East Elizabeth Street, Bethlehem, Pennsylvania. Contains an alphabetical list of United States and Canadian firms seeking college graduates; includes brief information on openings and the proper persons to contact; also includes alphabetical lists by majors and geographical locations, plus counsel for the serious job seeker.

Dun and Bradstreet Middle Market Directory. Names, addresses, telephone numbers, officers, products or services, number of employees, and alphabetical list of top management for about 33,000 firms whose net worth is $500,000 to $999,999.

Dun and Bradstreet Million Dollar Directory. Essentially similar coverage as for Middle Market, but focuses on firms with net worth over $1 million.

Fortune Magazine's Directory of Largest Corporations. Published annually in four parts. Includes industrials, financial services, retailing, transportation, and utilities.

Poor's Register of Directors and Executives; United States and Canada, published annually by Standard and Poor's Corporation, 345 Hudson Street, New York. Has an alphabetical list of over 27,000 leading business firms, their addresses, principal products, number of employees, directors, and key officers.

Thomas' Register of American Manufacturers. Thomas Publishing Company, 461 Eighth Avenue, New York.

Company annual reports, brochures, pamphlets, house organs, newsletters. (Get them in placement offices or by writing to the firms.)

Professional journals, business magazines, newspapers. Often periodicals have columns for both help wanted and position wanted. Sometimes special ads publicize openings. Also, occasional articles discuss companies' new ventures, expansions, additional products, and so forth. Such leads may suggest employment possibilities for you.

Besides these printed materials, you can get helpful advice and sometimes tips about good openings from persons familiar with work or companies in your chosen career. These may be useful sources of information:

Business librarians

Businesspeople and personnel departments in your chosen field or firm(s)

Chambers of commerce

Company representatives—traveling for various employers

Counselors—in your school placement office, faculty, and activity programs

Employment agencies—including national, state, city, and private bureaus

Friends and relatives

Desirable General Qualifications of the Applicant

Determining what the employers' (your buyers') needs and requirements are is an important part of your research about the job market. You will then be better able to focus on jobs that are in harmony with what you can contribute as an employee. Desirable general qualifications all employers look for usually include (in varying degrees, depending on the job) *the five broad areas listed in the self-appraisal,* pages 341–343. You will find detailed discussions on them later in this chapter.

In addition, employers also look for proper attitude toward employment. You will more likely make a favorable impression when your attitude shows a willingness to learn and work, sincere interest in the company as well as in the field, and reasonable attitude toward salary.

Willingness to Learn and Work

Especially if you are a recent college graduate, you should be willing to accept beginning or routine work within your chosen field. The many facts you've learned during perhaps 16 years of school before graduation, have been general enough to be useful for all types of businesses. On the job you will need to learn specific duties, procedures, and practices of the company that hires you. A college degree does open doors to employment, but you still have to prove your worth in your written application, interview, and actual performance on the job. You need to be genuinely willing to learn.

Sincere Interest in the Field and the Company

Show that you have a *genuine interest in your chosen field or job.* Employers expect you to know the type of work you prefer for a career. Don't expect the employer to decide in what areas you are best suited. You must reach your own conclusion.

Your *interest in the company* should also be sincere. After you have studied the company, you can state why you feel it is the type of organization in which you feel you can do your most productive work. Employers appreciate the applicant with *you-attitude and integrity.* Be sincere. In your résumé and letter try to *show how you can be helpful to the employer.*

Reasonable Attitude toward Salary

Do not emphasize your own self-interest, such as what fringe benefits and salary the employer will offer *you.* Generally it is better to consider a challenging opportunity more important than a large beginning salary. Emphasis on salary—in the first written job presentation—creates an unfavorable impression. In general, especially if you are just beginning your career, it is best not to mention desired salary in the letter or résumé. (This matter can be discussed during the interview.)

Desirable General Qualities for the Written Job Presentation

After you have evaluated your assets and researched job opportunities and employers' requirements, you are ready to prepare your written "sales promotion." The main purpose is to get an interview. You need to persuade the employer that you are the right candidate for the job. Many personnel directors have commented that only a small percentage of the hundreds of applications they receive each month are well written and appealing enough to warrant interviews. The rest must be discarded, for readers haven't time to figure out what the applicants have to offer. A sloppy, inaccurate message from an applicant supposedly trying to make a good impression causes the employer to wonder about that person's overall capability.

Your written job presentation—the letter and résumé—will make a more favorable impression on the prospective buyers if it has the seven C qualities. The following desirable *general* suggestions apply to both the résumé and the letter. Later in this chapter the separate sections on Résumé and Letter of Application illustrate *specific* ways to include your various qualifications effectively.

1. *Present your message concisely, clearly, honestly, with consideration for the reader.* Desirable length is usually a one-page letter and a one- or two-page résumé—unless you have many years of valuable experience pertinent to a top-level job. Focus on your credentials that show how you can help the employer in the job you seek.
2. *Include only positive specific information relative to the position.* Omit facts that may detract from your favorable qualifications. Emphasize the areas of job-related responsibilities in which you have a past record of excellence.
3. *Be yourself and don't use "canned" messages.* Your résumé and letter should reveal your individuality. Personnel executives easily recognize and react negatively toward canned messages that sound as if they've been copied from a textbook or written by an employment agency.
4. *Use an appropriate businesslike approach.* You should sound serious, rather than smart alecky or "cute." Avoid slang and novelties like: a burnt corner (to show "a burning desire" to work), an upside-down letter (saying applicant is not afraid to start at the bottom), or reference to yourself as "a product originating only 21 years ago"! Avoid overuse of the word *I*.
5. *Triple check for accuracy of facts and mechanics*—grammar, sentence and paragraph structure, organization, desirable headings, parallelism of items under each heading, punctuation, and spelling. Be especially careful to correctly spell names of persons, firms, and job areas.
6. *Make appearance attractive and professional-looking.*
   a. Paper for the letter and résumé should usually be 8½- by 11-inch white bond, of good quality.
   b. Typing of both letter and résumé should be with neat, black type; margins, ample for easy reading of uncrowded data; erasures or correc-

tions, unnoticeable. In the résumé, to emphasize key words and headings, you can use underscoring, capital letters, italics, "frames" with rule-line drawings, and other devices.

   c. Duplicating—by offset (such as multilith), print, xerography, or other neat professional methods (costing only a few cents per page)—is permissible for résumés, but *not* for letters. Each application letter must be individually typewritten.

7. *Personalize your presentation as much as possible.* Tailoring a résumé for a specific job or company is desirable. However, even if you are sending out numerous résumés (neatly reproduced), you should preferably address each accompanying *letter* to a specific person *by name* with correct title and use that name in your salutation. Address your letter to the person (chief accountant, sales manager, personnel director) who is in charge of employing applicants for the type of job you seek.

8. *Use good judgment in mailing your message.* Generally, be prompt. Sometimes it may be advisable to use special delivery to reach an executive at the best time, usually in the middle of a week. (However, some surveys show that letters answering a popular ad get better results if they arrive on about the eighth day rather than among the hundreds mailed the first seven days after the ad appears.)

RÉSUMÉ

Though the prospective employer will read the letter first, you should prepare the résumé first, for it includes facts on which the letter will be based.

The résumé gives a general, concise picture of *you*—what you have accomplished in your education, experience, and activities that will benefit prospective employers. Contents and layouts vary widely; there is no one best type. However, an important rule is to place your most impressive qualifications first whenever possible and desirable. Present your information under headings in phrases instead of full sentences, and avoid using personal pronouns.

This section discusses the possible contents and ways of presenting a résumé (also spelled "resume"). From the following checklist you can *select the parts that best fit your background and the job you seek.* Then arrange them in any desirable order. "Accentuate the positive" honestly.

CHECKLIST FOR A RÉSUMÉ

1. Opening section:
Your name, address, telephone number

Job or career objective

Summary of basic qualifications

2. **Education:**
   Advanced schooling and training—school names, locations; dates attended, degrees and certificates (include high school and military if significant)

   Major, significant pertinent courses (required or elective), academic honors, grade point averages; special skills; speeches, research, reports

3. **Work experience:**
   Employer names, locations; dates (month year to month year); titles and positions held; duties; supervisors (or number supervised); accomplishments

   Volunteer work, research, tutoring, publications, etc.

4. **Activities, achievements, awards:**
   School and community memberships, offices held, honors, publications; travel, languages, self-support, other facts

5. **Personal data—optional:**
   Birthdate, health, height, weight, marital status, military service, hobbies, date of availability

6. **References**

Opening Section

The information in the opening section (upper part of the résumé) gives the reader a general picture of the applicant—who the person is, what she or he wants, and what he or she offers.

Title

The résumé heading can range in content from your name alone to your name and the title of the job you are applying for to your name, address, and telephone number and/or the name of the firm receiving the job presentation. Also, you can choose other words besides *résumé,* as in these examples:

```
1. Résumé of Robert A. Fletcher for Retail Management
2. John O. Bowman
   1504 Lamb Avenue
   Peoria, IL 61610
   Phone: (309) 543-1072
3. Qualifications of Betty Jo Anderson for a Position as Business
   Teacher in the North Shore School District
```

Whatever title you choose, *include your address and telephone number on your résumé where your prospective employer can see and use them easily, preferably in the opening section.* A single person might have two addresses listed on the résumé—permanent (parents') address and temporary school address. You can include both if they serve a good purpose. If you prefer to omit address and phone number in the opening, you can include them in the Personal Data section.

Job or Career Objective

One entry that interests every employer is the job (or professional) objective. This statement is sometimes in the heading (see examples 1 and 3 above), or it is under a separate title. If you can do two quite different kinds of work—for instance, accounting and teaching—you should prepare two separate résumés, each with a specific objective and then feature different phases of your background in each.

Be careful to avoid inflexible titles or too narrow statements of objectives, because they decrease the scope of your availability. When your immediate goal is different from the ultimate goal, state both in your objective, as in the following:

```
1. An accounting position with a reputable public accounting firm
   which is a leader in its field. The position should eventually
   lead to management advisory services.
2. A sales representative position in a growing firm. Eventual goal
   is to become manager of the marketing department.
3. To work in your firm as an expeditor or coordinator with the
   eventual aim of a position in construction management.
```

Summary of Basic Qualifications

Immediately after—*or before*—stating your objectives (what you *want*), you can sometimes include a heading suggesting what you can *offer* for the job. The heading can be: Significant Professional Achievements; Summary of Basic Qualifications; Capsule View of Public Relations Background; or others. Such a summary statement is effective if you have two or more *outstanding* qualifications that are basic or especially important for the job, like those below. (Notice they are concisely stated in phrases or partial sentences.)

```
1. Offering six years of progressively more responsible experience
   in office management and business administration, in addition to
   a master's degree in policy and organization. Record of accuracy,
   integrity, and ability to work with people.
2. Associate of Arts Degree in Business--major in transportation; 3½
   years of full-time experience--specializing in in-bound cargo
   movement with steamship agency plus shipping department, order
   desk, and inside sales with manufacturing firm. (By a community col-
   ege graduate. )
```

3. Bachelor of Arts degree with a major in personnel management and with emphasis in psychology, sociology, and business. Four years of part-time experience working with people. Student counselor in Alaska, summer of (*year*).

4. A diligent worker with 10 years' successful job experience ranging from varied sales responsibilities to restaurant management. Proven ability to organize sales campaign and to supervise employees. (*This applicant had no college degree.*)

Education

The most important qualification you can offer for the job (or the job area) should be in the first major section following the résumé opening. If you are a recent graduate and education is your strongest selling point, cover this area first—in detail. The more years you are away from school, the less educational detail is required. But even applicants who have been away from school for a while should include (usually later in the résumé) names and locations of schools as well as dates attended and degrees earned.

If education is your main qualification, you may want to include all the items shown on the Résumé Checklist (page 349), provided this material strengthens your presentation. Include the name, location, dates attended, and degrees or certificates earned at all postsecondary schools you attended. (Even high school may be mentioned if its reputation or location of your achievements there somehow tie in with the job qualifications.) The number and kinds of courses to list vary with the type of work requested. Show that you have an acceptable background in the area of the requested work and also a broad understanding of the arts and sciences (if true). Also list useful elective courses related to your interest and the job. Good examples are courses in written communication, speech, and human relations; also others that helped you to reason objectively to a conclusion or to perform any skills needed for the job.

Grades are a controversial subject. If they are high—for instance, 3.8 on a 4.0 scale—they should be included. Grades indicate how well the graduate has mastered program studies and met numerous requirements. The importance of grades in the overall qualifications varies, of course, depending upon the type of job.

Illustrated below are various ways to show pertinent facts about academic background. Rearrange your own educational material so it best presents *your* preparation for the job you seek. List your most recent education first, and choose meaningful titles.

1. Concise listing of schools, with dates; then degrees, standing, major:

PROFESSIONAL TRAINING AND EDUCATION

University of Kansas	Lawrence, KS[1]	Business Administration	1982–84
Everett Junior College	Everett, WA	Liberal Arts	1980–82

[1] Abbreviations, if clear, are permissible on résumés.

```
U.S. Air Force School Denver, CO    Electronics          1977-79
Martin High School    Martin, WV     College Preparatory  1973-77

Degrees:   Bachelor of Arts in Business Administration, U.K., 1984
           Associate of Arts and Sciences, E.J.C., 1982
Standing:  Top 5 percent of class at both E.J.C. and U.K.
           Valedictorian, high school
Majors:    Operations Management and Finance
```

2. **Listing of courses functionally** (20-year-old community college graduate with no paid experience):

<u>Associate of Arts Degree—Technology/Accounting Major,</u>
<u>Metropolitan Community College, Syracuse, NY</u>

<u>Accounting Techniques</u>	Accounting Principles 1-2-3, Advanced Accounting, Federal Income Tax Accounting, Cost Accounting, Auditing, Governmental Accounting
<u>Business</u>	Business Organization and Management, Business Math, Business Law, Applied Economics, Business Statistics
<u>Communication Skills</u>	Written Communication, Speech
<u>Machine Operations</u>	Data Processing, Office Machines 1 and 2, Rotary and Electronic Calculators, Typing
<u>Working with People</u>	Introduction to Psychology, Office/Personnel Management, Public Relations, Psychology of Human Relations

3. **Inclusion of schools and grades with course information:**

```
Education
University of Illinois, Urbana—Sept. '80-June '84
Major: Accounting (43 quarter hours)
Grades: Overall—3.7 (possible 4.0)
        Accounting—3.9
```

Accounting courses:	Other relevant courses:
·Federal Income Tax	·Personnel Management
·Special Tax Problems	·Human Relations
·Auditing Standards and Principles	·Business Report Writing
·Case Studies in Auditing	·Principles of Economics
·Basic Accounting Principles	·Marketing Cases
	·Banking and Finance

```
Broadway High School, Waco, TX: Sept. '76-June '80
Major: General business and College preparatory
Grades: 3.8 (possible 4.0); top 5 percent of class
```

Work Experience

Any kind of work experience—related or unrelated—reveals information that helps the employer to evaluate the applicant. Work experience similar to that which you are applying for indicates you like the type of work in question and may shorten the training period. However, all types of work experience disclose pertinent facts about the applicant's work habits and personality, give a source for references, and perhaps show job preferences. If you are an older applicant with extensive experience, you will probably place Work Experience *before* Education. Also, you may prefer to include only the more recent jobs or those that best relate to the position you seek; employers appreciate conciseness, instead of a long list of irrelevant material.

Usually, for the standard "general" résumé, list your jobs in chronological order with the present or most recent first. Try to include at least:

1. Type of work performed and your title (supervisor, bookkeeper, and so forth)[2]
2. Name and location of company[3]
3. Time worked (month year to month year)
4. Whether job was part-time (otherwise employer will interpret statement as full-time employment)
5. Duties—work involving responsibilities, adaptability, similarity to what you're applying for, integrity, supervisory or budgetary functions, knowledge of products. Use *action words* like the following:

advised	delivered	expanded	maintained	produced
analyzed	demonstrated	improved	managed	reduced
coached	designed	increased	negotiated	researched
completed	developed	initiated	organized	sold
conducted	directed	instituted	planned	supervised
created	edited	instructed	prepared	trained
coordinated	established	invented	presented	wrote

Arrange the facts for each job in the most "selling" order. You can begin with your job title, or employer's name, or dates you held each job, or the functions you performed on each job.[4]

---

[2] Be honest. If you were a laborer, say "laborer." Don't try to put on airs by camouflaging the title. For example, don't say "sanitary engineer" if you were a garbage collector; say "garbage collector."

[3] If you are currently employed and do not wish to disclose your employer on your résumé, you can merely identify the firm by industry; for example, you might say "a medium-sized manufacturer of electronic equipment." That will give the reader some indication of your company without divulging its name and perhaps jeopardizing your job. If a firm's name is now different from what it was when you were employed there, state the present name and "formerly . . .)."

[4] Be sure to follow rules of parallelism—making two or more elements in a series similar in grammatical word structure. "Manager," "Representative," and "Bookkeeper" are all parallel to each other because each is a job title. "Managing"—which is a kind of work, not a title—would not be parallel to the other three titles. For duties: keeping, drilling, filing, typing are parallel; so are kept, drilled, filed, typed.

1. Job title first:

Service Representative, Upland Telephone Co., Norfolk, VA.; February
1982 to September 1984. Duties: assisted telephone customers regarding telephone installations, questions on bills, complaints,
selection of additional telephones.

Bookkeeper, Associated Hardware, Boston, MA; June 1978 to February
1982. Duties: figured discounts on statements, filed, typed, posted accounts,
wrote checks.

2. Employer first:

California State Highway Department 931 Ridgeway, Sacramento
Draftsperson, March 1982 to December 1983*
Duties: drawing roadway profiles and burrow sites
Personnel Assistant, May 1981 to March 1982*
Duties: keeping time and employee records for division and pre-
paring vouchers
Driller's Helper, January 1980 to May 1981**
Duties: drilling test holes for proposed highway routes

Illinois State Highway Department 210 Main, Springfield
Engineering Technician, November 1976 to December 1979*
Duties: processing traffic data and interviewing on truck surveys

*Part-time during school, full-time summers.
**Full-time.

3. Dates first:

June 1983 to October 1984	Legal Secretary––Took dictation, transcribed, typed, filed, received clients––for McGee, Strom, Burner, Attorneys 9988 Hightower Building Dearborn, Michigan 48121
School Year September 1982 to June 1983	Stenographer––Weekday mornings wrote shorthand, transcribed, filed, operated switchboard––for Barnes, Jayne, Jackson, Associates Ridley Tower Cincinnati, Ohio 45221
Other jobs before 1982[5]	Worked as cashier in a restaurant Fridays and Saturdays two months, typed business letters for high school principal, picked strawberries.

[5] To indicate industriousness previous to the earliest full job entry, ''Other jobs before (year)'' is
acceptable for applicants in their early twenties but may be regarded as inappropriate for older (30
or older) applicants.

4. **Functions first:**

Though similar to category #1, this arrangement focuses on skills or duties (functions) instead of job titles. The following example is from a high-level executive's résumé. He chose to omit employer names.

```
        FUNCTIONAL REVIEW OF WORK EXPERIENCE

General        As Vice President and General Manager of a highly di-
Management:    versified million-dollar company, was responsible for
1970-1984      six operating divisions. Reduced personnel turnover
               and increased profits by over 40%. Instituted tech-
               niques of modern creative management.


International  As Manager of International Operations of a company
Management:    whose sales exceeded six million dollars annually,
1962-1970      was responsible for the overseas sales and distribu-
               tion of four producing divisions. Products included
               plastics, pipeline coatings, wood products.


Consulting:    Conducted seminars on a worldwide basis for . . .
```

If you have had little or no paid employment but have done volunteer work, tutoring, or research (perhaps even published a report) without pay, you may list such responsibilities under Work Experience or under Activities.

Activities, Achievements, Awards

Participation in extracurricular and cocurricular activities is usually a good indication of an applicant's personality—ability to work with others, leadership, and emotional stability. When listing your activities, mention any offices you held as well as projects on which cooperation, teamwork, and sincere interest in other people (or projects) were needed. Include athletics, writing (such as journalism), speaking (such as debate), professional fraternities, student organizations, and community services that involve working with people.

Identify (in parentheses) any activity the employer might not know the significance of. However, if you are or were active in a church or political party, you need not identify them (because of civil rights); but do mention your responsibilities if pertinent.

Beta Gamma Sigma (national scholastic business honorary)

Beta Alpha Psi (accounting honorary)

Alpha Sigma Phi (social fraternity)

Helpers Club (a church youth group)

Statements like the following may be noteworthy:

1. Recognition, achievement, awards

```
a. Vice President, Senior Class, Central College
b. Most valuable student--Lion's Club Award
c. Mistress of ceremonies at Bay College Awards Assembly
d. Listed in the sixth annual edition of Who's Who among Students in
   American Junior Colleges
e. Eagle Scout
f. 3-year scholarship at Whitworth College
g. Dean's list for high scholarship (dates involved)
h. Two-year varsity basketball letterman
i. Outstanding senior male at (university)
j. High school salutatorian
```

2. Service

```
a. Assistant coach--Little League Football--(city, state)
b. Member of (year) World Service Team from my church. Sent to Yukon
   Territory, Alaska. Worked with high school, junior high, and pri-
   mary age children--teaching and counseling
c. Volunteer hospital work, day care
```

Personal Data

The category of personal information is now entirely optional. Civil rights laws state that one may not discriminate in hiring on the basis of race, age, religion, sex, marital status, national origin. Exceptions include occupational qualifications that are reasonably necessary to the normal operation of particular businesses, enterprises, or occupations. For example, some jobs in modeling, sports, teaching, and professional entertainment (TV, movies, etc.) may reasonably require certain personal attributes.

Though no law forbids applicants from volunteering personal information, they must be careful not to include items that could possibly be used for discrimination and harm their chances for getting an interview and a job. *Omit any information that might be considered negatively.*

Some applicants include under Personal Data a few significant facts pertinent to qualities needed for the job they seek. Among them might be: health, age, military service, hobbies, skills, expenses earned while attending college (to indicate determination, drive), travel (indicating knowledge of customs elsewhere).

Health

Good health is a prime requirement on most jobs because it determines both the physical and mental performance of the individual. You can indicate physical fitness in the Personal Data section or elsewhere by listing:

The sports you participate in. An active swimmer, football or basketball player, or a contestant in intramural activities must be in good condition.

Your hobbies that require activity, endurance, strength, and stamina. Examples include hiking, fishing, mountain climbing, boating, and bowling.

Age

If you think the employer may consider your age negatively (assuming that you are too inexperienced or overexperienced for the job you seek), but you feel you can sell her or him on your qualifications during an interview, *omit* age on the résumé. Or you can indicate your birthdate *after* listing your other excellent qualifications, so the employer reads them before seeing your age. (A federal law protects applicants ages 40 through 64 against age discrimination.)

Military Service

If significant for the job, military experience may be in a separate section or listed under Education, or Employment, or Personal Data. Here are suggestions:

1. Received Air Force commission on (*month day, year*). Air Force pilot from (*month day, year, to month day, year*). Received honorable discharge as Captain on (*month day, year*).
2. Serving eight years (*year to year*) in the Coast Guard Reserve with meetings every Thursday night and two weeks' summer training each year. Satisfactorily completed five years of service. Six months of basic training: (*month day, year, to month day, year*).
3. Six years in the Army Reserve (*month year to month year*). Active duty: (*month day, year, to month day, year*). Honorable Discharge.

Hobbies and Skills

If relevant to job qualifications, hobbies and/or skills may be listed under Personal Data or Activities (or sometimes under Education or Employment).

1. Requested work—studying the stock market, operating certain machines, speaking a foreign language, editing school paper, composing a report or article that was published
2. Mental activity—playing chess, reading
3. Creativity—designing clothes, tools, other useful items
4. Fine arts—music, crafts, drama, photography
5. Household tasks—cooking, sewing, knitting

Picture

Although including a picture on a résumé was formerly considered almost "standard procedure," this practice has been rare since the early 1970s. The best suggestion now is to *omit* the personal photograph, for it may trigger all kinds of unfavorable, harmful subjective reasons by the personnel representatives.

References

In general, if you are mailing your résumé to a list of employers, you'll be safer to omit references and state, "References will be sent upon request." (Then you won't risk having your references bothered by too many inquiries or being tired recommending you over and over again. Also, when you receive a request for references, you will know the specific kind the employer wants.) However, if you are writing to one employer (or a few) for a position you know is available, you can include references.

The least desirable reference is the "to whom it may concern" message you carry with you, and next are the references of friends. You (and the employers) know the references you choose will say only nice things about you; otherwise you wouldn't give their names.

Nevertheless, sometimes it will be to your advantage to list references if the names you list are well known and respected by the employers. They may be more interested in you even before the interview when they see the name of a person they know and have confidence in or who is considered an expert in a particular field, or perhaps even an executive in or an important customer of the company to which you are applying.

When you give references, list about three. The most appropriate names include present or former employers and professors. Also acceptable is a character reference whose name or occupation is respected. State each individual's full name, title, organization (if any), complete business address and telephone number. Since you obviously should get permission to use the names you're listing you need not say "with permission." Relatives should not be used as references.

Summary, with Sample Résumés

The résumé should contain selling facts about yourself in a neat, concise, easy-to-read, well-organized format that best indicates your value to the employer. Accentuate the positive by focusing on your strengths and minimizing any job-getting handicaps. If you have little job-related full-time work experience, sell your part-time or volunteer work, your useful thorough educational foundation, your knowledge of the product or firm, and/or your working-with-people experience that can be adapted to the job. On the other hand, if your formal college education is irrelevant or limited, sell whatever other job-related training you do have, plus your work experience, significant activities, and your dependability as well as additional pertinent personal attributes—with specific facts for examples.

```
                        QUALIFICATIONS OF LESLIE T. RYSON as
               STAFF ACCOUNTANT WITH TORGEN, SURGESS, AND ASSOCIATES

        Home address:    3982 Bula Drive, Pasadena, CA 91118    Phone 366-9876


    EDUCATION      Bachelor of Business Administration Degree, June 1985
                      University of California, Los Angeles

                   Associate of Arts Degree, June 1983
                      Central Community College, Seattle, Washington

                   A thorough understanding of corporation, partnership,
                   and proprietorship accounting and financial analysis
                   developed through these courses:

                   Accounting (40 quarter hours, with 3.8 grade average--GPA
                   scale top, 4.0):  Auditing, Public and Internal:  Cost;
                   Equity;  Consolidations:  Federal Income Tax;  Fiduciary

                   Related Courses (60 quarter hours, with 3.6 GPA):  Data
                   Processing, Business Communications, Business Law, Money
                   and Banking, Corporate Finance, Statistics

    EMPLOYMENT     June 1983-    Assistant Accountant, Purchasing and Personnel
                   Present       Dept.**  Doctors Hospital, Pasadena, CA

                   Dec. 1981-    Full-charge bookkeeper*
                   Dec. 1982     Marine Medical Clinic, Seattle, WA

                   June 1981-    Billing Clerk*
                   Dec. 1981     Cole Transfer and Storage, Los Angeles, CA

                   July 1977-    Bookkeeper and assistant to Secretary Treasurer**
                   Sept. 1980    Hillside Hospital, Burbank, CA

                    *Full time
                  **Part time during school;  rest, full time
                    Earned 80% of college expenses.

    ACTIVITIES     Member and Treasurer, Beta Alpha Psi, Accounting Honorary, UCLA
    AND HONORS     Chairperson, Student Association's Community Fund Drive, UCLA
                   Chairperson, Church Youth Activities Campaign
                   Hobbies:  tennis, swimming, golf
                   Award winner, Junior Scholarship Cup, Alpha Alpha Association
                   Dean's Honor Roll, UCLA School of Business Administration, 3 quarters

    REFERENCES     Dr. Albert Tyran       Ms. Nancy Green        Mr. James Black
                   Prof. of Accounting    Personnel Director     Manager
                   School of Bus. Admin.  Doctors Hospital       Marine Medical Clinic
                   University of California 909 University St.    944 Terry Ave.
                   Los Angeles, CA 90002  Pasadena, CA 91102     Seattle, WA 98104
                   (213)689-6666          (213)555-6666          (206)222-3333
```

Figure 12-1 *Personalized, one-page résumé*. Job objective and employer name are included in the heading. Applicant lists references; he knew there was a job opening for work he can do and he typed an individual résumé for that employer.

The foregoing discussions have included examples of various résumé sections. Figures 12-1 through 12-3 illustrate a variety of résumé contents and

```
                              Résumé of
                            Annette H. Bolles
                3261 Lakeside Lane, Gary, Indiana 46410   (219)726-8193


Professional Objective:  Business Education teaching position in an
                         Indiana Class-A secondary school


                    Education for Business and Teaching

Indiana University, Bloomington         September 1980 to August 1984

     Major:  Business Education, secondary school emphasis
             Courses in accounting;  business, government and society;
             business law;  secretarial procedures;  business communications;
             marketing;  teaching of typewriting, shorthand, and accounting

     Minor:  Economics
             Courses in macroeconomics, microeconomics, international
             economics, European and American economic history
     Grade Point Average:  3.9  (possible 4.0)
     Degree:  Bachelor of Arts in Business Education

     James High School, Waukegan, Illinois, September 1977 to June 1980
     College preparatory curriculum with emphasis on business and French
     Grade Point Average:  3.8  (possible 4.0)

                         Helpful Job Experience

Student Teacher  Broadway High, Bloomington, January to June 1984
     Supervisor:       Ms. Irene Grayson
     Courses taught:   Typing 2, 4;  Shorthand 2;  Vocational Office Practice
     Responsibilities: Supervised and planned three complete units for each
                       class, ranging from 20-30 students, with approval of
                       Ms. Grayson;  also worked with Mr. Ben Moor

     Title Clerk    Mason Ford Motor, 872 Raymon Avenue, Bloomington,
     and Secretary  January 1982 to December 1983 (part time during school,
                    full time summers); Mr. Charles Voney, Office Manager

     Responsibilities: Varied over the two years.  Operated switchboard,
                       typed reports and letters, checked titles, recorded
                       accounts payable and cash receipts, assisted office
                       manager as secretary and mail clerk.
```

Figure 12-2   *A general-purpose chronological résumé* (on two pages).

layouts—to help give you ideas of how you can arrange and sell your own qualifications.

Figure 12-2 is a chronological résumé with both centered and side headings. If work experience is limited, as it often is for recent graduates, the

```
Résumé of Annette H. Bolles - page 2


                        Helpful Job Experience (continued)

Assistant Claims Adjuster--Central Administrators, 559 John Street
                          Akron, Ohio, summer 1981
        Supervisor:       Mr. Mike Owen
        Responsibilities: Processed claims for health insurance, maintained
                          all billing files on customer accounts, and sent
                          reminders for premium payments

Part-time jobs before 1980--Waitress in Jolly Roger Restaurant, drug
                            store sales clerk, and library assistant

                        Honoraries, Clubs, Activities

College
        Phi Beta Kappa, academic national scholarship honorary
        Beta Gamma Sigma, national scholastic honorary in business
         administration
        Recording Secretary, Business Students' Association
        Vice President, Beta Beta Sorority
        Recipient of two academic scholarships:  from Faculty Wives and
         Panhellenic

High School
        National Honor Society and Torch Club--three years;  secretary one
         year
        President, Business Education Club
        Editor, Annual
        Outstanding Graduate 1980 (chosen by Indiana University Alumni Assn.)

                            Skills and Hobbies

Write and speak the French language
Office skills include:  Typing 60 wpm;  operating adding machine,
electric calculators, mimeograph, ditto, and copying machines;
taking shorthand (125 wpm).

Hobbies include:  bowling, hiking, working with people,
                  swimming, professional enrichment

                               References

                     Available with Credentials at
                     Placement Center, Indiana University
```

Figure 12-2   (Continued)   Second page of *general-purpose chronological résumé*.

applicants can detail their job-related activities, skills, and hobbies (as Ms. Bolles did on page 2 when applying for a teaching position). If it is desirable to have only one page, this résumé could be condensed by rearranging headings and facts and omitting some details.

```
Thomas R. Muchley              ******** OBJECTIVE ********
951 Compson Road               A line management position with responsibility
(city, state, zip)             for corporate or divisional profits.  Alterna-
(telephone)                    tively, responsibility for top level contract
                               negotiations or client development.

Major Qualifications     Offering 15 years of progressively more responsible
                         experience in Management, plus a Master of Business
                         Administration degree with a major and continuing
                         interest in this field.

                              EMPLOYMENT

Dates:
  Oct. 1974-Present      Standard Industrial Supplies, Inc.
  July 1964-Sept. 1974   ABC Products, International

Functional Review of Work Experience:

General          As Vice-President and General Manager, am responsible
Management       for six operating divisions.  Reduced personnel turn-
                 over and increased profits by over 40%.

Profit           Directed development of a successful analysis and
Planning         profit planning system to help with management
                 decisions on profit lines and areas.

International     As Manager of International Operations, was responsible
Management        for overseas sales and distribution of four producing
                  divisions.  Products ranged from intermediate chemicals
                  and pipeline coatings to treated wood.

Financial        Maintained financial relations with investment
Communications   bankers, security analysts, and clients through face-
                 to-face and written communications.

Report Edit-     Edited monthly Management Reports (printed for
ing and          distribution to 950 company managers). Wrote and
Writing          compiled award-winning annual reports.

Staff            As Assistant Manager of Personnel, supervised a staff
Management       of eight interviewers and testers for hiring both
                 office and warehouse personnel.  Devised policies for
                 training, rating, and disciplining staff employees.

                              EDUCATION

M.B.A. in Management, University of Illinois, 1980.
B.A. in Business Administration (Management and Organization),
     University of Kansas, 1964, cum laude.

                             PERSONAL DATA

Health:  Excellent    Languages:  Fluent Spanish; some German and French

         FURTHER DETAILS AND REFERENCES UPON REQUEST
```

Figure 12-3 *Functional résumé* (one-page).

The functional résumé is especially adaptable for the person with impressive work responsibilities related to the job sought or (like Mr. Muchley, Figure 12-3) with long job stability and few employers. It is also useful for applicants with little paid work experience but with considerable activities and job-usable skills (managing, selling, organizing, communicating, researching, helping people).

LETTER OF APPLICATION

The application letter is just as much a sales letter as any message selling a product or service[6]—and the résumé is an enclosure. In your letter you tell the prospective employer *what you can do for her or him and why you feel you are qualified.* You interpret only the important points in your résumé as they *relate to the specific job requirements.* Try to focus on what you can contribute to the employer (your "buyer"), not how much he or she can offer you. In just a few paragraphs—probably five—you must "sell" readers to the point where they want to know more about you. The checklist below may be a guide when you plan the content of your persuasive "sales" application letter—organized by the AIDA plan. Subsequent pages discuss ways to develop each item.

CHECKLIST FOR APPLICATION LETTER

A. Attention (1 paragraph)
   1. Businesslike beginning. Usually choose one or two:
      a. Summary—perhaps two or three outstanding qualifications
      b. Name—an individual or office the reader is familiar with or the publication in which the reader's ad appeared
      c. Question—for reader benefit
      d. News item—related to employer
      e. Other relevant reader-oriented statement
   2. Mention of specific job or field of interest

B. Interest, Desire, Conviction (2 or 3 paragraphs)
   1. Discussion of your qualifications from a reader-benefit or reader-interest viewpoint. Include your:
      a. Education and training—related to job requirements
      b. Work experience—related to job requirements
      c. Significant personal attitudes, interests, and/or qualities—related to job requirements
   2. Reference to résumé (once)

---

[6] The application letter should, however, always be individually typewritten, although other sales letters may be processed for mass distribution.

C. Action (1 paragraph)
  1. Request for interview . . . at reader's convenience, with suggestions when you will be available
  2. Easy action
    a. Phone number
    b. Hours you can be reached
    c. Reply envelope or card enclosed only rarely. Consider reader!

Opening for Favorable Attention

The application letter should begin with a businesslike paragraph that attracts the reader's attention. It should make clear that you are applying for a job—not inquiring about one or studying this phase for a school report. Also, identify the job (or job area) you're interested in.

As shown in the checklist above and the following examples, you have various choices for contents of the first paragraph. You can adapt these suggestions to your needs whether you write a "prospecting" (unsolicited) letter to firms that have not announced an opening or a "solicited" letter about a known available position. Also, if appropriate, you may combine two kinds of openings into your one first paragraph, as in some of the examples.

Summary Opening

One of the most effective openings is a summary of your two or three outstanding qualifications related to the job you seek. Like the first paragraph of a newspaper article, the summary states the important points you'll discuss in the message.

```
1. Retailing experience in a department store similar to yours,
   business knowledge gained academically, plus a sincere interest
   in these areas have helped me learn the basic requirements for
   running a department efficiently. I would like to contribute the
   practical skills I have acquired by becoming a part of your man-
   agement training program.
2. It is my understanding that a continuity writer for your station
   must have an interest in and knowledge of classical music. She or
   he must have ambition and a desire to achieve. Above all, this
   person must be able to write. I have these qualifications and
   should like to be considered for the job. (Applicant had no work expe-
   rience.)
```

Name Opening

If someone—especially a person well known to the reader—has suggested you apply to a particular firm for a job, you can use that person's name in the opening—unless he or she has asked you to keep it confidential.

If you are answering a job ad, refer to it and the name of the publication along with what you can offer. Avoid repeating requirements stated in the ad.

1. Dr. Horace Brann, professor of accounting and chairperson of the accounting department at (*university*), has informed me that your firm is looking for an accounting major who is interested in managerial accounting. I should like to be considered for the opening in your training program.
2. Your ad in the Sunday <u>Times</u> for an aggressive person to sell your graphic-communication products and services calls for qualifications that match mine very closely. With three years' successful selling as well as servicing of duplicators and electronic systems, plus genuine enthusiasm for selling and ability to solve complex graphic communications problems, I would like to join your staff as a sales trainee.

Question Opening

Another way to catch the employer's attention at the beginning is with a properly phrased question that shows understanding of a company problem or significant need and the applicant's desire to help.

For your tourist store in (*city*) do you need a reliable assistant store manager who speaks French and German fluently, has successful sales experience and a broad background of business training? I have these qualifications and would like to put them to work for you.

News-Item Opening

Sometimes you can mention a news event about a significant achievement of the employer or his or her company, or a contemplated change or new procedure—if it ties in with your desire to work for a certain firm.

1. In a recent (*name of journal*) article I read with interest that your firm is planning to open a branch office in Mexico. Because my college background and work experience, plus facility with Spanish, fit your basic requirements for a research assistant, I would like to apply for that job in your branch office.
2. Your firm's consulting activities, and especially its work in "information systems," may attract you to an individual with my qualifications and aspirations. My academic concentration on "open systems theory," coupled with practical experience, would enable me to perform well as a member of your management consulting staff.

Middle Paragraphs for Interest, Desire, Conviction

After your attention-getting opening, you present your qualifications for the job you're applying for. In the short space you have (perhaps no more than three paragraphs) you can't repeat *unnecessarily* what is on the résumé. You need to select and emphasize key points, considering carefully every word in every idea you include. *The emphasis is on how you can be helpful to the employer!*

As with most sales letters, *facts and figures* are more convincing than the writer's opinions. But these facts *must relate to the buyer's needs.* When you write each paragraph, ask yourself, *"So what?"* How do these facts relate to *the requirements for* this *job and* this *employer?* For example:

So what?	I am a recent graduate of City Community College.
Show how the facts relate to the job	The specialized textile training I received at City Community College will enable me to provide the expertise in fabrics your clients want.

In a solicited letter answering an ad, be sure to cover in a positive way every qualification the ad specifies. If you have a shortcoming (maybe you're too young or have no work experience), emphasize other positive qualifications to strengthen the reader's confidence in your capabilities.

The order in which you present these paragraphs is also important. If you use a summary opening, you'll organize the paragraphs in the same order as the qualifications are listed in the opening—with the most important qualification first. If you don't have a summary opening, you'll still organize by discussing the most important qualification first. So that the reader doesn't divert attention to the résumé before finishing the letter, don't refer to the enclosure until the next-to-last or last paragraph.

Education

Most recent college graduates consider education their most important qualification; if so, they should discuss it first—in the letter as well as in the résumé. However, an applicant must be careful not to imply that a college degree—even a master's degree—is the only qualification for the job. Employers who hire college graduates *look beyond the degree, to determine what the applicant can do or what the degree indicates about personality.* They appreciate such signs of intelligence as ability to think logically, sound judgment, mental alertness, and good grades. In the paragraph on education you can:

- Show that you have both a broad background in business (or arts and sciences) and also depth in a major or a certain area.
- Highlight your overall education by showing how your college studies prepared you for the work (or area) you seek.
- Explain how and why you supplemented your major with important electives outside your major.

Examples

1. Training I received in production control and planning at (*name*) College enables me to analyze, study, and recommend methods of work simplification in factory projects. Concepts learned about

time and motion studies will help me conduct a thorough investigation in any work area. Additional studies on person and
machine output rates, personnel relations, and business communications provided knowledge to make job analyses and to write
clear, concise reports.
2. The accounting courses I studied at the University of (state) emphasized up-to-date procedures, principles, and theory—that
provide a firm basis with which to grow in the auditing profession. Courses in data processing, in addition to my work
experience at a computer installation, have led me to be especially interested in the auditing of such systems.

Work Experience

The jobs you've held—full- or part-time, related or unrelated to the position
you're applying for—help strengthen your qualifications. Try to tell concisely
how you performed some functions and what you accomplished. By discussing
responsibilities you had in previous jobs, you can show:

- You gained experience that will help you understand (or learn faster) the
  special techniques required for the new job.
- You can adapt to people and like to work with them.
- You can handle responsibilities
- You're a hard worker.

Examples

1. For the past four summers while working in your office as a shipping clerk and assisting in the accounting department, I have
   gained considerable knowledge of the techniques and terminology
   unique to the accountant in this industry. This previous work
   experience with your company will enable me to adjust to your
   program with only minimum training.
2. During my employment at (name) Food Centers, I have ordered merchandise for a store operating at a volume of $40,000 a week,
   formulated pricing policies, supervised merchandise allocation of
   the shelves as well as the activities of about 25 employees.
   This background has helped me develop a working knowledge of the
   food industry and also the capacity to help make policy decisions
   on retail food-store operations.

Personal Attitudes, Interests, Qualities

In another paragraph or two you can highlight a few personal attitudes, interests, or qualities that relate specifically to the job requirements. You might
discuss (1) your ability to work with people; (2) your attitude toward employment—your interest in the field, company, or geographic area; or (3) your
personal qualities. If you are an applicant with little or no job experience (or
perhaps irrelevant education), these qualifications may be your main selling
points.

Ability to Work with People. If you genuinely like people and want to help them, you have a priceless quality to sell. You can convey to your prospective employer that you have this ability, as shown in the following examples:

1. As assistant manager of a Household Finance Corporation office and as a collection department supervisor for the National Bank of Commerce, I developed the ability to get along well with people. For both customer service and employee relationships it was necessary to exercise good judgment based on sometimes incomplete information, in varying situations or difficult circumstances. I enjoy opportunities to work constructively with people.
2. In several capacities I have been able to further develop my interest in communicating and working with people. Being the daughter of an Air Force officer, I have lived throughout the United States and in foreign countries and have spent most of my summers traveling. Furthermore, as hospitality chairperson of my sorority, I organized all affairs held at the house and acted as hostess for guests. As a result, I have learned to make friends quickly and to feel at ease with many types of people--attributes which will help me be beneficial in a retailing position.

Attitude toward Employment. Interest in the field, company, or area should be substantiated by proof.

Examples

1. My interest in construction developed in high school, working summers and part-time in residential home building. Upon graduation, I decided on a career in construction management, and consequently realized that a college background in business, combined with on-the-job experience, was essential preparation. As my interest and work experience indicate, I am very enthusiastic about a career in this field. Employment in construction completely financed my college education. Even in my spare time I am building a chalet, as the enclosed data sheet shows.
2. To supplement my marketing major, I sold men's clothing for three years part-time or full-time during school; this sales experience should give me a head start in your training program. I can sell, enjoy selling, and want to continue to sell. What's more, I proved my sales potential by winning the Arrow Shirt contest which I have mentioned on the enclosed data sheet. Selling stocks appears to be a challenge and I welcome that challenge.

Desirable Personal Qualities. By citing various parts of your background—schooling, jobs, and/or extracurricular activities, you can show you have personal qualities that are desirable for the job you seek.

Examples

1. As the enclosed résumé shows, I found it necessary to work while completing my college education. In fulfilling the respon-

```
    sibilities for the jobs and the courses, I learned to be punctual
    and to apportion my time--requirements also confronted by an
    "audit team" in completing an audit within a time and fee limita-
    tion.
 2. While attending the university, I worked part time or full time
    during the school year and up to 80 hours a week (on two or more
    jobs) each summer. I was entirely self-supporting throughout my
    college career, and feel I can offer your company qualities of
    adaptability, perseverance, and patience developed from working
    hard on many jobs with many kinds of people.
```

Usually in the next to the last paragraph but some times in the last paragraph direct the reader's attention to some data on the résumé (see example 1 above and the sample letters on the following pages).

Last Paragraph

The last paragraph of your letter usually asks for action—just as a sales letter does. Without begging or commanding, you ask for an interview and (if appropriate) say you will come to the employer's office when he or she suggests. Make action easy by giving your telephone number and hours to call if someone can't answer the phone throughout the day or evening.

Examples

```
 1. As I will be in (city) from April 20 to April 25, I will appreciate
    the opportunity to see you during that time to discuss further my
    desire to serve as one of your investigators. After you have re-
    viewed my qualifications and examined the enclosed résumé, will
    you please name a convenient time in a letter to me at my Seattle
    address?
 2. My class schedule allows me to come to your office any afternoon
    except Tuesdays. May I have an interview to answer any questions
    about myself that you might have? You can reach me by telephoning
    997-1234 before 10 a.m. or after 4 p.m.
```

Even if you're sending your job application hundreds of miles away, you might still ask for an interview if you think the company has a local representative who can screen you in person. You can ask the employer to send you the local representative's name or to arrange the interview for you with the local representative.

Example

```
Although the résumé and this letter give you some idea of my quali-
fications, I am eager to have a personal interview with you. Or per-
haps I could discuss my qualifications in greater detail with your
regional personnel representative. Please let me know how I can get
in touch with her or him.
```

Sample Letters of Application

The following application letters apply suggestions discussed in this chapter. Letter 1 illustrates both content and layout of an effective application letter that can accompany the résumé shown in Figure 12-1. Notice how well this applicant relates highlights of each paragraph to the job he or she seeks—staff accountant in a CPA firm which, the applicant knows, has an opening.

Letter 1

Solicited application for a staff accountant position. This letter accompanies Figure 12-1, page 359, personalized one-page résumé.

	3982 Bula Drive Pasadena, CA 91118 March 19, 198_

Mr. John Q. Torgen
Torgen, Surgess, and Associates
1520 Tower Building
Los Angeles, CA 90070

Dear Mr. Torgen:

Name; summary (attention)

Professor Albert Tyran has informed me that your firm is looking for a competent staff accountant. With thorough college training in accounting and related studies, varied bookkeeping experience, and proven ability to work efficiently, I feel I could be an asset to your staff.

Training (interest)

To prepare adequately for a public accounting career, I have completed 40 quarter hours of accounting at the University of California, with a grade point average of 3.8 (on a 4-point scale). Two electronic data processing courses I studied, in addition to the accounting, provided information that will be useful in working with your clients who use computers. My studies in speech and business communication enable me to present clearly the financial data and reports for superiors or clients.

Useful bookkeeping experience (desire; conviction)

Since your firm specializes in medical accounts, I believe I could be of special benefit to you because of my interest and work in this area. At age 18 I was preparing weekly payrolls for 60 hospital maintenance employees. This position included keeping time and equipment records, calculating payroll deductions, writing monthly labor-union benefit reports, and handling accounts payable. Later, as full-charge bookkeeper for a medical clinic and as assistant accountant in a hospital, accuracy and speed were necessary to meet deadlines at these fast-paced offices. My responsibilities included billing accounts receivable; monthly closing of general ledger; preparing financial statements, cost control data, and quarterly government tax reports. This experience will be useful in audits and analyses for cost control.

Personal qualities (conviction)

Serving as treasurer of the accounting honorary and chairperson of two charity drives required honesty, tact, and initiative. These qualities will be an important part of my code of ethics as a public accountant. By referring to the enclosed résumé and contacting former employers, you will be able to form a more complete idea of my personality.

Easy action

Will you call me at 366-9876 to name a time when I may come, at your convenience, to talk with you about being your staff accountant? I am usually home after 3 p.m. each weekday.

Sincerely,

Leslie T. Ryson

Leslie T. Ryson

Enclosure: Résumé

Letter 2 shows the content of an application from a 21-year-old college graduate seeking a teaching position in a high school business department. It is a prospecting letter, because the applicant does not know whether an opening exists.

LETTER 2

Prospecting application to a school superintendent for a high school teaching position. This letter accompanies Figure 12-2, pages 360–361, general-purpose résumé.

Dear Ms. Roberts:

Question and summary opening (attention)

Next September will one of your high schools need a business teacher who can make learning realistic and interesting for the students? If so, please consider me for the position. My qualifications include a liberal business background, work experience, and enthusiasm for teaching.

Liberal business background; specific courses (interest)

In August this year I will graduate from Indiana University in Business Education. Studies in business, education, and economics (my minor) have received special emphasis in my program. I am now prepared to teach any of these business courses that you offer on the secondary level: typing, shorthand (Gregg or Forkner), office machines, accounting, and business law or communications. If you are considering adding a course in economics to your curriculum, I will be happy to present to you my ideas about the advantages of teaching economics in high school.

Work experience (desire; conviction)

Two years of steady office employment and previous summer work have given me valuable insight into the growing needs of the business community for vocationally trained high school graduates. This practical experience expanded my knowledge of business education. I am better equipped to communicate to my students in an interesting manner the relationships between their goals and the requirements of the business community. The different positions I have held developed qualities of tact and adaptability, which I consider important when working with young people.

Personal attitudes and qualities (desire)

The past semester of student teaching—mentioned on the enclosed résumé—convinced me that high school teaching is my chosen career. I will work with the same zeal that helped me earn an A— overall grade average throughout college and high school.

Easy-action request

An opportunity to discuss further your requirements and my qualifications will be appreciated. To arrange a meeting, will you please contact me at the above address?

EXERCISES

1. This assignment helps you to know yourself better before you launch a job-getting selling campaign. Make a thorough self-appraisal by taking an inventory of all your employment qualifications. After rereading especially the suggestions on pages 341–343, list your accomplishments under these five main headings: (1) Work Experience, Skills, Aptitudes; (2) Education; (3) Activities, Achievements, Social Development; (4) Interests, Preferences, Attitudes; (5) Personal Characteristics. Add whatever subheadings are desirable. You might place check marks or asterisks by the qualifications you think are your strongest for the work you'd like to do. Support your personal qualifications with specific facts about your achievements.

   Type all your qualifications neatly under appropriate headings and subheadings; then insert them into a notebook. This information will help you to know what you have to sell. It is your "personal inventory" or "self-analysis."

2. Make a market survey to find what career opportunities and jobs are suitable for your qualifications. See suggestions on pages 343–345 regarding publications and people that can give you useful information.

3. The purpose of this assignment is to find out what qualifications the prospective employer looks for when screening you for your career job. Assume that in your market survey (Exercise 2) you discovered that sufficient existing publications are not available locally. So you will write to an organization of your choice (but not the firm to which you plan to send your application letter and résumé), asking for answers to your questions or arranging for an interview with the appropriate officer. Although you're not getting answers from the prospective employer, you *will* from a source that should reveal comparable information on the qualifications considered most important.

   Prepare a list of 10 (or more) questions you must know the answers to before you can write your application. All your questions must relate to a particular job or job area. (You may use the answers later for a report writing assignment.)

   Listed below are several questions that you should consider. They're possible springboards for the questions to which you must find answers.
   a. What are the basic qualifications that you look for when you screen a recent college graduate for a job in (your career area)?
   b. For this type of work what major do you think is best?
   c. Outside the major what courses (business or nonbusiness) do you think will be helpful on the job?
   d. What kind of previous experience do you look for in the applicant?
   e. How do you evaluate personality from a written job presentation?
   f. How important are grades?
   g. To get into this type of work, what initial job should I apply for?
   h. Do you prefer references in the initial written job presentation?

4. Prepare a letter of application with an accompanying résumé for the career job you plan to get into after completion of your college education. Address it to the firm of your choice and to the individual who should receive it. [If you cannot find the name of a particular person, you might want to direct it to a particular department within the firm or to the title the receiver possesses (such as "personnel manager").]

   To make this material as useful to you as possible, date the letter the month and year you actually plan to send it. For example, if you're graduating this year, the date of the letter should precede that of graduation by enough time (four to nine months) so you'll have the job when you're ready to go to work. But if you're a sophomore and have at least two more years of college and then two years of graduate school, use the date you'll actually be sending the letter.

   Use only facts, as far as possible, in both your letter and résumé. If you are dating the letter in the future, assume the activities (especially schooling, work experience, government service) that will most likely take place between now and then. This timing permits you to update the written job presentation when you're ready to revise, type, and actually send it.

   Try to make your message and résumé so convincing and selling that they will stand out from many others that may be received the same day. Both should be neatly and accurately typed—100 percent correct in spelling and accurate in facts and figures.

5. On the day your application letter and résumé (Exercise 4) are due to be handed in, bring them to class and exchange them (or copies) with a classmate—preferably one you do not know very well. Each of you will then evaluate the other's written job presentation. Assume you are the addressee of the letter, a stranger to the applicant. Would the letter and résumé convince you to invite the writer to your office for an interview? Why or why not? On a separate sheet write your answer to these questions. Also list (a) specific good qualities of the letter and résumé and (b) specific suggestions for improvements. Sign the sheet and return it to the writer, together with the letter and résumé. If your instructor wishes, each student will hand in these comments along with the letter and résumé. (No changes should, however, be made on these messages before the instructor reads them.)

6. Below are four application letters. Explain orally in class which ones will most likely result in an interview. Which are totally unacceptable? Why?

Letter A

Application to a grocery chain for accounting position.

> With my vast and diversified working experience in a *(town name)*
> Safeway store and my 5 years' college training in accounting and
> economics, I am well qualified to apply for an accounting position
> with Safeway Stores, Inc.

Having successfully completed studies in managerial and financial accounting while earning my degree at the University of (*state*), you will find that I can handle any accounting situation with ease and confidence.

While working in the many departments in Safeway in order to finance my college education, I became thoroughly familiar with every phase of operation of one of your stores. Because of my pleasing personality, my ability to get along well with others, and my excellent work record, I was chosen to supervise the night stock crew during the summers of (*year*) and (*year*).

My work experience with Safeway has been both valuable and enjoyable for me; therefore, I wish to continue working for your firm in my chosen field.

After you've had a chance to verify some of the things I've said about myself in this letter and on the enclosed data sheet, will you write me about the possibilities of working in one of your West Coast offices?

Letter B

Application to a firm for sales position.

Please consider my application for a position in your sales department. My qualifications are a bachelor of arts in General Business, a thorough and working knowledge of accounting and finance, and a sincere interest in selling.

I am seeking a position in your company in selling because I feel that I have the necessary qualifications to do a good job for the company, while learning the basic components of your needs. I selected your firm because it is the most rapidly expanding company in this industry and a leader in research and development, which I recognize as essential to maintain your present status. I feel that I can contribute towards these goals. I have studied the basic background of the transportation industry, and am deeply interested in furthering my knowledge, to the benefit of the company. I have enclosed a résumé of my personal background, complete with a transcript of my grades.

After you've had time to review my application and data sheet, will you please call me or write. My address and telephone numbers are on the enclosed data sheet. Thank you for your consideration.

Letter C

Application to home appliance firm as sales representative.

If hundreds of effective retail calls, thorough knowledge of point-of-sale and imaginative merchandising help make a home appliance representative, then I've begun to learn the business. I would like to put this practical field experience to work for Sack's Home Appliance Company.

Field work as an assistant district sales manager for the ABC Cleaning Products Company gave me an opportunity to plan and execute sales promotions that sold cleaners. I have proven ability to open nonbuying accounts, secure floor displays, sell additional packages and achieve point-of-sale dominance.

In addition, I have conducted route analyses, set up key account systems, and conducted sales training meetings for wholesaler personnel.

Frequent contact with retailers and consumers enabled me to handle consumer complaints and utilize a good layman's knowledge of various home appliances.

After you've had an opportunity to review some of the things I've said in this letter and on the enclosed data sheet, will you write me frankly about the possibility of beginning a career with Sack's Home Appliance Company?

I would appreciate an opportunity to discuss my qualifications.

Letter D

Application to a newspaper for position as assistant music and drama editor.

In reference to your advertisement in Editor & Publisher (3/14) for an assistant music and drama editor, the offer is worth an inquiry because of my deep interest in theater. But, very frankly, I'm afraid it would have to be an exceptional salary offer to lure me so far from the East Coast and what I'm convinced are its greater professional opportunities.

However, you will find samples of my reviews and a brief résumé attached. Should you desire to continue this corresponence further, I will send you references and other material customary to a job application.

My experience in motion picture-theater reviewing with the Sun has been limited to "filling-in" for the regular critic during his vacations or illnesses. Prior to that, I wrote a theater column in a weekly newspaper in Bath, Pa., a sideline to my daily reporting. I have engaged in all phases of amateur theater as an outside interest. I am not well versed in music——though I am confident in my critical capacities. Again, I have filled in at times for the Sun's music critic and, if need be, can also submit samples. I have handled general assignments and beats.

Your advertisement mentions "opportunity for advancement," without further elaboration. Your offer of the position of assistant music-drama editor would be considerably more attractive if coupled with a commitment to go to your Washington, D.C., bureau in two, or three, years or to whatever overseas bureaus the Daily Blat may sponsor, subject only to your complete dissatisfaction with the work produced for you.

The tendency, of course, of most newspapers is to fill the opening with the run—of—the—mill newsperson who is panting at the door and willing to accept chicken feed. Consequently, I have little reason to expect a favorable reaction to this letter. If I am mistaken, I hope you will advise me of the maximum salary you can pay for this position, the setup at the Blat and any arrangements that you would consider feasible. I hope we can discuss this matter further, but only with your understanding that I expect to drive a hard bargain.

My home address appears below and on the résumé. Please address your reply accordingly.

CHAPTER 13

Other Job Application Messages

The number of messages you'll send in getting your career job (or changing to another job) depends on economic conditions, need for graduates in your area, and your own qualifications and standards. If you're sending your job presentation when it's a seller's market and you have unusually good qualifications, you might get the job you want right away. But if the conditions are reversed, you can spend many weeks—even months—finding the right niche for yourself.

Preferably begin your job hunting at least four to nine months before graduation, and send your written job presentation with résumé to more than one firm. But don't send out too many (50 or 100) at one time. Limit the number to 10 or fewer and then wait for replies before you mail more.

This chapter discusses the job interview, follow-up messages from applicant to employer, and follow-up messages from employer to applicant.

THE JOB INTERVIEW

As you know, the goal of your application letter and résumé is to get an interview. Assume now that you achieved your purpose with your written "sales" presentation. The desired telephone call, letter, or telegram from the employer asks you to come for an interview on a certain day and time. That interview may be the most important step toward your getting the desired job. This section presents suggestions regarding preparation for the interview, conduct during the interview, questions frequently asked, negative factors to avoid, and notes after the interview.

Preparation for the Interview

Always prepare for an interview before you go to it. Remember that the interview is a two-way street. Your primary purpose is to get the best job suitable to your capabilities. The employer's goal is to get the best person available for the job. Take a look at yourself from the employer's point of view. In hiring you, the employer is making an investment that over a few years will mount to thousands of dollars considering salary, fringes, and taxes. Naturally the employer wants a quality product.

As the New York Life Insurance Company says so well in its booklet, *Making the Most of Your Job Interview:*

> The employment interview is one of the most important events in the average person's experience, for the obvious reason that the 20 or 30 minutes spent with the interviewer may determine the entire future course of one's life. Yet interviewers are constantly amazed at the number of applicants who drift into job interviews without any apparent preparation and only the vaguest idea of what they are going to say. Their manner says, "Well, here I am." And that's often the end of it, in more ways than one.

> Others, although they undoubtedly do not intend to do so, create an impression of indifference by acting too casual. At the other extreme, a few applicants work

themselves into such a state of mind that when they arrive they seem to be in the last stages of nervous fright and are only able to answer in monosyllables.

These marks of inexperience can be avoided by knowing a little of what actually is expected of you and by making a few simple preparations before the interview.[1]

Adequate preparation includes:

- Know yourself.
- Do some research on the company.
- List questions you want to ask as well as answers to questions you'll probably encounter.
- Pay attention to your appearance.
- Check details about the meeting place and time for the interview.

Know Yourself

The most important preparation relates to knowing yourself. But, then, you have already looked critically at yourself before you wrote your résumé and application letter. You should know the job or the job area you want to apply for, the requirements for the job, and how your qualifications (both your strengths and weaknesses) compare with the requirements. Take with you to the interview at least two copies of your résumé.

Do Some Research on the Company

Besides knowing yourself, get some facts about the company. Excellent references are available in your library or school placement office and from employees or annual reports of the company itself. Among other facts you should know are the age of the company, location of its plants, types of products and services, its growth over the years (especially the last few years), and its prospects for the future.

Prepare Questions and Answers

Another important step before the interview is to jot down questions you want to ask the interviewer if he or she doesn't first give you the answers. The questions you might ask relate to possible training the company offers after employment, company policy about moving your family to a new location, what type of management system the firm uses, the average age of the executives, whether they are promoted from within, why the person you'd replace left the firm, and perhaps also the company's profit picture (if you didn't find it in your research). The *last* questions may relate to fringe benefits and salary.

[1] *Making the Most of Your Job Interview,* New York Life Insurance Company. Copies of this 22-page booklet may be obtained in reasonable quantity without cost or obligation from any New York Life agent or office.

Also, you want to anticipate questions the interviewer will ask you, as discussed under Conduct during the Interview. Shown on pages 382–384 are questions frequently asked during the employment interview.

Be Careful of Your Appearance

The clothes you wear and your overall neatness affect your appearance. Wear conservative, neatly pressed clothes appropriate for the office, and clean your shoes. Use lotions or perfumes sparingly. Also see that accessories complement the suit or dress. Be sure your hair and fingernails are clean, your hairstyle is appropriate, and your breath is fresh. To project an image of quality and success, try to wear to the interview the best quality clothing you can afford.

Check Meeting Place, Time, and Other Details

Definitely know when and where the interview will be held—and be there at least 15 minutes early. Tardiness is generally considered inexcusable. Also, know the full name and address of the company, the interviewer's name and current title, and how to pronounce his or her name. Put a working pen or pencil along with a small notebook in your coat pocket or purse. If the job requires creativity or high grades, you might take along samples of your work or your transcript of grades—perhaps in a neat briefcase. Before you go into the room where the interviewer is, try to relax.

Conduct during the Interview

When you meet the interviewer, smile and greet him or her by name, pronouncing it correctly. If he or she offers to shake hands, do so—with a firm grip, but not a bone crusher. Also remain standing until invited to sit down; the only exception is when you're in a small room and the interviewer remains seated or sits down immediately. Look at the interviewer and keep eye contact throughout the interview.

The interviewer will be observing you carefully and listening to everything you say and do. The overall impression will be influenced by your appearance, oral communication ability, and your personality—qualities that can't be shown as clearly in the application letter and résumé. To make the best impression, you need to:

1. Show enthusiasm, vitality, interest. You can do so by the way you sit and look alert, by facial expressions, by questions you ask, and by the answers you give.
2. Be honest and sincere at all times. If you begin to exaggerate or fabricate details—and you're caught—the interviewer will be less likely to consider you as a favorable candidate for the job.

3. Be yourself. Don't try to put on airs. By being yourself, you'll seem more comfortable and be more at ease.

4. Be courteous. Don't chew gum, and don't smoke even if the interviewer invites you to do so.

5. Listen attentively and concentrate. Then you can receive valuable clues from the interviewer's statements and be ready to give better replies to the questions.

6. Accent the positive, with expressions that indicate you are competent and dependable. Avoid the negative attitudes or actions listed on pages 384–385 and also words such as *can't, won't, unable, hate, failure, incompetent.*

7. Use correct grammar and pronunciation; omit slang and expressions like *yeah, y'know, stuff-like-that.*

8. Never make a slighting reference about a former professor or employer. If you can't say something nice about a person, don't say anything.

After the warm-up period (exchange of pleasantries to develop rapport) be ready for the interviewer's first questions about your qualifications or interest. You might be asked, "Why are you interested in this company?" or "Tell me about yourself." When desirable, explain why you could help the company in this job and why you like doing this kind of work. (If useful, pull out of your briefcase some examples of your past work.) Your answer may include excerpts from your education, work, and/or activities showing competence, dependability, ambition, creativity.

If you have prepared adequately, you should be able to answer questions honestly and intelligently. The plain truth—even if it may seem a little unfavorable to you—is always better than exaggerations that may entangle you in contradictory answers to other questions. For a successful interview, here are additional suggestions to consider:

1. If you are strong in extracurricular responsibilities, and the interviewer hasn't mentioned that area, watch for an opportunity to ask, "Are you interested in my extracurricular activities?" The interviewer is not likely to say "no." Highlight those that relate to the job requirements, and, if pertinent, show leadership ability.

2. Also ask sincere questions about the company, because doing so shows interest and helps you perceive key problems or needs of that company as well as the interviewer's likes and dislikes.

3. Know the current beginning salary range for your type of work and experience. Try to postpone salary questions, if any, until near the end of the first or second interview—after you and the interviewer have discussed the job responsibilities and your credentials that affect your bargaining power. When you are asked how much salary you want, you can indicate that you're more interested in a job to prove yourself than in a specific salary. Most reputable firms will offer the standard salary for the type of job in question.

4. Even if you think the interview isn't going well and that you are rejected, don't let your discouragement show. Sometimes interviewers purposely appear disinterested just to test your reaction, self-confidence, and ability to respond.
5. Be alert for signs from the interviewer that the interview is about to end. And when you depart, be sure to thank the interviewer for seeing you.
6. Tactfully ask for some kind of commitment as to when the interviewer will let you know the decision.
7. If you are offered the job, you can accept immediately or ask for time to think it over.

Questions Which May Be Asked during the Interview

The following are 59 employment interview questions listed by Dr. Frank S. Endicott, director of placement (emeritus), Northwestern University in a copyrighted report published by the Northwestern University Placement Center.[2] Try to answer these questions orally or in writing *before* you go to an interview.

1. Why do you think you might like to work for our company?
2. What jobs have you held? How were they obtained and why did you leave?
3. What are your future vocational plans?
4. In what school activities have you participated? Why? Which did you enjoy the most?
5. In what type of position are you most interested?
6. What courses did you like best? Least? Why?
7. Why did you choose your particular field of work?
8. What percentage of your college expenses did you earn? How?
9. How did you spend your vacations while in school?
10. What do you know about our company?
11. Do you feel that you have received a good general training?
12. What qualifications do you have that make you feel you will be successful in your field?
13. What extracurricular offices have you held?
14. What are your ideas on salary?
15. If you were starting college all over again, what courses would you take?
16. How much money do you hope to earn at age 30? 35?
17. Do you think that your extracurricular activities were worth the time you devoted to them? Why?
18. What do you think determines a person's progress in a good company?
19. What personal characteristics are necessary for success in your chosen field?

[2] You'll find these questions in the New York Life Insurance Company's booklet, *Making the Most of Your Job Interview.* For suggestions to employers regarding interviewing see Chap. 21, and for a list of fair and unfair preemployment inquiries see Appendix A.

20. Why do you think you would like this particular type of job?
21. Do you prefer working with others or by yourself?
22. What kind of boss do you prefer?
23. Are you primarily interested in making money or do you feel that service to humanity is your prime concern?
24. Can you take instructions without feeling upset?
25. Tell me a story!
26. How did previous employers treat you?
27. What have you learned from some of the jobs you have held?
28. Can you get recommendations from previous employers?
29. What interests you about our product or service?
30. Have you ever changed your major field of interest while in college? Why?
31. When did you choose your college major?
32. Do you feel you have done the best scholastic work of which you are capable?
33. How did you happen to go to college?
34. What do you know about opportunities in the field in which you are trained?
35. Which of your college years was the most difficult?
36. Did you enjoy your four years at this university?
37. Do you like routine work?
38. Do you like regular hours?
39. What size city do you prefer?
40. What is your major weakness?[3]
41. Define cooperation!
42. Do you demand attention?
43. Do you have an analytical mind?
44. Are you eager to please?
45. What job in our company would you choose if you were entirely free to do so?
46. What types of books have you read?
47. Have you plans for graduate work?
48. What types of people seem to "rub you the wrong way"?
49. Have you ever tutored a freshman or sophomore?
50. What jobs have you enjoyed the most? The least? Why?
51. What are your own special abilities?
52. What job in our company do you want to work toward?
53. Would you prefer a large or a small company? Why?
54. Do you like to travel?
55. How about overtime work?
56. What kind of work interests you?
57. What are the disadvantages of your chosen field?

[3] Even with this negative, risky question you can focus on the positive—determination to further improve your strong qualities, and perhaps mention a non-job-related trait that needs improvement.

58. Are you interested in research?

59. What have you done which shows initiative and willingness to work?

Negative Factors to Avoid

Dr. Endicott, who compiled the questions that may be asked in interviews, also surveyed for negative factors evaluated during the employment interview.[4]

1. Poor personal appearance

2. Overbearing—overaggressive—conceited "superiority complex"—"know-it-all"

3. Inability to communicate clearly—poor voice, diction, grammar

4. Lack of planning for career—no purpose and goals

5. Lack of interest and enthusiasm—passive, indifferent

6. Lack of confidence and poise—nervous—ill-at-ease

7. Failure to participate in activities

8. Overemphasis on money—interest only in best dollar offer

9. Poor scholastic record—just got by

10. Unwillingness to start at the bottom—expects too much too soon

11. Excuses—evasiveness—hedges on unfavorable factors in record

12. Lack of tact

13. Lack of maturity

14. Lack of courtesy—ill mannered

15. Condemnation of past employers

16. Marked dislike for school work

17. Failure to look interviewer in the eye

18. Limp, fishy handshake

19. Sloppy application blank

20. Merely shopping around

21. Wants job only for short time

22. Little sense of humor

23. Lack of knowledge of field of specialization

24. No interest in company or in industry

25. Unwillingness to relocate

26. Cynical

27. Low moral standards

28. Lazy

29. Inability to take criticism

30. Lack of appreciation of the value of experience

31. Late to interview without good reason

32. Never heard of company

33. Failure to express appreciation for interviewer's time

34. Asks no questions about the job

[4] *Making the Most of Your Job Interview.*

35. High-pressure type

36. Indefinite response to questions

Notes after the Interview

Following the interview, record important or especially interesting comments of the interviewer and perhaps significant facts you learned about the company or the job. Also evaluate your success during the interview. On which of your answers did you feel the interviewer seemed disappointed or annoyed? Did you forget to mention any persuasive points that could strengthen his or her good opinion of you? How can you improve your presentation in future interviews? Keep similar records on all other interviews.

FOLLOW-UP MESSAGES FROM APPLICANT TO EMPLOYER

To strengthen your chances for the job you have applied for, follow up your application letter and résumé. Of the three ways to follow up—in person, by letter, or by phone—the written message is one of the most effective because employers can analyze the applicant's qualifications at their convenience. They can also more easily compare a large number of applicants—either on the job or at home in the evening. For several good reasons a written follow-up is effective. A written follow-up message . . .

1. Indicates courtesy and sincerity. If it follows an interview it serves as a reminder to the employer and permits better understanding of the applicant (through submission of additional information).
2. Impresses the employer favorably because only a few applicants—probably fewer than 10 percent—write a follow-up.
3. Shows the applicant is genuinely interested in the job or the company.
4. Indicates determination. Some firms won't reply to an applicant for a sales job until a follow-up arrives. Others intentionally mail the sales applicant a negative reply. The employer reasons that the applicant who follows up when applying for a sales job will follow up on prospects—even those who say no—when on the job in a sales territory.

This section first covers the two all-important and most frequently used types of initial follow-up messages and then presents other types involved in getting a job.

The Initial Follow-Up

The first follow-up you'll write is either (1) a follow-up after the interview or (2) an inquiry about the application letter and résumé when the employer hasn't replied.

Follow-Up after the Interview

For courtesy you should send the interviewer (or the appropriate company official) a written thank-you within two to five days after you have had your interview.[5] Remember, the interviewer spent valuable time to talk with you, and you need to acknowledge this time, attention, and consideration. Only when you are told during the interview not to write should you refrain from sending this message.

Usually this message is short—less than one page—and its organizational pattern is that of a good-news or neutral letter:

1. In the opening paragraph, state the main idea—express thanks for the interview or say you're returning a completed form. (If you don't thank in the opening, do so in the last paragraph.) Also, identify the job and perhaps mention the time and place of the interview.
2. In the middle paragraph(s) you discuss one or more of the following ideas:
   a. Mention how you *now* feel about the firm or a job with the firm—now that you have visited the plant, listened to the interviewer talk, and toured the facility. Of course, you write only honest, favorable responses.
   b. Add new material that might be helpful in determining your qualifications. For instance, report that you completed an assignment the interviewer gave you during the interview (such as to read a brochure, see someone, or take a test).
   c. If you think the interviewer questioned one of your qualifications or you think you might have made a negative impression concerning one statement during the interview, include honest, positive facts to rebuild confidence. For example, if the interviewer seemed to want an older person, convince him or her that you are mature because you've dealt successfully with all types of people on your various jobs; or you have assumed responsibilities; or you have had to allocate your time as student, spouse, and breadwinner. Or if you think you treated one or more areas unsatisfactorily, try to reestablish your credentials.
   d. Occasionally you can strengthen your presentation by stating: (1) your favorable reaction to points covered by the interviewer and (2) highlights of qualifications discussed during the interview.
3. In the last paragraph you can use one or more of the following:
   a. Offer to send additional information upon request.
   b. Thank for the interview (if not done in the first paragraph).
   c. Say you can come in for another interview.

[5] A Cincinnati executive, reviewing 35 different jobs in his company for which hundreds of applications were received, gives this tip: "In each instance the job went to the thoughtful applicant who followed up the interview with a sincere thank-you note." Numerous other executives as well as applicants have confirmed the effectiveness of these follow-up messages.

    d. Indicate hope (or confidence) that your qualifications fit the firm's requirements.

    e. Mention you're looking forward to a favorable decision.

    f. Ask for an opportunity to prove you can help the firm's sales, growth, and so on.

With this organizational plan in mind, study the following two examples of effective follow-up messages. Both applicants were successful in getting the job they sought though during the interview each appeared to have a shortcoming. In each case the employer stated that the follow-up letter helped greatly.

Message 1 is from a 22-year-old applicant seeking his first career job as a sales representative after college graduation. Notice how convincingly he surmounts what appeared to be a shortcoming by showing that his responsibilities *during* college were equivalent to two years' business experience *after* college.

Message 1

A successful after-interview follow-up, to a national industrial firm.

Dear Mr. Simonson:

Your interview with me yesterday was both enjoyable and informative. Thank you for your courtesies and the interest you took in my qualifications as a sales representative for your firm.

During the conversation you mentioned that you were particularly looking for a person who had at least two years' business experience since finishing college. I agree with you that the knack of working with people and the mature outlook gained from practical experience are valuable for a prospective sales representative. These qualities were firmly developed in me <u>during</u> my college years.

As my résumé shows, to obtain an Industrial Engineering degree I added an extra year of engineering and business courses to my studies. In various college activities my responsibilities were mainly with people. As Publicity Manager for <u>The College Engineer</u> magazine—after careful planning plus enthusiasm and drive—I increased sales 25% over the previous year. As president of our fraternity, I worked harmoniously with our 80 members and sold the alumni on the support we needed. My part-time and summer jobs during college ranged from clerking in a grocery store to tutoring first-year students. I believe these activities, jobs, and additional studies have given me a background of experience and judgment equivalent to the two years' business experience your firm would like its sales representatives to have.

You will find, I believe, that I can develop into one of your top industrial sales representatives, Mr. Simonson. Will you give me the opportunity to prove this statement?

Message 2 is from a 27-year-old recent accounting graduate applying for an accounting job in a community college. During the interview the college official was concerned whether the applicant—a quiet, soft-spoken individual—had adequate qualifications for leadership; she would have to supervise the work of six bookkeepers in the college office. This letter helped her get the job:

Message 2

A successful after-interview follow-up, to a college vice president and finance officer.

Dear Mr. Millard:

Thank you for taking time on April 4 to talk with me regarding my application for the accounting position in your office. As you re-quested, I am enclosing the transcript of my grades from the University of (*name*).

During my five years at the (*name*) Company I worked in a lead capac-ity with many people. The experience I gained would be useful for the job you outlined. For the first two of the five years I was re-sponsible for quality control in the Pensar Division. As one of my duties I supervised 10 employees and trained new people to visually and dimensionally inspect vendor-made parts purchased for use on the program. When I requested night-shift duty so I could carry 10 to 15 credit hours at Mason Junior College, I was given full respon-sibilities for the inspection duties on that shift, a position I held three years.

Four years of college studies (with no financial help) while holding full- and part-time jobs and raising a family indicate my per-severance. My school and work record of continuous four-year attendance (except for a three-day virus illness last summer) will assure you of my regularity and dependability on the job. We are buying a home in Blanktown and will enter our daughter in the school system here next fall; so my family is well established here.

I believe my education and 10 years of work experience will qualify me to assume the accounting and office responsibilities you pointed out to me. Please let me know your decision. You could depend on me to be a hard-working, mature staff member.

Inquiry about Application Letter and Résumé

If you haven't received a response to your written job application within three weeks, you are justified in sending an inquiry. Although it is unlikely your material was lost in the mail, it is possible the receiver misplaced or forgot about it. A well-run organization should acknowledge—and if it does not, you certainly should inquire.

This type of follow-up is usually shorter than the one written after the interview. Since many firms keep the written job presentation for six months or longer, all you really need do is give enough identification so that the employer can locate your material. The inquiry should include: identification of job sought, date of application letter previously sent, and (if appropriate) a request for an interview. In addition, some employers suggest you also include one or more of the following:

1. Interest in job
2. Date of availability
3. New material about qualifications
4. Reasons for wanting to work for the company
5. Status of application
6. Highlights of major qualifications already given in the application letter
7. Offer to send additional information upon request
8. Telephone number

Don't repeat information the employer already possesses. A personnel manager does not like to receive an application letter—and then one or two follow-ups—each with another copy of the same résumé. Below are two examples of acceptable inquiries, organized by the direct-request plan.

Message 1

Emphasizes identification of applicant's file.

Dear Ms. Bond:

On February 10, (*year*), I sent you my application letter and résumé for an opening in your management training program. Because I'm interested in your firm and its future, I'm inquiring whether you received this material.

Please let me know what information you wish about my background. And, of course, I can come for an interview whenever you suggest.

Message 2

Includes highlights of the applicant.

Dear Mr. Norden:

Perhaps you will remember I sent you my application for a position in your grain department on March 22. I am primarily interested in cash grain purchasing and the use of the futures market to assist in the operations of your company.

The principal points in my letter were that:

1. A research project I conducted on the use of the commodity exchanges by members of the state grain industry developed insights that I can use effectively for your company. I am now finishing the writing of the results for my master's thesis, also on aspects of the grain industry.
2. My college degree is in Business Administration, and I plan to receive a master of arts degree in June, (*year*), in marketing.
3. During 18 years on an Oklahoma farm, I became familiar with most of the grains in the grain industry.

I hope that you can use a person with my background. If you wish any further information, I will be glad to send it to you.

Other Follow-Up Messages from Applicant to Employer

A job-hunting campaign can include quite a few other types of follow-up messages in addition to those just discussed. The following pages discuss and illustrate some of them.

Answer to a Noncommittal Letter

Assume that you have sent your application letter with résumé—maybe even had the interview. Then you receive the following:

We were pleased to receive your excellent application for employment.

We are very much interested in your capabilities but regret that at the present time, we cannot make use of them; with your permission, however, we will keep your name on file and if anything should develop in the future, get in touch with you.

Thank you for your interest in our organization.

What should you do? At first you might interpret this message as a routine refusal. However, the employer has said, "with your permission . . . keep on file," and you should assume that the message is sincere and you will definitely be considered when an opening occurs. A short message like the following is a quite satisfactory reply:

Dear Mr. Lyons:

Thank you for your reviewing my qualifications for (*type of job*).

Will you please keep my name in your files so that you can consider me when a future opening in that field takes place? You can count on me to do a thorough, accurate job if I may join your staff.

```
I like what I read and hear about your organization--and hope some
day to be part of such a company.
```

If you receive a message that says essentially what Mr. Lyons wrote but does not ask your permission, a reply is optional.

Reply to Request for Additional Information

Occasionally an employer, interviewer, or school will request additional information about your background. If such a situation arises, analyze your background thoroughly, so that you will include all the important details to back up and strengthen your presentation, with your reader's needs in mind. Then organize and write. You'll probably use an outline like the following:

First paragraph: Thank for interview and express eagerness to tell about whatever is asked for. Also identify the topic(s) you are discussing.

Middle paragraphs: If asked about two qualifications (say interest in field and interest in company), write separate paragraphs for each. The discussion will be persuasive—quite similar to the middle paragraphs that create desire in the application letter.

Last paragraph: You might express:
1. Availability for another interview.
2. Any other idea that rounds out and strengthens the message.

The following letter was addressed to the director of a law school's admissions office. The applicant was asked to fill out the necessary form and, separately, to tell about her interests in law and give highlights of her background.

```
As you requested, I am returning the completed Form A and a brief
discussion of two questions you asked for: my interest in law and
highlights of my background.

Interest in Law
Before going into my background, I want to explain why I want a de-
gree in law. The need has been there since childhood. Unlike most
childhood fixations--teacher, doctor, and dancer--the desire to be a
lawyer has stuck with me since the age of twelve. More than a child-
hood dream is involved though. I feel that a law degree and the
ability to use it embodies one of the most valuable assets a person
can own.

To me law pervades every aspect of our society. Law is where the ac-
tion is. It is one of the few professions that enable a person to be
actively involved in forming her culture while at the same time en-
abling her to find a highly satisfactory role in life.
```

Specifically I plan to concentrate on corporate law with a later concentration on international legal business relationships. This area needs good lawyers, and I want to prepare myself to fill that need.

Background
Following is a brief sketch of my background that will help you in assessing my ability to study law. As the enclosed form shows, I was born in Germany. In (*year*) I became a naturalized citizen of the United States. I was reared in South Africa from the age of three and am bilingual, speaking and writing both German and English without any accent or faults in composition.

I used my undergraduate years to gain as wide a knowledge of as many disciplines as I could. My program emphasized political science, social sciences, some humanities with a later concentration on general business courses. This was, in my mind, the most useful road toward my eventual goal.

My transcript that you should have received by now shows I spent five years on my bachelor's degree. The extra year was necessitated by a scarcity of funds in my family. Part- and full-time jobs have put me through school and have allowed me to save enough money to attend law school. Although outside work has detracted from study time, I feel that the work discipline and the ability to communicate and work with all types of people more than offset any loss in academic learning.

If you should need any additional information to aid you in your decision, please let me know.

Acceptance of Invitation for Interview

Usually this message is conveyed by telephone; interviewers do not expect a letter. Whether you write or phone, your good-news reply will begin with thanks and acceptance. You might mention several possible times within a certain week when you could make the trip. Then the employer can choose the most convenient date and hour. The last paragraph should express sincere interest in the forthcoming interview. Message 2 on page 399 is a good example for an interview in a distant city.

Follow-Up if No Reply after Interview

If you receive no reply by the promised date, remember it takes time for the employer to interview all applicants, route the qualifications to interested officers in the organization, and make a final choice. However, if you have waited what you consider ample time and also *beyond* the promised date of notification—especially if another firm is waiting for your reply—you might want to write a nonpersuasive inquiry similar to the one that follows.

Four weeks have passed since I had the opportunity to talk with you about an opening in (*field*). At that time you said you'd notify me of your decision by (*date*).

Meanwhile, another firm has offered me a position and has requested a reply within the next 10 days. Before answering them, I would like to know whether you have reached a favorable decision as to my working for your company.

I sincerely prefer your firm, and will very much appreciate your reply before (*date*). You can reach me by phone weekdays between 9 and 11 a.m. at (*number*) or by letter at the above address.

Acceptance of Job Offer

When you receive an offer you want to accept, reply soon—perhaps within a week. Begin with the good news—that you accept with pleasure. In this first paragraph identify the job you're accepting; the next paragraph might give details about moving (if distance is involved) and reporting for work. Naturally what you say in this explanation depends on what the employer has already told you during the interview or in the job-offer letter. End with a rounding-out paragraph indicating you're looking forward to working for the firm. (See message 7, page 401, for a good example of an applicant's acceptance.)

Resignation from Present Job

Ideally you will have conferred with your present employer some time before accepting the new position. Though you may have orally told him or her the bad news that you are resigning, the employer may request a letter for company records. It should be dated at least two weeks or more before the effective resignation date, and may be organized by the direct plan, as in the following example dated May 1.[6]

As stated during our recent conference, I have accepted a position in the finance department of the International Products in (*city*). My reporting date will be June 11. Thus, please consider this resignation to be effective June 5.

In the meantime you can depend upon me to give my successor the help needed to ensure an effective transition here. I hope that you and my coworkers at Ace will continue to be my personal friends.

Again, thank you for your many kindnesses during the years I have worked in your firm. I wish you and Ace the best of good fortune in the years ahead.

[6] For an indirect-plan letter of resignation see pp. 252–253.

Messages to Others Concerned

After you have accepted a new position, inform other employers whom you have interviewed recently. Also notify your campus placement office (or any other agency that helped you) so they will know your decision and suspend their activities regarding your job application. They deserve your thanks and courtesy. Someday you may need them again, so maintain good relations with them.

Rejection of Job Offer

When you refuse an offer, you're writing a bad-news message. The organizational plan is: buffer; explanation; refusal (implied or expressed); and a friendly, positive closing. Even more important than the outline, however, is the attitude you have toward the company. Remember this firm seriously considered your qualifications and spent its time and money to bring you to the plant for an interview. If your refusal is discourteous and abrupt, you leave an unfavorable impression.

Shown below is one example of a well-written job refusal. Notice the outline, tactful tone, sincerity, positive approach, and genuine compliment to the firm. It is from a business administration graduate to a personnel director.

```
Thank you for offering me a position in your management training
program.

During my job hunting these last few months, I've sent applications
to several firms that I regard highly—only those I could be happy
working for. Fortunately for me, both you and another firm offered
me a job. Because my qualifications, interest, and background fit in
more closely with the other job, I have already mailed in my accept-
ance.

I do appreciate your consideration of my qualifications, the thor-
ough one-day interview at the plant, and the opportunity to meet all
department heads in production. I'll always think of your organiza-
tion as one in which management treats the employees as a highly
prized commodity.

Again, thank you for your consideration. I will always remember it.
```

FOLLOW-UP MESSAGES FROM EMPLOYER TO APPLICANT

You should not only be able to write messages the applicant must send, but also—since you will be in business someday—you need to dictate effective messages that will go to the applicants.

Invitations to Interviews

Depending upon circumstances, there are times when the employer writes direct to applicants to arrange interviews either at the company offices or plant or on a college campus near the applicants.

Applicant Invited to the Company for Interview

This message from you the employer is second in importance only to the job offer itself. Thus you must make the reader feel that you genuinely want a personal interview. Also clearly get across that you'll help in every way possible. For example, as in message 1, pages 398–399, you'll send a round-trip ticket (or a check), reserve a hotel room during the stay if necessary, and reimburse all incidental expenses. In addition ask which dates will be convenient for a visit. Maybe you will make responding easier by enclosing a card.

After you receive the applicant's acceptance of the invitation, you'll send a reply similar to message 3 on pages 399–400. You not only enclose a check for travel expenses, but give all necessary details and indicate interest in the forthcoming visit.

Employer Announces Impending Visit on Campus

Instead of asking applicants to come to the plant, you might notify them that you will come (or return) to the campus (or elsewhere) to interview. You're writing to the applicant because he or she is one of the graduates you particularly want to talk to. Qualifications on the application letter and résumé interest you. The example below tells of an impending visit and sincerely compliments the applicant on her qualifications.

Dear Ms. Webster:

Thank you very much for coming to the placement office at the University of (*state*) for an interview with (*name of firm*). Since you and I had our visit, I have interviewed on approximately 20 other college campuses and talked to approximately 200 students.

This has been my first opportunity to review the resumes of these students from which I have selected approximately 15% suggesting further interviews. Mary, you are included in this group of students whose scholastic ability, personality, grooming, motivation, and overall personality place you in the upper 15% of those I have talked to.

Our spring interview date at the university has not been definitely established at this time, but as soon as it has been, I will drop you a note; if you are interested, arrange to be placed on our spring interview schedule in the placement office. You may recall

that we select somewhere between 10 and 15 young men and women each
year to go through our Management and Underwriter Training Program,
which runs from the third week in June until the middle or end of
September.

Again we commend you for your fine scholastic record you have been
able to maintain and at the same time be responsible for 100% of
your college expenses. We look forward to visiting with you again in
the spring, for I feel certain we both have much to offer each other
by way of ability and opportunity for growth.

Follow-Up Messages from Employer after Interview(s)

As a personnel representative or officer concerned with employing applicants,
you will have a variety of other letters to write after interviews with applicants.
The following pages include suggestions for such messages.

Request for Further Information

During the interview you may have questions about the applicant's enthusiasm
or sincerity toward the company or toward his or her chosen field. Or you
might simply need additional information, as the letter below illustrates:

Dear Mr. Juntwait:

Recently we had the pleasure of talking with you in connection with
our college recruiting activity. Thank you for the time you gave us.

Our staff has had the opportunity to review your qualifications and
we are interested in learning more about you. Accordingly, will you
please complete the enclosed application and return it to me by
(*date*)? Also explain in an attached letter your interest in (*name of
field*). After this information reaches us, we will get in touch with
you on a more specific basis.

Thank you for your interest in (*name of firm*); we look forward to hearing from you in the near future.

Offer of a Job

When you send a job offer, begin by telling the good news in a friendly manner.
In the first paragraph also identify the job and state the salary (usually on a
monthly basis). In the following paragraph(s), try to anticipate any questions
the applicant might have—such as what moving expenses the firm will pay—
and answer them. (Naturally you won't go into detail about expenses until she
or he accepts.) Also, leave the door open for the applicant to ask questions
before making a decision. Be sure your tone is appropriate—convey that
you're interested in the applicant and sincerely want him or her to join your
organization. (See message 4, page 400.)

Grant of a Time Extension

If you believe an applicant has a sound reason for requesting more time to consider an offer (as in message 5, page 400), you may decide to grant the extension. Usually this matter is discussed conveniently by telephone. If you write a letter, grant the request in the first paragraph, explain (and in general terms set the cutoff date), express interest in the applicant, and end on a friendly positive note. (See message 6, page 401.)

Reply to Applicant's Acceptance

When the applicant has accepted your job offer, you still need to remember the value of public relations. The applicant doesn't expect a long letter, but a helpful you-attitude is always appreciated. (See message 8, page 402.) Sometimes an encouraging sentence can be included—*if true*—regarding the applicant's potential for broader responsibilities in line with the company's expected future growth.

Refusal of Job

The tone of your refusal is very important, for you want to avoid leaving the applicant with a lasting negative reaction to your firm. The individuals being turned down don't want weak excuses or outright false statements. They want honesty—but not discourteous blunt or crude expression. They will appreciate sincere, complimentary remarks about qualifications; consideration of background; and proper attitude.

In the first paragraph state a buffer—appreciate their interest in the firm or the opportunity to talk with them, or thank them for coming in for interviews. In the second paragraph, explain. First say something neutral (for example, that you have reviewed the qualifications) and then refuse in as positive a way as possible. One of the best explanations seems to be that several other candidates have overall qualifications more similar to your requirements. In the last paragraph, wish the applicants success, tell them you enjoyed talking with them, and thank them for their interest in the firm. Obviously you won't repeat in this paragraph what you said in the first.

Below is an effective refusal which follows the outline just discussed.

```
Dear Ms. Cotter:

Thank you very much for taking your time to be interviewed and
tested for the position of systems engineering representative with
(firm).

We have reviewed your educational background, work experience, and
aptitude tests, along with others we are considering for employment.
Our analysis indicates that there are several other candidates whose
overall qualifications are more in line with our requirements.
```

We enjoyed having the opportunity to interview you and sincerely appreciate your interest in (firm). Please accept our best wishes for
success in your chosen career.

Some taboos to be avoided in writing your refusal are:

1. Refusal in opening

We have considered your qualifications; however, we do not have a
position available for you.

2. Abrupt refusal in the first sentence of the second paragraph

Unfortunately we have no opening for you.

3. No reason for refusal

A review of your qualifications indicates that you have a background
which is commendable in many respects; however, we are not in a
position to further pursue the matter of your employment with (firm)
at this time.

4. Negative attitude ("sorry," "unable," "regret," "cannot," "not suited," "do not feel," "do not have," "delay")

In view of our needs, however, we regret we do not feel additional
interviews would be mutually beneficial or advisable.

SITUATION

In the preceding sections you studied separately various types of messages
employers and applicants use in securing jobs. The following situation illustrates how some of these messages were written by an applicant for an operations management position with a national firm and by the representatives of
the firm.

Message 1

*Mr. Taggat, supervisor of personnel services, invites applicant to interviews at
plant and head office about 1,100 miles from the campus.*

September 25, (year)

Dear Mr. Brown:

Following our recent interview on your campus, we invite you to
visit (name of firm) for interviews at our plant and head office. You
will receive the necessary expenses for air travel to (city), and return, as well as incidental expenses.

If you would like to make this visit, please let us know when you can come, and we will confirm a mutually agreeable date. A card is enclosed so that you can notify us of your decision. If possible, plan to spend one full day at the plant and office.

Thank you for the interest you have expressed in (*name of firm*). Upon confirming an interview date, we will forward a check covering your travel expenses, details for getting to the plant, and we will also reserve hotel accommodations in (*city*) if you so desire.

Message 2

Applicant's reply to message 1; acceptance of invitation.

October 1, (*year*)

Dear. Mr. Taggat:

Thank you for inviting me to visit your office and plant. I very much want to study your organization and operation.

Because of class schedules and previous commitments, the best dates are October 12–16, inclusive. Any one or more of these days permits ideal timing for the trip.

I'm looking forward to visiting your headquarters and talking with both management members and workers in production.

Message 3

Reply by certified mail to message 2; Ms. Jones, assistant supervisor of personnel services, gives details for visit and encloses check.

October 4, (*year*)

Dear Mr. Brown:

Thank you for informing us of your intended visit to (*firm*) for interviews. The date we have set is October 15. The enclosed check is to cover your plane fare, meals, and miscellaneous expenses. Please retain any receipts for air travel and lodging for our expense account purposes.

We have arranged prepaid hotel accommodations for you for Tuesday, October 14, at the Hilton Plaza Hotel, (*city*). You can come to the plant Wednesday morning in a company car which leaves our (*city*) office every morning at 7:10 a.m.

To get this car you should report by 6:50 a.m. to the lounge, Room 1420 Industrial Building, (*address, city*). Because of the early hour, you can plan on having breakfast when you reach the plant. You will be able to return to headquarters from the plant in the same manner, leaving there at 2:30 p.m. and arriving in (*city*) at about 3:10 p.m. for interviews here.

The interest you have expressed in (*name of firm*) is appreciated, and we look forward to your visit on the 15th.

Message 4

Job offer by Mr. Sawyer, general superintendent, following plant interview.

October 23, (*year*)

Dear Mr. Brown:

We are pleased to offer you employment as a management trainee, assigned to our industrial engineering department. Your starting salary on this position would be $--- a month.

Should you decide to join our organization, we will provide the cost of travel for you and your wife and move your household effects.

Thank you for the interest you expressed when you visited the plant. We hope you will decide to make your career with us. If you have any question concerning our offer or employment in general, please call Ms. M. A. Jones in the personnel office. Her telephone number is (area code 123), 555-4889.

Message 5

Applicant requests more time for final decision.

October 31, (*year*)

Dear Ms. Jones:

Mr. Sawyer sent me a job offer as a management trainee in the industrial engineering department and suggested that if I had any questions I should get in touch with you.

Before making a final decision concerning this offer, I will appreciate your allowing me until December 5 for my reply. My reason for requesting this extra time is to permit me to complete my interviews with several other companies that have already invited me to visit their plants.

Even with these other opportunities, I am at present more interested in (*reader's firm*) than all the others because many aspects of your company appeal to me. I was particularly impressed by the speed, efficiency, and precision of the manufacturing plant.

If you need my decision before the end of November, please let me know as soon as possible so that I will have the opportunity to make my final decision. Also, if you are giving me this extended time, please notify me to that effect.

Message 6

Ms. Jones gives applicant extension of time to accept offer.

November 7, (*year*)

Dear Mr. Brown:

As you requested, we will be glad to allow you additional time to decide whether you want to accept our previous offer to work for (*firm*).

We realize that you have many things to consider to reach a final decision regarding employment. Therefore, we want to allow you as much time as possible for your evaluation of all opportunities. So that we can establish the proper control on our recruiting activities and plans for the coming year, I will appreciate knowing your decision as soon as possible. However, inasmuch as you will not be available until March (*year*), your advising us a month from now will be quite acceptable.

We feel that you are well qualified for the career employment opportunities available within (*firm*) and hope you will decide to make your career with us.

If I can be of any further assistance to you, please write or telephone me. My number is (area code 123) 555-4889.

Message 7

Applicant's acceptance.

December 1, (*year*)

Dear Mr. Sawyer:

I am glad to accept your offer of $--- a month as a management trainee in your industrial engineering department.

Since graduation is Saturday, March 10, (*year*), my wife and I plan to leave (*city*) the following Monday, March 12. We should arrive in the (*city*) area the following day--Tuesday, March 13. Allowing a few days to locate living accommodations and to get settled, I should be ready to start work on Monday, March 19. Please let me know if this schedule is satisfactory with you.

I am very pleased in becoming a member of your organization. It is with great appreciation that I look forward to what I am sure will be a challenging future with (*name of organization*).

Message 8

Sawyer's reply to applicant's acceptance.

December 8, (*year*)

Dear Mr. Brown:

We are very pleased that you are coming with us, and we look forward to seeing you on March 19.

You will receive travel expenses in February, and we will contact you at that time regarding moving arrangements.

Please call on us if we can be of any assistance before that time.

EXERCISES

1. Below are four refusals to applicants by outstanding national companies. Evaluate by telling what you like and dislike about each message. Be specific in your discussion. Which one is the most satisfactory?

   a.
   Thank you for coming in to discuss employment possibilities during our recent visit to your campus.

   As you can appreciate, there is considerable competition for our limited openings. It is always a difficult task to select a few people from the many fine candidates we are given the opportunity to consider. After careful consideration of your qualifications with regards to our specific job requirements, we will be unable to offer you further encouragement.

   We do, however, appreciate your interest in (*firm*) and extend our best wishes for success in your business career.

   b.
   In reply to your letter of application dated January 5, (*year*), we do not have an opening on our staff. However, we shall be pleased to keep your application on file for future vacancies.

   Thank you for writing us.

   c.
   The delay in advising you regarding employment possibilities with (*firm*), following your interview with our recruiter, has been due to your application and file being forwarded to departments dispersed over a wide geographic area.

   Your background and qualifications have now been carefully reviewed by these various departments; but, we regret we are presently unable to offer you a position that would be of mutual advantage.

We appreciate your interest in (*firm*) and wish you every success in the future.

d.

Thank you for scheduling an interview with (*firm*), giving our recruiter, Mr. C. W. Lindenmeier, the opportunity to talk with you during our recent visit to your campus. He commented favorably about his conversation with you.

We have carefully reviewed all openings anticipated near your availability date which we believed might be of interest to you. I am sorry to inform you that we were unable to locate a position matching your background, training, and interests. We are, however, taking the liberty of holding your application on file should any appropriate openings develop in the near future.

I do regret that we cannot offer you more encouragement at this time. We appreciate your interest in our activities and wish you every success in beginning your professional career.

2. Evaluate the three messages below. The applicant is a graduating senior who sent her application letter with résumé to a large department store chain in a large city 1,000 miles from the campus. In the letter she mentioned she'd be in the city between winter and spring quarters (usually the latter part of March) and requested an interview, which she received.

Message 1

Applicant receives this offer after she returns to the campus.

As a result of our conversation with you, we are pleased to offer you the opportunity to join the (*firm*) Executive Training Program at a starting salary of $--- a month. Employment is contingent upon your passing a medical examination which will be given when you start work here in (*city*).

Enclosed for your perusal is a copy of our Annual Report, which we trust you will find of interest.

We look forward to receiving your favorable consideration of this offer, and I am sure you will find this a most stimulating opportunity.

Message 2

Applicant accepts job offer.

April 17, (*year*)

It is with pleasure and excitement that I accept your offer to join the (*firm*) Executive Training Program. I have been reading the Annual

Report you enclosed and am looking forward to working for as fine a company as (*firm*).

Will you please tell me when you want me to report after graduation, where, to whom, and at what time? I can be in (*city*) within two weeks after University of (*state*) commencement exercises June 13.

If you need any further information before giving me the details of my assignment, please write to me at my (*city*) address before June 9 and at my home address after that date.

Message 3

Reply to applicant's job acceptance and inquiry.

April 21, (*year*)

Thank you for your letter of April 17. We are pleased to know that you will be joining our Executive Training Squad this summer.

You may report for work any Monday convenient to you. You indicate that June 29 would be a convenient date. This is most acceptable, and we will look forward to your reporting at 8:55 a.m. to the personnel department, which is on the eighth floor. You may enter the building through the company entrance (on Westfall near Donson Street) and the guard at the door will direct you to the personnel department.

Enclosed is a booklet, which is given to all new Training Squad executives when they report for work, which may answer many of your questions. We are also enclosing a booklet given to every new employee, which will give you information as to dress regulations, etc.

Congratulations on your coming graduation. We look forward to seeing you again on June 29.

3. Assume you have written to a large corporation the application letter assigned in Exercise 4, page 373. Today you received an invitation for an interview next Friday (in your city). To prepare well for this interview study a copy of the firm's recent Annual Report. List information about its products, personnel, and other items of interest to help you answer pertinent questions. (See questions on pages 382–384.)

4. Assume you sent your application letter and résumé to the personnel manager of a particular firm; shortly afterward you received an invitation to come to his office for an interview. He is located in your city. During the 30-minute interview, he asked you questions about your qualifications and explained company policy, beginning salary, and other pertinent information. Write a follow-up for one (or each) of these possible outcomes:

    a. At the end of the interview he told you he'd notify you of his decision.

    b. At the end of the interview he asked you to write him why you want to get into the type of work you're applying for.

    c. At the end of the interview he asked you to visit the manager in one of the organization's several local retail stores. While there you should interview the manager and other employees to find out whether you want to make a career in this type of work. Then you're to write the personnel manager if you're still interested. Assume you are favorably impressed.

5. Assume you mailed your application letter three weeks ago but have received no reply. Send an inquiry to the firm.

6. Assume you received two offers for career jobs.

    a. Write the acceptance message.

    b. Write the refusal message.

7. As the employer, you must refuse a graduating senior the job she applied for because her qualifications aren't as good as those of the others you interviewed. Furthermore, one reference indicated this person is a troublemaker. Write the refusal message.

8. As a graduating senior, you received the following letter from Mr. Alexander, recruiting coordinator. Unfortunately you can't see the representative on January 30. However, you're very much interested in working for this company. Write the appropriate message to the coordinator, assuming any facts you wish as long as you don't alter the assignment.

> Dear (*your name*):
>
> Please forgive my resorting to a form letter to reach you—but time is getting short and I want to let you know that one of our executives plans to visit your campus soon.
>
> His primary purpose will be to interview (*year*) graduates for career employment with our newly merged organization. As you might imagine, we have an even greater horizon now to present to promising young people like yourself. Moreover, we have a number of good summer job opportunities for undergraduates this year.
>
> In any case, I have been alerted to your fine summer employment record with us and assure you our interest in you continues strong. Accordingly, if you want to explore a position with us, I urge that you sign up to see our corporate recruiting representative when he visits your placement office on January 30.
>
> If you cannot make that date, please drop me a line and let's try to arrange for you to visit some nearby branch office. I am en—

closing a return envelope for that purpose, together with a copy of our Annual Report and some other literature for your reference.

Meanwhile, accept our sincere best wishes to your forthcoming graduation.

9. Assume that three weeks ago you had an interview on campus with a representative of a national company whose head offices are 1,000 miles from you. Before parting, the interviewer asked if you would be willing to come to the head offices someday for further interviews, and you had replied that you would be glad to. Today you receive the following letter, dated February 2, from the personnel manager:

Dear *(your name)*:

It is with a great deal of pleasure that I confirm our invitation to visit us in *(city)* in order to pursue further the possibility of your joining *(firm name)*. We have arranged a schedule for which we would like to have you arrive at our executive offices at *(address)* at 1:30 p.m. on Monday, April 10; be prepared to stay with us through the following day.

As I pointed out during our brief meeting, at *(firm name)* we feel strongly that the matter of selection is a "two-way street," and we look forward to this chance of making you better acquainted with us and the opportunity we offer. Also, of course, we would like to review your qualifications more fully.

I know you have already accepted our invitation for further interviews, but we would appreciate a letter indicating that you still plan to come. It might be a good idea if you were to make airline reservations right away and let me know the flight numbers. I will then reciprocate by sending you an open ticket drawn on the airline you designate.

We will make a hotel reservation for you for the night of April 10, and for the night of the 9th too if schedules require you to come the night before. As a last point, please keep track of the incidental expenses incurred by your trip so that we may reimburse you for them.

That would seem to cover it, *(your name)*, but please let me know if you have any questions. I'll be looking forward to seeing you again.

Write the complete, thoughtful, friendly letter this invitation calls for. Before you do so, however, consider the kind of airline passage you should reserve. Should it be first-class? Coach? Economy? Why? Why do you think the employer leaves the choice up to you? You might also discuss in class the kinds of incidental expenses that will be appropriate for you to include in your later request for reimbursement—after this second interview.

10. If you and your classmates would like practice interviews, try this assignment. For one interview half the class members will volunteer to be job applicants and the other half will be employers' personnel representatives. For a second interview all students will switch roles.

    Each interview will be based on an application letter and résumé the applicant has written (as, for example, Exercise 4, page 373) and, presumably, mailed. In class students will merely exchange these papers.

    Each interview should preferably be about 20 to 30 minutes in length between students who do not know each other well. Both the applicant and the assumed personnel representative (or higher executive, if appropriate) should make all necessary preparations before the interviews. The applicant (interviewee) should review pages 378–385. The employer's representative (interviewer) will find helpful suggestions in Chapter 21, pages 643–651, regarding how to conduct an interview. He or she will, of course, also study the applicant's résumé before conducting the interview and know something about the company the interviewer represents.

CHAPTER 14

Collection Messages—
Written and Oral

Collection of past-due accounts is an important part of any business. After a borrower gets a loan or a customer purchases something on credit, payment should be made within a specified period—according to the terms of the agreement. When obligations are not paid on time, collection messages become necessary. Customer reasons for not paying are usually one or more of the following: they've overlooked the invoice or statement; they're dissatisfied with the merchandise, delivery, billing, or handling of a complaint; they're temporarily short of funds; they're chronic debtors.

Collection messages have an important, twofold purpose: to *get the money* and to *keep customer goodwill*. These messages may be delivered by mail, phone, personal visit, telegram, or Mailgram. To carry out the twofold function requires an understanding attitude and effective messages appropriately planned and timed throughout the collection stages. Most collection procedures have similar basic characteristics whether the messages concern retail credit (to customers) or mercantile credit (to business firms), and whether they are for open account or installment credit. For various reasons, they also have differences. This chapter discusses: the right attitude for effective collections, collection stages, and telephone collection procedure.

RIGHT ATTITUDE FOR EFFECTIVE COLLECTIONS

A debtor may be touchy about how and when the creditor asks for payment even though it is for a legitimate debt. The longer past-due the payment is, the more difficult the situation becomes. The right collection attitude for a creditor requires an understanding of human nature, careful choice of collection appeals, knowledge of the debtor's past credit record, as well as regulations affecting collection policies.

Understanding of Human Nature

When you send a collection message, remember you are communicating with a person, not with an account number. Each person has a different mental filter, with attitudes, prejudices, perceptions, and problems. All human beings have feelings and react negatively to offensive expressions, sarcasm, anger, and insults just as quickly as you do.

The fairest assumption to make is that your customers honestly want to pay as agreed. The majority of customers will pay when reminded. However, conditions change and with them the customers' ability and willingness to pay may also change. Some debtors conscientiously promptly write or telephone their reasons for lateness and explain when they will make their next payments. Some remain silent, and a few are repeatedly uncooperative.

A tactful, courteous attitude coupled with firmness and patience always collects more money in the long run than impolitely worded demands. As a collection manager you need to decide carefully *how* and *when* to contact customers about past-due accounts. If you're too lenient, some individuals may pay other bills that seem more pressing, and you won't get the money coming to you. On the other hand, if you threaten or harass customers, they may not pay either.

Tactless expressions like "you are delinquent" should not be used. Instead, phrases such as "two payments are past due" or "the delinquency of this account" are less offensive because they are impersonal. All the "C" qualities (Chapters 3 and 4)—especially consideration, concreteness, and courtesy—are important for effective collection messages. Also, the suggestions for proper attitude in bad-news letters (pages 225–226) apply to collections.

Choice of Collection Appeals

As you will read later in the discussion on Collection Stages, those collection messages which must be *persuasive* should include well-chosen appeals. These choices relate closely to the debtor's payment record. The following positive and negative appeals are effective in persuasive collection messages:

Positive appeals focus on cooperation, fair play, pride.

Cooperation, the mildest appeal, caters to one's desire to be considerate of others—in this case, loyal to the creditor who has been courteous and friendly in asking for what is rightly due. (This should not, however, be a whining "poor me" appeal.)

The **fair-play** appeal is usually developed by reviewing the facts—how long a payment has been pastdue—and showing that since the creditor has carried out his or her part of an agreement, the debtor (customer)—to be fair and honest—should keep his or her promise and pay. Resale on items bought is also effective.

The **pride appeal** should be subtle, not a high-pressure tactic. You can develop this appeal in various ways by referring to what you know the customer is proud of—a good credit rating, (sometimes) the items bought, or the respect and good reputation enjoyed in the community.

Negative appeals arouse debtor's emotions of self-interest and fear.

Individuals who care little about cooperation or fair play may be motivated to pay when you show what they will gain by doing so and will lose by further delay.

The **self-interest** appeal usually has two objectives—to show the value of the present advantages the customers have and to convince them that further delay may cause them to lose the advantages.

Fear appeal, instead of stressing the value of keeping various benefits, stresses the loss of such benefits (good credit standing or possessions). The past-due account will be reported to the credit bureau and turned over to an attorney or collection agency, or be taken to court as a lawsuit, which will be extra expense for the debtor.

You can use effectively one or a combination of these appeals in a persuasive message. Your choice of appeals is influenced by the debtor's payment record, your knowledge of collection policies, and the message's place in the collection stage.

Knowledge of Collection Policies and Laws

Besides understanding human nature and choosing collection appeals carefully after considering the debtor's past credit record, you and your assistants need also to know your firm's collection policies and government regulations. They may relate to various time limits on installment or mortgage late payments, foreclosures, and procedures regarding consumer credit and collections.

An effective collection policy necessitates bringing the debt to the debtor's attention *promptly* and *regularly,* with *increasing firmness* as the past-due period lengthens. Just how soon after payment due date the messages should be sent, and what you say in these messages, varies also according to the type of credit account, the particular debtor's situation, your firm's collection policies, and various legal aspects. (See Appendix A.) These factors also influence the time interval between collection messages and overall length of the collection process, as is discussed later in this chapter.

To summarize, the right attitude for collection messages requires tact, courtesy, consideration, fairness, firmness, and a positive viewpoint. It requires understanding of human nature, knowledge of collection appeals and the customer's past payment record, plus adherence to your firm's collection policies and government regulations.

COLLECTION STAGES

The first notification the customer receives after purchasing on credit or borrowing money on a loan is a statement (bill) or invoice showing the amount owed. This notification usually lists the transactions for the time period involved and states the terms and date of payment.

If the customer does not pay by the due date, you begin to send a series of messages called a *collection series.* Though the length, content, and collection methods of a collection series may vary according to circumstances, a well-planned series usually has three stages. The messages in each stage vary in number but usually follow a somewhat typical organizational plan and general assumption.

1. **Reminder** Stage	Plan:	Routine direct request
	Assumption:	Oversight
	Number:	Varies from 1 to 6 or 7
	Appeals:	None, usually
2. **Discussion** Stage	Plan:	Persuasive request (modified)
	Assumption:	Something unusual happened
	Number:	Varies from 2 to 5 or more
	Appeals:	Positive
3. **Urgency** Stage	Plan:	Persuasive request (modified)
	Assumption:	Debtor may need to be scared into paying
	Number:	Usually 1 or 2
	Appeals:	Negative; sometimes also a positive

Regardless of stage in the collection procedure or other differences, *all collection messages should make clear two facts–the amount due and the account number.* Also, an easy-action envelope, perhaps postpaid, is appreciated and often speeds the reply.

Reminder Stage

Messages in the reminder stage aim to jog the customer's memory. They are direct requests, ranging in number from one to six or seven. You first present the *main question or subject,* then *explain* (when necessary), and end the message by *requesting action.* You don't attempt to persuade or to use any appeals. Although some reminders—especially those sent to installment credit and the usually slow-pay customers—might have a personalized inside address, generally they are obvious processed forms to avoid any suggestion that you are questioning the customer's integrity or ability to pay. They usually range from one or more standard statements (usually not itemized), to computerized card-size messages, to an obvious form letter on company letterhead stationery.

The statement(s) following the first one might include rubber-stamped or hand-written messages that say "Please" or "Perhaps you have forgotten" on colorful stickers like the three shown on page 412 (which can be purchased in quantities from a printer).

Shown below are examples of a computerized message and a short letter reminder which is an obviously processed form on the firm's letterhead.

Reminder 1

A computerized form 3¾ by 6½ inches in size on green pastel paper. A large department store sends it to a customer along with a second statement (and sometimes a leaflet advertising new merchandise items–for sales promotion).

```
Customers say they appreciate being reminded when their accounts are
a little overdue.
So, we hope you will accept this reminder in the friendly spirit
with which it is intended.
If our letters happen to cross and your check arrives in the next
mail, please disregard this notice and accept our thanks for your
payment.
```

Reminder 2

A short form-letter request from an oil company to a credit-card customer who had previously received a statement and a form-notice reminder.

```
                        Dear Customer:
```

Main idea and amount due
```
It's easy to misplace statements and overlook form
notices.  That's why we're sending this letter to re-
mind you of your balance amounting to $———.
```

Action
```
The account is somewhat past due and we would appreci-
ate your sending us a check in the next few days.
```

Humor, witty short poems, anecdotes, and pictures that relate to the creditor's business or products can be quite effective—if they are used in the reminder stage—for small debts. Various humorous reminders can be purchased or specially designed. Good judgment and originality are necessary, of course, for appropriate humorous reminders. Consider seriously how the customer who owes money might react to the humor.

Discussion Stage

If you receive no response after the routine-request reminders you sent to the customer, you progress into discussion stage messages that are *persuasive* requests. In this stage you usually personalize your messages by using an inside address and a salutation with the customer's name. You assume that something unusual has happened. For some reason unknown to you the customer cannot or doesn't want to pay. (Do *not* revert again to the "oversight" assumption used in the reminder stage.) *Your purpose now is to get the debtor to send the payment or at least an explanation*—if there is a reason for not paying.[1] Then you may be able to make mutually satisfactory alternate payment arrangements.

Depending upon the type of debtor and account, discussion messages range in number from two to five or more. To get the customer to read your message, you will need to *attract attention* in the first paragraph. You try now to begin with a reader-interest theme—something beneficial, pleasant, interesting, and/or important to the reader.

Your *desire-conviction-proof* paragraphs may include facts, figures, and reasons why the debtor will benefit by doing as requested. Well-chosen *appeals* (see pages 410–411) will help convince the customer and stimulate a desire to do what is right. Usually your first message is an inquiry, asking if something is wrong and inviting the customer to send either an explanation or a check; the positive "cooperation" appeal may be effective. Successive messages become progressively stronger, ending with a hint of negative appeal in the last discussion message. You may also include more than one appeal in any message.

Some small business and professional firms that have no collection department may depend heavily upon using the telephone. Or they continue their collection efforts by merely attaching colorful discussion-stage stickers on their

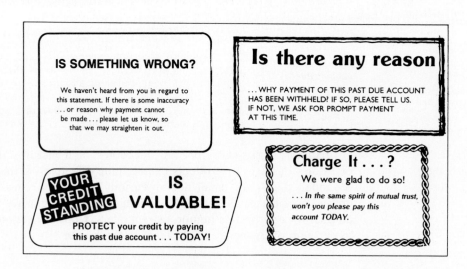

---

[1] Twice a year, according to the Federal Truth in Lending Act, creditors must mail to all credit customers a printed form titled, "In Case of Errors or Inquiries about Your Bill." (Creditors decide what months these will be sent; in large stores the mailing is automatically computerized along with two monthly statements a year.) This form explains rules about customers' rights and obligations if they question the accuracy of a bill. (See Appendix A.)

monthly statements that show amount due and account number. Stickers like those on page 414 can be useful in the early part of the discussion stage.

For more persuasive requests it is better to write personalized letters. If necessary, they can be essentially form messages—individually typed by computer or automatic or magnetic-card typewriters—identical for many customers but personalized by insertions of the date and other variable information, as in letter 1. Notice how skillfully this letter avoids suggesting a negative idea about the reason for nonpayment. It does *not* ask if something is wrong with the store's merchandise or service or billing; yet if any of these should happen to be problems, the customer is free to mention them and thus help "to expedite any possible adjustment." Easy action is provided by lines at the bottom for the customer's reply and by an enclosed envelope.

Letter 1

A tactful, persuasive, personalized form letter from a department store to a usually good-pay customer.

Dear (*Mr., Mrs., Miss, Ms. name*):

Attention (compliment)	The privilege of serving you is certainly our pleasure. For this, we extend our sincere thanks.
Appeal (cooperation)	You have always been cooperative in the past by keeping your account paid on time according to your credit agreement. As we have received no remittance from you for over three months, we wonder if you have a question concerning the balance.
Request for reason or check *Easy action*	Whatever information you request will receive our prompt attention, as we want to expedite any possible adjustment. A note at the bottom of this letter will do. Then just mail it—or your check for $_____—in the enclosed envelope.
Goodwill	Your cooperation will be greatly appreciated.

In letter 2 a wholesaler includes several appeals to the mercantile customer. By reviewing the facts about the overdue account and mentioning the high-quality merchandise plus a willingness to help, the writer makes a fair-play appeal. In addition, the compliments on the dealer's good-pay record and the reiteration of the value of a favorable credit rating develop both pride and self-interest appeals.

Letter 2

An effective personalized letter from a wholesaler to a mercantile customer.

Attention (agreeable comment)

It would be nice if we could get together in person to talk over your overdue account with us, but the demands of our businesses and the distance make this impossible.

Facts; compliment

Your account is 80 days past the final due date on our terms of 2/10, net 30. This is exceptional, considering your past prompt payment record with us; and we would like to know what is wrong.

Pride; self-interest appeals

You have worked many years to establish your favorable credit rating, Mr. Jones. It allows you to stock high-quality furniture such as the Allwood chairs when you need them and even take advantage of a discount if payment is made within 10 days. You can have an adequate supply of merchandise on hand at all times, without maintaining a large amount of cash for working capital. Your credit rating not only makes conducting of your business easier but also allows you to establish yourself with new suppliers quickly and easily.

Fairness appeal

Is there anything we can do to help you overcome a difficulty? We want to be fair with you. I'm sure we can work some kind of a plan for payment that will be compatible with your situation. Of course, the most satisfactory solution would be a full payment of the $629.57 in the return mail. If you cannot manage this, then send us a frank explanation of the problem you are facing and we will see what plan we can come up with to clear your account.

Easy action, with suggested time

The enclosed envelope is addressed to come directly to my desk unopened, Mr. Jones. I hope to see it again next week with your check for the full $629.57 inside. If this is not possible, then use the envelope to send me a full explanation of your situation so that we can help you find a solution.

The writer of the next letter uses the positive pride and self-interest appeals plus the negative loss-of-comforts-and-advantages appeal. Even though this borrower owes three payments, the letter (from a bank's lending officer) avoids a scolding tone and tries to keep the customer sold on the values of home ownership.

Letter 3

A bank lending officer's helpful, persuasive request to a borrower for a home loan.

Attention (pride appeal)

You have probably often heard the statement, "There's no place like home."

Appeals to self- and family interests

You and your spouse made a wise decision when you invested in your present four-bedroom home. Close to schools, your church, and stores, it has the ideal location for your growing family. Your loan department personnel here at (*name of bank*) were glad to help you with financing by extending you the loan you needed seven years ago.

Comfort, security

So that you can continue to enjoy the comfort and security of owning this home, it is important that you keep up your payments on your loan. Four messages have been mailed to you about the three payments that are now past due:

Easy-to-read facts

May 10	$272.00
June 10	272.00
July 10	272.00
Late charges	35.24
Total	$851.24

Economic self-interest and risk-of-loss appeals

It is easy to become so accustomed to a privilege that we take it for granted. You were fortunate to buy when you did, for today the same kind of home—even without the playroom and patio you have—would cost you at least $9,000 more, at a higher interest rate. You'll agree you can't afford to risk losing the comforts and advantages you now enjoy.

Action

So please send your check for $851.24 today or call me at (*number*) so we can discuss a satisfactory solution.

In any business you may find some customers who are repeatedly late in paying their bills. To such persons—who have in previous delinquencies received a variety of detailed letters from you (with inquiries and positive appeals), you may wish to concentrate on a negative appeal. The following letter emphasizes what the customer with a poor credit rating will experience.

Letter 4

A persuasive request with a strong fear appeal to the repeatedly late payer.

Attention

How valuable is your credit rating to you?

Self-interest appeal–positive

If you possess a good rating, you are able to buy on a charge basis whenever necessary. You can buy quality expensive items without paying the entire cost in cash at time of purchase. Also, if an emergency arises, your credit will be helpful.

However, if your record in various places shows you are a poor credit risk, this valuable possession of

*Self-interest–
negative appeal*
credit will be lost. You are likely to be subjected to the unpleasantness of drastic collection measures. In addition, your credit reputation will follow you wherever you go. It will take years to restore a good rating. You may be deprived of items you would like to purchase, because of the necessity for paying cash.

These are facts. We mention them only so that you will not take lightly the possible loss of your credit which may follow unless your account with us is paid.

Action
It is still possible to salvage your credit reputation. Please use the enclosed envelope to mail your check for $ (*amount*) today in payment of this account which has been overdue since (*date*). If you cannot pay it all immediately, you will find us willing to discuss a definite arrangement to take care of it. Please call me at (*number*).

For chronic ''delinquents'' you might omit the offer (in the last paragraph) to discuss a payment arrangement and simply ask for full payment.

Urgency Stage

During the reminder and discussion stages most messages may have been signed by someone in the credit or collection department. In the urgency stage—for greater impact on the past-due customer—messages may be signed by a higher executive, such as a vice president or even the president, in some firms.

These messages follow the persuasive-request plan and use the strongest negative appeal—fear. In addition, it is often desirable to include at least one positive appeal—giving the debtor a chance to avoid the drastic action and extra costs—before the account is turned over to a collection agency or lawyer or the merchandise is repossessed. The action request is firm and definite about the amount the debtor must send and the office to which it should be sent.

As the following examples illustrate, you can use one or two messages in the urgency stage. If two, the first one doesn't set a date for the drastic action, but the final message *always* sets the date.

Example 1

First of two messages in the urgency stage.

*Fairness; review
of facts*
The time has come when we must write the kind of letter we dislike very much. In previous letters we said about everything we could think of in urging you to pay your long-overdue bill, which is now $355.70. But we have received no replies to any of our requests.

Fear; self-interest; fairness

Must we now turn your account over to our attorney for collection? A lawsuit would require you to pay not only the bill but also the court costs. We don't want to do this without giving you one last chance to write and let us know your side of the story.

Self-interest; reader benefit

We have been good business friends for many years, (*name*). Please don't make it necessary for us to end our friendship in such an unpleasant way. Write us immediately—or better still, send us your check to pay this debt, now 115 days past due. But do it to-day, please!

If you are using only one letter in this collection stage, you can still use example 1, adding the following paragraph before the final one:

For that reason we will delay action for five days—until July 22— before turning your account over to Smith, Smythe, and Smothers.

If you feel that in the discussion stage messages you have given the debtor sufficient time to "discuss or pay" (especially when dealing with chronic late-payers), you might use a telegram or Mailgram as the first message in the urgency stage. According to Western Union, companies using Mailgrams report collection efficiency improvement of up to 70 percent.[2] You can, of course, send any length of message you wish. Here are two short messages that have shock value:

Example 2

Mailgrams as the first of two messages in the urgency stage–especially for chronic late-payers.

a. YOUR ACCOUNT #_____ WILL BE REFERRED TO AN OUTSIDE COLLECTION AGENCY. ONLY YOUR REMITTANCE FOR $_____ WILL STOP FORMAL CREDIT ACTION. SEND IT TODAY.

b. IMPORTANT YOU CALL COLLECT IMMEDIATELY (*TEL. NUMBER*) BETWEEN 8AM AND 4PM CENTRAL STANDARD TIME CONCERNING YOUR CREDIT CARD ACCOUNT NUMBER (_____). PLEASE TELL THE OPERATOR YOU RECEIVED THIS MES-SAGE.

Example 3

Final letter that sets a date. (Letter is signed by the collection manager or a vice president.)

Your account has just been referred to me, marked for "final ac-tion."

[2] *How to Excel in the Art of Friendly Persuasion*, The Western Union Telegraph Company.

> Because it is the policy of this company that every contact with our customers shall be one of courteous interest in their behalf, I am writing you this letter as a last appeal that you mail us your check for $623.02, or call personally to see us. I have withheld any action on your account and feel sure we can work out some mutually satisfactory arrangement for settlement.
>
> I shall hold your account on my desk for 10 days, hoping that you will attend to it at once. Unless I hear from you by June 25, I shall have no alternative but to assign your account for collection. I anticipate you will not force me to take a step that would have such a serious effect upon your credit reputation.

Some firms collect almost entirely by Mailgrams, using discussion-stage as well as urgency-stage messages. If you wish, you can store your collection-letter formats on a Western Union computer and file with that company the names and addresses of customers. Then you simply direct Western Union to send, for example, "format 31" to customers 10 through 50 and indicate amounts due. Each debtor gets a personally addressed Mailgram. A lending officer, for instance, might send a message similar to the following, which includes her or his name and "Assistant Cashier" at the end.[3]

Example 4

Mailgram that sets a final date for payment of overdue installments.

> REPEATED REQUESTS HAVE BEEN MADE FOR PAST-DUE PAYMENTS ON YOUR LOAN AT OUR OFFICE. YOUR MANNER OF REPAYMENT IS UNSATISFACTORY AND WILL NO LONGER BE TOLERATED.
>
> WE MUST RECEIVE YOUR OCTOBER AND NOVEMBER INSTALLMENTS INCLUDING LATE CHARGES AND SERVICE FEES NO LATER THAN NOVEMBER 25. FAILURE TO MEET THIS REQUEST WILL FORCE US TO TAKE WHATEVER STEPS ARE NECESSARY TO PROTECT THE BANK'S INTEREST.
>
> PLEASE MAIL YOUR REMITTANCE FOR $_____ TO (*bank name*), P.O. BOX (*number, city, state, ZIP*).

Example 5

Final message that sets a date. This printed form goes to customers who live within the city which is within the jurisdiction of the specific credit bureau.

---

[3] Courtesy of Tom Hardeman, sales representative, Western Union, Seattle, Wash. All employees handling telegrams and Mailgrams are (under the Communications Secrecy Act) bound to secrecy. They may not divulge content of any message or even that a communication was made between any two people. (For Methods of Sending Mailgrams, see p. 139.)

No. 1982

Please Read This Carefully

_____ 19 _ ____

To: _____

_____
Address   City   State

It is the purpose of this notice to inform you, as a matter of courtesy, of our

intention to assign your account to the **COLLECTION DEPT.,**   **(NAME) CREDIT SERVICES, INC.**

for collection unless your remittance is in our hands on or before _____ 19 ____

This can be avoided if **PAYMENT IN FULL** is made on or before the above date, but you must **ACT WITHOUT DELAY.**

The amount is $ _____

_____ (CREDITOR)

_____ (ADDRESS)

By _____

Pay your bills in full TODAY So that your Credit will be good TOMORROW

TELEPHONE COLLECTION PROCEDURE

As the preceding discussions indicated, both written and oral messages can be effective for collecting past-due payments. Basically, the goals, attitudes, and procedures are similar whether you collect by written communication or through oral contacts—face to face or by telephone. You need also to be aware of prohibited collection practices.

The following quotation expresses some advantages of the telephone method:

> Increasing use is being made of the telephone in collecting, both in early and late stages of the collection process, for this method, because of its directness, often succeeds where other methods fail. One of the chief advantages of this method is that it is somewhat surprising to the debtor and may, therefore, catch him unguarded with small alibis and grievances with which to excuse his delinquency. It furnishes the collector a good opportunity to impress him emphatically with the urgency of payment, varying the appeals as the need arises. Frequently, when the reason for nonpayment is understandable, although the failure of the debtor to communicate it is not, a plan of payment may be worked out, usually with a partial payment to be made immediately. Thus, by telephoning nearly all can be accomplished that could be gained by a personal solicitation. Telephoning, however, is often the speedier method, the more flexible, particularly in tracing skips, the less costly, even in the use of long-distance service, as long as it is used with efficiency and discretion.[4]

[4] Theodore N. Beckman and Ronald S. Foster, _Credits and Collections_, 8th ed., McGraw-Hill Book Company, New York, p. 533.

Because of the growing importance of the telephone in all three collection stages, this section focuses briefly on two special phases of telephone collection techniques: precall planning and the actual collection conversation.

Precall Planning

The steps a collector takes before an important telephone call—or a personal conversation—are similar to the first five planning steps before writing.

1. **Determine Your Purpose**
   Besides the general goal of collecting the money and keeping goodwill, you probably have a specific purpose too. Be sure to check all previous letters, calls, and any response to them. Is your purpose now to work out a special payment arrangement? Or to remind the debtor of a promise made recently but not kept? Or to urge the debtor to pay by a certain date? Or to present an important decision?

2. **Visualize Your Customer**
   First determine the right person to talk to. He or she should be the *only* one who is responsible for paying the bills. Try to judge whether the customer would respond better to a hard or a soft line. If the customer has just received the first overdue notice, your approach should of course be different from the approach to the customer who has ignored several previous contacts. Is the customer likely to be angry? Friendly? Cooperative? Hostile? The payment history is a good clue as to the way the customer will respond to your call.

3. **Collect All Necessary Facts**
   (a) Determine if your own company is at fault. Were shipments and billings correct? Were all payments recorded? If you find errors, take time to have them corrected before calling the customer to bring the account up to date. *(b) Check the past payment record.* How often were the customer's payments delinquent in the past? How long past due is the account now? If the customer has been late only once in the last year, he or she will probably more readily accept a payment plan than the customer who has been delinquent most of the year.

4. **Consider the Ideas to Cover**
   (a) Prepare the questions you'll ask the debtor to determine reasons for not paying bills on time. You'll want to make the customer feel that you are both on the same side. Plan open-ended questions that allow the customer to do the talking rather than merely answering "yes" or "no." Good questions begin with the five W's—who, what, when, where, why, and the H—how. *(b) Be ready to present a payment plan.* This is the heart of precall planning. The payment plan must account for all the overdue payments, not just one

or two; and it must include a *specific* schedule that will bring the overdue account to current status. Prepare to sell the plan to the customer in a positive way, without insulting or harassing statements.

5. **Plan and Organize**
   Prepare an opening statement and—at least in general—the order in which you'll present the material you want to cover.

Analysis of the Collection Call

Like the well-written collection letter, the collection call should likewise be tactfully persuasive. The conversation contains the following parts:

1. **Opening Statement**
   After identifying yourself and your firm, state the reason for calling. Then use a strategic pause—important in every call. If the customer is sincere in desiring to pay overdue bills, he or she will offer to pay or give a reason for not paying as soon as the reason for the phone call is given. Many collection calls are completed successfully immediately after this strategic pause.

2. **Fact-Finding Questions**
   As you hear the customer's answers to your preplanned questions, try to determine whether the payment plan you designed is realistic. Be ready to adapt it to meet the customer's situation. When you think that using either your original payment plan or a newly devised one will get the account current, and it meets your company policy, proceed to the next step.

3. **Presentation of Payment Plan**
   You might begin to focus the customer's attention on your plan by statements like these: "(Name), I've been thinking seriously about your account, and have come up with a plan of action that will get your account right back in good condition . . ."; or, "(Name), I'm glad you mentioned that you wish there were a way you could get your account paid up without having to do it today. I believe there is. How does this plan sound to you?" Now you have focused the customer's attention on the payment plan. If the final plan is a schedule of payments that will result in a paid-up account, it is a satisfactory arrangement regardless of who proposed the plan or how it is altered.

   You have been successful if the customer agrees to a plan. You can then move directly to closing the call. However, if the customer does not agree to all or part of the payment plan, you will need to overcome objections.

4. **Overcoming of Objections**
   Almost always, objections to a payment plan are based on a desire to postpone payments. Three basic steps you can take in overcoming objections are:

a. Determine specifically what the customer is objecting to. You can't overcome an objection until you know what it is.

b. Get agreement on those parts the customer is not objecting to. Maybe the customer's objection concerns only one of the payment dates in the plan. If so, get agreement on all the rest.

c. Work out the parts the customer objects to. If the objections are minor, you can compromise as long as the plan is specific and it gets the account current. However, if the customer's objections are serious, you should be sure the reasons are valid. Then stress the benefits to the customer of paying and keeping the account current.

5. Closing Statement

Summarize the payment plan and thank the customer, as in the following example. "Fine, Mr. White. Now let me summarize to make sure that I have everything straight. You will mail me a payment of $45.30 on Monday, the 18th. I should have that by the following Thursday. Then you will send another payment of $45.30 on Monday, the 25th, which I should receive by the 28th. That will bring your account up to date. Thank you very much, Mr. White. Good-bye now."

After the call is finished, write down for future reference everything that was said. Note the pertinent information on a card and file it with any other information on the account. (Of course, if the customer does not abide by the terms of the agreement, you or another collector must take further action.)

Prohibited Collection Practices

During the entire collection procedure—written and oral—creditors have, of course, the right to demand payment from debtors. However, they must be careful not to do anything illegal. The Federal Communications Commission released a public notice (70-609) reminding creditors that it is a violation of the telephone company's tariff to use the telephone to frighten, torment, or harass a person. The following practices are prohibited:

1. Calling debtors at odd hours of the day or night
2. Repeated calls
3. Calls to friends, neighbors, relatives and children, making threats
4. Calls asserting falsely that credit rating will be hurt
5. Calls stating that legal process is about to be served
6. Calls demanding payment for amounts not owed
7. Calls to place of employment

In addition, it is a crime under federal law when collecting private debts to use in any communication the words *national, federal,* or *United States (U.S.)* to convey a false impression that such communication is from a government-related department, agency, or bureau or in any manner represents the United States. Furthermore, various state laws condemn threats of violence to a debtor's person, property, or reputation; false accusation of fraud; threats of arrest; anonymous calls; deceptive or misleading representations regarding claims; and other unfair practices.[5]

SUMMARY

When a customer's account becomes past due, the creditor begins a collection series. Its goal is to collect the money and maintain goodwill. An effective collector must always treat the customer with consideration and courtesy. Though some customers do not always pay when they should, the collector should try in every way possible to help a defaulting customer arrange to pay an account. The creditor does not want to sue, because everyone but the collection agency or attorney loses.

The collection series is a preplanned but still flexible three-stage procedure to collect from the past-due customer. For the persuasive messages in the discussion and urgency stages, the collector may choose from five kinds of appeals. As the series progresses, each message makes greater pressure on the customer to pay. The length of the series and the insistence to pay depend on the credit record of the individual. Contacts with the customer can be by mail, telephone, wire, or personal visit. Messages by mail consist of statements, reminders, letters, Mailgrams, and wires. A collector who uses the telephone or makes a personal visit should plan carefully before each call and be tactfully persuasive during the call. In all collection procedures—both written and oral—creditors must be scrupulously careful that their practices are within both federal and their state laws, and in keeping with company policies (if legal).

EXERCISES

1. Evaluate the effectiveness of the following early reminders that follow the statement(s). Which ones do you consider appropriate? Which ones do you consider inappropriate? Why?

Reminder 1

Obvious form letter on letterhead stationery from an oil company (added are the personalized inside address and salutation).

```
We know it is easy to lose a statement or forget to pay a bill, par-
ticularly if it is a small one.
```

[5] Adapted from "Legal Phrases of Collections," *Credit Manual of Commercial Laws,* National Association of Credit Management, January 1979, pp. 543–545.

In case one or the other happened in connection with your account for $_____, will you consider this as a reminder to drop a check in the mail today?

Reminder 2

Personalized inside address and salutation with a typewritten body, on letterhead stationery from a bookstore.

We want you to know that we appreciate your patronage and we hope therefore that we will not offend you when we mention that we haven't received anything on your account since we sent you your statement. Evidently that was ignored. We feel you will readily understand our anxiety.

We would appreciate it if you could send us something this month.

Reminder 3

Obvious printed message on a 5½- by 7-inch paper from a weekly newsmagazine. There is no inside address or salutation.

Just a brief note to repeat our thanks to you for your interest in (*name of magazine*) and for your order that will bring you its quick, complete, and competent news briefing in the many eventful weeks ahead. I feel sure you'll find both pleasure and profit in its pages!

And may I add another thanks—in advance—to you for taking care of the enclosed bill promptly. I've sent this copy in case our previous invoice was mislaid or overlooked.

And from all of us at (*name of magazine*)—sincere wishes that your (*name of magazine*) subscription will mean the best of good news to you!

2. Below are unusual collection messages. Which do you consider appropriate to send as reminders? Which would you not send? Give reason(s) for your decision.

Message 1

Obvious form letter with no inside address. Attached is a real paper clip.

No! That little paper clip in the upper left-hand corner hasn't been left there by a careless stenographer. That's Elmer, our pet paper clip.

His sole purpose in life, as you know, is to hold two pieces of paper together. But our Elmer has enlarged his scope of usefulness

and has accepted two very definite tasks which we have asked him to
do:

1. To securely hold your check for $4,286.61 to this note, which
   will clear up that little account we've talked about, and . . .

2. by doing so, to bind the amicable relationship which exists
   between our two companies.

Let's get this little matter under the bridge. What do you say?

Message 2

Obvious form letter.

Dear Customer:

                                          Cordially yours,
                                          (*signature, etc*)

P.S. I'm practically speechless, but could whisper a hearty "thank
     you" for your check for $131.32 to clean up that balance on
     your June purchases.

3. Evaluate the following collection messages. What improvements can you
suggest in each for the discussion stage?

Message 1

Personalized letter throughout.

Dear Mrs. Larson:

This is not a dunning letter. Neither is it an attempt to gloss over
a serious situation with fancy language concealing a strong-arm attempt to pry money out of you.

Distance and time make it impossible for me to come to you for a
friendly chat, so I must ask you to accept this letter as the next
best thing. You owe us $99.50, long past due. You have always paid
your commitments promptly. Therefore, there must be some special
reason for your delay in this case.

I am not so much interested in the cause of this delay as I am in
how we can help you over the rough spot. If one can't look to
friends for help in times of stress, who on earth can one look to—

and I hope our past relationship entitles us to be classed among your friends.

We want our money, of course. But we also want to keep your friendship. I am sure we can accomplish both ends by being entirely frank with each other. What is wrong? What can we do to help you?

Please write me in full, in confidence. Perhaps between us we can work out some plan whereby you can take care of the past-due balance without crowding yourself too much and, at the same time, we can continue to make shipments to take care of your immediate needs.

Message 2

Obvious form letter with inside address and salutation typed in.

You must have a good reason for not having paid anything on your account after our recent letter. But we do not know the reason.

If only you would tell us what the situation is, no doubt some arrangement could be made that would relieve your mind of the worry of an over-due debt, and satisfy us, too.

If you can, send in a part payment with your answer. Whether you can do that or not, at least tell us just what is wrong. Give us a chance to help. What do you say?

Message 3

Personalized inside address and salutation, typewritten body. Dated May 31.

Over a hundred and fifty years ago Sir Walter Scott said, "Credit is like a looking glass which, when once sullied by a breath, may be wiped clear again; but if once cracked can never be repaired." The importance of a good credit rating has not changed today.

The barbecue you bought at Wardman's in January will continue to give many hours of enjoyment as you use it in your backyard this summer. We, however, have become concerned about your account listing that purchase. It is past due almost four months. Because of our satisfactory past dealings with you, we feel there must be something wrong, but you have not indicated this by a response to the other letters sent to you.

Because of your very active participation in community affairs, you can realize the importance of having a high credit rating in order to keep in good standing with the other merchants about town. Your good rating was given to us originally by the Lakeview Merchants' Credit Association, of which we are a member. Our agreement with these people requires that we report all those accounts that are seriously past due. Because this is such a serious action, we always wait with our better customers like you hoping for an explanation or, preferably, payment of the past—due account. In keeping with the Credit Association's requirements, we, however, will have to refer your name to them by June 5.

To keep your credit "glass" from being broken, just mail your check for $81.60 to us in the enclosed prepaid envelope. Then come to the store and see the new attachments and utensils for outdoor cooking, which you will continue to enjoy this summer.

4. Evaluate the following urgency-stage collection messages. Is the wording too strong or not strong enough? Is the writer still trying to help the individual? Does the message accomplish the twofold job of collecting the money and retaining the customer's goodwill?

Message 1

Personalized inside address and salutation, typewritten body. Dated March 8.

It seldom becomes necessary for us to turn an account over to an at—torney for collection. And on those few occasions when circumstances leave us no other alternative, we consider it only fair to tell the customer exactly what we intend to do.

Certainly, you must realize that we have made every effort to be fair and patient in requesting that you settle your January account of $205.40. We have written to you several times, asking that you let us know how we could cooperate with you in getting this indebt—edness straightened out.

Your continued silence leaves us no other alternative than to refer your account to our attorney for collection——a step that we sin—cerely regret. So won't you respond to this final appeal for your cooperation and thereby avoid a procedure that can only mean embar—rassment, inconvenience, and additional expense to you?

Unless we hear from you by March 22, we shall be compelled to trans—fer your account to the office of our attorney. Please use the enclosed reply envelope to let us hear from you.

Message 2

Personalized inside address and salutation, typewritten body. Dated Octo-ber 16.

A short time ago you and Ed Taylor registered in our hotel on Sep—tember 18 and stayed two days, checking out the 20th. The rate on this room is $80 per day. Our clerk, Mr. Newcomer, was on duty (his first day) when you checked out and he made an error and collected for only one day. You still owe us for that, and while Mr. Newcomer wrote you he would have to stand good for the $80 we thot you would send it to us. However you probably didn't give it much thot and perhaps have forgotten it. So we will appreciate your sending this to us at once.

For we are sure you would not intentially dismiss the subject and refuse to pay.

However, if this is not paid by November 1st, we are forced to turn the account over to the American Hotel Association and they would print your name in all the hotel magazines as one not paying hotel bill which would go to every hotel in the U.S.

I know you are a fine fellow and will take care of this. For we do appreciate the visit you made us and we want you to come back next time you are in (*city*). American (*name*) Show is now on. It's a wonderful show. Why don't you come see it.

5. The Denison Tire and Battery Company was established in your town (or city) to provide service stations and small garages with resale merchandise at low prices. You stock first-line merchandise at reduced prices so that your customers can more effectively compete with the large chain stores and discount houses. At the low prices you charge the service stations and garages, all understand that any purchases from you must be paid within 10 days of the delivery date. (Otherwise, you could not afford to keep the prices so low because of the high cost of doing credit business.)

    The CMT Service Station at 1001 Broadway, in a town 20 miles from you, ordered $371.89 worth of tires, batteries, and fan belts on July 14. Your truck delivered them on July 16 and you expected payment no later than July 26. It is now August 1 and the bill has not yet been paid.

    Write to CMT Service Station and remind the owners of the overdue account. Be strict, but remember this is the first time that CMT has been late in payments; perhaps a mere oversight is involved. Ask for payment by return mail; enclose a stamped, addressed return envelope; and try to keep the goodwill of the station management.

6. You are the manager of a swimming school that offers swim lessons as its main service. Nine sessions cost $36. Each class is small, no more than five children. Your office requires parents who sign their children up for lessons to pay a $10 registration fee and the balance—$26—on the first day of the lessons.

    Just recently Mrs. Richards signed three of her youngsters up for lessons. You had a terrible time getting her to pay the registration fee. Although you tell your customers that if they don't pay a registration fee, you cannot hold a space for them, you do not often follow through with the threat, since people usually pay the fee. Mrs. Richards finally did come through with the registration fee, but when the lessons began, she asked if she could wait to pay the $78 balance.

It is now the third lesson and she still hasn't paid. Furthermore, you learn that she placed a fourth child in a class on the second lesson, without paying the registration fee or balance. You checked with the instructor to find out how this happened, and he explained Mrs. Richards said that the office had told the child to be in the class. The instructor was new and didn't realize that such an action was highly irregular.

You must explain to Mrs. Richards that if she wants her fourth child in class, she will have to register and pay the balance. Also, you want to remind her of the outstanding balance. You have tried to telephone her, but no one ever answers. She didn't accompany the children for their last lesson, either. She owes you $114, including the fees for the fourth child, and you want to collect. Write a letter that will get the money and at the same time keep the goodwill of Mrs. Richards. You feel she has plenty of money because she lives in a very exclusive residential area and you notice her name often on the society page of the local newspaper.

7. As controller for Apex Corporation, manufacturers of plastic toys and specialties, you need today to write a personalized collection letter. You have just received today (July 25), from the U&I Distributors, a check for $182.37 in payment of your May 5 invoice of $213.16. You note they have deducted $4.26 cash discount, which you can't allow because of late payment. With terms of 2–10 E.O.M., this invoice should have been paid by June 10; but this customer's check was dated and mailed more than a month later. Also you need to know why they deducted the $26.53; so far as your records show, there is no such amount anywhere. Write them an appropriate inquiry and request for their payment in full.

8. You are a "collector" in a department store. The delinquent account of Mr. Jonah Y. Burns (228 Park Dr., Brooklyn, NY 11297) was turned over to you two months ago. At that time, Mr. Burns's account (#567-555-7601) was four months overdue and he owed the store $450.20 for purchases made five to six months ago.

Your first step was to call Mr. Burns for an explanation of why he had not made payment. Mr. Burns was apologetic and sounded somewhat embarrassed, as his account had never been delinquent before. He explained that his family had some unexpected medical bills and that he had been laid off his job in a manufacturing firm for two months because of a labor strike against a supplier. As a result, he had gotten behind in his payments to all his creditors.

As skillfully as you could, you tried to reassure Mr. Burns that your store wanted to be fair and could appreciate his problem. You offered to work out a repayment plan which would stop the collection messages and help him recover slowly. Mr. Burns agreed to pay $75 per month on the account until it was paid off. You confirmed the agreement in a letter and, the following week, you received a check from Mr. Burns for $75. However, you did not receive his check this month and your efforts to talk to him by phone have failed. (Either no one answers the phone or, when someone does answer, you are told that Mr. Burns is not available.)

Now you must write a letter to Mr. Burns to ask why he has broken his promise. Because you believe that Mr. Burns sincerely wants to take care of his account, you will offer to keep the agreed-upon repayment plan in effect if he sends you a check for $75 or more within a week and if he continues to send monthly checks until the account has been cleared. Write the letter, using the appropriate appeals.

9. You are credit and collection manager of the Uptown TV and Electronics Sales Company. Yours is one of the three major such stores in the city. Mr. Myron Jackson, a resident of your city, has been a credit customer of yours for six years, and his record is "good."

On February 10 this year, Mr. Jackson bought a portable tape recorder for $95.50 and charged it to his account. March 1 you sent him a bill for this amount, due March 10. April 1, since you had not heard from him, you sent a second bill. May 1 you sent a third bill, with a sticker at the bottom saying, "Did you forget? Please mail us a check now—while you have it in mind." On June 10 the account is considered 90 days overdue. Address a discussion letter to Mr. Jackson, offering to help any way you can. Make the basic purpose of your letter a reply from him—either a remittance, a letter, a phone call, or a personal visit. Prepare the letter as a form message with a personal inside address and salutation. Make it sound personal, but write it so that the body is applicable to any "good" customer with an account 90 days overdue.

10. Prepare a second urgency-stage collection letter for Mrs. James Underwood, 432 West College Avenue, Fort Washington, PA 19034. (You are assistant credit and collection manager for Millstream Contemporary Furniture Showcase of Allentown, Pennsylvania.) Millstream's policy is to repossess furniture after the fifth payment is missed unless the customer and you can agree on and implement a reasonable alternative payment plan.

Four weeks ago, you notified Mrs. Underwood that repossession of her dining room suite, according to the terms of her conditional sales agreement, would be the logical action to take if she did not bring her account up to date or make some other payment arrangements. She had missed four monthly payments of $120 each and since then has made repeated promises to make payments, but so far she has paid nothing. Now she is five months behind in her payments.

Your letter will be the last letter in the collection series. State clearly (but with an air of reluctance) that her dining room suite will be repossessed two weeks from today unless full payment of $600 is made, or another course of action is mutually agreed upon. For greater impact, this letter will be sent by certified mail and signed by one of the partners in the business. Although you must use the strong fear appeal and develop the unpleasant consequences of your drastic action, you still want to maintain Mrs. Underwood's goodwill as a potential cash customer. Therefore, incorporate one positive appeal.

11. Assume that you are the credit collection manager for the Skyway Airlines, whose air routes extend throughout the United States and overseas. The extensive routes that your planes travel make your airline very popular. In addition to the popularity that your airline already enjoys, your company has attempted to increase its passengers even further by offering a variety of credit plans to encourage travel.

    One plan that your company offers is a credit card that will allow a passenger to charge up to a limit of $800 for trips. The terms of the air travel credit card account are payable in full upon receipt of the bill.

    During the month of September, Ms. Cheryl Farmer, one of your credit card customers, charged several trips to her air travel credit card. The total amount of charges was $560. When Ms. Farmer mailed in her payment for September, she sent only $200 with a note that she would pay the remaining $360 in $120 installments.

    As credit collection manager, write Ms. Farmer a personal letter and request the full balance to be paid within 10 days. She has been a good-pay customer in the past, but you must reluctantly tell her that credit privileges will be withdrawn until full payment is made. After full payment has been received by your office, full credit privileges will be restored. In your letter, reexplain the terms of the credit card account, but try to keep her as a customer. Prepare this letter for the signature of the president of Skyway Airlines.

CHAPTER 15
Goodwill Messages

So far, the messages you have studied are necessary in the usual course of business. Their chief purpose is to take care of day-to-day problems through requests, replies, and announcements. In contrast, the letters and memos covered in this chapter are not absolutely essential or required for the operation of a business. *Their main purpose is to convey a friendly, usually unexpected, message that builds goodwill.*

Besides being friendly, unexpected, and outside the usual course of business, good-will messages have several other characteristics in common. Their organizational plan resembles *a good-news or neutral message*—most important idea first, then brief comments and details (if any), and a final cordial ending (if needed). Like all letters, good-will messages should be honest and sincere and avoid gushiness or wordiness. They can be sent to the reader's home or office. Depending upon their content, destination, and quantity, good-will messages may be typewritten, handwritten (for an extra, personal touch), or printed, perhaps on special paper appropriate for the occasion or season. Unlike most business letters, however, *genuine goodwill messages should not contain statements that try to sell the reader on buying additional products or services.* Most people dislike messages that pose as "goodwill only" letters but that actually have strings attached.

A genuine goodwill letter is almost always favorably received, for at least two reasons:

1. The writer presumably is not sending the message because of some business scheme.
2. The message comes as a pleasant surprise, for the recipient doesn't expect it. Bills will come if money is owed, but a thank-you from the seller for paying promptly or congratulations for winning an honor or celebrating a special anniversary aren't expected.

An unexpected benefit to firms that send goodwill messages is that they are remembered when the recipients want to buy products or services—sometimes months, even years, later.

Thoughtful persons—especially executives—often write messages designed to foster friendly relations with customers, suppliers, and others by:

Congratulating or giving deserved praise

Expressing appreciation

Conveying sympathy

Welcoming and/or offering favors

Showing continuing special concern

CONGRATULATING OR GIVING DESERVED PRAISE

A sincere, enthusiastic note of congratulations or deserved praise—sent promptly—can have an unforgettable impact on the recipient, especially because not many people take the initiative to send such messages.

Congratulatory Messages

The opportunities for congratulating are numerous, for congratulations may relate to any significant news about an individual's business, family, or personal achievements. For instance, you might congratulate a business executive when her firm has opened a new branch, reached its twenty-fifth or fiftieth anniversary, moved to larger quarters, attained a publicized milestone in total volume of sales, received a well-known award for distinguished service to the industry or community, or achieved special favorable publicity. You might congratulate an individual when he or someone in his family has made a significant achievement or won an honor. Among the events and activities that merit congratulations to an individual are: election to an office; promotion; graduation; birth of a child; winning a competitive contest, scholarship, prize; making an outstanding speech; writing a good magazine article or book; performing well in a theater, debate, or other public gathering.

When you write a congratulation, "talk" informally and enthusiastically—without flattery—as you would in a personal contact with the recipient. Focus on your reader instead of on yourself. And write promptly—as soon as possible after you learn the good news. The letters below are examples of various contratulatory messages.

Letter 1

A congratulatory note with good tone and word choice.

> Your promotion to vice president of General Construction Company was great news. I was happy to read about you in this week's Trade Press.
>
> If ever a person deserved company recognition, you do. Your courage and hard work in developing new ways to promote the services of your firm have won the admiration of many, including your competitors.
>
> Congratulations to you—and best wishes for your continued success!

Letter 2

A banker congratulates a businessperson on an election. (A similar note brought the banker who wrote it millions of dollars of business in installment loans.)

Congratulations, (*name*)

. . . upon being elected president of the Westside Lumber Dealers Association, as announced in yesterday's <u>Times</u>.

Under your capable leadership, this organization will reach a new high in activity and service.

Letter 3

A manager congratulates a customer for favorable publicity about the customer's business.

Heartiest congratulations to you on the splendid progress you have made with your poultry plant! It was a real pleasure for me to see your picture and read the feature article about your new cage house in the May issue of <u>American Poultry Journal</u>.

Verna Barns has spoken enthusiastically of your model operation and the excellent job you are doing. This article and its labor-saving suggestions have already been filed for future reference in our "idea" folder.

On my next field trip to Minnesota I want to meet you personally and visit your place. My very best wishes to you for your continued outstanding results with Erving's Chicks.

Sometimes, in addition to congratulating a person, you may want to send along a clipping of a picture or article published concerning the event. Some firms have specially designed folders to which such clippings may be attached with scotch tape or clips. Printed on the outside cover may be a message like "Congratulations," or "You're in the News," together with the company's trademark. For instance, the Carnation Company (dairy products) used a folder that pictured on the outside three carnations under the words, "Carnations to You!" On the inside is an attractive design and this message:

We Read With Interest . . . The attached clipping about you and thought you would be interested in receiving our copy.

At Carnation we are always pleased to read about those people who help make the Northwest such a wonderful place in which to live.

Sending an invitation or an inexpensive gift along with the congratulations, as in letter 4, can be an effective way to build goodwill. However, many other letters that begin with congratulations are actually not true goodwill messages, but disguised or obvious sales messages (with persuasion to buy the firms' goods or services).

Letter 4

A retail store sends layettes with congratulations to parents of twins. [Letter-head states: "Headquarters for clothes from crib to college." Salutation is "Dear Mr. and Mrs. (name)."]

May Barons add their congratulations to the many you have already received. It is a pleasure to send two layettes for your twin arrivals on April 23, 198—.

Your babies will no doubt model all garments beautifully. We are happy to send you these "double congratulations" for your doubly happy event—with compliments of Barons.

You can expect the layettes by mail within a few days. May you have many happy days and years ahead.

Praise for Unannounced Service

In addition to congratulating people for various achievements that are in the news, you may also find reason to give deserved praise for good service that has not been publicized.

For instance, you might compliment your employee(s) on exceptionally fine work—perhaps for achieving a new high record of sales or accuracy or attendance or other performance. Also, as a customer, you might write to a company executive to tell about unusually good service you received from his or her employee(s). Such sincere praise, judiciously given, is appreciated by both the executive and the employees; often the sincere compliments stimulate recipients to do even higher-quality work.

Sometimes your praise of employee service must be general, as in letter 8, because you do not know who performed the work for you.

Letter 5

A bank director praises a laundry's service by writing to its general manager.

You may be glad to know how much I like your Troy Laundry service on my shirts. Every morning I have a pleased grin as I pull one of your immaculately laundered shirts out of the smooth plastic case. Exactly the way I like it!

For the past dozen years or so I've tried several different laundries. But so far Troy has topped them all. I like the way your employees and machines roll my shirt collars neatly, press the shoulders without a wrinkle, AND sew on buttons whenever they're missing.

```
Your TV commercials first attracted Troy to me.  I'm glad to tell you
that I found everything those commercials say is true.  Congratula-
tions--and thanks!
```

Whenever possible, the person(s) you want to praise should be mentioned by their name(s) or identifying number(s). Military personnel also appreciate words of praise, as shown in the following example. A retired *Army* sergeant, after being treated in an overseas *Navy* hospital, wrote to the commanding officer of the overseas U.S. Naval Regional Medical Center, expressing grateful praise for the ''highly qualified and dedicated'' medical personnel. He included names of two doctors and three assistants and then praised also ''the unseen and unsung people in the laboratories, supply, kitchen, and other departments who help make things run smoothly.'' A few days later he received from the commanding officer the following pleasant reply, typewritten on official stationery in memo format:

Letter 6

(Memo) *A Navy commanding officer's reply to a letter of praise.*

```
Your letter in appreciation for the care you received has been for-
warded to all personnel concerned.  A copy will be available in the
appropriate records of those whom you named for commendation.

It is gratifying to know that there are recipients of our health
care delivery efforts who are not only appreciative of our endeavors
but also willing to express that appreciation in a letter.

You can be assured that your expression of satisfaction will enhance
the motivation of the involved staff members not only to continue
their good work but also to strive for improvement.
```

From time to time you will encounter employees—salespeople, bus drivers, police officers, teachers, clerks, and many others—whose service to you is far beyond the call of duty. A sincere note of praise written to the employee's superior has sometimes brought unexpected benefits to an otherwise unnoticed employee. One of many true stories with a happy ending began when an airline passenger wrote a letter to the company president praising an employee (Paula) who had traveled 26 miles in her own car and at her own expense to get medical care for a traveler sick in a Hawaiian town. The president showed the letter to the vice president, who wrote the employee a message of praise (letter 7); and less than four months later Paula received a long-hoped-for promotion. Though her advancement was no doubt earned through years of good work, Paula felt that a letter such as the one the passenger wrote first brought her to the attention of management.

Letter 7

Letter of praise from an airline executive vice president to an employee.

Attached is a copy of a letter President Jack Doe has just received which is indicative of the unusually fine job you are doing for us in (*name of town*). There is no question but that you made a life-long friend for Hawaiian Airlines.

Congratulations, Paula, on a job well done!

I am requesting Bob Cann to make this letter a part of your permanent personnel file.

EXPRESSING APPRECIATION

Everyone likes to know that his or her efforts are appreciated. Throughout your life you will have numerous occasions to express appreciation and thanks. As a business executive, you can express appreciation to customers, suppliers, employees, stockholders, and to many others whose activities relate to your business. Likewise, away from the office, you will have many opportunities to send such personal goodwill messages. Some of these messages will pertain to favors extended repeatedly over a period of time; others will thank for one-time kindnesses.

Appreciation for Favors Extended over a Period of Time

When you write to established customers, you can express appreciation for their patronage, for prompt payment of bills, for recommending your firm to friends, or for other courtesies. Some of these messages may be processed forms. Some contain both appreciation and praise, as in letter 1 below; some also include a small gift or a special privilege, as in letter 2.

Letter 1

Personalized form letter, individually typed, expressing appreciation for a prompt-pay record (sent once to each customer after a three-year good record).

Thank you, Miss Albrecht,

for the fine manner in which you have paid your bills year after year.

Such a customer as you, because of your spotless paying record, seldom hears from our credit department. But the manner in which you have handled your MacDougall account has often been noticed and appreciated. It has also established for you a credit record of which you may be justly proud.

We are pleased to have you as a MacDougall customer, and thank you sincerely for your splendid cooperation.

Letter 2

A computerized, personalized form letter sending appreciation and a lifetime privilege to a preferred credit customer.

We sincerely appreciate how promptly you have paid your (*company name*) account each month. Most certainly you can be proud of the excellent credit record you have established, Mr. Juntwait.

In appreciation to a preferred customer, your new credit card is now good for life!! Your card will be replaced about every two years. This will enable us to update the number of years shown on your card. Also, it will assure that your card remains clean, fresh, and attractive.

I hope you like your new card and that we may have the privilege of serving you for a lifetime.

Though messages such as letters 1 and 2 are usually personalized form letters—with matching insertion of the customer's name and address—some large companies have found it desirable to send printed thanks, as in letter 3. Customers usually appreciate even a printed message—unless the same message arrives every month for six months, tucked in with the monthly statement (as it did for customers of one firm).

Letter 3

A manufacturer's thanks for patronage—printed on special letterhead showing two hands clasped and the word THANKS at the top in red.

Too often in the rush of business life, we forget to say "THANK YOU" so that you can hear it, but you can be sure we always appreciate your patronage. It is our constant aim to please and satisfy you more each time.

Serving you is a real privilege and we are grateful for your confidence in us. Anytime we can be of service to you in any way, just pick up the phone and call us collect at (209) 887-6499.

Some firms send their expressions of appreciation along with seasonal greetings. If appropriate, you can send a seasonal message near a special holiday—New Year, Valentine's Day, Memorial Day, Independence Day, Thanksgiving, Christmas—or any other anniversary that may be meaningful to your recipients. Sometimes a small gift—calendar, ornament, picture—accompanies the greetings. In any case, the message should preferably be unique for the type of business as well as the season, and appropriately different from others the reader may receive during that season.

Letter 4

A company's greeting surrounded by 1-inch facial pictures and names of its 30 employees.

> One of the real joys of the Holiday Season is the opportunity for the expression of goodwill and the exchange of friendly greetings.
>
> In this spirit of friendship and with sincere appreciation for the pleasant business relations we have ejoyed with you, we extend the Season's Greetings and wish you Health and Happiness every day of the New Year . . .

The preceding examples of appreciation messages were sent by business firms. Also, it is good for every successful person to express gratitude to the individuals—perhaps a relative, coach, scout leader, teacher, or former employer— who have contributed something memorable to his or her life—especially if (as in letter 5) years have passed since they met.

Letter 5

A professional person thanks a former Army officer.

> Eight years ago, a young 1st lieutenant at Ford Ord, California, went out of his way to arrange transportation for a young staff sergeant who worked in his section. The transportation was for a unique purpose—not for a pleasure trip or for official duty, but for an education.
>
> Mr. Watters, I want you to know that the favors you did for me have had a great influence on my life. At the time you arranged for a jeep for my use in attending high school classes at Palo Alto, I thought it just another ordinary event in my life. Never did I dream that those twice weekly rides would become my first route on the road to higher education.
>
> The diploma I received was the ticket I needed for admission to college. However, I needed more than that. I needed someone to encourage me and show me the benefits that a college education would give to me. You were persistently trying to convince me of this value during my last days of duty. And though your work was filled with pressure and tension, you always managed to remain calm and ready to cheer me on.

You helped me in so many ways; I'm deeply grateful to you. You'll be glad to know that your wise words didn't go unheeded. I graduated from the University of (*state*) last June and am now in my first year of medical school. Thank you for starting me on the road to a better education. I hope some day to help other youngsters the way you helped me.

Such thank-you messages are an appreciated surprise to their recipients. Often they respond with sincere sentimental notes thanking the persons who wrote to them expressing appreciation for their favor.

Letters of appreciation are also due to people who have spent many hours on a worthy cause—like serving on committees, soliciting funds, or helping with an election campaign. To save expenses, a form letter similar to letter 6 is acceptable.

Letter 6

A successful candidate thanks volunteer assistants. [Instead of a personalized salutation, a general salutation such as "Dear (committee name) Member" could be used to further save time and expense.]

Dear Ms. Tomkins:

During the city campaign just closed, several hundred public-spirited citizens gave of their time and personal service to do the necessary mailing, telephoning, and campaigning which played so vital a part in the election. It is to you, one of these loyal workers, I want to express my sincere appreciation.

The fine work accomplished and the effort which no money can buy, come only from those who feel, as I do, a sense of responsibility for decent city government. I honestly believe that without the many tasks carried out by your committee the result would have been different.

Again I thank you for your part in the campaign and give you my sincere promise that I will do everything in my power to carry on in this city the kind of government for which you worked so diligently.

Thanks for One-Time Favors and Kindnesses

Thanking people promptly for any significant one-time courtesy is desirable for a successful business or professional person, as well as for everyone else with good manners. Whenever possible, a thank-you message should go to the person who: gives a speech without honorarium; writes a letter of recommendation for you; helps you win an honor or award; grants an informative, lengthy interview; sends you a letter of praise or criticism about you, your business, employees, or others in whom you are interested; donates money, gifts, or awards. Some firms even thank new customers for a first purchase or first use of a new charge account.

Of course, circumstances will govern the length and content of these thank-you notes, which may range from a few sentences to several paragraphs. Letters 7 through 10 are thank-you messages which thoughtful, courteous businesspersons have written on various occasions.

Letter 7

A program chairperson thanks a popular speaker–in an unusual, but gracious and sincere, letter.

> At the risk of contradicting the general theme of your talk on "The Freedom of Movement" at the Uptown Business Luncheon meeting last Thursday, may I say that you made captives of all of us.
>
> Believe me, I did not––after noting what was a record attendance for our meeting––speak lightly when I told you that your reputation as a speaker, a scholar, and, above all, a charming guest of honor had preceded you.
>
> I cannot resist adding, with all due apologies to Shaw––"What really flatters a man is that you think him worth flattering." On this point, certainly––and I speak with confidence for the club members and our guests––there is not the shadow of a doubt.
>
> We hope that your future will provide some respite from hard work and that you will be free to join us again. Thank you so very much.

When a customer compliments your firm or employees by letter, you should acknowledge the praise by writing a note similar to letter 8. [See also the commanding officer's memo (letter 6), page 439.]

Letter 8

A company president thanks a customer for her complimentary letter about an employee.

> Thank you very much for your warm and cordial letter of August 29. It is really a pleasure, upon opening the morning mail, to find a letter like yours.
>
> Nothing gratifies me more than to learn that the efforts of our employees are so thoroughly appreciated. Many people are quick to write criticisms, but seldom does anyone take the time to say something nice. So it is always pleasing to hear from the many, many people who are satisfied.

```
We will do our best to continue to provide you with the service you
like.
```

Criticisms should also be acknowledged courteously. A large, nationally known publishing firm, for instance, sends a card labeled "Post-o-gram" with this mimeographed message: "We appreciate your comments on (name of book) and the interest which prompted you to write. If we may serve you any time in the future, please let us know." Some acknowledgments of criticisms should include—in addition to thanks—also an apology and perhaps brief resale on the firm's products or services.

For thank-you messages that acknowledge money donations, the explanation section usually should include a few details telling the success of the campaign or how the funds are being used, so that the donors will feel good about having contributed. If you are an officer in an organization that must solicit donations year after year, appreciative messages similar to letters 9 and 10 may well serve as incentives for future donations.

Letter 9

(Memo) *A plant manager thanks employees for generous contributions.*

```
TO:      All employees
FROM:    John Mains, Manager, Plant 2
SUBJECT: Plant 2 UGN Contributions 198_

On behalf of the United Good Neighbor Fund I thank all of you who so
generously contributed to our UGN campaign.

This year, our plant had approximately the same number of contribu-
tors as last year, but a 21% increase in contributions! Our company
goal was a 9% increase. Obviously we have substantially exceeded
that amount.

Thanks again for your strong support at a time when it is needed
more than ever.
```

Letter 10

The president of a civic charity board thanks donors.

```
THANK YOU!     THANK YOU!     THANK YOU!

Words cannot adequately express our deep appreciation for the gift
you sent in response to our Christmas letter for the poor. Because
of kindhearted friends like you . . .

    Many hungry fathers, mothers, little children have enjoyed a spe-
    cial Christmas dinner—surely they are thinking, "THANK YOU."
```

```
And the shabbily dressed--as they left with a "change of clothing"
   bundle under arm--are surely thinking, "THANK YOU."

And the children--if you could have heard their cheers of joy as
   they opened their packages--are surely thinking, "THANK YOU."

They are all grateful there are "people who care." Thank you for
your generosity and thoughtfulness. You can take satisfaction in
knowing that your contributions have helped bring happiness to these
deserving people.
```

CONVEYING SYMPATHY

When people suffer a serious misfortune, they may be encouraged by messages of sympathy from business associates as well as from personal friends. Because they pertain to sad or unpleasant circumstances, goodwill letters of this type are much harder to write than those already discussed. However, in times of distress, the recipient may value these messages even more highly than expressions of congratulation or thanks.

You can express condolence to a customer, competitor, colleague, business friend, or employee. The occasion may involve a death, accident, loss of material possessions (such as a business wiped out by fire or flood), sickness, major operation, or other misfortunes that can happen to an individual. Expressions of sympathy can be shown by cards, flowers, attendance at a funeral, offers of tangible help, visits, written messages, or a combination of several. This section concentrates on the individual messages you can write expressing sympathy.

If you are writing for your company and the relationship is purely a business one, your secretary can type the message on letterhead stationery. Otherwise, use your own stationery and write (preferably not type) what you want to convey.

Although you *cannot mechanically follow a set outline* for expression of sympathy, here are *suggestions* to consider:

1. Begin with the main idea—sympathy and identification of the problem (such as accident, death, or loss of business).
2. Add only those details, if any, that are desirable for the circumstances. (For example, when writing to a survivor, you might express how much the survivor meant to the deceased.) Make all statements restrained and sincere.
3. Stress the positive—the good characteristics and best contributions of the deceased or ill person (if you knew him or her)—rather than the negative (pain, suffering, distress).
4. Offer assistance, if appropriate, but don't dwell on details. Perhaps you will offer to lighten a customer's monthly payments, move a due date forward, or make your warehouse available to a friend whose factory burned down.

Omit such business matters as the amount the customer owes you, how long a debt is past due, or similar subjects which can and should be taken care of in another letter.

5. End on a pleasant, positive, reassuring idea, perhaps looking to the future. Below are acceptable messages of condolence.

Message 1

Memo telling employees about the sudden death of a coworker.

```
TO ALL EMPLOYEES:

We are saddened by the death of Thor Bjornsen. Thor was killed in a
private-plane accident last Friday en route to a conference. Funeral
services will be held tomorrow at (name) funeral home, 1111 Broadway
Avenue, at 1:00 p.m.

Thor was one of the finest chaps in the company--always helping oth-
ers, especially newcomers. He was tops in his field and was generous
and kind. We will all miss him.

Thor's family does not want flowers for him; so arrangements have
been made with the Children's Orthopedic Hospital of (city name) to
receive sums for a memorial fund. Checks are to be made payable to
that hospital. Address contributions to Thor Bjornsen Memorial, 333
Ridgeway Road, attention of Mrs. Jackson.
```

Message 2

A personnel director's condolence to a widowed customer (whose wife he had never met personally).

```
With profound sorrow we have just learned of the death of your wife.

Though there is little one can say or do to lessen the grief that
must be yours, we want you to know the heartfelt sympathy of all
your friends at Boardson's is with you.

We hope that the cherished memories you have of your many years to-
gether will comfort you in the months ahead.
```

Message 3

Sympathy letter to a business friend whose store burned to the ground.

```
Dear Joan

The announcement on television yesterday about the widespread fire
in your buildings distressed us greatly. I want to convey our sympa-
thy to you and your employees.
```

```
If there's anything that I as an individual can do to help you at
this time, please call me (here at the office: 894-6666, Ext. 562,
or at home: 445-2323 evenings). Also you're welcome to use (at no
charge, of course), our company's Lander Street warehouse (about 500
sq. feet) to store any materials during your reconstruction period,
and our conference rooms for offices and meeting places as long as
you need them.

All the employees at the (name) Company join me in wishing you a
fast recovery.
```

If Joan were an out-of-town customer with an outstanding balance on her account, the sympathy message might have included an offer like the following to replace part of the second paragraph:

```
If we can help you by extending your credit terms and the payment
date on your account, just let me know. I'll consider it a privilege
to come to your aid to show——even in a small way——how much we have
appreciated your friendship and business through the years.
```

WELCOMING AND/OR OFFERING FAVORS

Some of the good-news messages discussed in Chapter 8—for instance, those granting credit or acknowledging first orders—include a welcome to the customer and some grant favors that the customer asked for. Also, many sales letters offer a favor or gift. All those messages are necessary in the daily course of business operations.

In contrast, the welcome and favor-offering letters discussed in this chapter are those "extra" messages that are not absolutely essential but are written mainly to build goodwill. The favors are freely offered, not written in answer to a request or to sell.

Sometimes these welcome messages go to persons who have not yet dealt directly with your firm or perhaps not with your department. Among them are messages you may send to newcomers in a city or state, to new employees in your firm, or to new "customers" of an organization whose work is related to that of your firm.

Letter 1

A secretary of state welcomes a new incorporator in the state.

```
Your name has been listed as one of the incorporators in a filing
just made in my office, and I am pleased to extend a warm welcome to
you.

It is a real pleasure to have been of service to you and your fellow
incorporators in a matter which reflects your confidence in the con-
tinued growth and prosperity of our state.
```

You have our sincere good wishes that you will find this confidence amply rewarded in the success of your venture.

A letter from an officer of any business firm, welcoming a distinguished newcomer to the area and offering assistance is usually a low-pressure *sales* message. Besides the welcome, it may include a city map, real estate guides, and a pamphlet or paragraph about the institution's services or products. Though such letters are useful for business, they are *not strictly goodwill* messages.

However, a welcoming message like letter 2 to a new customer can be considered strictly goodwill; it does not try to sell the reader on additional services but merely contains *resale* material (as in paragraph 2). Also, letter 3 is a goodwill message—to let a once "lost" customer know that renewed patronage is appreciated.

Letter 2

A savings and loan officer welcomes a new savings account customer.

It is a pleasure to welcome you to membership in our organization. Many thanks for opening a savings account with First Federal.

Here your savings are safeguarded by careful management, investment in sound home loans, and insurance of accounts by the Federal Savings and Loan Insurance Corporation, an agency of the United States government. At the same time, we maintain ample reserves for the purpose of meeting withdrawals, should you need all or any part of your savings; and in addition you earn an above-average dividend on your savings, compounded semiannually at the regular rate.

You receive the same personalized services at either of our offices—the Mountview Savings in the Southside Shopping Center or the downtown office.

Please call on me or any member of our staff when we can be of service to you. Our telephone number is 543-4444.

Letter 3

A credit manager welcomes back a long-absent customer.

The return of a good friend is as happy an occasion in the business world as it is in one's private life. Your recent purchase here at Baylor's was the first to be charged to your account for a considerable time . . .

and we take this opportunity to welcome you again to the Baylor Store. Thank you for your patronage.

```
You can be sure that it is our sincere wish to serve you to your
complete satisfaction.
```

The last example, letter 4, is an offer of a favor at "no charge or obligation" to noncustomers and customers. This message contains no direct sales plug for the writer's organization and does not ask the reader to buy or sell stock through the writer's firm. Thus, although the reason for the letter is probably to promote sales eventually, here it is mainly a goodwill message.

Letter 4

A stock brokerage firm's vice president offers a free current report. (A small, printed fill-in form is at the top of the letter; salutation is personalized.)

```
I'd like to offer you a Thompson Fynch service that many of the in-
vestors in (city name) have come to value highly: the opinion of our
research department about any stock listed on the New York Stock Ex-
change. If you'll just write the name of the stock on the form above
and mail it to our Central Information Bureau, I'll get an up-to-
date report from our research department back to you just as
promptly as I can.

Then, if you have any questions about the report, please call me at
(206) 555-2222. I'll be glad to make an appointment at your conve-
nience.

We are pleased to do this, (name), whether you have an account with
us or not. There is no charge or obligation for this service. In
fact, the only charge you ever pay at Thompson Fynch is the minimum
commission when you buy or sell securities.
```

SHOWING CONTINUING SPECIAL CONCERN

Another type of goodwill message shows that you are sincerely interested in maintaining confidence in your firm's goods and services. To demonstrate your concern, you can write various follow-up requests and announcements to customers, stockholders, suppliers, or employees. The purpose of these goodwill messages is to get feedback on products used or returned, to maintain the firm's good image, or to help the customer get the best use from your products which she or he has already bought.

For example, some firms systematically send messages similar to letter 1 to solicit comments from their product users and maintain quality control.

Letter 1

A manufacturer of outboard motors strengthens goodwill by inviting purchasers' comments.[1]

[1] Courtesy of Evinrude Motors, Milwaukee, Wisc.

HOW DO YOU LIKE YOUR EVINRUDE?

A good part of the boating season has slipped past since you bought your motor.

We hope you've had the opportunity to log a lot of pleasant hours with it. We're going to ask a favor of you—a report from you on the "good conduct" of your motor. (Or your frank criticism, if you have any you wish to make.)

For over 65 years our steady aim has been to make the most perfect outboard motors that can be built. We've spent millions on engineering, fine production facilities, and the most rigorous testing any manufacturer can give his products.

But there is one test that really tells how successful we have been. And that is your complete satisfaction, as the owner and user of our product.

Will you please send us your comments? For your convenience, a blue "stamped" envelope is enclosed—and if you like, simply jot your reply on the back of this letter.

Thank you—here's wishing you many seasons of happy boating.

If your corporation has a widely dispersed management group and a large number of stockholders, many of whom cannot attend the annual meetings, and you want to exchange viewpoints with these stockholders, you might consider writing a goodwill-building message similar to letter 2. (Each has a personalized salutation.)

Letter 2

The senior officer of a nationwide public utility invites stockholders to have an individual visit with a management representative.[2]

Across the nation in recent years, Bell System management men and women have met with over half a million AT&T share owners like you in their homes and offices for face-to-face discussions of the telephone business. Viewpoints have been exchanged, questions cleared up and in many instances assistance provided on matters of mutual interest.

These informal discussions have benefited our owners and your Company to such an extent that visits with share owners have been made a part of management's responsibility in Bell System Companies.

With over three million share owners we cannot hope to visit them all at once or in a short period of time. So, from month to month

---

[2] Courtesy of Mr. Charles E. Wampler, formerly vice president and secretary of American Telephone and Telegraph Company, New York.

```
and on a random basis, we select a number of share owners to be
visited.

We would like very much to visit you. I am arranging, therefore,
to have one of our Bell System management representatives in your
area get in touch with you in the near future for this purpose.
```

Still another excellent way to show concern for your customers (and others) is by anticipating (hopefully forestalling) complaints. If you discover that your company (or a supplier) has made an error which directly affects customers, you have the opportunity to admit the mistake to everyone who may be affected by it—before any customer finds it necessary to ask for an adjustment. Those who have done this (rather than staying silent, hoping only a few people will discover the error) have usually been pleasantly surprised at the loyalty, appreciation, and fairness of their customers.

Among the many examples of the goodwill-building power of announcements made to forestall complaints, two are mentioned below:

1. Following a serious storm a subsidiary of Bell Telephone Company sent an inquiry to customers asking them to name, on an enclosed reply card, the period for which they had no service and to state how many days they wanted the company to deduct from their phone bill. Most customers complimented the firm for its forthright message (and its "excellent emergency action"), and they appreciated but rejected the firm's offer to reduce the phone bill.
2. A candy department manager, upon discovering after Christmas that about 50 out of 200 charge-customer orders for a certain quality gift-box candy had been incorrectly filled with slightly lower-quality candy than ordered and sent to the customers' friends, wrote to all 200 customers offering to send a free replacement. As the store did not know which of the 200 customers had been incorrectly served, the manager invited everyone whose friend had received a gift box with a certain code number at the bottom to ask, on an enclosed reply card, for a free box of the ordered candy; she or he need not return the original. Although obviously at least 25 percent of the customers could have honestly asked for a replacement, less than 5 percent did so. All others who replied—including those whose friends had received the "wrong" candy—thanked the store, commented on the good-quality candy their friend enjoyed, and declined the free offer.

The managers who sent these messages were sure that the small cost of their letter was far outweighed by the resulting goodwill.

In the first paragraph of this type of announcement you frankly admit the mistake and sometimes announce the "good news" adjustment that you will make. The explanation section contains an apology (if it isn't in the opening) plus whatever details are desirable for showing how the error occurred. Like other adjustment-granting letters, this announcement should emphasize positive aspects and convey a sincere desire to serve the customer, as in letter 3.

Letter 3

The customer service manager of a national oil company announces credit to customers' accounts for an error made by a supplier (completely processed form).

Dear (*firm name*) Credit Card Customer:

We owe you an apology . . . and have credited your account for $9.83.

The hot tray that was shipped to you in response to your recent order was not the model pictured in the advertising brochure. This error on the part of the supplier of the hot tray has just recently been called to our attention.

Since you did not receive the correct merchandise, we are crediting your account with the total cost of the tray you purchased as a meaningful way of correcting this error. Please keep your hot tray as a small gift from (*firm name*).

If you would still like to receive the advertised hot tray, simply check the box and sign and mail the enclosed order card.

We will be glad to send the tray to you as soon as possible and bill you accordingly.

You can always depend on (*firm name*) for top quality.

SUMMARY

A goodwill letter is one that you don't *have* to send and that doesn't include a sales pitch or have strings attached. These messages congratulate, praise, thank, greet, sympathize, welcome, offer favors, or show special concern for the reader—without including any obvious sales material. The message plan is direct—main idea, details, courteous close.

EXERCISES

1. Below are two messages about free gifts the companies offer. Is each one truly a goodwill message? If not, why not? What do you like or dislike about each one?

   a. The Next Issue of (*name of free booklet*)

   will be mailed on Monday, October 25. The (*name of booklet*) is sent free each month to business firms employing three or more department heads.

   Before we address the envelopes for this issue, we want to make sure that our mailing list is complete and accurate. On the

sheet that comes with this letter, you will find reproductions
of <u>all</u> the Addressograph plates we have for members of your
staff.

Please take just a minute to go over the list. Make any corrections called for. Cross out the names of people who are no
longer there. Add the names of members of your staff for whom we
don't have plates.

The (*name of booklet*) is "different." Each issue is of direct interest to supervisors and managers working with people daily.

Please correct and mail the sheet today—in the enclosed envelope. No stamp is needed. You and your associates will then be
sure of getting (*booklet*) free throughout the year.

b. We know you will enjoy having this special edition of our 198_
color calendar, compliments of (*name*) Travel Service. We hope
that it proves to be both useful and convenient in your office.

This affords us the opportunity to let you know that we appreciate the privilege of serving as your travel agent. We thank you
for your past business and we look forward to hearing from you
whenever we can assist you with future travel plans in connection with business or pleasure.

We handle all forms of transportation—air, rail, steamship,
bus, as well as reservations for hotels, motels and U-drive service. Our daily delivery service to any downtown business office
is a time-saver for you and your staff, and we want you to feel
free to make use of it.

ONE CALL DOES IT ALL! – 333-0020

2. As assistant customer service manager of a national airline, you need to
write a letter to accompany a lost sorority pin which you are returning to its
owner. The pin had fallen under one of the coach seats on Flight #742 to
Chicago, June 29. No one wrote to report this lost pin; thus there has been
considerable delay in establishing ownership. You first had to identify the
sorority and then the chapter and where it was located, all of which was
time-consuming. However, you were eventually successful in learning this
traveler's identity through Joanne Jones, president, Alpha Chapter at
Texas State College.

   Ask the recipient of your letter to sign an attached lost property card
and return it to you. Will your reply be a goodwill letter with no strings
attached? Or will you include some sales talk and a look forward to future
business?

3. The following message was sent by the general manager of a hotel to all
business executives who had attended a national convention there seven

months earlier. Is this letter a goodwill builder? Why or why not? What improvements can you suggest? (Each letter has a personalized salutation.)

May I take this opportunity to thank you for your patronage to (*name*) Hotel, and all of us here sincerely hope that you enjoyed your visit to (*city*).

Have you any friends or business associates that might be coming to (*state*)? I would appreciate it very much if you would give me their names and addresses on the enclosed card so that I may send them a brochure of our hotel and invite them to stay with us while they are in (*state*).

The staff of the (*hotel name*) joins me in looking forward to your future visits with us.

4. Assume that one day six years from now you happen to read, in a professional or business journal, about a former college classmate of yours. She has been chosen to deliver the main address at the next regional convention of a national organization you belong to. You're pleased that she has gained a distinguished reputation as a technical expert in the field—all in the few years since her graduation. Write her an appropriate note of congratulation.

5. As manager of a wholesale hardware firm with customers in three states, you have just heard that Mr. Archie Oltimer will retire next month, after being in business for 45 years and your customer for 15. Mr. Oltimer's store is over 500 miles from your office—in a town not served by an airline—and you have never met him personally. However, his orders have come regularly through the years and his payments have been prompt. Now he has sold his store to a younger man. Write him a sincere message of appreciation.

6. Evaluate the following letter; is it candid, sincere, and businesslike, yet also a goodwill builder? Assume the firm is a national manufacturer of calculating machines. Salutation is "Good morning, Mrs. Mardon."

We got to thinking about you the other day, and we realized, though it hardly seems believable, that a whole year has whizzed by since we shipped you the two Model XX Comptometers! But the calendar says so, all right, and we are impressed with how times flies.

Now, on this first anniversary of your ownership of the two comp—tometers, let's just check to make sure they are giving you the service you had expected and paid for. We want you to know we think of you.

Are these machines doing their job, Mrs. Mardon? Do your operators like them? Have any problems with them? Any questions you want an—swered? Do the machines need a year's checkup?

```
Just jot down any remarks from your operators or yourself on the
enclosed, self-addressed card and shoot it right back to us. We'll
gladly help you promptly. And you'll be helping us to maintain the
quality you expected when you decided to buy your two Model XX's.
```

7. This assignment can be a message you will actually mail. (If your instructor approves, you can hand in your carbon copy and mail the original.) Write a sincere letter of appreciation to one person who has had a profound and lasting good effect on your life. Perhaps he or she encouraged you to stick with a job when you almost quit, helped pay your college expenses, or contributed in any other special way(s) to your well-being and achievements.

8. As manager of the foreign department of Your City Bank, write a congratulatory letter to Mr. Paul Mifford, recently elected president of Pan Xenia, international business honorary at his college chapter. Assume any other pertinent facts.

9. Rewrite the following congratulatory letter so that it has the appropriate you-attitude and tone.

```
I have just read that you have been promoted to vice president of
your company.

I am sure your attainment unequivocally substantiates the exemplary
service you are giving your employer. I believe you can be justi-
fiably proud of your outstanding performance in the industry.

I forward my heartiest congratulations and wishes for your con-
tinued success in your endeavors.
```

10. You are business manager of the Friedman Jewelry firm, registered jewelers in the American Gem Society. The largest bank in your city has just bought from you 35 of your $150 watches, which the bank will present to its employees who become members of the Quarter Century Club (25-year employees of the bank). The watches will be presented at a banquet two weeks from today. Your jewelry store has agreed to take care of all the service on these watches for one year free of charge. Write a letter of congratulation to be addressed individually to each new Quarter Century Club member, and include whatever goodwill-building material about your store is desirable. Make these people feel welcome to use your services.

11. Assume you graduated from college six years ago and have been successfully employed in work you like. You have also been active in a volunteer organization that helps a clinic for handicapped people in your community. Recently you were appointed chairperson of a fund raising committee which decided to send persuasive letters to three groups of people asking

for donations. Because you felt you needed some (free) expert advice on your three rough drafts, you phoned your former business communication instructor. Though that particular week happened to be a time when this professor was heavily involved with responsibilities and deadlines on previous professional commitments, he or she willingly devoted an entire evening to your drafts and rewrote one of them almost completely.

During the past three weeks since these letters were mailed they have already raised $2,400 in donations, and the committee plans to use them again and again for future fund raising campaigns. Write a letter of appreciation to your former professor for time and help given. Perhaps you can assume some definite equipment or services that the $2,400 have already purchased, and invite this professor to come visit the facilities at the clinic. Be sincere in your thanks and comments.

12. You are manager of a large sporting goods store located in a wealthy suburb of a large city. Many avid weekend hunters come into your shop. Every year you compile a record of names and addresses of customers who purchased shells and hunting equipment during that year. In the past the state game department has published annually a brochure listing the hunting season dates for the coming year. This year, to cut down on expenses, the state has eliminated these brochures, but has sent a complete brochure to all sporting goods stores explaining the regulations and the season dates. You would like to write a letter telling your customers the season dates and explaining to them that you have a complete listing of the regulations posted in your shop if they would like more information.

13. Write (or revise) a goodwill message that relates to one of the following situations.
   a. Condolence to the wife or husband of a long-time employee who died.
   b. Message to someone in the hospital because of an automobile accident.
   c. Thanks to a customer for being prompt in making loan payments the last three years. (Assume a bank or savings and loan association.)
   d. A message to accompany a clipping you're sending to a business friend.

14. As customer relations manager of the National Products Company, write a check-up letter to all business executives who have bought one of your machines to be used in their offices. (Assume any machine with which you are familiar.) Your letter is to be mailed one month after a machine is sold—to check on performance and to catch minor annoyances before they become major grievances. You want to make sure the machine is doing a good job for the reader, or you might want to know if the operators have any questions you can help answer. Will you enclose something for easy answering? Make sure your readers understand that your purpose is to help maintain the high standards for which your products have been famous, not to sell more machines.

15. The following letter from an auditor to the office manager of business firms he visited uses a play on words. Do you think the tone is appropriate and the message pleasingly unique? What do you like or dislike about the letter? It is dated December 18 and addressed individually, "Dear Mr. (name)."

        I enjoyed the friendly atmosphere of your office during the brief
        time I was with you this year. Then your financial statements were
        done and I was on my way——to another office and another short
        story.

        With 198_ almost gone it's time again for a statement——this time a
        personal one in which friendship and goodwill rank high.

        As I look back over my own accounts I know that many things have
        been left undone. With the end of the calendar period coming near,
        it's time to stop and credit them to your account.

        I wish to enter my appreciation for the courtesies you and your
        staff showed me, the pleasure I felt in working with all of you,
        and the "thank you" I thought of but might have left unsaid.

        Let me record all these, so my thoughts will be clear, while I send
        you BEST WISHES for a HAPPY NEW YEAR.

16. You are public relations manager of a firm that manufactures lighting fixtures. Yesterday you read in *Illuminating News,* a trade journal, that one of your good customers—Patrice O'Leary—has just opened her fifth lighting goods store in Florida this month. The article states that the store is considered the largest and most modern store of its kind in the Southeast, in keeping with the tremendous growth of the area. You recall that eight years ago, when you were credit manager, you first opened Ms. O'Leary's charge account with your factory; she then had only one store. Through the years she has placed increasingly larger orders with your firm and has paid them all promptly. Though your lighting fixtures have had a part in her success, resist the temptation to claim credit yourself or to dwell on the merits of your products. Write Ms. O'Leary a letter of congratulations.

Reports

PART FOUR

CHAPTER 16

Business Reports:
Types, Preparation, Presentation

Thousands of modern businesses need various reports to carry on efficient operations. In almost any kind of responsible business job—whether you are a management trainee, a salesperson, an accountant, a junior executive, or a vice president, you may have to write reports. Your communication effectiveness and, often, your promotion and salary increases are affected by the quality of reports you write.

Three chapters in this text are devoted exclusively to written reports. As you proceed in your study of reports, you will see how some parts of Chapters 1 through 6 and Appendix B also apply to reports. You may occasionally find a brief review of them helpful, because a sound understanding of the communication process, business writing principles, planning steps, and formats of related business messages is desirable for effective report writing.

This chapter provides a general overview of business reports. It includes: what reports are and how they are classified; how to plan, prepare, organize, outline, and illustrate the report body; and how to achieve the C qualities in written reports.

Chapter 17 illustrates short, informal reports; and Chapter 18, long, "formal" reports.

MEANING AND CLASSIFICATION OF BUSINESS REPORTS

Because of the wide variety of reports, they can be and have been defined and classified in a variety of ways.

What Is a Business Report?

Although the following statement is only one of many good ways to define a report, it covers adequately the types of reports presented in this book: A business report is an impartial, objective, planned presentation of facts to one or more persons for a specific, significant business purpose. Usually a report pertains to a more complex topic than is covered by the typical one-page factual business letter or memorandum. It requires more attention to organization, visual aids, and other techniques for improving readability. Also, to be impartial and objective a report presents accurate, reliable information logically, without emotional appeals.

Reports travel upward to supervisors and management policymakers; downward and horizontally to those who carry out the work and policies; and outward (outside the firm) to stockholders, customers, the general public, and perhaps to government officials. A report may be written or oral, but most significant reports are written. The report facts may pertain to events, conditions, qualities, progress, results, investigations, or interpretations. They may help the receiver(s) understand a significant business situation; carry out operational or technical assignments; and/or plan procedures, solve problems, and make executive decisions.

How Are Business Reports Classified?

You can classify business reports in at least six different ways—according to:

1. *Origin:* . . . whether authorized or voluntary; also whether private or public. Authorized reports are requested or authorized by another person. The voluntary report you write on your own initiative. The private report originates in a private business firm; the public report originates in a government, school, or other publicly financed office.
2. *Function:* . . . whether to inform or to analyze. The informational report merely presents the facts and a summary—without analyzing, interpreting, drawing conclusions, or making recommendations. Among the informational reports that have special names are "progress reports."

   The analytical report presents facts, analyzes and interprets them, and makes conclusions as well as recommendations if needed. Some analytical reports have special labels—such as "recommendation report," "proposal," and "justification report." They usually end with a recommendation.
3. *Subject Matter:* . . . usually in keeping with the department from which the report originates. Examples include: accounting, advertising, collection, credit, engineering, finance, insurance, marketing, operations, personnel, production, statistical, and technical reports.
4. *Frequency of Issue:* . . . whether periodic or special. The periodic report comes out at regular intervals, such as daily, weekly, monthly, or yearly. The special report involves a single occasion or unique situation.
5. *Formality:* . . . whether formal or informal. Formal reports are generally long and about complex problems. Informal reports are generally short. However, meanings of the terms "long" and "short" vary depending upon circumstances as illustrated in Chapters 17 and 18. General differences in the main parts of formal and informal reports are noteworthy here.

   Formal reports always include—in addition to the body—some or all of these prefatory and supplemental parts:

   Prefatory parts—cover; title fly; title page; letters of authorization, acceptance, approval, transmittal; acknowledgments; table of contents; table of tables; synopsis, abstract, or executive summary

   Body—introduction, text, terminal section

   Supplemental parts—appendix, bibliography, index

   Informal reports usually include only the body. Some informal reports, however, may have a title page, transmittal, and appendix.
6. *Type or Appearance:* . . . mainly influenced by report length and formality. Reports **a, b, c,** below, are popular types of informal, short reports; **d** is the formal, long report.

    a. *Memorandum report* uses memo format with TO, FROM, SUBJECT, DATE heading; is usually single-spaced, and sent within the organization.

    b. *Letter report* uses letter format with letterhead, inside address, salutation, complimentary close, signature area, and reference section; is usually single-spaced; and may go outside or inside the organization.

    c. *Printed report* has printed headings, instructions, blank lines, and spaces for the writer to fill in pertinent specific facts and figures. It is used both inside and outside the firm, is a timesaver, and is adaptable to a tremendous variety of uses. Among well-known examples are: salespersons' expense vouchers, job application forms, Internal Revenue Form 1040, automobile accident reports, insurance claim reports, employee appraisal reports.

    d. *Formal report* is usually longer than the **a, b, c** reports, above, and includes parts other reports don't have. It is used both inside and outside the organization.

In some reports a *standardized format* may be desirable. For example, the report writer may use the same standardized headings repeatedly for any one type of report, but begin with a blank sheet of paper, not printed sheets. This method is especially useful whenever the same type of information is needed in every report but the facts under each heading are likely to vary significantly in length and space needed, depending upon each situation.

    You have probably noticed that the various classifications do not place reports into mutually exclusive categories. In fact, one report may be part of all the categories—as, for example: an authorized monthly analytical memo report from the marketing department, written in a standardized form.

PREPARATION BEFORE WRITING REPORTS

As with letters and memos, you want to consider the planning steps before you begin to write a report. This planning process is, of course, much more detailed for long, formal reports than for shorter presentations. Nevertheless, for all reports adequate preparation *before* writing involves the following *six important steps* regarding purpose, reader, ideas to include, facts to collect, interpretation, and organization.

Define the Problem and Purpose

The first planning step is to analyze the problem involved and know the purpose of your report. Ask questions like "*What* is wanted?" "*How much?*" "*Why?*" "*When?*" The answers will help you determine your problem, purpose, scope, limitations (in time and perhaps funds), and title of the report. Then try to write your purpose in one concise, clear sentence.

    The central purpose of many business reports often is to help the receiver solve a problem and/or make a decision. For example, if your firm is experiencing too great a turnover of employees, that's a problem. The purpose of the report may be to find out what causes the high turnover and—better yet—how to keep the employees after they have been hired. Your scope might include surveying all employees or a random sample; you might also need to find out how other firms have solved similar problems. Or, in other reports, your problem may be concerned with an investment and a choice between two or more methods, machines, or policies. Your question might be: "Which proposal is better?" "Should we buy, rent, or lease?" "Should we choose *x*, *y*, or *z* machines?" and so on. Thus, the problem and purpose of your report can influence its length, content, and style.

Consider Who Will Receive the Report

Visualizing your reader and his or her needs is an extremely important step in business report writing. Who wants (or needs) this report? Who will read it? How much detail do they prefer? What is the reader's point of view? Experience? Knowledge? Prejudice? Responsibility? Is the recipient an officer of your firm? Stockholder? Customer? Government official? Will the report be sent to several—or perhaps hundreds—of persons at the same time? Will it be passed on from the primary reader(s) to secondary readers? What are their needs and interests?

If your report goes to say, your department supervisor, you can use technical terms and abbreviations used in your area. But if it is routed to other departments within your firm—or if it goes to someone outside the firm, or to your stockholders—your language may have to be nontechnical, with intricate explanations.

Determine Ideas to Include

In short reports this third step may involve merely writing down the general ideas and main topics you'll need to develop in order to accomplish the report's purpose. In long reports a detailed working plan is desirable. For some reports, formulating hypotheses is desirable (even essential) as a basis for determining what information you'll need; and then you will jot down the tentative topic headings in a preliminary, tentative outline.

For instance, if your purpose is to find out what causes the high turnover within the company, you might first jot ideas like these: working conditions, supervision, salaries, promotion policies, fringe benefits. Then you might consider subdivisions of these topics. Working conditions might involve ideas about physical environment (location of offices or factory, conveniences such as desks, chairs, temperatures, lighting, employee lounge, cafeteria), and intangible factors (such as noise, odors, and transportation). This step helps guide you to kinds of facts you'll need to gather.

Collect Needed Material

The fourth step in report preparation is to gather needed facts thoughtfully from reliable sources. For some reports you may have all the data in your head or nearby records. For others you may have to do extensive secondary and/or primary research involving "legwork" in addition to brain work.

Secondary Research

Research through published material is *secondary research*. Publications already in print—books, magazines, newspapers, pamphlets, government documents, atlases, reports, encyclopedias—are known as *secondary data*. A good start for your research may be in company, city, or college libraries, to find relevant materials that have been gathered and reported by other persons. Some researchers have saved their company hundreds of hours—and dollars—by avoiding unnecessary duplication of research and reporting because they first consulted already printed materials. *Caution:* Check your sources' reliability carefully; not everything is true just because it is in print!

Words of advice from experienced researchers and report writers are: Collect all possible data that might be needed. Record your notes on cards or sheets of paper any size you prefer, usually with only one fact or idea on each.

Perhaps you already have your own good system of preparing note cards; that's fine! If you need suggestions, you might find these helpful:[1]

1. At the top of the sheet (or card) place the heading under which the information will be filed. (See your preliminary outline, made in step 3, page 465.)
2. Next, write the data source—author, book name, or title of article and magazine name; edition, publisher, city, state, date, page numbers. (If you already have this biographical information on a master list of sources, you need to write on your notecards only the source number and page. For example, 5:82 means source 5, page 82.)
3. Record (with any of your own abbreviations) the facts you need. To avoid plagiarism carefully indicate whether you are quoting verbatim, paraphrasing, or merely recording the gist in your own summary words. When in doubt, write a little more than you'll need—rather than statements so inadequate or vague that you must discard them later.

Primary Research

To collect *primary data* (that which you "dig up" firsthand from unpublished information), you may use—with permission:

1. Records from your organization's files
2. Original letters, diaries, minutes, reports
3. Questionnaires—mailed, telephone, or taken in person

---

[1] If you need additional details on research methods, see books such as the following which specialize on report writing: Leland Brown, *Effective Business Report Writing,* Van Nostrand Reinhold, New York, 1980; Raymond V. Lesikar, *Report Writing for Business,* 6th ed., Irwin, Homewood, Ill., 1981. Also an extensive bibliography on business and technical writing in *The Journal of Business Communication,* published by the American Business Communication Association, University of Illinois, Urbana, Winter 1975, pp. 33–67, may be helpful to you.

4. Interviews
5. Personal observations—such as counting cars in a parking lot at different hours of the day, observing mannerisms of individuals as they approach a cashier to pay their bills, or witnessing a car accident
6. Experiments—such as comparing two groups in which all factors, except for one variable factor with which you are "experimenting," are the same. This method is common in measuring effectiveness of advertising and communication media.

Sort and Interpret Data

In this fifth step the amount of brain work depends of course on the complexity of your research as determined by purpose and reader needs. In a short, informational report this step may take only a few minutes. In a long, analytical report based on masses of detailed data from many sources, this step may require weeks of study, arranging, and analysis between the first sorting and the final interpreting of data. Your analysis and interpretations should of course be objective, free from your own personal bias (if you have any).

If some (or all) of your facts came from questionnaires, you will need to rearrange and analyze the data after you have tabulated the answers. Column after column of figures, perhaps on computer printouts, are meaningful only after they are carefully analyzed so they can be grouped under appropriate headings. *Always* consider what information is most important to the reader and what is not applicable.

Prepare any desirable charts, graphs, and tables (in rough draft) before beginning to write the report.

Now is also the time to reconsider the logic of your hypotheses and whether any main ideas in your original, tentative outline (in step 3) should be revised. Occasionally, after investigating your primary and secondary sources, you may find that some points in your tentative outline are not logical or possible to complete. Conversely, some areas which should have been included in the outline were omitted. And so you now revise, add, and delete topics where necessary.

Organize Data and Prepare Final Outline

After careful analysis and interpretation, you will organize the findings and make the final outline. But before preparing this important outline, you need to know what constitutes the report body and consider methods of organizing and outlining. These areas are discussed in the next two sections of this chapter.

PARTS OF THE REPORT BODY

One part that every report has is the body. This part includes (or implies) three sections—introduction, text, and terminal section.

Introduction: Eleven Elements

The purpose of the introduction is to orient the reader toward better understanding of the report. You can include in the introduction any of the following elements if they are helpful to the reader(s) and apply to your report:

Authorization	Methodology	Limitations
Problem	Sources	Brief statement of the results
Purpose	Background	Plan of presentation
Scope	Definition of terms	

1. *Authorization* names the person (if any) who requested the report. If it is a voluntary report, this introductory element is omitted. But when you include the authorization, use conversational language—such as, "as you requested" or, "as (name), (title) authorized" rather than stilted words like "pursuant to your request."

2. *Problem* is usually defined early in the introduction. In fact, many introductions begin with the problem and then proceed to the purpose—which is often determined by the problem (see step 1, pages 464–465).

3. *Purpose* must appear in every introduction. It is the most important single element because it should determine what the writer includes in the report. Among other names for purpose are: "objective," "aim," "goal," "mission," "object."

4. *Scope* relates to the boundary of the investigation and of the report. For instance, if you are inquiring by questionnaire what married women customers between 25 and 35 years of age with three or more children think about something—that's your scope. You don't include anyone else.

5. *Methodology* means the method(s) of collecting information. You might get data by reading library materials, by interviews, by survey, by observation, or by experiment. In production reports, you may need to describe apparatus and materials used for experiments.

6. *Sources*—primary and/or secondary—are those that furnished the main information for your report. You may include publications, company records, letters, minutes, documents, interviewees, employees, homeowners, and so forth.

    If you are writing a report of your own experience, you are your own source for the statements made in the report. But if you consulted other sources, you mention them—usually in a general summary statement. (Specifics come later, in the text section and bibliography.)

7. *Background* (or history) of the situation being investigated is sometimes included if the reader needs the information to grasp the overall picture and clearly understand the present discussion.

8. *Definition of terms* is necessary if you use any terms that have several possible interpretations. You need to tell the reader the exact meaning you have in mind. You can define terms in three different places—in the

introduction, in a glossary at the end of the report, or within the text of the report. The introduction is the best place when you have only a few (one to three) terms to define and the meaning dominates throughout the entire report. If you have many definitions, a glossary is the best. Defining each word as you develop the text is also quite acceptable—especially when the discussion of each word being defined doesn't prevail throughout the report.

9. *Limitations* refer to restrictions such as time, money, research assistance, or available data. Without sounding negative, the writer should mention those factors that precluded further investigation.

10. *Brief statement of the results* tells the decision—whether or not to buy, which machine is the best, who is your choice of applicant. Then as the reader reads the details in the text, he or she knows how the facts affect the decision. This element is appropriate only when the terminal section comes at the end of the report body and when revealing the decision before the discussion is psychologically sound.

11. *Plan of presentation* tells the reader in what broad areas (major divisions) the text is developed and in what order the topics will be presented. This preview is usually at the end of the introduction; in a one-page report it may be omitted because the reader can see at a glance what the report covers.

Try to include in your introduction all elements that are desirable for giving your reader the orientation needed, but omit all unnecessary elements. If one or more lengthy elements tend to make the introduction disproportionately long, you can take them out of the introduction and place them separately under specific headings or as part of the appendix.

In short reports the few needed elements may be combined into one or two paragraphs with or without the title Introduction. In some short, periodic reports (especially those covering the same topics every period) you might even omit the introduction if its contents are the same each period and your reader knows them.

For long formal reports the introduction may occupy several pages, but usually less than one-tenth of the entire report. In these long reports the introductory section always has a title—Introduction or a meaningful substitute. Also, subheadings (for example: Problem and Purpose, Scope, Background, Methodology, Plan of Organization) should always be used whenever such guides would be helpful to the reader.

Text: All Necessary Explanation

The longest portion of any report body is the text. In fact, sometimes (in short, routine, periodic reports) the text may be the whole report—if introduction and terminal section are omitted. In this section you discuss and develop the necessary details that help you fulfill the report's purpose. As with all good business writing, include pertinent facts and trim away nonessentials. Anything you think your reader will want to see immediately while reading the text should be in this section. Other materials—such as copies of questionnaires, supporting documents, long lists of figures (except for statistical reports), should be in the appendix.

The text is never labeled Text. Its title may be Discussion, Findings, Data, or other meaningful words. Or, instead of one main title for this section, you may use a series of headings throughout the text, corresponding to the main topics discussed in it. Both Chapters 17 and 18 illustrate various headings for the text portion.

The content, organization, language style, and visual aids of every report should be adapted to the reader's needs. The *longer and more complex the content, the greater the need for careful organization, headings, transitional devices, and other qualities that aid in readability*. Because these aspects are so important for the entire report as well as for its longest section, the text, they are discussed separately later in this chapter and illustrated in Chapters 17 and 18.

Terminal Section: Summary, Conclusions, Recommendations

Whether the terminal section appears before or after the text, it should definitely add to its value. Its functions are to summarize clearly the highlights of the whole report. This terminal section should be based on the text discussion and should include no new material. It summarizes, concludes, and/or recommends.

The terminal section for an *informational* report is usually called Summary. For an *analytical* report, it is usually called Conclusions, or Recommendations (or a combination—such as Conclusions and Recommendations). The terminal section is never labeled merely Terminal Section.

1. *A summary* condenses the text discussion, but not necessarily the entire text. Sometimes only the main points, strong and weak points, or benefits and disadvantages are summarized.
2. *The conclusions* evaluate facts discussed, without including the writer's personal opinion. Actually it's impossible to completely filter out personal opinion, but you should be careful to make your evaluation only from data in your text. Disregard your own biases or desire for a particular outcome.
3. *Recommendations* suggest a program of action based on the conclusions. If you make recommendations throughout the report, you will probably summarize them here. (The same is true for conclusions.)

In some reports an unusual title such as Benefits or Suggested Action is appropriate for the terminal section. Among other possible titles are: Probable Developments, Pertinent Suggestions, Merits of the Plan, Final Decision, Forecast (as an economist might make), and Important Precautions.

ORGANIZATION AND OUTLINE OF REPORT BODY

The way a report is organized has a distinct bearing on the manner in which it will be received and acted upon. The report's reader(s), purpose, and subject matter must be considered when you choose the organizational plan for the entire report body and the text section. Then you will need to outline the topics correctly.

Plans for Organizing Report Body

The two main ways to organize the three sections of the report body are: inductive and deductive.

Inductive Arrangement

The words *indirect* and *known-to-unknown* highlight the inductive organizational plan. It is basically the same indirect plan you have used for bad-news and persuasive-request messages (as outlined in Chapter 5, pages 97, 99–100). You present *explanation before* the *main idea(s)*. For reports, the three sections are arranged in this order:

> Introduction
>
> Text (discussion and explanation)
>
> Terminal section

When should you choose inductive arrangement for a report? In general, you may use this plan if you estimate that your reader:

1. Must have a detailed explanation first in order to understand the conclusions and/or recommendations; for example, in scientific and technical reports
2. Is the type who will fight your decision unless he or she is first given complete details and becomes convinced by logical development of facts
3. Will consider your conclusions bad news, because they are contrary to the expected outcome of the study
4. Might feel less bias toward conclusions and be more likely to accept them if first given an analysis of important factors
5. Needs to be encouraged to read the entire report, not just the terminal section . . . and/or
6. Prefers that this report (or all reports) be organized in this order

Deductive Arrangement

The word *direct* briefly describes the deductive organizational plan. It is comparable to the direct plan you used for direct requests and good-news messages. (See Chapter 5, pages 97–99.) You state the *main idea(s) before presenting the explanation*. For reports, the three sections may be arranged in one of these two ways:

Terminal section		Introduction
Introduction	or	Terminal section
Text (discussion and explanation)		Text (discussion and explanation)

In a lengthy report readers usually prefer the deductive arrangement because it gives them an overall picture before they delve into the mass of details. If the terminal section *isn't* at the beginning, some readers skip to the end of the report, read the terminal section, and then return to the beginning. Even in the one- or two-page memo report, many business executives prefer the deductive to the inductive order. In general, you may (or should) use this plan if your reader:

1. Is a busy executive who wishes to know only what the conclusions are or what action is to be taken, where, and who has the responsibility
2. Prefers to determine quickly whether to scan the text for confirmation of conclusions or recommendations and whether the rest of the report is worth reading
3. Will consider your conclusions good news or neutral information
4. Can better analyze data if conclusions or recommendations are given first
5. Wants the writer's point of view promptly
6. Dislikes suspense and prefers to see the recommended action first so that the discussion then substantiates it . . . and/or
7. Prefers that the report (or all reports) be organized in this order

Ways to Organize Report Text Section

One of the most challenging tasks in report writing is to decide upon the best way to organize the mass of details in the text section. You must make this decision before you prepare the final outline (step 6) and, of course, before you begin writing the report. You can develop the text in one (or more) of the following ways:

1. *By Criteria* or *Topics*. Your main headings may be the standards, factors, or characteristics—criteria—on which a decision rests. For example, if your report's purpose is to determine whether the firm should buy, rent, or lease trucks; or whether to open a new branch in City X or Y; or which applicant to hire for a management job, and so on, you first decide which criteria are important for the decision. You use them as headings; also, you try to determine subtopics (subheadings) which relate to them.

2. *By Order of Occurrence.* Agendas, minutes of meetings, convention programs, progress reports, and write-ups of events or procedures may follow this chronological arrangement. The time periods may be hourly, daily, seasonal, yearly, or whatever best fits the subject matter.

3. *By Order of Location.* This organization is useful for any orderly description focusing on space locations of units—whether they are in a house, factory, office building, shopping center, or international firm with branches widely distributed geographically. For instance, the main divisions in a report on a national firm's operations could be by regions—Northeast, Southeast, Central, and so on. A realtor's description of a house might be by rooms—living room, dinette, ...

4. *By Order of Importance.* First present the most important ideas, events, or topics and proceed to the less important points. If all items are of almost equal importance, arrange them by some other reasonable plan, perhaps alphabetically. Also, when you organize your text by criteria, you can arrange them by order of importance, if desirable.

5. *By Order of Familiarity.* Always proceed from the simple or familiar to the complex or unfamiliar, because the reader can comprehend better what is known than what is not known. Likewise, begin with present circumstances and then proceed to the proposed situation.

6. *By Sources.* This method is less desirable unless you are sure your reader is most interested in what each source revealed rather than in the criteria or other important ideas. You can use this way if, for example, you are reporting on prominent experts who spoke at the convention your firm asked you to attend (at company expense).

Methods of Outlining

After you have decided how to organize the body and the text, you will arrange the headings and subheadings in an outline. A good outline, especially for reports two or more pages long, is an essential tool and a real time-saver. It will become your guide for writing the report. In a long formal report, it also becomes your table of contents.

The outline helps you—before you write the report—to see the relationship between topics, compare proportions and headings, check for loopholes in logical order, and eliminate overlapping. Before you word and set up the headings in your outline, you need to consider types of headings, formats of outlines, and parallelism in headings.

Types of Headings

For the wording of headings, you can choose from three heading types: *topic, sentence,* or *variant.* Topic headings are the most common. They consist of single words (nouns), a few words, or short phrases. Sentence outlines use complete sentences for the headings. A variant of the complete sentence drops the subject and begins with a verb form. Compare these examples of different ways to write one heading:

Topic headings
Preparation   *or*   Preparation before Writing

Sentence headings
Preparation Is Essential   *or*   A Writer Should Prepare before
before Writing Reports   Writing Reports

Variant headings
Prepare before Writing   *or*   Preparing before Writing

A good heading should clearly indicate the subject matter below it, preferably using no more than seven words. If you choose a one-word topic heading, be sure it doesn't indicate broader discussion than actually is included under it. For instance, the heading Students would be far too broad for a report on the living expenses of college seniors at a particular college.

Formats of Outlines

Having chosen your organizational plan and the wording of your main headings, you next choose a way to show levels (degrees) for the various items in your outline. For short outlines (of only three or four headings and subheadings), you may prefer a format of simple indentations. Longer outlines will be clearer if you use either the traditional popular *numeral-letter combination* or a *decimal system* (favored in scientific and some business reports). Compare the formats in Figure 16-1 for numbering up to five degrees of headings.

When arranging your headings and subheadings in the outline of the report's text, remember these five *important cautions:*

1. Place most important ideas (for instance, your criteria) in the highest degrees of headings possible, considering report length, subject matter, and reader.
2. Try to balance the sections as well as possible. For example, if Section II-A, in Figure 16-1, had 12 subheadings and section II-B had no subheadings, the the proportion would be lopsided. You might then try to narrow the scope of heading II-A (by rewording it and by rearranging facts) and broaden II-B.
3. Have at least two subheadings if you divide any topic; for example, A-1 and A-2; *never* merely A-1.
4. Use good judgment in the number of section headings for readability—neither too many (which could be annoying) nor too few. (Usually three to seven main sections are considered desirable.)
5. Never use the report title as a section heading.

Degree of Heading		Numeral-Letter Combination			Decimal System	
1st	(INTRO-	I.			1.0	
2d	DUCTION)[2]		A.		1.1	
2d	"		B.		1.2	
2d	"		C.		1.3	
2d	"		D.		1.4	
1st	(TEXT)	II.			2.0	
2d	"		A.		2.1	
3d	"			1.	2.11	*ADD ANOTHER DECIMAL POINT*
3d	"			2.	2.12	
3d	"			3.	2.13	
2d	"		B.		2.2	
3d	"			1.	2.21	
3d	"			2.	2.22	
4th	"			a.	2.221	
4th	"			b.	2.222	
5th	"			(1)	2.2221	
5th	"			(2)	2.2222	
1st	"	III.			3.0	
2d	"		A.		3.1	
3d	"			1.	3.11	
3d	"			2.	3.12	
2d	"		B.		3.2	
3d	"			1.	3.21	
3d	"			2.	3.22	
3d	"			3.	3.23	
1st	"	IV.			4.0	
2d	"		A.		4.1	
3d	"			1.	4.11	
3d	"			2.	4.12	
2d	"		B.		4.2	
3d	"			1.	4.21	
3d	"			2.	4.22	
1st	(SUMMARY	V.			5.0	
2d	or CON-		A.		5.1	
2d	CLUSIONS)		B.		5.2	
2d			C.		5.3	

Figure 16-1 Two ways to number heading degrees in report outlines.

Parallelism in Headings

For parallel—and consistent—construction, all headings of the same degree within any part of an outline should be parallel to each other. This means they should have the same grammatical form—all nouns, all phrases, or all clauses

[2] This sample column is arranged for an inductively organized report. For deductive organization the introduction and terminal section will be I and II; the text will be III, IV, V.

or sentences. For example, in the Figure 16-1 numeral-letter outline the following headings should be parallel to each other: I, II, III, IV, V; A, B, C, D under I; 1, 2, 3 under II-A; 1 and 2 under II-B; a and b under II-B-2, and so on. However, subheadings 1, 2, 3 under II-A need not necessarily be parallel with subheadings 1 and 2 under II-B, nor with other 3d-degree subheadings in parts III and IV. Compare the following headings for parallelism:

Parallel (all topic headings —phrases)	*Parallel* (all sentence headings)	*Not parallel* (topic, variant, and sentence headings)
Types of Headings	Select Heading Types	Types of Headings
Formats of Outlines	Choose Outline Formats	Choosing Outline Format
Parallelism in Headings	Make Headings Parallel	Make Headings Parallel

VISUAL AIDS

To help improve both readability and appearance of a report, good writers use headings and—when desirable—also graphic materials. Because of their importance, these visual aids deserve special attention both before and during the actual writing of the report.

Headings as Directional Signs

The headings you have selected for your final outline will be directional signs for the reader of the finished report. Use headings within any report if they will help direct the reader(s) through the entire presentation. Whenever a heading has subheadings, always first tell your reader what subheadings are included under that heading *before* you discuss them. See, for example, the various transitional introductory sentences and paragraphs in this chapter (and throughout the text) after all headings that have subheadings. Notice the transitions come before the subheadings are used.

The boxed material below shows one popular system of placing the degrees of headings you may need for various lengths of reports. Other styles of placement and typing (or printing) of headings may be acceptable too, but the chosen style must be used consistently throughout the report. If your typewriter has variable type, you may of course choose different type sizes and styles (including italics—with or without underscoring) as printers do.

```
                    FIRST-DEGREE HEADINGS


In a report that requires four or five degrees of headings (as in
Figure 16-1) you can use first-degree headings for the main
parts--introduction, text main divisions, and terminal section.
```

Typed in all capitals, they are centered and placed usually with three blank lines above them and two blank lines below them.[3] For the title of such a report you may use this all-capitals heading—underlined or typed with S P A C E D   C A P I T A L S.

Second-Degree Headings

If your report's title is the all-capitals first-degree heading, you may use second-degree headings for main sections—introduction, text main divisions, and terminal section. These headings are centered and typed with or without underscoring.[3] You capitalize the first word and all others except prepositions with less than five letters (such as *to, of, with, on*), conjunctions (for example, *and, but, as, when*), and articles (*the, a, an, this*). Leaving at least two blank lines above these headings and one blank line below is desirable.

If in a long report you use first-degree headings for the main sections, then the highest-level subheadings within those sections will have these second-degree headings.

In a short report that has only two or three degrees of headings, you may if you wish use a second-degree heading for its title. Then the subheadings will be third-degree and lower.

Third-Degree Headings

Placed flush with the left margin, third-degree headings are underscored (in typing). Leave a blank line before them and (usually) a blank line after them. Capitalization can be the same as for the second degree (as in this example), or only the first word need be capitalized. (Then *D* in *Degree* and *H* in *Heading* would be in lowercase)

Fourth-degree headings.—When you need a fourth level for subheadings, you can type them just like the third-degree headings except that they are indented, usually five spaces, from the left margin and followed by a period. (Adding a dash is optional.) These headings are always underscored if regular type is used. The paragraph begins on the same line as the heading, which is typed with one blank line above it.

Fifth-degree headings consist of merely the underscored (or italicized) first key word or words of the first sentence in the paragraph. Use this degree of heading when the report requires all five degrees or when you started with third-degree and are using third-, fourth-, and fifth-degree headings.

---

[3] If you have extra-wide left margins, you may place first- and second-degree headings in that margin, as was done in this book, instead of in the center.

Graphic Materials for Quantitative and Other Data

Whenever you must present numerous figures (quantitative data) or describe a technical process or a procedure, well-planned graphic materials can help give your reader the picture more quickly—and interestingly. Graphic aids (also called visual aids or illustrations) include *tables, charts, graphs, pictograms, maps, pictures, and other display materials.* They help you avoid cluttering your paragraphs with masses of figures. They also improve the physical appearance of the report, making it more interesting and inviting. This section suggests ways to correctly present visual aids for quantitative data and then illustrates several popular types.

Essentials for Correct Presentation

The following brief suggestions give you a general overview of essentials for correct presentation of graphic materials in your reports:

1. *Placement.* Usually the best place for each illustration is within the text discussion if it is directly relevant and the reader will need to refer to it while reading the report. Place it as close to the discussion as possible—preferably in the same paragraph or page (or, if it is long, on the immediately following page).

   Two other possible placements are: (a) in the appendix—if the information is only supplemental to the discussion and/or extremely lengthy (as, for instance, a five-page table); (b) in a footnote—if the illustration is small and concerned with the discussion but is not vital to it.

2. *Introduction and Interpretation.* Always introduce the reader to the illustration *before* you show it. This can usually be done in one to three sentences. Emphasize the highlights, averages, extremes, or other significant aspects of the illustration—whatever is most important for the report you are developing. But don't detail all the minute data, for such unnecessary repetition will be boring and wasteful of space and reading time. Also, if the graphic is so simple that its meaning is obvious, omit interpretations because they may be insulting to the reader's intelligence.

3. *Lead-in Sentence.* The sentence just before the visual aid may end with words like, "as the following table (chart, picture, graph) shows (or illustrates)." If the visual aid is in the appendix, refer to it in the introduction and/or in the text.

4. *Numbers.* Normally, do not number small tables, charts, graphs, and so forth when they are placed within a paragraph and occupy only a few lines (perhaps under ten). However, in longer reports if you have several formal illustrations with complex data, these should be numbered—Figures 1, 2, 3; Charts 1, 2, 3, 4; Tables 1 and 2; Maps 1, 2, and so on. If you have several graphics but only one or two of each kind (figures, charts, tables), you may number them all in one series, naming each a "Figure." All illustrations should have meaningful titles. If desirable, the titles can then be included in

separate lists of tables and/or charts after the table of contents, for easy reference.

5. *Expression of Figures.* Express important figures as simply and meaningfully as possible—perhaps in percentages, ranks, or rounded-off numbers. For example, your reader can more easily compare 3 percent with 75 percent (or $8,000 with $200,000) than $8,243.21 with $206,080.25. (If you are multiplying figures, do *not* round off *before* multiplying, for the results may be distorted.) Put figures in context: "Profits rose 9.9% last year, the highest rise in our company's history."

Following are illustrations and brief explanations of these popular graphic aids: tables, bar graphs, pie charts, line graphs, and pictograms.[4]

Tables

When you need to present quantitative information systematically in rows and columns, use a table. Titles of the rows are usually called "stubs" and titles of the columns are "captions," as marked in Figure 16-2.

Mortgagor's Net Effective Monthly Income	1983		1984	
	Properties Acquired %	Total Insured %	Properties Acquired %	Total Insured %
Less than $300	2.7	2.4	1.3	1.8
$300 to 399	25.8	19.2	23.7	16.9
400 to 499	33.3	28.8	34.5	21.9
500 to 599	20.5	21.8	21.4	25.3
600 to 699	10.5	13.5	10.8	16.2
700 to 799	2.5	7.4	4.3	9.4
800 to 899	3.7	3.6	2.0	4.5
900 to 999	.2	1.5	1.5	1.9
1,000 to 1,999	.4	1.2	.5	1.4
1,200 or more	4	.6	—	.7
Total	100.0	100.0	100.0	100.0

Table 3 Percentages of Properties Acquired and Insured 1983 and 1984

Figure 16-2   Illustration of a numbered table.

Bar Graphs

Easy to construct and understand, the bar graph is one of the most common and adaptable types of graphic presentation. The bars of equal width but

---

[4] The emphasis in this book is on presentation. If you need help in constructing tables, charts, and graphs, you can find detailed chapters in texts devoted entirely to statistics or report writing.

varying lengths help to show changes and comparisons in certain areas. Careful labeling is necessary for the bars and the units in which the values are measured. Though there are several other variations of bar graphs, three types you will probably use most often in your reports are the vertical, horizontal, and subdivided bar graphs—illustrated here.

Vertical Bars. When a time factor is considered, vertical bars are especially useful. Notice that in Figure 16-3 the dates are placed across the bottom scale. Millions of dollars beginning with zero at the bottom are listed upward at the left, to help determine the height of each bar. A figure above each bar shows its total.

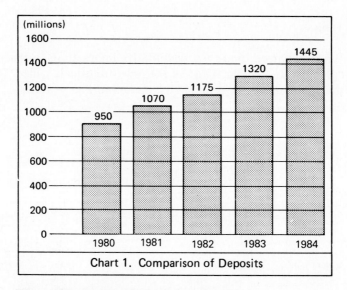

Figure 16-3 Example of a vertical bar graph.

Horizontal Bars. Many uses and variations are possible with horizontal bar charts. They may include single bars (as in Figure 16-4) or multiple bars (Figure 16-5), which compare two or three variables within each single bar. The scale at the bottom line may list percentages (as in both figures, page 481), dollars, tons, barrels, miles, or whatever is the basis for comparison. Each horizontal bar begins on the vertical line at the left and each has a name. For example, if the report compares total exports of five states in millions of dollars, each bar represents a state, named at the left. In Figure 16-4 each bar names an area of energy use. In Figure 16-5 each double bar represents a use of plastic cards—compared for the years 1982 and 1983.

For extra clarity, you can have both a bottom scale and figures within the bars. With or without a bottom scale, every bar must be in exact, correct proportion according to a specific scale. Among other variations are showing

The number at the end of each bar helps readers to see easily the exact percent for each area. A lead-in sentence in the report states that the graph "helps to identify the areas of energy use where conservation measures can accomplish the most significant savings: Transportation, heating, and industrial processes." As this is a spot graph within the report, it is not numbered.

Source: U.S. Energy Prospects: An Engineering Viewpoint, National Academy of Engineering, Washington, D.C., 1974, p. 26.

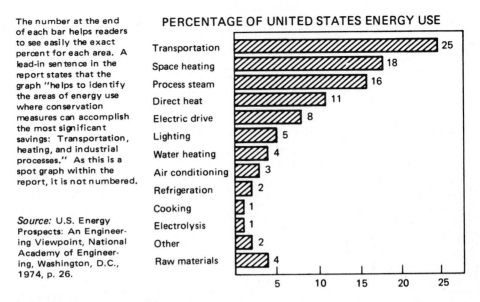

Figure 16-4 A horizontal bar graph.

To distinguish the years in each double bar, cross-hatching, shading, or colors may be used. The key to the years (or whatever the variables are) is placed wherever space is available.

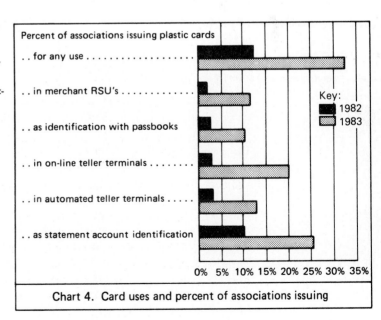

Figure 16-5 A horizontal multiple-bar graph.

totals and/or percentages at bar ends (Figure 16-4) or listing these figures in nearby columns, as in Figure 16-6.

Subdivided Bar Graphs. To show the constituent elements or parts of a whole area or subject which is being compared with other subjects, a subdivided (component) bar graph is helpful. Each part of a bar has a certain color, shading, or cross-hatching—as in Figure 16-6—to distinguish it from the other components. A legend explains the markings on all parts. Notice that in Figure 16-6 the dates are across the bottom. All bars except two contain figures within the segments (components); for the two smallest the figures are outside at the right.

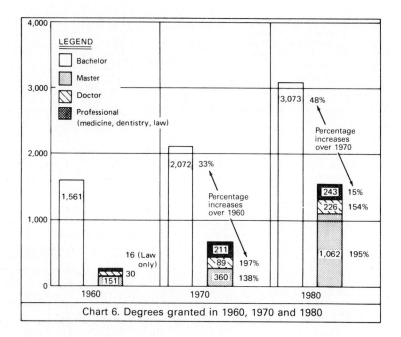

Figure 16-6   A subdivided bar graph.

Pie Charts

When you want to show relative sizes of parts in a whole or group, pie charts are effective. To make a comparison of facts easier, the pie segments (pieces) should be shown in percentages, as in Figure 16-7 and perhaps also total figures, if useful. With this pie chart the total dollars for each segment were listed in a separate column below the pie. Notice that each piece of the dollar (pie) is clearly labeled, with labels inside the larger pieces (starting at the 12 o'clock position) and labels outside the smaller pieces.

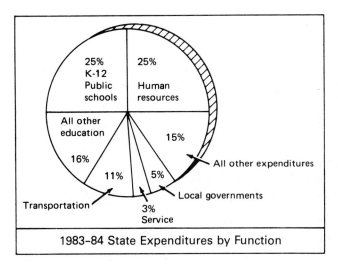

Figure 16-7 Example of a pie chart.

Line Graphs

When you want to portray a trend or series of figures covering a large number of time periods, the line graph is useful and fairly easy to construct. In a line graph, the time scale is usually across the bottom and the magnitudes are placed near a left-hand vertical line, as in Figure 16-8. One extra feature of this graph is that the peaks are clearly marked with figures.

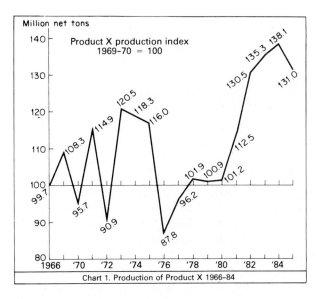

Figure 16-8 Example of a line graph.

Pictograms

You can present the same types of data in pictograms as in horizontal or vertical bar graphs. The main difference is that in the pictogram—instead of using lines to outline the bar rectangles, you insert simple small pictures that represent the data. Depending upon your subject matter, the pictures might be people (👥) or moneybags (💰) or houses (🏠) or any other simple, pertinent sketches. As in the pictogram shown in Figure 16-9, all units should be identical. Notice that each car represents the same number of units, 1 million vehicles. Pictograms are often used—because they are interesting and attractive—in reports to the general public, annual reports to stockholders, company advertising booklets, and magazine articles.

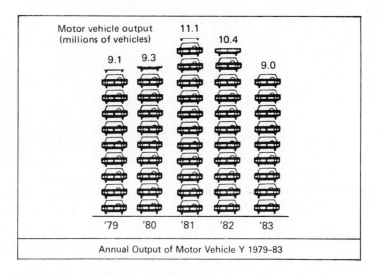

Figure 16-9   Example of a pictogram.

Maps and Other Visual Aids

Maps help reveal geographic facts and comparisons. They can show locations of natural resources (as in Figure 16-10), company offices, transportation routes, environmental or weather patterns, quantities of products sold in certain areas, and various other data. The map in Figure 16-10 uses crosses and triangles to mark locations of two products. Other ways to show facts on a map are by use of different colors, shading lines, cross-hatching, dots, numbers, or various sketches or pictures.

Among other visual aids that help enliven a report are cutaway drawings (like those showing parts of a machine), organizational charts, flowcharts, and photographs.

Figure 16-10 Example of a map showing deposits of two natural resources.

QUALITIES OF WELL-WRITTEN REPORTS

After you have completed your outline and any needed visual aids (in rough draft), you are ready to write the report. And then—before you transmit it—you'll revise wherever necessary. The way you write the report often determines whether it will be accepted by the management people involved.

Actually, all the business communication principles you studied in Chapters 3 and 4 also apply to reports. Because reports must be objective as well as interesting and because they are generally longer and more complex than letters or memorandums, they require special attention to all areas.

The following checklist summarizes ways to achieve the seven C qualities for good report writing. Chapters 17 and 18 provide additional details and examples about various parts, procedures, and requirements referred to in this checklist.

CHECKLIST OF C QUALITIES IN WELL-WRITTEN REPORTS

A. Completeness and Conciseness

1. *Include—in the body (introduction, text, terminal section) all facts needed to answer both primary and secondary readers' questions relevant to report's purpose.* Use an appendix for relevant facts too detailed to be in the body.
2. *Cover the what, why, when, where, who, and how* whenever appropriate for purpose and reader(s).

---

3. *Give the person who requested the report what he or she wants—* detailed descriptions and figures or mainly highlights with minimum supporting data.

4. *Trim the report to essentials that fit purpose and reader requirements. Omit all irrelevant material* even if you devoted many hours (perhaps days) to gathering and preparing it.

5. *Avoid, wordy, trite expressions, unnecessary repetitions, and overuse of articles and prepositional phrases.* Instead of "Analysis *of the* data shows," write "Data analysis shows." Good business writing averages only one prepositional phrase to every 11 words.

6. *Present both favorable and unfavorable factors* that affect the situation your report covers.

7. *Include whatever prefatory and supplemental parts are desirable,* depending upon the report's complexity, length, and "formality." Avoid unnecessary overlapping with the report body (as, for instance, in the transmittal letter and the introduction).

B. Concreteness, Conviction, Objectivity

1. *Use specific words and figures* ("52 percent" or "8,100 employees" instead of "many" employees), because they are essential for fair and convincing reports.

2. *Identify information sources* within the introduction, text, and/or a supplemental list. Include appropriate documentation.

3. *Substantiate a source's reliability (if necessary for reader conviction),* by stating truthfully (briefly) whether the source is a recognized authority; where, when, how, and under what conditions the person made the quoted statements; and whether they are likely to be biased.

4. *Be sure you yourself are objective in your quotations, paraphrasing, and abstracting.* Do not quote a source out of context or slant statements with your own intentional bias or opinion. Try to make the abstracted material a fair representation of the whole situation or area from which you abstracted.

5. *Consider carefully the bases for your inferences.* Inform your readers as to what portions of your statements are mere assumptions. Distinguish between verifiable facts, inferences based on facts, and your own assumptions.

6. *Avoid emotional writing,* with glowing adjectives and adverbs based on your opinions.

7. *Present facts impartially, showing both sides whenever necessary. Don't discolor facts with your personal feelings and prejudices.*

8. *Use concrete nouns as subjects of sentences.* Whenever possible,

avoid beginning sentences with abstract, intangible nouns or with expletives (*it* is, *there* are, etc.).

9. *Place action in verbs, not in nouns.* Instead of "The function of this department is the *collection* of payments and *notification* of . . ." say "This department *collects* payments and *notifies* . . ."

10. *Use mostly active–not passive–verbs.* Instead of the passive verbs in "An observer *was sent* around the plant to . . . , and it *was found* that . . . ," use active verbs: "Management *dispatched* an impartial observer to officially record incidents of. . . . He (or she) *discovered* that. . . ."

11. *Avoid the subjunctive whenever possible,* because it conveys contrary-to-fact ideas in the reader's mind. Instead of *would, could,* and *might* (all subjunctive), use *will* (future) or *can* and *may* (present tense). For example, instead of: "For better product distribution your firm *would need* three branch stores; each *would have* a manager who *would* . . . ," write: "For better . . . , your firm *needs* three branch stores; each *will* (or *can*) *have* a manager who *can.* . . ."

12. *Write in present tense whenever possible.* Besides using present tense when you refer to the present, use it also when stating a fact that was true in the past and is still true: "The manager informed the employee that promptness *is* (not *was*) expected." Furthermore, use present—not future—tense when referring to something that seems to be happening in the future but actually exists now:
    a. In the introduction write, "This report *shows* . . ." (not "will show"), because the reader has the completed report before him or her and whatever you're referring to is present now.
    b. Instead of future tense: "Two years of challenging work *will be* ahead for those who *will enter* this program. They *will spend* six months in each area . . . ," write in the present tense: "Two years of challenging work *are* ahead for those who *enter* the program. They *spend* six months in. . . ."

13. *Base your conclusions (if any) or your summary statements on adequate facts and be sure your written presentation is logical.* Avoid unwarranted, hasty generalizations.

C. Consideration and Courtesy

1. *Apply integrity in your research, analysis, interpretation, organization, and presentation of all facts, figures, comments.*
2. *Choose your organizational plan (inductive or deductive) for the most effective reader reaction.*

3. *Organize text topics after considering what will be most meaningful for the reader.* If possible, place favorable aspects before the unfavorable and the simpler ideas before the complex.

4. *Adapt writing style and formality to the reader* by using one of these choices:

   a. *In all memo and letter reports and* in other *informal* reports use the same informal style as in letters and memos—personal pronouns (I, we, you).

   b. *In longer, formal reports*—for instance to top company, public, or government officials or to the general public (and sometimes also in reports with controversial subject matter) you can use impersonal style in which you never refer to yourself at all. (But try to avoid overuse of passive verbs and expletives with this style.)

   c. *In a more formal report style*—seldom necessary or desirable in business reports—you might refer to yourself as "the author" and your assistants as "the research staff," "committee," or a similar title.

5. *Handle disagreeable material tactfully and courteously.* If you know your findings are contrary to the reader's opinions or expectations, you might precede your unfavorable statements by a tactful statement like, "Although one might have expected a different outcome, nevertheless . . . ," or, "Considering your previous experience, a study of these data leads to an unexpected conclusion. . . ."

6. *Watch your tone and logic,* to establish or reinforce the reader's confidence in you, the writer.

7. *Base your recommendations, if any, on logical conclusions resulting from objective presentation* of facts—*and not on emotional appeals.*

8. *Omit your own opinions unless the reader asked for them and you clearly label them.*

9. *Make your report interesting as well as readable* by using topic sentences; headings; and tables, graphs, charts, pictures, or other graphic aids if they will be helpful. Also, occasional questions, pertinent stories, and examples spark interest—if appropriately related to the report's purpose.

10. *When a decision is close, present in the terminal section both the pros and cons;* list favorable aspects (advantages) before the unfavorable (disadvantages), usually in the same order as in the text discussion.

D. Clarity

1. *Phrase all statements so the reader can easily understand them.*

Keep average sentence length within 17 to 20 words; paragraphs, average 7 to 8 typewritten lines. Include a topic sentence for each paragraph.

2. *Include definitions of any technical terms*—in the introduction, text, and/or appendix.

3. *In comparing figures, use percentages, ranks, ratios, or rounded-off figures for easier reader comprehension.* But show exact figures somewhere in the report, perhaps in a table right in the text or the appendix.

4. *Use graphic aids*—charts, graphs, pictures, etc.—whenever they help clarify your presentation of quantitative data.

5. *Discuss a graphic aid briefly (highlights) before you present it.*

6. *Use headings to guide the reader, but be sure your writing is clear and coherent without them.* In the sentence immediately following a heading, do *not* refer to the heading by the word *this* or another pronoun.

7. *Use transitional words and phrases* (such as "also," "on the other hand," "similarly," "for example,") *to link sentences* and tie ideas together. (For a list of transitional words and phrases see pages 731–732.)

8. *Use transitional sentences with forward or backward references to link paragraphs or sections.*

   a. A *forward* reference is placed at the end of a paragraph. For example, the last sentence in a paragraph about education might lead to the next paragraph this way: "Thus education of the recent college graduate is important, but so is attitude toward employment."

   b. A *backward* reference sentence can effectively begin a paragraph and serve as both a transition and a topic sentence of that paragraph. In the previous situation, the attitude-toward-employment paragraph could begin with a topic sentence that ties the two paragraphs together, like this: "Not only is education an important job qualification for a recent college graduate, but so is attitude. . . ." (Do not use both (a) and (b) in consecutive paragraphs.)

9. *Use introductory, summary or concluding, and transitional paragraphs to tie together sections of a report.*

   a. The *introductory* paragraph of a section serves a section the same way a topic sentence serves a paragraph. If a section has two or more subdivisions, always introduce them to the reader before you discuss them.

   b. A *summary or concluding* paragraph can be effective if a section is quite long—say, three or more typewritten pages—but this final paragraph must definitely be helpful to the reader.

   c. A *transitional* paragraph is especially helpful in a very long report—perhaps with 30 or more typewritten pages. You add this paragraph somewhere in the middle of the report body to tell the reader where she or he is; it tells what has been covered and what is yet to come.

10. *List and number conclusions or recommendations* if you have more than one.

E. Correctness

1. *Double-check accuracy of facts, grammar, nondiscriminatory expressions, spelling, parallel structure;* relationship of prefatory and supplemental parts (if any) to the text; typing; and mechanics.
2. *Distinguish clearly between facts, opinion, inferences* throughout the text and in the terminal section.
3. *Observe the five important cautions* (page 474) regarding arrangement of headings and subheadings.
4. *Word your conclusions accurately,* with conservative, unexaggerated statements. If they are based on an estimate, state the basis.
5. *Check to see that your report has all the other good qualities* of report language, readability, and objectivity already mentioned in this checklist, and that important ideas are correctly emphasized (by adequate details, placement, headings, and other visual aids).
6. *See that report layout is attractive and uncrowded,* with pleasing margins and white space.
7. *In a long report, check for accuracy of all prefatory and supplemental parts* (Chapter 18) as well as of the body, and see that all parts are placed in correct order.
8. *Include no new material in the terminal section.* It must be based on facts in the discussion section.

EXERCISES

1. Revise the following sentences so they conform to the C qualities for well-written reports. Which of the numbered suggestions in the above Checklist does each violate?
   a. This corporation adheres to a policy of nonacceptance of gratuities from firms or their representatives with which the company has, has had, or may have business agreements, contractual or otherwise.
   b. Following the request outlined in your memo of April 5, the warehouse was surveyed for the availability of space for storage.
   c. In January it was observed that many of the drinking fountains were left running continuously. It was also noted that lights were left on by many of the supervisors in offices while they were in the shop. And although not as prevalent, many of the

lights are left burning throughout the noon hour. Finally it was observed that even on cold days many of the outside windows in the various departments were left open. Since most of the rooms have thermostats, the heating system is overloaded in trying to maintain constant temperatures.

d. During the planning activities involved in constructing and implementing the project, and Supply System has, and will continue to, recognize and consider in a systematic and interdisciplinary fashion the technical, economic and environmental factors associated with the proposed project.

e. If you paint the shop in light colors, you can expect the following advantages: (1) reduced lighting costs, (2) increase the productivity, (3) the shop will appear larger.

f. An explanation by the interviewer gave the indication that a trainee usually will become acquainted with the marketing procedures of the firm when he will work with an experienced salesman. Sometime before six months will be up the trainee will take over the responsibilities of a supervisor.

g. There were a good many people interviewed for this report. Employees in the trucking industry constituted the largest percentage.

h. Production increased during the last quarter because there was less absenteeism, improved working conditions in the laboratory, metal shop, and factory, and equipment was maintained better; also we had more effective quality control procedures. It was found that greater tensile strength was developed under high temperatures.

i. Pursuant to the Atomic Energy Act, as amended, and the U.S. Nuclear Regulatory Commission's regulations in Title 10, Code of Federal Regulations, an application, with an accompanying Environmental Report, was filed by the (name) Public Power Supply System (herein referred to as the applicant) for construction permits for two generating units designated as the (name) Nuclear Project 1 and (name) Nuclear Project 4 (WNP-1 and WNP-4) (Docket Nos. 50-406 and 50-513), each of which is empowered by a pressurized-water reactor and is designed for initial operation at approximately 3,600 megawatts thermal (MWt) with a net electrical output of 1,218 megawatts electric (MWe).

2. Assume the paragraph just before the one below discusses the firm's tax difficulties. In each blank space insert a transitional word or phrase from the list on pages 731-732 (or any other source). The words in parentheses guide you toward the intended meanings.

Wages. Labor relations present an even more pressing problem. The cost-of-living index is rising; (result), the company's wage policy may have to be reexamined. It is true that the ABC Amendment permits wage raises to be passed on to the consumer. (contrast), many branches of the company will not recover the increased costs. The appliance division (instances) would encounter heavy sales resistance. (addition), management will have to consider the effects of price increases or labor difficulties in an election year. (summary), negotiations with labor will have to be taken with caution.

3. Evaluate the following report by answering these questions:
   a. What improvement can you make in the subject line?
   b. Does the introduction orient the reader to the material that follows? Why or why not? What elements do you find in the introduction? Should it have a heading?
   c. What is the purpose of the introductory paragraph immediately following the Discussion heading? Can you suggest a way to improve it?
   d. If the writer had chosen to omit the heading Discussion and instead had placed the titles of the three reports as second-degree headings, what change would this choice have required in the introduction? Which setup do you prefer?
   e. What degrees of headings does this report have? What degrees would it have if the change suggested in (d) were made?
   f. Is the text organized inductively or deductively?
   g. Underline all passive verbs. How many do you find?
   h. Circle the active verbs. Does the report have more active than passive verbs?
   i. Does each paragraph have a topic sentence?
   j. Is the terminal section correctly labeled? Does it satisfactorily carry out its function? Why or why not?
   k. Can you suggest any other corrections or improvements?

```
TO:       Malcolm Greene                      November 10, 19--
FROM:     Thomas Jones
SUBJECT:  Installment Credit Department Reports
```

As you requested, I have compared reports written by one commercial bank here in (*city*). I interviewed Diana Whitelon, assistant cashier at State National Bank, concerning business reports used in her organization. As you are especially interested in installment credit, I have limited my discussion to reports prepared and used by the Installment Credit Department.

Discussion

The three types of reports used in this department and discussed in this report are the Interoffice Memorandum Report, Statistical Report, and Memorandum Report for the Credit File.

Statistical Report

Employees of the installment credit department compile the statistical report monthly under Miss Whitelon's supervision. The report is a statistical presentation of the total loan balance of each of the department's individual accounts. These individual accounts are then divided between punctual and delinquent accounts.

The purpose of a statistical report is to inform the department manager and the branch manager of the quantitative and qualitative aspects of the department's operations. The branch manager consolidates this report into a branch report, which she or he then sends to the divisional manager and ultimately the executive vice president in charge of operations.

To provide quick evaluation of the department's performance, the report is presented in table form. It shows delinquent accounts, but these are given closer examination in the interoffice type discussed next. Little or no discussion is included, because only statistic are emphasized.

Interoffice Memorandum Report

The interoffice memorandum report is written by Miss Whitelon or employees in her department to supply credit information to upper management and any other bank officer, concerning any of their installment credit accounts. The most important are the upper-management reports concerned with delinquent accounts.

All bank officers receive report writing training that provides standard guidelines for credit appraising. Delinquent account credit reports are evaluated by upper management by thorough application of these guidelines and the validity of corrective action taken.. The reports are usually one page or less in length.

Credit File Memorandum Report

Any bank officer may write the credit file memorandum report. Whenever a bank officer contacts an installment credit account, he or she makes a report of any new information that has been acquired. This report is then included in the credit file account and provides the bank with a more detailed picture of the account. This procedure guards against the possibility of one officer being the sole contact with an account and also enables any other officer to become familiar with that account quickly and easily by reading the credit file.

Copies of these reports are sometimes sent to other interested bank officers although the credit file memorandum becomes part of an account's file. For example, sometimes there is a person who mentions over lunch that she or he wishes to organize an employee trust fund. The officer, upon learning this information, then makes a comment on a memorandum-for-credit-file form. A subject line is provided for the account name, and a colume is provided for the date and origin of the report. In the column the bank officer places the date and his or her name, and any persons to recieve copies, in this case the Trust Department. The comment is entered opposite the date and is usually no longer than two lines.

Summary

The Installment Credit Department of State National Bank uses three types of reports: statistical report, inter-office memorandum report, and memorandum report for the credit file. The statistical report is an operating report to upper management for the department with little or no discussion, while the other two are written reports concerned with individual accounts. The inter-office

memorandum is used mostly for delinquent account evaluation for upper management, while the credit file memorandum contains any
pertinent information about an account. A copy of the credit file
memorandum is retained in the account credit file to build a more
complete file, but all three reports go outside the department.

4. When you evaluate the report below, answer the following questions:
   a. Does the subject line clearly identify the subject of this memo report? If
      not, how can you improve it?
   b. Why should a writer initial the report?
   c. What improvements can you suggest for the format and spacing of the
      TO-FROM-SUBJECT lines?
   d. Does the introduction orient the reader to the material that follows? Why
      or why not? What elements do you find in this introduction? What
      improvements can you suggest?
   e. What degrees of headings does this report have? Are they appropriate?
   f. Do you like the three major divisions of the text or would you prefer only
      two? If two, and they were Skills Needed and Training Needed—what
      would be the two subdivisions under Skills Needed? How would these
      changes affect the degrees of headings in this report?
   g. What improvements can you suggest for the format and spacing of the
      numbered items?
   h. Is the terminal section correctly labeled? If not, what better heading can
      you suggest?
   i. Circle the active verbs and underline the passive verbs. How many of
      each do you find? What derivatives of "to be" and "to have" do you
      find?

Date: April 21, 19—

TO: Superintendent Robin James
FROM: Roberta Cutting, High School Placement Counselor RC
SUBJECT: Communication Skills Audio-Visual Center Needs

On April 12, as you requested, I asked Mr. Eric Mott, management
representative of the Audio-Visual center in (*city*), what communication skills high school people need to work for his company. This
report will give the results.

Students need training in both oral and written communication,
according to Mr. Mott. Even though new workers may not be responsible immediately for writing, their writing skills are considered at
this time of employment and during their early days on the job.
This is because the Audio-Visual Center generally advances personnel
from within the company.

Oral Skills Needed

Because the Audio-Visual Center hires most beginning workers in
clerical positions, they must be able to communicate orally in the

following ways. (1) Talking and listening on the telephone, (2) Receiving and introducing callers, (3) Working well with many other people.

Although these are beginning jobs, the employee is responsible for the image of the company and must be able to communicate clearly and tactfully with customers and other employees.

Written Skills Needed

The beginning worker needs to write more and more as he or she advances. However, even a beginner's duties could include the following. (1) Taking telephone messages, (2) Filling in office forms, (3) Writing routine letters, (4) Addressing envelopes.

If an employee advances to a supervisory position, he or she needs to write periodic evaluation reports on the people in the unit.

Training Is Needed

The Audio-Visual Center does not have any in-service training or company manual. Therefore, applicants must get their training in school. There are several specific areas that Mr. Mott thinks the schools should be teaching.

1. Students should learn correct telephone techniques
2. Everyone, including young men, should learn to type
3. Students must learn to write legibly
4. All future employees should learn to spell correctly and use a dictionary
5. Learning desirable business attitudes

The last item is perhaps most important. Students must be aware that regular attendance, punctuality, appropriate dress, and getting along with others are every bit as necessary as their skills.

Conclusions

Teachers cannot assume that students can communicate well; they must teach them to speak, listen, and write. The Audio-Visual Center feels that these are qualifications for even the most basic job.

CHAPTER 17
Short Reports

What business executives look for in a report is concise, accurate, unbiased material with appropriate supporting evidence to help them make needed decisions. The preceding chapter can serve as your general guide for good work in planning, organizing, and writing the body of any report, regardless of its length. However, short, informal reports require fewer elements in their introductions, fewer transitional devices for continuity, fewer headings, and a more personal writing style than do long, formal reports.

This chapter begins with a checklist of suggestions for writing short business reports, and then it illustrates those which are most frequently written in business-memorandum reports, both analytical and informational; letter reports; and other short reports.

CHECKLIST FOR SHORT REPORTS

1. **Subject line.** In a memo report or letter report, state the subject on the subject line.
2. **Introduction.** Explain the problem (if there is a problem), and clearly state the purpose. Also include other introductory elements that are necessary to orient the reader to the material that follows.
3. **Text.**
   a. *Present all relevant facts accurately and impartially,* for both sides of a situation. Do not allow your personal feelings and prejudices to affect the facts.
   b. *Organize* your report by the inductive plan or the deductive plan.
   c. *Emphasize important ideas* by showing more details; placing them in prominent positions (with the highest degrees of headings that are appropriate); and/or using mechanical means such as capitalization, underscoring, visual aids, more space, and repetition.
   d. *Use headings* to guide the reader through the report, but write your sentences and paragraphs so they can stand alone—as if the headings didn't exist. Usually headings range from second- or third- to fifth-degree, with not more than two or three degrees of headings in any one short report.
   e. *Use topic sentences* for your paragraphs, *and* use *an introductory paragraph at the beginning of a major section that contains two or more subdivisions.*
   f. *Apply the seven C writing principles.* Throughout, make your writing easy to read. Use understandable words, sentences averaging 17 to 20 words, concrete nouns, few adverbs, few adjectives, and paragraphs whose average length is about seven typewritten lines.
4. **Terminal section.**
   a. Be sure that your terminal section is an integral part of the report and *results logically from the facts already presented in the text.*

    b. *Remember that a summary condenses the text, conclusions evaluate the text, and recommendations offer specific courses of action.*

    c. Don't include any new material in this section of the report.

    d. Usually list summary points in the same order as topics are discussed in the text.

    e. If you have more than one conclusion or recommendation, list and number them. You might do the same in a summary, if desirable.

    f. Support your conclusions or recommendations with ample appropriate facts that are up-to-date and accurate.

5. Appendix. Put in the appendix material that belongs in the report but would clutter the text and isn't vital to its development or presentation.

ANALYTICAL MEMORANDUM REPORTS

To show you one way of planning, organizing, and writing an analytical memo report, the following discussion presents first a step-by-step analysis of a specific situation. Thereafter it includes three ways to organize justification reports and illustrates two periodic reports with figures.

Steps in Preparing an Analytical Personnel Report

Assume that Gene Mohr, manager of your bank's head office savings department has asked you (assistant manager of the personnel department) to help find a replacement for a teller who is quitting work and moving to another city. You advertised and 15 people applied for the job. After carefully checking their application forms, test scores, and your own interview notes, you narrowed your list to the five best applicants. Then you wrote to their references for recommendations. After receiving the replies, you have chosen the three best-qualified candidates. Your task now is to evaluate each of the three in a memo report to Mr. Mohr. He likes you to analyze the facts for him—and rank the applicants—but he wants to make his own recommendations and decision.

Here are facts about the three applicants:

Helen True:
One year business college; high school graduate with a 3.0 (out of a possible 4.0) grade point average; completed in high school an office machines course with a grade of B; typing, 60 words per minute; arithmetic aptitude, excellent; neatly groomed for business appearance; excellent references—"highly dependable, courteous, and honest"; excellent health; 11 years of business experience—all with one company.

James Mace:
High school graduate with a 2.6 GPA; completed in high school an office

machines course with a grade of C; typing, 50 wpm; arithmetic aptitude, good; fairly neat and well groomed; good references—"Dependable, tactful"; good health; six years of business experience with two different firms; two years' military service.

Beth Astor:
One year at the local four-year university, with a 3.1 GPA; high school graduate with a 3.2 GPA; completed in high school an office machines course with grade of A; typing, 65 wpm; arithmetic aptitude, excellent; very neat, well groomed; references—"good worker but has difficulty getting along with others"; fair health; three years' business experience with three different firms; attendance irregular in two.

With all these figures facing you, where do you begin? One way is to group these facts under headings representing *criteria* (see item 1, page 472) you will be using to measure the three people's qualifications. Notice that if you merely group them by their names as in the above list, comparisons are difficult. After some juggling, you decide that all the data fall under the headings of Education and Skills, Personal Qualifications, or Probable Permanency with Firm. (Many times when organizing you have material that could fit under more than one heading: health is an example. So you organize such material the best way you can; in this report it can fit under Personal Qualifications or Probable Permanency with Firm.) You can now arrange the backgrounds of the three applicants in working tables like the following:

	True	Mace	Astor
Education and Skills			
Education	High school graduate 1 year business college	High school graduate	High school graduate 1 year at university
Grade point	3.0	2.6	3.2 in high school 3.1 at university
Arithmetic aptitude	Excellent	Good	Excellent
Typing	60 wpm	50 wpm	65 wpm
High school grade in machines	Grade B	Grade C	Grade A
Personal Qualifications			
Appearance	Neat and well groomed	Fairly neat; well groomed	Very neat and well groomed
Dependability	Excellent	Good	Fair; but good worker
Compatibility	Excellent	Good	Fair; difficulty working with others

Probable Permanency with Firm

Number of jobs	1	2	3
Years of work	11	6 plus 2 military	3
Health	Excellent	Good	Fair
Attendance record	Excellent	Good	Fair (irregular in two firms)

Now you can begin to analyze and interpret the material. Suppose your interpretation results in the following ranks and points for these candidates (assuming you decide to assign 6 points for first place, 4 points for second place, and 2 points for third place):

Criteria	True Rank	Points	Mace Rank	Points	Astor Rank	Points
Education and skills	2d	4	3d	2	1st	6
Personal qualifications	1st	6	2d	4	3d	2
Probable permanency	1st	6	2d	4	3d	2
Total scores		16		10		10

From this analysis Helen True wins first place; and although Mace and Astor are tied for second place in scores, it is obvious that Mace is ahead of Astor in two of three criteria. Thus he wins second place; and Astor, third.

Your next step is to write the report, in rough draft. You know you'll be sending a memo report because that's the form you use between individuals within an organization. And you'll use the inductive organizational plan because Mr. Mohr told you once he preferred that plan for all memo reports.

The following discussion assumes you have already studied and interpreted the data in the tables shown above. You decide to leave the first table as it is and to place Appearance as the third item in the second table. In the Probable Permanency table you decide on these new criteria titles and arrangement order: Experience (instead of Years of work); Previous jobs (instead of Number of jobs). You have omitted such items as marital status and ages because the hiring decision is based on other criteria.[1] With that groundwork completed, you begin to write—first the *subject line,* which should contain no more than five to seven words, preferably. You decide on "Evaluation of three teller applicants." Then you write the introduction, next the major divisions in the text, and finally the terminal section.

Introduction

The following list shows which of the 11 introductory elements (pages 468–469) you should include in this particular report. (The others are irrelevant.)

---

[1] Although Title VII of the Civil Rights Act does not specifically mention marital status, this topic is closely related to and often interpreted under sex discrimination. Furthermore, many states have laws that employers may not discriminate against applicants on the basis of marital status, age, or sex preferences.

Element	*Comment*
Authorization	Mr. Mohr asked you to assume the assignment.
Purpose	To evaluate the three applicants' qualifications for one opening as teller.
Background	From 15 applicants you selected three.
Methodology/sources	You used application blanks, test scores, your own interview notes, and recommendations from references.
Plan of presentation	You will develop the text according to the three criteria for a teller.
Brief statement of your decision	Optional. You may tell Mr. Mohr that Mrs. True ranks highest of the three candidates: or wait to tell this only in the terminal section. Your choice will depend upon what you think Mr. Mohr prefers.

When you put these five or six elements into words and sentences, you might have an introductory paragraph like one of the following:

```
As you requested, here is the report concerning evaluation of candi-
dates for a suitable replacement for your retiring teller.  On the
basis of company test scores, screening initial applications, my
personal interview with each applicant, and recommendations from
references, 3 final candidates have been chosen from 15 who ap-
plied.²  In evaluating the candidates, I have placed primary
importance on (1) education and skills, (2) personal qualifications,
(3) probable permanency.  On the basis of these considerations, Mrs.
True rates the highest of the 3 candidates.
```

or (for the reader who fights your decision before reading the text):

```
Here is the report you requested concerning the evaluation of candi-
dates for a teller as a replacement for the employee who is resign-
ing.  Through careful screening of application forms, test scores, my
own interview notes and recommendations from references, I have se-
lected 3 out of 15 applicants for your final consideration.  Mrs.
Helen True, Mr. Thomas Mace, and Miss Beth Astor were chosen on the
basis of their teller proficiency, personal qualifications, and
probable permanency of their employment with our bank.
```

² Previous chapters in this book have adhered to the Rule of 10 regarding numbers. As discussed in Appendix B, p. 721, you should write out (with exceptions) numbers one through nine; but beginning with 10 you use the figure. Departing from the Rule of 10, this chapter uses—in informal reports and messages—figures for all numbers—except one. Because of a trend in business toward writing figures for all numbers (unless the number begins the sentence), you can decide for yourself what you prefer and act accordingly—in *in*formal reports and messages.

Main Divisions of the Text

You will use three main sections for your text—one for each criterion. You will study each table (which you prepared in rough draft) and analyze the facts. If your reader wants all the details, you will include each exact table or a variation of it within the text. The following discussion concentrates on the section labeled Probable Permanency. Your procedure for the other two sections will, of course, be similar. What are the most important facts you can pull from the table? Avoid saying in sentence form before or after a table everything that's in the table; that wastes time and is monotonous. After careful thought you might write a paragraph like this to place before the table:

> Mrs. Helen True's experience and her previous job responsibilities show a background and future potential for a greater degree of permanency with our organization than either Mr. Mace or Miss Astor. The following table shows that both Mr. Mace and Miss Astor might have a greater tendency to leave since they have less stable past employment records and they do not possess the excellent health that is preferable for the teller work.

After the table you might include comments like these:

> Mr. Mace rates as a second choice. His two jobs in 6 years and good health are a better record than that for Miss Astor. Also in his favor is the fact that he plans to make a career of working with people.

Terminal Section

Will you choose a summary or conclusions? The decision depends upon what Mr. Mohr prefers. Because he asked you to analyze the facts and present your evaluation and he wants to make his own recommendations, your terminal section should include conclusions, not merely a summary, and you'll omit recommendations.

The following illustration (memo report 1) is one of several ways this completed report may be worded. It is typewritten on your bank's memo stationery, addressed to Mr. Gene Mohr, without his title as manager of the head office savings department. This title could, however, be included if company policy so dictates or when the organization is large enough to justify a title for clarification. (Usually memos and memo reports don't include the title of the individuals because the people involved know one another and don't need any identification other than the name itself.) When you're writing to a superior, it may be wise to include the courtesy title ("Mr." here).

Notice that the introduction for this memo report doesn't require a heading, but the main sections within the text and the terminal section have headings—second-degree, parallel grammatically. Also, the headings and subject line should be underlined for emphasis.

Memo Report 1

A personnel department officer's analytical report to a savings department director.

M E M O R A N D U M   (*bank name*)

TO: Mr. Gene Mohr   DATE: March 15, 198_
FROM: (*your name*)
SUBJECT: Evaluation of Three Teller Applicants

Here is the report you requested concerning the choice of a replacement for your teller who is resigning. On the basis of
information obtained from applications, test scores, personal interviews, and recommendations from references, I have selected 3
out of 15 applicants for final consideration. Of these 3, I feel
that Mrs. Helen True best meets the job requirements of permanency, education and skills, and basic personal qualifications, as
discussed below.

Probable Permanency

Mrs. Helen True's background of experience and previous job responsibilities indicate future potential for a greater degree of
permanence with our organization than either Mr. Mace or Miss Astor. The following table shows that both Mr. Mace and Miss Astor
have less stable past employment records and they do not possess
the excellent health that is preferable for the teller work.

Criteria	Helen True	James Mace	Beth Astor
Experience	11 years	6 years	3 years
Previous jobs	1 firm	2 firms	3 firms
Health	Excellent	Good	Fair
Attendance record	Excellent	Good	Fair (irregular in 2 firms)

Mr. Mace rates as second choice. His 2 jobs in 6 years and good
health are a much better record than that for Miss Astor. Also in
his favor is the fact that he plans to make a career of working
with people.

Education and Skills

On the basis of education and skills, Miss Astor is an outstanding
applicant. The table below provides facts in which Miss Astor
ranks consistently higher than the other 2 in education, grades,
and skills.

Criteria	Helen True	James Mace	Beth Astor
Education	H.S. graduate, 1 year business college	H.S. graduate	H.S. graduate, 1 year at university
Grade point	3.0	2.6	3.2 in H.S., 3.1 at university
Arithmetic aptitude	Excellent	Good	Excellent
Typing	60 wpm	50 wpm	65 wpm
H.S. grade in machines	Grade B	Grade C	Grade A

Although Mrs. True's results are not as high as those of Miss Astor, she shows a more than adequate proficiency in her skills. She should prove just as efficient and capable as Miss Astor in a teller's position.

Personal Qualifications

Mainly on the basis of references from past employers, Mrs. True has the personality that best fits the performance and image of the position. As the following table shows, she is the only applicant of the 3 who has excellent references with no additional qualifying statements by those references.

Criteria	Helen True	James Mace	Beth Astor
Dependability	Excellent	Good	Fair; but good worker
Compatibility	Excellent	Good	Fair; difficulty working with others
Appearance	Neat and well groomed	Fairly neat; well groomed	Very neat and well groomed

The references of Miss Astor are somewhat disturbing because of former employers' comments about her ability to get along with her fellow workers.

Conclusions

1. Mrs. Helen True is the best qualified to fill your teller vacancy. She rates highest in degree of expected permanence and in personal qualifications for the job. Although her professional ability does not rate highest of the 3 applicants, she ranks second and shows a more than adequate proficiency.

2. Mr. Thomas Mace rates as a good second choice, mainly on the basis of his expected permanence and his compatibility. Although he does not rank as high on skills and grades as either of the other 2 applicants, his education and scores indicate he can perform the job adequately.

3. Because of the questions raised in her references, I feel Miss Beth Astor is definitely in third place among these 3 candidates for this position. Another less desirable factor is her "fair" health and the uncertainty of her permanency with our organization. Her outstanding professional ability is too greatly outweighed by these 2 factors.

With this memorandum report, Mr. Mohr can quickly glance through the facts and decide whom he should hire.

Justification Reports

Many analytical memorandum reports in business have a special purpose—to justify an expenditure or a change in procedures. Among various reasons for such reports are specific suggestions to help the organization increase profits, save time and money, reduce accidents, reduce employee turnover, and improve customer goodwill. Often these reports are voluntary—written by the suggestion maker; but sometimes they are authorized (requested)—for a thorough study to be made of a suggestion an employee left in a company suggestion box.

Reports 2 a, b, and c show three ways to organize such a report; plans 1 and 2 are preferred because they give the busy executive the main ideas (conclusions) first.

1. *Deductive plan:*
   Conclusions before or after the introduction but always before the discussion
2. *Variation of deductive plan—*
   commonly called "Justification Report"—for top management: Purpose, cost and savings (sometimes also method of installation if an intricate system), conclusions, discussion
3. *Inductive plan:*
   Introduction, discussion, conclusions

The discussion section in any of these reports usually is 50 percent to 75 percent of the entire body.

Memo Report 2a

Organized by deductive plan.

DATE: May 3, 198_

TO: William David, Director, Purchasing
FROM: Joan Swanson, Assistant Manager, Electrical
SUBJECT: Justifying Purchase of Wire-measuring Machine

<u>Conclusions</u>

1. A capital outlay of $300 for a wire-measuring machine will save us $744 gross or $444 net the first year and $3,420 net for the 5-year guarantee period.
2. The machine will save the clerk the cumbersome job of coiling up the wire and also free the customer's time and our clerk's time by 10 minutes for each wire purchase.

<u>Introduction[3]</u>

Recently I became aware of a costly procedure in the electrical department--a procedure of hand measuring wire which we should change because it is costing us about $740 of unnecessary expense each year. In addition to possible dollar savings, this report shows a convenience to both the clerks and the customers with the purchase of a wire-measuring machine manufactured by the Ace Tool Company.

<u>Possible Savings</u>

In our downtown hardware store we can expect savings in wages and in elimination of losses due to measurement errors after we change from the present hand measurement system to machine measurement of wire. (Similar benefits may be expected for our branch stores, but this report covers only the downtown store.)

Possible Savings on Wages

Presently we are hand measuring the electrical (copper) wire on a yardstick that is permanently affixed to the counter. I made a random check of 100 purchases and found it takes an average of 15 minutes for one clerk to measure, coil, and price 50 yards of wire. The measuring machine can perform the same job in 5 minutes--a savings of 10 minutes or 1/6 of an hour for every 50 yards of wire.

Since our business volume requires that we always have to hire extra help throughout the year, time saved in measuring means money saved in wages. We sell an average of 2,000 yards of wire a month or 24,000 yards yearly and clerks' rate of pay is $6 an hour. With a measuring machine there is a possible annual savings of $480 in wages, as shown below:

---

[3] Introduction could also come before the Conclusions. The heading Introduction may then be omitted if the introduction is only a paragraph or two.

Estimated time saved: $\dfrac{24,000}{50} \times \dfrac{1}{6}$ 80 hours

Estimated savings in wages: 80 × \$6   \$480 yearly

Possible Savings on Measurements

During the past 6 months, in my quarterly inventory checkups, I have found that an average of 50 yards had left the store but was not accounted for over each 3-month period. This 50-yard loss was attributed to errors in measurement, although we have had no complaints of short measurement nor reports of excessive measurements.

At 44 cents a foot (or \$1.32 a yard) for the wire, we can save annually an additional \$264, as the following figures show:

50 × 4 (quarters) × 1.32 = \$264 savings realized if we eliminate shortage loss caused by hand measuring

We can realize a total gross savings of \$744 (\$480 and \$264) yearly with the measuring machine. And because the machine sells for \$300 and carries a 5-year guarantee, we can save \$444 net the first year or \$3,420 within 5 years——\$444 + (\$744 × 4).

Convenience Factor

In addition to the dollar savings, both the clerks and the customers will appreciate the convenience factor of the machine. Because the wire comes in spools of 1,000 yards, the clerks now have difficulty in hand measuring less than a whole spool——but a large quantity, say, 150 yards——of wire. They must measure off 150 yards and then coil it in some fashion so that it won't tangle and will be easy to carry.

As a contrast, the machine measures wire of all diameters, meters up to 1,000 yards, and includes 3 parts:

1. A spindle to hold the spool of wire to be measured
2. A meter that measures and prices the wire
3. A spindle to receive and coil the wire that has been measured

Thus, this machine will not only eliminate mistakes in measurement and pricing; it will also save the clerk the cumbersome job of coiling up the wire and also free the customer's time by 10 minutes for each wire purchase.

Memo Report 2b

Variation of deductive plan.

TO: *Same as 2a*   May 3, 198_
FROM: *Same as 2a*
SUBJECT: *Same as 2a*

Purpose

To show the dollar savings and convenience factor with the purchase of a wire-measuring machine for the electrical department.

Cost and Savings

For a capital outlay of $300 for a wire-measuring machine, we can save an estimated $3,420 in 5 years.

Conclusions

1. Possible savings: $3,420 net for the 5-year guarantee period
2. Convenience factor: For both clerks and customers

Discussion

Recently I became aware of a costly procedure in the electrical department. By purchasing a wire-measuring machine manufactured by the Ace Tool Company, we can save money and at the same time assure convenience to both the clerks and customers.

Possible Savings
(Same as that section in the deductive plan. If two subheadings are used, they will be 4th-degree headings.)

Convenience Factor
(Same as that section in the deductive plan.)

Memo Report 2c

Organized by inductive plan.

TO: *Same as 2a*   May 3, 198__
FROM: *Same as 2a*
SUBJECT: *Same as 2a <u>or</u> change to noncommital*
            (See number 1 below)

Recently I became aware of a . . . . *(same introduction as for deductive plan, but the title "Introduction" is omitted because this section is the first part of the report body.)*

Possible Savings
(Same as that section in deductive plan.)

Convenience Factor
(Same as that section in deductive plan.)

Conclusions
(Same as those shown in deductive plan.)

In the introduction for report 2a you let the president know your results—that a wire-measuring machine will save both money and convenience. But suppose you are a management trainee and you're writing to a 65-year-old penny-pinching owner whose usual reply when someone suggests a change that costs money is, "We've been doing all right so far; why should I spend more money to buy something new?" When you write to this person (or to anyone else who will begin to fight you if the decision is given before the facts), you'll need to change the report in the following ways.

1. You'll need a *noncommittal* subject line:

   Cost Comparison of Hand and Machine Wire-Measuring Methods

2. You'll need a noncommittal introduction:

   Recently I became aware of a costly procedure in the electrical de-
   partment--a procedure of hand measuring wire. This report compares
   cost and convenience factors of two alternatives--continuing with
   the present hand method or buying a wire-measuring machine manufactured by the Ace Tool Company.

3. Text (same as above)
4. Conclusions (same as above)

   With this presentation, you don't indicate the conclusion until the terminal section—until you have given all the facts to the reader.

Two Periodic Reports with Figures

Reports with many figures in the text require special attention for clarity, as the next two examples illustrate.

Memo Report 3

Hard-to-read report with many figures.

TO: Sarah Dewey, Vice President   DATE: November 8, 198__
FROM: Loren Konel, Treasurer
SUBJECT: Treasurer's Savings Analysis Report

The following schedules provide an analysis of the number and balances of the association's savings accounts in groupings of $1,000
for the month of October, 19___. These schedules were obtained as a
supplement report of our regular monthly trial balancing of savings
accounts. The accounts were processed October 29 and 31 and reflect
balances at those dates.

Total savings accounts were 5,097 with balances of approximately
$20,900,000. The average account balance for all classes of savings
accounts is $4,100.

A gain of 503 accounts has been registered since the October 19___
analysis, for an increase of 10.97%. Account holders with balances
of $5,000 or more make up 35.79% of our savers. These savers hold
81.58% of the association's total savings dollars. Savers with balances of $10,000 and over make up 17.65% of our total account
holders and they hold 52.21% of the total dollar value. This compares to 48.78% of one year ago, for an increase of 3.43%.

Savings balances have increased $2,341,334 (including the crediting
of $568,850 in dividends) for the 12-month period October 19___
through September 19___. This represents an actual gain of
$1,772,484 or 9.55%. Accounts with balances of $1 through $4,999 in-
creased $53,110 while accounts with balances of $5,000 or more
increased $2,288,224. Accounts in the $5,000 to $5,999 grouping
showed an increase of approximately $500,000 and in the $15,000 to
$15,999 category gained $620,679. Savings certificates which have
been issued since January 2, 19___, totaled $4,005,000 or 19.16% of
total savings. New money invested in savings certificates was
$1,347,572 (gross $1,414,572 less withdrawals of $67,000) while
transfers from existing accounts equaled $2,657,428.

As a welcome contrast to report 3, the following revision not only orga-
nizes the many figures in table format but also includes headings to show two
comparisons—first by number of accounts and percentages, then by dollar
balances. This revision permits the reader to grasp the data more quickly and
more thoroughly. Notice that this monthly analytical report adds "A Few
Highlights" heading for a brief terminal section before showing comparisons
and analyses of various totals.

Memo Report 4

Revision of report 3 illustrates effective organization of many figures.

TO: Sarah Dewey, Vice President   DATE: November 8, 198_
FROM: Loren Konel, Treasurer
SUBJECT: Treasurer's Savings Analysis Report—October 198_

The following schedules provide an analysis of the number, percentages, and balances of the association's savings accounts in
groupings of $1,000 for October 198. These schedules were obtained
as a supplement report of our regular monthly trial balancing of
savings accounts. The accounts reflect balances on October 29
and 31.

A Few Highlights
    Our 5,097 savings accounts totaling $20,900,000 as of October 31
    include 503 new accounts opened since October last year. Four-
    fifths of our association's total savings dollars are held by sav-
    ers with account balances of $5,000 or more.

Comparisons by number of accounts and percentages
Total number of savings accounts 5,097
Gain of accounts since October 19__ (previous year)   503
% of increase in number of accounts 10.97%
% of savers with account balance $5,000 or more 35.79%
% of our association's total savings dollars that
   these savers hold 81.58%
% of savers with account balances $10,000 or more 17.65%
% of our association's total savings dollars that
   these savers hold 52.21%
% of increase over last year 3.43%
% that savings certificates are of total savings 19.16%
% that savings balances increased (actual gain) 9.55%

Comparisons by dollar balances
Total balances of all 5,098 savings accounts $20,900,000
Average account balance for all classes of savings
   accounts $4,100
Increase in savings balances Oct. 19__
   through Sept. 19__ $2,341,334
Dividends included $568,850

Actual gain (9.55% minus
   dividends) $1,772,484
Increase for savings account holders with balance of:
   $1 – $4,999 .... $53,110
   $5,000 or more 2,288,224
   $5,000 – $5,999 .... (approximately)   500,000
   $15,000 – $15,999 620,679
Total of savings certificates issued since
   Jan. 2, 19__ $4,005,000
New money invested in savings
   certificates (gross) $1,414,572
   Less withdrawals   67,000
Net new money invested in savings
   certificates $1,347,572
Transfers from existing accounts $2,657,428

If you wish to discuss any part of this report with me, please let
me know. I'll come to your office at your convenience.

Numerous other analytical periodic reports are written in business. They
of course vary widely—in periods covered (daily, weekly, monthly, yearly) as
well as in subject matter and purpose.

INFORMATIONAL MEMORANDUM REPORTS

In contrast to analytical reports, which give conclusions and/or recommendations, informational reports merely present and summarize facts. Obviously,

information reports vary widely in content, depending upon the type of business, purpose, topics discussed, and readers' needs. The following examples illustrate three kinds of often-used information reports: conference reports, progress reports, and monthly reports.

Conference Reports

The subject matter of conference reports ranges from summaries of personal conferences to write-ups of meetings attended by hundreds of persons.

For example, an advertising account executive may write a conference report after every meeting between the agent and a client. Its purpose is to record all decisions made concerning a campaign. A credit or collection manager may make similar reports after conferences with customers. Likewise, many other employees as well as executives may be responsible for writing reports after any significant conferences with individuals or committees. *The text of such reports is usually organized by topics discussed.* Some firms have standardized headings for the often-written reports to assure that the same information or main topics are recorded in all of them.

In a different situation, a company's delegate to an important convention may be asked to present a report to superiors. Its purpose is to inform other management personnel of significant happenings, decisions, or topics discussed. How would you organize the text of such a report? You might choose to *organize by order of time, topics (criteria), importance, or sources.* In report 5 the sales manager (who attended the firm's regional conference of sales managers) used *a combination of the first three choices.* The three main topics and their subtopics serve as *guides (or criteria)* for planning this particular sales campaign. Headings 1, 2, and 3 are the *main topics in order of importance.* Under the Open Houses heading, items (a), (b), (c) are *arranged by order of time.* This report uses third- and fourth-degree headings.

Memo Report 5

A sales manager's report on a regional conference.

```
TO:    Martha Gerbman           DATE:  June 5, 198___
FROM:  Matt Deaning          SUBJECT:  Open Houses and Promotion

cc:    Frieda Dinson    Bill Campbell    Pete Mallon
       Terry Moran                       Tyna Green
       June Donaldson   Erick Brown      John Raney
```

The following is a report on the items we discussed during our recent meeting in (*city*) regarding our XL product. They pertain to the scheduled open houses, our promotional programs, and the signs and identification of our products. The names of those who were asked to be responsible for the various parts of these plans are listed in the right-hand column below.

1. Open Houses
   Here is the tentative schedule that was established, subject primarily to availability of dignitaries at the ribbon-cutting
   ceremony.

   a. Employees' Meeting – Thursday, July 20   Terry Moran
      (1) Families will be invited, and sandwiches
          and refreshments provided.
      (2) This will provide an opportunity to dry run
          the tours being conducted on successive
          days.

   b. Ribbon-Cutting Ceremony – Friday, July 31   June Donaldson
      (1) Dignitaries to be invited need to be agreed
          upon. We generally agreed that, as this
          occasion presents an exceptional oppor-
          tunity to publicize the growth of new and
          nonpolluting industry in our state, as well
          as an opportunity to gain state and re-
          gional publicity for the expanding
          capabilities of our company in the XL prod-
          uct business, an effort should be made to
          include those state officials most capable
          of gaining this type of publicity.
      (2) Additionally, press invitations need to be
          extended and press releases developed.

   c. Distributor Event – Saturday, August 1   Martha Gerbman
      (1) Begin tour at 10 a.m. followed by lunch at
          Ritz Plaza Hotel.
      (2) Develop a program to impress upon the dis-
          tributors our program for XL Product
          Division.

2. Promotional Programs

   a. The XL product brochure was reviewed and rela-   Frieda Dinson
      tively minor changes agreed upon. Another draft
      will be sent to Bill Campbell for approval
      prior to setting type. Bill Campbell will pre-
      pare and forward guarantee copy to agency.
      This project is to proceed as rapidly as possi-
      ble. The agency will prepare a list of names
      for the prefinished RM product line.

   b. Introduction Brochure   Erick Brown
      (1) We agreed that a brochure to familiarize
          our customers with the operation of the XL
          will be desirable.
      (2) We agreed that the procedure used formerly
          in materials showing photographs of the
          various personnel will be a good approach.
          Agency will develop layout.

(3) Those to be included in this brochure will
    be Tyna Green, Martha Gerbman, Bill Camp-
    bell, Frieda Dinson, Pete Mallon, Erick
    Brown, Terry Moran, June Donaldson, and
    John Raney, the sales secretary.

c. Advertising and Direct Mail   Frieda Dinson
   (1) A direct mail program directed to builders   and
       needs to be developed, perhaps in conjunc-   Matt Deaning
       tion with local distributors.
   (2) We agreed that advertising regions should
       be expanded to cover the entire region.
       This project will be further developed.

3. Signing and Identification   Matt Deaning

   a. Unit Signs
      White cardboard unit signs which will fold over
      the top edges of XL products displayed will be
      printed at the Print Shop. Design approved was
      forwarded to the Print Shop for production and
      delivery to the plant by June 23.

   b. Property Signs
      Building and property signs were agreed on and
      covered in a separate memo.

In report 6 the assistant manager organized the conference report by *sources*, because the division manager was mainly interested in the presentations of the three national experts in the field. Second-degree (centered) headings are used. (Perhaps to save space, no blank lines were left after these headings.)

Memo Report 6

An assistant manager's conference report (organized by sources, logically).

TO: Anthony Bloome   DATE: October 2, 198_
FROM: Verna Bennett
SUBJECT: Summary of St. Louis Regional Conference

Here is a brief summary of the St. Louis meeting that I attended
September 30 on coin service at military installations. Because you
are mainly interested in the presentations of John Klinest, Wardman
Jones, and Kathy Cummings, I am focusing this report on their contributions to this conference.

                    John Klinest's Presentation
John Klinest conducted our meeting and introduced the subject. Because of the current situation at military posts, coin service at

these posts will be a problem for years to come. It's important to improve our service because:

1. The need is there. The present military situation requires more coin service.
2. Many of the young men and women on these posts are making their first real acquaintance with public telephone service. Their opinions of our service now are likely to be lasting.

A series of slides shown by Klinest pointed out that coin conditions around the country vary from very bad (standing in mud puddles to use coin kiosks) to very good. The coin center at (*name*) is so plush it is used as a reception center for guests.

Wardman Jones's Presentation
Wardman Jones talked about some of the revenue characteristics of military coin service . . . .

> *(Three paragraphs follow, including itemized facts and figures.)*

Kathy Cummings's Presentation
Regarding the traffic considerations, these were enumerated by Kathy Cummings. She emphasized that . . . .

> *(Two paragraphs follow, highlighting her suggestions.)*

Plan of Action
John Klinest recommends the formation of an interdepartmental district team to evaluate our coin service at (*names*) and report its findings to higher management. The team will use the attached checklist.

Progress Reports

As the name implies, progress reports show "progress," accomplishments, or activity for a certain period or stage of a major assignment. The organizational plan is usually inductive, including topics similar to these:

Introduction (purpose, nature of project)

Description of accomplishments during the reporting period

Unanticipated problems (if any)

Plans for the next reporting period

Summary (overall appraisal of progress to date)

The example below is a general chairperson's progress report to the executive vice president of the company, which is hosting the first purchasing

managers' regional convention in that city. It uses the inductive organization
plan, with third- and fourth-degree headings.

Memo Report 7

A general chairperson's progress report on convention plans (inductive).

TO: Bruce Boyne, Vice President   DATE: November 9, 198_
FROM: Vivian Porte, Convention Chairperson
SUBJECT: Progress Report on Purchasing Managers' Convention,
              January 26, 198_

To keep you informed about the activities of our planning committee
for the first regional purchasing managers' convention to be held in
our city, here is a brief report of our progress so far. Because
some plans from now on will depend upon funds available and your
preferences, you will also find a few questions on which we will appreciate your suggestions and approval.

Date, Time, and Place

The Tower Oaks Hotel offices are holding the following reservations
for us:
Date: Tuesday, January 26, 198_
Informal luncheon: 12:15 - 1:30 Regency Room--for up to 100 persons
Conference rooms: 9:00 - 4:30 Mezzanine rooms 202, 203, 204--each
                                accommodating up to 40 persons plus
                                exhibit tables.

Tentative Program

So that the convention will have an appropriate official opening,
the committee members are delighted that you have agreed to express
the opening welcome--as executive vice president of the company that
is sponsoring the convention.

    Keynote Speaker.--You will probably be glad to hear that for key-
noter we can count on having Jonathan Harrison, vice president and
general manager of National Products Company. The topic he has
chosen is "The Challenge Ahead for Purchasing Shortage Items."

    Other Participants.--As the attached tentative program (Exhibit
A) shows, we will have 10 outstanding business leaders on panel discussions in the morning and afternoon sessions. A 15-minute coffee
break is planned for 10:30 a.m. and 3 p.m.

Publicity

Our first announcement in newspapers (local and in three states)
will be early in December. One or two other news stories should appear during January.

If funds allow, we would like to mail two letters to all purchasing managers in this region, along with a colorful brochure of the conference program, exhibits, film specials, and evening entertainment for those staying in the city overnight. Exhibit B shows the planned layout. The ABC Printer has quoted a price of $ for 200 copies and $ for 150 copies.

Estimated Financial Requirements

Exhibit C, attached, is a suggested tentative budget. The estimated total of $ excludes the cost of stationery, typing master copies, and mailing services. Norma Henry has assured me that these expenses can be taken care of through our company's usual supplies and postage budget and need not be itemized here.

We will appreciate any suggestions you may have about our estimated expenses and your approval of the needed funds. Then we can proceed to make the necessary arrangements.

Summary

To date many persons have already assisted our committee with their expressions of preferences and suggestions. We have hotel reservations, firm acceptances from keynote speaker and panelists, price quotations on a brochure for mailing, and tentative publicity plans.

You will receive from us a definite program soon after plans are completed and another progress report on December 10. We expect to devote many more hours to planning and writing. After that we can all look forward to an interesting and successful convention.

In the meantime, your preferences regarding publicity brochure, estimated financial needs, and any other suggestions you may have will be sincerely appreciated.

VP:wh
Attachments: Exhibits A, B, C

cc: Susan Rader
    Timothy Blythe

Monthly Reports

Included in this section are only those informational reports that are written monthly in memorandum report format. (As you know, there are numerous other monthly reports; many are analytical—mentioned in the preceding section; many others are presented on special printed forms. When a memorandum report is written each month about the same department and to the same reader(s), an introduction and terminal section are unnecessary. Report 8 keeps the home office informed about certain activities at a branch. The text headings help the reader grasp the main topics quickly and easily. Instead of the signature and typewritten title after the report's last paragraph, Mr. Bell could have initialed or signed his name near his typewritten name after FROM. Also, a blank line after each heading and paragraph would improve the report's appearance.

Memo Report 8

This monthly memo report—from a branch manager to an official at the bank's home office—does not include an introduction or terminal section.

```
TO:       David Bell                        DATE: October 2, 198_
FROM:     Paul Roe
SUBJECT:  Branch Activities--September 198_
```

```
Personnel Training
1. September 1 marked the beginning of the second phase of the Bank
   Offices' training program.  Training is progressing satisfactorily
   and on schedule.  With Marton Harrington's resignation, we need to
   make a slight alteration in the program, but don't expect any
   postponement of training.
2. Martin's termination will advance the training of Harriet Samson
   and Andria Mines.


Business Development Activity
1. I again contacted Ann Dean, surgeon, regarding transfer of funds
   from Regional Association of Neurosurgeons, of which she is trea-
   surer.  She says she has received permission to transfer about
   $10,000 more to National Bank after December 1.  This additional
   amount brings the total to about $55,000.
2. Although 3 employee vacations and one prolonged illness have dis-
   rupted my outside business-call activity, I have aimed to
   converse regularly with every broker, real estate agent, insur-
   ance agent, and attorney that comes into the office.  Although it
   is difficult to assess results from the little additional time
   and effort spent on this form of intraoffice business develop-
   ment, numerous phone calls for loan information and a couple of
   loan commitments were a direct result of this activity.


Customer Comments and Action Taken
1. An unusually high number of customers in September complimented
   us on the friendly and courteous service of our personnel.
2. We had a complaint from a large checking account depositor re-
   garding a check on which he had stopped payment too late (his
   creditor had already cashed the check).  Meanwhile our depositor
   had mailed to his creditor a second check (with a slightly dif-
   ferent amount), which was also cashed.  Both were paid by our
   bank.  He blamed us for allowing this situation to happen and con-
   demned our system for not catching the stop-payment in time.  He
   quizzed Jean Warde unmercifully until I interfered.  When he
   started swearing, I invited him to leave the office.  Finally he
```

```
calmed  down,  listened  to  my  review  of  the entire  matter,  apolo-
gized  for  his  error,  and  left,  still  a  friend  of  the  bank.

Building,  Equipment,  and  Parking  Lot  Comments
1. We  encountered  the  usual  autumn  heating  problem  in  the  office--
   cold  in  the  morning  and  hot  in  the  afternoon.  Blower  fans  are
   turned  off  at  noon  each  day.  We  have  told  Doner  Company  of  this
   circumstance  many  times,  but  they  cannot  rectify  the  situation.
2. Interior  clock  does  not  keep  correct  time.  Maintenance  department
   knows  about  the  trouble  with  this  clock  and  will  take  care  of  it.
```

(signature and title of branch manager)

In summary, although one of the distinguishing features of memo reports is the three-part body (introduction, text, and terminal section), sometimes the introduction and/or terminal section may be omitted. When you understand the three basic plans for memo reports, however, you can adapt to the special formats and headings you'll encounter on the job.

Furthermore, for the often-used reports, many business firms develop printed forms and/or standardized headings for reports. These all save time—for those who must present the needed information in the reports and for those who receive them. They assure uniformity and completeness of coverage and permit the receiving officer to know what to expect so he or she can compare it by periods. Also, the suggested format makes it easy for the report writer to include the data the receiver wants. The writer merely adds the needed information under each heading, without worrying about what headings should be used.

LETTER REPORTS

As the title indicates, a letter report uses the format of a letter—with date, inside address, salutation, body (different from a letter), complimentary close, signature, reference section. It is typed on the firm's letterhead. Often is has a subject line typewritten a line or two below the salutation. Its length may range from two to five (seldom more) pages. The heading for pages beyond the first is the same as for a letter—reader's name, page number, date.

Though the general format of the letter report is like that of a letter, its body requires some of the special qualities of short reports, as discussed below.

1. *The first paragraph* usually includes the following elements found in an introduction:

Authorization (if any, mention date of request)

Purpose (always)

Problem (if one exists)

Statement of the results (optional)

Plan of presentation (depends on length of report)

Examples:

a. As requested in your January 7 letter, I have investigated the delivery service department, with regard to reducing its operating cost.

b. While auditing your books last month, I noticed your firm does not have a centralized receiving department. The purpose of this report is to explain the present setup and then show how a receiving department will benefit your organization.

c. It is a pleasure to report to you our progress in the year just completed and look ahead with you for this year just started.

2. *The middle paragraphs* comprising the text should present *objectively, without emotional appeals, all pertinent facts—both favorable and unfavorable.* Sources and methods should be mentioned along with emphasis on findings or results. Headings, visual aids, and transitional sentences are also included wherever desirable.

3. *The last paragraph* brings the letter report to a pleasant, friendly close, as for letters. If you need to conclude or recommend, do so just before the last paragraph. If appropriate, offer to discuss further or to come to the reader's office.

One use of letter reports is to answer inquiries. For example, in letter report 1 Mr. Mains, graphic services manager of a corporation with 23 branches, informs Ms. Golden, vice president of a corporation in another state, about his firm's one-year experience with the Compugraphic composition system. Ms. Golden wrote that the manufacturer had given her Mr. Mains's name as an example of a new (one-year) customer. She said she is especially interested in Mr. Mains's comments on performance and dependability of this system.

Letter Report 1

A manager's report on his firm's use of a graphics system.

Dear Ms. Golden:

Regarding your inquiry July 15, I am glad to tell you our experience with the Compugraphic system. We have been pleased with its performance, advantages, and dependability. It has given us better technology and also new types for copy and headlines.

Performance

By using the keyboards with video display terminals our operator can see the copy as it will come out and can easily plug in any changes. When the type is set in these Editwriters, it is run out on a related machine that does fast, high-quality typesetting. It has produced our bulletins, charts, forms, illustrations, and other non-standard graphics in a much more efficient manner than was possible with our previous old equipment.

Advantages

An important feature of this equipment is its storage capability. Everything can be stored on disks and can be called up later when needed. This new system has saved us considerable time because it allows us to typeset documents without rekeystroking. Now, although work volume in the department is up significantly, the projects are getting done, more of the corporate need can be met in-house, and we are producing more professional-looking products efficiently. Graphics users throughout our corporation are seeing new capabilities and results.

Dependability

This new system has served exceptionally well the needs of several departments this year. It has required only one minor repair, which the factory serviceman took care of promptly. The scheduled six-month checkups also were thorough and dependable.

Three quarterly reports to the board of directors, plus the chairman's key item reports, have been completed on the new equipment, with very satisfying results. Also, our monthly News Bulletin has received unsolicited compliments from many readers since we've used the new equipment. It also gives dependable service for our profit planning forms. They can be stored on disks for reuse next year, and any changes can be quickly plugged in.

Major users in our headquarters and branches are the communications and publications departments. In trying to meet everyone's needs we have found that prescheduling is very important because of the number of projects we're involved in. If a department is doing its own graphics, this new equipment is a dependable helper, timesaver, and producer of quality end products.

Ms. Golden, please feel welcome to write again or phone me if you have any other questions regarding our use of the Compugraphic system. It is a pleasure to help you.

Perhaps you have already noticed that a letter report like the one above about a system or machine is organized the same way as a letter of recommendation you might write about a person—his or her work for you or credit record with your firm. In fact, basically a recommendation is a confidential report. If the inquirer asks you several (five or more) questions about broad areas and doesn't furnish a printed report form for your answers, you will need to write a long, factual, objective message that is really a letter report. If your answers require more than one paragraph under each question, you should of course number the questions and/or use headings to help improve readability. Your own good judgment should guide you in choice of headings and format.

Besides writing letter reports to answer inquiries about persons or about products you don't sell, you may also need to write letter reports about the products (or services) your firm does sell. In general, the same care and techniques you use for planning and writing any other objective report should be used for these letter reports, whether they go to a government agency, customer, or other inquirer.

Another popular use of letter reports is the annual message the company president sends to stockholders. In many firms—especially the larger ones— this letter report is part of the printed annual report. However, in other firms the president's letter report is mailed on company letterhead stationery along with enclosed financial statements.

Though many letter reports go outside the company, they may also be used inside. For example, in some firms traveling salespersons write letter reports back to their firm from the field.

In addition to the various kinds of letter reports already mentioned, one more deserves mention here. It is the *progress report.* If you are a management consultant, an independent researcher, or a representative of a firm doing work under contract on a long-term (perhaps yearly) project for another company, you should report your progress periodically—in letter-report form. Under some agreements such reports must be made monthly, quarterly, semiannually, or annually. Basically, the general topics discussed in a progress report in letter form are similar to those outlined for a progress report in memorandum format on page 515.

OTHER SHORT REPORTS

You will also see—and write—in business other short reports besides the memo report, letter report, and printed or standardized reports. The three most significant are annual reports, "dressed-up" short reports, and proposals.

Annual Reports

Every organization—business, government, religious, athletic, and so forth— has annual reports that summarize activities and financial affairs. For some small concerns the report is exceptionally "short"—consisting of perhaps a brief transmittal letter with one or two pages of financial statements. For other organizations—especially corporations which must report to their stock- holders—the annual report may begin with a top official's letter report. Some- times the letter is the entire report (perhaps eight or more pages). If not, then the report body discusses operations and activities; and of course every annual report should have a balance sheet and statement of earnings and expenses.

Some reports also include pictures of officers, employees, products, machines, operations—plus charts or graphs and easy-to-understand explanations in nontechnical terms.[4] Financial statements also may have simplified discussions understandable by any stockholder with little knowledge of accounting. To see examples of various annual reports, you might write to selected corporations or consult your business or general library—or your campus placement office.

"Dressed-Up" Short Reports

In some situations a comprehensive, important memo report or letter report would be more impressive if it had some of the "dress-up" features of a long report. If your report is, for example, four or five single-space typewritten pages long and has several attachments, you might consider using: a title page, transmittal letter or memo, the report body (typed in single- or double-space), plus an appendix for the attachments. (For discussion and illustrations of these prefatory and supplemental parts, see Chapter 18.)

To give you an idea of how one of the short reports already discussed in this chapter might be dressed up, let's look again at memo report 1 on pages 503–505. Suppose you were also required to attach to this report confidential copies of recommendation letters and test sheets for each of the three tellers. Your report would then have 12 pages of attachments plus three single-spaced or five double-spaced pages of body (tables would remain single-spaced). If you decide to add a title page, it will include the TO, FROM, SUBJECT, DATE information attractively set up in these three parts: (1) Evaluation of Three Teller Applicants, (2) Prepared for Mr. Gene Mohr, Manager, Savings Department; and (3) By (your name), Assistant Manager, Personnel Department, March 15, 198_. You will then omit this information from the first page of the report. If you use a transmittal memo, you'll also make a few changes in the first paragraph of the report introduction (as discussed on pages 553–555, in Chapter 18). Your 12 pages of attachments can become the appendix; pages will be numbered consecutively after the last page of your report. For example, if your report body (double-spaced) ends on page 5, the appendix first page will be page 6, and so on through page 17.

Short Proposal Reports

A special type of report that has become increasingly important in business and industry as well as in government and education is the proposal. In a survey of the chief executives for nearly 50 randomly selected manufacturing firms with

---

[4] For some large national and international corporations annual reports are often elaborate, colorful brochures printed on glossy paper with 40 or more pages. As such, they are outside the scope of this chapter, for they are not "short." Actually, they are impressive advertising brochures for the public as well as stockholders. They also are informative for college graduates and others seeking jobs with reputable firms.

$1 million minimum annual sales volume, 65 percent reported that proposals play an important part in the operations of their firms. Of these, over 50 percent said the part is "great" or "crucial."[5]

Like other reports, some proposals are short and informal; others are long and formal. The present section discusses an informal short report proposal. Usually it is in letter-report form, with attachments. Its purpose is (a) to get a project accepted and/or (b) to get your company—or you—accepted for work on a project. The proposal illustrated here is a sales presentation a firm makes to a prospective buyer. (Do not consider it a model of perfection; it is, however, an example of a fairly typical informal proposal to sell an installation product. You can probably suggest ways to improve it.) Before sending the proposal, the seller has visited the company's place of business, studied its present setup, and discussed its needs.

The proposal consists of:

Transmittal letter (in the usual letter format)

Attached report on: Explanation of Spacefinder Filing System
Advantages of Spacefinder System
Present System Now in Operation
Proposed System
Cost of Proposed Equipment

This letter and the attachment are comparable to the application letter and résumé; the letter sells, while the enclosure or attachment presents pertinent facts effectively. Notice that the letter follows the AIDA formula for sales letters. The first paragraph catches the reader's attention; the second and third paragraphs create desire by referring to facts and figures in the attached report (about present system and benefits of the Spacefinder System); the last paragraph asks for action.

The attached report permits the writer to streamline the letter without cluttering it with details. As with any good sales pitch, the report leads the reader through explanation and advantages of Spacefinder, details of the present system, and proposed system before it mentions cost. The letter and the report together constitute the proposal which is to convince the reader to convert to the new system.

Dear Mr. Jaysen

The attached proposal is for a conversion by your firm from drawer files to TAB PRODUCTS' Spacefinder Filing System. This conversion will result in significantly increased filing efficiency and a sav-

---

[5] Bill G. Rainey, "Proposal Writing: A Neglected Area of Instruction," *The Journal of Business Communication,* vol. 11, no. 4, Summer 1974.

ing of floor space. It is a proven fact that the Unit Spacefinder Filing System does increase filing efficiency up to 50%.

The system you now use in the vault on the third floor is sketched on the enclosed quarter-inch grid paper. The vault is drawn to exact scale and the drawer files now being used are placed in their present position. Using the overlay you will notice how much space you can save in this vault when you have the TAB PRODUCTS' Unit Spacefinder Filing System. It also increases efficiency in locating records and returning them to the file. Furthermore, you can use this floor plan in the future to expand storage in the same area.

The attached pages explain the Spacefinder System and quote figures showing advantages to your firm in floor space savings and efficiency. You are welcome also to see time studies made by other firms that achieved 50% increased efficiency.

If you need further information, please call upon me for assistance. My telephone number is 111-2222. Thank you for this opportunity to quote on TAB PRODUCTS Unit Spacefinder Filing System.

PROPOSAL

to (*name of receiver's firm*)

for conversion to **TAB PRODUCTS'** Unit Spacefinder Filing System

Explanation of Spacefinder Filing System

The Unit Spacefinder Filing System differs from shelf and drawer filing in many respects. Listed below are the efficiency factors of Unit Spacefinder:

1. You file in a container, not in a drawer, on a shelf, or in a cabinet. The unit box is 4" wide. This means that the documents have support every 4". This need is one of the most important required in lateral filing. The more support, the easier it is to "in-file" and pull records. (See sketches attached.)

2. The unique "stair-step" effect, caused by the angle in which unit boxes are hung, gives you easier accessibility never before possible. This accessibility is an exclusive feature of Unit Spacefinder. Every folder is easy to reach and easy to see.

3. You get flexibility. You can rearrange and expand without a lot of time-consuming bother, such as in the case of drawer files or shelf files. You create space where you need it simply by sliding boxes easily along rails. There is no need to transfer records handful by handful.

2

Advantages of Unit Spacefinder Lateral Filing System

1. The "stair-step" effect allows folders to be readily identified, removed, and replaced with the least effort.

2. The unit boxes can be removed from the racks, a feature which
   allows:
   a. Work with the records at a desk for purging or for check-
      ing, etc.
   b. Fast fleeting of records by rearrangement of the unit
      boxes.

3. Visibility is a definite advantage. All folders are exposed
   to the file clerks and with proper indexing can be located at
   least 50% faster than when the folders are used in drawer
   files.

4. A 50% increased efficiency by record staffs handling their
   work load has been proven in many filing areas, both large
   and small. Efficiency means saved person-hours, which in
   turn, means saved dollars.

5. Flexibility of the Unit enables us to assure you we can tai-
   lor the Unit Spacefinder framework to fit your needs. It is
   freestanding and does not have to be anchored to the walls or
   floor; therefore, if you need a different configuration to
   fit a particular location, we can easily meet your desires.

6. You get more filing space in less than half the floor space.

3

Present System Now in Operation

12 ea. 5-Drawer legal-size files
 8 ea. 4-Drawer legal-size files
 Total filing inches   2,300"
 Total floor space   122.11 sq. ft.
   (including drawer pull)

Folders used are 3d cut, top position right-hand side, legal.
Filed in numerical sequence.
   a. Conversion factor — use same folders
   b. Use Colorvue Guide Cards, which reveal inserted number on
      both sides.

Proposed System

Use combination of 42" and 30" Single Face Sections of Unit
Spacefinder against wall and double-face Unit Spacefinder
spaced 42" to provide ample aisle space.
Total filing inches 2,380"
Total floor space   47.02 sq.ft.

```
                                                              4

Conversion
Present folders can be used.  Right-hand tab allows easy identi-
fication of numbers.
Guide Cards should be inserted in file every two to three feet.

Summary
1. Increase in filing inches - 80"
2. Floor space released for expansion or other purposes--
   75.09 square feet
3. Efficiency increase - minimum 35%

Cost of Proposed Equipment
1 ea. 5422  Initial 45" legal-size single    $---.--   $---.--
2 ea. 5334  Additional 42" legal-size with
            workshelf, single                 ---.--    ---.--
3 ea. 5404  Additional 30" legal-size single  ---.--    ---.--
1 ea. 5430  Initial 45" legal-size double
            with two workshelves               ---.--    ---.--
1 ea. 5408  Additional 30" legal-size
            double                             ---.--    ---.--
                                                       _____
                                                      $-,---.--
```

SUMMARY

The preceding illustrations and discussions have indicated the wide variety of subject matter, uses, and formats for memorandum reports, printed and standardized reports, letter reports, and other special reports. Yet, basically, all short reports have various characteristics in common. If you think logically and objectively, consider your purpose and your reader(s), use good judgment with facts, plan and organize carefully, and achieve the qualities of well-written reports as suggested in both Chapters 16 and 17, you will turn out commendable short reports on the job.

EXERCISES

Rewrites

1. The following letter report (answering an inquiry) is quite good. Your job is to make it even better. Assume the customer asked about all the topics mentioned; thus, keep all the ideas but improve the report in these ways:

a. Insert headings—second- and third-degree or third- and fourth-degree headings.
b. Show more you-attitude.
c. Change at least five passive verbs to active voice (and of course make whatever subject changes are necessary).
d. Tabulate some listed details—for easier reading.
e. Make any other minor changes desirable for good business writing.

Thank you for your request for information relating to INSURED savings accounts in this association. This reply includes facts concerning types of savings plans, security of savings, withdrawal of funds, and necessary forms for opening an account. I am also enclosing a copy of our latest financial statement and several pamphlets of general information which give you essential facts you desire about us and the savings accounts we issue.

We have two types of savings plans available--a passbook savings account and a 6-month savings certificate.

Briefly, an insured passbook savings account may be opened for any amount at any time. Upon receipt of your remittance, we issue to you our savings passbook with the amount credited inside. Additional sums may be added in any amount and at any time you desire. Interest earnings are credited to passbook savings accounts on March 31, June 30, September 30, and December 31 of each year. This is done automatically on these dates whether you send in your passbook or not. Gold Bond stamps are given as an extra bonus to passbook savers, as outlined on the enclosed card. The current rate of dividend on passbook savings is $5\frac{1}{2}\%$ per year, compounded daily.

In addition to our savings passbooks, we also issue insured 6-month savings certificates. Designed to offer larger, longer-term investors the maximum rate for insured savings, these certificates are issued for a minimum of $1,000, with larger amounts in multiples of $100. They differ from passbook accounts in several respects. Earnings on certificates begin on the day of purchase and are paid at the end of each 6 months on maturity dates. The certificates are in certificate form, and checks are mailed to the certificate holders every 6 months from the date of issue, instead of being automatically credited to the account as is done on passbook accounts. Of course, if you have a passbook savings account with State Federal, the dividends on your savings certificate may be automatically credited to your passbook account upon your request. For your convenience, savings certificates are automatically renewed on the maturity dates for an additional 6 months unless you are notified at least 30 days prior to a maturity date. The current interest rate on six-month savings certificates is $8\frac{1}{4}\%$ per year.

Savings in this association are INSURED up to $100,000 by the Federal Savings and Loan Insurance Corporation, Washington, D.C. We are also members of the Federal Home Loan Bank System, a reserve

credit system for associations. We lend our funds upon the security of selected monthly reducing first mortgages on homes. So,
you will see, there is really exceptional security for savings
placed with us.

You will probably wish some information concerning withdrawal of
your funds. It has always been the policy of this association to
pay withdrawals in PART OR IN FULL without notice. We have followed
this policy ever since organization in 1926. However, a savings and
loan association may require notice of withdrawal if necessary. If
the country should again experience an economic emergency such as
prevailed in 1932–33, it is possible that we would require notice.
Under such circumstances it is quite likely that every financial institution would necessarily restrict withdrawals. This provision in
the savings and loan laws is a wise one for the protection of the
customers.

For your convenience I am enclosing a signature card which may be
used either for an individual or a joint account. If you desire to
open an account in your own name alone, you should use Form 100.
If, however, you wish to open an account in your name jointly with
some other person, probably another member of your family, you
should use Form 200, on the reverse side of the card. If you desire
a six–month savings certificate, the same signature card may be
used.

We also have trust accounts, frequently used by parents in carrying
savings accounts for children, or by persons who desire to hold
funds in trusts for another. Signature card forms for this type of
account will be mailed to you upon request.

I thank you kindly for your inquiry and extend to you a cordial invitation to use the facilities of this association.

2. Given below is a report to shareholders. Assume this message appears on
   one side of an 8½- by 11-inch sheet and the annual statement of condition
   appears on the opposite side. Rewrite so that the information is easier to
   read. For example, can you put in table form some or all of the figures and
   dates given in the first three paragraphs? And can you list the names and
   titles in the last two paragraphs? Also, add an appropriate rounding-out last
   paragraph.

Report to the Shareholders
We ended our 61st year May 3, 19___, which proved to be a very good
year. Our assets totaled almost $12,000,000 being $11,997,728.90,
representing an increase of $430,315.75 which was due principally to
the increase in home loans of $538,622.30.

Savings accounts reflected a total of $11,013,074.26, representing a
gain for the year of $385,321.70, which was substantially greater
than the gain in the previous year. During the year the association

repaid $265,000 to the Federal Home Loan Bank and had no notes pay-
able May 3, 198_. Net operating income, after expenses, amounted to
$558,293.40, reflecting an increase of $32,423.01 over the prior
year. The operating ratio of the association for the fiscal year
was 17.87% of gross operating income, which was substantially lower
than the national average, which is in excess of 27%.

During the year, $42,000 was added to reserves, $495,810.52 was distributed as earning on savings accounts, and $20,482.88 was added to
undivided profit. Total reserves were $514,000 and undivided profit
$87,505.03, making a total of $601,505.03, representing over 5% of
total liabilities. Our reserves and undivided profit places us in a
rather enviable position and leaves no question, in my opinion, of
our ability to continue at our present rate of return to our savings
accounts.

At our Shareholders Meeting held Monday, April 5, the following were
elected to serve as directors for the ensuing year: William E.
Brady, Robert E. Becker, Stephen G. Mills, Mary A. Aitken, Daniel A.
Roberts, Lisa L. Gifford, and Louise G. Hulett.

At the Directors Reorganization Meeting, immediately following the
Shareholders Meeting, the following officers were elected: Chairperson of the Board of Directors and President, Judy E. Brady; Vice
Chairperson, Robert E. Becker; Executive Vice President, Secretary
and Treasurer, Stephen G. Mills; Vice President and Assistant Secretary and Treasurer, Louise G. Hulett; and Assistant Secretary,
William A. Dugger. Sylvia Reddie was reappointed Savings Officer
and Bonnie Whittemore was appointed Head Bookkeeper. Fred L. Sharp
was reappointed attorney.

Problems

1. *(Informational memo report with table or other comparisons)* Your employer is interested in expanding the business and asks you to prepare some
   information about these cities: Jacksonville, Florida; Toledo, Ohio;
   Oklahoma City, Oklahoma; Charlotte, North Carolina; and Charleston,
   West Virginia.

   He or she is interested in many geographic and demographic items, but
   asks you to begin your study with only six. Make brief (but complete)
   comparisons, on the topics listed below, for each of the cities. Use whatever
   form, headings, tables, and content you believe necessary for a complete
   answer. Keep your memo report to no more than two typewritten pages.
   Your report will compare

   a. Population
   b. Area size
   c. Transportation facilities
   d. Health facilities

     e. Educational facilities

     f. Major industries

One of the best places to find such information is one of the several almanacs which are available; or perhaps you can find it in a standard encyclopedia. Whichever source you use, be certain that you footnote the reference for your employer's information and that you use up-to-date material.

Finally, you should remember that if you do a complete job for him or her on this report, you will probably be called on to do additional research on the project. With that in mind you might want to make some appropriate mention of willingness to do future research.

2. *(Informational letter report)* Assume you have received a letter from the Assistant Dean of Students, Dr. Jean Inquire, Administration Building, your college or university, stating that you have been selected in a random sample to take part in a survey. The information gathered will be included—without student names—in an orientation booklet for entering students. She asks you to answer these questions regarding your course costs for this quarter (or semester):

     a. What is your year in college and major?

     b. How much did your textbooks cost you? Please mention course names and book titles, too.

     c. What other required course materials did you have to pay for and how much did they cost? (Include lab fees, if any, but exclude tuition fees.) Figure only prices of new texts and materials (but you may mention any savings you gained if you bought used items).

     d. What relation, if any, do you find between these total course costs and the number of credit hours your courses carry?

     e. What relation, if any, do you find between these total course costs and the college (Arts & Sciences, Engineering, etc.) or department (Business, Education, Art) in which they are offered? (Answer this question if you are taking courses in more than one department or college of this institution.)

The only data you need are the prices of *new* books and materials plus lab fees, if any—for each course you are carrying *and* the credit hours of each course.

In case you feel that this quarter or semester is exceptional for you (perhaps because you are taking only one or two courses), you may, if you wish, include information for both last quarter and this one. Indicate clearly the costs and credits in each.

Suggestions: Write your report in good business letter-report form—with heading, inside address, subject line, salutation, and closing. Use well-chosen headings to mark the main divisions of your report. Construct a table that includes your courses, credit hours, book titles, and costs of the required books. Keep your report factual, objective, and well-organized.[6]

3. *(Analytical memo report)* You are the new assistant to Mr. James Rohn, regional manager of employee relations and education (name company). Two days ago you received the following memo from him:

> Will you please look into the film "*(name)*," review it, and report to me what you think of it? Specifically, I'd like (in a concise written report) to know:
>
> 1. What are the main ideas of the film?
> 2. What are its technical (and other) aspects—length, photography, method of presentation, quality, cost?
> 3. How useful would it be to our company and our branches?
> 4. What do you recommend we do—purchase, rent, or forget it?

Your office selects, from time to time, various instructional materials, visual aids, and other teaching materials for use in your management training program at the main office (your city). In addition, they are also available to the four branches whenever requested and when not used at the headquarters office. Each branch has its own trainees. Your company has 2,000 employees, of whom 900 are working within a radius of 300 miles from the home office. About 30 percent of your employees are in some kind of supervisory or management capacity. They communicate not only orally, but also through letters, memos, and reports.

The one communication film that the company now owns is a sound filmstrip, in black and white, shown for the past 10 years, regarding essentially letter writing. Most of the older executives think it is still adequate. It's *Dear Mrs. Somebody*. Mr. Rohn (age 59) is always on the lookout, however, for the newest and best materials regardless of cost, as long as they can be justified as to their usefulness for the firm.

Assume that yesterday you reviewed this color film about which he asked you to report. If your instructor can show a film to the entire class—or if you have seen a film in another course—use the facts and title from that film for this report. If no film is available for class showing, assume you previewed *Management Communications* at the Audiovisual Services Center in your city.

This morning Mr. Rohn, in passing your desk, casually remarked he had heard of this film (the one you previewed) through a manager who sat next to him at a luncheon recently. Mr. Rohn's comments indicated, indirectly, what his hopes and preferences are about the use of this film in your company. After seeing the film, you now realize that your own honest

---

[6] Actually, for a survey of this type the inquirer should send a questionnaire form on which each respondent merely fills in answers. However, for purpose of this assignment, let's assume she sent merely a stamped envelope and that she is also interested in seeing how well college students express themselves in written reports. Make yours one of the best!

conclusions and recommendations are contrary to Mr. Rohn's expectations. (This realization guides you in selection of an organization plan for your report.) Regardless of whether you report on *Management Communications* or another film you saw yourself in a class, you are free to recommend whatever you wish, provided you objectively consider all facts.

Facts about the film *Management Communications:*

25 minutes long: produced and sold by BNA Incorporated. Bureau of National Affairs, 1231 24th St., N.W., Washington, D.C. Assume it costs $450. You've also discovered that the local Audiovisual Services Center rents it for a three-day period at $18 plus postage. They require at least 24 hours' advance notice, and they will ship the films anywhere across the country, except to Hawaii and Canada.

Your rough draft notes on main ideas of the film are these:

Shows a series of modern office scenes with a manager and one, two, or three employees who are under his management. Scenes show good and bad techniques of communication by the manager. A narrator helpfully explains the differences in techniques. Color, excellent; acting, amateur.

Major viewpoints are empathy and credibility on part of management toward subordinates and customers. Empathy is crucial. The manager must be able to put him- or herself in another person's place. To change a person's viewpoint, the manager must show that the person will benefit through the change. The manager must find out what customers' or fellow employees' beliefs are, how they will change or resist the information given, and what are their interests.

To be credible the manager must be competent, dependable, and enthusiastic. Competence is attained from a communication aspect. The manager must keep well informed and communicate necessary facts to subordinates so they in turn can transfer information to their subordinates. When possible, he or she should let them make suggestions before decisions are made; let them participate.

Being dependable requires that the manager not shirk managerial duties. The manager must not "pass the buck" by assuming no responsibility for actions or blaming them on another person. If he or she has an unfavorable management decision to pass on to the subordinates, it must be done in a way that assures them they can depend on the manager to help in every possible manner.

The manager must be enthusiastic and have enough energy to see things carried through to the end without complaining when work demands are heavy. The last four letters of "enthusiasm" may stand for "I am sold myself" (on whatever topic the manager is discussing), but the manager must be sincere.

Make any other necessary assumptions for your memo report; indicate them in a separate note clipped to the top of the report you hand to your instructor.

This is the first report you've been asked to write for Mr. Rohn. Write it in memo-report format; be sure it is well organized, with appropriate headings and subheadings. Mr. Rohn likes concise and complete reports. Try to keep this one within two typed pages (elite type), single-spaced, and trimmed to basic but important essentials. Show facts and figures regarding relative costs for renting or buying; consider home office and branch needs. Try to construct and refer to a table including the number of showings, days, and time periods needed and the rental costs for the head office and branches.

4. *(Informational memo report)* You are a management trainee for Central Advertising Agency, in which the ability to write good reports is an important qualification. Two days ago Mr. James Sorgens, training director, asked you to find out what types of reports are written by account executives in this firm. He suggested you interview Ms. May Emerson, vice president/account executive at Central and then write him the best report you can about your findings. Yesterday during your interview with Ms. Emerson you jotted down the following notes (with her permission). Ms. Emerson also gave you a sample of each of the four reports most often written in the company and she added general comments on agency reports.

Account executive writes reports when directly involved in the situation. Otherwise, person involved and a/c exec decide together who writes report. In all cases concerning client, however, a/c exec is ultimately responsible for reports concerning client's campaign.

Bulk of reports written by a/c exec: job memo, memo report, conference (or meeting) report, and recommendation report.

Job memo report—most important in the office. An intraoffice report written to all depts. of the agency. Written by a/c exec as often as necessary whenever any action on client's campaign is called for. They give authorization and instruction concerning client's campaign. Generally, a/c exec writes these daily.

Memo report written as often as necessary—usually daily. Short (usually one page)—to communicate information to a specific person within agency. This report concerns information dealing with many facets of client's advertising campaign needed by the a/c exec in performing his job or her job.

Recommendation reports—most extensive and comprehensive report by a/c exec. Written perhaps once or twice a year; gives client agency's recommendations, marketing plan, budget analysis, and advertising approach for campaign.

Agency and client both have copy of this report; many are 20–30 pages long. Not only does a/c exec receive a copy, but so does head of agency and heads of all depts. involved with a/c.

Important that a/c exec and client understand always where ad campaign stands and how it is progressing. So that each one has a record of all the decisions made concerning the campaign, the conference report is used. Written immediately after a conference or meeting between agency and client. Purpose: clarify discussion and the decisions made at the meeting.

General comments:

General purpose of reports—no matter what type—is to ensure and expedite communication between agency and client or between depts. of agency. Emerson pointed out several items she thought this agency's reports could be improved upon. Also those items she thought made for good reports. Also provided information on format this agency uses for reports and what they have done to improve quality of their reports.

Too many reports not concise. Tend to be wordy and too long; lack clarity; and negative. Ms. E. thought that if reports were more objective and emphasized positive rather than neg., they wd. help communication more. Also desirable factors: brevity and conciseness. In general, reports should communicate entire message in fewest words possible without sounding abrupt.

Format—no particular order or format is strictly adhered to. Whether text or terminal section comes first is not a written policy, but main points of discussion should ideally precede the discussion to expedite reading of report.

Company does not use any printed forms for reports, *except* for the job memo report. Nature of a/c in question dictates form used for recommendation or conference reports. Headings are used to assist reader of report.

Because of volatile nature of advertising business, no formal school in better report writing techniques is conducted. However, the American Assoc. of Advertising Agencies does provide some bulletins on better writing techniques. These help improve agency reports. Also, the a/c exec attempts to stress qualities of conciseness, clarity, and other desirable points of report writing in informal discussions with other execs and their subordinates.

Organize these rough draft notes into a complete, well-written, concise memorandum report. Use inductive plan and two degrees of headings. Assume you are attaching the four exhibits; be sure to refer to them appropriately within your report text. Remember to use topic sentences for paragraphs and to introduce subheadings properly.

5. *(Analytical memo report)* One of your duties as manager of Jaycy's Manufacturing is to check the plant's suggestion box. Recently a number of complaints have appeared about the unsightly, unsanitary mess in the washroom. Some employees have been careless about using and disposing of paper towels. Each dispenser has a built-in trash basket and even a sticker to remind employees to place used towels in the basket. However, the problem still persists.

As a solution, you have decided to replace paper towels with a hot-air hand dryer. At your request, Haworth Inc., makers of the Jetaire Hand Dryer, sent a salesperson to evaluate your needs. The salesperson made a cost analysis of your situation and also presented an estimate of the cost for changing to the Jetaire Hand Dryer. Jaycy's has 200 employees and each employee visits the washroom an average of 4 times a day. The average number of paper towels used each visit is 2½ towels at a cost of $0.003 a towel. Assuming 22 working days a month, a 3-year cost figure for towels alone was derived. Haworth's salesperson also pointed out that there are "intangible" costs involved with paper towels. These include time spent in filling out purchase orders and the cost of mailing the order; cost per square foot of storage of the paper towels; costs in distributing, collecting, and carting away paper towels; and plumbing expenses for toilets and sinks clogged with paper towels. These intangible costs usually amount to 50 percent of the 3-year total cost of paper towels for any business.

According to the salesperson, each of the four washrooms in your plant should have three Jetaire units. The units cost $140 apiece and together use about $4.50 in electricity per month. There is also an installation fee of $95 (for all machines).

Because the estimated acquisition cost of the Jetaire Hand Dryers is over $800, it is necessary to receive authorization from Mr. Steve Larson, the plant superintendent. He is a very busy person and often does not have the time to sort through a lengthy cost analysis report. He likes to know immediately what the cost and savings are in the company. Write a memo report bringing to Mr. Larson's attention these points as well as other facts such as employee benefits. Include in your discussion section two concise, easy-to-read columns of labeled figures showing calculations that lead to your important totals. For your organizational plan will you use 2(a), (b), or (c) pages 505–509?

6. *(Analytical memo report)* As assistant sales manager, you have been delegated the responsibility of evaluating sites for the company's sales conference in your city. Each April your company's 225 sales representatives from all over the state attend a four-day sales meeting to study product improvements, discuss marketing strategies, set sales quotas, and develop selling techniques. You are to investigate two hotel-motels and evaluate each on suitability of facilities. The sales manager will use your analytical memo report to make her own decision and recommendations.

The sales manager has narrowed the choice down to two sites—one downtown, the other suburban. She has prepared these criteria on which each facility will be evaluated:

a. 100 double rooms, 30 single rooms, 2 bedroom-living room suites.
b. Banquet facilities and staff to accommodate 250 persons for breakfasts, luncheons, dinners—either sit-down or buffet. Provision for coffee breaks and hospitality hours.
c. Conference facilities for large group meetings of 250. Small meeting room facilities for five groups of 50. Rooms may be multipurpose (large group, small group, banquet) if set up ahead of the opening session and preparation requirements permit efficient scheduling.
d. Exhibit area of approximately 5,000 square feet.
e. "Break-out" areas for informal discussion and relaxation—lounge areas, spacious lobbies, and corridors.
f. Audio-visual equipment: film projection equipment and screen in large meeting area; overhead projectors, screens, and lecterns equipped with microphones for sound amplification in each meeting area. Capable staff for setup of all equipment and operation in the case of film projector.
g. Diversified menu, well-prepared food, good food service.
h. On-site entertainment and relaxation facilities.
i. Bar service.
j. Parking for 200 cars.
k. Adequate security, especially in exhibit and parking areas.
l. Efficient, courteous staff.

You do not need to consider cost factors in your analysis. Your company attempts to project a first-class image, and both site options fulfill that requirement. Your main concern is providing for the actual space, facility, and service needs of the sales meeting as well as possible.

Select a downtown and a suburban hotel-motel in your city; and using these criteria, systemmatically gather the relevant data on each facility through meetings with their conference and banquet managers and/or their promotional literature. Develop a graphic display in which you logically organize your facts and rate or rank each site on the 12 criteria.

Because your superior prefers the deductive approach, you will use this organizational pattern. Therefore, present your conclusions first, then your introduction, and finally your discussion of each facility's strengths and weaknesses relative to the selection criteria. Headings should orient the reader, and graphic aids will be useful for presenting your comparative data.

7. *(Memo and informational memo report)* So far you have been reading the text's discussion of reports and listening to your professor's interpretations. You will now find out for yourself the types of reports you'll be writing on the job after graduation. Select an organization similar to the one you hope to be associated with after graduation and interview someone who has a job similar to the one you want. If you can't interview this person, consider her or his superior.

In preparation for this assignment, hand in to your professor your answers to the following in memo format. (The purpose of this screening is so your professor can make sure you ask appropriate questions and that no more than one student in class goes to the same firm.)

a. The name of the company. If you plan to be an accountant in a C.P.A. firm, choose a C.P.A. firm; if you intend to get into personnel work, choose an organization that has a personnel department.

b. Name of the individual you'll interview and/or that person's title. Be sure to choose someone who can tell you the types of reports you'll be writing on the job after graduation.

c. Purpose of the interview. To be sure the questions you'll ask fulfill the purpose of the assignment, jot down in one sentence the purpose of the interview: "The purpose of the interview is to find out all I can about the types of reports I'll be writing on the . . . job in my chosen career." Keep this purpose in mind as you select your questions. All questions should relate directly to this purpose.

d. List at least 10 really pertinent questions you plan to ask the officer you will interview. Consider questions to which you want answers and arrange the questions in the order you'll be asking them. Given below are a few examples of questions you might want to ask.

(1) What types of reports does your (firm) prepare? (Please specify whether memo report, letter report, formal report, or printed form report.)

(2) Which of the above-mentioned types of reports are written most frequently? least frequently?

(3) Who usually prepares the report? (Individual versus group, lower echelon versus upper echelon.)

(4) What are some common weaknesses in these reports?

(5) What make(s) a good report?

(6) What is the most frequent arrangement for the body of the report—inductive (logical) or deductive (psychological)?

(7) How long a time, on the average, is spent preparing each type of report?

(8) Do employees work on the report more during working hours or more at home?

(9) What is the difference between a report going upward to management and downward to the workers?

(10) In what way do you feel your (firm's) reports may be improved?

Write a memo report to your professor about your findings. Be sure to include a subject line, body (all three parts), and necessary headings. The text should include more than one main division but perhaps no more than two or three. Also, you might need subheadings for one or more of the major divisions in the text.

8. *(Informational letter report)* Assume that your employer's public relations department sponsored a volunteer program one year ago to show the firm's concern for helping with certain needs of people in the community. You have become active in one phase of that program—as chairperson of a special tutoring committee that works with foreign students at a nearby college.

Yesterday you received a letter from Mr. Lawrence Centro, public relations manager of a business firm in a nearby city. Having heard about your program, he asks you for information about it because he is interested in setting up a similar project.

The aim of your committee is to give foreign students the individual help they need in their conversational English. One volunteer employee is assigned to each foreign student seeking help. These two agree to meet at least once a week for a 10-week period. Some volunteer–foreign student pairs have sessions that last longer than one hour a week. No sessions are scheduled during company working hours.

Publicity is important to keep the program going. Notices in the firm's employee News Bulletin and in the college newspaper are instrumental in recruiting volunteers and informing the foreign students. (Occasional write-ups by city newspapers have brought unsolicited favorable public relations publicity to your firm.)

Due to the intrinsic appeal of this program, many people volunteer. So far you have kept up with the foreign student demand. Some tutors are poor. Some say they will help and don't; others contribute a lot of time and effort.

In addition to meeting with the foreign student one hour a week, each tutor

is required to meet with the other tutors and your company's public relations director one Saturday morning each month (in the company lounge).
They discuss problems and ways to add variety in their sessions with the
foreign students. As a result, you made a list of activities—including sports,
recreations, studies, trips, shopping, games that require practicing English.

You give both the tutors and the students a way to end the relationship if
they don't get along. The students are free to terminate the meeting arrangements at any time and ask for a new tutor. Also the tutor can ask for a new
student. Strict confidence is maintained in this matter; a lot of juggling does
occur. Volunteers have paid their own expenses for the sessions. However,
recently the company has established a small fund to cover some general
costs—including a semiannual reception or luncheon for the participants.

On the whole, the program has been a great success. Many new and lasting
friendships have resulted. The tutors also learned a tremendous amount
from the foreign students. The cultural exchange has helped both the students and the tutors.

Reply to Mr. Centro's request and report your experience. Under appropriate headings, mention both the good and the difficult areas in organizing and
operating the program.

9. *(Analytical memo report)* One month ago Max Huber, manager (since 1964)
of the appliance department, Mason's Department Store, announced his
upcoming retirement. As the supervisor of all departments, you were asked
by Lisa Mason (vice president in charge of personnel) to recommend a
suitable replacement. For three weeks you have been interviewing applicants and compiling profiles on currently employed personnel that are
qualified to handle the position. Mason's has no seniority policy for hiring
departmental managers. Emphasis is placed on individual qualities of leadership, ability to work with others, and a general knowledge of business
operations. Previous management experience is not necessary, since most
of the daily management routine can be quickly learned on the job.

Having carefully considered all 25 qualified employees and applicants,
you have narrowed the field down to three main candidates, one of whom
you must recommend—in an analytical memo-report—to Ms. Mason. On
the basis of your recommendation, she will make the final decision.

In your report consider the following three candidates' qualifications:

Thomas Osborne:
Tom, a high school graduate, received an honorable discharge after
serving six years in the Army (two years as a master sergeant), worked
four years in construction and then seven years selling magazines on
the road, and has worked in Mason's appliance department the last

twelve years. Now 48, he has the most seniority among the clerks. Often when Mr. Huber was absent because of illness or for business reasons, Tom was asked to act as manager. Company policy requires that each departmental manager keep a personality and efficiency inventory on all employees in her or his department. In the inventory Mr. Huber praised Tom's ability to handle the managerial duties in his (Huber's) absence, but he also noted that Tom had trouble in getting along with some of the employees. At times Tom was "bossy" toward new employees, even when he was not acting as manager.

Carol Barlow:
Carol has a B.A. degree in history and English, taught high school English eight years, worked in Mason's home furnishings department for two years and in the appliance department the last four years. She is now 36. The principal of the high school where Barlow taught told Mr. Huber by letter he has no unfavorable criticism of the job done at any time, but Barlow quit teaching because she had disciplinary problems. However, both faculty and students in high school liked her. In the personality and efficiency inventory, Mr. Huber wrote that Carol is one of the best workers he has ever managed. She never questions any request given her by Mr. Huber or by any of the other employees. Carol also gets along with all employees and seems to be the most popular among them. She has never been in a managerial position, but she does have a sound knowledge of the operations of the appliance department.

Don Page:
Next month Don will receive his master's degree in marketing. From Don's résumé and an interview with him, you know he is a capable leader and has the type of personality that will get along well with employees in the department. In college he was captain of the track team. Most of Don's working experience has been part-time or full-time summer employment. For the last six years he has worked in an appliance store in the university district. A reference from the store manager was complimentary and noted especially Don's ability to keep himself busy when there were no customers to wait on. He is now 28.

The formal (sometimes called "long") report is merely an expansion of the shorter one. The body of both a short report and a formal report consists of an introduction, a text, and terminal section organized either inductively or deductively. Both have headings and other visual aids when desirable. *Formal* merely means the report includes certain prefatory and supplemental parts; it does not mean the level of language is formal. You should continue to use easily understood words and apply the C Qualities in Well-Written Reports (summarized on pages 485–490).

The formal report generally covers a more complex problem than the "short" report. Consequently, the needed preliminary investigation plus gathering, sorting, and interpreting data, as well as the writing and editing, are often far more time-consuming and costly than for short reports. This chapter presents additional information you will need regarding the following aspects of formal report writing: proposals; working plans; prefatory parts; supplemental parts; documentation and explanatory notations; plus writing, editing, revising, and typing.

PROPOSALS

In business, industry, government, and academia, proposals have a significantly important part. They range in length from short proposals of three or four pages—as shown in the preceding chapter—to long "formal" documents of 50 or more pages. Many projects require proposals with comprehensive, detailed, elaborate presentations regarding various intricate problems involved.

A business or industrial firm (also an individual) that seeks the award of a large contract from a government agency or another firm must submit a proposal (bid) before being considered. Also, a researcher who needs a grant before undertaking a costly project or study culminating in a long formal report must write a proposal to the funding agency. Likewise, department heads who require extensive remodeling of their employer's facilities must usually present proposals to the executives concerned with approving funds.

In general, the best advice for writing proposals is to be sure your objectives match the philosophy and requirements of the funding individual, agency, or company. Follow *meticulously* the proposal requirements of the funding source. It may require for all proposals certain headings, details, format, number of copies, deadlines, and so forth. Adhering honestly and accurately to all requirements will work to your advantage. Whenever possible, use the outline and same words the agency has in its literature or guidelines. Don't use jargon that only you and your assistants can understand. The following suggestions for outlines, formats, and writing style are adaptable to various formal proposals.

Outline

Among the topics listed below are those you will often need to include in your proposals for complex research studies and for major business proposals regarding sales of your company's (or your) services, equipment, or extensive installation facilities. Of course, only very long, comprehensive proposals may include all (or almost all) these topics. Obviously smaller projects will require discussion on only a few—perhaps five or six—topics. For others, the total presentation may cover 30 or more topics and subtopics. Information required for a $2 million grant or sales contract will surely be longer and more profound than for a $200 allowance. Therefore, *consider carefully which topics are desirable for your specific proposal outline*.

1. Problem

Clearly define the problem. If it's a community problem, is it specific for the local area or a general one? If it's a company problem, does it concern a certain branch or area—such as shipping delays, shoplifting, inventory control, poor customer relations, excessive purchase returns, inadequate communication, or what?

Background . . . what led up to the problem. Be concise.

Need for solution. Is it urgent? critical? why?

2. Purpose (Objectives)

State objectives concisely and clearly. Are they measurable? achievable?

What reader benefits, if any, should be emphasized?

Avoid including too many objectives or too broad a purpose.

3. Scope

Define the boundaries of your project. If you're proposing a research study, will you study one area of a community, company, department, or severe problem? What boundaries are you setting to accomplish your objectives? If your proposal is for service or equipment you are selling, in what areas will it serve the prospective buyer?

4. Procedures

What specific methods will you use? Are they scientifically sound?

What are you going to do? How?

Who is involved?

What is your plan of attack? Can your methods solve the problem?

Identify specific activities and state your time schedule for each. (For a research project state your initial plan and organization, search of literature, interviews, correspondence, questionnaires, experiments.) Include estimated calendar dates if possible.

Consider and identify variables, if any, in the project.

Make clear your sequence of steps in the project.

Allow sufficient time for data collection and for unexpected problems.

5. Equipment and Facilities Available

Show you have thought deeply enough to realize what facilities will be needed. (For a research project, state what equipment and facilities you already have for use and assure that you can get the rest. Depending upon the type of project, you might, for example, need a movie camera, computer, programmer, 10 desk calculators, a nearby library, typewriter(s), duplicating machines and services for questionnaires, etc., even a car, truck, boat, or small plane!) If your proposal is for your company's bid on an enormous construction job, probably several departments will cooperate with you in presenting needed facts and figures.

6. Personnel Qualifications

Include an organization chart; perhaps a flow chart, if desirable.

Show job descriptions, names, and one-page résumés for top personnel (with their permission) who will assist on your project.

State your own experience and past successes with similar projects. Include dates and references (with permission) so that the prospective funder can verify your statements.

7. Evaluation

State how data generated in your project will be handled and stored.

If you are planning a community or a company project, state what factors will determine whether your project can be done again in another community or company branch.

If you are proposing a research study, show how you will evaluate how well the project is working while it is under way and how you'll determine whether to continue it, change directions, or terminate it.

State the likelihood of success. Do not promise more than you can do. Can you guarantee a solution within stated boundaries? Some problems (crime, cancer, drug abuse, etc.) may be so complex that no one expects any one researcher to solve them. In your proposal, protect yourself from charges of misrepresentation by honestly estimating (conservatively) what probable outcome can be expected. Even a partial solution of an adequately limited problem may be a step in the right direction.

8. Budget

If you're applying for a research grant, do *not* overbudget; funding sources quickly reject a padded budget. Be realistic.

List: Salaries and fringe benefits for all staff assistants and yourself
Equipment and consumable supplies needed to reach objectives
Travel requirements (estimate miles, type of transportation, number of persons who will be traveling)
Miscellaneous expenses and indirect costs
Allowance for the unexpected
Provide justification for each budget item.

If you're bidding on a job for your company (or yourself), consider all aspects of the proposed work (perhaps with advice of experts) to be sure your proposed price is competitive as well as economically feasible.

In general, before you agree to work on a lengthy project for any firm or agency, see that a suitable written agreement covers your costs, hours of work, time schedule; and make sure you understand what penalties, if any, apply for delayed performance or nonperformance. Sometimes consulting a qualified financial counselor is advisable.

Format

After you have written, in rough draft, your answers to all pertinent topics, arrange them in a coherent order. If your discussion under one topic is too brief, you may need to expand on it, or perhaps group the information under another, broader heading—unless of course the agency's guidelines prescribe exact headings and order of arrangement.

The format of the proposal includes many of the parts found in formal reports. Here is one possible suggested format for a formal research proposal:

1. *Prefatory parts*
Title page
Letter of transmittal
Table of contents

List of tables (if any)
List of figures (if any)
2. *Body of proposal*
Introduction
    Problem
    Need
    Background
Objectives/Purpose
Procedures
    Methods and sources
    Plan of attack
    Sequence of activities
    Equipment and facilities available
    Personnel qualifications
Evaluation
Budget
3. *Supplementary parts*
Agency forms
    Budget justification
    References
Tables or figures (if any)

Writing Style and Appearance

You will be wise to apply all business communication principles and report writing techniques when writing the proposal—whether it is for a research grant or for a million-dollar sales contract by your company. Placed on top of the proposal, usually, is a transmittal letter with an appropriate message.

In its digest on proposal writing, the Washington State Office of Economic Opportunity includes the following excellent advice:

> First impressions are very critical. None is more so than that first impression your proposal gives to the reader when submitted to an agency or foundation for consideration. Many proposals are lost at the first look by the reader. He appraises the proposal immediately in terms of:
>
> 1. General appearance
> 2. Neatness
> 3. Specific appearance of:
>   a. Table of Contents
>   b. List of Figures
>   c. Title Page
>   d. Maps
>   e. Graphs
>   f. Charts
> 4. Consistency of style

5. Title—is it grandiose or does it properly describe the project?
6. Completeness
7. Professionalism

Therefore, you cannot afford to skimp on the time you spend in "polishing" your proposal. Each item must be checked and re-checked. Since you have spent many hours developing the proposal idea, and further hours researching and writing before your first draft, why risk your investment over poor typing, proofing, graphics, etc. Some of the most important time spent working on the proposal will be that spent on the final draft.

If you are not an artist it might be advisable to employ one to prepare the cover, charts, graphs, etc. The cost is minimal when you consider the potential return.

Be sure you and your typist are familiar with an appropriate typing style. Learn it well and be sure to follow it consistently. . . . Select one which best fits your needs and adopt it for all your proposals.

Don't accept or be satisfied with sloppy typing or art work. Make sure it is reworked until satisfactory. You want all the final copy to be neat and clean prior to submission.[1]

The preceding suggestions on proposal outline, format, and writing style can be adapted to all kinds of proposals. If, instead of seeking funds for a comprehensive research study, you are writing a proposal which is your company's bid on a $3 million sales or construction contract, the basic characteristics of the formal proposal are similiar. You will of course need to know the capabilities of your firm's products and services and be scrupulously accurate.

So important are proposals for some firms that they have spent thousands of dollars to equip their own company libraries with individual study rooms and up-to-date research facilities plus a staff of typists and designers. Their main purpose is to help their marketing representatives turn out top-quality, winning proposals. For example, one marketing executive's 28-page (single-spaced) successful major proposal has on its colorful cover an accurate sketch of the prospective customer's buildings. The proposal is attractively bound and protected by a plastic cover.

Here is the body of that proposal's considerate *transmittal letter* (with changed names), typed on the company's letterhead and bound in the report:

```
Thank you for the opportunity to review the communication needs of
the Sun City Administrative Services Center.

In the past few years this administrative center has grown rapidly
in both staff and services to the community. Because your communica-
tions system has not kept pace with your growth, a number of
communication-related problems have developed.
```

[1] Lon F. Backman, Program Development, *A Digest on the Elements of Proposal Writing*, Washington State Office of Economic Opportunity, Olympia, December 1971.

> Your department heads, receptionists, and employees have been most
> cooperative during our discussions to determine major communication
> problem areas. The problems uncovered, and the solutions to them,
> are discussed in the following pages.
>
> Metrodynamic Communications looks forward to providing a telecom-
> munications system which will grow and expand as your Center ex-
> pands. To meet that goal, we recommend a Direction PBX. The Direc-
> tion PBX features stored program control combined with time division
> switching, which provides exceptional versatility for today's needs
> and is easily adaptable to future requirements. As an alternative
> Centrex II will also respond to your needs, with capabilities some-
> what different from the Direction System.
>
> Either system will provide the Sun City Administrative Services Cen-
> ter with an efficient, flexible, versatile system for today and
> tomorrow. I am looking forward to working with you on a continuing
> basis.

This proposals's table of contents lists: Objectives, Communications Problems, Direction Benefits, Explanation of Contract, Direction Pricing, Summary
of Direction Features, Centrex Benefits, Centrex Pricing, Optional Services,
Summary of System Features, Appendix. Many of these topics have subheadings, too.

The body of the proposal is neatly, accurately typed (single-space) with
helpful headings (second-, third-, and fourth-degree). Colorful illustrations and
pictures help emphasize that the proposed system is "efficient, economical,
flexible." Important figures, rates, charges, and other details are shown in
tables both within the text and in the appendix.

WORKING PLANS

When someone—inside or outside of your company—requests that you investigate a problem and write a report, you first make sure you know what the
person wants or needs. Be sure you are told, orally or in writing, clearly what is
expected of you.[2] You should know the problem, purpose, scope, procedure to
follow in collecting data, and deadline for completion. If your employer (or
whoever has requested the report) doesn't give you complete information, you
need to ask questions until you understand the assignment thoroughly.

After you receive the assignment, you use the given facts for informal talks
with authorities on the subject and people associated with the problem, preliminary review of materials existing in libraries, study of company records, and so
on. Use whatever sources will give you the necessary background and understanding to proceed further with the investigation—through the first three

---

[2] In a formal report of a public nature, the one authorizing or commissioning the report notifies the
report writer in a letter called a "letter of authorization." The message will be bound with the
formal report's prefatory pages, usually just before the transmittal letter.

planning steps (discussed on pages 464–465). Given here are a suggested working plan outline and a sample plan.

Outline

The culmination of preliminary investigation is a working plan that you'll present to the person who asked you to make the report. If no one authorized you to take the assignment, you still should make out a working plan for your own benefit. In this working plan—perhaps a memo to the employer in your own organization or a letter to someone outside the firm—you'll include:

1. Problem
2. Purpose
3. Scope
4. Limitations
5. Use of the report
6. Type of reader(s)
7. Tentative outline (your main text and terminal section headings)
8. Method(s) of collecting data
9. Work-progress schedule

The whole idea of the working plan is to tell the one who authorized the report (or yourself) the way you understand the problem, the purpose, the use of the report, and so on, and to make sure you see eye to eye. Be sure you understand who your readers will be. Do you have both primary and secondary readers? Are they familiar with the subject or will they need background material? Are they biased, antagonistic, or favorably inclined toward the subject?

In the outline you want to show the areas you'll investigate and discuss in the report—and, if possible, subdivisions for each major area. Also indicate the type of terminal section you'll have—summary, conclusions, and/or recommendations—and whether you are arranging the parts logically or psychologically.

Example

The following working plan is from a researcher in a management consulting firm to a department head. It is typewritten on the firm's intraoffice memo stationery, in memo form.

```
TO:       Nina Vandeline                    DATE: April 12, 19___
FROM:     Tom Browne
SUBJECT:  Working Plan for Study on Treelane Homeowners Association

Confirming our conversation of April 8, here is my working plan for
the study you requested concerning Treelane Homeowners Association,
a development in south XY County.
```

Problem
The association's programs are not meeting the needs of its members.
The benefits the association affords are rarely taken advantage of
by homeowners. They share assets consisting of a clubhouse, park,
swimming pool, and fishing pond. In addition, the association has a
charter which outlines rules and guidelines all homeowners are supposed to follow for (1) making changes in their property, (2)
general regulation of pets, and (3) use of the common area.

However, rules are often ignored. Social activities are rarely attended by many homeowners. Business meetings have a very poor
attendance record. Communication is poor. Some owners are hostile.

Purpose and Objective
I will determine the causes for the above-stated problems and make
recommendations to help Treelane become a more effective organization.

My plan is to find the attitudes and interests of individual homeowners and apply my findings to aid officers in modifying the
organization. My findings and proposals will hopefully lead to an
organization which involves homeowners and helps them to receive
benefits they are paying for.

Limitations
My evaluations must be limited to programs which are useful and
stimulate interest and to modifications of property within the budget. The study is limited in time, in that the recommendations are
needed one month from today.

Scope
I will evaluate only those changes which are practical and feasible
and which have apparent potential for bettering Treelane.

Procedures for Gathering Data
A questionnaire will be sent to all homeowners. In addition to the
replies received from homeowners, I plan to interview all officers
and to examine--with your permission--the records of the association.

Division of Problem and Tentative General Outline
The problem will be divided into three parts: (1) social activities,
(2) physical property, and (3) rules.

First a questionnaire must be prepared to find out what preferences,
dislikes, and ideas property owners have. The data will be analyzed,
and selected recommendations will be evaluated by talking with officers and looking at the budget.

Tentative Conclusion
The homeowners association needs social activities which will involve more property owners. This change will stimulate interest in
the organization and decrease the hostilities now present.

```
Work-progress Schedule
Data will be collected by Friday, April 22; organized and inter-
preted by Monday, May 6. Report outline will be ready by May 9. The
final report will be submitted by May 12.
```

After completing the preliminary investigation—the authorizer and the report writer might have further consultations if warranted and appropriate. These additional contacts might occur: (1) at the completion of the investigation—after the writer has collected and studied the material and determined the results; (2) after the writer has made the final report outline; and (3) after the writer has written the report but before he or she officially submits the finished report to the receiver.

PREFATORY PARTS

One of the distinguishing features of a formal (or long) report is that it has some or all of the following prefatory parts that are placed before the report's body: cover, title fly, title page, letter of authorization, letter of transmittal, table of contents (contents), table of tables, abstract.

Cover Design and Wording of Title

Many reports combine the cover and title page for the top page. But often for a formal report you can use a separate cover to which the reader will react favorably. Sometimes a simple hard cover (both for the front and back), with a properly placed title, will suffice. You can type the title on a gummed label, or type or print it directly on the cover itself. However, for some subjects you can—with a little imagination—design a more attractive, special cover to tie in with the material being discussed. For example, assume you're writing a report in which you're suggesting that the firm switch from its present printed personnel form to a more effectively worded and comprehensive form. The cover can consist of parts of both forms with a title superimposed.

The report's title should indicate concisely and specifically what the report covers. Choosing correct wording and arrangement requires careful thought. Here are a few suggestions:

1. Include whichever of the five W's—*who, what, when, where, why*—are pertinent. For instance, suppose your report discusses detailed marketing procedures that the ABC Company should adopt to increase its sales in Canada during a certain year. To select the title you might begin with this analysis:

   who: ABC Company
   what: Marketing procedures
   when: 1986

where: Canada
why: To increase sales

Thus the title could be: "Marketing Procedures for Increasing ABC's 1986 Canadian Sales." Or, to emphasize increased sales, these words could come near the beginning: "Increasing ABC's 1986 Canadian Sales by New Marketing Procedures."

2. Keep title length preferably within a maximum of about eight or nine words. Omit "the," "a," and "an" whenever possible. (For some reports you may need to add a subtitle.)

3. Avoid vague, extremely short, too-broad titles. For example, "Marketing Procedures" or "Increased Canadian Sales" would both be inadequate and misleading titles for the report mentioned in suggestion 1 above. Also, "Agriculture in (state)" is too broad if you're discussing only grains, vegetables or fruits.

Title Fly and Title Page

Only when you have both a cover and title page can you use the *title fly*—usually a blank sheet of paper located between the two parts. As in books, it acts as a buffer or relief when the reader opens the book.

The *title page*—attractively arranged—usually contains the title, names of the recipient and sender, and the completion date—each of which may have a separate focal point on the page. It may be in four sections, as illustrated on page 577. If you arrange it in three sections, you combine date with author's identification. If appropriate, you may add pertinent facts about the individuals involved, such as title, department, and organization. Date of completion must agree with the date on the letter of transmittal.

When used with a separate cover, the title page is the same weight paper as the text sheets. As a combination cover and title page this part might have a heavier weight paper.

Letter of Authorization

The person authorizing or commissioning the formal report notifies the report writer in a letter called a letter of authorization. In a formal report of a public nature, this message becomes one of the bound prefatory pages. Although it is often omitted from the business formal report, it may of course be included.

When you are in the position of authorizing a report, organize your message by the direct-request or good-news plan. And be sure to make clear just what you are authorizing.

Letter of Transmittal

The message that conveys the report from the writer to the reader is the letter of transmittal. In some formal long reports—especially those written to a large group of readers—the author's message is labeled "preface" (as in books) or "foreword."

The letter of transmittal is usually worded in conversational language (with first- and second-person pronouns—I, we, you) as you would talk if you were handing the report to the recipient in person. Only if you are writing to a formal distinguished group—for instance, top government officials—might you use impersonal language and "the writer." Even prefaces may use the first-person pronoun.

Organization of the transmittal letter follows the direct, good-news plan: main idea, explanation, courteous ending. The following are topics that may be included—arranged in any appropriate, desirable order.

Main idea

Transmittal (usually omitted in preface and foreword)

Authorization

Purpose

Need or use of report

Explanation and/or highlights

Perhaps a brief indication of outcome—in general only. Indicate conclusions and/or recommendations *if* you think the reader will consider them good (or neutral) news and *if* an abstract or terminal section with the same information doesn't appear at the beginning of the report—just a few pages after the transmittal.

Maybe a comment or two to help the reader use and appreciate the report.

Background, methodology, limitations sometimes—stated briefly.

Courteous ending

Acknowledgments to people who assisted. (In some formal reports acknowledgments are in a separate section instead of in the transmittal or preface.)

Indication that later reports may be necessary or forthcoming.

Willingness to discuss, do additional research, or assist with future projects.

Expression of appreciation for the assignment.

You need to be careful not to include the same elements in both the transmittal and the introduction, or the transmittal and the abstract or executive summary, if any, for the needless repetition would be annoying.

The example that follows is a transmittal for a 33-page analytical formal report. Notice it briefly indicates the outcome and the writer's recommendation. (The terminal section is on page 32.) The letter is typed on this marketing consultant's letterhead stationery in the usual letter format.

Dear Mrs. Larson:

Here is the report you authorized October 18 regarding a survey of market potential on Bigg Island. The purpose of this report is to present an analysis of data collected about the possible implementation of home-care service at Bigg View Convalescent Center.

You will be pleased to learn that our survey indicates a generally favorable reaction to the project. The report includes survey results in five areas:

Social structure
Age range
Percent over age 65
Financial structure of persons over age 65
Preferences for convalescent care

On the basis of the survey made, I recommend that Bigg View Convalescent Center initiate a home-care service and a program of extensive informal education of the island's population.

I have enjoyed making this study and appreciate the opportunity to help you reach a reliable decision concerning the home-care service. Please call me if you have questions or if I may assist you in any further analysis.

Sincerely yours,

(*signature, typed name, title*)

Table of Contents

You should include a table of contents as a prefatory part of your long report whenever such a table would be a helpful guide for your reader. The table of contents lists the main headings of the report outline plus page numbers showing where the sections begin in the finished report. This table is especially useful for the reader who wants to see a concise overview of the report's contents and needs to read only a few scattered, selected sections or parts.

Figure 18-6, page 579, illustrates a table of contents with two degrees of headings. These are preceded by the Roman numerals (I–V) and alphabetic letters (A–E). Including the numerals and letters is optional. (Notice that the Roman numerals are typed so that their last digits are aligned.) For reports that have also third-degree headings, these too may be included in the table of contents, but doing so is optional.

Though the table of contents is placed before the report body, you must, of course, prepare the table after the entire report is typed—so you will know the correct page numbers. Use leaders (dot, space, dot, space, dot) to lead the eye from the name of each entry to the page column on the right. Every entry shown in the table of contents should appear exactly as it does in the body. But not every heading in the body has to appear in the contents. Usually you show no more than three degrees (first, second, and third) of headings.

If the appendix includes several different entries (questionnaire, reprint of a statute or regulation, various tables, or other visual aids) you can show them in one of two locations: (1) as subdivisions of the appendix on the contents page if you have only a few entries; or (2) as subdivisions of the appendix on a separate appendix title page if you have a rather extensive appendix.

Table of Tables

The label for this prefatory part depends upon the type of formal visual aids shown throughout the text. If the illustrations are all tables, you can label the page Table of Tables or List of Tables. Follow the same procedure for charts, pictures, and so forth. If you have a mixture of tables, charts, and other visual aids, consider a title that encompasses them all; perhaps a Table of Illustrations will suffice.

This prefatory page serves the same function for the visual aids as the contents page does for the sections covered in the report. Whether the table of tables is placed on the same page with the table of contents or by itself on a page, the layout is similar to the following:

Table of Tables

Table		Page
1	(title)	6
2	(title)	9
3	(title)	11
4	(title)	23

Abstract, Synopsis, Executive Summary

The informative abstract (also labeled synopsis, executive summary, epitome, précis, digest) performs a vital timesaving service for the reader. It is a condensed, concise, accurate statement of what is important in the report. Usually its length is between 5 and 10 percent—or less—of the whole report. The busy manager, after scanning it, can determine whether she or he wants to read further.

This prefatory part may be organized inductively (introduction, text, terminal section) or deductively (terminal section before the text). Either way, it includes purpose, scope, methods, data sources, sometimes committee members (if significant for the reader), major facts and figures, statement of results, conclusions, and/or recommendations. Generally it is placed on a separate page between table of contents and report body. If short (five or six lines), it may be at the bottom of the title page; in published articles it often appears above the title.

Besides being a useful prefatory part of a long, formal report, informative abstracts also serve other important functions. Some firms circulate to all their management personnel only the abstract *without* the report. (The person who originally authorized the report of course gets the complete, original report.) Those who receive only the abstract can decide whether they need the original report, which is then sent to them upon their request. This practice saves much time and expense, especially when reports are 50 or more pages long.

Another important use of abstracts is for reports, articles, documents, and such that are published. A well-written abstract can communicate contents to hundreds, even thousands, of business associates. In brief reading time colleagues can scan abstracts in their professional and business journals, thus keeping up to date on literature in their special field. The quality of an abstract may determine who and how many ever see the full document. Those who find interest in the abstract may send for the original write-up.

Though the informative abstract length varies somewhat in proportion to the report length, it should be confined to fewer than 500 words (preferably on one page). To show you how abstracts vary, here are three examples:

Example 1

An informative abstract of an energy conservation report (parts of that report are shown on pages 577–582.)

> This report analyzes the energy conservation effort at Central Diesel, Inc., in three dimensions--based mainly on interviews: usage before the shortage, usage currently, and projected usage after proposed changes within separate areas of special concentration.
>
> Before last winter's energy shortage, the firm, like many others, had no conservation policy. After realizing an energy crisis existed, all departments cooperated. Savings totaling about 14% energy usage were made by reducing temperatures, removing unnecessary lighting tubes, and reducing heat-loss sources plus excessive wastes in convenience electricity and company vehicles.
>
> Five recommendations for future improvements to achieve estimated 35% total savings include: installing certain access doors, repairing an air compressor, replacing one inefficient heating system, changing diesel generator testing procedures to cut fuel consumption, and replacing older vehicles with smaller economy models.

Example 2

A short abstract on a 75-page published report.

To determine the basic vocabulary of written business communications, a computer count was made of 2,504 letters, memorandums, and business reports, submitted by 1,411 companies representative of the population of industries nationwide. A total of 606,496 running words and 15,522 different words were identified, with the 100 most frequently occurring words accounting for one-half of all word occurrences. Major differences between this list and previous lists were noted.[3]

Example 3

Executive summary of a student-group analysis of a problem.

Our group approached the problem assigned to us under the following purposes:

- To enhance students' effectiveness in small group decision making
- To increase students' awareness of current political, social, and economic issues
- To promote students' persuasiveness in presenting a solution to a problem in both oral and written form.

Our committee analyzed this topic: "Orphan Drugs: What Policy Should the United States Adopt to Ensure Availability of Drugs with Limited Commercial Value?"

Six specific aspects of the problem were identified by their respective presenters as follows:

Definition of the Problem	Dawn Wong
Drug Development Process	Bob Westphal
Ethical Drug Industry	Tom Washburn
Role of Government	Cori Staley
Causes of the Problem	Fran Morel
Importance of the Problem	Joseph Haviv

Preparation work was done over a period of five weeks, with each member contributing information to the other members. Data and information were gathered from various sources: Congressional records, government reports, journals, periodicals, personal interviews. Special emphasis was placed on personal interviews—with six doctors and three pharmacists.

The committee unanimously felt the solutions to the above problem should be derived from at least one of the following areas:

1. Individual pharmaceutical companies

---

[3] Scot Ober, "The Basic Vocabulary of Written Business Communications," Alpha Sigma Chapter, Delta Pi Epsilon, Arizona State University, Tempe, 1981.

2. Nonprofit organizations or consortia
3. The federal government

<u>Final recommendation</u>: to change the current FDA regulations and introduce economic incentives, consisting of three components:

- A reduction in current FDA regulations on orphan drugs
- An introduction of economic incentives
- A public recognition program of the problem.[4]

One more, popular use of abstracts should be mentioned here. If you are invited to present a report at a business meeting (planned perhaps eight months in advance), the chairperson may ask you to send an abstract for distribution before the conference. The abstract may be requested even before you have started writing your report or talk. The well-planned abstract you write for the chairperson can contain the topic sentences you will use later to develop your report and talk. In this situation the abstract is written before, not after, the complete report.

DOCUMENTATION AND EXPLANATORY FOOTNOTES

When your report contains quotations, paraphrases, and/or specific facts from various sources, you must cite these references for documentation to establish the trustworthiness of your statements. In addition to sources, some reports (as well as articles, chapters, or books) may have cross-references and various explanatory footnotes. To help you use footnotes correctly, this section focuses on their kinds, purposes, contents, and placement.

Kinds and Purposes of Footnotes

The three kinds of footnotes are source, cross-reference, and explanatory. They meet the following purposes:

1. *Source footnotes give credit to sources you used.* Any quotations and important factual statements that are not common knowledge or based on your experience must be supported by references to your sources. If you quote someone else's statement verbatim or you paraphrase it in other words and you don't credit that source, you are plagiarizing. Penalties may be severe. By citing sources you not only give credit where credit is due, but also you help convince your readers that your data are trustworthy and you are willing, to let them examine the sources.

2. *Cross-reference footnotes direct the reader to another place within the report.* For instance, they may mention a detailed discussion, examples of

---

[4] Report completed at The Graduate School of Business, University of Michigan, Ann Arbor, by the students mentioned in the abstract.

important principles, or perhaps a page in the appendix. These footnotes help to emphasize significant points without unnecessary repetition.

3. *Explanatory footnotes discuss, explain, and/or give additional information.* This material relates to an idea in your report text, but is incidental; too long, complicated, or technical to include in the text discussion; or shouldn't interrupt the flow of thought.

Contents of Footnotes

The following discussion begins with superscripts, which precede most footnotes; then the section concentrates on guidelines and examples of footnote contents, especially for source footnotes.

Superscripts

To refer your reader to footnotes and to number them, you may use superscripts. These are usually *Arabic numerals* placed slightly above the line. You can number these superscripts consecutively throughout the report or begin a new series with each chapter—the recommended practice—(as in this book).

Place superscripts consistently where they will be easily noticed by the reader and fair to the sources. To avoid interrupting the reader's attention, the superscript is best placed at the end of a sentence or a title. (See, for instance, superscripts 5 and 6 below.)

Superscripts in tables and figures should be symbols (asterisks, daggers—the * and †), or *lowercase alphabetic letters,* not Arabic numbers. The same symbols are used repeatedly for all tables or figures in an entire report (or article or book). Thus this method differs from the numbering of superscript numerals, which continue consecutively throughout a manuscript or chapter.

Content of Source Footnotes

The choice of content in source footnotes varies somewhat depending upon whether the report includes a bibliography, whether the source footnote is used the first time or repeated, and also which authority you are following.[5] To avoid confusing you with several alternatives, this section summarizes briefly the main items included in one popular (and simplified) method. Remember that others may be equally desirable for different situations. Use whatever is pre-

---

[5] Space in this book allows only highlights about bibliographies and footnotes. For additional details on numerous variations in content and setup, you will find these publications helpful: William Giles Campbell and Stephen V. Ballou, *Form and Style: Theses, Reports, Term Papers,* 5th ed., Houghton Mifflin Company, Boston, 1977; *MLA Handbook for Writers of Research Papers, Theses, and Dissertations,* Modern Language Association of America, New York, 1977; Kate L. Turabian, *A Manual for Writers of Term Papers, Theses, and Dissertations,* 4th ed., University of Chicago Press, Chicago, 1973; *United States Government Printing Office Style Manual* (abridged, revised edition), U.S. Government Printing Office, Washington, D.C., 1973. If your report uses other sources and it is to be published, be sure you abide by copyright laws to avoid infringement. Information is available on "Publications of the Copyright Office," Register of Copyrights, Library of Congress, Washington, D.C.

ferred by your instructor, employer, industry, business, editor, (or by you) and be consistent.

Source Footnotes *without* **Bibliography.**[6] Footnotes citing sources the first time should always contain complete information if the report has no bibliography. When the same source is repeated in later references, these footnotes may be shortened. Sources may be either published materials or unpublished information.

You get most of the information about a book source from title and copyright pages. For a periodical—published quarterly, monthly, weekly, or daily—you'll find needed information on the cover page and the article itself. Though your reference materials will vary in content, try to include whatever items are available and helpful to specifically identify each source for your reader(s). Then arrange the items in the sequence shown in the following checklists and examples.

For published materials the following checklists outline briefly the items that may be included *in first-time full footnote references when the sources are books, periodicals, or newspapers.* You can use these guidelines also for sources in other publications—encyclopedias, almanacs, annual reports, government documents. Of course, not all these items are available or essential for every footnote.

CHECKLIST GUIDELINES FOR FIRST-TIME FOOTNOTES ABOUT PUBLISHED SOURCES

A. Books	B. Periodicals	C. Newspapers
1. Superscript	1. Superscript	1. Superscript
Facts about the Composition		

2. Author name(s)
a. 1 ⎫ normal
b. 2 or 3 ⎭ order
c. over 3:
    1st author plus
    "and others" or
    "et al."
3. Author capacity:
(Used only if not really the author)
a. editor—typed "ed."
b. translator— "trans."
c. compiler— "comp."
	2. Author name(s)
	a. 1 ⎫ normal
	b. 2 or 3 ⎭ order
	c. over 3:
	    1st author plus
	    "and others" or
	    "et al."
	d. Sometimes no person's name given
	e. A bureau may be author
		2. Author name(s)
		a. 1 ⎫ normal
		b. 2 or 3 ⎭ order
		c. over 3:
		    1st author plus
		    "and others" or
		    "et al."
		d. If no name, maybe state section (Editorial, Business), if any

[6] Bibliographies are discussed in the next section, Supplemental Parts.

A. Books	B. Periodicals	C. Newspapers

4. Book title
   a. typed: all capitals
      or underlined
   b. printed: italics
5. Edition number or
   name (if not the first)
	3. Article title
	   a. typed $\Big\}$ in
	   b. printed quotation marks
		3. Article title
		   a. typed $\Big\}$ in
		   b. printed quotation marks

Facts about the Publication		

6. Publisher name
7. Publisher location
   (usually headquarters
   city; add state if not
   well-known city; add
   country if foreign)
   Note: Items 6 and 7
   may be reversed—
   City: Publisher.
	4. Periodical name
	   a. typed: underlined
	   b. printed: italics
	5. Publisher location—if
	   desirable to include,
	   same as A-7
		4. Newspaper name
		   a. typed: underlined
		   b. printed: italics
		5. City and state may be
		   inserted if not in name

8. Date of Publication—
   year of latest edition
 	
9. Volume number, if
   more than one vol-
   ume
10. Page(s) of the cita-
    tion
	6. Date of volume or issue
	7. Volume number, if any $\Big\}$ 6 and 7 may be reversed
	8. Page(s) of article
		6. Date of newspaper—
		   month, day, year
		
		7. Page(s) of article

For *unpublished sources—minutes of meetings, speeches, letters, theses, interviews*—you will find a variety of different citations used. However, as a *general guide*, the minimum items to include are:

Superscript
Name of author or sponsoring organization
Title or kind of material
Date
Page numbers, if these would be helpful to the reader.

The following examples illustrate various first-time full source footnotes about published and unpublished materials. In the first footnote example the small italicized numbers in parentheses after each item are inserted merely to help you identify easily which items on the book checklist are included. Can you identify the items in all the other footnotes by comparing them with the checklists?

Books

¹ *(1)* Richard Wincor *(2a)*, <u>Contracts in Plain English</u> *(4a)* McGraw–Hill Book Co. *(6)*, New York *(7)*, 1976 *(8)*, pp. 82–85 *(10)*.

^{2}John R. Willingham and Donald F. Warders, A Handbook for Student Writers, 2d ed., Harcourt Brace Jovanovich, New York, 1978, p. 293.

^{3}Charles Burden and others (eds.), Business in Literature, David McKay Press, New York, 1977 (paper), pp. 176–177.

Periodicals

^{4}J. E. Weinrauch and J. R. Swandra, Jr., "Examining the Significance of Listening: An Exploratory Study of Contemporary Managers," The Journal of Business Communication, 13:1, 1975, p. 25.

^{5}"Discretionary Justice," Business Week, March 16, 1982, p. 15.

Newspapers

^{6}Editorial in Los Angeles Times, February 1, 1983, p. B–7.

^{7}Associated Press Dispatch, "Economics Seen behind Cancellation," The Jamaica [New York] Chronicle, November 30, 1979, p. 3–C.

Unpublished Materials

^{8}H. Greenbaum, "The Appraisal of Organizational Communication Systems," unpublished manuscript delivered to the International Communication Association, Atlanta, 1972, p. 3.

^{9}Report of the National District Attorneys Association Symposium on White Collar Crime Enforcement, conducted at Battelle Seattle Research Center, 1982, p. 12.

Source Footnotes *with* **Bibliography.** When the report includes a bibliography, the footnotes may (but not *must*) be shortened to these items:

Superscript
Surname(s) of author(s)
Title of book, article, report, or manuscript
Page number(s) on which the information appears

For example, source footnotes 1 and 4 shown on the preceding page and this page could be shortened as follows:

^{1}Wincor, Contracts in Plain English, pp. 82–85.

^{4}Weinrauch and Swandra, "Examining the Significance of Listening," . . . ., p. 25.

Because the bibliography gives the complete citations, readers can refer to it if they wish more details about any source.

Repeated Source Footnote References. When you need to cite the same source more than once in a paper, the citations after the first time are usually shortened. Two methods are acceptable ("a" is usually preferred).

a. Superscript, author(s) surname(s), page number(s).

or

b. Standard Latin abbreviations (which many readers do not understand, but which may be required for some academic papers):

Ibid. (meaning "in the same place")—refers to the immediately preceding footnote, but a different page. Content is: Superscript, *ibid.*, page(s)—as for footnote (fn) 2 in Examples below.

Op. cit. ("in the work cited")—refers to a previously cited footnote that is followed by at least one intervening footnote about another source. Content is: Superscript, author(s) surname(s), *op. cit.*, page(s). See fn 4, below.

Loc. cit. ("in the place cited")—refers to same page in a previously cited footnote:
(1) when one or more other source footnotes intervene, use: Superscript, author(s) surname(s), *loc. cit.* See fn 5, below.
(2) When no other source footnote intervenes, use: Superscript, *loc. cit.* See fn 6.

The following examples show how to shorten source footnotes by using methods **a** or **b** whenever source references are repeated:

¹Richard Wincor, <u>Contracts in Plain English</u>, McGraw-Hill Book Co., New York, 1976, pp. 82–85.

(*Method a*)	(*Method b*)
²Wincor, p. 89.	²Ibid., p. 89.

³J. E. Weinrauch and J. R. Swandra, Jr., "Examining the Significance of Listening; An Exploratory Study of Contemporary Managers," <u>The Journal of Business Communication</u>, 13:1, 1975, p. 25.

(*Method a*)	(*Method b*)
⁴Wincor, p. 100	⁴Wincor, <u>op. cit.</u>, p. 100.
⁵Weinrauch and Swandra, p. 25.	⁵Weinrauch and Swandra, <u>loc. cit.</u>
⁶Weinrauch and Swandra, p. 25.	⁶<u>Loc. cit.</u>

Content of Cross-Reference and Explanatory Footnotes

As you know, besides the source footnotes discussed in detail above, you may also use footnotes for cross references and for additional discussion, as mentioned under "purposes," pages 559–560. For examples of content, see the following (and other) footnotes in this book:

> Cross References: footnote (fn) 6, p. 561; and fn. 3, p. 420, which includes both a cross reference and discussion.

> Explanatory: fn. 5, p. 560; fn. 2, p. 549; fn. 5, p. 386.

Placement of Footnotes

Three alternatives are frequently used for footnote placement: at the bottom of pages, within the text itself, and in a list at the end of the report.

Bottom-of-Page Footnotes

The traditional, preferred placement of footnotes is at the bottom of the same page on which they are cited by superscripts—the method used in this book. When typewritten, they are separated from the text by a typed solid line 1½ or 2 inches long—a double space below the last line of the text—beginning at the left margin. Each footnote is typed single space, usually indented three to five spaces on its first line and even with the left margin on all succeeding lines. Double-space between footnotes, as shown in Figure 18-1.

An advantage of bottom-of-page footnotes is that the reader can easily read them without turning pages to find a list at end of the report. A disadvantage is for the typist, who must plan enough space to correctly insert footnotes at bottom of pages.

Within-the-Text Notations

Another method of documentation is to place a source right within the text. Sometimes you can weave into a sentence the minimum essentials of a citation. For example:

```
According to Lewis Benton (Supervision and Management, McGraw-Hill Book
Company, 1972, p. 54), absenteeism can be controlled by . . . .
```

or

```
Another writer--Leslie Bernstein (in "How to Right a Report," Business
Management, September 1978, pp. 46-48)--states that. . . .
```

This placement of the citation within a sentence or paragraph is convenient for both reader and writer, but it has limitations. If the citation is long, the

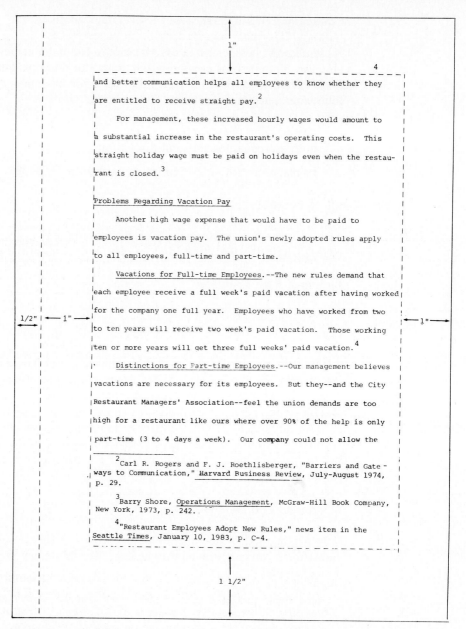

Figure 18-1 A long-report page (double-spaced) showing placement of three superscripts and three complete footnotes.

sentence also becomes undesirably long and the thought is interrupted by the notation.

Some writers place in parentheses only the author's name and page number(s)—(Bernstein, pp. 46–48)—within a paragraph. Then when readers turn to the bibliography, alphabetized, they discover the Bernstein complete citation and know information came from it on pages 46–48.

In addition to citing sources within text sentences or paragraphs, you can also place some cross-references and short explanatory comments there. For example, you might insert a parenthetical sentence like: "(See item 4, pages 52–53.)." Inserting the explanatory parenthetical statements is permissible if they are short—usually not more than a line or two.

List after End of Report

A third way to place footnotes is the terminal method, in which all notations are in a list after the body of the report, not in footnotes on the same pages as the superscripts. This placement, used by many professional journals and academic writers, is discussed in the next section, Supplemental Parts.

In summary, as with everything else for good report writing, use good judgment in your choice of documentation, footnote content, and placement; then be consistent. Various methods have advantages in certain situations. Consider the type and length of note or reference and whether your reader would prefer reading it immediately, or as a footnote, or at the end of the report. Furthermore, if any material is definitely irrelevant, *omit* it entirely from your report text and footnotes. If you are writing a report for publication in a journal, use whatever documentation method the journal editors require.

SUPPLEMENTAL PARTS

The special parts that are added after the body of a report are called supplemental or appended parts, or addenda. They may include a bibliography or other list of references, an appendix, and an index.

Bibliography or Other Appropriate List

List of Sources

The bibliography is a list of all sources you cited in the footnotes as documentation and also other relevant references you consulted for the content of your report. Among the published sources included in a bibliography are those from books, government publications, yearbooks, public documents, encyclopedias, pamphlets, bulletins, magazines, and newspapers. It is possible that a report, article, or other paper may have footnotes but no bibliography; also that a bibliography may be included without any footnotes.

You can present bibliographic entries in a single alphabetic list under the one heading, Bibliography, or under various pertinent subheadings. For example, if your list is long and varied, you might arrange sources within broad groups such as books, periodicals, and government publications—as in Figure 18-2.

If you consulted also unpublished sources such as manuscripts, interviews, responses to surveys, and organization letters or documents, the title of your list of sources may be "Sources Consulted," "Reference Sources," or whatever adequately covers its contents. For example, see Figure 18-9, page 582.

The popular way to arrange bibliographic entries is in *alphabetic order by authors' surnames*. These source entries usually differ from the footnote setup in the following ways, as shown in Figure 18-2:

1. The first word of each entry begins at the left margin and all other lines are indented—usually three to five spaces. For footnotes, as previously shown, the opposite setup is used: each first line is indented and all succeeding lines start at the left margin.
2. The author's surname is listed first, for alphabetizing. If a source includes two or three authors, only the first author's name is reversed. (An alternate arrangement by some writers is to reverse all authors' names, not just the first name.) If more than three authors are involved, reverse the first author's surname but don't list the other names: "Thompson, Robert, and others," or "Thompson, Robert, et al."
3. For books and other bound volumes the total pages are stated, not the pages of parts consulted.

Some bibliographies are *annotated*. They contain, just below the composition and publication information about each entry, a brief statement about its content and value. For example:

```
Concentrates on basic principles and techniques of writing technical
reports. Focuses on data gathering, data analysis, and the scien-
tific method. Contains good examples.
```

List of Notes, References, Sources

If a report includes also cross references and incidental explanatory notations in addition to sources, and the writer chooses the terminal method of listing notations, the list after the report is usually quite different from those discussed under Bibliography. Entries appear on the list in the same numerical order that the citations and superscripts occur in the report; author names are not arranged alphabetically. The list may be titled Notes and References, or List of References, or, sometimes, merely Endnotes.

Figure 18-3 is an example of 13 entries—a cross reference (#3), an explanatory note (#7), and the 9 sources listed on pages 562–563. Notes 11 and 13 are shortened because they are repetitions of sources #10 and 12, respectively, except for page citations.

BIBLIOGRAPHY

Books

Burden, Charles, and others (eds.) Business in Literature, David McKay Press, New York, 1977 (paper) 318 pp.

Kornblum, Allan N., The Moral Hazards, D. C. Heath and Company, Lexington, MA, 1976, 179 pp.

Willingham, John R., and Donald F. Warders, A Handbook for Student Writers, 2d Edition, Harcourt Brace Jovanovich, Inc., New York, 1978, 348 pp.

Wincor, Richard, Contracts in Plain English, McGraw-Hill Book Co., New York, 1976, 148 pp.

Periodicals and Newspapers

Associated Press Dispatch, "Economics Seen behind Cancellation," The Jamaica (New York) Chronicle, November 30, 1979, p. 3-C.

"Discretionary Justice," Business Week, March 16, 1983, p. 15-

Editorial in the Los Angeles Times, May 4, 1983, p. B-7.

Weatherly, Richard, Michael Lipsky, and Thomas Jones, "Street-Level Bureaucrats and Institutional Reform," Harvard Educational Review, May 1977, p. 172.

Weinrauch, J. E., and J. R. Swandra, Jr., "Examining the Significance of Listening; An Exploratory Study of Contemporary Managers," The Journal of Business Communication, 13:1, 1975, p. 54.

Government Publications

Consumer's Resource Handbook, The White House Office of the Special Assistant for Consumer Affairs and the Postal Service, U.S. Government Printing Office, Washington, D.C., 1980, 77 pp.

International Postal Rates and Fees, United States Postal Service, U.S. Government Printing Office, Washington, D.C., 1981, 41 pp.

Figure 18-2 A bibliography. This one shows how seven source footnotes illustrated on pages 562-563 are rearranged alphabetically under three subheads, and it includes two additional sources (Kornblum; Weatherly, Lipsky, Jones) that were not in the footnotes, as well as two government publications.

References and Notes

1. Richard Wincor, Contracts in Plain English, McGraw-Hill Book Co., New York, 1976, pp. 82-85.

2. John R. Willingham and Donald F. Warders, A Handbook for Student Writers, 2d Edition. Harcourt Brace Jovanovich, Inc., New York, 1978, pp. 293-4.

3. For a list of documents, see pages 21-22.

4. Charles Burden and others (eds.), Business in Literature, David McKay Press, New York, 1977 (paper) p. 176.

5. J. E. Weinrauch and J. R. Swandra, Jr., "Examining the Significance of Listening, and Exploratory Study of Contemporary Managers," The Journal of Business Communication. 13:1, 1975, p. 25.

6. "Discretionary Justice," Business Week, March 16, 1979, pp. 15-16.

7. In an industrial setting, such as an assembly line, little discretion is exercised by the laborer. Consequently, the generalization concerning the exercise of discretion, on the street-level, applies only to occupational settings like social service agencies.

8. Editorial in the Los Angeles Times, May 4, 1983, P. B-7.

9. Associated Press Dispatch, "Economics Seen behind Cancellation," The Jamaica (New York) Chronicle, November 30, 1979, p. 3-C.

10. H. Greenbaum, "The Appraisal of Organizational Communication Systems," unpublished manuscript delivered to the International Communication Association, Atlanta, 1972, p. 3.

11. Greenbaum, p. 4.

12. Report of the National District Attorneys Association Symposium on White Collar Crime Enforcement, conducted at Batelle Seattle Research Center, 1982, p. 12.

13. Report . . . . , p. 14.

Figure 18-3 List of references, notes and sources. Numbers are in same order as in text discussion. *No* footnotes appear on text pages. List of 13 includes 9 different sources, 2 repetitions (#11 and #13), a cross reference (#3), and a discussion note (#7).

Appendix

You put materials into the appendix when you need to include them somewhere in the report, but they aren't essential in developing any part of the text. The appendix permits you to avoid cluttering the discussion (text) with exhibits, copy of a questionnaire, and pamphlets that are unnecessary to read for the right understanding of the report but which may be useful as reference or as supporting information.

With short reports, you merely add the appendix sheets directly to the report. But for a formal report, you place a sheet of paper (the appendix title page) between the last page of the body and the first page of the appendix. If you have enough material in the appendix to justify a separate table of contents, show the contents below the title on the appendix dividing sheet, in order of the page arrangement. (See, for example, the appendix dividing sheet in this text, page 703.)

Each separate entry (sample forms, detailed data for reference, table, picture, questionnaire, chart, map, graphic representation, blueprint) in the appendix naturally requires an identifying title. As a rule you should refer the reader to every entry in the appendix in the report body (within the discussion itself or in a footnote).

The last page of the appendix is the ideal place for any table or illustration the reader will need to refer to throughout the report. You can set up this table on a pull-out sheet and tell the reader about the sheet in the letter of transmittal or introduction. Such an arrangement permits the reader to keep this master table—or whatever is on the sheet—in full view at all times.

Index

The index lists topics alphabetically and guides the reader to various places that discuss certain subject matter in the report. Only in very long reports will you need an index if it is necessary to help the reader find specific subjects and items alphabetically.

PRESENTATION OF THE FORMAL REPORT

Before you begin to write your formal-report body and other parts, you should, of course, have completed all preliminary work. You have defined the problem and purpose, collected all needed material, sorted and interpreted data, organized the final outline, and prepared visual aids. If it's required or desirable, you may also have presented a working plan for approval by whoever assigned the report. The next steps are: writing, editing, revising, and typing the report.

Writing the First Draft

With your research materials close at hand—sorted in piles or in folders under your outline headings—you can now begin writing. Perhaps you'll start with a section you consider easiest for you: That's a good way to feel comfortable with the job. Writing a long report will seem easier if you think of it as a series of short reports (your main report sections), linked coherently by your well-planned outline and appropriate transitional devices.

In the first draft just get your ideas down on paper without stopping to correct spelling, punctuation, or grammar. While writing your rough draft, leave wide margins and plenty of space between lines for later revisions. Also, make your first draft as complete as possible. Later, when revising, you'll find it is easier to delete material if necessary than to insert new material. Generally, it is better to allow several days to write a long report. Don't try to cram it all into one eight-hour session, for exhaustion and rushing will adversely affect the quality of the report.

You can begin with the introduction; or finish the text first. Either way is acceptable. Be sure to include those elements in the introduction that will best orient the reader to the rest of the report. For a 15- to 25-page double-spaced typewritten report the introduction should be no more than 1½ or 2 pages. If, for example, it is four pages long because the problem or background material has required three of the pages, take the problem or background material out of the introduction and make it the first main section of the text.

The text for a 15- to 25-page report probably shouldn't have more than three or four major divisions. If you have more than that, look critically at your outline to see whether you can and should regroup or combine sections. Although the divisions don't all have to be the same length, every main division should include enough substance and length to justify its position of importance. Of course, a report with a hundred or several hundred pages will have proportionately more main divisions; in fact, it may have "chapters," each with its own main divisions and subdivisions. Remember to insert documentation where necessary, too.

The terminal section should be a logical outcome of the material in the text. As you know, you may label it Summary, Conclusions, or Conclusions and Recommendations; or you may want to consider one of the other possible titles, such as those listed on page 470.

Besides completing your first draft of the report body, you should also write a draft of the abstract, letter of transmittal, and bibliography or endnotes list, if you'll have one. You can also set up the table of contents and the table of tables (if any) in rough draft; but only after the final typing is finished can you know correct page numbers for these tables.

Editing and Revising the Rough Draft(s)

After you have finished the first draft, lay it aside for at least one day. Doing this will help you look objectively at the material and to see more clearly the weaknesses in the draft. Editing requires objective self-criticism. What seemed right in the first writing may seem seriously out of place upon second reading. Remember too that the best writers revise and rewrite several times, when necessary!

A few handy supplies are useful when you revise a long report. You'll need a pencil (perhaps a red pencil, too), a stapler, cellophane tape, extra paper, and a pair of scissors or a razor blade. As you read your draft critically, you can use your pencil(s) for small corrections in the margins and between lines, or to cross out unneeded sentences. However, if you find a section that needs major reorganizing, use your scissors (or razor). A paragraph out of place on one page may be cut out of that page and stapled or taped to another page after you have cut it apart at the place where the insertion belongs. (Use a backing sheet underneath each cut page if necessary.) Likewise you may need to write an entirely new paragraph; you can insert it, too, into a section after you have cut the sheet at the right place.

Just rereading each word of the report isn't the best way to approach the all-important job of editing and revising. Instead you should:

1. Check critically the title, abstract (or synopsis or executive summary), introduction, and terminal section. The title should tell concisely what the subject of the entire report is. The abstract (or synopsis, executive summary), if any, should reveal the problem, purpose, sources used, results (usually), and whatever else is pertinent. The introduction should include all needed elements. The terminal section should contain no new material and should stem logically from the information in the text.
2. Compare the letter of transmittal, introduction, and terminal section (if it precedes the introduction and text); avoid repetition. The reader who has to read the same information two or three times in close sequence will react unfavorably.
3. Check the table of contents to make sure that all major and minor sections match the headings in the text. But not all headings in the text (such as fourth- or fifth-degree headings) need to appear in the table of contents. Check also to see that you have indicated correctly the relation of major and minor parts and that headings of the same degree are parallel.
4. Check footnotes, if any, for consecutive numbering and correct placement in the bibliography, or whatever endnotes list you have.
5. Now edit the entire report for the C qualities. Read again the pertinent items in the checklists on pages 485–490. If your report violates any, try again to improve it wherever possible.

Typing the Formal Report

After you have revised the draft(s) to your satisfaction, the report is ready to be typed (by yourself or your secretary). Although various authorities have different rules for typing this material, the suggestions here are for one of the acceptable methods. Whatever method you use, be consistent. An appropriate, consistent typing style is very important for the overall appearance of the report. The report should make a favorable impression in its overall appearance, spacing, margins, and pagination, in addition to its well-written content.

Overall Appearance

Regardless of how well written your report is, if its appearance is untidy, it will create an unfavorable impression in the mind of the reader.

To achieve the correct initial impression, see that the cover is appropriately attractive, that typing is neat and on quality bond paper, that visual aids and footnotes are correctly placed. Avoid smudges, streaks, curled ends, wrinkled paper, and any other distractions that might divert your reader's attention from the message.

Double Spacing versus Single Spacing

Reports may be typewritten with double or single spacing. Those who prefer double spacing feel it is easily read; it is also preferred by printers. (Another reason, though not generally admitted, is that double spacing makes a report appear longer.) Single-spaced reports have become popular in recent years not only because they save paper, but also—with fewer pages for the same amount of report data—they save in several other ways: (a) typing time, (b) filing space, (c) expense of both duplicating time and materials when multiple copies of a report are needed, and (d) reading time, because readers have fewer pages to turn and the line spacing on them is similar to that on printed publications which they are accustomed to reading.

If you double-space the report, the first word of every paragraph should be indented (usually five spaces). In a single-spaced report paragraphs may be indented or begin at the left margin. However, always double-space between paragraphs and both before and after long quotations, visual aids, and footnotes.

Regardless of whether the report is typed in double or single spacing, the following parts should be single-spaced:

1. Transmittal letter—typed on company letterhead if you are writing it as an employee of the firm. And, of course, the letter is centered attractively on the page.
2. Quotations and examples of three or more typewritten lines. If this material consists of two or more paragraphs, double-space (leave a blank line) between them. Also, indent margins of the quote five spaces to the right and left of the double- or single-spaced text material. Use ellipses (. . .) to indicate omissions if you are quoting only parts of an author's paragraph. In long quotations you can show lengthy omissions by either a full line of periods or by four periods at the end of the paragraph before the omission.
3. A list of items you want to set off or emphasize.

4. Footnotes (but double-space between them).

5. Some tables and other visual aids.

Margins

In addition to the following suggested margins, you need to add ½ inch for binding on each page. Although the report is usually bound on the left-hand-side—like a book—you can bind at the top. Acceptable margins are as follows:

> *First page of each prefatory part* (preface or letter of transmittal, table of contents, table of tables, abstract), *body,* and *supplemental parts* (appendix, bibliography or endnotes, index): Top margin of 1½ or 2 inches.

> *All other pages:* Top, bottom, and side margins are 1 or 1½ inch (plus the ½-inch allowance for binding at either left side or top).

Pagination

Every page in the report—except the cover and title fly—should have a number but not all numbers are actually typed on each page. For the prefatory sheets use small Roman numerals; for the body and supplemental sheets use Arabic numbers, according to these guidelines:

1. *Prefatory parts page numbers* are centered and placed ½ inch below the imaginary line that frames the bottom of the typewritten material. Count and number the prefatory pages as shown below.

Cover and Title fly	don't count or number
Title page	count (i) but don't insert number
Letter of transmittal	count, but usually don't insert, number. A one-page letter is page ii at the bottom; a second page of the transmittal is page iii.
Table of contents	count and number each page
Table of tables	count and number
Abstract	count and number

2. *Body and supplemental parts page numbers*

   a. If your report is bound at the left, page numbers are usually placed near the upper right corner of the page, aligned with the right margin and ½ inch (or a double space) above the top imaginary line that frames the typewritten material. The exception is that the numbers for first pages of parts are either omitted (though counted) or placed ½ inch (or a double space) below the imaginary line that frames the bottom of the typed material. They are centered with the typing on the page (as for prefatory parts pages).

b. If your report is bound at the top, page numbers are placed usually in the center at the bottom of the page, ½ inch or a double space below the imaginary line that frames the bottom of the typewritten text.

EXAMPLE OF PAGES FROM A FORMAL ANALYTICAL REPORT

The following pages from an energy conservation report within a company apply many of the suggestions in this chapter and Chapter 16 for writing a formal report. They are illustrated not as models of perfection but as one way of presenting parts about which students most often have questions:

> Title page (Figure 18-4)
> Letter of transmittal (Figure 18-5)
> Table of contents (Figure 18-6)
> First and second pages of the text (typed single space) (Figures 18-7 and 18-8)
> List of sources consulted (Figure 18-9)

Succeeding pages in the text section of this report are arranged and numbered as shown on its page 2. The main headings—III, IV, and V—are centered (horizontally) on pages 3, 12, and 18 as stated in the table of contents. They do not begin new pages, but merely follow the preceding text paragraphs. Subheadings for them are third-degree headings placed at the left margin like those on its page 1—Authorization and Purpose, The Problem at Central, and Sources of Data.

Though the report is a long formal report with prefatory and supplemental parts, the wording throughout is appropriately informal because the writer is a staff assistant in the company discussed by the report. It is typed single space in keeping with his company's preference. (The broken lines and arrows are inserted in these illustrations only to show you the widths of the imaginary margins.) The bibliography is titled Sources Consulted, because most of the information came from interviews rather than publications. If you are wondering how footnotes are typed on single-spaced pages, the answer is that they are placed at the bottom of pages with the same spacing as shown in Figure 18-1—though it is a double-spaced report. (See also Placement of Footnotes, on pages 565–567.) To protect anonymity, in the energy conservation report the names of persons and of the company as well as some numbers in the illustrated pages have been changed.

In summary, the formal business report is "formal" because of its parts—not because it uses formal language. Each prefatory and supplemental part should serve a useful purpose for the reader; if it doesn't, it should not appear in the report. Writing a formal report becomes easier for the writer when the writer has performed carefully and thoroughly the research steps before writ-

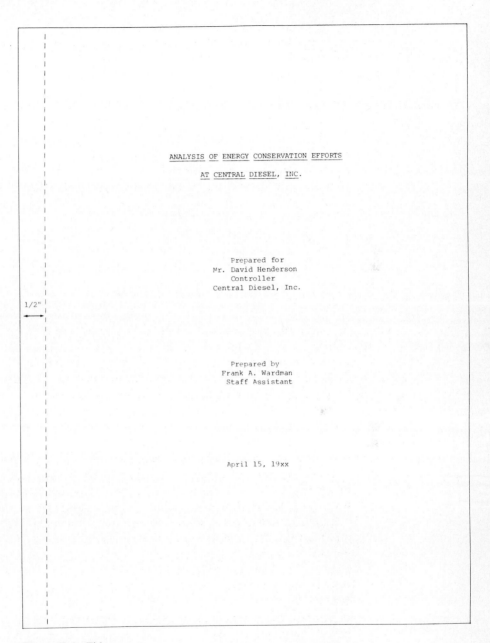

Figure 18-4   Title page.

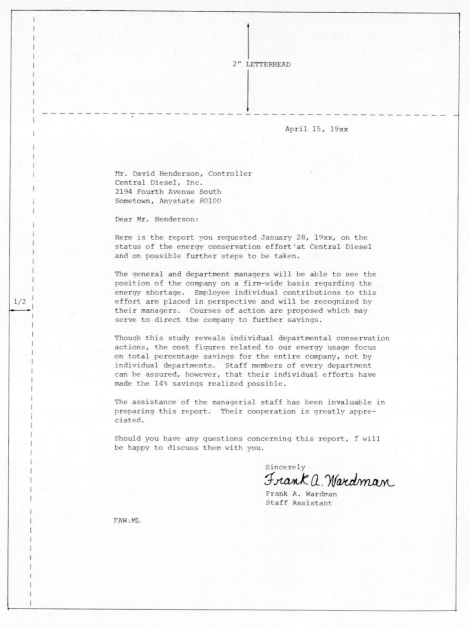

2" LETTERHEAD

April 15, 19xx

Mr. David Henderson, Controller
Central Diesel, Inc.
2194 Fourth Avenue South
Sometown, Anystate 80100

Dear Mr. Henderson:

Here is the report you requested January 28, 19xx, on the
status of the energy conservation effort 'at Central Diesel
and on possible further steps to be taken.

The general and department managers will be able to see the
position of the company on a firm-wide basis regarding the
energy shortage. Employee individual contributions to this
effort are placed in perspective and will be recognized by
their managers. Courses of action are proposed which may
serve to direct the company to further savings.

Though this study reveals individual departmental conservation
actions, the cost figures related to our energy usage focus
on total percentage savings for the entire company, not by
individual departments. Staff members of every department
can be assured, however, that their individual efforts have
made the 14% savings realized possible.

The assistance of the managerial staff has been invaluable in
preparing this report. Their cooperation is greatly appreciated.

Should you have any questions concerning this report, I will
be happy to discuss them with you.

                                    Sincerely

                                    Frank A. Wardman
                                    Frank A. Wardman
                                    Staff Assistant

FAW:ML

1/2

Figure 18-5 Transmittal letter.

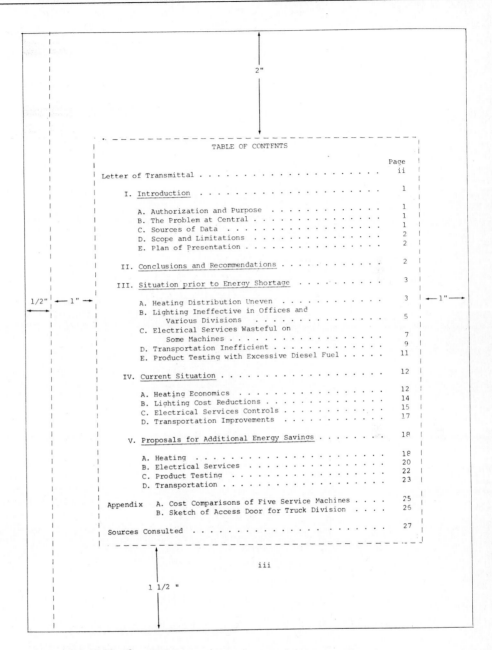

2"

1/2" ← 1" →   ← 1" →

iii

1 1/2 "

Figure 18-6 Table of contents.

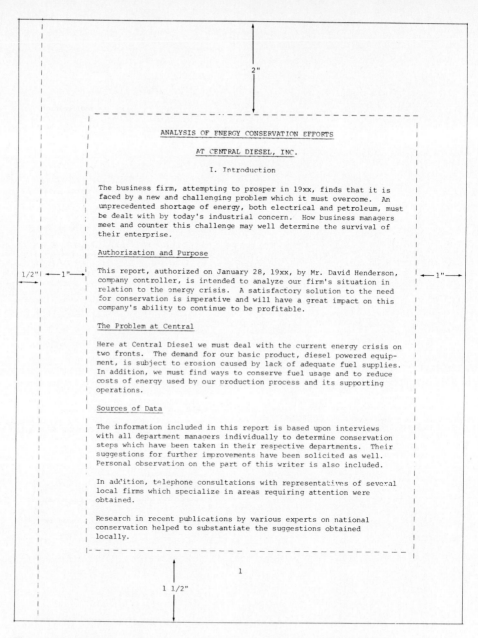

The content shown within the figure:

2"

ANALYSIS OF ENERGY CONSERVATION EFFORTS

AT CENTRAL DIESEL, INC.

I. Introduction

The business firm, attempting to prosper in 19xx, finds that it is faced by a new and challenging problem which it must overcome. An unprecedented shortage of energy, both electrical and petroleum, must be dealt with by today's industrial concern. How business managers meet and counter this challenge may well determine the survival of their enterprise.

Authorization and Purpose

This report, authorized on January 28, 19xx, by Mr. David Henderson, company controller, is intended to analyze our firm's situation in relation to the energy crisis. A satisfactory solution to the need for conservation is imperative and will have a great impact on this company's ability to continue to be profitable.

The Problem at Central

Here at Central Diesel we must deal with the current energy crisis on two fronts. The demand for our basic product, diesel powered equipment, is subject to erosion caused by lack of adequate fuel supplies. In addition, we must find ways to conserve fuel usage and to reduce costs of energy used by our production process and its supporting operations.

Sources of Data

The information included in this report is based upon interviews with all department managers individually to determine conservation steps which have been taken in their respective departments. Their suggestions for further improvements have been solicited as well. Personal observation on the part of this writer is also included.

In addition, telephone consultations with representatives of several local firms which specialize in areas requiring attention were obtained.

Research in recent publications by various experts on national conservation helped to substantiate the suggestions obtained locally.

1

1 1/2"

1/2" 1" 1"

Figure 18-7 First page of this formal report. (Either single or double spacing is acceptable.)

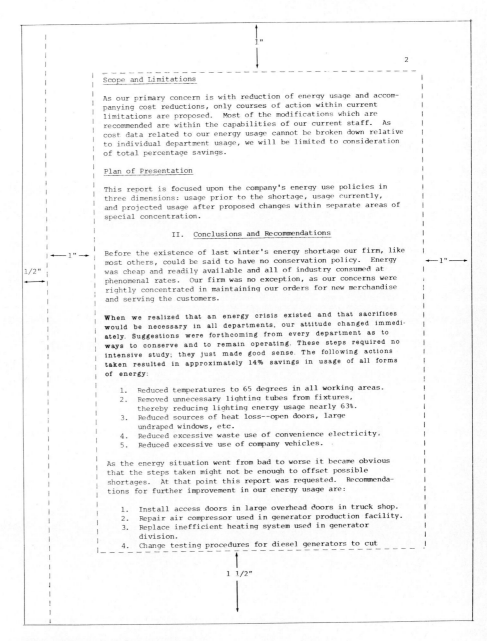

2

<u>Scope and Limitations</u>

As our primary concern is with reduction of energy usage and accompanying cost reductions, only courses of action within current limitations are proposed. Most of the modifications which are recommended are within the capabilities of our current staff. As cost data related to our energy usage cannot be broken down relative to individual department usage, we will be limited to consideration of total percentage savings.

<u>Plan of Presentation</u>

This report is focused upon the company's energy use policies in three dimensions: usage prior to the shortage, usage currently, and projected usage after proposed changes within separate areas of special concentration.

II. <u>Conclusions and Recommendations</u>

Before the existence of last winter's energy shortage our firm, like most others, could be said to have no conservation policy. Energy was cheap and readily available and all of industry consumed at phenomenal rates. Our firm was no exception, as our concerns were rightly concentrated in maintaining our orders for new merchandise and serving the customers.

When we realized that an energy crisis existed and that sacrifices would be necessary in all departments, our attitude changed immediately. Suggestions were forthcoming from every department as to ways to conserve and to remain operating. These steps required no intensive study; they just made good sense. The following actions taken resulted in approximately 14% savings in usage of all forms of energy:

1. Reduced temperatures to 65 degrees in all working areas.
2. Removed unnecessary lighting tubes from fixtures, thereby reducing lighting energy usage nearly 63%.
3. Reduced sources of heat loss--open doors, large undraped windows, etc.
4. Reduced excessive waste use of convenience electricity.
5. Reduced excessive use of company vehicles.

As the energy situation went from bad to worse it became obvious that the steps taken might not be enough to offset possible shortages. At that point this report was requested. Recommendations for further improvement in our energy usage are:

1. Install access doors in large overhead doors in truck shop.
2. Repair air compressor used in generator production facility.
3. Replace inefficient heating system used in generator division.
4. Change testing procedures for diesel generators to cut

Figure 18-8   Page 2 of this formal report.

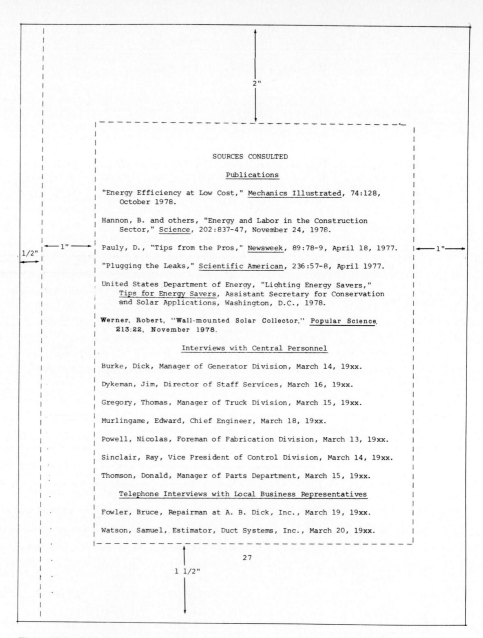

```
                          SOURCES CONSULTED

                            Publications

"Energy Efficiency at Low Cost," Mechanics Illustrated, 74:128,
     October 1978.

Hannon, B. and others, "Energy and Labor in the Construction
     Sector," Science, 202:837-47, November 24, 1978.

Pauly, D., "Tips from the Pros," Newsweek, 89:78-9, April 18, 1977.

"Plugging the Leaks," Scientific American, 236:57-8, April 1977.

United States Department of Energy, "Lighting Energy Savers,"
     Tips for Energy Savers, Assistant Secretary for Conservation
     and Solar Applications, Washington, D.C., 1978.

Werner, Robert, "Wall-mounted Solar Collector," Popular Science,
     213:22, November 1978.

                 Interviews with Central Personnel

Burke, Dick, Manager of Generator Division, March 14, 19xx.

Dykeman, Jim, Director of Staff Services, March 16, 19xx.

Gregory, Thomas, Manager of Truck Division, March 15, 19xx.

Murlingame, Edward, Chief Engineer, March 18, 19xx.

Powell, Nicolas, Foreman of Fabrication Division, March 13, 19xx.

Sinclair, Ray, Vice President of Control Division, March 14, 19xx.

Thomson, Donald, Manager of Parts Department, March 15, 19xx.

       Telephone Interviews with Local Business Representatives

Fowler, Bruce, Repairman at A. B. Dick, Inc., March 19, 19xx.

Watson, Samuel, Estimator, Duct Systems, Inc., March 20, 19xx.

                                27
```

Figure 18-9 List of sources consulted, including both published materials and interviews.

ing. And he or she is certain to have a better piece of writing when he or she has properly revised the first draft and considered the importance to the reader(s) of the report's overall presentation.

EXERCISES

1. Assume that after graduating from college you have worked in a responsible job related to your chosen major field. Because of your high-quality work in a certain area, your employer gave you more and more responsibilities helping other employees. The past two years this firm has paid you a generous extra salary for conducting seminars two evenings a week for various groups of employees (5 to 15) that need to improve their skills in. . . . (Choose an area in which you can excel. For example, it might be memo or letter writing, English fundamentals, selling, accounting, a technical skill, or even an indoor sport activity helpful in the company's employee recreation program.) Recently your company's vice president personally complimented you on your good seminars (which are now completed) and on the substantial improvement he has noticed in the work of employees who attended them.

   Your success has also come to the attention of an executive friend in another firm that has been considering a similar training program for its employees. You have conferred with this executive, thoroughly assessed that company's needs, and decided you would like to conduct a seminar for its employees. Now you must prepare a well-written proposal that will win the contract for this consulting job.

   Begin by reviewing the suggestions in this book regarding outline, format, writing style and appearance of well-written proposal. Choose the topics that apply to your particular proposal. You might also provide answers to these and similar questions:

   a. Specifically what will your seminars or workshops cover? And *how will they meet the needs of this firm's employees?* Be careful not to promise more than you can accomplish, and do not bind yourself to too many specific functions that you may find later are unnecessary. You will be legally bound to fulfill your commitments to the firm's satisfaction.
   b. Will you require a textbook or any other purchases by the participants?
   c. Will you provide handouts as needed?
   d. How many total hours will you probably devote to these seminars? Consider hours for:

   Teaching or consulting—two nights a week, two hours for each session

   Preparation before each session

   Reading and commenting on employees' work

Conferences with individuals or small groups (three or four) on their specific problem areas

e. Because the workshop will meet in a classroom within the employer's building, what facilities will you need? (Consider blackboard, chalk, screen, projector, tapes, tables, armchairs, etc. Will you need use of that firm's Xerox or other duplicating equipment to reproduce materials for class discussion?)

f. What will you charge for your services? This is, of course, a difficult and very important decision. You want your price to be reasonable, neither too high nor too low. (Assume the firm is well able to pay most any fair amount, and that your present employer paid you $40 an hour even though you were a ''beginner'' at consulting.)

g. What other legitimate expenses should your client expect to meet? (Consider transportation costs, meals, materials, duplicating, typing, etc.)

h. What payment method does this firm prefer? Will you be expected to submit an itemized statement monthly and to be paid shortly thereafter; or will payment be a lump sum at the end of the workshops or perhaps a part payment before they begin?

i. What parts of your own training and experience should you include in your résumé?

After a complete analysis you will write, revise, and type the final copy of your winning proposal. Include a letter of transmittal and follow the other pertinent guidelines on pages 543–549.

2. Choose a problem which you can solve by experimentation, survey, and/or observation, and write your proposal to the organization that is concerned with the problem. Or (if more appropriate) assume your proposal goes to a funding agency whose philosophy is in keeping with the problem you propose to research. Here are suggestions for topics—but feel free to choose your own.

a. Try to solve a problem related to a firm's product development; plant expansion; improvement of a sales, accounting, or purchasing system; or curtailment of shoplifting.

b. Analyze a problem in your community—crime(s) in a certain area, a traffic snarl situation, poor citizen involvement in local issues, need for attracting new industry or keeping young, educated persons in the community.

c. Undertake a project in one of your college classes—or survey a sample of the student body regarding an important campus problem.

Follow thoughtfully the suggestions in this chapter regarding proposal writing. Organize your topics under appropriate headings and write a proposal that meets all requirements as to content, format, and writing style. Then submit your complete proposal to (a) your instructor and/or (b) your class in an oral presentation. Be prepared to defend your proposal and to have the class critique it.

3. If you need practice in organizing topics under meaningful headings, try this assignment. Assume the sales manager of ABC New Car Agency in your city has asked you, a management consultant, to review and evaluate the agency's sales system. The internal control seems to be weak and something is causing problems.

   The main purpose of your study is to determine the strength of the internal control and its effect on the financial papers for new-car sales.

   You have just finished both secondary and primary research. Two new accounting books (assume names) substantiate your concept for internal control. In your primary research you interviewed four middle managers and 15 or 20 employees. You studied the personality of the sales staff and the viewpoints of other personnel. You observed the personnel performing their duties and their interactions. Up to now you have information under the following topics, jumbled and in no useful order.

   File clerks' job

   Keypunch operator's responsibility

   Dealership's environment

   Title clerk's functions

   Salesperson's personality

   Internal control by buyers' orders

   Personnel system's internal control

   Dealership's history

   Sequence of signatures in sale of a car

   Accounting clerks' duties

   Control system's procedure

   Title clerk's work

   Sales staff's functions

   Flowchart of new vehicle sales system (you have drawn this on seven pages)

   Dealership's new vehicle sales system

   Introduction

   Conclusions

   Sales manager's part

   Bibliography

   Choose the main headings for the text of this report (three or four should be sufficient). Then organize these 19 topics under the main headings and wherever they belong in a complete outline of the well-planned formal report.

4. Your assignment is to write a formal report whose body is approximately 15 to 25 double-spaced pages. Choose a topic that is broad enough to justify the length. Yet beware of a topic so broad that it would require volumes. If possible, consider a subject that you know something about, or one that especially interests you.

Try to find a topic that involves a business problem. (For example, you might know there's too great a turnover of employees in a certain department.) From the problem, and with some thought on your part, you can determine the purpose of your report. Other ideas that you can use as a springboard for a topic are listed below, pertaining to problems involved in:

Accounting, credits, collections

The accountant's role in cost reduction and analysis

Computer programming and errors in monthly statements

Problems and progress of accounting in X Company

Accounting contributions to the effective management of X Company

Problems involved in a bank's converting to a computerized operation

Policy or procedure and degree of communications used by X Company in collecting retail accounts.

General management and/or labor

The functioning and problems of your campus student-body governing organization; accomplishments and recommendations for greater effectiveness

A profit-sharing plan for X Company

Would hiring handicapped workers be charity or good business for X Company

A program for achieving optimum discipline in X Company

Business outlook for Y industry or X Company

How X Company (or your campus) has met the energy crisis and what should still be done

A proposed program (or plan) for hiring and training of minority groups in X Company

Development of a profitable ski area on a certain mountain

Suggestions for X Company's response to Z Union's attempt to organize workers

Recommendations for a formal salary scale for X Company

Personnel administration

Development of a personnel testing program for X Company

Analysis of the merit rating system of X Company

A safety program for X Company

The performance of women in top executive positions

Survey, interpretation, and recommendation—after a study on attitudes toward certain recent troublesome problems:
a. Opinion of X Company's employees regarding wages, working hours, parking, food services, promotion plan
b. Opinion of students in your school regarding grading, credit hours for certain courses, student parking, housing
c. Opinion of X Organization's members regarding membership dues, requirements, privileges, new clubhouse

Marketing

A promotional program for introduction of X product

A new plan for X Company to offer incentives to sales personnel

Where should X Company locate its next supermarket

How can X Company measure effectiveness of its advertising

How downtown merchants can cope with suburban shopping centers

After you have clearly determined the purpose of your report, state it in one sentence. Continue your preliminary investigation (steps 1, 2, and 3 on pages 464–465). At this point in your research submit to your professor (or anyone he or she suggests) a memo report of your working plan. Be sure to include in this memo at least the following: problem, purpose, methodology, readers (both primary and secondary), and suggested outline. In this outline show the order for the introduction, major divisions of the text, subheadings for each major division, and the type of terminal section.

After you have approval of your working plan, you can begin to collect your data; then organize this material and interpret it. With the completion of this last stage—interpretation—you can draw conclusions and make recommendations. Naturally if you're writing an informational report, you'll skip interpretation of material and merely summarize. Also at this time you should prepare (at least in rough-draft form) your tables and any other necessary visual aids. If your professor requests it, submit the final outline that you'll follow in writing your report—the one that will become your table of contents.

Now you should be ready to write. Choose the right time and place and follow the rules outlined in the chapter—both for the first draft and the revision. After your final revision, you can type (or have typed) the body of the report in final draft, or you can first write the necessary prefatory and supplemental parts. In this report assignment include at least the following: cover, title fly, title page, letter of transmittal (or preface), and table of contents. Also, you'll need to include other parts—especially appendix and bibliography—if your report requires them. If the transmittal may affect part of what's included in the body, you should at least plan the transmittal before the final typing of the body.

Although the content and presentation of the material are most important, also remember the role that mechanics play. Be sure you have nothing that detracts your reader from concentrating on what you want to tell. Thus, be sure the spelling, grammar, punctuation, and appearance are acceptable.

PART FIVE
Oral Communications

CHAPTER 19

Successful Speaking and Listening in Business

The ability to communicate effectively orally as well as in writing is highly valued in business. In fact, speaking, writing, and listening represent the core of business communication.

Throughout each working day you as a business or professional person communicate orally with customers, colleagues, associates, supervisors, employees, inquirers, and others. Besides speaking with individuals face to face or by telephone, you will at times also be asked to address various groups of people; in other words—to make a speech. You will also need to listen to the ideas of many persons.

This chapter briefly covers various essentials for improving your oral presentations within groups and for effective listening skills.

IMPROVING YOUR ORAL PRESENTATIONS

Whether the group to which you speak consists of 10 colleagues around a conference table, 30 students in a class, a thousand in an auditorium, or a wider television audience, the ability to speak effectively is important (sometimes crucial) for your success.

The objectives of this section are to give you an overview of:

- Various kinds of oral presentations
- Essential steps for preparing effectively
- Methods of delivering the message
- Suggestions and requirements for the speaker

Kinds of Oral Presentations

The types of talks and speeches given daily throughout the United States are of course so numerous that only a few highlights can be included here.

Short talks may range from 1 to 10 minutes in length. Many are periodic brief progress or committee reports. Some talks introduce new managers or employees (usually during special events), or they may introduce distinguished guests or speakers and panel members at conferences. Other short talks are presentations of awards to people who have earned recognition and thanks for outstanding work on the job, in the community, in sports, in school, or whatever. Still others may be words of welcome to visitors touring your plant or attending the organization's anniversary reception. Or you might be asked to give a short cordial welcome to the audience gathering to hear how your company's products protect the environment; and so on and on.

Long, or formal, presentations may vary from 10 minutes to 1 hour. Some organizations observe 20- or 30-minute time limits for speeches. Often long oral reports or proposals are presented within the organization at important management or staff meetings. They usually include statements of significant main points on complex problems that are detailed in long written reports.

Also, long speeches are frequently scheduled at regional, national, or international conferences of business, professional, religious, social, political, and other associations. Their subject matter varies widely, ranging from information on research studies and projects to discussion of controversial issues.

Essential Steps for Preparing Talks Effectively

Careful planning is essential for successful speeches, short or long. The better you prepare in advance, the more confidence you will have on stage. Preparation usually requires the following seven steps. Most of them include important concepts similar to those for writing reports, letters, and memos (as discussed in previous chapters, especially 2, 3, 4, 5, and 16).

1. Determine the purpose.
2. Analyze the audience and the situation.
3. Choose the ideas for your message.
4. Research your topic thoroughly.
5. Organize the data and write your draft.
6. Plan visual aids if desirable.
7. Rehearse the talk and revise where necessary.

1. Determine the Purpose

Each speech has a general and a specific purpose. Usually the general purpose of business talks is one of these: to inform or instruct, to persuade, to entertain. The specific purpose is to achieve a definite, particular result.

To Inform or Instruct. In short talks to introduce a speaker, to welcome visitors, or to confer an award, the general purpose is obvious. The specific purposes are usually related to building goodwill—so that the listeners sense a need to know the information presented. In short committee reports the specific purpose is generally to inform executives and employees (or other group members) about significant activities during a particular period. Sometimes the aim is to teach a new procedure.

For longer informative speeches, state your specific purpose in a precise, concise infinitive phrase.

Vague specific purpose	*Infinitive specific purpose*
•Logo styles	•To inform the committee on various logo styles prepared by our marketing group
•Health care	•To compare advantages and disadvantages of HMOs versus Blue Cross–Blue Shield

●Foreign sales trip
                                    ●To explain results of conversa-
                                    tions with representatives in
                                    Germany and Switzerland

The relationship between a talk's title, general purpose, and specific purpose is as follows:

Title: What Happens after 55?

Purpose: To inform

Specific purpose: To review changes in our organization's retirement
                    policy for employees over 55

To Persuade. The goal of persuasive speaking is to get your listeners willing to act or accept your beliefs. In business you do this through logically proving your contention, policy, resolution, or claim. Infinitive phrasing will channel your thinking into a precise statement of purpose:

Vague specific purpose

●Coal-fired power plant

●Teleconferencing

Infinitive specific purpose

●To recommend that our organization move from gas, nuclear,
and hydro options to a coal-
fired power plant

●To convince the group that our
own in-house teleconferencing
equipment will be cost-effec-
tive as opposed to renting such
equipment

The following compares a title, purpose, and specific purpose:

Title: This Year's Red Cross Drive

Purpose: To persuade

Specific purpose: To give reasons and provide incentives to all employees for contributing to this year's Red Cross community drive

To Entertain. As businesspersons you will sometimes (though less often) be asked to give speeches that entertain. The occasions may be retirement or promotion parties or celebrations of some anniversary of the organization, committee, or persons.

Title: Happenings in 30 Years: How to Succeed in Business with
         Really Trying

Purpose: To entertain

Specific purpose: To recount humorous events in the 30-year work of
our retiree, Tom R.

2. Analyze Audience and Situation

As emphasized in previous chapters, the message—whether oral or written—should be adapted to the audience. If your talk is within your organization, you will have some idea about who and how many will be in the audience, their occupations, educational level, approximate ages, interests, and the occasion. You will know, too, whether employees attend on their own volition or because their supervisors request them to attend, for various reasons.

When your talk or speech is outside your organization—to a business, public, or social group—less information is available. You need to find out the size of the group, age range, interests, goals, occupations (at least in general). Usually you can get this information from the person who asked you to speak and from other members of the group. If permissible, you might also attend a previous meeting, to see the surroundings, size of room, and facilities you will have for your speech.

Background information about the audience will help you use words and illustrations that are meaningful to your listeners. For example, you will prepare a different talk to college students than to managers or to retirees, even if the general subject is the same. Also, if all in your audience have the same occupation, for instance, computer specialists or purchasing agents, you can use appropriate technical expressions and illustrations.

Whenever possible, estimate the audience's attitudes and prejudices toward your subject. Are they sympathetic? Indifferent? Critical? Hostile? If yours is a controversial topic or bad news, you need to choose tactful opening statements that will get you in step with the audience, without irritation, so they will listen attentively. Begin with ideas about which there is agreement.

Information you gather about the situation is useful for planning your speech and visual aids, if any. Will the meeting be held in a large auditorium, small meeting room with listeners seated around a table, or outdoors with you and other speakers on a raised platform?

3. Choose the Ideas for Your Message

4. Research Your Topic Thoroughly

When you know your purpose and something about the audience interests and level of understanding, you proceed to choose the ideas and collect needed facts. For research, the speaker follows the same procedure as the writer does when preparing a written report.

5. Organize the Data and Write Your Draft

After you have gathered all needed information, you should organize your speech and write the draft. A good speech has three parts—introduction, body (usually called "text section" in reports), and summary or conclusions. You can organize in either the direct (deductive) or the indirect (inductive) order. The choice usually depends upon consideration of your listeners' knowledge and attitudes toward your subject matter. If you are planning an oral report, you may find helpful suggestions on pages 471–476, because steps in organizing oral and written reports are similar.

Introduction. The opening statements should capture your listeners' attention and help create their confidence in the speaker. Thus the introduction has special importance, for it assists in getting your listeners into the right frame of mind. Here are some speech beginnings that help capture audience attention:

1. Telling an anecdote, appropriate joke, or good-natured story related to your subject

   ```
   "Let me begin with a story of an event familiar to most of you, as
   it concerns those over age 30."
   ```

2. Using a quotation that establishes background for developing your subject

3. Greeting your audience sincerely

   ```
   "Two places I especially enjoy coming to are: home and your commu-
   nity. It's good to be with you."
   ```

4. Making a startling statement

   ```
   "By the end of my talk 2,000 people will have been born; 1,800
   others will have died. . . ."
   ```

5. Asking a question that makes audience start to think

   Always include whatever introductory elements are needed to adequately orient your listeners to your talk. State the problem (if any) and your purpose—always. If you are reporting on a research study, briefly describe your methodology and perhaps the importance and timeliness of the subject. Define (here or in the body) any terms that are technical or need clarification. State limitations, if pertinent.

   For the transition to the main part of your speech, state your plan of presentation.

   ```
   "Our goal now is to focus on regulations affecting employment of the
   handicapped. Let us look at that topic in three ways. . . ."
   ```

Body (Text Discussion). The main part of your speech must present whatever material is necessary to achieve your specific purpose. If you are giving a short talk to introduce a speaker or to present an award for an outstanding achievement, you can use that person's résumé as a basis of your text. Sincerely highlight the attributes; *don't* just read everything on the résumé! Try also to add some interesting incident that the audience will enjoy hearing.

Developing an oral report is similar to the way you develop the text of the written report—organized under appropriate headings, followed by facts to support your main points. However, because of a specified time limit for the speech, you usually must omit much detailed data of a long written report and concentrate on perhaps one to three topics.

To organize this main section you can choose from several ways:

- By criteria or topics: The subject itself suggests natural divisions.
- By time: Movement is chronological—from earliest time to later times.
- By location: Spacial movement may be from east to west, north to south, top to bottom.
- By order of familiarity: Proceed from the simple or familiar to the complex or unfamiliar.
- By problem solution: First section states problem; second section offers solution.
- By cause to effect: State probable causes that produce certain results.

The evidence you present depends upon the aims and complexity of your speech and the nature of your audience. Controversial statements demand evidence—authoritative material for supporting your assertions. You have these options:

- Examples and illustrations. Brief, concrete incidents can help clarify and support a point.
- Quotation or testimony. Rarely will you·be the sole expert on your speech topic. To improve your credibility cite verbatim the words of a recognized authority or expert who agrees with your position.
- Analogy. Sometimes you can support your assertions by comparing things that are unlike in appearance or form and yet similar in behavior, relationships, or properties. For instance, you might point out the analogy between the heart and a pump.
- Statistics. Business speaking demands precise figures instead of statements like "some," "a small part," or "a large percent." But avoid stating too many figures, for they readily confuse an audience. Written figures on handout sheets or projected on a screen help to give a comparison quickly.
- Visual aids. As discussed in Chapter 16 and later in this section, appropriate visual aids can be convincing evidence to support your statements.

Summary or Conclusions. The last part of your speech presents briefly the key points or perhaps repeats a quotation that best emphasizes what you wanted to convey. Words like "In closing, . . ." or "One last point is . . ." are appropriate signals for the ending. The last one or two sentences might produce special applause.

6. Plan Visual Aids if Desirable

To help get your message across to the audience, you may also need to plan meaningful visual aids for display at appropriate times. First decide whether you will distribute handouts for each person in the audience or whether you will display all visual aids from one spot. The latter procedure is usually better, because your audience will focus attention on what you are displaying instead of shuffling papers and reading when you would rather have them listen. (However, if you think they would benefit from taking copies home, you can distribute them after your talk.)

The most common devices for "one spot" displays are chalkboards, flip sheets, cards or posters, and projectors. Each has some advantages, depending upon subject matter and audience size.

Chalkboards. When you wish to write brief, significant points or figures either before your talk begins or while you are talking, a chalkboard is useful. If you will have much material for the board, plan if possible to place it there before your talk session begins. The board can be covered until you wish to reveal your display. However, if you prefer to draw or write as you talk, do it without turning your back to the audience. The chalkboard visual aids are usable only, of course, when the audience will be seated near enough to see and easily read the notations on the board.

Flip Sheets. A variety of material on large separate pages can be on flip sheets, fastened at the top and attached to an easel or stand the right height for easy audience viewing. The size of sheets as well as the words, charts, tables, or drawings on them can be modified somewhat, in keeping with expected audience and room size. Even so, of course, their use has limits, for they may be hard to read in large auditoriums seating hundreds of people.

One advantage of using flip sheets instead of a chalkboard is that you can prepare them before you come to the room where you'll be speaking. Another is that they can be larger and of better quality when prepared with colored markers than when material is written with chalk. Also, you can skip pages or add facts on sheets whenever desirable. You can even insert small handwritten notes—not for the audience, but as cues for yourself to guide you to the next topic. And if you are speaking to a small group around a conference table, you can use smaller "table flipsheets" easily read by your audience. Furthermore, during your talk you need merely flip pages in any order you wish and more quickly focus your eyes again on your audience.

Cards or Posters. To serve the same purpose as flip sheets, cards or posters are also useful. They can display the same kinds of drawings and materials, provided they are large enough to be easily read by the audience. An advantage is that you can arrange them easily in any sequence. They are not attached to an easel. Disadvantages are that when they are large and of heavy posterboard, they are cumbersome both to carry and to hold up for display.

Pointing to pertinent parts is also difficult unless the speaker has someone else to help hold the poster while he or she talks.

Projectors. Most adaptable for displaying business materials are the opaque and the overhead projectors. Both project images on a screen or wall for clear viewing by any size audience.

With the opaque projector you can use any typewritten, handwritten, or printed materials or various specimens just as they come from your files. You can project the exact charts, tables, letters, graphs, or pictures from your written report. And you can write on them or point to the parts of them as they are projected on the screen. The opaque projector must be used in a darkened room. You should arrange to have an assistant turn room lights off and on when necessary (and shut off annoying background music or a howling P.A. system.) To read your notes if the lectern has no light, even a pocket flashlight may be useful.

The overhead projector has the advantage of being usable in daylight or a lighted room. To use the overhead you must first convert your display materials into transparencies. These can be prepared quite inexpensively, in a few seconds, on your company's spirit duplicating or Xerox machine, on one of the various other modern transparency makers, or by professional photographic methods. While projecting the transparencies to your audience you can write on them (with marking pens or pencils). You can add overlays of more draw-ings when necessary—as, for example, when explaining the development of a certain manufacturing or marketing process. Also (as with the opaque) you can cover up and reveal your display material point by point so your audience can't read ahead or jump to a conclusion.

The risk of equipment failure on any projector need not worry you if you prepare adequately. Check the machine beforehand. Have an extra bulb and an extension cord available. Check the best placement of screens and know which electric outlet is nearest the podium or lectern.

7. Rehearse the Talk and Revise Where Necessary

After you have considered the preceding six steps, you are ready to apply them by rehearsing your talk. And you will revise wherever improvements are needed. Some executives go through numerous drafts before presenting an important speech.

To develop confidence, you should know the subject better than anyone else in the audience. Are you concerned about stage fright? All good speakers and actors, even professionals, experience some stage fright symptoms—wobbly knees, trembling hands, "butterflies" in the stomach. Actually, the uneasy feelings are the body's ways or providing extra emotional and physical energy to help a person rise to the occasion. With thorough knowledge of your subject and after thoughtful adequate rehearsals, assure yourself that you can present your speech confidently and with enthusiasm.

When rehearsing, stand and deliver your speech out loud—maybe in front of a mirror. To get the feel of the volume level you will use for the presentation (in case the lectern will have no microphone) talk so that a friend (real or imaginary) in the back row can easily hear you.

- Always imagine the audience in front of you.

- Use transitional phrases and sentences to show your listeners the relationships between sections of your report.

- Take each of the main points one at a time and learn to present each with its supporting material as a unit.

- Include the visual aids you'll use—and mark your notes where each aid should be presented.

- Anticipate questions from the audience. Jot them on paper and consider thoughtful answers.

- Stop at the allotted time. Then cut and revise the speech accordingly until you can deliver it entirely well within the time limit—allowing also for a question-and-answer period.

How many times should you rehearse? A president delivering a Christmas greeting rehearsed four times; a vice-president making a presentation to a Congressional committee went through his talk three times; a vice president at a new car announcement rehearsed five times; a president of a foreign subsidiary visiting the home company rehearsed eight times; some speakers go through still more rehearsals and revisions. The decision is up to you.

Four Methods of Delivering the Message

To make your oral presentations you have four choices of kinds of speaking:

1. Extemporaneous Method

With the extemporaneous method—which is usually preferred—you speak from a previously prepared outline or notes. Your outline may be detailed with some comments, quotations, and statistics—all typed on 8½-by-11-inch paper, with pages numbered. For short talks, your notes may be on numbered 3-by-5-inch cards; but usually the larger 5-by-8-inch cards or sheets are preferred, especially for the longer speeches.

Use this extemporaneous method of speaking whenever possible, because it permits more eye contact with the group and you can more easily establish rapport with your audience. After you have given numerous oral presentations, you will be able to use fewer notes and feel more at ease and more confident than a beginning speaker. Also, you will likely prefer to deliver your talks extemporaneously.

2. Manuscript-reading Method

For some long speeches it may be necessary to read parts of your manuscript. The technical data and certainly also quotations from authorities will be read verbatim. Be sure to look at the audience often. Do avoid reading the entire speech word for word.

Occasionally some top-level executives and government officials find it necessary to read their speeches. If they will be filmed on television or quoted in news media, ad-libbing could sometimes lead to problems. Also, of course, laws and rules must be read verbatim. In these cases reading is safest and acceptable; but the reader must still maintain eye contact with the audience.

Large type, wide margins, and double or triple spacing between lines are helpful aids when you must read from the manuscript. In the margins you can write any last-minute comments added before you go to the lectern. You might also underline important words with a red pencil and write cues like "show slide 2" or "turn flip chart 4" at appropriate places.

3. Memorization Method

The beginning speaker might memorize a short talk, but the delivery should be made to sound spontaneous. Rarely ever should a long speech be memorized.

Some of the best speakers memorize—but *not* word for word—the purpose statement and main points of their speech. Try to memorize not the exact words you will use but the *ideas*. Also it may be helpful to memorize your first sentence—especially if you are inclined to feel stage fright at the beginning.

4. Impromptu Method

When you are called upon for comments without prior notice, you will speak impromptu—on the spur of the moment, without specific preparation. In routine business meetings and conferences this request may occur frequently.

Suggestions and Requirements for the Speaker

Communicating successfully before an audience demands actions and qualities not found in writing. Both physical and vocal behavior are important.

Physical Behavior

The speaker's posture, movement, facial expressions, appearance, and gestures all convey external nonverbal cues. Some of the negative impressions to avoid are sketched in Figure 19-1.

1. Posture. Stand erect, relaxed, with weight on both feet. Avoid leaning and slouching. Also, standing on one foot or on your heels or with feet wide apart may impress listeners negatively.

Figure 19-1   Undesirable attitudes and postures for speakers and meeting leaders. (*Source:* B. Y. Auger, *How to Run Better Business Meetings: An Executive's Guide to Meetings That Get Things Done*, Minnesota Mining and Manufacturing Co. (3M), St. Paul, 1979, pp. 64–65.)

2. Movement. Here are four suggested reasons for body motions during an oral presentation:

Move to hold attention. At large sessions lecterns restrict our movement. In business meetings the audience may be smaller, thus permitting you to stand behind a desk or table. Move more often from side to side rather than back and forth. But don't move continuously, like a caged lion!

Move to get rid of nervousness. A way of decreasing stage fright is to move physically, especially in the beginning of your talk. Even the manner in which you approach the lectern tells something about you. Are you slow and plodding, or do you move with assurance, determination, enthusiasm? The latter gives a confident feeling while decreasing some of your initial nervousness.

Move to suggest transitions. Cues for transitions in writing include headings, words, and numerical hints as (1), (2), (3), or (a), (b), (c). In your talk, you visually supplement the oral words of transition by physically moving when making a direction shift. The audience follows you more easily.

Move to increase emphasis. In writing we use exclamation points following emphatic statements. In speaking, a movement toward the audience, accompanied by a gesture, can imply you are stressing a point. Emphasis through movement suggests idea importance and holds group attention.

3. Facial Expressions and Appearance. When you smile or laugh, your face suggests that your topic is of interest to you. A frowning or glaring facial expression may convey nonverbal impressions that you are worried, angry, or perhaps ill at ease. Show enthusiasm and vitality. You must not only *feel* but *show* your interest in your ideas. Sincerity is important. Your enthusiasm must reflect your sincere belief in your ideas and a sincere desire to share them with your listeners.

Regarding appearance, the speaker should of course be dressed appropriately for the occasion and groomed neatly. Clothing that is sloppy, gaudy, or loud in color may negatively affect your audience and distract them from listening to your speech.

4. Gestures. Briefly, gestures are movements of the hands, arms, head, shoulders. Hand and arm gestures are used for several reasons:

To emphasize. For example, the clenched fist emphasizes a point by either hitting the palm of the hand or shaking it upright before an audience.

To point. The index finger calls attention, indicating either locations or directions.

To reject. A sample phrase accompanying this gesture would be "I can't believe the actions of our competitors." Here the hand may go to the side in an act of rejection.

To describe. Clearly, though your hands cannot give the precise picture of the idea or thing you are speaking about, even an approximation of size is worthwhile.

Head and shoulders drooped or turned to one side indicate different nonverbal messages than if these physical parts are erect and the speaker faces the audience—the desired stance.

A few suggestions regarding gestures are noteworthy:

Vary gestures. Using the same action repetitiously is boring to the audience and suggests lack of creativity on your part.

Avoid continuous gestures. Visually we need a rest from the frequent movements of a speaker and gestures. Using continuous gestures weakens the emphasis.

Watch timing. The gesture should accompany the oral thought, not precede or follow.

Adapt gestures. Seated at a table is not the time for broad, all-inclusive gestures. On the other hand, a large audience would not see a small gesture. Adapt to the size of the group.

Vocal Behavior

Your voice during communication is a major contributor to impressions about you. You can use it more effectively in business speaking by following a few suggestions regarding quality, pitch, rate, volume, and pronunciation.

1. Vocal Quality. Here are words to describe voice: husky, throaty, loud, vibrant, dynamic, moving, weak, strong, harsh, shrill, effeminate, masculine, gentle, squeeky, muffled, falsetto. We perceive people in great measure by their voice quality, that indefinable something which distinguishes their voice from others.

The size and shape of these parts of our body affect voice quality: mouth, tongue, lips, teeth, sinuses, palate, and nose. Good voice quality is helped by deep breathing and a conscientious attempt at relaxing the throat for an unrestricted resonating chamber such as the mouth, throat, and nasal cavities.

2. Pitch. A simplistic definition of pitch is the highness or lowness of your voice. But first look at some problems in pitch:

Monotone. A sameness in pitch level. An occiliscope of your voice in a monotone range would show a rather flat line: little variation, little rising or falling of the voice.

High or low. An excited speaker would be in the upper range (during a heated conversation between people), while the dull, monotonous speaker would rest at the lower level of pitch.

Lack of word value. Each word, regardless of its importance in a thought group, receives the same pitch emphasis, the speaker not distinguishing between important and unimportant words in a sentence.

To remove these problems, pitch changes are accomplished through steps and glides—from a higher to a lower level, abruptly. Say this sentence out loud: "Tom, don't do that!" On which word did you raise your pitch? That sentence can be said four different ways, each word receiving a higher pitch depending on the precise word you wish to stress.

Usually we end strong declarative thoughts with downward pitch changes, giving the feeling of finality, determination. A rising inflection is more appropriate to asking questions or suggesting indecision.

Variety in pitch is necessary. Not to use variation is risking being called a monotonous or uninteresting speaker.

3. Rate. The speed or rate at which people speak varies. Sameness in rate also enhances monotony. A speaker may be considered dull when the rate is slow and unvarying, even though that speaker's content may be superior. Conversely, the fast speaker also causes discomfort: we wish the staccato speaker to slow down so that we can digest the thoughts. The key words are variety and pause.

Communication experts suggest the range for public speakers lies between 80 and 160 words per minute. For some people conversing informally, the rate may range from 80 to 250.

4. Volume. To utter the admonition "speak up, please" from the rear of the room demands listener courage. But to sit passively while unintelligible words flow by is a disservice to the audience and to the speaker. Volume is the loudness or softness of your voice. How do you improve it?

By contrast in emphasis, louder or softer volume. How would you express the following thought at the end of an oral proposal presentation?

```
And with that we conclude our remarks. Personally, I look forward to
working with you and the other members of your project team. I can't
forget that at one time I was asked to join your firm. Now I'm on
the other side, offering a proposal which I hope you'll accept. Re-
gardless of your final decision, we wish you to know that we enjoyed
this morning with you."
```

The man who gave that statement lowered his voice, made it a moving personal appeal at the end of a rigorous three-hour interview. His soft volume matched the intimacy of his thoughts.

You can also accent syllables, as well as important words you feel should orally stand out.

By controlled breathing. Unless you breathe deeply, from the diaphram, your shallow breaths will not generate a strong volume. Your lungs must be filled with air to produce a pressure level high enough to propel the air force-fully past your vocal folds. Incidentally, slow deep breathing before beginning to speak also relaxes you, decreasing some stage fright symptoms.

Certainly you must adapt your volume level to the size of the audience and room. Speaking to 50 people in a room without an amplification aid would surely demand more volume than when you speak to 5 people.

5. Pronunciation. We decry persons who mispronounce our name. In fact, we all subconsciously register a reaction when any word is mispro-nounced—by our concept of how it should be pronounced. We may be wrong, the speaker right.

Within your organization you will also learn jargon pronunciations. The danger lies in using these in-group pronunciations outside your group, with inevitable quizzical nonverbal reactions from your listeners. Several problems of pronunciation need to be mentioned:

Varied regional accents. In some words, for example, Southern pronun-ciation and accents differ from those in Chicago or Boston. For most words, however, there is a common standard throughout the states, as it must be for us to understand, quickly.

Added or omitted sounds. Speakers should, of course, be careful not to add such sounds as "uh," "hm," "y'know," "er," "OK" between words or sentences. Other bad habits of adding and omitting may also affect pronuncia-tion. For example, the preferred pronunciation is second in the following:

Adding		*Omitting*	
po-a-sture	posture	mangr	manager
pot-a-purri	potpourri	blong	belong
idear	idea	gonna	going to

Adding		*Omitting*	
athalete	athlete	watcha say	what did you say
arthuritis	arthritis	meetin	meeting

Misplaced accent. Here are examples of improper accents, followed by the preferred accents:

u ʹnited / unit ʹed   hor ʹizon / hori ʹzon
respite ʹ / res ʹpite   compar ʹable / com ʹparable

Suggestions for improving pronunciation are:
Listen to the educated and cultured people of your community. You can usually assume that their standard is correct and acceptable for their region of the country. A public speech by a respected businessperson is also a good guide.

Consult a recent dictionary. More options on pronunciation of words are included in recent editions. When in doubt get a consensus from your class members or your instructors.

IMPROVING YOUR LISTENING

"Nobody listens to me" is a common complaint. It is so common that businesses spend large sums of money teaching their employees how to listen. All of us spend much of our lives speaking, writing, *and* listening—the last far in excess of the other acts of communication. The subject is important.

Most of your listening, as a learner, is comprehensive listening; that is, you're seeking to understand (and, sometimes, to evaluate) information given you orally. You, and many others, also engage in enjoyable, relaxed listening, as at a movie or theatre, or to music or television.

So you're already engaged in the kind of listening you will do in business, namely, trying to absorb as much information as possible—through your ears. Thus, even now, it pays to improve your listening ability. It can be of crucial importance in business, whether you are an executive or a subordinate employee, as the following statement from a company's management brochure indicates:

Poor listening habits can keep an organization from functioning properly. Verbal information can be misunderstood. Those with public contact may misinterpret what a customer wants. A manager who doesn't listen efficiently cannot pass along instructions, and subordinates who don't listen well often have difficulty carrying out instructions.

The benefits of applied listening skills are impressive. Good listeners make a company a more effective organization. They have better rapport with others, they get more out of meetings and are more effective in conferences, and they are better at understanding the needs of others.[1]

Common Faults of Listening

Studies agree that our listening efficiency is no better than 25 to 30 percent. That means, foremost, that considerable information given us orally is lost. Why? Some reasons follow.

1. Prejudice against the Speaker. Perhaps you have heard this quotation: ''Who is saying it shouts so loudly that what is said is easily forgotten.'' We are distracted because who the speaker is conflicts with our attitudes. For example, can you maintain attention when the speaker's position, attitude, or belief is entirely contrary to your own?

2. External Distractions. The preceding fault was more of an internal distraction. Some nonverbal cues are strong external distractions. Does the speaker stammer? Wear loud clothing? Dress sloppily? Walk or gesture excessively? Reek of perfume or cologne? All of these and more cause persons to tune out on speakers.

Actually, the entire physical environment affects listening. Among the negative factors are: noisy fans, poor or glaring lights, distracting background music, overheated or cold or oddly shaped or gaudily decorated rooms, excessive draft from a window or register, and so on. Also, sitting near disturbing individuals in the audience might distract a listener's attention from the speaker's message.

3. Thinking Speed. An assertion sometimes heard is that most of us speak between 80 and 160 words per minute. But others allege people have the capacity to think at the phenomenal rate of up to 800 words per minute. That leaves time on the listener's hands (or his or her head). What do you do between the time you hear the words and your much faster thinking time? Do you go off on tangents, focus your attention elsewhere, begin to daydream, shift your attention? Soon you can be off, far away from the words of the speaker—missing some important points.

4. Premature Evaluation. How many times have you interrupted persons before they completed their thought? Finished their sentence? Stated *their* conclusions? Directly as a result of our rapid thinking speed, we race ahead to what we feel is the conclusion. We anticipate. We arrive at the concluding thought quickly—often different from what the speaker intended.

5. Semantic Stereotypes. As certain kinds of people bother us, so too do their words. An interesting class interchange occurs when discussing this

[1] Pacific Northwest Bell, *Management Report,* Issue No. 122, pp. 2–3.

question: What is your favorite word, and why? Opposite to that question is: What words bother you, and why?

Internal, reaction words vary from person to person, each list influenced by feelings, attitudes, prejudices, biases we carry inside ourselves. (See the communication model in Chapter 2.) Hence, some words cause negative reactions. We tune out the speaker because the word annoys us; it shouts so loudly in our brain that effective listening is impaired.

6. Delivery. A monotone can readily put listeners to sleep—or cause them to lose interest. Sadly, some teachers speak in monotones. So do significant people in government or business. How a speaker delivers his or her message does annoy some people—and they become bored, uninterested, and critical of the message. ''He's a bore'' is more a critique of delivery than an assessment of a speaker's mental abilities.

Good listening is hard work—and important. It is easier to listen to what we enjoy, and to those we enjoy—more quickly following arguments and ideas which link with our own way of thinking.

Effective Listening Habits

At this point you may feel that the burden for idea clarity rests primarily with the speaker: it is his or her responsibility to keep you interested and informed. Wrong. You, as a listener, can help ensure receiving the intended message by doing the following:

1. Be Prepared. For a class this means completing your reading and assignment responsibilities. For an outside speaker you can learn something about the speaker, the topic, the audience, the situation even before attending. In a sense you are preparing yourself to listen.

2. Accent the Positive. ''If you have to do it, do it with a positive attitude'' is a centerpiece of many modern self-help books—and a good model for life. In listening, too, we ought to leave our negative baggage at home, taking along only a constructive attitude. Find something interesting or useful in the message.

3. Listen to Understand, Not Refute. Respect the viewpoint of those you disagree with. Try to understand the points they emphasize and why they have such feelings (training, background, . . .). Don't allow your personal biases and attitudes regarding the speakers or their views to influence your listening to their message. To deny hearing a view with which you disagree is to possess a closed mind and ear.

4. Focus Your Attention. Tune out internal and external distractions by facing and maintaining contact with the speaker. If you experience some negative environment factors (mentioned on page 607), you can, sometimes, move to another location in the room. Blot out your meandering thoughts and focus on what is being said.

5. Concentrate on Content. Search out the main ideas. Construct a mental outline of where the speaker is going. Listen for transitions and the progression of ideas. Look for supports which develop the thesis.

6. Take Notes. If you focus on content, the physical act of writing main points reinforces the mental outline you are constructing. Jot down ideas. Even incomplete sentences or single words will later be a memory jogger of what was said. But avoid trying to record entire sentences verbatim, for while you are writing them you may miss the next significant points the speaker is presenting. Note the general principles and record the supporting facts for them whenever possible.

7. Curb the Impulse to Interrupt. This suggestion applies to interviews, conferences, job instructions, and meetings. Listen attentively until the speaker invites questions. Don't assume conclusions (perhaps wrongly) before the speaker has stated them.

8. Summarize and Evaluate. Restate—in your own words—just what you think was said. You should also question evidence used, and mentally test the validity of evidence in support of a proposition. Furthermore, during the speech, you can also note nonverbal cues (gestures, eye contact, tone) that help indicate whether the speaker appears to be sincere in his or her statements. At the conclusion of the talk, during a question period, it is your right to ask questions about material presented.

Results of Good Listening

Positive, purposive listening—to speakers in discussions, in interviews, in speeches or in one-on-one situations—pays valuable dividends:

1. Leads to helpful, positive attitudes—by understanding the hindrances which lie in the way of good listening.
2. Permits the speaker and listener(s) to improve communication because each side is more aware of and receptive to the other's viewpoint.
3. Indicates by feedback to the speaker that listeners are interested; in turn, the speaker tries harder to give his or her best presentation.
4. Helps listener(s) obtain useful information on which they can make accurate decisions.
5. Creates better understanding of others and thus helps listener(s) to work with others.
6. Assists the speaker (especially in an interview) to talk out a problem. A person needs to receive as well as give help.

SUMMARY

When you can communicate effectively orally, you have an important skill to help you advance in business and professions. For short talks you may be asked to present periodic brief progress reports, introduce various persons, present awards, and occasionally welcome visitors or meeting attenders. The longer speeches may be presentations of proposals or highlights of research reports or complex problems—to audiences within or outside your organization.

Careful planning is essential for successful speeches, short or long. Steps for preparing effectively require thoughtful consideration of purpose, audience and situation, ideas, research, organization, visual aids, and revisions. An important extra step is rehearsals—to build confidence and reduce or eliminate possible stage fright.

The general purposes of speeches businesspeople give are to inform, to persuade, or (less often) to entertain. The specific purpose of each speech is best stated in an infinitive phrase that ties in with your speech title and focuses on your precise goal to meet the audience and occasion. Organization and evidence are logical parts of good business speaking. To neglect either is to wander aimlessly and to employ unsupported generalizations.

The extemporaneous method of presentation is usually preferable to reading from the manuscript and memorization. The former allows more visual and nonverbal contact with an audience. Posture, movement, facial expressions, appearance, and gestures convey nonverbal cues that give vitality and sincere meaning to any presentation. Variety and enthusiasm are key words relating to voice usage in pitch, rate, and volume.

Good listening is demanding, requiring omission of personal biases as well as external distractions. With a positive attitude and active involvement through personal summaries and evaluation, you can have a fruitful listening experience.

EXERCISES

1. Assume the Business and Professional Club in your city has invited you and six other students to a dinner meeting. Each of you is to present an informative five- or six-minute talk on how the current curriculum in your chosen major field prepares students for successfully filling jobs in business or a profession. Choose at least three main topics for your talk, and back them up with specific facts. Adapt your carefully organized talk to your listeners' interests. Talk with sincerity and enthusiasm, mindful of your physical and vocal behavior.

2. For a four-minute talk, select any topic you are familiar with—a sport, favorite food, event, place, gadget. Introduce yourself to the class, tell

what your topic is, develop it in any instructive or entertaining way you wish, and summarize your talk. After you have finished, your class members will make constructive suggestions.

3. For this assignment each student will give a short (three- to five-minute) talk to introduce a member of the class as either a speaker or an award winner. First, choose a classmate (by any method your instructor suggests). Then exchange résumés with that person. Confer with each other to get acquainted. (Your classmate needs information to introduce you, too.)

   You may each assume that your classmate is a speaker about a certain topic at a meeting of a business, professional, campus, or other club of which you are both members. You have been chosen to introduce him or her. If you prefer, instead of introducing your classmate as a speaker, you may assume you were asked to present an award to that individual for special recognition.

   Whichever specific purpose you choose for your talk, select from your classmate's résumé at least four pertinent facts—with his or her approval. All statements in your talk should be true—except of course the assumption that this classmate is a speaker or award winner. To support either of these assumptions you may need to add a few "made-up" incidents. For instance, if you will present an award, be sure to mention clearly the (assumed) noteworthy achievement—on the job or in scholarship or in community activities, sports, music, or whatever. Organize your talk well and present it enthusiastically to your audience.

4. Prepare an informative presentation that makes an idea clear or explains a process. This speech should be about four to six minutes in length. Criteria are organizational clarity, a good delivery; and content that supports your ideas. Try also to use visual aids. You may choose from these topics or others:

   The steps involved in buying stock

   What is meant by the "invisible hand" in business

   Characteristics of rejection letters

   How a word processor works

   What is meant by first in/last out in the accounting field

5. Prepare a five-minute oral statement on a controversial topic that you wish to defend before the class. You will make but one main point. Clearly, you will have to present evidence so the group will accept your proposition. Your support (evidence) should come from reliable outside sources and individual investigation. Prepare an outline similar to the following:

Title of one-point proposition: _____

General purpose: To persuade

Specific purpose: _____

Specific one main point: _____

    1st support: _____

    2d support: _____

    3d support: _____

Some sample one-point assertions are these—and others:

- Age should be left off résumés.
- Writing is more effective than oral communication for communicating reprimands.
- Some good-paying jobs do not require a college education.
- English is the language of business throughout the world.
- Nonverbal communication is as effective as oral communication.

6. Rewrite into specific infinitive phrases the following general purposes for speeches to persuade:

Unions in the United States

Social Security reforms

Retirement at 62

Government bonds

Advertising in the Yellow Pages

Telegrams versus letters

Lawyers make significant contributions to business

Communicating effectively in business

Surveys gather information

Dress affects the listener

7. Assume you have been asked to present your long formal report orally at an informal conference attended by 10 managers in your company. (See Exercise 4, pages 586–588). Their work is closely concerned with the subject matter of your report. Prepare your report presentation thoughtfully. Usually a mere "summary" of the report is not the best method, because it may be too general to be meaningful to your listeners. In addition, if appropriate, select specific highlights about the problem and its solution. Choose the ideas that are most likely to be of interest and importance to your audience. For example, you might introduce to them

the three or four most important factors you considered in the report. Be well informed about the overall highlights of your report and be prepared to defend your findings in a question-and-answer session (by your class members) immediately after you have presented your report. (In your presentation, you will of course, *not* read many parts of the report to the audience.) Make your talk businesslike with the right tone; it may be 20 or more minutes in length.

8. Prepare a persuasive oral presentation for members of the class, who will assume the role of salespersons attending a sales meeting. They are present to gain helpful tips on how to be persuasive when giving sales presentations.

   As the basis for your persuasive talk, use a sales letter you prepared in Chapter 11. Or you may sell any product on which you can gather sufficient information—using popular ads; sales letters you or friends have received; facts about the product's content, price, advantages; and your own first-hand knowledge or use of that product. Remember to attract favorable audience attention, and create interest, then desire. Emphasize specific benefits the customer will receive. Use visual aids to stress the importance of creating a desire in the customer to do what it is you want done. The visual aids you could use might include one or more of the following: transparencies, flip charts, posters, chalkboard, projector, slides.

   The following is a sample persuasion problem for your talk:

   Make a presentation to a group of college students and extend to them an invitation to become a subscriber to a popular magazine. Place emphasis on items such as the savings of 50 percent off the regular newsstand rate; features in the magazine; how it will supplement their textbooks; and the ease in placing the order.

9. The corporate annual report is perhaps the best-known and most widely circulated business report. Virtually every public, college, and university library receives copies of annual reports from business and industrial firms. Some libraries catalog the printed reports and store them in filing cabinets; others store annual reports in some other form, such as microfiche or microfilm.

   Your assignment here is to make an oral report, using information collected from corporate annual reports. You will concentrate on a comparison of certain key financial ratios for the company or companies chosen. Information on computing ratios (such as the current ratio, the acid test ratio, the net profit to net sales ratio, and the inventory turnover ratio) can be found in most financial management textbooks or in *Key Business Ratios,* a booklet available free from Dun & Bradstreet, Inc.

   You have your choice of two options in making the comparisons. The first option is to choose *one* company and make a comparison of at least three ratios computed for each of two recent years. Of course, you will compute the ratios yourself. Obviously, your comparisons must be between ratios which compare the same things. For example, you could choose to compare the current ratio, the acid test ratio, and the inventory turnover ratio for Company X for the two most recent years.

The second option is to compare the ratios computed for *two* companies, using annual reports for the same fiscal year. For example, you could compare the current ratio, the acid test ratio, and the net profit to net sales ratio for Company A for the most recent year to the same ratios of Company B for the same year.

To make your presentation complete, explain how the ratios were computed and what the ratios mean. For this purpose, you should prepare a visual aid (such as a poster or a transparency for use with an overhead projector). A visual aid should also be used to enhance your comparison of the ratios computed.

The time limits for your report will be assigned by your instructor. In most instances, the report called for here will fall in the four- to six-minute range.

10. The purpose of this assignment is to make you more aware of cues which one receives nonverbally, without words, without oral communication. Each day for seven days keep a log, noting nonverbal cues you feel communicate something to you. Note any situations you wish, but you should have at least three examples per day for seven days. In addition to the discussion on nonverbal cues in this chapter, you may also find useful suggestions in Chapter 2, Nonverbal Communications.

   a. Keep a Nonverbal Communication Log, which you will hand in to your instructor on a prearranged date.

   Divide your paper into two columns: on the left put the heading *Situation,* and on the right *Conclusions*. Under Situation describe the incident observed and under Conclusions draw some inferences as to what you felt was communicated.

   b. Be prepared to discuss the assignment orally in class.

11. Attend a speech on campus or in your local community. This speech may be either to inform or persuade. Complete the following analysis form for that presentation:

   Title of speech: _____

   General purpose: _____Speaker: _____

   First major point: _____

   Kinds of supports (evidence) used to back up first major point:

   a. _____

   b. _____

   c. _____

Second major point: _____
Kinds of supports used to back up second major point:

    a. _____

    b. _____

    c. _____

What statements, if any, were merely the speaker's opinions, not true and verifiable facts? _____
_____

What were the speaker's conclusions? _____
_____

Your evaluation of speech: _____
_____

Successful Business Meetings

Every week across the United States thousands of meetings are held—in educational, business, industrial, professional, government, athletic, religious, and other organizations. Well-planned, productive group communications are essential for conducting modern business. But too often we hear the remark ''That meeting was a boring waste of time.'' Because time is valuable, meetings should be held only when absolutely necessary—to achieve objectives and results that cannot be accomplished effectively in any other way.

The cost of business meetings is, of course, influenced by many factors. If ten supervisors meet two hours every week on company time and their salaries average $25 an hour, each meeting represents at least $500 weekly salary cost; $26,000 for 52 meetings a year. To this should be added the time devoted for planning and presentations; secretarial time for typing agendas, handouts, minutes; overhead expenses for meeting room facilities; and travel expenses if some representatives come from distant branches. When you add these meeting costs to those of the numerous other time-consuming meetings business executives and employees attend, the figures are surprisingly high. Do the results justify the investment?

The purpose of this chapter is to suggest how your meetings can be more successful when leadership and participant skills are of high quality. Four topics are discussed:

- Meetings in business
- Methods of solving problems
- Leadership responsibilities
- Participant responsibilities

MEETINGS IN BUSINESS

This section considers briefly the definition and purposes of meetings and the importance of oral communication in them.

Definition

Numerous writers have wrestled with their definition of a meeting. Perhaps you have heard this negative comment from some attendants: ''A meeting is an event at which minutes are kept and hours are lost.'' In contrast, let us use this positive definition:

> A business meeting is a gathering where purposive discourse occurs among three or more people who exchange information on a common topic or problem, for better understanding or for solving the problem.

The key words are *purposive, understanding,* and *solving.*

Meetings are useful when the group leader and participants know the reason—"specific purpose"—for a meeting. What is your evaluation of the following memorandum announcing a meeting?

```
To:      Members of personnel staff
From:    J. Rankin
Subject: Meeting on the 5th

   You're asked to join the heads of our three personnel departments
for a discussion on compensation. Hope to see you August 5th, at
11:00.
```

You may say—rightly—"I don't have the foggiest idea what that meeting will be about." The memo has no precise, clear statement of purpose.

The word "understanding" in our definition suggests learning from the information presented at a meeting. You will gain something if there is an effort to understand, through asking questions or listening.

"Solving" a problem is the most common reason for a business meeting. The action steps leading to this goal are discussed later.

Purposes and Kinds

As implied in the above definition, meetings are held for two basic purposes: to present information and to solve problems. Usually three types of meetings help achieve these objectives.

Informational Meetings

In the environment of an informal group setting, informative meetings are held to disseminate information and check on the understanding of those who attend. For example, the following notice appeared in an employee bulletin:

All department purchasing clerks should attend a meeting on Thursday, December 4, at 3 p.m. in the Personnel Conference Room. The topic will be the new staff categories approved by the Personnel Office.

At that meeting the clerks learned, asked questions, understood the new categories. No problems were solved, no recommendations for change in policy occurred; rather, each person gained an improved understanding of the issue.

Other informational meetings may be held to brief employees on certain revised procedures; to provide or clarify essential information for relief of tension; to inform on use of new equipment—to assure understanding by all present. Only when a check on understanding is necessary should an informational meeting be called. Otherwise, a written memo suffices.

Suggested Solution Meetings

The simpler of two kinds of problem-solving meetings is used when the executive has a solution to suggest. Usually a preliminary analysis may have shown it has outstanding merit. The leader presents the suggested solution at the beginning of the meeting. Thus discussion revolves about the suggestion, with the participants contributing their ideas.

Problem-Solving Meetings

Meetings which result in decisions for action predominate in the business world. When the executive has no adequate solution for a problem, he or she seeks suggested solutions in a problem-solving meeting. The problem is presented at the beginning by either the executive or someone previously appointed to prepare a written report on it. The meeting participants suggest solutions, discuss and evaluate them, and arrive at a decision on which action is to be taken.

Because the problem-solving meeting requires the most careful planning and presiding by the leader, as well as challenging participation by those attending, the remainder of this chapter focuses on this type of meeting. You can use most of the suggestions, of course, for all types of meetings.

Importance of the Oral Communication

Whether one is the meeting leader or a participant, the movement of ideas in a meeting is oral. The suggestions for successful speaking and listening discussed in Chapter 19 are equally important for participating in a group, particularly when you wish to persuade others.

In a meeting, problem-solving discussion leads to a decision. Then that decision is defended and supported orally against opposition by others. Persuasion and debate occur; you defend your position; listen to others' views; and argue logically for the group-supported decision.

METHODS OF SOLVING PROBLEMS IN MEETINGS

How do you think through a problem? Some of you may use intuition (rapid insight into a problem); rationalization (justification based on feelings); trial and error (numerous attempts over time); or scientific, reflective thinking (logical progression) to come to an answer. The latter is the method discussed in this section.

To aid you as a meeting chairperson or participant, moving from a felt awareness of a problem to its eventual solution, some of John Dewey's ideas on problem solving (in his book *How We Think,* D. C. Heath, Boston, 1909) are adapted here. Four stages are involved in problem-solving meetings: background analysis, solution discovery, solution evaluation, and choice of action.

Background Analysis

You feel a problem exists; you are confused, frustrated that something is not going well in your organization. This stage has three steps, similar to the planning steps discussed in Chapters 5 and 19 for written and oral communication.

1. State the Problem in the Form of a Question

When answered, this question should help solve the problem. Stating the question must meet the rules of language discussed earlier in this text—particularly conciseness, concreteness, and clarity:

```
What should be the policy of our company regarding alternate sources
of energy?

Which data processing system should we use in our product parts
warehouse?
```

2. Define and Limit the Problem

The preceding questions are concise, but they demand some clarification. For example:

```
By alternate sources we mean coal, atomic energy, water, solar, oil,
gas. . . .

By system we suggest at least three alternatives before making a de-
cision.
```

3. Collect Facts on the History of the Problem

What you consider in this step can be suggested by possible questions:

```
• What is the history of the problem?
• What are some symptoms of the problem?
• What is the extent and seriousness of the problem?
• What is the size of the problem?
• What are some possible causes and effects of the problem? (For ex-
  ample, management, labor unions, government.)
• How do other companies handle the problem?
```

Your thoughtful examination of background material will have helped to prepare you for the role of either leader or discussant. And, if you have prepared written material that is read by others, it will serve as background material to prepare for the next stage—Solution Discovery.

Solution Discovery

Two steps occur in identifying solutions to a problem.

1. Establish Criteria

Basically this means setting up criteria by which to judge solutions, weeding out alternatives which do not fit the criteria or goals set. Frequent criteria for assessing solutions include workability, feasibility, acceptability, positive/negative consequences.

In response to the question "What should be the policy of our company regarding alternate sources of energy?" a discussion group might set up the following criteria for judging alternatives:

```
Is the solution equitable--from the environmental perspective and
from the company's position?

Can the solution be easily implemented? Societal and structural mod-
ifications should be minimal; legislation required, if any, must
receive majority support.

Is the supply of the source consistently adequate for our company's
production program in three plants?

Does the solution provide economic advantages? Manufacturers' incen-
tives to comply with the proposed solution, industrial incentives to
innovate and improve efficiency must not be inhibited.
```

Thus alternative solutions are measured against criteria, the process moving logically toward a decision. Interestingly, some criteria may change during a meeting, or different weights may be attached. You, as chairperson, must adapt to those group proposed changes.

2. List Possible Solutions

Most of us are eager to get to this step in solving a problem. The nonthinking person will offer only one solution, blind to other possibilities, insisting (wrongly) that the problem can be solved only one way. The careful chairperson and participant considers several solutions that may vary from the practical to the daring to the innovative. Important in this step is advice not to judge; simply list—perhaps on a blackboard—alternatives on how a problem might be solved.

Solution Evaluation

The preceding step was simply formulating a list of *tentative* suggestions on solving a problem. Now you must evaluate those suggestions in light of your stated criteria. In other words, you begin testing, locating pro and con reasons about a solution, answering whether a preferred solution truly will solve a problem, or create new ones. As you work through the process in a discussion you may end with selecting one of your tentative proposals, create an entirely new solution, or combine parts of several solutions. Your responsibility is this: you should arrive at a solution during this evaluation phase.

A series of questions can serve as hints to what you could be asking, for example, on this problem: "What health programs will best meet the needs of the American worker?"

- What will be the consequences of adopting one of the tentative so-lutions?
- Will any of the solutions introduce new dangers, new problems?
- Will all the causes of the problem be removed?
- How do each of the solutions meet the criteria established for judgment of the solutions?
- What are the advantages and disadvantages of each solution?
- What effect will the solution have upon the future?

In each of us are hidden, secret reasons why we support or do not support a given solution. Often these are based on personal attitudes, opinions, bias, or prejudice, as discussed in Chapter 2. But the rational person will try to apply a reasoned approach to problem-solving meetings. Consensus, or formal vote, then determines the solution to be accepted. You have one more thing to decide.

Choice of Action

This step answers the question "How will the solution be carried out?" In business meetings a specific office or person should be empowered to implement the decision; funds are allocated, time schedules are set. Frequently a board of directors makes the policy decision, with implementing details to be carried out by administrative units.

Example of Complete Outline Using Scientific, Reflective Process

Assume for this example that you are an employee of an automotive organization and that your superior asked you to do two things: (1) prepare a written report and (2) lead a discussion on the general topic of productivity improvement in the auto industry. Your complete outline—a mix of the written and oral—could progress in this manner.

    I. Background Analysis
       A. Problem in form of question
          "What can be done to increase productivity in the American
          automotive industry?"
       B. Defining, limiting problem
          1. Productivity may be defined as "the percentage change in
             output divided by a percentage change in input."
          2. A limiting factor is that productivity is rarely constant

in the automotive industry because of variances in models, schedules, or the like.

    3. Input we define as labor, invested capital, materials, or the effort or ingenuity of management.

C. Background, history of problem

    1. Importance of the problem is seen in the declining productivity effects on the American household.

    2. Automotive production history

        a. 1955–1958   c. 1965–1970

        b. 1958–1965   d. 1970's–

    3. Possible causes of productivity decline

        a. Management is confronted with unpredictable long–run costs; financial markets; foreign competition; stockholders.

        b. Workforce problems include boredom and frustration; job movement; absenteeism; high turnover rate.

        c. Labor unions: rates higher than in Japanese auto plants; restriction on output; cost of living allowances.

        d. Government: excessive regulation in the seventies; tax structure for business; devalued asset allowance.

    4. The Japanese approach to productivity

        a. Culture and philosophy of Japanese people

        b. Workforce of Japan's auto companies

        c. Organizational structure of Japanese auto industry

        d. Use of automation in Japanese auto industry

    5. Effects of productivity decline

        a. Poor quality of product

        b. GNP affected; one–fifth of GNP auto–related

        c. Competitive edge lost

        d. American dollar decreased in value

II. Solution Discovery

A. Establishing criteria

    1. Low cost: costs may be dollar costs or social costs

    2. Time: time before solution implementation and time before measurable results obtainable

    3. Effectiveness: must produce measurable, positive results for consumer, worker, manager

    4. Feasibility: affordability and practicality of solution

B. Possible solution

    1. Motivation of the worker

    2. Use of improved technology

    3. Management changes

    4. Labor and their unions

    5. Government: law and regulations

III. Solution Evaluation

A. Advantages of solutions 1, 2, 3, 4, 5

B. Disadvantages of solutions 1, 2, 3, 4, 5

C. Acceptance of solution: combination of all five solutions

IV. Choice of action

A. A committee of five persons, selected by the chairperson, will contact (1) legislators, (2) American Association of Manufacturers, (3) labor leaders.

B. Committee will submit cover letter and full report, with final recommendation, to groups named above.

LEADERSHIP RESPONSIBILITIES

So far, the focus has been on the procedure for solving a group problem. From here on the emphasis will be on you as either leader or participant in the oral world of a business meeting. Knowing the different kinds of meeting leadership and its functions—before, during, and after the meeting—can help you be a more effective leader.

Kinds of Leadership

Keep in mind that leadership functions may move from the appointed leader to group members, each contributing ideas that influence the meeting. The following analysis focuses only on the person appointed as leader. Leadership kinds range from authoritarian to democratic to leaderless.

Authoritarian

The behavior of the autocratic leader could range from leader suggestions which must be accepted to commands which must be carried out. A leader in this position has quiet contempt for participants; dominates the thinking of a group; manipulates others to his or her advantage; praises those who agree with his or her position; resents questions; issues orders and commands; puts self above all.

Other characteristics may be added. This type of leadership is obviously contrary to our democratic way of thinking and should be avoided.

Just a step above the autocratic leader is the strong supervisory leader who keeps the *group* under tight procedural control, while the autocratic leader is more interested in *self*. Paternalistic describes strong supervisory behavior.

Leaderless

On the other end of the continuum is the person who gives up all leadership functions to the group, even in a formal meeting. This person believes that shared leadership is appropriate to problem solving, and thus the formal meeting has no leader. Certainly you have chance meetings where quick discussions occur without a leader. Sometimes such leaderless groups are successful with high-ability people who need little direction and control. Yet even they do depend on someone finally offering guidance and a summary of what they achieved.

Democratic

The ideal leadership role for your business meeting is the democratic. The role lies between the two extremes noted previously and seeks to win cooperation of the group as it moves toward a solution. The democratic leader realizes that the group has final authority; knows that groups vary in their ability to make decisions; helps the group make the decision rather than forcing decisions upon it; facilitates productive group discussion; promotes minority opinions; evaluates unsupported generalizations; clarifies vague statements.

Democratic leadership takes time; that is, democratic discussion is slow. It takes patience to listen to the opinions and views of others. Autocratic leadership is faster, the leader making many decisions with or without approval of the group. In the end, however, it is you as a democratic leader who best guides the group, through the following functions.

Planning Steps before the Meeting

The leader's responsibilities before the meeting pertain to planning for the purpose; audience; meeting date, time, place; announcements and agenda; physical arrangements.

1. Consider the Problem and Determine Purpose

First, the leader must decide whether the meeting should be called at all. In one sentence he or she should write the problem and specific purpose. If the purpose can be better attained by telephone, memos, letters, or video teleconferencing (when available), the participants should not be called together for a meeting, especially if long trips by some would be required.

A good meeting topic must be timely, genuine, really important, and meaningful for the conferees. It must present a difficulty or controversial question that is within the experience of the meeting attendants. Also, it should be limited adequately so that conferees are able to solve it—at least partially— within the conference time. It should be about a matter that can be acted upon after the group has arrived at a solution or conclusion.

2. Decide Who Should Participate

Secondly, unless this is to be a regularly scheduled department or board meeting, the leader should consider whom to invite. If the meeting is to solve a difficult, top-level problem, the invitees should be those who can make special contributions; who have positive attitudes, preferably some experience related to the problem, and good judgment for solution evaluation; and who are dependable in carrying out responsibility.

Usually, the deeper the problem, the smaller will be the group—sometimes five or fewer. But if an executive needs mainly a list of possible solutions from a "solution discovery" meeting, perhaps 10 to 20 participants would be desirable for a brainstorming session. To review and discuss regular department activities, 30 might be invited. And for some informational meetings hundreds may be interested and gain useful explanations.

3. Arrange for Meeting Date, Time, Place

Date and Time. Generally, the better days for meetings are Tuesdays through Thursdays. Considered poor times are Monday mornings, Friday afternoons, and immediately after lunch. Good times are 9 to 11 a.m. and 2 to 4 p.m., but some leaders have found that to keep a one-hour meeting "on the beam," 11 a.m. is psychologically a desirable starting time. Participants then work more alertly to help accomplish the goals of the meeting so that it will end on time for their lunches.[1]

Place. Depending upon audience size and makeup (and purpose of the meeting), the chosen place may be in the executive suite, a company conference room, an auditorium, a hotel, or convention center.

4. Notify Participants

Most often it is the meeting leader who words the question, with precision, and prepares the agenda so the participants know in advance the direction of the meeting. The announcement should be sent early enough to give them adequate time to prepare their understanding and thoughts on the matter.

Wording the Question Properly. Three types of problems underlie discussion: fact, value, and policy or procedure.

"Fact" questions are concerned with what is true and what are the facts, as in these examples:

```
What are the procedures for selling products overseas?

What are our competitors' plans regarding rebates?

What were the labor, management, and insurance costs of our last
contract?
```

"Value" questions depend on words implying appraisal and judgment of the goodness-badness, rightness-wrongness, saint-sinner, merits-demerits of a person, place, or thing. Value words as "fair," "justify," "worth," and "values" in the following questions steer discussants to a judgment based on a mixture of factual content and feelings about an issue:

---

[1] Virginia Johnson, market development supervisor, Visual Products Division/3M, speaker on "More Effective Meetings" at the International Convention of the American Business Communication Association, New Orleans, Oct. 22, 1982.

Is the current system of bonuses fair for salespersons whose gross sales are in excess of $50,000 a month?"

Can we justify our current mileage allowance in contrast to other firms of a similar size?

What is the worth of continuing our in-house programs on team building?

What are the merits of sending a common rejection letter to all interviewed students who don't fit into our plans?

"Policy" or "procedure" questions are the main concern in most business meetings. What should be done? What action should we take? Who should carry out the actions? Implicit in these questions is the idea of options—with reference during the discussion to factual and evaluative observations.

What should be our policy on building our own motors for our heart-lung machines?

Which office should handle training of personnel assigned overseas?

What are our options regarding procedure for distributing our Christmas profit-sharing checks?

You as a leader, manager, caller of the meeting will get off on the right foot when your worded questions are short, clear, unbiased. Poor questions like the following should never be used:

What's the problem in personnel?—*Unclear referent*

Why are our salespeople so poor in comparison with others in the firm?—*Prejudgment*

Our company letters stink; what can we do about it?—*Prejudgment, bias*

How do we get out of the problem of inflation?—*Broad, vague topic*

Preparing the Agenda Announcement. Five ingredients make up a good agenda announcement: topic, date, time, place, responsibilities of participants. For some meetings it is also desirable to stimulate participants' interest in the problem by stating its importance before they come to the meeting. The following memo begins with mention of a related news item.

	To: Warehouse salespeople	October 7, 19___
	From: Chris	
(Title of topic)	Subject: Computer market for homes	
(Importance)	Electronic Topics suggests in the October issue that a potential market exists for increased sales of computers in the home.	
(Topic question)	Will each of you please give thought to the question of how to increase sales of our personal computer	

(Responsibilities)   hardware and software in our area? This will be the
first meeting on the issue; we'll assign more responsibilities at the meeting.

(Date, time, place)   We'll meet two weeks from now, Tuesday, October 21,
19___, in my office, at 9:00 a.m.

In addition to the five ingredients listed above and "importance" of the topic, you may also—when desirable—include suggested reference materials, as sent with this announcement:

To: Product Planning Committee   May 22, 19___
From: RNS, President

(Date, time, place)   Subject: Monthly meeting Wednesday,
June 6, 10:00 a.m., Rm. 816

(Responsibility)   Two questions are to be discussed in our monthly
meeting:

(Specific topic questions)
1. What other uses can you suggest for our disposable tubing?
2. What policy should we follow about producing intra-venous suckers which use internal wiring for support?

(Responsibility)   Beyond these two questions we will have a review of
progress on our redesigned modules—by Mike S. and

(Responsibilities of group)   Tom G.—and the usual monthly review of our ongoing
new product items, by all of you.

(Responsibilities of group)   My staff has prepared the background and history of
the two questions above. I ask you to come prepared
to recommend options. Suggested reference material is
enclosed with this announcement for the meeting.

If the agenda is not announced in the call to the meeting, a good chairperson comes prepared with a handout to be distributed—as a first item of business. In essence the agenda is a simple listing of topics to be covered. One such sample is illustrated below:

Agenda for Meeting
of Executive Committee

10 a.m., September 4, Conference Room

1. Welcoming remarks   Morgan B.
2. Relevant background information to topic: What
   should be our policy on building our own motors   Morgan B.
   for our heart-lung machines?
   a. Definition of the problem   Janice T.
   b. Causes of the problem   David J.
   c. Importance of problem to firm   Paul H.
   d. Tentative proposals by Engineering   Frank R.
   e. Tentative proposals by Manufacturing   Bryson M.
   f. Alternative solutions   Harry S.

```
3. Question and answer period
4. Discussion—by all members
5. Summary                                           Morgan B.
6. Date of next meeting
```

5. Take Care of Physical Arrangements

As the last step before any specially scheduled meeting, the leader should consider such physical arrangements as seating, materials, equipment, atmosphere.

Seating. Someone should be appointed to arrange chairs—perhaps in a circle, or around a conference table, or in a diamond or "U" shape, so all conferees can easily see one another . . . and the chairperson. (For large general, informational meetings of 30 to 100 or more persons, seating may, of course, be on parallel rows of chairs or on one side of tables placed horizontally.)

Materials, Equipment, Atmosphere. Items to consider are: chalkboard(s), chalk, eraser, pencils, paper, charts, microphone, lectern, projectors, visual aids (charts, tables, graphs). Drinking water, glasses, and ash trays (if smoking is allowed) should be handy. Name cards may be desirable if participants come from different firms or widely separated departments and are not personally acquainted. The room itself should, of course, be adequately lighted, heated, ventilated, and quiet so it is conducive to free discussion. A secretary—or someone else—should be asked in advance to take minutes at the meeting.

Procedures during the Meeting

For success of the problem-solving meeting the leader's attitude and efficiency—from the beginning statement through the entire discussion—is critically important. The leader should be well prepared, able to think and act quickly, get along with others, respect their opinions, know objectives of discussion and the reasoning process, be patient, and have a sincere interest in the values of cooperative group action.

1. Begin with Appropriate Opening Statement

Obviously, you should prepare your introductory statement before the meeting, but neither memorize nor read it. Present it informally and naturally—in one or more of these suggested ways:

Stating the problem

```
We're here today for an analysis of this question: "Which divisions
are not meeting the strategic goals set last January?"
```

Indicating importance of problem

```
At no time in the history of this company have we faced more serious
problems. Without exaggeration, I suggest that we must come up with
a firm answer to the question I put on the agenda: What should be
our position on expanding our overseas data processing operations?
```

Suggesting issues

```
It appears three issues relate to our question of overseas expan-
sion: (1) what is the political base of those countries in which we
wish to expand; (2) what is the economic base; and (3) under what
conditions should we consider moving more production to foreign
countries.
```

Using a quotation

```
Jobber News' editorial has this comment: "Reversing a ruling last
year by an administrative judge, the Federal Trade Commission has
ordered Tenleso, Inc., to sell off its Martoe Equipment Co. unit."
That opening comment is a good springboard to our meeting today:
Which units in our organization are possible targets for court ac-
tion?
```

Stating cause for discussion

```
The Citizens' Lobby in the House is prepared to offer two bills on
the issue of regulating content and sale of dread disease insurance
policies. They were kind to send us copies of those two possible op-
tions, and wish our suggestions for change. To begin our discussion
I suggest we examine both versions, then move into our discussion.
```

Other possibilities are open to you as chairperson, but the above are some of the most common. Some chairpersons have also used visual aids, case analysis of a situation, or video-taped statements by superiors.

2. Stimulate Discussion for Solution Discovery

In general, try to encourage all conferees to participate, and do keep the discussion moving forward. Write the criteria on the chalkboard (or projector) to help spark discussion on each topic. List on another board the possible solutions of the problem as conferees suggest them. Ask questions and keep participants from wandering onto irrelevant paths or from chatting among themselves while someone else is expressing his or her views. Get conferees to analyze their own thinking as much as possible. Sometimes if the original contributor of an idea cannot add to it, another conferee may be able to carry it further. If a participant's statement is vague, rephrase it clearly before you write it on the board.

Maintain an atmosphere of goodwill and cooperation throughout the conference. If a situation becomes tense or some members are reluctant to speak or are annoying or antagonistic, apply the techniques you have learned for handling bad-news situations. Try to be tactful, considerate, understanding; and show a sense of humor. Sometimes an appropriate interesting or humorous short story can quickly revive flagging interest. Here are other tips for handling difficult conferees:

The Reticent, Nonparticipating Member. First ask this person a question he or she can answer by a simple "yes" or "no." Then whenever possible, ask this member to give the conferees some information which he or she is sure to know because of job, training, or experience. Thank and praise the person as much as you can; he or she may then be more likely to enter the discussion confidently.

The "Know-It-All." This individual may be asked to justify every statement he or she makes. Whenever possible, ask other conferees for their opinions of these statements. Sometimes, if necessary and you feel the majority are annoyed by this person's arrogance, you may tactfully quiet the person by asking for a show of hands from the group, which strongly outvotes these suggestions.

The Long-Winded Conferee. You may thank this talker when he or she is at the end of a sentence, and then recognize someone else. Or you might move the discussion to another highly important point, perhaps with a statement like, "Well, we have two more points to consider before we wind up this meeting, so let's move along to the next topic now."

The Erroneous Member. If the other members—out of respect—are reluctant to correct this person, an especially tactful comment by you, the leader, may be required. As with any bad-news message, avoid direct criticism, sarcasm, or ridicule. Shield the person's pride. "When praising people, single them out; when criticizing them, put them in a group." Perhaps analyze a similar case, without referring to the speaker personally.

The Conferee Who Shows Personal Animosity. Though rare, sometimes an angry member shouts hateful, tactless comments toward another member or members. You can show an attitude of calm understanding and turn him or her off by directing a question to another conferee.

3. Sort, Select, Interpret Data for Solution Evaluation

After you have listed conferees' suggestions on the board, encourage participants to consider advantages and disadvantages of each suggested course of action. List them separately on the board. As leader, be careful not to impose your own opinions on the group. Encourage each group member to feel a sense of responsibility for the success of the analysis. Good listening by everyone to what others offer is extremely important.

Get members to feel they are working as a group toward the collective solution to the problem, rather than allowing each member to force his or her views upon the rest. Regroup suggestions, as desirable; get the group to select the important ones, to interpret them, to compare, and to evaluate—in line with the criteria. Invite the conferees to determine the order of importance of the facts. Some suggestions may belong together under a main heading; some may need to be eliminated entirely because of irrelevance or disadvantages. Depending upon the problem, conferees may have to consider various criteria—costs, safety, employee relations, union rules, and so forth before they make a decision.

4. State the Conclusion and Plan of Action

As with any written analytical report, the terminal section is of crucial importance. Before you dismiss the conference, review what the group has accomplished. Summarize what part(s) of the problem conference members have solved or partially solved. Mention only the highlights. Don't merely repeat the details of the discussion or those on the chalkboard. State the decision (conclusion) clearly and definitely. You might begin your statement of the conclusion by saying, "You have agreed . . ." or, "You have suggested . . ." rather than, "I think this is what should be done." If the group arrived at several conclusions, list them, preferably in order of importance.

Make some statement about how the solution the group decided on will be carried out. Appointments may be made then or announced later in a memo regarding the action.

Throughout the meeting as an effective leader you should also, of course, follow the suggestions and requirements for successful speaking and listening discussed in Chapter 19. Try to eliminate any distracting mannerisms, such as tossing chalk or twirling eyeglasses or chains, and undesirable postures like those shown in Figure 19-1. Always keep in mind your function as a conference leader—to encourage the group's thinking and assist them in clarifying and formulating their own thoughts rather than insisting that they conform to yours. Encourage teamwork by maintaining an atmosphere of goodwill and cooperation while the meeting is in session. Try to begin and end the meeting on time.

Follow-Up after the Meeting

Two functions after the meeting are distribution of the minutes and—most important—seeing that responsible committees, departments, or individuals are appointed to carry out the chosen action. In some situations the meeting leader may have to confer with other executives of higher authority before appointments are made regarding policy decisions.

Copies of the minutes your secretary or assistant prepared should be sent to the meeting participants soon after the meeting. They usually should include:

Name of the organization, department, or group

Date, time, place of the meeting

Names of members present and those who were excused

Names of any others present as invited visitors

Name of chairperson and (at the end) recording secretary

Brief summary of reports, if any, by those listed on the agenda

Highlights of solutions presented and decision(s) made

Time of adjournment

PARTICIPANT RESPONSIBILITIES

Implicit in the preceding section was the idea that some leadership functions may be assumed by participants. If it were not so, the leader could be accused of being autocratic. But more often you will be a discussant.

Preparation for Meetings

You will surely bring to the meeting some general knowledge and innate understanding. The more specific preparation, however, will occur in terms of a precise problem and the expressed purpose of the meeting.

As part of your preparation you will gather evidence, the raw material on which to base generalizations and logical comments. Examples, statistics, quotations, definitions, and analogies will make up much of your data, ready to be injected into the discussion.

You cannot be overprepared for a meeting. The phrase "I don't know" in response to your supervisor's question will communicate more than the fact that you are not prepared. That negative answer can be avoided if prior to a meeting you observe, interview experts on the issue, listen well, and spend time with written sources on the topic. In brief, some kind of research is needed for you to make a significant contribution.

Effective Participant Roles in Meetings

Having collected information beforehand, you can express your ideas objectively in meetings and listen open-mindedly to ideas others present. With a positive attitude you can have the following nine participant roles, suggested by

William M. Sattler and N. Edd Miller in a definitive text on discussion and meeting process.[2]

1. Organizer

Business meetings, with little difficulty, get away from their central topic. When you assume the role of organizer you make comments which steer the group back to main issues. You suggest procedure, note points that have been discussed, or summarize where the group has been. Procedural comments may be these:

```
"I'm sure we're interested in your personal reminiscences, but we
seem to be losing sight of our major purpose. I suggest we get back
to the main problem."
```

```
"Could I pause a moment and see if I know where we are. I understand
two issues face us: What will be the reaction of our stockholders
and what will be the response of the stock market?"
```

Such procedural suggestions—by you if the leader does not do so—are of inestimable value to keep a group on the right path.

2. Clarifier

In the role of clarifier you point out misunderstandings and clarify complex or foggy ideas. Your statements could be similar to these two examples:

```
"Well, it seems we've gotten lost in understanding the meaning of
the term 'strategic.' Some of you are speaking of it as those plans
under one year while others are out at least three years. I suggest
we first get at a common definition."
```

```
"Let me add one comment: some of you are talking about the foreign
rate of exchange on the German Mark two months ago while the rest of
you are speaking in terms of today when the rate is 15 cents higher
on each dollar. That 15 cents will make a lot of difference in our
overseas budget of eight million. Let's agree on a common time frame
so that we're all talking about the same thing."
```

3. Questioner

Often your question will ask for further information. You wish to fill in the knowledge gaps for yourself and for the group, some of whom also do not know but are too hesitant to ask.

[2] William M. Sattler and N. Edd Miller, *Discussion and Conference*, Prentice-Hall, Englewood Cliffs, N.J., 1966, pp. 338-340.

One danger in asking questions is that they may be too broad. The result is answers that come back with such diversity that time is wasted before zeroing in occurs. Knowing the difference between the vital and the inconsequential will help you to be a productive participant.

4. Factual Contributor

A thorough preparation permits you to make substantive contributions. A caution is not to monopolize or suggest in an overbearing manner that you have *the* information. The tone of your oral statement will say as much as the content. A few desirable comments follow.

```
"Your point is interesting. I wonder if I may add some data from a
study appearing in the December issue of the Journal of Business
Communication."
```

```
"Concerning the length of memorandums, Mr. Paul Blank, President and
Chief Executive of (name) Chemical Company, made this statement:
'Memorandums crossing my desk should be limited to one page.' My in-
ference is that here is a busy man who demands brevity in written
communication."
```

```
"I like what you say, but my information based on Forbes gives these
data. . . ."
```

5. Energizer

Sometimes you can keep the discussion moving, stimulating the members to reach their goals when gloom or frustration has set in. You suggest there is light at the end of the tunnel when some feel the problem is incapable of being solved.

```
"We're almost there. If we give it another half hour I'm sure we can
arrive at a consensus on the issue."
```

```
"I suggest a brief recess, say ten minutes. Then let's come back and
show the exec committee we can come in with a proposal on time."
```

6. Idea Creator

When you play this role your comments may be offered in this manner:

```
"After listening to the discussion I feel we have at least four op-
tions. . . ."
```

```
"Before coming to the meeting I made several phone calls for others'
ideas; here are their comments on the issue before us. . . ."
```

> "My guess is we're working so hard on a single solution that we're
> blind to the possibility of combining all our options. . . ."

And so on. Creativity in problem solving means you are capable of thinking through hypotheses amidst a potpouri of seemingly disorganized data. But out of this disorganization you are able to synthesize, arriving at a solution you were deliberately seeking after, one you discovered accidentally, or one you were bright enough to see arising out of the discussion. With the ability to suggest creative responses you will be looked upon as an invaluable member of any group.

7. Critical Tester

One of the more significant roles in a meeting is that of critical tester—evaluating the strengths and weaknesses of contributions. You, and every member, may challenge data and opinions if you think any misleading or inaccuracy has occurred. For instance, a single example should not lead to a definitive conclusion. Here are some questions to keep in mind:

- Were a sufficient number of facts given on which to build a conclusion?
- Is the information consistent, or do some contradictions get in the way of accepting the information?
- Are the facts—and the language—clear?
- Are the sources of information and the statistics reliable?
- Is the information recent; can one see the source and verify the evidence given?
- Was the cause sufficiently powerful enough to produce the alleged effect?

You must challenge the unsupported assertion, the unclear referent. Not to do so is to omit a responsibility when reading a report or participating in a discussion.

8. Conciliator

Mutual interaction can turn into violent disagreements as pro and con opponents debate an issue. Deadlocks may result. Positions can become so polarized that losing face in addition to losing the argument is at stake. You as a conciliator seek to find a middle ground, seek to restructure positions that are acceptable to the opposing parties. Some examples are these:

> "Here's my suggestion: Instead of a four-year term of office the
> compromise might be a two-year term, with an evaluation for a longer
> term to occur at that time."

> "Let me suggest a way out of this impasse: We've heard arguments

```
from the two main groups. I suggest a drafting group, two from each
of the opposing groups and three from the rest of the body, to come
in with a merger of the positions. Let's look at that, then make a
final decision at our next meeting."
```

9. Helper of Others

A final suggestion is that you can help other participants as well as the leader. Sensitivity to others through tactfulness and cooperativeness characterizes this role. You do not seek to embarrass but rather to help those who feel inadequate or frustrated, giving them the feeling of being accepted and wanted. You might do that in several ways:

```
"We've heard from most of us around this table. I'm eager to hear
what Paul has to suggest on this topic." (invitation to participate)
```

```
"Mr. Chairman, you may have misunderstood. What I think Kathy was
saying was this. . . ." (clarification and further support for her idea)
```

```
"That's a superior suggestion, Donna. Let's take a couple of minutes
and see what others think." (praise of member)
```

You rarely will use all of the preceding nine roles in a single meeting, nor should you be expected to. But to be proficient in perhaps four of them would be making a significant participant contribution to a group meeting.

SUMMARY

1. Two basic purposes of business meetings are to present information and to solve problems. Many business meetings are based on written reports or statements submitted in advance. Such information includes material leading to the solving of a problem; then oral discussion takes over.
2. The rational, logical, reflective pattern of solving problems is most effective in business meetings. You begin with background material on a problem; arrive at a tentative list of solutions; evaluate those solutions; and decide ultimately on a plan of action.
3. In a meeting the democratic leader is most desired. The authoritarian leader is concerned with self and is dogmatic, while a leaderless group has little guidance and shares leadership functions.
4. Effective leadership requires careful planning before the meeting—to consider the problem and purpose; participants; meeting date, time, place; wording of the question for the meeting; preparation of agenda announcement; and physical arrangements within the meeting.
5. During the meeting the leader has responsibilities of beginning with an appropriate opening statement, stimulating discussion for solution discovery, evaluation, and choice of action. The chairperson also encourages

minority opinions, tests unsupported generalizations, clarifies vague statements, and maintains an atmosphere of goodwill and cooperation.

6. After the meeting, functions include distribution of the minutes and seeing that responsible appointments are made to carry out the necessary action.

7. Desirable responsibilities as a participant include thorough preparation for a meeting followed by effective role participation in that meeting. The participant may be organizer, clarifier, questioner, factual contributor, energizer, idea creator, critical tester, conciliator, and helper of others. All these roles may be used in a meeting, or you may use all these roles successively or perhaps only four or five. Regardless, you will be making a positive contribution to the group.

EXERCISES

1. Supply definitions for the following terms which have a relationship to meetings and group discussion:

Conference	Colloquy
Symposium	Committee
Panel forum	Parliamentary procedure
Debate	

2. Attend a meeting on your campus or in your community; report back on the following questions:
   a. Was the purpose of the meeting clear?
   b. What were some actions by the chairperson:

   - How was the meeting begun?
   - Was the chairperson democratic, or were other roles exhibited?
   - What was done to move the group along toward a decision?
   - How was the decision regarding a problem announced?

   c. What roles were played by participants?

   - Were negative characteristics exhibited by some members? If so, what were those characteristics?
   - What kinds of support did members bring to the discussion? How did they support their ideas?
   - Describe the most useful member in the group; what made that person effective?

3. The following questions have been posed by other students as they considered topics for a discussion. Their goal was to have a problem-solving discussion before the class. Evaluate these questions; which are satisfactory and which are not?

    a. New products for next year?

    b. What's the problem with our new administration/education building?

    c. Is our economy getting better or worse?

    d. What should be the policy of the government on allowing banks to sell securities?

    e. Oral communication in business—what makes it effective?

    f. What steps can business take to improve business relations with third world countries?

    g. The BBA students should go on in school and obtain their MBA degree.

    h. Which of the Big Eight accounting firms is the most respected in our state?

4. Wording the question for a meeting is important. Write at least three questions each on fact, value, and policy. Bring those to class; defend your questions as being of fact, value, and policy.

5. Attend a public meeting of a local school board, a city council, or a student organization. Use the following evaluation form for determining the number and kinds of contributions made by the participants. Bring that form to class for a report on the roles participants played in the meeting.

PARTICIPATION FORM

Discussion group: _____

Date: _____

Tally in the appropriate category the type of contribution made by each of the participants. (See discussion of participant roles in textbook.)

Type of contribution   *Participant*

	#1	#2	#3	#4	#5	#6	#7
Organizer							
Clarifier							
Questioner							
Factual contributor							
Energizer							
Idea creator							
Critical tester							

	#1	#2	#3	#4	#5	#6	#7
Conciliator							
Helper of others							

Which type of contribution was made most often? Why? _____

_____

_____

_____

6. The information below summarizes the basic requirements of this oral/written assignment involving extensive group work on employing the scientific-reflective method.

   a. Each member of the class will be assigned to a group.

   b. Each group will select its own chairperson; set its own meetings outside of class; meet the deadlines imposed; select its own problem for the assignment.

   c. Each group will present to the class and instructor the following information:

      (1) *On day prior to background-analysis presentation,* distribute to the class—or announce—topic to be discussed in the following class period.

      (2) *On day of informative, background-analysis statement* about the group problem

         (a) Distribute agenda for the meeting.

         (b) Chairperson introduces group members, sets out direction for the meeting.

         (c) Each member in group orally presents one part of the background, location, recognition, description of the problem chosen by the group.

            ● Definitions needed to understand discussion
            ● History of problem
            ● Effects of problem
            ● Causes of problem
            ● Importance of problem
            ● Evolution of problem (early period; late period)
            ● Comparison of problem

(d) Chairperson concludes presentation and allows questions and discussion with members of class.

(e) A secretary can take minutes on the presentations of group members.

(f) The meeting is adjourned.

(3) *On day of persuasive, solution presentations* about the group problem

(a) Minutes of preceding meeting may be presented to the class for approval.

(b) Chairperson of group summarizes preceding background presentation of group.

(c) Each member in group orally offers his or her own solution to the group problem.

- Criteria for evaluating alternatives to solving the problem
- Overview or range or listing of solutions available to solve the problem
- Solution A
- Solution B
- Solution C
- Solution A/B
- Solution C/D

(d) Chairperson concludes presentation by summarizing the alternative solutions presented and allows questions and discussion with group members.

(e) A secretary may record the presentations of the group members.

(f) The class/group may or may not decide on a single solution.

CHAPTER 21

Interpersonal and Other Nonwritten Communications

Within business, professional, and government organizations many activities are carried out orally on an individual, one-to-one basis. Your work will likely include interviewing, telephoning, and dictating. This chapter presents suggestions for handling these communications more effectively as you apply principles of good speaking, listening, and writing.

INTERVIEWING

Used in a wide variety of situations by many different types of business and professional people, the interview is an important method of carrying out necessary functions successfully. Though specific objectives vary widely, the steps in planning and conducting interviews have basic similarities. This section includes some highlights of various company interviews and then focuses especially on the interviewer's responsibilities for employment interviews.

Definition

The interview is a two-person conversation with a predetermined purpose: to accomplish a certain goal. The general purpose is to inform, to persuade, and/or to solve a problem. During an interview two people exchange information, attitudes, and feelings in a spirit of goodwill, and through discussion they may work toward solution of a problem if that is part of their objective.

Often, the two persons are within the same company. They may have the same status (both supervisors, both project coordinators) or different status (department head interviewing a subordinate).

In other interviews the persons may be representatives of different companies. A bank officer interviews a credit manager of a local firm that wants a loan. An account executive presents vital sales data to inform and persuade the purchasing director of another organization.

Still other frequent interviews are held by professional people or company representatives who interview individuals that need advice on personal problems. Examples are: attorney/client, doctor/patient, adjustment manager/ customer, IRS counselor/taxpayer, and so on.

Essentials for Successful Interviews

To be effective, interviews require preparation beforehand, efficient, thoughtful procedures during the discussion, and follow-up afterwards.

Preparation before the Interview

As emphasized often in this text regarding written and other oral presentations, careful preparation is essential. Whether you are interviewer (the one who conducts the interview) or interviewee, you should usually go through the following planning steps.

1. Know the specific purpose at the time the appointment is made.
2. Find out as much as will be useful about the person you will be interviewing—name, position, attitude, work, needs, biases, background.
3. Collect all facts and materials necessary for attaining the objective.
4. Plan questions you will ask, and consider answers you may give to questions the other person asks you.

The place chosen for the interview should be appropriately quiet, comfortable, and without distracting interruptions.

Procedures during the Interview

1. Begin with sincere, pleasant comments that establish harmony—goodwill; get "in step" with each other.
2. State the purpose of the interview.
3. Present facts and questions in language that follows the seven C principles. Be concise, complete, considerate, concrete, clear, courteous, correct. Allow time for the other person to speak before you proceed to the next point. This discussion is the main part of the interview—comparable to the body of a speech and text section of a report. However, an important added responsibility in the interview is the tactful interchange of ideas as the discussion progresses.
4. Listen attentively to each other's views, be receptive to suggested solutions, and be courteous also when you disagree.
5. Notice meaningful nonverbal cues that sometimes are different from the spoken words (a forced smile on the outside, crying or anger inside?).
6. Work to achieve agreement on action to be taken—what, when, why, where, by whom, and how.
7. Before closing, summarize the main points and make sure that both persons understand the conclusions.

Follow-Up after the Interview

The need for and extent of follow-up activities depend upon the specific purpose of the interview and the decisions reached in it. Whatever future actions are agreed upon, these should be carried out within the scheduled time. The interviewer (or a dependable assistant) should check upon them. Other interviews may be necessary and should be scheduled.

Kinds of Interviews

Obviously, among the thousands of business and professional interviews held daily there are many different kinds, for a variety of reasons. They can be grouped broadly according to their specific purposes. The discussion here focuses briefly on interviews you may have as a manager or employee within your company. As you read about them, consider how the essential steps discussed above regarding preparation and participation can be adapted to these interviews.

Employment Interview

If you are a recruiter or personnel director, you will interview applicants (interviewees) to evaluate their qualifications for a particular job in your organization. Details on procedures for this type of interview are presented later, in the next section.

Training and Instructional Interview

Every new employee needs information about the specific job duties and company policies. In addition to general group training sessions, one-to-one instructions and demonstrations may be given by a supervisor or by another employee holding a position similar to that of the new trainee.

Whenever you have the responsibility of training someone in the duties for a job, be sure you have a clear understanding of the job description. Preferably write it out clearly first and then present it orally step by step, according to the C principles. Demonstrate, whenever desirable, and help your listener to understand your instructions.

.Too often new employees are ''trained'' by an employee whose explanations were ''as clear as mud.'' He or she raced through incoherent, faulty, inadequate, confusing comments. And the trainee was reluctant to ask questions. To help the listener follow instructions, you should welcome questions by asking, ''Now, what questions do you have?'' Then answer them tactfully. Many needless, costly errors can be avoided by invited questions and helpful answers.

Counseling Interview

A supervisor, personnel officer, or professional counselor may be asked to interview an employee who has work-related questions or a personal problem (financial, health, family). In such cases the interviewer must listen, analyze carefully, praise when possible, suggest solutions, and tactfully work with the interviewee to evaluate the solutions for the benefit of the interviewee and the company.

Work Evaluation Interview

In many firms, managers or supervisors interview their subordinates periodically to review and evaluate their performance. Such purposeful interviews help to exchange useful information about quantity and quality of work, dependability, cooperation, and ability to work effectively with supervisor and fellow employees. They may encourage the employee to improve and set new goals for future advancement. Tact, good judgment, and accuracy are especially important. Usually a printed personnel appraisal form is filled out at the end of the interview and signed by both the supervisor and the employee.

Disciplining Interview

In contrast to the regular periodic evaluation interviews, a special consultation may be necessary for some employees if their behavior or actions deserve reprimanding. In such a bad-news situation, the interviewer usually needs to shield the employee's pride, retain goodwill, and stress the positive rather than the negative aspects. Instead of harping on what the employee *failed* to do and what he or she did *wrong*, the interviewer should, usually, first tactfully restate specific instructions that show how and why something *should* be done—the *right* way—for the benefit of employee, company, and customers. The interviewer must listen also for the interviewee's comments and reactions. Ultimately, if successful, the two try to reach an agreement for future behavior that will help avoid the problem in the future. (Of course, for a several-time "repeat offender" the interviewer will have to use a sterner method.)

Complaint Interview

Sometimes an employee wishes to express a complaint about an annoying situation within the firm. If so, the facts should be carefully thought out and presented to the supervisor (interviewer) without malice or anger against any person. The goal usually is to persuade that certain changes should be made. Even if the employee is mistaken, the interviewer after listening explains the situation and clarifies what can or cannot be done—and why. The result should be that the employee at least feels better about the matter because someone in authority has shown an interest in the request, has listened, and has relieved tension.

Job Termination (Exit) Interview

When employees terminate their employment—voluntarily leave the company—someone in the personnel department should conduct an objective exit interview with them. Their reasons or observations about some company procedures and policies (whether marketing, salaries, ethics, working hours, environment, production, or others) can be helpful for improving employee relations and decreasing turnover in the future. Some employees will be reticent to state their true feelings; some may be bitter. The interviewer's empathy, tact, and assurance of confidentiality often help gain their cooperation. Carefully worded open-end questions sometimes get specific, helpful suggested solutions from some interviewees.

Interviewer's Responsibilities in Employment Interviews

As promised earlier, this section presents detailed suggestions for the interviewer—recruiter—who interviews job applicants. The following topics are included: objectives, preparation before the interview, procedures during the interview, and evaluations afterward. In Chapter 13 you can reread suggestions for the interviewee—the job applicant. Appendix A mentions some legal aspects regarding interview questions.

Objectives of the Patterned Interview

Considered most effective in getting truthful responses from the job candidate, the patterned interview is used most often. The interviewer guides and controls the conversation but encourages the interviewee to speak freely and at length about relevant topics.

The interviewer's threefold objective for the patterned interview of a job applicant is to:

1. Help evaluate job qualifications that other sources cannot assess as well.
2. Give the applicant essential facts about the job and the company.
3. Create and promote goodwill toward the company.

Interviewer's Preparation before Employment Interview

If you are an interviewer of job applicants, you will need to prepare in the following ways before the interview:

1. Know your company's organizational structure; also know the requirements and work environment of the job about which you are interviewing applicants. Read each applicant's résumé before the interview.
2. Decide what information you need from each applicant. Usually the areas pertain to character, personality, work experience, training, interests, and activities.
3. Know the current regulations—national and those in your state—regarding fair employment practices.
4. Carefully plan the questions you will ask. Be sure they are within the laws concerning marital status, age, race, sex, religion, and other matters. (For a brief list of suggestions, see Appendix A.)
5. Also make your questions clear, free from personal bias, and essentially the same for all candidates you will interview for the same position. The last point is important to your making fair comparisons. For a list of 59 questions which may be asked during the interview, see pages 382–384.
6. Whenever possible, choose a quiet, distraction-free room for the interview. (If you are interviewing on a campus, you will of course adapt to whatever facilities are available.)

7. Arrange your schedule so that no one will have to wait long. A comfortable waiting room with chairs and business magazines is relaxing for the candidates you have planned to interview.

Warmup Period of the Interview

At the beginning of the interview you as interviewer should greet the applicant in a cordial way—with a handshake, warm smile, and a friendly tone of voice. To put the applicant at ease and to establish rapport it is usually desirable to chat—perhaps three to five minutes—about some current topic. It may be the weather, an event of the day, an item relating to the applicant's hobbies (athletics, music, sailing), or whatever is appropriate.

Main Content of the Interview

After the brief warmup, you make clear the purpose of the interview and the topics you plan to cover. You encourage the applicant to do most of the talking, but you control the interview and see that it does not wander aimlessly. You ask appropriate planned questions and use desirable methods throughout the interview.

Asking Appropriate Questions. You might begin by inquiring about the applicant's education, then move to the work history and off-the-job activities. Focus on relevant information that cannot be obtained as well from other sources.

Open-end questions are usually preferred because the applicant can give you more information—both verbal and nonverbal. Among useful open-end questions you might ask are those that begin with "what," "why," or "how," —like some of the suggested questions on pages 382–384.

> What courses did you like best? Least? Why?
>
> How do you feel about overtime work?
>
> Why are you leaving your present job? (*If the applicant mentions "problems with my supervisor" or other vague reasons, you may tactfully probe for clarification.*)

Open-end job-related questions similar to these can reveal important qualities of an applicant regarding personality and character—attitudes, trustworthiness, temperament, interests. You may need also to check drive and aspirations (willingness to work hard), social effectiveness and emotional balance (relations with others and self). If relevant to the job, some questions might relate to physical vigor and energy or willingness to travel or to make permanent moves.[1]

---

[1] Theodore Hariton, *Interview: The Executive's Guide to Selecting the Right Personnel,* Hastings House, New York, 1970, pp. 25–34.

Dead-end questions (also called "closed") usually ask for only "yes" or "no," or other one-word answers.

```
How many accounting courses did you have in college?  Which of
your college years was the most difficult?
```

They elicit quick responses that are easy to tabulate. But the information may be less helpful than that from open-end questions—unless you probe for an explanation or reasons for the answers.

A few cautions regarding wording of questions are noteworthy. To be fair, avoid questions that invite a given response or that show your own preferences. They may tempt a tense applicant to slant answers accordingly, especially if he or she is reluctant to admit having no knowledge of the matter at all.

```
Are you in favor of . . .?

What is your opinion of the unfair ruling our state legislature
recently made regarding . . .?
```

Questions should be neutral and not about provocative, controversial issues or personal matters that will embarrass the applicant and are irrelevant to the job.

Using Effective Methods. The following checklist is included here to help you review whether your procedures during the interview are desirable:

1. Try to make the applicant feel at ease and favorably impressed with you and your company.
2. Ask questions that are tactful, legal, unbiased, pertinent to the information you need, and mainly open-end—so the interviewee can give you more information, freely.
3. Listen to all verbal answers; when necessary prod for details: "What happened then?" or "Can you explain that in a little more detail?"
4. Notice also nonverbal cues and behavior that may tell much about personality and social skills. Among the nonverbal messages that can be as revealing as anything the applicant says in words are: blushing, stammering, casting eyes downward, shouting in angry tone of voice, gestures, hesitations, and general conduct.
5. Respect the applicant's feelings even though you might consider the person wrong; keep your opinion to yourself; avoid frowns and expressions of disapproval.
6. Let the interviewee do most of the talking; but tactfully control the direction of the interview.
7. Give the applicant opportunities to ask questions; answer them honestly and courteously.
8. Save most note taking until after the interview. (Sometimes you may jot

brief notes on important points, but avoid doing so when the applicant is under stress or giving unfavorable information.)

9. Be adequately aware if the applicant anticipates your preferences and responds according to them instead of stating his or her true feelings.
10. End the interview courteously, indicating what the applicant should do next or when a decision may be expected.

Avoiding Pitfalls. If you place the word "DON'T" in front of the "Effective Methods" suggested above, you will have a list of ten pitfalls to avoid. Then add to them the following biases, prejudices, and other weaknesses to be avoided:

- Don't form an overall opinion about the applicant based on a single aspect or a few surface clues.
- Don't judge the applicant's character, mental ability, or attitudes by handwriting, outward features, birthdate, handshake, number of letters in the name, lines on palm of the hand, or shape and bulges of the skull.
- Don't be discourteous, rude, critical, argumentative, or cold toward the applicant.
- Don't leave unexplored gaps or form conclusions before carefully probing for meaning and accuracy.

Evaluation after the Interview

Immediately after closing the interview, write notes on all important points. Using the information you have obtained from the candidate during the interview, you later must supplement it with vital facts from other sources and then form an overall opinion. In your evaluation of the interview, the following clues should prove useful to indicate the applicant's state of mind and general makeup:[2]

1. Behavioral and psychological symptoms

Positive	*Negative*
a. Early arrival	**a.** Late arrival
b. Alert, responsive attitude	**b.** Inattentive, dull attitude
c. Emphatic attitude	**c.** Condescending or withdrawn attitude
d. Relaxed manner	**d.** Tenseness, fidgetiness, body tremors
e. Smiles	**e.** Frowns
f. Clear voice	**f.** Choked voice, mumbling

---

[2] Hariton, *Interview: The Executive's Guide to Selecting the Right Personnel*, p. 58.

2. Verbal symptoms

a. Sticking to the main point	**a.** Changing the subject
b. Incisiveness	**b.** Overgeneralizing or too much detail
c. Relevant responses	**c.** Irrelevant responses
d. Well-organized presentation	**d.** Disorganized presentation
e. Appropriate use of humor	**e.** Uncalled-for levity
f. Spontaneous replies	**f.** Long pauses before replying
g. Speaking well of people	**g.** Criticism of others
h. Candor	**h.** Rationalization, evasiveness

After the interview you may prepare an "interview write-up," consisting of a one- or two-page report with a paragraph on whatever areas are pertinent to the interview. It may cover such items as education and training, work experience, current off-the-job life, personal characteristics, and overall summary. The beginning of the report shows interviewee's name, date, the topics considered, and name of interviewer. At the end (you might call it "conclusion") is a scale where the interviewer checks his or her overall rating of the applicant or others interviewed.

Choosing the right candidate for the job is a serious responsibility. If the person chosen has ability far above or below the job level, the result can be a disservice in three ways—to the applicant, who may not remain on the job long; to the company, which will need to search for and train another employee; and to the interviewer, who will lose respect because of an inadequate evaluation. On the contrary, if the chosen person matches the job level and requirements closely, the advantages can be far-reaching.

TELEPHONING

For business and professional use the telephone is a versatile, effective oral communication tool and one of the most important channels of communication. This section discusses its importance, the variety of equipment and uses, and suggestions for effective telephoning.

Importance of the Telephone

Often a telephone conversation can take the place of two written messages or a face-to-face interview between two persons. The importance of telephones is indicated partly by the number in use and their advantages.

Number of Telephones

In the United States an enormous telecommunications network links over 110 million telephones and handles more than 20 million long-distance messages daily.

Throughout the world the number of reported telephones connecting foreign sources with the United States surpassed the half-billion mark— 508,286,000—as of January 1981, according to an AT&T statistical compilation. During the decade ending in 1980, the number of reported telephones increased by an astonishing 237.6 million, or 87.8 percent, unadjusted. An informal survey of several sources suggests that unreported telephones could number as many as an additional 15.9 million.[3] Each year telephones are added for wider international communicating. Furthermore, a study by Thorngren showed that some European firms handle 60 to 80 percent of their total business by telephone.[4]

Advantages of Telephoning

Before we consider the telephone's advantages, let us remember that written communications and some face-to-face interviews are essential for countless business and professional communications. In some situations, even after a phone call or interview is successfully completed, a written memo or letter should be sent to confirm the decisions made. The following discussion of telephone advantages relates to the many other business matters that can be effectively handled, almost entirely, by the telephone—with substantial benefits in time, money, and goodwill.

Saving Time and Goodwill. If you have questions, for example, about a product, price, or delivery date, or a complaint about a billing error or other relatively easy-to-discuss matters, a telephone call may give you a response in a few minutes. The prompt, pleasant cooperation of the businessperson who helps you reinforces your confidence and goodwill feeling toward the company. Exchanging written messages on these matters might take several days, and traveling to a personal interview also takes much longer than a phone call.

Saving Money. According to the oft-repeated statement, "Time is money." The time that phone calls save to handle certain kinds of inquiries and business is valuable for both the callers and the respondents. Furthermore, the prompt phone replies can help other employees in the callers' organizations to act promptly on the information gained instead of having to wait several days for the needed answers. And their prompt actions may in turn help them to serve their customers more efficiently—with quick "turnaround" time on shipments and orders.

The actual cost of a phone call, of course, depends mainly upon whether it is local or long distance. Local business calls are usually made without extra charge on the monthly phone bill. But the set flat monthly service rates may, in

---

[3] *The World's Telephones,* Overseas Department, AT&T Long Lines, Morris Plains, N.J., July 1982, pp. 1 and 26.
[4] Bertil Thorngren, "Silent Actors: Communication Networks for Development," in Ithiel de Sola Pool (ed.), *The Social Impact of the Telephone,* MIT Press, 1977, p. 381.

fairness, be higher for firms making, for instance, 500 local calls a day than for those making only 50.

The costs of long-distance calls must also be considered before concluding that phoning saves money. Let us compare average letter costs with specific figures on some of the longest long-distance calls within the United States.

For example, regarding letters—according to the Dartnell Target Survey, the cost of an ''average'' 175-word business letter dictated face to face to the stenographer was $7.11 in 1982. If dictated to a machine, the letter cost $5.33. The time it takes to dictate the average business letter is about eight minutes.[5] Because in the exchange of needed information two letters must be written— the inquiry and the reply—these estimated costs will be approximately doubled.

Regarding long-distance call rates, according to Telephone Directory figures for the same year (1982) an eight-minute long-distance phone call across the United States between the two most widely separated time zones—Pacific and Eastern—cost $4.17. (Mountain and Central Zones are less.) This cost was based on the 1982 highest Weekday Full Rate coast to coast, as the following figures show:

Weekday M–F Full Rate 8 a.m. to 5 p.m.		Evening M–F Discount 40% 5 p.m. to 11 p.m.		Night and Weekend Discount 60% 11 p.m. to 8 a.m.	
First minute	Each additional minute	First minute	Each additional minute	First minute	Each additional minute
.74	.49	.44	.30	.29	.20

On the assumption that the average person's speaking rate is between 80 and 250 words per minute, even if we use a conservative estimate of only 150 wpm, two people can exchange about 1,200 words during the eight-minute $4.17 call. If they ask and give all the information needed, they have achieved their purpose in eight minutes. In contrast, if they had written letters, they would have had to wait a few days for the mail each way before reading each other's message (dictated in 16 minutes and costing an average of between $10.66 and $14.22 for the two). A 16-minute phone call would cost $8.09 plus tax.

You can save still more on long-distance calls by intelligently planning the time you place them. For instance, in the Pacific Time Zone many businesses that communicate often with firms in Eastern cities have their communicators

---

[5] ''Dartnell Target Survey,'' The Dartnell Institute of Business Research, Chicago, 1982.

come to the office at 7 a.m. Any calls they complete to those cities before 8 a.m. are billed at the lowest rate—with 60 percent discount.[6] Cost-saving calls from Eastern Time Zone cities to the Pacific could be made starting at 5:01 p.m. (2:01 p.m. Pacific Time) and receive the evening discount of 30 to 35 percent.

Earning Money. In addition to saving time and money, well-planned telephone calls also help make (earn) money. Many firms sell their products or services regularly through local and long-distance calls to new prospects, long-time customers, and marginal accounts. By keeping their sales people on the phone instead of on the road, they contact more customers more frequently, at lower costs, and earn money from their sales.

Variety of Telephone Equipment and Uses

During the past decade amazing new electronic technological advancements have widely expanded the ways telephones can be used. Still further significant inventions are progressing rapidly each year. (See also Chapter 22.) The following is just a brief sample of some popular kinds of special telephone equipment for efficient oral communication. (These are listed alphabetically.)[7]

- *Advance Mobile Phone Service* (AMPS) enables people to make local and long-distance calls to cars, trucks, aircraft, boats, and ships that have phones. Calls can be completed by dialing direct or calling Operator.
- *Automatic call sequencers* answer numerous incoming calls, play a recorded message to the callers, place them on "hold" (sometimes with music background), and forward each call to the first available operator. These are especially useful in a telemarketing environment—for airline and hotel reservations, credit and adjustment inquiries, department stores and any other offices having a high volume of incoming calls.
- *Data Communications* can electronically route information spoken into a special recorder from the sender's telephone terminal, through computers or other equipment, to various named persons who may receive a printed-out message.
- *800 Service* lets out-of-town customers dial businesses without charge; they can place orders, ask questions, or check on orders.
- *Facsimile telecommunication equipment* transmits drawings, graphs, pictures, and written messages long distances through data impulses and signals by means of the telecommunication network.
- *Gemini 100 electronic blackboards* can be tied in on teleconferences so that the information participants in one city write on their blackboard is commu-

---

[6] Robert Hankins, manager of business services, Pacific Northwest Bell, Seattle, Nov. 17, 1982.
[7] *Telephone Techniques* and *Teleconferencing,* Bell System, AT&T, 1982; *Affordable Business Improvements from Pacific Northwest Bell* and various other brochures, courtesy of Sue West, manager, Business Telemarketing Center, Pacific Northwest Bell, Seattle, November 1982.

nicated through the telecommunication network to the blackboards of participants in other cities.

- *Intercoms* enable persons within an organization to have direct telephone connections with each other simply by dialing one- to four-digit code numbers. There's no need to walk to see coworkers; participants can stay at their own desks with all information needed right at their fingertips.
- *International calls* can be placed to practically any country in the world either by direct dialing or by assistance from an Operator.
- *Message-Holding service* flashes a light on the user's phone, indicating that a message is being held while the person is away. This system is especially useful for hotel guests as well as for executives and everyone else who needs to know who called during his or her absence.
- *Outdoor phones* protected in weather-resistant housing are for emergency calls on highways, construction sites, forestry stations, streets. A new, additional "911" service in communities that have it will automatically route calls to the nearest speedy emergency service.
- *Paging equipment* broadcasts messages (by a loud speaker voice or beeps) to various locations within the organization, to locate "missing" persons in the office thus giving better service to callers.
- *Pocket pagers* alert their users to calls when they are in a meeting, restaurant, or anywhere within miles from their offices. The pagers are 24-hour conveniences with an optional dual tone feature that lets users distinguish between emergencies and routine calls; they also have built-in memory to collect messages and relay them when users turn them back on.
- *Private Branch Exchange* (PBX) switchboard and its extensions serve as a telephone exchange performed by operators within an organization, enabling speedy, direct inward dialing and forwarding of incoming calls.
- *Recording equipment* automatically answers incoming calls, states a prerecorded message to the caller, records the caller's message, and disconnects.
- *Remote Call Forwarding* (RCF) is a unique telephone service that gives out-of-town customers a local number to a firm's home office. For the business firm it's like having a branch office in any or all of 350 markets nationwide—at a mere fraction of the cost. Listings can be in local directories wherever the service is available, and customers call as easily as a local call.
- *Special attachments for handicapped* listeners convert telephone sounds into comprehensible signals for those who have impaired or lost hearing, sight, or speech.
- *Teleconferences* among three or more people in two or more locations widely separated geographically can be valuable savers of travel time, fuel, and money when used in place of face-to-face meetings.
- *Videoconferencing* among three or more people in two or more locations has the added advantage that participants *see and hear* those who are in the meeting—on their respective home premises or on telephone company property or leased premises that have the needed equipment.

- *WATS* (Wide Area Telecommunication Service) enables persons to call from a WATS access station line to other stations within a designated service area. WATS customers pay a set (reduced) monthly fee up to a maximum number of intrastate or interstate calls. WATS can be used for outward calls as well as inward.

Suggestions for Effective Telephoning (One to One)

As with all other successful written and oral communication, telephoning requires preplanning by the caller and desirable behavior during the conversation by both persons who are conversing. As the commercials advise, "Reach out and touch someone." Though you are not meeting face to face, your conversation will be voice-to-voice and you want it to be as favorable as possible.

Preplanning by the Caller

1. Know the specific purpose of your call.
2. Know the name and occupation (if pertinent) of the individual you are calling.
3. Consider the best time to phone, from the standpoint of that person and of your company. Usually, avoid calling just before lunch or at closing time. For some executives the best available time may be between 10:30 and 11:30 a.m.; for others between 4 or 5 p.m.. For prospects you call at home, Monday or Tuesday evenings between 7 and 9 p.m. are usually preferred. If you are calling long distance be sure to notice time zones; consult your Phone Directory map and choose discount times whenever possible and desirable.
4. Plan your opening statement.
5. Jot down the questions you want to ask. Try to limit your call to one main point. If you are calling to sell something, know your sales psychology and have factual suggestions for listener benefits. The suggestions for unsolicited sales letters—in Chapter 11—may be helpful for your phoning, too.
6. Have paper and pen handy for note taking; also place near the phone any figures, files, former correspondence, or whatever may be necessary for reference during the conversation.

Behavior during the Telephone Conversation

When You Are the Caller. Introduce yourself, and if you are calling long distance, say so at the beginning. Secretaries are more willing to interrupt their bosses if they know you are calling from out of town. Person-to-person calls add importance and a feeling of urgency. If the individual you are calling is not in, ask whoever answers the phone for the best time to reach that person. Or you can leave a message with your number to have your call returned. Even if you reach the desired individual on your first call, it is courteous to ask if this is a good time to talk. The person may be interviewing someone in the office or preoccupied with a rush job, making it difficult to give you full attention. If so, find when would be the preferred time for a call-back.

1. At the beginning of your conversation with the desired individual, smile. Though your listener cannot see you, the tone of your voice will sound more pleasant when you smile.
2. When speaking, hold the phone mouthpiece about ½ inch from your lips.
3. Establish rapport—preferably with some item of interest or benefit to your listener.
4. State the purpose of your call and proceed—with a clear, enthusiastic, tactful voice—to one of your questions or to the main point to be discussed, unless it is bad news that should come only after other material has been tactfully presented.
5. Listen to the other person's views, ideas, and suggested solutions; don't interrupt.
6. Listen also for the tone of the other person's voice; if it sounds annoyed, negative, angry, try to be helpful without arguing immediately.
7. If you are trying to sell something, never read a sales pitch word for word. It will sound insincere and canned. Adjust your presentation to your listener as well as possible. Be sincere and truthful.
8. Before closing, summarize the main decisions, if any, that were made and check that your listener agrees with your statements.
9. Thank your listener, and let him or her hang up before you do.

When You Answer a Phone Call. With a clear, pleasant voice answer promptly, usually with your name and department. If you are answering for your employer or a coworker, you might say, ''Mr. Brown's office, Peggy Smith speaking. May I help you?'' If Mr. Brown happens to be in another office, you might transfer the call (with the caller's permission) or suggest when Mr. Brown can be reached in his office.

DICTATING

Up to now the discussion in this chapter has focused on direct oral conversations between two persons speaking either face to face in an interview or voice to voice in a telephone conversation. Dictation is also oral communication—to an intermediary who transcribes the spoken words into a written message that is to be sent to an addressee. Because a frequent complaint of secretaries pertains to the poor dictating habits of executives, this section focuses on both the importance of good dictation and suggestions for better dictation.

Importance of Dictation

The person who can dictate messages clearly and quickly (instead of writing them all out in longhand) saves time and money for the employer and also, indirectly, helps build goodwill with customers.

The importance of good, clear dictation is especially noteworthy when one considers the enormous costs of errors resulting from poor dictation. Transcription errors because of dictators' lack of care have ranged from embarrassing or comical to costly and disastrous. Four examples are mentioned here.

1. A department supervisor, intending to write to the Dungeness Crab Company, began his dictation (to a new secretary) with this statement: "Send the following letter to Dungeness Crab Co." (He pronounced the last word as "ko.") The result? His letter—which he unfortunately signed and mailed without reading the inside address—was addressed to "Mr. Dunjen S. Crabco."
2. An insurance agent with a southern accent found that a secretary had transcribed what he dictated as "Mr. Robert's heart murmur" as "Mr. Robert's hot mama."
3. Another dictator's poor enunciation and omission of spelling on an unusual name resulted in a $4,000 damage suit. Her firm's wrecking crew—instead of razing an empty house at 560 McDonough Street—had begun to tear down an empty house at 516 McDonald Street!
4. A chief engineer had a habit of uttering "huh" and "er" between phrases while dictating into a microphone, and of dropping off word endings— saying, for instance, "hund" instead of "hundred." On one important materiel requisition for this international construction company a new typist misinterpreted this engineer's "uh" for "hundred," and thus she typed 111,000 feet of a certain dimension of lumber instead of the intended 11,000 feet. The requisition with the unnoticed error was duplicated and mailed to the company's 50 construction engineering branch offices. Can you estimate the cost of that error causing all those offices to buy 100,000 extra feet of unneeded lumber?

Suggestions for Better Dictation

Before you dictate, prepare! Know your purpose. Visualize your reader, and consider also your secretary who will listen to your oral message and transcribe it. Collect all material and facts you will need for the content of your message. Prepare an outline—with key words or phrases. If you are answering a letter, you might jot main points in its margin. Set aside sufficient time so you are not pressured and are free from interruptions—especially if your dictation is directly to a stenographer instead of to a machine.

Here are good oral practices to follow while dictating:

1. Dictate from your outline, using language that follows the C principles and good organization as discussion in previous chapters of this book.
2. Enunciate clearly. Very few persons can speak clearly with candy, gum, or cigarettes in their mouths. Be especially careful with plurals, and figures that sound similar, such as fifty and sixty. (''five o'' and ''six o'' are much more definite.) Distinguish clearly between similar sounds like p and b, m and n, f and v, t and d. Sometimes you need to say ''T as in tape,'' or the like.
3. Spell unusual words and names when using them for the first time. Also be especially careful with the many English words that are similar in sound but different in meaning and spelling. Here are a few examples:

accept, except	practical, practicable
addition, edition	principal, principle
affect, effect	residence, residents
allusion, illusion	right, rite, write
assistance, assistants	sight, site, cite
brake, break	stationary, stationery
cease, seize	straight, strait
coarse, course	their, there, they're
council, consul, counsel	to, too, two
formally, formerly	vice, vise
its, it's	waive, wave
latter, ladder	weather, whether
ordinance, ordnance	who's, whose

4. Dictate—at the beginning of the message—any special instructions such as extra carbon copies for certain persons, unusual tabulation of figures, or your desire for a rough draft only. For a complicated message—report, letter, memo, speech, etc.—you will surely want to edit and revise before it is mailed. Thus be sure to ask for a rough draft, double-spaced. Otherwise your assistant may unknowingly type the usual, say, four carbon copies. Your correct instruction can save precious time as well as paper and supplies.

   If your office has a magnetic card or magnetic tape typewriter, you and your typist can save still more time. You can then make changes or additions easily without having an entire report draft retyped. Text as originally draft-typed is ''played out'' automatically to each point of revision. Changes or additions are typed manually, and then automatic playout of the corrected copy resumes.
5. Always dictate as much punctuation as your transcriber needs to turn out an accurate, attractive message quickly. At least dictate ''paragraph'' to indicate each new paragraph; ''quote,'' ''unquote''; ''parenthesis,'' ''close parenthesis.''

6. Dictate at a normal rate, as you talk. Avoid long pauses followed by rapid dictation. It is thoughtful to slow down a little when reading, for instance, an inside address or a policy number. Overall rate may be 60 or more w.p.m.

7. Let your secretary use his or her initiative as to grammar corrections, additional punctuation, and arrangement of your letters, memos, and reports.

8. When dictating a reply to a letter received, you can save both your time and your stenographer's time if you dictate only the name of the addressee. Your stenographer can later copy the full address from the letter you return after you have dictated your reply.

9. Especially when dictating by telephone or on a machine (not face to face to a secretary), be sure to omit any side comments that are neither for the operator's instructions nor for your addressee. For instance, some careless dictators have found statements like "That guy is really nuts," or "I don't believe what this darn customer wrote" within the transcribed letter. Naturally, it had to be revised, with wasted time by the assistant and embarrassment to the dictator who had expressed, aloud, feelings that were not to be in the letter.

10. If you have many important figures to be tabulated, write them on paper from which the stenographer can copy them.

11. Keep the mail you are answering in an orderly pile by turning each letter (or memo) upside down when you have finished answering it. After all your dictation is completed, your entire pile of answered incoming correspondence will be in order for your stenographer to obtain needed information, attach file copies, and so forth.

12. In addition to these dictation tips, you can save yourself and your company time and money by having definite dictation periods (for instance, a set time each morning and/or afternoon) with no interruptions by telephone or callers.

13. Standardize basic instructions and put them in writing for your transcribers—to eliminate needless repetition. Develop simple code words to indicate frequently used instructions—such as "CEPO" for "Send a carbon copy with enclosure to our Portland office."

14. Dictate less and delegate more. Develop effective interchangeable form paragraphs and use them wisely to handle your repetitive situations. Dictate only the basic ideas and let your subordinate compose the routine letters. Be sure he or she has adequate information.

Example of Dictation

The following opening and closing sections from a goodnews reply to a phoned request for product information simulate how an orally dictated letter might "sound" to the transcriber. If you dictate to the secretary face to face, most of the words below in italics will be omitted. If, however, you use one of the voice-recording instruments described briefly in the next chapter, your instructions to the transcriber may be similar to those in italics below. Of course, voice inflection conveys additional (unspoken) instructions—for instance at the end of each sentence.

Good morning, operator. This is Robert Bridges in the Consumer Service Department, Extension 507. Please transcribe this letter addressed to Mr. Phillip *P-h-i double l-i-p* Jones, Department four two, Harrington *H-a-double r-i-n-g-t-o-n* Corporation, one six zero zero Avenue of the Americas *plural*, New York, New York, one zero zero three eight. Dear Mr. Jones.

Thank you for your inquiry about our *operator next two words all caps* ELEC-TRO *hyphen* SPEED *operator cap M as in Mary* Model 28 *operator cap T* Typewriter. Yes, *comma* indeed *comma* this model has proved very popular in such applications as yours in which *operator one word* downtime must be minimized. *Paragraph.*

(. . . Middle paragraphs dictated in similar fashion. . . .)

Our sales representative in the *cap E* Eastern *cap T* Territory *comma* Tanya *T-a-n-y-a* Brickler *B-r-i-c-k-l-e-r comma* will call you next week to set up a meeting to discuss your needs more specifically *semicolon* she will then be able to inventory your needs and give you a price quotation. To help you investigate our product line more thoroughly *comma* I have enclosed six colorful brochures *period Parenthesis.* Note the blue leaflet which describes the automatic *quote initial cap N* Never *hyphen initial cap F* Forget *end quote* one zero zero *hyphen* character memory system *period close parenthesis. Paragraph.*

Please call me at six two one *hyphen* double nine eight seven if we can answer additional inquiries about our typewriters. Cordially yours, Robert Bridges, Customer Service Representative. Enclosures, six.

SUMMARY

The interview is a face-to-face conversation by two persons for a predetermined specific purpose. The general purpose is to inform, to persuade, and/or to solve a problem. When grouped according to their specific purposes, interviews within a business firm may include: employment, training and instruction, counseling, work evaluation, discipline, complaint, and job termination interviews. Successful interviews require adequate preparation beforehand; tactful presentation of questions, facts, solutions, summary during the interview; and—whenever desirable—follow-up afterwards.

The main objective of the employment interview is to find the best applicant for the job. It must also inform each interviewee adequately about the job and build goodwill toward the company.

The job interviewer's preparation should include knowing pertinent facts about the company, job requirements, applicant's résumé (if available), and fair employment laws; also preplanning appropriate job-related questions. During the interview—after a brief, friendly warmup period—the interviewer should courteously ask preferably more open-end than "yes"/"no" questions, and should listen impartially for both verbal and nonverbal messages before evaluating the applicant.

A telephone conversation can often (but surely not always) take the place of two written messages or a face-to-face interview between two persons. The importance of telephones is indicated partly by the number in use and their advantages. Throughout the world more than a half-billion telephones in foreign countries connect with the United States telecommunication network of over 110 million telephones. Advantages of telephoning include saving time, saving money, earning money (in sales), and building goodwill. Whenever possible, comparative costs of letters and long-distance telephone costs (including night and evening discount rates) should be considered.

Numerous electronic technological advancements have widely expanded telephone usage. The list of special supporting equipment ranges from internal devices providing business conveniences, automatic recording, paging, and message holding, to external transmission of spoken and written messages between two or more persons in teleconferences and videoconferences. For effective telephoning the caller must preplan regarding purpose, listener, best time to phone, opening statement, questions, and supplies to have nearby. During the telephone conversation both caller and called should observe the C principles in their behavior and language while expressing ideas. Attentive listening and cooperation are essential.

Dictation is oral communication to an intermediary who transcribes the spoken words into a written message that is to be sent to an addressee. Careful preparation includes many of the essential planning steps recommended also for interviews and telephoning. In addition, the dictator must also consider the intermediary (secretary). Dictation should preferably be from an outline of key words or phrases. Desirable dictation practices include clear enunciation, spelling of unusual words (when appropriate), and adequate instructions to the transcriber—especially in machine dictation.

EXERCISES

1. This project involves an interview (for information-gathering purposes) and an oral presentation (for information-dissemination purposes). Your first task is to identify and interview a person who has a type of job or career which you hope to enter upon graduation. The purpose of the interview is to determine what kinds of communication activites that person must engage in during a typical week. You should cover not only the types of written messages sent and received, but also determine the volume or frequency,

the job title of the originator of the incoming messages, and the disposition of the messages (what does your interviewee do when he or she receives each type of message?). Don't forget to cover oral communication messages (verbal orders or directives, telephone requests, etc.). For outgoing written or oral messages, find out to whom (title of person) the messages are directed. Unless the interviewee keeps a log of such activities, you will have to depend on the interviewee's estimates for some of the information.

The second part of this assignment requires you to make a formal oral report of your findings in class. A three- to five-minute time limit should be sufficient; however, your instructor may wish to establish other limits.

2. For efficiently handling a situation in which your oral communication skills are important to a company, you must do some preliminary planning and practice.

Assume that you work for a firm with high employee turnover. Your responsibility is to gather informaton that will be useful to management in determining why so many employees leave. This information will be gathered in an exit interview procedure used by your company and conducted with every employee who leaves. You are to establish specific objectives to be followed during the interview, set up strategies that can be followed, and develop a specific list of questions that you will ask during the interview.

Try these questions out in an interview setting in class, using another member of the class as the employee who is leaving the company. In your interview, you should first express appreciation to the employee for his or her service. (This should be done in order to set the tone for a positive and relaxed interview.) You should then emphasize to the employee that in no way will the information gathered be used against the employee when seeking employment elsewhere. Stress the fact that the information will be used to help management improve working conditions in the company and perhaps help cut down on employee turnover. Use any technique that you believe will assure a nonthreatening situation.

Your primary functions during the interview are to solicit the information your company needs and to provide informaton that will be helpful to the employee.

3. For this project choose two questions from the list of preemployment questions on pages 382–384 and assume your interviewer has asked you to answer them. Then prepare a three-minute presentation to your class (or to smaller groups). Your instructor and/or your class members will "interview" you on what you said or on any other pertinent question. They will offer constructive criticism on your persuasiveness in answering the two questions that you assumed they asked you, and will comment on both your verbal as well as nonverbal expressions. An alternative to this assignment is to divide the class into groups of two to five persons. Each student will then

be "interviewed" by the group or by one student interviewer instead of by the whole class. The other members of each group will take turns being the interviewee—to present their three-minute talks answering their two chosen preemployment questions.

4. You are correspondent for a company with a centralized word processing department. By dialing a special number, you dictate correspondence from your desk telephone. This dictation is recorded in the word processing department on tape for later transcription. The typed document is routed to you for signature and mailing—or editing and retyping if necessary.

    Dictate a solution for a letter-writing exercise in Chapter 7 or 8. To simulate dictating to a word processing department, use a tape recorder. Experienced dictators can dictate routine correspondence from nothing more than a mental outline; however, you probably will need to consider the best organizational pattern to use, jot down a brief outline with major points for development, and then dictate. Be sure to indicate your name and department. Then, using the dictation suggestions on pages 658–661, dictate your letter from inside address to name and title.

5. Present to the class a five-minute instructive explanation on how to perform the duties of a particular job you are familiar with. After you finish, call on a class member to tell as well as possible what she or he learned. (This procedure tests not only your instruction clarity but also the listener's attentiveness.)

PART SIX

Significant Concerns for Effective Business Communicators

CHAPTER 22

Modern Office Technology for Business Communication

Before the invention of the typewriter, business letters that a manager dictated to a secretary were recorded in shorthand, then written in longhand; and the handwritten message was sent by mail to the addressee. Obviously, much hand work and time were involved in sending a message. After the typewriter was placed on the United States market in 1875, that machine gradually became part of office equipment. It speeded up the business communication process and—with a good typist—turned out more legible products. Later, with the advent of carbon paper, storage of the original message became easier.

Your office world in the 1980s has changed considerably since the 1880s, and even since the 1960s. Furthermore, office technology is continuing to change rapidly. Progressive business communicators need to keep up to date on the automated office and how modern technology can help to affect business communication favorably.

This chapter presents an overview of the electronic communication process; inputs into communication systems; machines to process, store, retrieve, reproduce, and disseminate information; and teleconferences, videoconferences, and video cassettes.

OVERVIEW OF ELECTRONIC COMMUNICATION PROCESS

Today, and in your future, whether as an office worker or a manager, you will work in a high-technology office. You will be part of an office technological revolution, all in the interest of improving office productivity.

A simple schematic of what occurs in an office may look like this:

Your vocabulary today includes word processors, dictation equipment, automatic typewriters, floppy disks, CRTs, computers, micrographics, reprographics, duplicators, electronic mail, TWX, facsimile, teleconferencing, and a host of other terms.

INPUTS INTO COMMUNICATION SYSTEMS

In a high-technology office you will have various instruments available for dictating or otherwise "inputting" information before it is transcribed into written form. However, regardless of whether you use technological input methods or orally dictate face to face to a secretary, careful preplanning is essential. Know your purpose, consider your audience, organize ideas, and choose language that meets the C principles, as emphasized throughout this book. (For suggestions on dictation, see Chapter 21.)

Voice-Recording Instruments

Though some executives still prefer to write their messages in longhand first and/or dictate them to a secretary face to face, many other dictators are using various modern instruments that electronically record the voice. An advantage of "machine" dictation is that it saves time. The secretary can be doing other tasks while the executive is dictating. Also such recording machines can be used effectively while the executive is away from the office.

Basically, three general types of dictation instruments are available (in many different models): desktop, portable, and central recording systems.

Desktop Machines

Several desktop voice-recording machines have been available for many years. (The first dictation machine was invented by Alexander Graham Bell in 1888; many improvements have been made since then.) The media on which these dictation machines record ideas are cassettes, floppy disks, or belts. With any of these media the dictators can listen back to their spoken words, make changes, then easily remove the media and give them to the typists for transcribing on their transcribing machines. The media can be filed for future reuse and/or "erased" for new dictation on them anytime. These machines are especially useful for persons who have a heavy volume of dictation or long, complex documents.

Portable Recorders

Hand-held portable recorders make it possible to record dictation on microcassettes, magnetic belts, or disks, which can be sent to typists for transcription. Small enough to fit into a pocket, these recorders can be carried easily by travelers while in remote locations such as in cars and planes. Also some employees working in the field or factories use them to communicate information to the home office.

Central Recording Systems

In companies that have central recording systems the dictators may use the standard telephone, portable recorder, or a microphone specially wired for dictation in the office, at home, or out of town. To start dictation on a telephone within the office, for instance, the dictator merely picks up the telephone receiver, dials one to four prescribed digits, and waits for a tone signal that dictation can start. This method also allows for pauses and replay for review or changes. The spoken words are recorded on the firm's central recording system located in a "steno pool" or office where typists receive and transcribe spoken messages from various dictators.

Input Machines

Information can also be fed directly into word processing systems on special input machines—without the oral dictation mentioned above. Across the United States and in many other industrialized countries around the world word processing (WP) has become a popular way to significantly increase communication efficiency.

Word processing is a system to produce and process written communications speedily and accurately by using an efficient, economical combination of people, procedures, and special business equipment.[1] One important function is to accept input of ideas and information—for typical typewritten office documents such as letters, memos, forms, and short reports.

Automated typewriters can now perform many word processing functions. When you use an automated typewriter with a small TV-like display screen, you can compose any messages or other documents and see them on the screen before they are on paper. This system has three parts: keyboard, screen, printer.

a. *Keyboard.* The typewriter has a standard keyboard plus various additional keys to enable you to make corrections and changes easily.

b. *CRT Screen.* A cathode ray tube screen above the keyboard displays your material for editing. Thus, before the material is typed on paper you can from your keyboard electronically correct errors, insert material, rearrange spacing, or make various other changes.

Automated "intelligent" typewriters are being marketed with built-in memories, permitting a typist to include repetitive material at the press of a key. Each machine contains its own minicomputer, capable of storing banks of paragraphs, phrases, addresses. It can edit for spelling, readability, grammar, and other errors, flashing them on the screen automatically. It can also align decimal points and rearrange horizontal spacing. For example, material originally keyed in one column can be rearranged in two narrower-lined columns without retyping by the operator.

c. *Printer.* When you are satisfied with the display copy on the screen, you can press a certain key to instruct the printer to automatically begin typing the message on paper. And if you have, for instance, a two-page letter, the printer can be typing the first page while you are keyboarding the second page.

MACHINES TO PROCESS, STORE, AND RETRIEVE INFORMATION

After the input of information, the next important step is, of course, to have the material typewritten—processed—on paper. Machines are equipped to not only process but also make storage and retrieval easier and more efficient.

[1] For further reading on Word Processing, see Susannah Ganus, "List of Books and Subscriptions on Word Processing," *ABCA Bulletin,* June 1979, vol. XXXXII, no. 2, pp. 23-25. Two newer texts that are particularly good for an overview of the modern technological office are Shirley A. Waterhouse, *Word Processing Fundamentals,* Canfield Press, San Francisco, 1979, and William Saffady, *The Automated Office: An Introduction to the Technology,* National Micrograhics Association, Silver Springs, Md., 1981.

Word Processing Systems

The final printing of typewritten messages that have been keyboarded on automated typewriters will be accomplished quickly by the printers of word processing systems, at speeds ranging from 150 words to over 600 words a minute. Some offices use separate printers with word processing systems so that printing can be done while the message composer (or operator) is inputting other additional information on the keyboard.

Form messages are also easy to process. For instance, if you wish to send the same letter to 500 persons and have individual names with addresses inserted, the machines accomplish the task quickly after you punch a few keys. They help process "complete," "fill-in," or "paragraph" form messages (discussed in Chapter 6).

Storage with Micrographics

The storage space needed for filing typewritten materials is significantly smaller with modern technology. Central memory units are replacing vertical files. Data that were formerly stored in several volumes on shelves or in file drawers now might fit into one small file cabinet—or less. With micrographics the size of any typewritten materials can be reduced by placing them on small sheets of film like microfilm or microfiche for storing.

"Examples of specific types of micro forms include role microfilm, microfilm cartridges, microfilm jackets, microfiche, aperture cards, and fiche-size card jackets. The images they contain are properly called *micro images,* and they may be created by filming paper source documents or from machine-readable, computer-processible data via computer output microfilm (COM) technology. Their content may consist of either textual or graphic information."[2]

With automated typewriters the size of documents can also be significantly reduced. For example, magnetic cards can store 1 to 3 pages of text; tapes can store 10 to 16 pages; cassettes, 30 to 125 pages; and floppy disks, 60 to 128 pages.[3]

Some businesses now store their written material—both inactive and active records—in micro form. Law enforcement agencies store criminal records with fingerprints and photos; banks and many other firms store customer transaction records; hospitals store patient records; libraries usually store out-of-date periodicals or books.

Electronic Retrieval

Micrographics and electronic file searching are replacing manual retrieval. Retrieval systems involve a micro computer which searches a microform index keyed to filed documents. In other words, to find a stored document that you

---

[2] Saffady, *The Automated Office: An Introduction to the Technology,* p. 89.
[3] Waterhouse, *Word Processing Fundamentals,* pp. 111–112.

are looking for, you key in information that is mentioned in the document. For example, it may be names of sender and addressee, title, file number, and/or date. All documents with those references will be called up and you then select the one you need.

This process is also useful if you need to reread, for instance, all the messages that Ralph Jones wrote to Jane Doe during a certain month and year. The material can then be retrieved in micro form. When you place the microfiche in a reader with a small TV-like screen, the material is enlarged and you read it on the screen or light-sensitive background. Any material you want typewritten on paper can then be reproduced as you wish.

Today it is possible for you to work with a single word processing machine (available in various models) to perform electronically all the inputting, editing, processing, storing, and retrieving functions. In fact, you could work overseas and via a keyboard system link up with a satellite, connect with your home office in the United States, and have your material electronically ready for reading by your colleagues at the press of a key. In brief, any company work station in the United States or abroad can access—except for security measures—the same material, for analysis and decision making.

REPRODUCTION

"Reprographics" is a term referring to the process of reproducing or duplicating documents by modern techniques. The process may use automated typewriters, copying machines, duplicating machines, or phototypesetting equipment. (Formerly carbon paper was the main means of getting extra copies. But the number of neat legible carbon copies that can be typed on a traditional ordinary typewriter at one time is limited to about five or six.)

Many modern offices, as already mentioned, use automated typewriters and printers to produce and reproduce materials. In addition, your office will likely have one or more types of duplicating systems as described in the following.

Copying Machines

This popular copy-machine method makes copies of an original and electrostatically transfers them to ordinary paper. Machines like Xerox, IBM, Kodak, and others are simple to operate and produce copies in a few seconds. Many copiers can also copy on both sides of the paper, copy colors, feed document sheets into the machine automatically, collate pages in correct order, line the copied pages up evenly, and staple them.

Duplicating Machines

Two traditional machines that have been popular many years, especially in the smaller offices needing 15 to 80 or so copies, are the mimeograph and the ditto. Your high school or college offices probably ground out many copies of documents from a familiar inked drum using a master typed mimeograph stencil. Or perhaps your office still uses spirit duplicators like the ditto machine, which reproduces from ditto-carbon copies placed on a smooth metal drum. Once a mainstay of reproducing copies, these machines are being replaced by electronic machines.

Offset Printing

Offset printing machines are useful when several professional-quality copies are needed of, for example, manuals or booklets with many pages. They require a specially trained operator. (One of the early kinds of offset printers was the multilith.) Nowadays firms that need such copies only seldom and cannot afford to buy a machine, use the services of private professional printing or copying businesses.

Phototypesetting Machines

By this phototypesetting process the typewritten characters of a manuscript (for a booklet, manual, or other printed documents) are transferred directly from the initial keyboarding through a phototypesetting machine. That machine converts the material into ''camera-ready'' copy (on special paper) for printing and binding. This process saves both time and paper. It eliminates the need for typesetting and proofreading the same material twice—because the document does not have to be retyped in the printer's office.

Graphics

Converting data into colored graphic form was usually a time-consuming task: collecting figures; sending that data to an art department; integrating that material by hand into a graph or chart; rechecking and correcting the data with the originator; then making a slide, transparency, or copy. Often there were last-minute changes. Time, energy, and money were spent.

You will have it easier. Today computer graphic instruments permit bar graphs, pie charts, or word charts to be prepared literally in minutes, along with a choice of colors which are almost infinite. Moreover, you can also choose type styles, format, and see the final product before you have it printed as a slide, transparency, or color print.

DISSEMINATION

Up to now this chapter has discussed inputting (and editing), processing, storing, retrieving, and reproducing documents. One step remains in office technology: sending the material. This process, too, has seen significant technological improvements that speed delivery of messages—via telecommunications, satellite, and the U.S. Postal Service.

Telecommunications

Telephones are probably the most-used communication tool in any office. The Bell System and other independent telephone firms have in recent years provided many additional money- and time-saving electronic features. (For brief descriptions of some popular kinds of special telephone equipment, please see the list on pages 654–656.)

The following section introduces you to electronic mail—telecommunications—for sending and receiving typewritten messages over telephone lines. Two kinds of machines are mentioned here. Other telecommunication methods are included later in this chapter (under E-COM and conferences).

Telex and TWX Machines

Because they can send and receive messages via telephone, the Telex and TWX machines are referred to as teletypewriters. To call the receiving person, an operator merely uses the telephone dial on the keyboard of these machines. The message can be received in typewritten form or as a tape that may be fed into a computer.

Facsimile Machines

When you need to send photos, graphs, or other drawings over telephone lines, a facsimile machine is necessary. With this machine, after the operator dials and is connected with the receiving machine, each page of the information is communicated via telephone lines to the receiving machine in two to six minutes. Some of the recent facsimile machines are equipped to automatically dial and receive messages day or night without operator assistance. As you know, evening and night long-distance telephone rates have substantial money-saving discounts.

Satellite Communications

The most recent method of communications is via satellite. Many firms with word processing and facsimile for their mail find this method reliable, fast, and more economical than other systems. By this process a messsage is beamed from an office on earth to a satellite located thousands of miles above the earth. The satellite then beams the message to the receiving destination on earth—in less time and with less cost than by telephone lines. Being developed are amazing additional facilities that will carry data, voice, and graphics all on the same channel through a satellite system, at tremendously increased speed.

U.S. Postal Service and Modern Technology

In at least two popular ways the U.S. Postal Service has been helping significantly to increase speed and decrease costs of electronic mail deliveries.

Mailgrams

Each Mailgram message is routed electronically by the Western Union network to a post office near your addressee and printed out individually. Usually the next day after the message is sent, sometimes the same day, it is delivered by the Postal Service in a Western Union blue and white Mailgram envelope. For information on costs, see page 139. (Telegrams, too, can be delivered to the addressee by mail, though most are delivered, faster, by telephone. For costs see page 141 or Western Union.)

E-COM[4]

Over the years, the post office has moved mail by horseback, wagons, steamships, trains, trucks, and planes. Now it also moves mail electronically. The U.S. Postal Service began E-COM (Electronic Computer Originated Mail) January 4, 1982.

With E-COM the Postal Service provides two-day delivery of electronic computer-originated messages of up to two pages in length anywhere in the continental United States. A system of 25 serving post offices (SPOs), strategically located in large United States cities (see map below), are equipped with computers to convert the electronic E-COM messages into hard (paper) copy. That copy is then automatically trimmed, folded, enveloped, and delivered as first-class mail. E-COM service reduces delivery time by bypassing the internal

---

[4] Statements about E-COM are adapted from "Computer-Originated Mail Comes of Age with E-COM," "Presenting E-COM," and "E-COM Customer Information Booklet," plus sample enclosures, all by *United States Postal Service Publications* January 1982 through October 1982; also from the Newsletter by and interviews with Richard P. Casmier, E-COM Sales and Service Representative, P.O. Box 9000, Seattle, WA 98109-9602, December 1982.

Figure 22-1 E-COM Serving Post Office Locations and Service Areas. (*Source:* United States Postal Service; Richard P. Casmier's Newsletter, November 1982.)

mail preparation system and submitting messages to SPOs via electronic communication lines. Customers can access the nearest SPO by public telephone lines or other private telecommunications anytime; lines are open 24 hours a day, seven days a week.

E-COM users must send a minimum of 200 messages per transmission. E-COM will accept messages in three different formats:

1. Single Address Messages (SAM). These include the destination address and a unique (personalized) text to produce each complete mail piece.
2. Common Text Messages (COT). These are identical letters sent to multiple addressees. (They are "complete" Form Messages, as discussed in Chapter 6 of this book.)
3. Text Insertion Messages (TIM). These are "fill-in" form letters with similar text to any number of addressees, plus unique information "plugged in" to a "skeleton." The address list and unique information must be provided with the transmission.

With E-COM service you can send almost any kind of one- or two-page messages (even charts, bar graphs, tables of figures, or agendas) for just 31 cents for two pages; only 26 cents for one-page messages. The 1982–1983 price includes not only postage but also the paper, attention-getting blue and white envelope, printing, and labor for preparing the mailing.

E-COM service can be useful for messages from executives and any departments such as sales, credit/collections, payroll, customer services, and others. It is considered ideal for monthly statements, billing, invoices, fund raising, intracompany correspondence, price lists, recall notices, advertising messages, and other computer-generated mail.

TELECOMMUNICATIONS, VIDEOCONFERENCES, AND VIDEO CASSETTES

More and more large firms have their own telecommunications and/or video network for conferring with colleagues in distant offices and for a wide variety of other uses.

Conferences by Telephone

Multiparty calls for conferring by telephone have been possible for several years. You can hold meetings with local or out-of-town associates without any of you ever leaving your offices. For expanded group participation a Speakerphone used with a Microphone/Loudspeaker combination can be placed, for example, on a long conference table. All people sitting around it can hear the incoming voice(s) within 12 feet—without anyone holding a telephone receiver. The group members can also participate in the conference discussion.

For successful teleconferences it is desirable, whenever possible, to choose in advance a date and time suitable for the conferees. If the participants are expected to contribute useful information (instead of just listening), they should prepare in advance, as for any other effective conference. A leader can help steer the conference so that several people don't all try to talk at once. When well planned in place of face-to-face meetings, teleconferences can save both time and money.

Visual/Oral Conferences via Television and Cassettes

With a video network, colleagues in distant offices can confer both visually and orally for various business reasons.

Videoconferences

Instead of traveling to the home office for a conference, you can sit in a local conference room or studio which includes TV screens, cameras, microphones, and perhaps an electronic blackboard. Your colleagues are in a similar studio, linked via satellite, cable, or special telephone equipment. Hotel and motel chains realize the potential of the videoconference and are equipping their facilities for such meetings.

For you as a business communicator in a video conference there are certain implications regarding important communication skills:

1. Your speech becomes a significant carrier of the message.
2. Your ideas demand tight organization.
3. Your nonverbal appearance or cues will support or hinder your credibility.
4. Your visual aids must be brief and instantly clear to your distant viewer(s).
5. As a leader you will have to maintain tight control along with good summaries; as a participant you will have to contribute positively along with relevant remarks.

Video Cassettes

Another useful oral/visual communication method for persons in various locations is by video cassettes. Many company managers are sending video cassettes in place of written reports to their employees in out-of-town branches or even in widely separated departments within the same large company. Those who receive the cassettes can insert them individually on a video machine if they have one in their office. More often, groups of employees gather—perhaps during a coffee break or lunch hour—in a room that has a video machine into which the cassettes can be inserted for viewing on a TV screen.

For example, the chairman of the board or other management members might appear on the video cassettes in extended interviews with various employees who probe with questions. Or a "FYI" (for your information) video report might be sent periodically to update or train employees with various kinds of information.

Current Video Usage

A review of the popular video uses is seen in the following table:

Current Video Applications in Ranking Order of Use by Total Respondents (N = 326)*

Video Application	Percentage of Total Respondents
Basic skill training	72.7
Specific job training	70.6
Employee orientation	63.5
Supervisory training	62.3
Employee information	59.2
Management communications	56.1
Management development	54.9
Sales training	50.9
Safety/health	50.6
Employee benefits	49.4
New product demonstration/introduction	47.2
Sales meetings	32.5
Community relations	31.3
Proficiency upgrading	31.3
Annual reports/meetings	27.9
News programs (regularly scheduled)	27.6
Point-of-sale programs	21.8
Economic information/education	17.8
Labor/government relations	13.8
Security analyst presentations	8.6

* Judith M. and Douglas P. Brush, *Private Television Communications: Into the 80s,* International Television Association, Berkeley Heights, N.J., 1978, p. 55.

While skill and job training rank high, you as a participant or viewer will in the future probably be involved, through video, in the following ways:

- Working with or viewing a company weekly newsletter
- Viewing live or on cassette the annual stockholders' meeting
- Listening to a personal statement from the CEO or president of your organization
- Viewing a taped conference held by your company out of the country
- Learning about the annual report as discussed by major contributors to that report
- Orienting yourself to specific problems on the basis of a previous teleconference—at which you could not be present

SUMMARY

1. The process of technological changes affecting business communication involves inputting information, processing, storing, retrieving, reproducing, and disseminating information.

2. You will, in the technological office, become involved in procedures using word processors, automated typewriters, computer equipment, micrographics, electronic retrieval mechanisms, and various machines for reproducing written communications; and you will be involved with electronic mail through use of telephone lines, satellite, and/or the Postal Service's E-COM.

3. Technology will also involve you in teleconferences and video technology.

4. A concluding statement by an expert in office automation technologies emphasizes well the underlying requirement for successful communication:

> Regardless of the future technologies, the basic principles for creating effective business communications will apply. If people have a good grounding in the principles, then they will be able to adapt to whatever technology may bring. If they do not have a good grasp of the basics, then they will continue to produce *ineffective* business communications. The only differencee will be in the speed with which the ineffective communications are created, distributed and retrieved.[5]

EXERCISES

1. For a fuller understanding of some terms used in the modern office, provide a definition and statement of how the following terms and phrases relate to the modern office:

Basic	Microfacsimile
Boilerplate	OCR
Correcting typewriter	Reprographics
CRT	Stand-Alone System
Dictation systems	Teleconferencing
Electronic mail	Text editor
Facsimile	Word processor
Floppy disk	Xerographic process
Intelligent typewriter	

2. Read the *Wall Street Journal* or another daily or weekly publication. Look for advertisements which feature the different types and kinds of word processors on the market. Then discuss in class the similar or different capabilities of the various manufacturers' products.

[5] Raymond W. Beswick, "Business Communication in the Automated Office: Some Thoughts on Integrating Information Systems and Communication," Harwick Word Processing Consultants Ltd., Edmonton, Alberta T5J 2Z2, Jan. 8, 1982.

3. Visit a local organization which has its own teleconferencing facilities. Speak with some of the persons in that organization who have participated in a teleconference. Find out what were some of the positive aspects of the experience and some of the negative. Report to the class.

4. Write to the director of corporate communications at a large company and determine whether it produces videotapes. Ask to view one of its tapes specifically produced for employees, the public, or distributors. View that videotape in class; offer comments on how this form of technology is a type of business communication. What made the program effective or ineffective?

5. Review for the class an article on some aspect of modern technology in the office. Your subject may be similar to any discussed in this chapter: inputting systems; analysis, storage, and retrieval of information; reproduction of material; and dissemination of information.

6. Obtain permission to attend a video or teleconference at a local motel or hotel equipped to send or receive such a conference. The emphasis in your report should be on the process, not the content: What made the meeting effective or ineffective? What were the problems you saw as an observer? Who was the leader of the meeting? What was the physical setup for the meeting? How long did the session last?

7. The following terms relate to teleconferencing and are a mix of technical jargon and terms which will arise as your office moves into the future. Provide a brief definition for each:

Anik	Monitor	Satellite
Audience	Network	Symbols
Audio line	Origination site	Westar
Feedback	Originator	
Media	Reception site	

8. Visit a word processing center of an organization near you. As you tour the office, be prepared to report on the following questions:

In what form does the input material arrive in the office?
What type of machines text-edit the material?
How many machines and persons are involved in the office?
What are the capabilities of the machines?
How is the printed, final-form material delivered to the originator of the message?
Conclude this assignment by drawing a floor plan of the office you visited.

CHAPTER 23

Communication on Social Issues

Forecasting social issues which affect you in your job is risky. Issues can change rapidly, so rapidly that concerns vary from year to year.

Why then this chapter? Because you may be asked to speak or write on social topics, special societal problems arising in your area of work or within your organization.

You will then have to argue and explain social issues for your coworkers inside your organization and to a society outside which is becoming more vocal, concerned, and interested in answers. In short, the letter, memorandum, report, and speech will still be main vehicles for moving ideas. But in the future you may contribute to issues in forms that go beyond the typical kind of business communication noted so far in this text.

Thus the goal is to view the rapid rise of social issues in business communication by defining external and internal communication, considering current social themes, looking at methods of communicating those themes, noting additional purposes and styles, and focusing on implications for business communicators.

EXTERNAL/INTERNAL COMMUNICATION

External Communication

Once upon a time the main type of company communication to outside groups was the annual report. That yearly document, in early years a brief and unembellished statement, was supposed to meet the needs of investors, financial analysts, students, government regulators, and others interested in the company. Originally it included few pictures, scanty financial information, and little reporting on social concerns.

But by the 1960s society demanded an accounting of business, suggesting that social concerns were legitimate as exemplified in this question: What is the social cost of the economic development of a company?

A pilot study of selected annual reports of 1964 and 1979 indicates that social concern topics increased by the percentages shown in the table at the top of page 683.

One reason—some say the compelling reason—for increased communication about the environment and energy was the rise of environmental groups and others under the "consumerism" heading. Business was under siege. Like any other group, business began to defend itself and used the annual report as one vehicle for disseminating information to many disparate groups outside the company. This method and others are discussed later in this chapter.

Internal Communication

What do you think are the most common ways management communicates with employees? Many employers use the bulletin board. Others use interviews and personal letters. Still other popular methods (to be considered later) are newsletters, magazines, and annual reports.

**Categories as a Percentage of Total
Reporting for 1964 and 1979***

	1964	1979
Environment	3	10
Fair business practices	20	23
Personnel	53	21
Community involvement	23	17
Products	—	8
Energy	—	22

* See H. W. Hildebrandt and Kathryn Rood, "Social Responsibility Disclosures: Communication in Selected Annual Reports," Working Paper No. 263, Division of Research, Graduate School of Business, University of Michigan, Ann Arbor, 1981.

An internal-communication analysis based on a survey of 45,000 employees suggests—in the following table listing 17 subjects—that employees have a strong interest in "meaty" topics in place of lightweight material such as birthdays and anniversaries. Though employees do wish to hear or read the usual personnel-oriented material about their organization, they are also interested in subjects which affect them and their quality of life.

**Internal-Communication Subjects of Interest to Employee
Survey Respondents***

Rank	Subject	% Very Interested and Interested
1	Organization's future plans	95.0
2	Personnel policies and practices	90.3
3	Productivity improvement	89.7
4	Job-related information	89.4
5	Job advancement opportunities	88.4
6	Effect of external events on my job	87.6
7	Organization's competitive position	87.1
8	News of other departments/divisions	85.9
9	How my job fits into the overall organization	85.6
10	How the organization uses its profits	83.2
11	Organization's stand on current issues	83.1
12	Organization's community involvement	82.2
13	Personnel changes/promotions	81.4
14	Financial results	79.3
15	Advertising/promotion plans	78.2
16	Stories about other employees	72.2
17	Personal news (birthdays, anniversaries, etc.)	57.4

* Joyce A. Gildea, "45000 Employees Judge Effectiveness of Internal Communication," *Journal of Organizational Communications* 2 (1981), pp. 3–11.

Social Disclosure Themes

In your work it is likely that you will contribute some material on social concerns—either by writing a section of a report or as a speaker for your organization. The topics may include one or more of these: environment, fair business practices, personnel, community involvement, products, energy, and perhaps still others. The following examples appeared in external and internal publications.

1. Environment

Few issues have produced such a torrent of words and cold statistics as environment, given heat through emotional rhetoric. Often it is directed at business and its profit motive and it demands a response. The following examples suggest that reports, both to external and internal groups, include environmental concerns:

- "A majority of NDCC employees surveyed listed air and water pollution as being, in their opinion, the two most important environmental problems facing the U.S. today." (*Dispatch,* National Distillers and Chemical Corporation, August 1981)
- "Our attention has focused on environmental concerns, particularly forest management, and air and water quality matters. . . ." (*Consolidated News,* Consolidated Papers, Inc., January–February 1981)
- "Keeping the Good Earth Good" (*Think,* IBM, September–October 1981). The article is the third part of a special report on what the company is doing to protect its people and preserve the environment.

Other reports include concerns with pollution control in the manufacturing process, product improvement to reduce pollution arising from the product's use, or conservation of natural resources.

2. Fair Business Practices

This generic phrase relates to statements on the doctrine of fairness, that business is treating employees according to merit regardless of race, creed, color, sex, or national origin. Inherent, too, is the awareness of business ethics, that a written or unwritten creed of honesty pervades the organization. Company documents attest to a continuing and increasing concern with stating an ethical doctrine.

- "The Wisconsin Electric Power companies have a longstanding policy of conducting their business activities with the highest standards of honesty and integrity." (*The Outlet,* Wisconsin Electric Power, April 1981)
- "Minority Business Is Good Business" (*View,* Carrier Corporation, Fall 1980)

- "Affirmative Action: Much More than Words and Numbers" (*Dialogue,* Perkin-Elmer, November 1981)
- "1981 Minority Purchasing Goal Exceeded" (*Gas Lines,* Boston Gas, no. 9, 1981)

You will also read and possibly write about your organization's employment and advancement of minorities, the employment and advancement of women, the employment of other special interest groups, the support for minority businesses in the United States, and compliance with governmental regulations for equal employment.

3. Personnel

The preceding societal concern with fairness is carried over to all workers: their well-being, their safety, their families, their way of life. The trend in annual reports of 1964, for example, was to report the usually drab statistics on number of workers, their years of employment, their benefits, their safety record. A close reading suggests that these concerns are no less today, and in great measure have increased as organizations disclose to workers, and in turn to the outside public, actions taken affecting the well-being of the employee. Examples include the following:

- "*Squibbline* held a background session with several Squibb scientific and commercial executives to discuss 'Science, Medicine, and the Quality of Life. . . .'" (*Squibbline,* Winter 1981–1982)
- "Population, Technology Change," discussion of older people and their need for health care (*Baxter Travenol World,* October 1981)
- "Industrial Hygiene," discussion of industrial hygienist seeking to meet government regulations and determine if workers' well-being such as health, comfort, and efficiency is affected. (*Dispatch,* National Distillers and Chemical Corporation, November 1981)

The entire range of topics affecting you as an employee would include compliance with Occupational Safety and Health Administration standards. OSHA is concerned with employee health and safety, employee training, programs for retraining and placement of displaced workers, efforts to lessen unemployment owing to economic conditions, and general disclosure of socially responsible industrial relations policies.

4. Community Involvement

A kaleidoscope of topics has been distributed to the public, in response to internal and external groups, answering this question: What has an organization returned to society as a result of what it obtained from that society?

A report by the Exxon Corporation is a good example of an attempt to rearrange false intuitions. Undoubtedly it required the writing input of many individuals, so much so that the *Dimensions 80* report covered 97 pages. The preamble is worth quoting:[1]

> This year, in our fifth annual report on Exxon and its affiliates' financial contributions to public interest organizations, we describe the activities of eight such groups that received funds from the company in 1980.
>
> Each group's story is quite different and reflects the diversity of our company contributions program. One article tells how women are exchanging welfare checks for paying jobs. Another describes an effort to alert young people to the need to preserve the ecological balance of Chesapeake Bay. Others discuss a center for Middle East studies, health and social services that are being brought into the home. . . .

That same report has these major divisions: public broadcasting programming, health, the arts, public information and policy research, community services, environment, list of contributions in the United States, contributions outside the United States, and the Exxon education foundation report.

Similarly, other companies have included topics such as donations of cash, products, and employee services to community activities; health-related activities; education and the arts; and other general community activity disclosures.

In addition to community involvement in the many ways listed above, one other matter is significant. It concerns the growing need for key officers of business corporations to upgrade their role in public policy. For example, during an ongoing series of seminars planned by the Public Affairs Division of Seafirst Corporation for its senior officers, a recurring message was the importance of understanding how public policy arguments are formed in America and how the officers can help guide public policy for the benefit of both the public and the business. Too often in very complex issues the public has only inadequate or biased information. Many people have changed their thinking after they understand the honest message from business. As Seafirst Vice Chairman Joseph Curtis stated in *Seafirst News,* April 2, 1982,

> We must do better at discussing, thinking and forming bank policy around the many public issues of our time, whether they be local affairs or world affairs. . . . We must not only know more, but also use what we know to make better decisions, be more confident in our reasons, and more willing to discuss them even in unfriendly surroundings. . . .

Examples among the many *Seafirst News* topics pertinent to provocative public issues and policies are the following:

> "Constitutional Challenge to Initiative 394 Calls for Major Communication Effort"; "Know What You're Signing if Petitions Come Your Way"; and "Initiative 412 Would Restrict Available Credit."

---

[1] *Dimensions 80*, A Report on Exxon's 1980 Contributions in the Public Interest and the Exxon Education Foundation Report, Exxon Corporation, New York, 1980, p. 1.

5. Products

A lesser though not less important number of public statements relate to product safety and improvement. More often these product discussions are mentioned in internal publications, as in these examples:

- Conservation of energy is explained in an article on use of a disc system (*Info-systems,* sponsored by Memorex Corporation, May 1981)
- "Sarns will continue to focus its resources, human and material, on developing and maintaining a *total* system of safe, reliable, and effective medical products for use during open heart surgery." (*Sarns 1981 Year-End Newsletter,* January 1982)

6. Energy

From almost zero discussion of energy in 1964 annual reports to 22 percent in 1979 implies a breakout of a topic far in excess of any other societal concern. Even small firms, begun by entrepreneurs, have succumbed to society's call for some statement on energy conservation. A myriad of topics have appeared, only a few of which are indicated here:

- "Spinning Wind into Gold," the use of windpower as a potential energy source. (*CBI News,* Chicago Bridge and Iron Company, vol. 4, 1981)
- Consumer responsibilities in energy crisis. (*Annual Report, 1980,* Delta Drilling Company)
- "Energy Ideas at Work." (*View,* Carrier Corporation, Summer 1977).
- "Energy." (*The Lamp,* Exxon Corporation, Winter 1981).
- "The Language of Energy." (Mobil Oil Corporation, 1981)

To the above examples can be added categories such as presence of an energy conservation program, expenditures on energy conservations, amount of energy conserved, nuclear energy, or energy savings attributed to products. You could list other topics and expand the list. The point is this: You will communicate with a society that seeks to have business respond to its concerns.

Methods of Communication

Business communication on social issues is both written and oral, though the emphasis is primarily on the written methods. This section presents some of the popular variations used to communicate externally and internally on social issues.

1. Annual Reports

As mentioned in the first section of this chapter, businesses now use the annual report to convey both financial information and topics of social concern to many different groups outside their organizations.

"Employee Annual Reports Rarely Shine" is the headnote for an article in the *IABC News* 11 (December 1981, p. 1ff.). The article suggests that reports to employees are still the stepchildren of the full-blown annual report to outsiders. Yet progress is being made.

Through humor and concise writing employee annual reports condense voluminous data into eminently readable prose, with employees still given the option to read the detailed annual report if that is their desire. A few samples follow.

- *Annual Report to Employees, Nabisco, Inc. 1979.* This most innovative report is in the form of a checkbook with various checks indicating the amount spent, for example, on payroll; supplies and services; maintenance, repairs, and depreciation; advertising and marketing; and other company costs.
- Employee Annual Report in *Consolidated News,* Consolidated Papers, Inc. Two speeches—those delivered at the stockholders' meeting—are included in the regular employee publication.
- *Report to Jobholders, 1981,* Pitney Bowes. The president's opening line adequately summarizes: "This annual report to the employees of Pitney Bowes Business Systems has been prepared to review our achievements and problems in 1980, and to provide background information for jobholder meetings. In addition, the annual report to stockholders is being mailed to your homes to provide further information."

While devoid of much financial data, the annual employee report becomes both another writing and reading opportunity. As budgets increase for internal communication, this method may be more popular in organizations.

2. Meetings with Employees

This category of communication between management and employee builds on the idea mentioned above by Pitney Bowes; namely, meeting with employees after they receive a written document. The annual jobholders' meetings are a 30-year tradition where employees ask questions of management ranging from personal work conditions to detailed financial inquiries.

For you the employee there will be many other firms that provide opportunities for communication, both written and oral. Indeed, many employee publications provide feedback opportunities via questions, survey questionnaires, even hot lines, where you can write or speak on a personal concern. Management replies may be published in the employee newsletters, mailed direct to employees, and/or presented orally in meetings.

3. Specialized Reports

You could be asked to supply brief sections of a total report—as for instance in this diverse series of topics in Exxon's Background Series on *World Energy Outlook*:

World Economic Growth
Energy/GNP Ratio
World Energy Demand
World Energy Supply
Electric Power Outlook
World Nuclear Energy Outlook
World Coal Outlook
World Gas Outlook
World Oil Demand
Rates of Discovery of World Oil and Gas Reserves
Synthetic Fuels and Very Heavy Oil Outlook
Renewable Energy Outlook
United States Energy Outlook
Europe Energy Outlook
Centrally Planned Economies Energy Outlook
Developing Countries Energy Outlook

Furthermore, some employee publications, though not specialized, devote entire issues to a limited topic, either in response to a questionnaire or a theme selected by the editor. Hence the National Standard Company published a tabloid which summarized 505 worker responses to 15 questions; Hewlett-Packard in an issue of *Measure* summarized 7,966 employee responses to more than 100 topics, some of which included pay, pay philosophy, benefits, management concerns, training, affirmative action, and communications.

4. Speeches

Speakers' bureaus are a part of numerous firms' attempts to reach the public, either for giving information about the firm or for providing speakers on a variety of topics. A look at *Vital Speeches* indicates that management members take their view to the public in national forums or before special interest groups.

When getting a message across to a wide public audience is crucial, business executives also have hundreds of interviews with the press and appearances on special TV or town meeting programs. Topics may include social concerns like those mentioned previously under "Social Disclosure Themes" or still others that may affect public policy and business.

Some companies use outside speakers as their cadre of persons to represent the company, while others depend entirely on company employees. To prepare yourself for being a company speaker, remember to hone your oral communication skills, know your subject matter thoroughly, and understand and react tactfully to the interests of various audiences.

5. Letters

Some companies are so small that they have no budget for any detailed reports, internal or external. Some of these firms send letters on a quarterly basis to employee homes. That may not sound unusual except that many persons contribute to each letter, adding comments and information on their section of the company. Hence the letter is a group effort, with the president of the firm acting as the chief editor.

6. Magazines, Newsletters, Newspapers

Two professional organizations (American Business Communication Association and International Association of Business Communicators) exist in part to assist employees who collect, gather, write, edit, produce, and send internal employee magazines to employees and outside readers.

These internal news media help management to keep in touch with employees both informally and formally. They weave together information about the firm along with the usual personal photos, anniversaries, birthday celebrations, and retirements. Over the years, however, less space has been devoted to the personal, family side of employees and more to topics of a more substantive nature—including also staff surveys and management responses on various issues.

Many of the examples in this chapter were taken from employee publications, for they are prolific indeed. For a fuller listing of publications refer to Craig T. Norback, *Corporate Publications in Print*, McGraw-Hill, New York, 1980.

Additional Purposes and Styles

When we examine annual reports to outside groups and internal employees, we can easily observe that their contents go beyond the purpose of informing. Yes, financial facts are included and information about social themes has increased. But additional purposes exist, as indicated below.

For instance, the 1980 requirements of the SEC (Securities and Exchange Commission) include these specifications regarding annual reports:

- Expanded discussion, along with analysis of the financial condition of the company; a detailed look at the operations of the company.
- Requirement that firms report data for five years, to include: net sales, net earnings, earnings per common share, dividends per common share, total assets, and long-term debt obligations.
- Mandate a three-year income statement, along with footnotes to cover that period.
- Requirement for two audited balance sheets, for the last two fiscal years.

Those are the legal requirements that accompany the social disclosure statements and examples in the annual reports. As a potential accountant, financial analyst, marketing person, policy and control employee, or personnel officer, you may have to contribute, in writing, to the annual report.

An analysis of recent employee magazines and annual reports indicates those documents are multipurpose. They meet the requirements of the SEC and do communicate with employees, but go beyond. How?

- By including innumerable photographs which are slick and in good magazine format. Many companies, for example, even have photography contests, the results of which are published in company publications.
- By including advertisements of company products. Some publications include the very advertisements found in popular periodicals—amid required financial data.
- By showing pictures of employees at work, in a desirable environment. Hence employee documents and public reports may be used for recruiting purposes, as witness the reports and publications available in college placement offices.
- By combining public relations with financial data. Unwise is the company which does not try to promote its wares and personnel in a widely distributed document. It is reported that some companies divide costs of the annual report between the financial and public relations areas.
- By following a central theme. Major cover stories pervade an entire document, along with pictures that support that theme.

We as business communicators welcome stylistic changes that improve clarity of words, permitting laypersons other than financial analysts to comprehend an annual report. Consequently the humor in the 1980 spoof of *The Barrel-Proof Co.* by National Distillers and Chemical Corporation, the 1980 annual report of the Delta Drilling Company, complete with cartoons, or the 1975 Orange Bowl Annual Report, with horns, champagne glass, and streamers, makes for informative and interesting reading. Casualness, as exemplified by the delightful pictures of the board of directors of the American Crystal Sugar Company sitting in tractors or kneeling in a grain field, along with prose that is clear, correct, and concise, reflect the new sense of creativity. Likewise strikingly interesting is the publication *Round Robins International* by A. H. Robins, in English, French, German, and Spanish.

IMPLICATIONS FOR BUSINESS COMMUNICATORS

Forty-five thousand employees suggested (in the 1981 survey report by Gildea and others) that they were interested in more substantive topics than were normally found in employee publications. That such topics are being included is seen in both annual reports and employee publications. For you, the employee and/or manager of the future, there are these implications:

1. You will—perhaps on occasion—be asked to contribute material beyond your area of expertise.
2. You may have to do research on topics of social concern beyond your functional competence and relate those topics to your competence.
3. You may be asked to speak, to participate in discussions, to represent the company to the public on social topics—sometimes also business-related public or political issues—which society is interested in.
4. You may be required to provide feedback, in employee meetings or via questionnaires, in response to company policies or directives.
5. You may wish, or be asked, to contribute an article for a publication on a topic of social concern that represents your point of view.

Letters, memorandums, proposals, reports, and speeches will still be your main means of communication. But as a good communicator you will be able to contribute information beyond the usual, by being effective in representing yourself and your company to the public.

SUMMARY

Beginning in the 1960s society demanded that business communicate externally and internally on topics suggesting the social impact of doing business.

Major social themes, for both external and internal communication, include environment, fair business practices, personnel, community involvement, products, and energy.

Annual reports, employee meetings, special reports, speeches, letters, and magazines, newsletters, and newspapers continue to be the usual methods of communicating with employees or the public. To reach wider public audiences another method is through speeches on radio or television or at various public meetings.

EXERCISES

1. Look at an annual report of a major corporation. Note these usual parts: Letter to Shareholders by either the CEO or the president, or both; Financial Highlights; Report on Operations; Selected Financial Data; Consolidated Financial Statements; Notes to Consolidated Financial Statements; and Notes of Certified Public Accountants. Headings in other reports will be similar.

   Either within a group or as an individual assignment, complete the following on the basis of an annual report adapted to the employees:

   a. Write a brief letter to employees (instead of to stockholders) of that corporation.
   b. Condense the annual report using similar headings or new ones of your choosing.

2. Assume you are an employee in a functional area of an organization. Your expertise is the area of marketing, finance, accounting, or whatever. But your superior knows you have an interest in topics of social concern. Your supervisor gives you this assignment: write a statement which represents your view on one of the following topics, either informative or persuasive.

   a. Air pollution
   b. Water pollution
   c. Nuclear power
   d. Ethics in business
   e. Product safety
   f. Business and the community
   g. Needs of the community
   h. Improving health and safety of the employee
   i. Special interest groups
   j. Or others . . .

   Your statement will appear in a regular employee newsletter with your signature, and represents your personal view.

3. Choose any five annual reports. It is better if your choice involves reports from different industries. Then write or present orally a brief report on this topic: ''Possible Audiences for the Annual Report.'' As you prepare your paper, keep these questions in mind for each of the five annual reports:

   What evidence is there that the report goes beyond the immediate stockholder?

   What does the company do to suggest that the products are acceptable to the public?

CHAPTER 24
Intercultural Communication

Your chances for foreign travel or overseas work are increasing. Even small companies export goods abroad. Their salespersons, marketing managers, and strategic planners are in evidence throughout the world. The President's Commission on Foreign Language and International Studies found that 6,000 American companies have overseas operations; 20,000 American concerns export products or services to foreign markets.[1]

Another recent study suggests that nearly 21 percent of 1,661 career executives have spent time overseas.[2] Working and communicating in another culture is not easy, as these three quotations suggest:

> . . . A few American companies have attempted to take their uniquely American approach to management and transplant it in Japan. Without exception, every attempt has been a complete and total disaster.[3]

> Ethnocentrism . . . a habitual disposition to judge foreign peoples or groups by the standards and practices of one's own culture or ethnic group. A tendency toward viewing alien cultures with disfavor and the resulting sense of inherent superiority.[4]

> You've got a choice: either you go back with me or I return home alone. (*Statement of some spouses*)

This chapter introduces you to basic ideas you need for overseas work. It discusses two topics:

Some cultural variables you face when working abroad

Suggestions to prepare yourself for overseas work

CULTURAL VARIABLES

What is your concept of time? What is your concept of space? Food? Acceptable dress? Language? Religion? Manners? Decision making? Education? Politics, economics, ethics? Values and norms? People of other nations may have some similar and some very different concepts, as the following examples indicate.

---

[1] *Strength through Wisdom: A Critique of Capability/A Report to the President* from the President's Commission on Foreign Language and International Studies, Government Printing Office, Washington, D.C., 1979, p. 125.
[2] Floyd A. Bond, Herbert W. Hildebrandt, Edwin L. Miller, and Alfred W. Swinyard, *The Newly Promoted Executive: A Study in Corporate Leadership,* University of Michigan, Ann Arbor, 1982, p. 12.
[3] William Ouchi, *Theory Z,* Addison-Wesley, Reading, Mass., 1981, p. 14.
[4] Webster's *Third New International Dictionary of the English Language,* unabridged, G & C Merriam, Springfield, Mass., 1971.

Concepts of Time

Persons in Latin America and the Middle East treat time more casually than do Americans, who usually prefer promptness. Germans are time-precise; rarely do you wait for an appointment in Germany. In Latin-America—and Buddhist cultures—you may wait an hour, your host not showing disrespect thereby, just having a different concept of time; arriving late is a socially accepted custom. In some cultures businesspeople take afternoon naps, close shops, and postpone times for business meetings and dinner. Some countries speak of the rainy and the dry season; Americans think of spring, summer, fall, winter.

Concepts of Space

How close may people approach before you feel uncomfortable? A foot, two feet, five feet? Most Americans feel uncomfortable if a stranger comes closer than 18 inches; comfortable at 5 feet. How will you react in Saudia Arabia when someone's breath brushes you in conversation? How will you feel crowded into a train in Japan or India where you are so close you cannot fall down?

Americans demand more room; we need a larger territory around us. Our cone of space varies from person to person—family members to complete strangers—but for some cultures physical closeness to the message receiver is entirely appropriate.

Concepts of Food

Young American students visiting Hong Kong, Tokyo, or Paris, for example, rush off to the ubiquitous McDonald's, to the chagrin of the nationals. Off the beaten path or in many communities of the world, food, its preparation, its meat cuts, its cleanliness will vary. Pork is forbidden in Middle East countries; beef is hard to find in India; veal is plentiful in Europe; rice is ever-present in Hong Kong.

In the Far East tea is a national drink—they also have good beer—while in Europe workers enjoy a glass of wine with lunch, often a stated codicil in a labor contract. Cheese may be dessert in France, part of a sandwich in Denmark, or an hors d'oeuvre in Germany. Your palate must adapt as well as your view of time and space.

Concepts of Acceptable Dress

The Western business suit for males and dresses or suits for women are the common uniform for doing business. The British businessman may wear a bowler along with a dark suit and an umbrella.

Ask foreign students what is the dress of American students and they respond "jeans." But with the worldwide market for jeans the youth culture has taken hold overseas as well.

In the Middle East long cotton coats are acceptable. In some situations you may see the Hawaiian muu muu, the Polynesian sarong, the Japanese kimono, or the Iranian chador.

Concepts of Language

English is a world language—and to some extent the language of business. *But* you will do a better job overseas if at a minimum you know some basic vocabulary of your host country. Your informal contacts and your off-the-road visits and travels will take you to places where ''no speak the English'' will be heard. Younger people overseas know English; fewer older people do. Yet interpersonal bonds are forged between yourself and your hosts by your trying to learn the language—with all your errors. Each language has its own sentence patterns and vocabulary. In addition, gestures are often important nonverbal communicators.[5]

Concepts of Religion

You could, with some class discussion, arrive at the similarities among the Protestant, Catholic, and Jewish faiths. All three religions are found abroad— sometimes in the minority. Also Shintoism, Buddhism, Hinduism, and the Moslem religion are found in many parts of the world, affecting values (and attire) of the people who profess these faiths. Know the religion of your host country.

Concepts of Manners

Some cultural anthropologists suggest you should observe children in foreign cultures, for by watching them you learn the behavioral habits of elders. Children shake your hand in Germany; hug you in Italy; are often in the background in India. In fact, the ritual of the greeting and the farewell is more formal overseas with adults and with children. You bring a gift when visiting most homes in Europe, or in Japan. If you bring flowers, you avoid gifts of red roses in Germany, white chrysanthemums in France, Belgium, and Japan. Knowing the manners of a country means a two- to three-hour lunch in Europe is acceptable, if you can call up your patience.

In Saudia Arabia you will learn that sons defer to their fathers; that age is paramount; that a junior prince is silent when a senior enters. At the heart of their system is the family, the House of Saud. To know even these cultural manners is to begin understanding this developing giant in the Middle East.

---

[5] Desmond Morris et al., *Gestures: Their Origins and Distribution,* Stein and Day, New York, 1979. The book researches nonverbal gestures in foreign countries, for better understanding on the part of employees going abroad.

Concepts of Decision Making

Americans are accused of being brusk; we wish to get to the point—fast. "Getting down to business" is a trait of our Western culture. The Germans, Swiss, Dutch, and Scandinavians are similar, quickly getting to the issue. The Italians, French, and British prefer more leisurely social amenities.

When one reaches Japan, decision time is held back as group consensus moves you toward a decision. Participation, by many people, is the touchstone. You can imagine that much time, therefore, is spent in reaching an answer. That is what frustrates Americans; that is where we throw up our hands. Unhappily, we do not try to understand that for the Japanese the system of participative decision making works, that the *ringi* process (stamps of approval by many people on a proposal) means underlying agreement is obtained in advance of beginning an action.

Thus patience, inside a business environment and within a foreigner's home, is demanded. The song line "stop and smell the roses" may be telling us more than we realize.

Concepts of Education

Happily all of you have the opportunity to attend a college. In some European countries only the best students, with high examination scores, are admitted to college. Those are dark days when an able student is denied admittance and must select a vocation without a college education. There just is not enough room.

Japanese desire to study in the United States; so do many foreign students from around the world. But getting into the right school abroad is hard, so hard that parents in Hong Kong sign up their children in good church schools at age 3 or 4, begin teaching them early to have them pass their entrance exams—into grade school. Some young Indian students, for example, are sent away from home to private schools. Education is not so easily obtained as in the United States.

Concepts of Politics, Economics, Ethics, Values, and Norms

The list of questions is almost endless. These additional topics and suggestions under the preceding questions are but a start at understanding another culture. You may say you have problems coping with your own culture; add the foreign element and the problems are compounded. Try to learn about the foreign culture before entering a job. Study. Learn the language. Do your research.

PREPARATION FOR OVERSEAS WORK

No magic formula is available for success in foreign work. Try to learn the language, know communication differences, do some research to find all you can about the culture before entering a job.

Learn the Language

The most often heard request by foreign businesspersons is that American students should know more foreign languages. The rapport between you and your foreign colleagues increases when you attempt to speak their language. Your foreign friends will forgive your grammatical errors—perhaps one of the few times in your life—when you make attempts at communicating in their tongue.

If you are like most students you may have had one year, perhaps two, of a foreign language. Which language should you learn? Germans advise German; French suggest French; Chinese propose Cantonese; Japanese hint Japanese; and South Americans counsel Spanish. When you know in which country you will work, begin language training—not only for yourself but for other members of your family as well. Numerous private companies offer language training via cassettes or through total emersion, from 60 to 80 hours; or your company may hire a tutor to prepare you in basic language familiarity.

Obtain copies of documents and types of correspondence you will work with overseas. Take these documents to your language class and learn the form, style, and basic rudiments of what to expect. Emphasize the oral as well. The written will take more time, often demanding assistance from a bilingual secretary or assistant.

Know Communication Differences

While the letter has similarities the world over, in short and long reports differences occur. Germans have much background information, while some Chinese reports are general and vague, lacking specificity. Foreign reports are often consistent from month to month, simply having spaces for figures, giving little chance for interpretative comments. You may actually do less writing of formal reports overseas than in your home country.

Learn the rules for handling written material. For example, in the United States one signature is sufficient on letters, while in Germany some letters require two signatures, often with completely illegible names. Learn due dates for major reports. Foreign countries have more holidays than we do. You may be completing a report for your United States office on a day when everyone in the foreign country is celebrating a national event—unfamiliar, uninteresting, or unknown to you.

Of course the hardest problem will be merging your English with the language of your host country. A usual route is this: You receive a request in English from the States; it is translated into the language of your host country. Discussions on the response occur both in English and the language of your host. An answer may first be written in the foreign language, then translated into English. You may be the outsider when discussions occur in your host's language, you becoming informed only when the answer appears in your tongue. Again, knowing the basic language will improve your communication ability.

Visual aids, audio aids, and visual supports for ideas are as good overseas as in the United States; conference rooms are equipped with everything to make your oral presentation succeed. You will be more of a success if you know your host's language.

Do Some Research

Four suggestions pertain to reading, speaking with returnees, visiting the country, and asking questions.

Spend Time with Published Material

Probably your company will have a collection of material on the various countries in which it does business. Read from the general to the specific; that is, first get an overview of the country before looking at specifics. For example, know about the major goods and services before studying the monetary system in detail. The following organizations may also help on specific countries:

American Society for Training and Development
P.O. Box 5307
Madison, Wisconsin 53705

The Business Council for International Understanding
The American University
Washington, D.C. 20016

Intercultural Communications, Inc.
P.O. Box 14358
University Station
Minneapolis, Minnesota 55414

Overseas Briefing Associates
210 East 36th Street
New York, NY 10016

Additionally, these publications will provide useful information:

The Bridge, Review of Cross-Cultural Affairs and International Training, Center for Research and Education, Denver, quarterly.

Casse, Pierre, *Training for the Cross-Cultural Mind,* Society for Intercultural Education, Training and Research, Washington, D.C., 1980.

Harris, Philip R., and Robert T. Moran, *Managing Cultural Differences,* Gulf, Houston, 1979.

Kohls, Robert L., *Survival Kit for Overseas Living,* Intercultural Network, LaGrange Park, Ill., 1979.

Post Reports (for major countries), U.S. Department of State, Government Printing Office, Washington, D.C.

Terpstra, Vern, *The Cultural Environment of International Business*, South-Western, Cincinnati, 1978.

Speak with Returnees

If the persons you consult have had a positive experience, you can benefit immensely. Conversely, negative reactions can also teach: what you should avoid, how to adapt, what were the specific problems.

Visit the Country in Advance

Large multinational corporations consider money well spent sending you and your spouse overseas for a brief period. Sample the environment. It is better to know in advance that you cannot adapt rather than finding this out later— costing you and your company considerable money.

Ask Questions; Find Answers

A useful list of questions comes from Joan Wilson of the Foreign Service Institute, U.S. Department of State. Some of her queries are adapted as possible probes for thinking about overseas work:

- Who are the country's national heroes and heroines?
- What is the attitude toward gambling, drinking, dope, religion, education?
- What things are taboo in this society?
- Which colors are positive in tone? Which are negative?
- What are the special privileges of age and/or sex?
- What are the important holidays? How is each observed?
- What sports are popular?
- What is the normal work schedule? How does it accommodate to environmental or other conditions?
- How will your financial position and living conditions compare with those of the majority of people living in this country?
- What is the history of the relationship between this country and the United States?
- Where are the important universities of the country? If university education is sought abroad, to what countries and universities do students go?

SUMMARY

Your effectiveness abroad will depend on many factors, not the least being your ability to adapt. The adaptation cycle may take you several months; some never adapt. To be successful demands trying to understand the other culture with its differences and then meeting that culture at least halfway. Prepare yourself by learning the language, knowing the rules for handling written communications, and doing research to help you answer many questions pertinent to successful overseas work.

EXERCISES

1. After reviewing the definition of ethnocentrism, list examples of those values you consider significant and representative of the culture in your native country. You could use these headings and others: politics, economy, manners, higher education.

2. List what you consider to be the characteristics of the people of a country you know about or have read about. Clearly, no generalization will hold for an entire nation, but some surface qualities may appear with some consistency.

3. While numerous differences exist between cultures, there are also high degrees of commonality. One sees this commonness when comparing idioms or sayings between two cultures. We in the United States are familiar with the idioms in the left column. Match them with their Chinese counterpart in the right column.

	Familiar to U.S.	*Familiar to Chinese*
a.	It's the bad apple that spoils the barrel.	___ The head of the cow does not fit the mouth of the horse.
b.	It takes two to tango	___ It's impossible to clap with only one hand.
c.	Speak of the devil	___ Paper cannot wrap up fire.
d.	It's like building castles in the air.	___ One hair from nine oxen.
e.	You bite off more than you can chew.	___ The wood has already been used in making the boat.
f.	A drop in the bucket	___ You ride a tiger and find it hard to get off.
g.	As ye sow, so shall ye reap.	___ To dig a well only after one is thirsty.
h.	To lock the barn door after the horse is gone.	___ Like ants on top of a hot cooking pot.
i.	It's water over the dam.	___ If one plants melons, one gets melons.
j.	Where there's smoke, there's fire.	___ Like climbing a tree to catch a fish.
k.	Like comparing apples and oranges.	___ The horse that leads the herd astray.
l.	On pins and needles	___ Blow on the hair and search for tiny sores.
m.	Picky, picky, picky.	___ When you speak of Ts'ao Ts'ao, Ts'ao Ts'ao arrives.
n.	The truth will out.	___ There are no waves if there is no wind.

APPENDIXES

APPENDIX A
LEGAL ASPECTS OF YOUR BUSINESS COMMUNICATIONS

When you apply integrity, honest consideration for your reader, and the golden rule in your business communications, you should be safe in the eyes of the law. Yet as a cautious, sensible businessperson—and as a consumer—you need to realize that there are legal dangers even in some true statements. On the other hand, not all untrue words that appear to be libelous will lead to a lawsuit.

Thousands of statute laws and court decisions have been passed in the 50 states and our federal government. The laws of one state have no effect in other states, but federal laws apply throughout the country and have precedence over conflicting state laws. The U.S. Constitution is the supreme law and takes precedence over conflicting statutes passed by Congress. The right to freedom of speech versus the individual right not to be libeled have led to various legal privileges under various conditions. Furthermore, changing social and business conditions necessitate changing laws from time to time. Thus, even while books about laws are being prepared for publication, many new laws may be enacted. No single chapter or book can begin to cover even partially all specific legal interpretation applied to business communication.

The purpose of this appendix is to call to your attention some of the legal risks and complications that may occur in business communications. An overview of pertinent legal concepts should be helpful to you both as the writer and the recipient of business messages. Remember, however, that statutes in various states differ, that numerous new laws and interpretations are made from time to time, and that each legal case must be analyzed individually upon its facts. Ignorance of the law excuses no one. For advice on specific details that apply to some complicated situations, you may need a lawyer. The discussion here is necessarily a brief general introduction only; no liability is assumed for its completeness. Yet if you are aware of the risks discussed here, you can avoid harmful utterances and costly misunderstandings regarding:

- Defamation
- Invasion of privacy
- Fraud
- Some pertinent laws regarding employment, credit, and collections
- Other areas of caution

Defamation

The unconsented and unprivileged "publication" of a false and malicious statement which tends to injure one's character, fame, or reputation is *defamation*. Oral defamation is *slander*. Written defamation is a *libel*. Truth is usually an acceptable defense to a defamation suit, but there are exceptions. Also, some false statements may be either absolutely privileged or conditionally privileged. Because the words *publication* and *privilege* have important legal significance, they are discussed first; then follows a sampling of defamatory terms.[1]

Publication

In the legal sense, the unconsented intentional or negligent communication of defamatory matter to a third party is *publication*. Any means of communication by which some

---

[1] Unless otherwise footnoted, this discussion on defamation is based on Arthur B. Hanson, *Libel and Related Torts,* vol. 1, The American Newspaper Publishers Association Foundation, New York, 1969, pp. 21–195; Harold J. Grilliot, *Introduction to Law and the Legal System,* 2d ed., Houghton Mifflin, Boston, 1979, p. 501.

third party (anyone other than the person attacked) actually receives the defamatory idea can effect a publication.

If you tell Mr. X to his face privately that you consider him incompetent or a swindler, you are within your legal rights; only he has heard your statement. But if you intentionally communicate the defamatory statement to at least one other person who is not "privileged" (as defined later), you can be in serious trouble. The derogatory qualities that make a statement defamatory are the same for libel and slander. Because libelous statements are more permanent, laws pertaining to libel are more severe than those about slander. The writing (for libel) may be any permanent communication—such as a letter, postcard, telegram, circular, picture, photograph, cartoon, newspaper, recorded tape, or phonograph record.

Even a sealed letter addressed and mailed to the person you are accusing can result in actionable publication if you knew or should have known that it would be intercepted by or shown to a third person. For this reason, a letter containing unfavorable information about a person (or organization) and any collection message about pastdue payments should be mailed only in a sealed envelope and addressed so that it will be read only by the addressee. Adding the words *Personal and Confidential* or *Personal* is a good precaution. Another precaution is to use an opaque envelope and to fold the message into the envelope in such a way that it cannot be easily read when held up to a light.

Accidental communications to third persons (by eavesdroppers or unauthorized letter readers) are not actionable unless you knew of or should have foreseen such possibilities. A mere possibility that someone may have seen or overheard the statement is not enough.

Dictation to a stenographer is considered by most authorities to be a publication which is conditionally privileged with respect to matters reasonably related to the ordinary conduct of the business.

Privilege

A legal right to communicate defamatory information in certain situations is *privilege*. The privilege may be "absolute" or "conditional."

Absolute Privilege

In these three general areas absolute privilege applies: judicial proceedings, legislative proceedings, and the acts of important government officials, usually executives. The privilege is concerned with statements by and about various persons.

Defamatory Statements by Officials. Judicial officers, attorneys, and all parties participating in a judicial proceeding are absolutely privileged to make defamatory statements and to file such papers during and as part of the trial, if they bear some relationship to the matter under consideration. Letters between parties or attorneys relating to a controversy are also privileged. However, defamatory statements about a case made outside the ordinary course of a judicial proceeding, such as comments to reporters in the hallway, are not entitled to the absolute privilege for judicial proceedings.

Similarly, legislators and government officials are absolutely privileged to make defamatory statements in the performance of their official functions, but not if the statements are irrelevant to the public matter then under consideration. For example:

A member of the highway commission in New Mexico made a defamatory statement about a highway contractor at a commission meeting with reporters present. A superintendent of banks in California made libelous statements concerning his former attorney. In each case the Supreme Court of the respective state held that these public officials were protected by an absolute privilege in the exercise of their executive function. In contrast, a public official would not be absolutely privileged to defame his subordinates when publicly explaining why he dismissed them.[2]

Criticisms of "Public" Persons. The risk of liability for criticism of public persons decreased significantly in the United States after the Supreme Court decided the *New York Times* case in 1964. Under the *Times* rule, public officials cannot recover libel damages unless they prove actual malice. Criticism or comment about the public conduct or fitness for office of public officials and statements about the public conduct of other voluntary public figures are privileged even if they are based on or include erroneous material—unless there was actual knowledge of falsity or reckless disregard for whether the material was true or false. Two prongs to the rule are:

1. Inclusion of both fact and opinion within the privilege of fair comment
2. The degree of "malice" (intent to injure) necessary to defeat the privilege, constituting knowledge of falsity or reckless disregard for truth

The Supreme Court has included within the public official designation: a city commissioner; a group of parish judges; a county attorney and chief of police; an elected court clerk; a deputy sheriff (and others). The "public figure" to which the rule applies is a person "intimately involved in the resolution of important public questions" or one who by reason of his or her fame shapes events in an area of concern to society at large, and as a result, already has as much access to the mass media "both to influence policy and to counter criticism" of his or her views and activities as does a "public official." The Supreme Court has found a university athletic director and a retired army general who was actively involved in a federally enforced school integration to be within the class of public figures covered by the *Times* rule.

However, the news media have been on more uncertain ground (particularly during the decade 1972–1982) in comments on private individuals who are involved in matters of public or general concern. Increasingly, persons complaining of being libeled have convinced judges that they are not public figures.

In a 1974 case (*Gertz v. Robert Welch, Inc.*, 418 U.S. 323) the U.S. Supreme Court held that private citizens are not public figures unless they have achieved general fame or notoriety in the community. In 1979 (*Wolston v. Reader's Digest*, 443 U.S. 157) the ruling was that to be public figures individuals must have voluntarily thrust themselves into the forefront of the public controversy. In another 1979 case it was declared that a research scientist who receives federal grants is not necessarily a public figure, even though research is of public interest. In still another libel suit the decision was that a campaign consultant to a candidate for the U.S. Senate was not a public figure.

Among private individuals who have won multi-million-dollar jury awards in libel suits was a building contractor awarded $9.2 million (later settled, reportedly for somewhat more than $1 million).

In a 1982 meeting of the American Society of Newspaper Editors, a Dow Jones lawyer warned that "megaverdicts are going to be a fact of journalistic life for years to come."[3] The media are, however, preparing better to fight back.

Conditional (Qualified) Privilege

In several kinds of situations a conditional (qualified) privilege applies when the interest of either the participants or society dictates that communication in good faith should not

---

[2] Paul P. Ashley, *Say It Safely: Legal Limits in Publishing, Radio, and Television,* University of Washington Press, Seattle, 1966, pp. 43–47.

[3] "How Media Are Fighting Back," Legal Affairs, *Business Week,* June 14, 1982.

be hampered by fear of lawsuits. Thus defamatory statements made in the ordinary commercial activity are qualifiedly privileged, whether they are interoffice messages or sent to persons outside the company, when the recipient has a lawful interest in the topic of discussion. This aspect of conditional (qualified) privilege is significant regarding recommendations of applicants.

Requested Recommendations. *The person who answers an inquiry about the performance of an employee or the credit record of a customer is obligated to take reasonable precautions that the information sent is accurate.* He or she must *avoid intentional deceit or malice.* "In a personnel report it is generally believed that the writer owes a moral duty to state what is known about a former employee. What is stated honestly and in good faith is privileged communication even if it is subsequently shown to be untrue."[4]

Thus whenever you send requested information to an inquirer (prospective employer or creditor, for instance, who might suffer a loss if he or she employs or lends to an unworthy applicant), make every effort to *tell the truth and to reply in good faith without malice.* If a respondent intentionally or carelessly misleads the inquirer who seeks information about another person (for instance, a job or credit applicant), he or she may be sued for damages. The reply should neither mislead the recipient into hiring or lending to an unworthy applicant nor maliciously deprive a worthy applicant from being considered fairly for employment or credit.

Writing letters of recommendation is a serious responsibility. A failure of true candor resulted in a highly publicized court trial after a hospital hired a physician who had been praised in four glowing recommendation letters by his senior colleagues. They neglected to mention job-related legal difficulties (concerning rape and assaults of patients). In the words of a respected pediatrician, "If the person you recommend doesn't measure up, your future credibility is zero."[5]

When the truth about an individual or an organization is unfavorable and directly related to a question you are asked to answer, try as much as possible to protect the good name of the one involved. Also indicate in your reply that the information was *requested* and ask that it be kept *confidential*, if possible. Remember, however, that under public disclosure laws some information cannot be kept confidential.

Some employers have been reluctant to state unfavorable but true and relevant information about an employee because they fear facing a lawsuit threatened (or implied) by the applicant. Nevertheless, the prevailing view is that the employer's right to freely express his or her opinion should not be restricted by another person's insinuations. If an employee threatens legal action in an attempt to restrain an employer from stating or committing to writing what is true, the threat is a baseless attempt to intimidate. An employer certainly can state "It is my opinion that the employee has failed to live up to the quality of work we require at this institution. We have certain standards and we feel he (or she) did not meet those standards." It is necessary, of course, to specify what the expected standards are and to have records and documentation which will support the statements made.[6]

When you *request* someone *to send you information* about another person, show in your letter that you have an interest to protect and promise to keep the received information confidential if this is permissible. Also, to receive all the important facts you need, it may be advisable to include a question like, "Do you have any other information (or . . . know of any personal habits) that might help or hinder this applicant's success in the position for which we are considering her (or him)?" Such statements help protect the informer against a libel suit.

[4] Iris I. Varner and Carson H. Varner, Jr., "Business Communications and the Law," presented at the International Convention of the American Business Communication Association, Atlanta, Dec. 28, 1978, pp. 7 and 8; reviewed Dec. 1, 1982.
[5] "Importance of Being Frank," *Newsweek,* Oct. 5, 1981, p. 87.
[6] S. G. Tenney, Assistant Attorney General, University of Washington, interview, Nov. 29, 1982.

Unsolicited Information in Recommendations. *Is it illegal to provide unsolicited information* in a personnel report (or recommendation letter)? No, but in this case the standard for truth is higher. Dr. Carson Varner has presented the following example:

> Suppose you are writing a recommendation for an employee who has worked as a janitor and is applying for a job as bank teller. The inquiry to which you are responding is: "How has the candidate been as an employee?" You know the janitor has been in jail, and it is generally believed the janitor was convicted twice for embezzlement, and you write this in your recommendation. Suppose it turns out the janitor has been in jail for involuntary manslaughter not embezzlement (the distinction might be critical for a bank job) and the janitor sued you for libel. Normally, the recommendation is privileged, but does it apply here? Here you were only asked to comment on the janitor's performance on the job and not about the background; therefore the information is not privileged, but subject to another standard.
>
> Were you careless or negligent in stating what you knew? If so, you could be held liable for damages caused. On the other hand, let us assume the janitor had started the rumor or everyone had believed it for years and the janitor had made no attempt to correct the rumor. In this case the jury could find you were not careless in your statement and therefore not liable.[7]

In summary, if one responds to an inquiry, one should basically have no fear of saying what one knows or adding relevant information in good faith. The response to such an inquiry is qualifiedly privileged, and truth is generally an adequate defense. But if one speaks or writes maliciously (for example, because of a desire for personal gain against a competitor or to hold an applicant up for ridicule), one may be held liable in any case. Privilege does not extend to defamatory statements unrelated to the purpose of the particular privilege (as, for instance, defamatory remarks not relevant to job qualifications). Also, the former employer may lose the privilege if the response uses such violent or abusive language that the real motive in the reply is evidence of malice or some other improper purpose. Furthermore, if the former employer knows the statement is false, clearly the privilege is defeated. If he or she is negligent or unreasonable in believing it to be true, jurisdictions differ as to whether the privilege is lost.

Privilege does not apply to unreasonable disclosure and publication of particulars concerning a debtor to his or her employer, relatives, and to the public by such devices as "deadbeat lists" or obvious communications forms which may be read by others who have not requested the information and have no immediate need of it.

Defamatory Terms

Among the terms that have been judged libelous, the following are a representative (but incomplete) sampling of words to be avoided or used with caution when you refer to a person or an organization:

bankrupt	drug addict	incompetent	quack
blackmailer	faker	inferior	racketeer
Communist	falsified	insolvent	shyster
corrupt	forger	kickbacks	swindler
crook	fraud (fradulent)	misappropriation	thief
deadbeat	gouged money	misconduct	unchaste
dishonest	grafter	misrepresentation	unworthy of credit
disreputable	hypocrite	profiteer	worthless

[7] Varner and Varner, *Business Communications and the Law,* pp. 7–10.

Some statements are defamatory because they malign a characteristic necessary in a person's work (provided the occupation is legal). Thus, in most jurisdictions, it is defamatory to impugn the financial responsibility of a merchant, but not of a teacher, because ability to obtain credit is essential only to the merchant. Also it has been held defamatory to attribute communist sympathies to a public official, but not to an engineer. And, as already discussed, it is defamatory to impugn the competence of an employee to perform duties required by his or her job. But such statements may be conditionally privileged if made in the ordinary course of business activity, as discussed above under Privilege.

The truth is usually adequate defense in a libel suit, especially if there is no evidence of malice. But if the writer cannot prove his or her unprivileged statements to be true or prove that there was adequate reason for writing them, he or she may have to pay large money damages.[8]

Invasion of Privacy

The unconsented, unprivileged, and unreasonable intrusion into the private life of an individual is *invasion of privacy*. Unlike defamation, privacy can be violated although no publication to third persons takes place and even though the matters delved into are true or not particularly harmful to reputation. The concept of right of privacy is analogous to that of trespass, which gives one the right to keep unwarranted intruders off one's land not because of any resulting emotional distress or loss of rents, but merely to ensure the solitude of landowners. Though the boundaries in this concept have not been definitely determined, its primary concern is the protection of a mental interest—such as freedom from mental anguish resulting from invasion of one's privacy.[9]

This section discusses two aspects of invasion of privacy: use of a person's identity without permission; and physical surveillance of records, reports, and letters by persons not entitled to examine them.

Use of a Person's Identity

If a person's name, photograph, or other identity is used without permission on a sales letter or advertisement (or other permanent publication—not word of mouth), that person may have cause for legal action because his or her right of privacy has been violated.

Recovery and monetary awards have also been granted for publication of x-rays and other medical pictures, for pictures of a deformed infant, and for undue publicity of a delinquent debt.

Furthermore, the personal information customers are required to give when they apply for credit, insurance, medical care, or a job should be accurate and kept confidential. Unfortunately, in some cases the data collection methods result in incorrect, misleading, unfounded, or outdated information. (Some private investigating agencies gather information by questioning neighbors, landlords, and friends about lifestyles, health, and traits of applicants.) Some individuals who have been turned down on their application have found it necessary to sue when they discovered that incorrect personal information about them was filed (perhaps computerized) by a firm and then passed on to other firms without the customers' knowledge or permission. Customers should have the right to privacy.

Yet, not every use of another's likeness or identity is actionable. In some states it must be unreasonable under the circumstances, as well as unprivileged. Using pictures of an all-American football team on a beer company's calendar which also contained

---

[8] Philip Wittenberg, *Dangerous Words: A Guide to the Law of Libel,* Columbia University Press, New York, 1947, pp. 282-308.
[9] Hanson, *Libel and Related Torts,* pp. 197-206.

advertising was held (in one case) not to be an invasion of team members' privacy, because they were public figures and there was no false implication of endorsement. But using a person's picture to illustrate a story about dishonest tactics of cab drivers would shed false and unfavorable imputation on the person and would be an invasion of privacy.

Unreasonable publicity of private life may also result in legal action and costly money awards to the offended person, as in these two cases:

> A former prostitute and the acquitted defendant in a notorious murder trial had reformed, married, and pursued a respectable life in a new community which knew nothing about her former life until the defendant revealed the whole story in a movie, using her name. She was allowed a cause of action for publication of these true but embarrassing personal facts.[10]

> In the "pink letter case" a suggestive letter bearing a woman's signature was mailed to 1,000 men. Handwritten in a feminine hand, the letter was mechanically reproduced on pink stationery and mailed by a mailing agency. The name signed to the letter was that of the principal character in a motion picture the letter was advertising. Unfortunately, it also turned out to be the name of a woman living in Los Angeles—the only person by that name listed in the City Directory or the telephone directory. When the letters began arriving (in hand-addressed, pink envelopes), many wives must have looked at their husbands with a quizzical eye. But it was worse for the plaintiff, who began getting telephone calls from the men. She also worried for fear that some irate wife might shoot her—for the letter invited the men to meet the signer in front of a certain theater on a certain day and to look for a girl "with a gleam in her eye, a smile on her lips and mischief on her mind." The court felt that the plaintiff should be compensated for invasion of right of privacy.[11]

If you wish to use the picture or identity of an individual for your advertising or sales letters, for instance, be sure first to get previous consent and make clear just how the picture or identity is to be used. An individual may have indicated consent by willingly posing for a photograph, but alteration of the photograph or using it in a way to carry objectionable implications is an invasion of privacy. Photographers should carry releases (permission to use photos) in their camera case so that on-the-spot permission may be obtained.

Physical Surveillance of Records, Reports, and Letters

The right of privacy may also be violated if records, reports, and letters are read by persons not entitled to examine them.

Powerful binoculars, long-range telephoto cameras, and "zoomer"-type television cameras have been used effectively (and illegally) in recent years to look through windows at important papers lying face-up on desks, at models of new products and designs, and at charts displayed at conferences. These techniques have become so common in certain areas of industrial espionage that elaborate security precautions are taken to keep designs and models in windowless rooms and to keep blinds drawn at all times in certain offices.

Modern technology has added to these existing situations the possibility of passing visible light or reflected infrared energy through an envelope and taking pictures of the contents. These pictures can then be read (deciphered) by persons skilled in reading handwriting or typing where lines are inverted or superimposed. Also available is a

---

[10] Hanson, *Libel and Related Torts*, p. 203.
[11] Kenneth and Irene Donelson, *When You Need a Lawyer*, Doubleday, Garden City, N.Y., 1964, pp. 245–249.

needle-thin "flashlight" that can be inserted in a sealed envelope to "light it up" for quick reading by a trained investigator. You can help to greatly reduce or even prevent this type of surveillance by using—when desirable on certain very confidential material—envelopes with a random pattern inside them to make them opaque and/or inserting more than one sheet of paper in them.[12]

Fraud

The intentional misrepresentation by one party to a contract of a material existing fact which is relied upon by the other party to her or his injury is *fraud*. Both as a seller and a buyer you need to be aware of the elements of fraud as well as the significance of warranties so that you can better detect and avoid fraudulent practices.

Elements

Fraud in the law of contracts requires that the party alleging it prove these elements:

1. A *misstatement* was made with the *intent* to deceive.
2. The misrepresentation was of a *material existing fact*.
3. The deceived person was justified in *relying* on the statement.
4. This person was *damaged* (in the legal sense) by the false statement.

If the misstatement was innocent misrepresentation, the victim may rescind the contract.

The misrepresentation need not be a direct falsehood for fraud to be present. In fact, failing to reveal defects or confirming false impressions by remaining silent can be sufficient. Any physical act intended to conceal true facts is in effect a misstatement. For example, a seller who sets back the mileage on a car conceals an important fact and asserts an untruth as effectively as if she or he were speaking. To be actionable fraud (for lawsuit), the misrepresentation must be of a *material* fact. False statements of opinion or of conditions to exist in the future do not constitute fraud. Before a false statement can be considered fraudulent, the person to whom it was made must reasonably believe it to be true and rely on the statement to his or her damage (injury). If he or she investigates before entering into the contract, and the falsity is revealed, no fraud exists.

Section 5 of the Federal Trade Commission (FTC) Act as amended, outlaws practices which deceive or are otherwise unfair to consumers. Included are (among others) false advertising regarding prices, performance capability, quality, and character of goods or services. Also included are endorsements by persons misrepresented as "experts" or "doctors," and many other misstatements intended to deceive.[13] A test for fraud is to ask, "Would the other party have entered into the contract had he or she known the truth?"

Warranties

In most sales contracts the seller undertakes certain obligations concerning the nature, title, and quality of the goods being sold. When these obligations are expressly stated or implied and when they actually induce the sale, the obligations are called *warranties*.

[12] Alan F. Westin, *Privacy and Freedom,* Atheneum, New York, 1967, pp. 78–79. Copyright 1967 by The Association of the Bar of the City of New York. Reprinted by permission of Atheneum publishers, USA.
[13] Robert N. Corley, Robert L. Black, O. Lee Reed, *The Legal Environment of Business,* 4th ed., McGraw-Hill, New York, 1977, pp. 515–520, and Michael P. Litka, *Business Law,* Harcourt Brace Jovanovich, New York, 1970, pp. 152–153.

They are guarantees by the seller with respect to the goods sold. Warranties may be "express" or "implied."

An *express warranty* affirms a fact or a promise the seller made to the buyer in bargaining concerning the nature of the goods—description, grade, or model. Such a promise becomes a basis for the contract even though the term *warranty* or *guaranty* is not used.

Implied warranties are considered part of the bargain even though the parties themselves say nothing about them. For instance, the seller warrants that he or she is conveying a good title to the goods. Also, under the Uniform Commercial Code (adopted by all 50 states) if the seller is a merchant with respect to goods of that kind, he or she warrants that the goods are salable and are fit for the ordinary purposes for which such goods are used. If the seller knows the buyer intends the goods for a particular purpose and that the buyer is relying on the seller's judgment as to their suitability, there is an implied warranty of fitness for that particular purpose.

The federal law on warranties (enacted in 1975) requires that warranties on products costing $5 or more must disclose the warranty terms in simple and readily understood language. For products costing over $15 the warranty must be labeled "full" or "limited." "Full warranty" products must be repaired or replaced by the seller without charge within a reasonable time if there is a defect. If a warranty is limited, the limitation must be conspicuous so that buyers are not misled. Since passage of the new law, many sellers have chosen the limited warranty. Some have even eliminated their warranty entirely, rather than become involved with all the law's requirements.[14]

Mail Frauds

According to the U.S. Postmaster General, in the Post Office Department's informative booklet *Mail Fraud Laws,* fraudulent schemes sent through the mail are costing American consumers an estimated $500 million a year. Among the many dishonest practices to trap the unsuspecting consumer are: fake contests, home improvement offers, auto insurance frauds, charity appeals, missing heir schemes, fake business opportunities, worthless medical cures, and fake correspondence-school programs promising "exciting, high-paying jobs."

The U.S. Chief Postal Inspector lists the following ways you can help enforce mail fraud laws:

> To stop a dishonest scheme, inspectors must find that you and others buying a product or service were cheated as a result of claims the seller made in an intentional effort to defraud. Mail fraud violations occur when a general scheme or pattern of fraud exists.
>
> When you believe mail fraud exists, hold all letters, including envelopes and other evidence related to the questionable scheme. See if your neighbors or business associates have also received similar material.
>
> Bring such information to the attention of a postal inspector in your area by contacting him directly or through your postmaster.
>
> Inspectors cannot investigate a case simply to force a supplier to speed up deliveries, obtain refunds, or to otherwise act as an intermediary in settling unsatisfactory transactions. In such instances the dissatisfied buyer should:
>
> Seek an adjustment or settlement with the seller.

[14] Corley, Black, and Reed, *The Legal Environment of Business,* pp. 524–528.

Bring his complaint to the attention of the Better Business Bureau, Chamber of Commerce, Trade Association, or publication which carried the ad.

Seek relief through civil suit if a breach of contract may be involved.[15]

Most states now have consumer protection divisions in the Attorney General's office, and they can be very helpful too.

Some Pertinent Laws regarding Employment, Credit, and Collections

Here are some of the acts that affect business communications in various ways.

Employment—and Preemployment Inquiries

Title VII of the Civil Rights Act of 1964, with amendments in 1972 and 1978, prohibits discrimination in employment as to hiring, firing, compensation, termination, and conditions or privileges of employment on the basis of *race, color, religion, sex,* or *national origin.* (Exceptions are allowed in some businesses or enterprises—such as church organizations, modeling agencies, entertainment producers—when religion, sex, or national origin may be bona fide occupational qualifications necessary for normal operations.)

The law forbids discrimination, *not* the asking of certain questions. But some questions may be unfair or risky to ask because they appear to be for the purpose of discriminating, and in fact do discriminate. They might later be the basis for legal action. Even if an employer wins the court case, the damage in public relations may be extremely serious. Thus many firms have policy guidelines with narrow rules on what recruiters may or may not do when interviewing.[16]

The following list of general suggestions for fair and unfair preemployment inquiries[17] meets the federal *Uniform Guidelines on Employee Selection Procedures.* Some states, as well as cities and counties, may have stricter regulations regarding a few of the preemployment inquiries. Thus, because of variations, it is advisable to check your own local and state laws or consult a counselor when in doubt.

Subject	Fair Preemployment Inquiries	Unfair Preemployment Inquiries
a. Age	Inquiries as to birthdate are permitted in some states; in others, only whether applicant is of legal age.	Any inquiry which implies discrimination (without job-related justification).
b. Arrests (See also Convictions)	None.	All inquiries relating to arrests.

[15] *Mail Fraud Laws: Protecting Consumers, Investors, Businessmen, Medical Patients, Students,* U.S. Post Office Department, Washington, D.C., June 1969.

[16] Varner and Varner, *Business Communications and the Law,* pp. 9–11.

[17] Excerpts from *Pre-employment Inquiries and Screening,* Washington State Human Rights Commission, July 1977 and November 1982.

Subject	Fair Preemployment Inquiries	Unfair Preemployment Inquiries
c. Citizenship	Whether applicant is prevented from lawfully becoming employed in this country because of visa or immigration status. Whether applicant can provide proof of citizenship, visa, or alien registration number after being hired.	Requirement before hiring to present birth certificate, naturalization, or baptismal record. Any inquiry which would divulge lineage, ancestry, national origin, descent, or birthplace.
d. Convictions (See also Arrests)	Inquiries concerning specified convictions that relate reasonably to fitness to perform particular job being applied for, provided that such inquiries be limited to convictions for which date of conviction or of prison release is within seven years of job application date.	Inquiries that would divulge convictions which (a) do not relate reasonably to fitness to perform the particular job or (b) do not relate solely to convictions for which date of conviction or of prison release is within seven years of job application date.
e. Family	Whether applicant can meet specified work schedules or has activities, commitments, or responsibilities that may prevent meeting work attendance requirements.	Specific inquiries concerning spouse, spouse's employment or salary, children, child care arrangements, or dependents.
f. Handicap	Whether applicant has certain specified sensory, mental, or physical handicaps that relate reasonably to fitness to perform particular job. Whether applicant has any handicaps or health problems that may affect work performance or that employer should take into account in determining job placement.	Any inquiry which is not based on actual job requirements.
g. Height and Weight	Inquiries as to ability to perform actual job requirements. Being of a certain height or weight will not be considered to be a job requirement unless the employer can show that no employee with the ineligible height or weight could do the work.	Any inquiry which is not based on actual job requirements.
h. Marital Status (See also Name and Family)	None.	Whether applicant is married, single, divorced, separated, engaged, widowed, etc.; whether Mr., Mrs., Miss, Ms.

Subject	Fair Preemployment Inquiries	Unfair Preemployment Inquiries
i. Military	Inquiries concerning education, training, or work experience in the armed forces of the United States.	Type or condition of military discharge. Experience in other than U.S. armed forces. Request for discharge papers.
j. Name	Whether applicant worked for this firm or a competitor under a different name; if so, what name. Name under which applicant is known to references if different from present name.	Inquiry into original name where it has been changed by court order or marriage. Inquiries about name that would divulge marital status, lineage, ancestry, national origin.
k. National Origin	Inquiries into applicant's ability to read, write, and speak foreign languages, when such inquiries are based on job requirements.	Inquiries into applicant's lineage, ancestry, national origin, descent, birthplace, or mother tongue. National origin of parents or spouse.
l. Organizations	Inquiry into organization memberships, excluding any organization the name or character of which indicates race, color, creed, sex, marital status, religion, or national origin or ancestry.	Requirement that applicant list all organizations, clubs, societies, and lodges to which he or she belongs.
m. Photographs	May be requested *after* hiring for identification purposes.	Request that applicant submit photo, mandatorily or optionally before hiring.
n. Pregnancy (See also Handicap)	Inquiries as to duration of stay on job or anticipated absences which are made to males and females alike.	All questions as to pregnancy, and medical history concerning pregnancy and related matters.
o. Race or Color	None.	Any inquiry concerning race or color of skin, hair, eyes, etc.
p. Relatives	Names of relatives already employed by this company or by any competitor.	Names and addresses of any relative other than those listed as proper.
q. Religion or Creed	None.	Inquiries about applicant's religious denomination or affiliations, church, pastor, parish, religious holidays.
r. Residence	Inquiries about address to the extent needed to facilitate contacting the applicant.	Names or relationship of persons with whom applicant resides. Whether applicant owns or rents home.
s. Sex	None.	Any inquiry.

Credit and Collections

Because of the widespread use of credit by consumers, the federal government and the states have enacted a series of laws to protect consumers and try to assure that they are treated fairly in credit transactions. Because state statutes vary, you will need to investigate those in your state. Space here allows only a brief introduction to some of the federal laws. They are detailed in the United States Statutes at Large. (Volume and page numbers are in parentheses after each act described below.)

Equal Credit Opportunity Act requires that financial institutions and other firms engaged in credit extension make that credit equally available to all creditworthy customers without regard to sex or marital status. Subsequent amendments have extended the act's protection to all persons regardless of race, color, religion, national origin, or age. The credit extenders have certain rights to make necessary inquiries for determining credit worthiness. (88:1521-5) (1974)

Fair Credit Billing Act aims to protect the consumer against inaccurate and unfair credit card practices. The act specifies procedures for consumers to challenge any charge-account statements they believe are incorrect. It states procedures for creditors regarding acknowledging, investigating, problem solving, account closing, collecting, and reporting debtors to credit-rating offices. It includes penalties for creditors that don't conform to the rules. Creditors must send to customers printed instructions twice a year explaining the procedures. (88:1511-17) (1974)

Fair Credit Reporting Act requires that consumer reporting agencies (credit bureaus; investigative, detective, and collection agencies; computerized information-reporting firms; lenders' exchanges) adopt impartial, fair procedures for meeting the needs of consumers regarding consumer credit, personnel, insurance, and other information. It specifies guidelines with regard to confidentiality, accuracy, relevancy, and proper use of such information. It stipulates the circumstances under which consumer reporting agencies may furnish consumer reports, the type of information they may and may not furnish, and the requirements for disclosing to the consumers the substance and sources of information as well as for reinvestigating to correct disputed information or errors. (84:1114-16) (1970)

Fair Debt Collection Practices Act states what bill collectors (other than creditors and attorneys) can and cannot do. In the collection of debts or in attempts to collect any claim alleged to be due or owing, the collector should not unreasonably oppress, harass, abuse, or intentionally cause mental distress to any person. Harassment and abuse include abusive language, anonymous or repeated telephone calls at odd hours, anonymous c.o.d. communications, or any that look like messages from a credit bureau, government agency, or court summons. (91:874) (1978)

Federal Truth in Lending Act aims to assure meaningful disclosure of credit terms so that consumers will be able to compare more readily the charges by different credit sources. It requires lenders and creditors to disclose the terms, conditions, finance charges, and service or carrying charges (including annual percentage rate) before a consumer signs a contract. It also gives a consumer the right to rescind within three business days after signing a contract that will result in a security interest being acquired in his or her residence. If the transaction is rescinded, the borrower (consumer) has no liability for any finance charge. (82:146-158) (1968)

Other Areas of Caution in Business Communications

Noteworthy also are a few highlights regarding some mailed items, and cautions on copying of documents and copyrighted material.

Unmailable Materials and Unordered Items

Suggestions on how you can help enforce mail fraud laws are listed under Fraud, in this chapter. Among the many other *unmailable materials* that may violate United States postal laws are letters and printed matter concerning lotteries, obscene literature, extortion threats, and solicitation of illegal business. Space does not permit discussion of these items here. You can obtain booklets on most of these subjects through your local postmaster or the U.S. Government Printing Office, Washington, D.C., 20402. And if you are in doubt about the mailability of any particular material, you may submit a request to the Office of the General Counsel, Mailability Division, Post Office Department, Washington, D.C., 20260. A ruling will be furnished as promptly as circumstances permit.

The sending of *unordered merchandise* through the mail does not violate postal laws unless it is sent c.o.d. However, persons receiving such unordered items can:

If the package has not been opened, write "Return to Sender" and put it back into the mails.

If the article is not wanted, set it aside for a reasonable period of time and if unclaimed, destroy.

Treat unordered merchandise as an unconditional gift if living in a state where the laws apply.

The sending of *unsolicited credit cards* is illegal, as specified in the Consumer Credit Cost Disclosure Act.

Copied Documents

Another caution pertains to the copying of certain documents. Congress, by statute, has forbidden the copying of the following documents and items under certain circumstances: United States government obligations or securities, such as Treasury and Federal Reserve notes, National Bank currency, certificates of indebtedness, silver and gold certificates, paper money, and others; also United States savings bonds (except for campaign publicity for their sale), Internal Revenue stamps (except in copying for lawful purposes a legal document on which there is a canceled revenue stamp), postage stamps canceled or uncanceled (except for philatelic purposes, provided the reproduction is in black and white and is less than ¾ or more than 1½ times the linear dimensions of the original); postal money orders; bills, checks or drafts for money drawn by or upon authorized officers of the United States; and other representatives of value issued under any act of Congress.

Among other materials that may not be copied are certificates of citizenship or naturalization (except foreign naturalization certificates); passports (except foreign); immigration papers; obligations or securities of any foreign government, bank, or corporation; draft registration cards, selective service induction papers bearing certain information; badges, identification cards, passes or insignia carried by military, naval personnel, or members of the various federal departments and bureaus such as FBI or Treasury (except when ordered by head of such department or bureau). In some states copying auto licenses, automobile certificates of title, and drivers' licenses is also forbidden. For these items—and others not listed here—penalties of fine or imprisonment are imposed on those guilty of making illegal copies.

Copyright Material

The new U.S. Copyright Law which went into effect January 1, 1978, forbids the copying of copyrighted material without permission of the copyright owner—except for certain limited "fair use" privileges and single copies made for noncommercial purposes, as specified in the bill. It includes details about permissible uses of single or multiple copies from books, articles, essays, poems, graphs, charts, cartoons, pictures, and so on, and states when written prior permission must be obtained.

Summary

As a final caution, in general, remember to:

Be honest and fair in all your business transactions and correspondence.

Avoid any statements and acts that may be considered defamation, invasion of privacy, or fraud. When answering requests for recommendations of former employees, customers, or others, include relevant facts truthfully without malice. As a seller or buyer of merchandise, be aware of federal and state laws regarding warranties; also be aware of how to help curb fraudulent schemes sent through the mail.

Keep yourself well informed on responsibilities regarding laws pertaining to employment, credit, collections, and other areas of concern—based on both federal laws and those in your state. Recognize the importance of honest, prudent actions by yourself and your subordinates.

Consult an attorney when in doubt about the handling of any complicated situation that might involve legal risks. Each case must be analyzed individually.

Exercises

1. Choose one of the following acts (or perhaps any other related to your major field of interest). Then consult the U.S. Statutes at Large for details about that act.

   - Equal Credit Opportunity Act
   - Fair Credit Billing Act
   - Fair Credit Reporting Act
   - Fair Debt Collection Practices Act
   - Federal Truth in Lending Act
   - The new Copyright Law
   - The new Bankruptcy Act

   Prepare a short report or oral presentation with information that will be useful to your class members—and yourself.

2. The purpose of this assignment is to broaden your knowledge of guidelines for ethical practices among advertisers. You can obtain information from the Fair Practice Code of the Council of Better Business Bureaus, from the Direct Mail/Marketing Association, and from some pamphlets by the U.S. Postal Service regarding laws, regulations, and mail fraud. Write a short (two- to four-page) memo report to your instructor, stating highlights of your findings.

APPENDIX B
MECHANICS AND STYLE

Abbreviations

In business letters and reports, abbreviations are appropriate for the following titles: Mr., Mrs., Ms., Messrs. (as for a law firm of Messrs. White, Green, and Black). Other common abbreviations are: Jr., Sr., Mt. (Mount), St. (Saint), Inc. (Incorporated), Ltd. (Limited), D.C. (District of Columbia); compound directions, NW or NW. or N.W. (Northwest) with similar variations for SW, NE, SE; and the professional degree symbols such as B.B.A., Ph.D., M.D., C.P.A. The title Dr. (Doctor) is usually abbreviated, especially when the first name or the initials are used with the surname. [Some authorities suggest abbreviating "Doctor" when the first name or initials precede the surname (Dr. John Brown) but spelling it out in a salutation (Dear Doctor Brown). Businesspersons, however, feel that applying two rules is impractical, and they abbreviate "Doctor" in both situations.].

The following words should be spelled out whenever possible: *president, superintendent, honorable, reverend, professor, building, association, department*; as well as *street, boulevard, avenue, east, west, north, south*. City names should also be spelled out. It is best to use abbreviations sparingly within messages. A good rule is: "When in doubt, spell it out." However, if you are using the U.S. Post Office Department two-letter state abbreviations on envelopes, you should preferably also abbreviate the state the same way in the inside address for consistency. The Post Office recommends use of the following two-letter abbreviations—two capitals without periods or spaces.

Alabama .... AL	Louisiana .... LA	Ohio .... OH
Alaska .... AK	Maine .... ME	Oklahoma .... OK
Arizona .... AZ	Maryland .... MD	Oregon .... OR
Arkansas .... AR	Massachusetts ..... MA	Pennsylvania ...... PA
California .... CA	Michigan .... MI	Puerto Rico .... PR
Colorado .... CO	Minnesota .... MN	Rhode Island ...... RI
Connecticut .... CT	Mississippi .... MS	South Carolina ..... SC
Delaware .... DE	Missouri .... MO	South Dakota ...... SD
District of Columbia DC	Montana .... MT	Tennessee .... TN
Florida .... FL	Nebraska .... NE	Texas .... TX
Georgia .... GA	Nevada .... NV	Utah .... UT
Hawaii .... HI	New Hampshire .... NH	Vermont .... VT
Idaho .... ID	New Jersey .... NJ	Virginia .... VA
Illinois IL	New Mexico .... NM	Washington .... WA
Indiana .... IN	New York .... NY	West Virginia ...... WV
Iowa .... IA	North Carolina ..... NC	Wisconsin .... WI
Kansas .... KS	North Dakota ...... ND	Wyoming .... WY
Kentucky .... KY		

Dangling Participles

A *participle* is a word that ends in "ing" or "ed" and looks like a verb; yet it actually is an adjective that must modify a specific noun or pronoun. If it doesn't, it is called a *dangling participle*.

The three most common forms of dangling participles are caused by the writer not observing the following rules:

1. The participle should be placed close to the word to which it refers, and there should be no intervening noun to which the participle might seem to refer.

Unclear: A complete *report* is submitted by our branch office, *giving* details about this transaction. (*"Giving" is the participle; it should modify "report," but it seems to modify the intervening noun "office."*)

Clear: Our branch office submitted a complete *report, giving* details about this transaction. (*Now the participle clearly modifies "report."*)

2. A participle at the beginning of a sentence (or at the beginning of a second independent clause in a compound sentence) should refer to the subject of the sentence or independent clause.

Unclear: *Having* been boiled for the proper length of time, the *homemaker* took the shrimp off the stove. (*"Having" modifies the subject "homemaker" when the participle should modify "shrimp."*)

Clear: *Having* been boiled for the proper length of time, the *shrimp* were taken off the stove by the home- maker. (*Now "having" modifies the right word—"shrimp," which is the subject of the sentence.*)

or

After the shrimp had boiled for the proper length of time, the home- maker took them off the stove. (*This sentence discards the participle.*)

Here's a simple way to see if the participle beginning the sentence properly modifies the subject: State the subject ''shrimp'' and follow it with the participial phrase, ''having been boiled for the proper length of time.'' If the two parts give you the meaning you want, ''shrimp, having been boiled for the proper length of time,'' then the participle is modifying the right word. But if you are boiling the homemaker, something is wrong.

3. A participle following the main clause should refer to a definite noun, not to the general thought expressed by the clause.

Unclear: These accounts disappeared from the vault, thus causing us very much worry. (*Instead of modifying a particular word, "causing" modifies the entire clause that appears before the comma. Suggestion: Reword so that you don't have the participle in the sentence.*)

Clear: Because the accounts disappeared from the vault, we are very much worried.

Clear: These accounts disappeared from the vault, a fact which caused us much worry.

Exercises

Identify all dangling participles in these sentences, tell whether each one violates form 1, 2, or 3 just discussed, and then correct all errors.

1. Being an old customer, we know that you are familiar with our Christmas displays.
2. The check arrived six days late, causing me to write a collection letter.
3. Realizing our mistake, a new check was immediately sent to replace the first one.
4. Being larger and more attractive, these offices should make your work more pleasant, thus enabling you to work better.
5. Being a savings association, our customers do not have checking accounts here.
6. Please go down to the main office, and lying on the manager's desk you will find a copy of the latest report.
7. Having been run through the computer, the clerk used the figures for his report.
8. Changing your monthly loan payments, it will be necessary to get approval from the loan department.
9. Having been an outstanding keynote speaker, we can offer you this special award.
10. Enjoying 5% earnings, a savings account should be opened.

Numbers as Figures or Words

In general—use the figure instead of the word, because the reader can more easily read the figure and grasp its meaning. In invoices, tabular materials, purchase orders and the like, always use figures. In letters and reports—use the rule of 10 (spell out numbers 1 through 9; use figures for numbers 10 or higher) except for amounts of money and for isolated cases, as shown below.[1]

1. *If a sentence begins with a number, express the number in words:* This rule is used when the sentence cannot be effectively revised.

   Fifty applicants were interviewed for the position.

2. *When a number standing first in the sentence is followed by another number to form an approximation, express both in words:*

   Fifty or sixty will be enough.

   Note: Try not to begin a sentence with a number. Rewrite the sentence to place the number within or at the end of the sentence.

   The confirmation request was answered by 559 businesses.

3. *When a sentence contains one series of numbers, express all members of one series in figures.*

   We had 25 applicants from Arkansas, 15 applicants from Texas, and 6 applicants from Oklahoma.

4. *When a sentence contains two series of numbers, express the members of one series in words and those of the other series in figures:* If this rule is not followed, confusion results because of too many groups of numbers.

   Five students scored 95 points; seventeen students scored 30 points; and eleven scored 75 points.

---

[1] Most of these rules have been adopted by the Committee on Teaching Materials and Aids of the American Business Communication Association.

Three senior accountants made $100 a day; twelve semiseniors made $80 a day; and five junior accountants made $40 a day.

Note: For clarity, tabulate more than two series of numbers.

Name of Accountant	Daily Rate	Estimated Working Days	Total Estimated Earnings
Barlow, Helen	$80	3	$240
Dickinson, Al	70	2	140
Oman, Charles	80	1	80

5. *When one number immediately precedes another number of different context, express one number in words; the other, in figures:*

The specifications call for twenty-five 2 x 4's.
The deposit slip listed four 5's as the only currency.
You ordered 275 three-inch bolts.

6. *When an isolated number is below 10, express it in words.* This rule does not apply to exact dimensions or amounts of money.

The new salesperson sold eight refrigerators last month.
She hit a 6-foot pole.
This paper is 8½ inches wide.

7. *When numbers are expressed in words, as at the beginning of a sentence, use a hyphen to join the compound number, twenty-one through ninety-nine:* A compound number usually acts as a compound adjective.

Fifty-six accounts; twenty-one women; ninety-three men.

8. *When a numerical quantity contains more than four digits, each group of three digits should be set off by a comma (starting at the right).* (Obviously, this rule does *not* apply to dates, street numbers, serial numbers, and page numbers.)

1,000; 1,021; 5,280,000; 60,000; 600,000

9. *Express amounts of money in figures.* The following practices are recommended.
   a. *When an amount of money consists of dollars and cents, always express the amount in figures:* The dollar sign should precede the amount (unless in a tabulated column).

The invoice total was $5.51. The bonds were sold at $999.50.

   b. *When an amount of money consists only of dollars, omit the decimal point and the double zero:* Exceptions: (1) When the amount is tabulated in a column which includes both dollars and cents, include the double zero.

The invoice is $150. The check is for $5.

$ 250.80
200.00
312.70
286.50
$1,050.00

(2) When a series of money amounts contains mixed figures, include the double zero for consistency on all even figures.

The committee raised amounts of $15.00, $33.75, and $75.00 in the three rummage sales.

c. *When an amount of money consists only of cents, write the amount in any of the following ways:*

```
The piggy bank yielded $.57.  The piggy bank yielded 57¢.
The piggy bank yielded 57 cents.  The piggy bank yielded 9 cents.
```

d. *As a rule, do not write an amount in both figures and words. This procedure is necessary only in legal and financial documents.*

```
The check is for $7.        The total assets are $23,000.50.
```

In financial and legal papers write:

```
Ninety-five dollars ($95.00)
seven dollars ($7.00)
twenty-three and 42/100 dollars ($23.42)
twenty three dollars and forty-two cents ($23.42)
```

10. *Express the following numbers in figures, unless otherwise indicated:*
   a. *Dates:*

```
October 3, 1980
3d of October
Your letter of October 3 was most welcome.
```

b. *House or room numbers:* (except number one)

```
1503 Thomas Street
One Lenox Drive
```

c. *Numerical names of streets:*

Over 10:	315 69th Street or 315 – 69th Street (*Note two spaces or space hyphen space to separate house and street number.*)
Under 10:	2930 Third Avenue or 2930 3d* Avenue

* Many people prefer to use figures for all street numbers.

d. *Numbered items such as page numbers, chapter numbers, figure numbers, table numbers, chart numbers, serial numbers, and telephone numbers:*

```
Page 10        Table X                      Policy #V9109815
Chapter 10     Table 10                     Policy V9109815
Chapter X      Chart 10                     Claim No. 13189756
Figure 8       Chart X                      Telephone 543-1111
Fig. 8         Service Serial No. 01845283  Phone (206) 333-1111
```

e. *Decimals:*

```
10.25     3.1414     .3535
```

f. *Dimensions and exact age:*

```
8½ x 11 inches    2 x 4 inches    He is 24 years, 5 months,
8½ by 11 inches   2 by 4 inches   and 8 days old
```

g. *Time:*

```
7 A.M. (reserved for headings)   7:35 P.M. (reserved for headings)
7 a.m. (more commonly used)      7:35 p.m. (more commonly used)
seven o'clock                    seven in the morning
```

h. *Percentages*

35%	6%
99.99%	6 percent
0.09%	

i. *Fractions:*

1/32	one-half	4 3/4
3/64	two-thirds	or
25/64	one-fourth	4.75
25/100	three-fourths	1/2 or ½

Exercises

Listed below are sentences that contain numbers in the form of figures and words. If any number is used incorrectly, cross out what's wrong and add the correct usage directly above the error. Don't mark any number that is used correctly.

1. 5 policies lie on my desk.
2. Two men and 8 women work in this office.
3. The insured's car hit a 10-foot pole.
4. 10 men scored 94 points, 17 men scored 110 points, and 3 men scored 143 points.
5. May I have 100 12-inch rulers?
6. This morning I answered 17 letters.
7. You'll find the answer on page 8.
8. Mary came home at 7 o'clock.
9. She works from 8 a.m. until 5 p.m.
10. Thanks for the $50.00 loan.
11. The car hit a ten-foot pole, rolled over, and then fell down a 20-foot embankment.
12. The gate is six feet, three inches tall.
13. Your lot is 45 feet wide and one hundred thirty-two feet deep.
14. Please send the policy to 1 South Fifteenth Street.
15. Thank you for your check for twenty dollars.
16. Please buy 17 3-cent stamps.
17. The 3 items are on sale for $15, $16.95, and $20.

Punctuation Makes Sense

Punctuation is important because it helps the reader understand what you are saying. That's the whole purpose of commas, periods, dashes, and all those other little marks— to make reading easier and clearer.

Comma Is Used:

1. When you address the reader directly.

   Please let me know, Mr. Jones, when you will be in Tucson.
   I'll certainly appreciate your taking care of this assignment, John.
   Ms. Smith, that was a fine speech you gave to our group last week.

2. When you mention a person's title after his or her name or the name after the title.

   This person is Mrs. A. B. Jackson, President of Acme Company.
   Mr. Julius Roller, Jr., has done a splendid job.
   Our representative, Ms. Hall, will see you next week.

Note: You omit commas in an expression like "my brother George" when a one-word name ("George") follows the title ("brother") and you have more than one brother. If you have only one brother: "my brother, George, ..."

3. When the year follows the month and the day.

```
On October 4, 1978, I started working for this company.
```

but

```
I was born in July 1958.
```

4. When the sentence contains a series or list of more than two things or persons.

```
He raises turkeys, chickens, and geese.
Mr. Smith, Mr. Snow, and Mrs. Hull appeared in court.
```

But in the names of business firms, follow the usage of the particular firm.

```
Merrill Lynch, Pierce, Fenner & Smith, Inc.
```

5. When you can add "and" between two words that describe something.
You are an efficient, hard-working fellow. *(You are an efficient and hard-working fellow)*

but

```
A right mental attitude makes for happiness.
```
(It doesn't make sense to say "A right and mental attitude makes for happiness.")

6. When a sentence has two clauses separated by "but." (A *clause* is a group of words that includes a subject and verb; on the other hand, a phrase is a group of words that does not include a subject and verb.)

```
I like this car, but it is too expensive for me.
```

7. When a sentence has two clauses separated by "and" and one clause or both clauses are long.

```
You need a thorough knowledge of forestry, and you can get that
knowledge from on-the-job training.
His name is John, and he told me some of the most fascinating tales
about the South Pacific.
```

but

```
I like you and you like me.
```
(No comma is necessary when both clauses are short—say, usually no more than five words each.)

8. When a sentence begins with a long dependent clause (one that cannot stand alone and that starts with such words as *although, since, because, as soon as, after, when*).

```
As soon as your letter reached me this morning, I called Mr. Doe.
Although his plan was incomplete, he received general approval.
```

but

```
His plan received general approval when the president read favor-
able comments to all his department heads.
```
(When the dependent clause comes after the main clause and is closely connected with it, no comma is used.)

9. When a word or clause that follows the name of a person or thing isn't necessary to identify that person or thing.

```
This man, who went without sleep for two days, fell asleep at the
wheel.
Boston, the capital, is the largest city in Massachusetts.
```

but

A man who went without sleep for two days fell asleep at the wheel.
(*Here the "who" clause is necessary to identify "man."*)
Buy the book *Investments* the next time you go to the bookstore.

10. When a sentence includes a loosely connected word or phrase, called a parenthetical word or expression.

You will agree with me, however, that he is a great risk.
Yes, I agree with you.
You did a fine job, to be sure.

11. When two verbs come together.

Whatever is, is right.

12. When two figures come together in a sentence.

In 1979, 432 employees took their vacations in July.

13. When two sentence elements may be misunderstood or look strange if read together.

Wrong: Ever since we have enjoyed working with him.
Right: Ever since, we have enjoyed working with him.
Confusing: That that is is that that is not is not.
Clear: That that is, is; that that is not, is not.

14. When a sentence contains a quotation.

"Rules," he said, "are made to be broken."
He said, "Rules are made to be broken."

15. When the first word of a sentence ends in "ing" and modifies the subject.

Looking into this man's record, we find he was arrested twice.

16. When a sentence omits a word (usually a verb).

One of the persons involved in the accident is a mill operator; the other, a logger.

17. When the state follows the city.

Denver, Colorado, is called the mile-high city.

Period Is Used:

1. To end a sentence.

This firm has several branches throughout the state.

2. To show omission of words from a quoted sentence. (Periods indicating the omissions are called *ellipses*.)

"Fourscore and seven years ago our fathers brought forth on this continent a new nation, ... dedicated to the proposition that all men are created equal . . . ." (*The fourth period stands for the period that ends the sentence.*)

3. To indicate abbreviations. *But* omit period after many organizations or government agencies.

Mr. Dr. Inc. a.m. p.m. N.E. NE. J. E. Doe
AFL, RCA, TVA, AT&T

4. For decimal sign.

```
13.5%, .04, $374.22.
```

5. In tabulation.

```
1.
2.      ( only one space after the period. )
3.
```

Semicolon Is Used:

1. Between clauses that can stand alone and the second clause begins with words such as *however, nevertheless, consequently, therefore, moreover, hence, likewise, furthermore,* and *namely.*

```
He has an excellent background in education and work experience;
however, I cannot find much information concerning his extracurricu-
lar activities on or off campus.
```

2. Between closely related clauses that can stand alone and don't have any word between them.

```
I prefer a person who has worked her or his way through school; he
prefers an individual who has devoted the entire time to schooling
and has a high grade point average.
```

But, you may use a comma to separate very short main clauses not joined by words listed in number 1 above.

```
I stopped, I aimed, I fired.
```

3. Before expressions such as *for example, that is, namely, for instance,* and *in fact* when they fall in the middle of the sentence.

```
Three of our offices have been redecorated; namely, Everett, Long-
view, and Bellville.
```

4. When a comma is in at least one of two clauses, both of which can stand alone and a word such as *but, and,* or *or* lies between the clauses.

```
On January 16, 1984, you mailed your report to us; but it didn't ar-
rive until January 27.
```

5. When a sentence contains a series and at least one part of the series has a comma.

```
The speakers included Ms. Roberta Jule, Vice President of Sales; Mr.
Dennis Greiner, Secretary; and Mr. Jack Blue, Comptroller.
```
Note: You could place a colon after "included."

Colon Is Used:

1. To introduce any lengthy quotation, list, or a table after such words as *the following, as follows, as, these, this*—stated or implied.

```
This is what he said: "Choose a job you'll enjoy living with for the
rest of your life, and then. . . ."
That house has four rooms: front room, dining room, kitchen, and
bedroom.
```

Note: To show emotions or greater emphasis, you should use dashes instead of colons.

2. To separate hours and minutes.

```
4:50 a.m.
8:35 p.m.
```

3. After the salutation in a business letter.

```
Dear Mr. Jones:
```

Dash Is Used:

1. To emphasize.

```
When you don't know how to spell a word——use a dictionary.
```

2. To set off a series within the sentence.

```
These people——Mr. Smith, Mr. Jones, and Mrs. Peterson——asked me
about this type of account.
```

Hyphen Is Used:

1. To break a word at the end of a line.

```
sub-        knowl-
stantial    edge
```

2. To tie together words thought of as a unit, except when the words follow the noun.

```
well-written report;    but    report is well written
letter-writing contest  but    contest for letter writing
up-to-date rule         but    rule is up to date
secretary-treasurer
his take-it-or-leave-it attitude
40-foot pole
short- and long-run objectives.
```

But, don't hyphenate when the first word is an adverb ending in "ly."

```
slowly moving object
```

3. In numbers 21 through 99 when spelled out.

```
fifty-five
ninety-nine
one hundred seventy-six
```

4. To separate "ex," "elect," and "self" from the next word.

```
ex-president  ex-President Ford
president-elect
self-control
re-cover (cover again)
```

5. To avoid an ambiguous or awkward combination of letters.

```
re-address, pre-election (Some authorities use readdress, preelection)
```

Exclamation Mark Is Used:

To indicate strong emotion.

```
What a beautiful car!
What a mess!
```

Question Marks Are Used:

1. For direct question.

What have you found out about this individual?

But, use a period or a question mark after a request.

May we hear from you within the next 10 days.
May we hear from you within 10 days?

2. To show doubt.

In 1592 (?) Columbus discovered America.

Quotation Marks:

Here are three good suggestions to remember about punctuation before and after quotation marks.

1. All periods and commas go within the quotes.
2. Semicolons and colons always go outside the quotes.
3. Question marks, exclamation marks, and dashes
   a. Go outside the quotes when they punctuate the entire sentence.
   b. Go inside the quotes when they punctuate only the quoted matter.

Quotation Marks Are Used:

1. Around a direct quotation.
2. Around unusual, substandard, or inexact terms.
3. Around titles of magazine articles and book chapters (but not titles of magazines, books, and pamphlets).
4. Around words to be set off.

The "please" in a request. . . .

Apostrophe Is Used:

1. To show possession.

child's, women's, anybody's, Jones's, Moses', father-in-law's, someone else's

2. For omission of a letter or number.

I'll, you'll, we've, don't, can't, hasn't, o'clock, isn't, it's
the blizzard of '79

3. For plural of figures,   7's look like 9's
             letters,   p's and q's
             words used as words. You have five "hope's" in this letter.

Sentences to Punctuate:

1. The price is high but the quality is low
2. Washington Lincoln and Franklin Roosevelt were well known presidents
3. Youll find up to date information in that book
4. My sister Mary now attends college
5. The person who finds my watch gets a $20 reward

6. The boys are smiling the girls are laughing
7. As we agreed on the telephone this policy will run until May 6 1984
8. What system of bridge do you play
9. The price is high and the quality is poor
10. You did a fine job John in handling this situation
11. When you come to the meeting you should see Mr. John Narver our personnel manager
12. It is wise therefore to trade with reputable merchants
13. A stitch in time saves nine says an old proverb
14. You can be certain Ms. Corbett that you'll have our answer within a week
15. In 1970 72 persons from our office enrolled
16. Among those at the conference were Mr. A B Moe Superintendent Mr. Harris Lobe Sales Manager and Ms. Rollow Butts Educational Director
17. Having read the policy twice he was familiar with its contents
18. There was nobody there in fact when I arrived
19. His suggestion was this Think before you write
20. I always thought he was looney
21. This person who found my watch gets a $20 reward
22. When she talks she lisps her ss and rolls her rs
23. Enclosed is a copy of our letter of February 12 1979 regarding the endorsement dated January 30 1979
24. Seattle Washington is the largest city in the Northwest
25. Please send the following Form A Form B and Form C
26. Be certain to read pages 4 15 17 22 and 30
27. This is your desk that one is mine
28. Nothing has been done according to Joe to change the picture
29. John said that he would do it
30. It takes guts to publish that report
31. As Pete ate John gave him an account of the accident
32. For the next two weeks send my mail to 441 South Estelle Wichita Kansas
33. I saw this man hit that pale blue four door automobile
34. In 1939 when World War II started you were only several months old
35. People who live in glass houses shouldn't throw stones
36. They asked me whether I had taken any courses in finance
37. My sister you will be pleased to hear is now an accountant
38. A person who is honest will succeed
39. Three students Henry Pete and Mary invariably have their assignments well prepared every day
40. Its true that plenty of practice with proper guidance will improve your writing ability

Syllabication (Division of Words)

Syllabication is the division of words at the ends of lines to avoid a ragged right margin. In general, avoid this division of words, because the material isn't as easy and as clear to read. The following rules will help you to syllabicate words correctly.

1. Divide words between syllables only. Examples: prod-uct, knowl-edge.
2. Do not divide at the ends of more than two consecutive lines of typing.
3. Limit the number of syllabicated words to no more than four on a full page of typewritten material.

4. Divide hyphenated words at the hyphen only. Examples: self-control, half-brother.
5. Never divide words of one syllable or words pronounced as one syllable. The addition of past tense does not necessarily add an extra syllable. For example, "guessed," "slammed," "learned," "backed," "seemed," and "glanced" cannot be divided, because they are all one syllable.
6. Do not divide a four-letter word. If possible, avoid dividing words of five or six letters. Examples: upon, final, avoid.
7. In words having three syllables or more, a one-letter syllable should be typed on the preceding, rather than the succeeding, line. Example: sepa-rate, not sep-arate.
8. Avoid separating a one- or two-letter syllable at the beginning of a word from the rest of the word. Example: apti-tude, not ap-titude; enough, not e-nough. Exception *if necessary*: two-letter prefixes—ad, de, en, ex, im, in, re, un, up, etc.
9. Never carry just two letters of a word to the next line. Example: newly, not new-ly.
10. When two vowels coming together are pronounced separately, divide between the two vowels. Example: cre-ated, gradu-ation.
11. As a rule, divide between a prefix and the rest of the word. Examples: trans-pose, con-sign.
12. As a rule, divide between suffix and the stem of the word. Examples: lov-able, announce-ment.
    a. Note that in such words as "ame-na-ble," "fea-si-ble," and "de-fen-si-ble," the termination is "ble"—and the vowel preceding it is considered a part of the preceding syllable.
    b. When a root word ends with a double consonant, separate the suffix from the root word. Examples: guess-ing, tell-ing.
    c. When a final consonant is doubled before a suffix, the additional consonant goes with the suffix. Examples: trip-ping, strag-gling, stop-ping.
    d. Note that the endings "cian, cion, gion, sion, and tion" are kept as syllables, regardless of word derivation. Example: expres-sion.
13. When a consonant is doubled within a word, divide the word between the consonants. Examples: fer-ret, tal-low, shut-ter.
14. Do not divide the last word on a page.
15. Do not divide abbreviations, contractions, figures, or proper names.

Transitional Words and Phrases to Help Tie Sentences Together

Addition:

again	equally important	in addition	next
also	finally	last	others
and	first	lastly	secondly
and then	further	likewise	thirdly, etc.
besides	furthermore	moreover	too

Cause and Result:

accordingly	because of	hence	thus
as a result	consequently	therefore	unless
assuming	for this reason	thereupon	

Comparison:

better yet	in like manner	similarly	an even greater sum . . .
here again	likewise	still worse	even more important

Contrast:

although, even though	however	on the other hand
and yet	in contrast	on the contrary
at the same time	nevertheless	still
but	notwithstanding	yet

Instances, Lists, Explanations:

in particular	for example	for instance	to illustrate

Place:

adjacent to	here	on the opposite side
beyond	nearby	opposite to

Summary:

as has been stated	for instance	in short	to be sure
as I have said	in brief	in sum	to sum up
for example	in other words	on the whole	

Time Sequence:

afterward	during	in the meantime	soon
at the same time	following	meanwhile	then
before	immediately	previously	while

Trite Expressions to Avoid

advise (when you mean "tell" or "inform")	has come to hand
allow me to	I have your letter of (date)
and oblige	in re
assuring you of our prompt attention, we remain	in reply wish to state
attached please find	kindly (when you mean please)
attached hereto	party (when you mean a person)
avail yourself of this opportunity	please be advised that
beg to (state, advise, inform)	please do not hesitate to
contents noted	please find enclosed
Dear Madam, Dear Sir, Dear Sirs	receipt is hereby acknowledged
dictated but not read	re your letter of recent date
don't hesitate to (call, write)	said (the said individual)
e.g. (avoid this and other Latin abbreviations)	same (as a pronoun—thank you for the same)
enclosed please find	thank you in advance
esteemed	the writer
even date	we are in receipt of
favor (meaning letter)	we transmit herewith
	wise (cost wise, product wise, personality wise)

Index